FEATURE	SHORTCUT	FEATURE	
Document Initial Codes	Shift+F8 DC	Full Justification (paragraph)	
Document Summary	Shift+F8 DS	Full Justification (all lines)	Shift+F8 LJA
DOS (go to)	Ctrl+F1 G	Generate Auto-References	Alt+F5 G
Dot Leader	Alt+F6 Alt+F6 or Shift+F6 Shift+F6	Go To	Ctrl+Home
Dot Leader Character/Spacing	Shift+F8 CL	Grammar	Alt+F1 G
Double Indent	Shift+F4	Graphics Box	Alt+F9 B
Double Underline	Ctrl+F8 AD	Graphics Line	Alt+F9 L
Double-Sided Printing (duplex printers)	Shift+F8 PO	Graphics Mode	Ctrl+F3 G
Double-Sided Printing (non-duplex printers or Booklet)	Shift+F7 M then O (or B)	Hanging Indent	F4 Shift+Tab
		Hard Page Break	Ctrl+↵
		Headers	Shift+F8 HH
Drag-and-Drop	Drag, click, drag, release	Help	F1
		Help (coaches)	F1 O
E-mail	See *Mail*	Help (macros)	Alt+H M
Endnote	Ctrl+F7 E	Hide Text	Alt+O H
Envelope	Alt+F12	How Do I...	Alt+H H
Equations	Alt+F9 BCY ➤ Equation Box ➤ SE	Hypertext	Alt+F5 H
		Hyphenation	Shift+F8 LY
		Import Text	Shift+F10
Exit Document	F7	Indent	F4
Exit WordPerfect	Home F7	Index	Alt+F5 M or D
Export Text	F10 (R)	Info (document)	Alt+F1 D
Fax	Shift+F7 X	Info (WP)	Alt+H W
Figure (retrieve)	Alt+F9 Shift+F10	Insert/Typeover	Insert (Ins)
File Manager	F5	Install Hardware/Driver	Install (from DOS)
Flush Right (all)	Shift+F8 LJR	Italics	Ctrl+I
Flush Right (line)	Alt+F6	Justification Limits	Shift+F8 OPJ
Font	Ctrl+F8		
Fonts (install)	Ctrl+F8 Shift+F1 I	Kerning	Shift+F8 OPK
Footers	Shift+F8 HF	Keyboard Template	F1 (Template)
Footnote	Ctrl+F7 F	Keyboard Layout	Shift+F1 K
Force Odd/Even Page	Shift+F8 PF	Labels	Shift+F8 PL

For every kind of computer user, there is a SYBEX book.

All computer users learn in their own way. Some need straightforward and methodical explanations. Others are just too busy for this approach. But no matter what camp you fall into, SYBEX has a book that can help you get the most out of your computer and computer software while learning at your own pace.

Beginners generally want to start at the beginning. The **ABC's** series, with its step-by-step lessons in plain language, helps you build basic skills quickly. Or you might try our **Quick & Easy** series, the friendly, full-color guide.

The **Mastering** and **Understanding** series will tell you everything you need to know about a subject. They're perfect for intermediate and advanced computer users, yet they don't make the mistake of leaving beginners behind.

If you're a busy person and are already comfortable with computers, you can choose from two SYBEX series—**Up & Running** and **Running Start**. The **Up & Running** series gets you started in just 20 lessons. Or you can get two books in one, a step-by-step tutorial and an alphabetical reference, with our **Running Start** series.

Everyone who uses computer software can also use a computer software reference. SYBEX offers the gamut—from portable **Instant References** to comprehensive **Encyclopedias**, **Desktop References**, and **Bibles**.

SYBEX even offers special titles on subjects that don't neatly fit a category—like **Tips & Tricks**, the **Shareware Treasure Chests**, and a wide range of books for Macintosh computers and software.

SYBEX books are written by authors who are expert in their subjects. In fact, many make their living as professionals, consultants or teachers in the field of computer software. And their manuscripts are thoroughly reviewed by our technical and editorial staff for accuracy and ease-of-use.

So when you want answers about computers or any popular software package, just help yourself to SYBEX.

For a complete catalog of our publications, please write:

SYBEX Inc.
2021 Challenger Drive
Alameda, CA 94501
Tel: (510) 523-8233/(800) 227-2346 Telex: 336311
Fax: (510) 523-2373

SYBEX is committed to using natural resources wisely to preserve and improve our environment. As a leader in the computer book publishing industry, we are aware that over 40% of America's solid waste is paper. This is why we have been printing the text of books like this one on recycled paper since 1982.

This year our use of recycled paper will result in the saving of more than 15,300 trees. We will lower air pollution effluents by 54,000 pounds, save 6,300,000 gallons of water, and reduce landfill by 2,700 cubic yards.

In choosing a SYBEX book you are not only making a choice for the best in skills and information, you are also choosing to enhance the quality of life for all of us.

Mastering WordPerfect 6 for DOS

Special Edition

Mastering WordPerfect® 6 for DOS®

Special Edition

ALAN SIMPSON

San Francisco • Paris • Düsseldorf • Soest

SYBEX®

ACQUISITIONS EDITOR: Dianne King
DEVELOPMENTAL EDITOR: Steve Lipson
EDITORS: Sarah Wadsworth, Savitha Varadan, Carol Henry
TECHNICAL EDITORS: Sheldon M. Dunn, Maurie Duggan, Tanya Strub
BOOK DESIGNER: Suzanne Albertson
SCREEN GRAPHICS: John Corrigan
PAGE LAYOUT AND TYPESETTING: Len Gilbert
PROOFREADER/PRODUCTION COORDINATOR: Catherine Mahoney
PRODUCTION ARTIST: Lisa Jaffe
INDEXER: Matthew Spence
COVER DESIGNER: Archer Design
COVER PHOTOGRAPHER: Mark Johann
COVER PHOTOGRAPH ART DIRECTION: Ingalls + Associates
Screen reproductions produced with Collage Plus

Library of Congress Card Number: 93-84821
ISBN: 0-7821-1180-7

Manufactured in the United States of America
10 9 8 7 6 5 4 3 2 1

To the million-or-so of you
who bought my previous WordPerfect book. This one's for you.
(My wife thanks you too. She gets the money.)

ACKNOWLEDGMENTS

THANKS to Elizabeth Olson, my #1 perfection-demanding, co-authoring sidekick on this ambitious project. Thanks also to Virginia Andersen, Mac Dunn, and Clinton Hicks for their authorial contributions.

Thanks to Martha Mellor who, as always, fielded problems and made cool heads prevail through yet another stress-ridden time.

Thanks to everyone at SYBEX who changed this book from my original WordPerfect manuscript into the beautiful finished product you're now holding in your hands. In particular, thanks to Steve Lipson, Developmental Editor; Sarah Wadsworth, Savitha Varadan, and Carol Henry, Editors; Len Gilbert, Typesetter; Catherine Mahoney, Proofreader; John Corrigan, who produced the screen graphics; and Lisa Jaffe, Production Artist.

Also at SYBEX, thanks to Rodnay, Alan, Rudy, Barbara, and Dianne, for giving me the opportunity. (Dianne—we're all going to miss you terribly. Can we get you to change your mind?)

Thanks to WordPerfect Corporation for creating the best word processing program in the universe. And for supporting me and my work.

Thanks to Bill Gladstone and the gang at Waterside Productions, my literary agency. It's been over a decade now, gang.

Thanks to John Vorhaus-rhymes-with-(never mind), writing instructor extraordinaire. Your two-day seminar at UCSD Extension taught me to lighten up and enjoy my work once again.

And of course, thanks to Susan, Ashley, and Alec, for cutting Daddy loose for a few weeks, to pound the keyboard night and day. Again.

Contents

AT A GLANCE

CONTENTS

PART TWO   **...AND THE START OF EVERYTHING ELSE**

PART SIX   **OFFICE TOOLS**

PART SEVEN   DESKTOP PUBLISHING

29 Adding Equations to Your Documents 1035

APPENDICES

INTRODUCTION

FIRST of all, thanks for buying this book. If you just borrowed it from someone else, then thanks for giving it a chance. I appreciate it. Now with gratitude aside, let's get to specifics.

Whom This Book Is For

You. That is, this book is for every WordPerfect user, from the absolute beginner to the experienced WordPerfect wizard who wants to take full advantage of everything WordPerfect has to offer. Here's a little guidance on how to get started with this book, depending on which of those two types of people you are.

Road Map for Beginners

If you're new to WordPerfect, you might want to take this route to get up to speed in a jiffy:

- The five quick hands-on lessons in Chapter 1 will teach all you need to know about creating, printing, saving, retrieving, and editing documents with WordPerfect.

- Read Chapters 2 through 4 to get a broader, and deeper, understanding of the features you learned about in Chapter 1.

- When you're working on your own and feel stuck, lost, or confused, look to Appendix C for quick first aid to common problems.

Road Map for Experienced Users

If you're already a WordPerfect wizard, but you've recently upgraded to (or are considering upgrading to) Version 6.0 for DOS, try this route:

- Browse through Appendix B for a quick overview of Version 6.0's best new features.
- Skim through the first three chapters, if you wish. And take a close look at Chapter 4. There you'll learn about the new graphical interface, Button Bars, and other hot new features.

Road Map for Everyone

Once you've gotten your bearings, use the book to find answers to questions, and solutions to problems, as they arise. No, I *don't* expect you to read this entire book. Nobody (except an author like me) needs to know *everything* about WordPerfect.

After all, if you don't use equations in your documents, why learn about equations? If you have no interest in desktop publishing, why read Part Seven? On the other hand, if you know the basics already, and you enjoy being creative, you certainly wouldn't want to miss Part Seven.

Features and Structure of This Book

This book has one goal. To make the time you spend at the keyboard with WordPerfect as productive and enjoyable as possible. WordPerfect is loaded with information. And here's how that information is organized to help you get to what you need, when you need it.

Glossary, Table of Contents, Index

Like any book, this one has a Table of Contents up front and an index at the back to help you look up the information you need. I've also added a glossary to the back of the book, so you can look up any unfamiliar terms you might come across.

Step-by-Step Instructions

Within each chapter, I typically describe a feature by first identifying it with a heading, such as "Starting WordPerfect." That's usually followed by a brief description of the feature. The description, in turn, is usually followed by step-by-step instructions for using the feature.

When you're in a hurry, feel free to skip the paragraph under the heading, and jump right to step 1 to put that feature to work.

Fast Tracks

Fast Tracks at the beginning of each chapter summarize the main features discussed in the chapter. Use these for an overview of things to come, or as reminders after you've learned about a feature and just need a quick nudge on how to get to it.

First Aid for Common Problems

I've summarized the most common day-to-day problems and confusions in Appendix C. There you can look up a problem and find a solution in a hurry. If that doesn't do the trick, you can always use the index or table of contents to find more in-depth information about a way to solve the problem.

Quick Reference Charts

We've got a lot of quick-reference type information inside the front and back covers of this book. If you just need to remember how to get at a particular feature, you may be able to find the answer right there inside the covers.

For beginners, I offer a couple of simplified reference charts near the end of Chapter 1. Feel free to make copies and keep them near your keyboard for quick reminders on using the more common day-to-day features of WordPerfect.

Notes, Tips, and Warnings

My Notes and Tips provide references to related topics in the book, short-cuts, good ideas, and tips on using the feature in conjunction with other features.

The Warnings point out actions that, if taken carelessly, might not be too easy to "undo" (such as deleting your entire document from disk!). Think of a warning as a way of saying "Hmmm.... You better think before you act here."

Sample Documents

Sometimes the best way to learn something new is to look at something someone else has created and then find out how they did it. Because of that, this book is loaded with sample documents. We cover everything from your basic business letter to professional-quality newsletters.

If you'd like to see some of the more advanced and particularly fancy sample documents I've dished up for you experienced (and soon-to-be-experienced) WordPerfect mavens, thumb through Chapters 5, 7, and 26–28.

If you did just go and peek at those sample documents, you may be thinking "I could never do *that* one." *Au contraire!* If *I* can do it, *you* can do it. It's simply a matter of knowing which features to use and when to use them. And that, ultimately, is *really* what this book is all about.

Perhaps I should mention that I typed all the text in this entire book with WordPerfect, before sending it to the publisher. And, except for a little custom artwork here and there, I created virtually all of the sample documents in this book with WordPerfect, too.

I did take the liberty of using fonts and clip art beyond those that come with the WordPerfect program. I did so under the assumption that if you're going to be creating more advanced documents, you too will probably use additional fonts and clip art. Chapter 10 explains how to expand your font collection. Chapter 26 talks about expanding your clip art collection. It's remarkably inexpensive to do these days. So it's pretty hard to resist!

Installing/Upgrading to Version 6.0

If you (or someone else) hasn't already installed WordPerfect on your computer, you'll need to do so before you can do anything in this book. You can refer to Appendix A for installation instructions.

About WordPerfect Interim Releases

WordPerfect occasionally puts out *interim releases* of their products. These interim releases fix minor bugs or improve features as users offer up their suggestions.

An interim release has the same version number as the initial release. If you want to be sure that you're always using the latest and greatest release, you can contact WordPerfect's Software Subscription Service to learn about the various programs they have for keeping you up to date. The phone number is (800) 282-2892.

Additional Support

Part of the success WordPerfect has enjoyed stems from the fact that they're serious about offering telephone support to their customers. WordPerfect Corporation phone numbers for answers to specific questions are listed below:

Orders	(800) 321-4566
Installation	(800) 533-9605
Features	(800) 541-5096

Graphics/Tables/Equations	(800) 321-3383
Macros/Merges/Labels	(800) 541-5129
Laser/PostScript Printers	(800) 541-5170
Dot Matrix/Other Printers	(800) 541-5160
Networks	(800) 321-3389

There's also the monthly magazine titled *WordPerfect the Magazine*. For more information, contact

WP Magazine
Circulation Department
270 West Center Street
Orem, UT 84057-9927
Voice: (801) 228-9626

One Last Pep Talk for the Technically Timid

One last pep talk for those of you who are still feeling a little skittish. Keep in mind that like everything else in life, from driving a car to skiing down a mountain, WordPerfect is only confusing and intimidating when you're at the very bottom of the learning curve—that disorienting time when you're struggling to get your bearings and figure out how to work the darn thing.

WordPerfect is not an evil menace. Nor is it solely for the use of Nobel prize–winning scholars and other assorted geniuses. Nope. It's a writing tool that *everyone* can use. I promise you: Once you get a little time "behind the wheel," the fear and intimidation will melt away, as it does in *every* endeavor we humans undertake. So do what I always do: Quit worrying and start *enjoying* yourself already!

PART ONE

The Least You Need to Know...

CHAPTER 1

WordPerfect in an Evening: A Hands-On Guided Tour

IF YOU'RE new to WordPerfect, probably the first thing you want to know is "how do I work this pup?" At the very least, you might want to type up a letter or memo without getting stymied, baffled, or totally lost.

In this chapter we'll go through five quick lessons that will teach you how to do just that. You'll learn to use WordPerfect well enough to get a job done without getting stuck. You can probably complete these lessons in an evening. That's a lot better than spending weeks fumbling around in the dark.

Notice I said you can *probably* complete the lessons in an evening. If you can't type worth beans, it might take you a little longer. But don't worry. If you only make it to the end of Lesson 2, you can stop for as long as you wish then pick up with Lesson 3 later.

If you're an experienced WordPerfect user, you'll probably find most of the material in this chapter to be too basic for you. Not to worry. There's plenty of more advanced stuff later in the book. In this chapter, you might want to familiarize yourself with the new ways of setting up your screen and getting help (see Lesson 4) and then continue with Chapter 3.

Lesson 1: Typing Your First Document

The first step is to start the WordPerfect program on your computer. The following section explains how.

Starting WordPerfect

HANDS ON!

Turn on your printer, screen, and computer in the usual manner (switch all the "off" switches to "on," or from 0 to 1). Then...

- If (and when) you get to the DOS command prompt (which looks something like **C>** followed by a flashing cursor), type **wp** then press ↵.

- If you get to a menu system when you first turn on your computer, choose the WordPerfect option.

You should see a brief message announcing that WordPerfect 6.0 is on its way. That's followed by a screen that has something like this in the lower-right corner:

Doc 1 Pg 1 Ln 1″ Pos 1″

That just tells you where the *cursor* (the blinking marker) is currently positioned on WordPerfect's imaginary page (you'll find out more about this in Chapter 3).

If you're not sure whether you're in or out of WordPerfect, glance down at the lower-right corner of the screen. If you see the **Doc Pg Ln Pos** thing, it's a sure-fire guarantee that WordPerfect is up and running on your computer. If you *don't* see that **Doc Pg Ln Pos** business, chances are you're in some other program, such as DOS.

If, when you try to start WordPerfect, you get the message "Bad command or file name" or some other bogus message, please see "Starting Word-Perfect" in Chapter 2 for additional help.

Typing with WordPerfect

Typing with WordPerfect is practically identical to typing on a typewriter except that you type on a screen before you type on paper. The advantage is that it's much easier to make changes and corrections on your computer screen than it is on paper.

These are the other main differences between typing in WordPerfect and typing on paper:

- WordPerfect lets you back up and correct your text on the spot by pressing the Backspace key. (The Backspace key usually has a ← arrow on it, and it's usually located above the ↵ key.)

- When typing 1 (one) and zero (0) with WordPerfect, you need to get in the habit of using the 1 and 0 keys above the letters on the keyboard. Don't use the letters "l" and "o".

- If you type *John Smith* and it comes out as *jOHN sMITH*, it means your Caps Lock key is on. Press the Caps Lock key once, then press Backspace until you've erased all the mistyped text. Then type the text again.

- When you're typing a paragraph with WordPerfect, *don't* press ↵ to end each line. Instead, just keep typing off the right edge of the screen, and let WordPerfect break the line for you.

T I P

If you need extra help finding certain keys on the keyboard, see "Using Your Keyboard" in Chapter 2.

Key+Key Combination Keystrokes

Sometimes you'll need to press *combination keystrokes* to make WordPerfect do what you want. You'll know when you need to press a combination keystroke when you see a + sign between two keys, like this: *key+key*.

To press a combination keystroke, *hold down* the first key, *tap* the second key, then *release* the first key. Don't try to hit both keys at once, and don't press the second one first. For example, to press Ctrl+F1, hold down the Ctrl (Control) key, press and release the *function key* labeled F1 (usually at the top or left side of your keyboard), then release the Ctrl key.

You're Probably Not Stuck

Contrary to what you may feel from time to time, you're rarely ever "stuck" in WordPerfect. When you think you're stuck or lost, try pressing the (appropriately named) Escape key (sometimes labeled Esc or Cancel). Press the

Escape key repeatedly until you get back to familiar territory. (In fact, if you pressed Ctrl+F1 in the preceding section, you can now press Escape to get rid of the *dialog box* that popped up on your screen.)

Typing a Letter

HANDS ON!

OK, let's try some things out. Together, we'll type up the letter shown in Figure 1.1. Here goes!

1. Type **Wanda Bea Tuna** (if it comes out as *wANDA...* it means your Caps Lock key is on, as explained earlier).

2. Press ↵ to end that line and move to the next line.

3. Type **123 Oak Tree Lane** and then press ↵ to move to the next line.

4. Type **Hollywood, CA 91234** and press ↵ twice (once to end the line, then again to put in a blank line).

5. Type **Dear Ms. Tuna:** and press ↵ twice.

Now you should see something like this on your screen:

Wanda Bea Tuna
123 Oak Tree Lane
Hollywood, CA 91234

Dear Ms. Tuna:

FIGURE 1.1

The sample letter you'll be typing in this lesson

```
Wanda Bea Tuna
123 Oak Tree Lane
Hollywood, CA  91234

Dear Ms. Tuna:

    Rumor has it that you are an expert on TV script writing.
Therefore, I'm hoping you can answer a simple question for me.
Why is it that actors and actresses never say "Goodbye" before
hanging up the phone? I always say Goodbye (or at least 'kay-
bye). Why don't you make the actors do that to, you know, make it
more realistic like? This has always puzzled me, and drives me
crazy becuase I can't stop noticing it.

Thanks in advance for your reply:



Willie B. Goode
```

Don't worry if it's not perfect. I'll show you how to make corrections later.

Typing Paragraphs

When you're typing a paragraph that's longer than a single line (as most paragraphs are), don't press ↵ at the end of each line. Just type right off the edge of the screen, and let WordPerfect *word-wrap* the line for you.

WARNING

If you *do* press ↵ at the end of each line, and then you make changes to the paragraph later, Word-Perfect won't be able to reformat the paragraph on its own. This can be a major pain.

1. Press the Tab key (usually to the left of the Q) to indent about half an inch.

2. Type the paragraph below (including mistakes) as though it were one long line. Don't worry if the paragraph wraps differently on your screen—just don't press ↵.

   Rumor has it that you are an expert on TV script writing. Therefore, I'm hoping you can answer a simple question for me. Why is it that actors and actresses never say "Goodbye" before hanging up the phone? I always say Goodbye (or at least 'kay-bye). Why don't you make the actors do that to, you know, make it more realistic like? This has always puzzled me, and drives me crazy because I can't stop noticing it.

3. After you've typed the whole paragraph, press ↵ twice (once to end the paragraph, a second time to put in a blank line).

4. Type **Thanks in advance for your reply:** and then press ↵ about five times to insert some blank lines where your signature will go.

5. Type your own name, or **Willie B. Goode,** or whatever tickles your fancy.

Now your letter should look something like the one in Figure 1.1.

What Happens to Text at the Top?

We're going to keep this sample document short, just to make life easy. But don't think you're limited to typing only as much as there's space for on the screen. You can type as much text as you want. In fact, I typed this whole book using WordPerfect!

As you type off the bottom of the screen, some text will scroll up out of view, off the top of the screen. The text isn't gone for good. It's just out of your way for the time being.

As you'll see, you can use the Page Up (PgUp) and Page Down (PgDn) keys to scroll from page to page in your document. Since our sample letter fits on less than a page, however, those keys will just move the cursor to the top and bottom of the letter.

Lesson 2: Printing and Saving Your Document

Assuming your printer is turned on, hooked up, and online (according to the manufacturer's instructions), you can now print a copy of the letter that's on your screen. You're also ready to save the document.

Printing Your Document

HANDS ON!

To print the document that you're looking at on the screen, follow the steps below:

1. Press Alt+= to get to the *menu bar* (remember, hold down the Alt key, press the = key, then release both keys). The menu bar appears as a row of commands across the top of the screen, like this:

   File Edit View Layout Tools Font Graphics Window Help

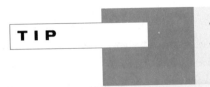

TIP There are lots of different ways you can work with the menus. I'll discuss these under "Using the Menus" in Chapter 2.

2. Tap the letter **f** to choose File. A *drop-down menu* (also called a *pull-down menu*) will appear.

3. Type the letter **p** to choose the Print/Fax option. You will be taken to a *dialog box*. This one is the Print/Fax dialog box (the name of the dialog box always appears centered at the top of the box).

4. Type the letter **r** to choose the Print/Fax option (or, if you have a mouse and know how to use it, move the mouse pointer to the Print command button and then click the left mouse button).

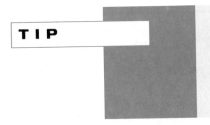

TIP For the most part, using the mouse is optional in Word-Perfect. If you don't have a mouse, or you don't know how to use your mouse yet, don't worry. "Using a Mouse" in Chapter 2 defines basic mouse terminology and describes how to use the mouse.

After a brief delay, the printed letter should roll out of your printer. It will probably have 1-inch margins, which is the default margin size for all WordPerfect documents. (You can change the margins in your document at any time, as you'll learn in Chapter 8.)

Saving Your Work

HANDS ON!

In the best of all worlds, your letter would be perfect just as it is and wouldn't need any more work. But in reality, we often need to go back and make changes to things. For that reason, you want to *save* a copy of most of the documents you create.

When you save a document, you store a copy of it on disk with a *file name* that you can remember (that way, you can find the letter when you need it later). The steps to follow are listed below.

WARNING Right now the letter on your screen is in *memory*, or RAM (Random Access Memory). Anything in memory is wiped out the moment you turn off the computer or leave WordPerfect. That's why you always want to save your work before calling it quits.

1. Press Alt+= then type **f** to pull down the <u>F</u>ile menu.

2. Type **s** to choose Save (or click on the Save command using your mouse).

3. Now you need to enter a file name. The basic rule of thumb is that the file name can be no longer than eight characters, followed by a period, followed by an extension up to three letters long (for example, MyLetter.wp6 or SpareMe.wp). In general, you should stick with letters (other than the one optional period) and don't use punctuation marks like +, /, \, ?, *, and so forth. Case doesn't matter: MyLetter.wp is the same as myletter.w*p*, which is the same as MYLETTER.WP.

   If you can't think up a good name right now, type **myfirst.wp** (with only one period—never type a period at the end of a file name). Whatever name you type in, write it down in a safe place, *exactly* as you typed it on the screen. (If you don't have a pen handy, memorize that name *exactly*.)

TIP If you give all your WordPerfect documents the same extension, such as .wp, it'll be easier to identify them later when you're looking at a long list of files. (Files and file names are discussed in more detail in Chapter 20.)

4. Press ⏎ (or choose OK by clicking the OK button with your mouse pointer).

It's possible that you'll see a message like this:

Replace C:\WPDOCS\MYFIRST.WP?

That means there's already a file with that name on disk. If it's just an earlier copy of the same file, or you're *certain* that whatever is in that file isn't important, choose Yes (by typing **y**) to replace that file with what's on your screen right now. Otherwise, choose No (by typing **n**), then type a different file name and press ↵.

Exiting Gracefully

HANDS ON!

You always want to *exit* WordPerfect before you turn off your computer. Forgetting to do so is the leading cause of lost work and *misocomputerism* (a term I just made up for "hatred of computers"). Exiting is easy—you just have to remember to do it!

1. Press Alt+= then type **f** to choose File (or click the right mouse button, then click on the File option, if you prefer to use the mouse).

2. Type **x** to choose Exit WP (or click that option with your mouse).

3. You should see a dialog box that looks something like this:

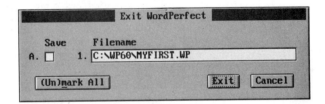

4. Choose Exit (or Save and Exit) by pressing ↵ or clicking that command button with your mouse.

If you've never saved this document, you'll need to type in a file name now, as described under "Saving Your Work," above. If WordPerfect asks you about replacing the previous copy, you can choose Yes (by typing **y**).

You'll be returned to the DOS command prompt (**C>**) or wherever you were before you started WordPerfect. The document you created in this lesson is safely stored on disk under the file name you assigned to it (for example, MYFIRST.WP).

WARNING Contrary to what you may have heard in the rumor mill, pressing Ctrl+Alt+Del is not a graceful way to exit any program.

If you want to take a break, now is the perfect time to do so. If you like, you can turn off your computer. Just pick up with Lesson 3 whenever it's convenient.

Lesson 3: Opening and Editing Your Document

At this point in the chapter you've started WordPerfect, you've created, printed, and saved a document, and you've exited WordPerfect. Now let's suppose that after reading through the printed copy of your letter, you decide to make some changes to it.

Since you created the document in WordPerfect, the first thing you need to do is get WordPerfect up and running again so you can *open* (get into) your document.

Starting WordPerfect (Again)

As I mentioned at the beginning of this chapter, most people just need to type **wp** and press ↵ at the DOS command prompt (**C>**) to start WordPerfect. Go ahead and do so now. (Or, if you've found some other way to start WordPerfect, do *that* now.) You should see WordPerfect's opening graphic followed by the now-familiar **Doc Pg Ln Pos** indicators in the lower-right corner of your screen.

It Says "WordPerfect Stopped without Exiting Properly..."

If you see a message telling you that WordPerfect stopped without exiting properly, it means that you (or somebody else, or some*thing* else—like a power outage) turned off the computer before exiting WordPerfect. And, WordPerfect automatically saved *some* of your work before that improper exit happened.

NOTE

WordPerfect automatically backs up your work every ten minutes or so. But don't rely on that as an excuse for not saving your work and exiting properly. Chapter 19 talks about automatic backup in more detail.

You can see what's in that saved file by choosing Open (just type the letter **o** or click the Open button with your mouse pointer). Of course, you don't need to bother with this right now because you exited WordPerfect properly at the end of Lesson 2. Right?

Opening a Document

HANDS ON!

Now that WordPerfect is up and running again, displaying a blank editing screen, how do you open the document you created earlier? Easy: Choose File ➤ Open by following these steps:

1. Press Alt+= to get to the menu bar.

2. Type **f** to choose File, or click on File.

3. Type **o** to choose Open, or click on Open. You'll be taken to the Open Document dialog box which looks something like this:

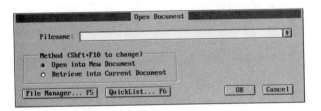

4. Here you can tell WordPerfect which file to open using either of the methods below:

   - Type in the name you entered and jotted down back in Lesson 2 (be sure to type it *exactly*). Then press ↵ and skip steps 5–9 below.

   - If you want to look around a little, or if you don't feel like typing the whole file name, choose File Manager by clicking that button with your mouse pointer or by pressing the F5 key.

5. Press ↵ to skip over the next dialog box that appears (or click on the OK button). You'll see a list of all the files that are stored along with the document you saved in Lesson 2. Notice that one of the file names is highlighted.

6. To move quickly to the file name you want, choose Name Search by typing **n** or clicking on Name Search.

7. Type the first few letters of the file name you entered back in Lesson 2 until WordPerfect highlights the name of the file you want to open.

8. Press ↵ to stop the Name Search.

9. Notice command number 1, near the top of the screen, Open Into New Document. That's the command you want to choose. Press ↵, type **o**, or click that command with your mouse.

The document should appear on the screen looking exactly like it did when you last saved it (unless, of course, somebody else used the computer and changed or deleted the document). Neither the computer nor WordPerfect will change (or lose) a file on its own.

Basic Everyday Editing Skills

Now, suppose you want to make some changes to your document. Before you get started, let's cover some of the basics. Go ahead and experiment with these techniques. You can't hurt anything. Honest!

Moving the Cursor

The first thing you need to do is to place the cursor where you want to make changes. Use any of the following methods:

- Move the mouse pointer to where you want to put the cursor, then click the left mouse button.

- Use the →, ↓, ↑, and ← keys to move around a line or a character at a time.

- You can "exaggerate" the arrow keys by pressing Home once or twice first. For example, press Home ← to move to the beginning of the current line or Home → to move to the end of the current line. (You can also press End to move to the end of the current line.)

- Press Home Home ↑ to move to the top of the document. Press Home Home ↓ to move to the end of the document.

NOTE Remember that the + sign between command keys means "hold down the first key while pressing the second key." A series of key names *without* the + sign, such as Home Home ↑, means to tap each key individually in the order shown.

For a more complete list of cursor-positioning keys and techniques, see "Moving the Cursor" in Chapter 3.

"My Arrow Keys Don't Work— They Type Numbers!"

If you need to use the arrow keys or other special keys on the numeric keypad, keep in mind that they'll only work when the Num Lock key is turned off. If pressing ↑ ↓, ←, →, and so forth typed numbers into your document, then your Num Lock key is turned on. In that case, press Num Lock once, then use the Backspace key to erase any numbers that you typed by accident. Now you can move the cursor with the arrow keys and the other special keys.

"I Can't Get the Cursor Past the End!"

The mouse, arrow, and other cursor-positioning keys only move through existing text. They won't move the cursor past the end of the document.

When you're at the end of the document, you can press ↵ to insert another line and then move the cursor into that line. Likewise, you can move to the right by adding spaces (press the spacebar) or by indenting (press Tab).

If you insert blank space or lines into your document accidentally, use the Backspace key to back up and correct the mistake.

Deleting Text, Spaces, and Lines

You can delete anything that's on your screen using the Delete key or the Backspace key:

- Press Delete (Del) to delete the character, space, or line break that's right at the cursor position.
- Press Backspace to delete the character, space, or line break that's just to the left of the cursor position.

If you forget to position the cursor before pressing the Backspace or Delete key, and you end up deleting the wrong text, you can "undelete" using the Escape key. For more information, see "Undeleting Text" in Chapter 3.

"Whoops—What Did I Just Do?"

If you're not really paying attention, and you mess up your document without even knowing what you did to mess it up, all is not lost. There's a good chance that you can undo whatever you just did. Try pressing Ctrl+Z, and see if that does the trick.

For more on the joys of Undo, see "Undoing a Recent Change" in Chapter 3.

Breaking (and Unbreaking) Lines

If you want to break a line (for instance, to split one paragraph into two), move the cursor to where you want to make the break. Then press ↵ (twice, if you also want to insert a blank line).

If you break a line by accident, pressing Backspace right away will usually fix the problem. But even if you've moved the cursor since breaking the line, it's still easy to join the lines again. Just move the cursor to the very end of the top half of the broken line (use the ↑, ↓, and End keys, as necessary). Then press Delete (Del) to delete the hard return that's breaking the line. (The hard return is not visible on your screen.)

Adding More Text to the Document

You can add more text to a document at any time:

- To add text to the bottom of the document, move the cursor to the end (Home Home ↓), then start typing. (Press ↵ first if you want to move to the next line before typing.)

- To add text to the top, move the cursor to the beginning of the document (Home Home ↑). If you want to insert a line at the top, press ↵ and then ↑ to move the cursor into that new blank line. Then just start typing.

- If you want to add text within existing text, move the cursor to the point where you want the new text to appear, and then start typing.

You can either *insert* or *type over* (replace) text at the cursor position. How do you know whether WordPerfect will insert or type over *before* you start typing? Easy. Look down toward the lower-left corner of the screen. If you see the word "Typeover," then anything you type will *replace* whatever is to the right of the cursor. If you don't see "Typeover" (but you see a file name or something else instead), WordPerfect will *insert* the new text you type.

This brings us to the next question: How do you tell WordPerfect whether you want to insert or replace text? Simple, just press the Insert (Ins) key.

The Insert key acts as a *toggle*. When you're in Insert mode, pressing the Insert (Ins) key switches you to Typeover mode (and "Typeover" appears in the lower-left corner of the screen). If you're in Typeover mode, pressing Insert switches you back to Insert mode (and removes the Typeover indicator from the screen). Go ahead and try it. Press Insert (Ins) a few times, and keep your eye on the lower-left corner of the screen.

When you're done experimenting, leave WordPerfect in Insert mode. For more information, please see "Inserting and Replacing Text" in Chapter 3.

Editing the Document

HANDS ON!

Now you need to try out some of the awesome editing features you've heard so much about. Figure 1.2 shows a copy of the original letter, marked up with some changes and corrections that need to be made. I'll bet you could make all those changes yourself, right now, using the skills you've learned in the last few minutes (and assuming you can decipher my editorial scribbles). But I'll walk you through it since this might be your first time at a keyboard.

FIGURE 1.2

Our sample letter marked up with some corrections

```
                            ←——— Insert date

        Wanda Bea Tuna
        123 Oak Tree Lane
        Hollywood, CA  91234

        Dear Ms. Tuna:
                                     world-renowned
        ←——Rumor has it that you are an expert on TV script writing.
        Therefore, I'm hoping you can answer a simple question for me.
        Why is it that actors and actresses never say "Goodbye" before
        hanging up the phone? I always say Goodbye (or at least 'kay-
        bye). ¶Why don't you make the actors do that to, you know, make it
        more realistic-like? This has always puzzled me, and drives me
        crazy because I can't stop noticing it.

        Thanks in advance for your reply:



        Willie B. Goode
```

Inserting the Current Date

First, we need to insert the date and a blank line at the top of the page. I'll show you a shortcut for typing the current date:

1. Move the cursor to the top of the document (press Home Home ↑).

2. Now, rather than typing the date yourself, try this little maneuver: Press Shift+F5, then type **t** to choose the T̲ext command.

3. Press ↵ three times to place the date on a line by itself and insert two blank lines.

The date that appears is your computer's current *system date*. (I'll talk more about that little shortcut for typing the date in Chapter 4.)

Un-Indenting a Paragraph

Some people like to indent the first line of every paragraph. Others prefer to put a blank line between each paragraph and not indent. You're free to do whatever you want. But for the sake of our example, let's say we decided to use the latter method.

First, since we're near the top of the document at the moment, we'll delete the indent:

1. Using your mouse or arrow keys, move the cursor to the beginning of the line that starts with "Rumor has it," like this:

   | Rumor has it...

   or like this:

   _Rumor has it...

NOTE Whether the cursor is horizontal or vertical depends on which of WordPerfect's *display modes* you happen to be in. Don't worry about it now. I'll get to that in Lesson 4.

2. Press the Delete (Del) key.

WordPerfect removes the indentation in one quick stroke. (If, in spite of what I said earlier, you indented with spaces rather than a tab, you'll need to press Delete once for each space.)

Adding Words to a Sentence

Next, since we're in the general vicinity, we'll insert the words "world-renowned" and change the "an" in front of expert to "a":

1. Use the arrow keys or your mouse to move the cursor to the *n* in "an":

   you are a<u>n</u> expert *or* you are a|n expert

2. Press the Delete (Del) key to delete the *n*.

3. Take a look at the lower-left corner of the screen and, if you see the word "Typeover" there, press the Insert (Ins) key once to switch to Insert mode.

4. Press the spacebar to insert a space.

5. Type **world-renowned** and notice how WordPerfect automatically squeezes it in, reformatting the rest of the paragraph as necessary.

Splitting the Paragraphs

Now let's split the big paragraph into two, where I've marked it with a paragraph symbol (¶) back in Figure 1.2:

1. Position the cursor just after the period following "'kay-bye).":

   'kay-bye).| Why   *or*   'kay-bye)._ Why

2. Press ↵ twice: once to break the line, a second time to insert a blank line.

3. Press Delete (Del) to delete the blank space at the start of the paragraph.

Deleting Text

Next we'll get rid of the unnecessary words in the penultimate sentence.

This is an easy one:

1. Use the mouse or arrow keys to move the cursor to the comma after "do that to":

   tol, you know   *or*   to, you know

2. Press Delete 11 times, and watch it gobble up those characters on the screen.

3. Now position the cursor just after the word "realistic" (the cursor may end up at the end of the line if the word "like" is on the next line):

   realisticl like?   *or*   realistic_like?

4. Press Delete five times to delete the five characters to the right of the cursor.

Correcting a Misspelling

Now we just have one last job to do: Change "becuase" to "because":

1. Use your mouse or arrow keys to move the cursor to the *u* in "becuase":

   becluase   *or*   becuase

2. Type **a**.

3. Press → to move over the letter *u*.

4. Press Delete to delete the old letter *a*.

That was easy enough. You see, editing in WordPerfect is simply a matter of putting the cursor where you want to make a change, then typing the change (or deleting text, pressing ↵, or whatever else it takes).

At this point, your letter should look something like the example shown in Figure 1.3. (It may look a little different because different printers use different *fonts*. I'll explain about fonts in Chapter 6.)

And that, believe it or not, is about all you need to know about WordPerfect to type perfect letters, memos, and other short documents. Almost painless!

```
Wanda Bea Tuna
123 Oak Tree Lane
Hollywood, CA  91234

Dear Ms. Tuna:

Rumor has it that you are a world-renowned expert on TV script
writing. Therefore, I'm hoping you can answer a simple question
for me. Why is it that actors and actresses never say "Goodbye"
before hanging up the phone? I always say Goodbye (or at least
'kay-bye).

Why don't you make the actors do that to make it more realistic?
This has always puzzled me, and drives me crazy because I can't
stop noticing it.

Thanks in advance for your reply:


Willie B. Goode
```

Other Ways to Edit a Document

The basic editing techniques described in the preceding sections will allow you to correct any mistake or make any change to any WordPerfect document you want. However, there are zillions of other editing techniques that you can use as well. Some of these techniques are very powerful, and you'll want to learn to use them if you're going to be working with large documents or you plan to do a lot of heavy-duty editing.

These industrial-strength editing techniques include…

- Selecting specific amounts of text to delete, move, copy, print, or reformat (Chapter 3)

- Moving and copying selected text (Chapter 3)

- Searching and replacing throughout a document (Chapter 9)

- Having WordPerfect automatically check and correct your spelling (Chapter 11) and grammar (Chapter 12)

- Changing line spacing, margins, and alignment with just a few keystrokes (Chapter 8)

- Sprucing up with **boldface**, *italic*, and special characters (Chapter 6)

And WordPerfect 6.0 offers much, much more, as you'll learn in upcoming chapters.

Saving Your Recent Changes

HANDS ON!

Keep in mind that whatever you're looking at on the screen is the *copy* of the document that's in memory (RAM). The copy that's on the disk is the original copy. That original version "knows" nothing of the changes you've been making since you reopened the document.

To save your changes, just resave the entire document. Resaving replaces the previous copy on disk with the updated copy you've been working on. Here's the quick and easy way to do it:

1. Open the menu bar (press Alt+= or click the right mouse button).

2. Choose File, then choose Save (by clicking each command or typing **fs**).

As long as you've already saved the document and given it a name, WordPerfect won't bother to ask you for a new name. Instead, it will flash a message indicating that it's saving the current copy. If your computer is close by, you might even hear a little reassuring disk activity and see the drive light on the computer blink as WordPerfect writes the new copy of the document to disk.

You can print a copy of the current version of the document using the same technique you used to print the first copy. (Wanna take the shortcut? Press Shift+F7, then type the letter **r** to choose Print.)

Now, you might want to stick around and leave that document on your screen as you move on to Lesson 4. But if you've had enough for the time being, you can exit WordPerfect using the same technique you used to exit earlier in this chapter. (Here's another shortcut. If you don't want to go through the menus, just press Home F7 to exit WordPerfect.)

Lesson 4: Controlling the Beast

Now I'd like to depart from the typing-and-editing tutorial to teach you some of the basics of getting along with WordPerfect. You might want to experiment with these techniques while you have WordPerfect up and running on your own screen.

Have It Your Way: Setting Up the Screen

WordPerfect offers three different ways to view your document while you're typing and editing:

Text mode   Only text appears on the screen. Graphic pictures, fonts, print attributes, and other things you'll learn about later are represented by colors and boxes.

Graphics mode   On computers that have EGA or VGA displays and sufficient memory, Graphics mode displays the document exactly as it will look when printed, but without the top and bottom margins.

Page mode   Page mode is the same as Graphics mode, but it displays the top and bottom margins.

Figure 1.4 shows a fancy document in Text mode. Figure 1.5 shows the same document in Graphics mode. You probably don't know how to create anything that fancy yet, but don't worry. I'm just showing you this fancy document so you can see the difference between Text mode and Graphics mode.

After comparing Figures 1.4 and 1.5, your first thought might be "Why would anyone want to use Text mode?" There are several answers to that question:

- It's exactly the same as earlier versions of WordPerfect, which several million people are already familiar with.

FIGURE 1.4

A fancy document in Text mode

```
 File  Edit  View  Layout  Tools  Font  Graphics  Window  Help




     This is one of those fake newsletters I use as an      answer soon. N
     example. The text here doesn't have anything to do     cell activity
     with the title. Some authors just fill in this part    feature only t
     with fake latin. But we can use this space to          whatsoever!
     wrestle with a profound universal question from           It's calle
     our own field.                                         be a better te
                                                            is no fast eas
     The Big Question
     The big question, that almost everyone asks about      Practical Matt
     computers is, "Why don't they just make comput-           Now, onto
     ers and programs simple, so anyone can use             writer knows,
     them?"                                                  truthful, and
         You want to know the answer to that question?      It's gotta be
     Really? Are you sure? OK then brace yourself,          people have to
     here it is... "Because they didn't create the whole    Readers, who a
 F:\PROJECTS\WP60\01-04.WP                               Doc 1 Pg 1 Ln 0.25" Pos 1"
```

FIGURE 1.5

The same document shown in Figure 1.4, but in Graphics mode. (You can see a full-page printed copy of this document in Chapter 28.)

File Edit View Layout Tools Font Graphics Window Help

American Fungiblist

This is one of those fake newsletters I use as an example. The text here doesn't have anything to do with the title. Some authors just fill in this part with fake latin. But we can use this space to wrestle with a profound universal question from our own field.

The Big Question

The big question, that almost everyone asks about computers is, "Why don't they just make computers and programs simple, so *anyone* can use them?"

You want to know the answer to that question? Really? Are you sure? OK then brace yourself, here it is... "Because they didn't create the whole technology just for you personally."

Oh the pain of truth. Reality rears its ugly head and faces us with the fact that there are other peo-

answer soon. Not to mention all the time and brain cell activity required to learn about some obscure feature only to discover that it's of no use to you whatsoever!

It's called being at the bottom (the *dregs* might be a better term) of the learning curve. And there is no fast easy cure.

Practical Matters

Now, onto more practical matters. As every writer knows, good writing is accurate, succinct, truthful, and above all, a certain number of words. It's gotta be a certain length because A) Production people have to fit it into some finite space and B) Readers, who always peek ahead, won't read it if they decide that it's too *many* words.

Word count isn't the only way to get stuff to fit on a page. You can use some of WordPerfect's

F:\PROJECTS\WP60\01-04.WP   Col 2 Doc 1 Pg 1 Ln 4.82" Pos 4.63"

- Text mode is by far the fastest for basic typing and editing (especially with documents that contain graphics).

- Not everyone has the kind of equipment it takes to use Graphics mode and have it work at a decent speed.

Choosing a View

HANDS ON!

Assuming your machine has what it takes to display any of WordPerfect's modes, here's how to switch from one to the other:

- Press Ctrl+F3, then choose either Text, Graphics, or Page by typing **t**, **g**, **p** or by clicking the option you want with your mouse.

- Or, press Alt+= or click the right mouse button. Then choose View by typing **v** or clicking that command. Next choose Text Mode, Graphics Mode, or Page Mode by typing **t**, **g**, or **a** or by clicking with your mouse.

Personalizing Your Screen

HANDS ON!

Figure 1.6 shows some optional doodads that you can use to simplify your work. I'll talk about how to use these things in Chapter 4. But for now, I'll just show you how to display them or hide them if they're in the way.

To display or hide a doodad and set up the screen to your liking, follow the steps below:

1. Press Alt+= or click the right mouse button to get to the menu bar.

2. Choose View (by clicking that command or typing **v**).

3. Choose Screen Setup (by clicking or typing **n**). You'll be taken to the Screen Setup dialog box (in Graphics mode), shown in Figure 1.7. (This example, like most in the book, is in Graphics mode.)

At this point, you just want to concern yourself with the two *option groups*: Screen Options and Window Options. Notice that within each option group there are several *check boxes*—hollow squares or squares with ×'s inside.

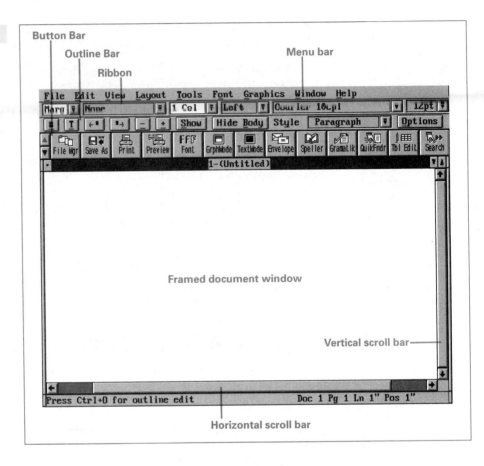

FIGURE 1.6

The WordPerfect screen in Graphics mode, with all the optional doodads displayed

To select (turn on) an option, you need to put an × in its check box. To clear (deselect or turn off) an option, you need to clear the × from its check box. Either way, here's what to do:

- Click the check box you want to select or clear.

- Or, type **s** to choose <u>S</u>creen options, then use the ↑ and ↓ keys to move the highlight (or outline box) from option to option within a group. To turn the option on or off, press the spacebar or type the underlined (or boldface) letter in the option name. When you're done choosing options within a group, press Tab.

- You can also type **w** to choose <u>W</u>indow options, then use the ↑, ↓, and spacebar keys to turn options on and off. You can also type the underlined (or boldface) letter in the option name.

FIGURE 1.7

The Screen Setup dialog box lets you choose which optional doodads you want to display on your screen. To get here, choose <u>V</u>iew from the menu bar, then choose Screen <u>S</u>etup.

- When you're finished with the Screen Setup dialog box, choose OK by clicking the OK button with your mouse or by pressing Tab until the OK button is highlighted (or framed) then pressing ↵.

You'll be returned to the *document window*—the place where you do your typing and editing—with the doodads you selected visible on the screen.

NOTE

If you select the <u>P</u>ull-Down Menus and <u>A</u>lt Key Activates Menus commands from the Screen Setup dialog box, you won't need to press Alt+= or click the right mouse button to display the menu bar. With these options selected, you can just press and release Alt to move the highlight into the menu bar or click any command using the left mouse button. There's more on this in Chapter 4.

Getting Help

HANDS ON!

When you need information on the spot, here's all you have to do:

- Press F1 (Help).
- Or, open the menu bar (Alt+=) and pull down the <u>H</u>elp menu (click <u>H</u>elp or type **h**).

If you press F1, WordPerfect will present its *context-sensitive* Help. With context-sensitive Help, the information that appears is relevant to whatever you were doing when you pressed F1. If you weren't doing anything special at the time, you'll be taken to the general Table of Contents for WordPerfect's Help system.

Your best bet is to explore the Help system on your own. Try the various options, and see if you can get the hang of using Help based on what it tells you on the screen. (You can also learn more about the Help system in Chapter 4.)

If you enter the Help system using the Help command in the menu bar rather than the F1 key, you'll see this drop-down menu:

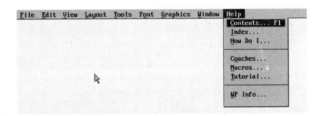

Choose any option by clicking or pressing the bold or underlined letter in the command you want. The Help options are summarized below:

Contents... Takes you to the Table of Contents for the Help system.

Index... Takes you to an index where you can use the mouse, arrow keys, and ⏎ key to look up a topic.

How Do I... Takes you to a list of procedures that answer the question "How do I...?" For example, the first option under Basics (Use Help) answers the question "How do I use Help?"

Coaches Like <u>H</u>ow Do I...? but better because it actually coaches you through the exact steps required to accomplish a task, even when you're working on a document of your own. This way, you can learn while you're getting real work done. *Definitely* worth a try!

N O T E

If you have trouble using the dialog boxes in Coaches, see "Getting Along with Dialog Boxes" in Chapter 2.

<u>M</u>acros... Describes advanced macro techniques. This one is for advanced users who know what macros are all about. If you don't know a macro from a mackerel, don't worry about it.

<u>T</u>utorial... Takes you to WordPerfect's hands-on workbook, where you can take lessons right at your keyboard.

<u>W</u>P Info... Takes you to a screen that displays the current version number, date, and other technical information about your computer and the WordPerfect program.

You can get around in the Help system by moving the highlight with the ↑, ↓, →, and ← keys, then pressing ↵ when the option you want is highlighted. Or, if you know how to use your mouse, you can double-click on any item, or click the item once then choose the <u>L</u>ook button.

The bottom of the Help window contains some command buttons to help you get around. You can click any button with your mouse to select it. Or, type the underlined (or boldfaced) letter on the command button you want to choose. In general, you can choose from among the following command buttons:

<u>N</u>ame Search Choose this option when you're in the Help Contents or Index if you want to type in a topic to look up.

<u>C</u>ontents Takes you to the Help Table of Contents.

C<u>o</u>aches Takes you to the Coaches section (described above).

<u>L</u>ook Takes you to the section or topic that's currently highlighted above the buttons.

Previous   Takes you to whatever Help screen you just left (if you left one).

Cancel   Takes you out of the Help system. (You can also choose the Cancel button by pressing Escape.)

The Help system is fairly self-explanatory, so I encourage you to explore it on your own and learn about it at your own convenience. If you need help working with the dialog boxes, please read "Getting Along with Dialog Boxes" in Chapter 2.

Getting Out of Help

The down side to online Help is that it temporarily covers up whatever you've been working on. You can get out of Help and return to your document by pressing Escape or clicking the Cancel button with your mouse. If a dialog box asks whether or not you're sure you want to exit Help or Coaches, choose Yes.

Lesson 5: Using the Rest of This Book

Believe it or not, what you've learned in these few lessons could very well be most of what you really need to know to get along with WordPerfect. "So then," you might ask "why are there about a jillion more pages after this one?"

Good question. The answer is that WordPerfect is a big program with lots of *options*. (Note the word "options"—as in "not mandatory.") You may find some of those options extremely handy from time to time. So this book is here to help when your work requirements, curiosity, or creative desires go beyond the basics you've already learned.

Finding What You Need

When you're learning to use WordPerfect, you need to know what's available, and you need answers to questions and solutions to problems as they arise. Otherwise, you'll end up doing everything the hard way. Therefore, I suggest the following course of action for using the rest of this book:

- Browse through the Table of Contents at the beginning of this book to get a general idea of what's in WordPerfect and what's in this book.

- When you have a specific problem or question, you might want to check out WordPerfect's online Help first, since it's right there on your screen. Or, check the index at the back of this book. Chances are, you'll find the answer you're looking for soon enough.

- Browse through this book and look at the pictures to get some good ideas or learn new tricks. The sample documents were created with the very same WordPerfect program you're using. (Of course, I did use fonts and clip art that I purchased separately, but the samples are WordPerfect documents nonetheless.)

- Last, but not least, read the Introduction at the front of this book. Many people skip introductions because they think they're just so much blathering. But in this kind of book, we authors generally use the Introduction to explain how the book is organized and how to use the book effectively.

The Five Commandments of WordPerfect

Figure 1.8 summarizes the rules of thumb you need to remember about typing and editing in WordPerfect. If you're new to word processing, maybe you should make a copy and keep it near the keyboard until you get the hang of things.

FIGURE 1.8

The Five Command-
ments of WordPerfect

Five Commandments of WordPerfect

I. Thou shalt start WordPerfect *before creating or editing a document, by typing* **wp←** *at the DOS prompt. Or, on my computer:*_____
_____ Chapter 2

II. Thou shalt not press ← when typing a paragraph *until I get to the very end of that paragraph — Chapter 2*

III. Thou shalt not use the Spacebar to indent. *Better to use Tab, Indent (F4), Center (Shift+F6), Flush Right (Alt+F6) and so forth — Chapter 5*

IV. Thou shalt position the cursor *using arrow keys or mouse button <u>before</u> typing or deleting text — Chapter 3*

V. Thou shalt save thy work often *using File ► Save. And also shalt remember to exit WordPerfect (Home F7) before turning off or rebooting the computer — Chapter 3*

from Alan **Simpson's**
Mastering WordPerfect 6.0 for DOS

WordPerfect Survival Guide

Figure 1.9 summarizes WordPerfect's most frequently used features. Many of these go beyond what we've covered in this chapter. When you need more information, just look up the topic in the index at the back of this book.

	Feature	*Shortcut or Menu*
B	Boldface	`CTRL`+`B` or F**o**nt ‣ **B**old
	Center	`SHIFT`+`F6`
	Columns	`ALT`+`F7` `C`
	Envelope	`ALT`+`F12` or Layout ‣ En**v**elope
	Erase	`DEL` or `←`
	Escape	`ESC`
	Exit WP	`F7` or **F**ile ‣ E**x**it WP
	File Manager	`F5` or **F**ile ‣ **F**ile Manager
	Flush-Right	`ALT`+`F6`
	Font	`CTRL`+`F8` or F**o**nt
	Full Justify	Layout ‣ **J**ustification ‣ **F**ull
	Help/Coach	`F1` / **H**elp ‣ **C**oaches
	Indent	`F4` or Layout ‣ **A**lignment
	Indent All	`SHIFT`+`F4`
	Indent First	`TAB`
I	Italic	`CTRL`+`I` or F**o**nt ‣ **I**talics
	Left Justify	Layout ‣ **J**ustification ‣ **L**eft
	Line Spacing	`SHIFT`+`F8` `L` `S`

FIGURE 1.9

WordPerfect 6.0 for DOS Survival Guide: the most frequently used keys and techniques (continued)

Feature	Shortcut or Menu
Margins	[SHIFT]+[F8] [M]
Move/Copy	Select text, Edit ▸ (option)
New Doc.	File ▸ New
Open Doc.	[SHIFT]+[F10] or File ▸ Open
Print Doc.	[SHIFT]+[F7] or File ▸ Print/Fax
Save Doc.	[CTRL]+[F12] or File ▸ Save
Screen Setup	View ▸ Screen Setup
Search	[F2] or Edit ▸ Search
Select Text	Drag or [ALT]+[F4] or [F12]
Special Char.	[CTRL]+[W]
Speller	[CTRL]+[F2]
Start WP	(from DOS) WP ↵
Tables	[ALT]+[F7] or Layout ▸ Tables
Undelete	[ESC] or Edit ▸ Undelete
Underline	[CTRL]+[U] or Font ▸ Underline
Undo	[CTRL]+[Z] or Edit ▸ Undo
Window	[F3] or Window ▸ (option)
Zoom	[CTRL]+[F3] or View ▸ Zoom

So What Can WordPerfect Really Do?

If you'd like to know where all of this is leading, what's under the hood, and what WordPerfect can *really* do, why not check out some of the sample documents in Chapters 7, 26, 27, and 28. If you're intimidated by them, don't be. They're a lot easier than they look. And besides, what do you care? All you really *need* to do is whatever your job requirements, curiosity, or creative needs demand. Right?

On the other hand, if you're really into it, and you want to create some dazzling documents, you've come to the right place. I don't think you'll be disappointed when we get into the more advanced stuff.

It's fun. So enjoy it already!

CHAPTER

2

Getting Around in WordPerfect

fast **TRACK**

IN THIS chapter and the next chapter, we'll look at basic skills and options in more depth. Feel free to breeze through the section headings and skip over any information you already know. Zero in on topics that seem confusing or unfamiliar to you.

Starting WordPerfect

If you took the guided tour in Chapter 1, you should now know how to start WordPerfect. But just in case you had problems there or you skipped that chapter, here's the standard routine:

1. Turn on your computer, monitor, and printer in the usual manner.

2. When you get to the DOS command prompt (typically C>) type **wp** and press ↵.

If you get a message like "Bad command or file name," try switching to WordPerfect's home directory first by following these steps:

1. Type **c:** then press ↵ (the Enter key).

2. Type **cd \wp60** then press ↵.

3. Type **wp** then press ↵.

If those steps don't work, either WordPerfect is not installed on your hard disk or you need to ask your local network manager or other know-it-all for alternative startup instructions.

NOTE If you're having startup problems and you *are* the local know-it-all, refer to Appendix A for startup switches that might help.

When you first start WordPerfect, a copyright notice will appear, followed by the WordPerfect Document window. The exact appearance of that screen depends on which display mode WordPerfect was in the last time someone exited it. You can easily choose the mode, as you'll learn a little later on in this chapter.

Opening a Document at Startup

If you want to start WordPerfect and open a previously saved file in one fell swoop, you can follow the **wp** command with a space and the name of the file you want to edit. For example, the command **wp myfirst.wp** starts WordPerfect and opens the document named MYFIRST.WP (if it exists).

Of course, once you're in WordPerfect you can open any document you want by selecting File then Open, pressing Shift+F10, or pressing F5 (you'll learn about these commands in Chapter 3). It's not *necessary* to open a document right at startup, though.

Using Your Keyboard

If this is the first time you've used a computer, you'll probably notice that the keyboard is different from that of a standard typewriter. The computer keyboard is divided into several areas: the function keys, typing keys, numeric keypad, and cursor-movement keys. Figure 2.1 illustrates some common computer keyboards.

FIGURE 2.1

Popular computer
keyboards

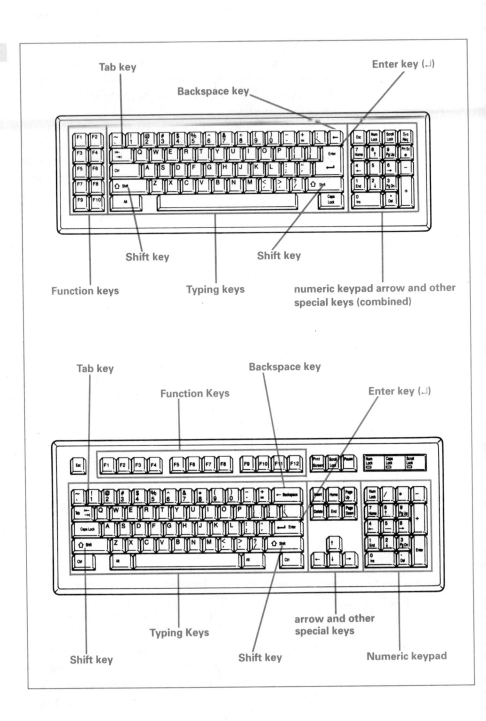

Figure 2.1 also points out the locations of the ↵ (Enter), Tab, Backspace, Escape, and Shift keys. Be aware that different keyboards use different symbols for some keys. For example, the ↵ key is sometimes labeled Enter or Return. Refer to the figure if you have trouble locating the ↵, Tab, Shift, Backspace, or Escape keys.

The Enter (↵) key, shown at left, is the computer's equivalent of the type-writer's carriage-return key. On some keyboards this key may be labeled simply ↵, Enter, or Return. In general the ↵ key is used to "inform" the computer when you've finished typing a line of text or to select a currently highlighted item.

As mentioned in Chapter 1, when typing in WordPerfect you use the ↵ key to end short lines of text, insert blank lines, and end paragraphs. You do not need to press ↵ to end each line of text within a paragraph, as you do with a typewriter.

The Escape key, as the name implies, is sort of a universal "Get me outta here" key. Usually, it lets you escape from the current situation back to wherever you just came from.

TIP Mouse users can also use the right mouse button as a "Cancel key."

In earlier versions of WordPerfect, the Cancel key (F1) played the role that's now played by the Escape key. WordPerfect actually lets you choose whether you want to use F1 or Escape as the Cancel key. I'll talk more about this later on in the chapter.

As you'll learn in Chapter 3, the arrows and other cursor-movement keys are useful for editing text. (They don't do anything until you actually have some text on your screen to edit.)

On many keyboards, the cursor-movement keys are independent of other keys. But on some laptops and older keyboards, the cursor-movement keys and numeric keypad are combined. In that case, the cursor-movement keys work only when the Num Lock key (shown at left) is turned "off" (and there's text to edit on the screen). In general, you'll want to keep

Num Lock off so you have ready access to the cursor-positioning keys. You can always use the numbers across the top of the keyboard instead of the numeric keypad.

Caps

The Caps Lock key (shown at left) works much like it does on most type-writers. When Caps Lock is on, letters are typed in uppercase. When Caps Lock is off, letters are typed in lowercase. The Caps Lock key has no effect on numbers or punctuation marks.

Shift

The Shift key (shown at left) serves the same purpose in WordPerfect as it does on a standard typewriter: It's used to type uppercase letters and special characters. For example, to type a single capital letter A, you hold down the Shift key, type the letter A, and then release the Shift key. To type an asterisk (*), hold down the Shift key and press the * key (the number 8).

The Shift key works in reverse when Caps Lock is turned on. That is, when Caps Lock is on, letters are typed in uppercase. If you hold down the Shift key when Caps Lock is on and then type a letter, that letter will appear in lowercase.

Tab

The Tab key (at left) plays the same role on the computer keyboard as it does on a typewriter: It indents to the next tab stop. Press Tab whenever you want to indent the first line of a new paragraph.

N O T E On some keyboards the Tab key is marked with two opposing arrows. Usually it's to the left of the Q.

The Tab key is also very useful for controlling other types of indentations and alignments. In general—and this is sort of a cardinal rule in word processing—you want to use the Tab key, rather than spaces, to do any kind of indenting. I'll discuss this in depth in Chapter 5.

The Backspace key (at left) lets you back up and make corrections as you type, much like the backspace key on a typewriter with correctable ribbon does. On many keyboards, the Backspace key does not have the word "Backspace" on it, but is marked only with an elongated ←. Backspace is typically located above the Enter key.

Don't confuse the Backspace key, which is in the typing-key area, with the ← key, which is one of the cursor-movement keys. The Backspace key erases text as the cursor backs up. The ← key simply moves the cursor backwards without erasing anything.

Typematic Keystrokes

All the computer's keys are *typematic*. This means you can repeat a keystroke simply by holding down the key. You can see this for yourself by holding down any letter key on the keyboard for a few seconds. To erase the letters you typed, hold down the Backspace key for a few seconds.

Key+key Combination Keystrokes

When you see two keystrokes separated by a plus sign (+), you need to *hold down the first key, tap the second key, then release the first key.* You don't need to hit the two keys at the same moment. For example, to press Alt+F1 you would hold down the first key (Alt), then tap the second key (the F1 function key), then release both keys.

Experimenting with combination keystrokes may bring up menus you aren't familiar with yet. If this happens, just press Escape to cancel the selection. As you may already know, combination keystrokes can often be used as shortcuts to the menus.

Using a Mouse

A mouse is optional with WordPerfect 6.0, so don't worry if you haven't got one attached to your computer. On the other hand, some tasks truly *are* easier with a mouse, and some super shortcuts are accessible *only* with a mouse. Furthermore, there is a general trend in the software industry toward applications that use mice. So if you don't already have a mouse, you might want to think about installing one on your system.

If you *do* have a mouse installed on your computer, here's how to use it: Place your hand on the mouse so that your index finger rests on (but doesn't hold down) the left mouse button, like this:

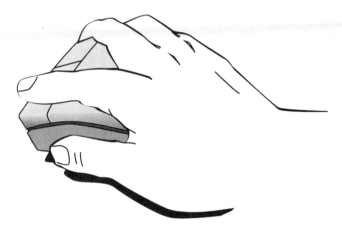

As you slowly roll the mouse around, you should see the mouse pointer on your WordPerfect screen move in the same direction. (The mouse works best if you roll it around on a rubber mouse pad instead of on a slick desk surface.)

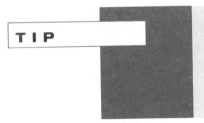

T I P

If the mouse pointer doesn't move around on your screen, see "Mouse Problems" in Appendix C. You can also use techniques described under "Customizing the Mouse" in Chapter 19 to fine-tune a working mouse to your liking.

In this book, I'll use the following standard mouse terminology:

Mouse pointer   The square or arrow that moves around on the screen as you roll the mouse on your desktop.

Mouse button Whichever button on the mouse works. Typically this is the button where your index finger naturally rests—the button on the left if you're right-handed.

Click To *click* an item, move the mouse pointer to that item on the screen, and then press and release the mouse button.

Double-click To double-click an item, move the mouse pointer to the item on the screen, and then press and release the mouse button twice in rapid succession (as fast as you can: *click click!*).

Drag To *drag* an item on the screen, move the mouse pointer to the item, *hold down* the mouse button, roll the mouse to drag to some other location, then release the mouse button.

Right-click To right-click an item, move the mouse pointer to the item and click the button on the right if you normally use the left mouse button; click the button on the left if you normally use the right mouse button.

Using the Menus

Like menus in a restaurant, the *menus* in WordPerfect, present you with choices. The options on the menus (called *commands*) tell WordPerfect to do something. When the *menu bar* is active, you'll see commands listed across the top of the screen, something like this:

File Edit View Layout Tools Font etc...

You can activate the menu bar and choose commands using either the mouse or the keyboard.

Choosing Menu Commands

Mouse To choose menu commands with the mouse, follow these steps:

1. If the menu bar isn't already visible, click the right mouse button to activate the menu bar.

2. Click whichever command you want to choose.

If you make a mistake and want to back up, click the right mouse button or press the Escape key or Alt key.

Keyboard If you prefer to use the keyboard rather than the mouse, you can select menu commands like this:

- If the menu bar isn't already visible, press Alt+= (hold down the Alt key, tap the = key, then release both keys).

- Type the highlighted or underlined letter of the option you want (such as the F in File). Or, use the ←, →, ↑, or ↓ keys to move the highlight to the option you want, then press ↵ to select that option.

- If the menu bar is already visible, you need not press Alt+= to display it. Instead, hold down the Alt key and type the highlighted or underlined letter of the command you want. For example, if the menu bar is already visible, you can press Alt+F to open the File menu.

Changing Your Mind

When you're first learning to use WordPerfect, you may choose commands that lead you to other commands, that you don't understand. To back up into familiar territory, try any of the following techniques:

- Click the right mouse button to cancel the command.

- Press Escape until you get back to familiar territory.

- Press and release the Alt key to deactivate the menus.

What's on the Menu?

When you open a menu, it will look something like the example shown below (depending on whether you're in Graphics mode or Text mode):

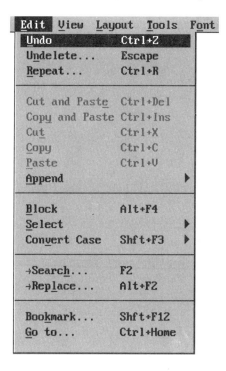

Menus also provide information about alternative shortcuts and what to expect next. Here's a summary of what you'll find in a typical menu:

... This symbol next to a command indicates that selecting the command will take you to a *dialog box*. (Dialog boxes are described a little later in this chapter.)

Key **name** A key name (such as Escape or F3) or a combination keystroke (such as Ctrl+F5) next to a menu command is the shortcut for activating that command. For example, instead of choosing Undo from the Edit menu, you can just press Ctrl+Z.

Dimmed Commands Any dimmed commands on the menu aren't relevant to the current situation and therefore can't be selected.

✓ or *   A check mark or asterisk to the left of a command indicates that the command is a *toggle*, and it is currently "on."
(Toggle commands can either be on or off. Choosing the command changes it to the opposite setting.)

▶   This symbol next to a command means that choosing that
command will take you to another menu.

What's That ➤ Symbol For?

In this book I use the ➤ symbol to separate a series of commands you select from the menus. For example,

Choose Tools ➤ Writing Tools ➤ Document Info or press Alt+F1 D

means the same thing as

Open the Tools menu, choose Writing Tools, then choose Document Info from the next menu. If you prefer, you can press Alt+F1
and then press D as a shortcut.

This shortcut notation is just easier to read. Note that the underlined letter in each command is the same as the *hotkey* (or shortcut key combination) that appears in the menu. You can use any of the mouse or keyboard
methods described earlier in this chapter to choose menu commands. The
choice is a matter of personal preference, and you should feel free to use
whichever method is most comfortable for you.

If you just did those menu commands listed above, you're now at the
Document Information dialog box. You can ignore the information in this
dialog box for now. Just press Escape or click the OK button to leave the
Document Information dialog box.

Text, Graphics, and Page Modes

Perhaps the most important new capability of WordPerfect 6.0 is that you
can work with your documents in any one of three different modes: Text
mode, Graphics mode, and Page mode.

Text Mode

Experienced WordPerfect users are familiar with Text mode. In Text mode, only text appears on the screen (no graphics are displayed). This display is the fastest to work with, but it shows font attributes as colored characters and graphics merely as boxes. Figure 2.2 shows a sample document in Text mode.

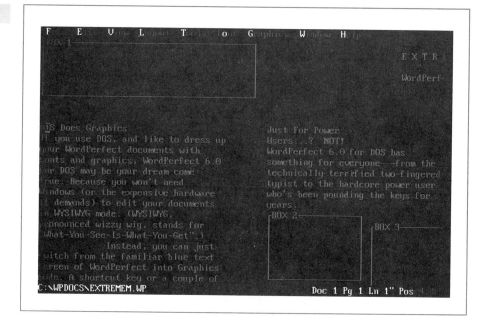

Graphics Mode

Graphics mode and Page mode offer *WYSIWYG* (pronounced "wizzy wig," short for "What You See Is What You Get"). This means that the screen looks like the printed output, right down to the fonts and graphics. Figure 2.3 shows the same document that appears in Figure 2.2, but in Graphics mode rather than Text mode.

Experienced WordPerfect users might compare Graphics mode to the old View Document mode. The difference is that you can actually edit your document in Graphics mode.

FIGURE 2.3

The sample document shown in Figure 2.2 after switching to Graphics mode

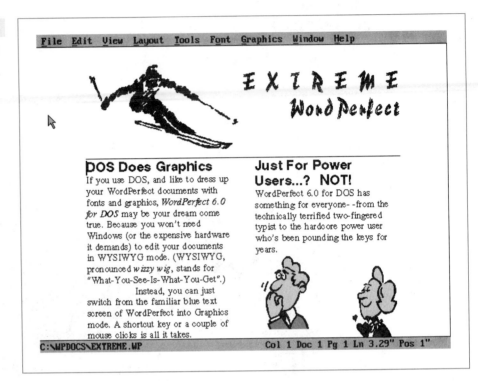

Page Mode

Page Mode is the same as Graphics mode, but it displays top and bottom margins, headers and footers (if there are any), and other page design elements. (See Chapter 4 for more about Page mode.)

Switching between Text and Graphic Modes

It's easy to switch from one mode to the other. Use either of these techniques:

- Choose <u>V</u>iew from the menu bar, then choose <u>T</u>ext mode, <u>G</u>raphics mode, or P<u>a</u>ge Mode—whichever you prefer.

- Press Ctrl+F3, then choose Text, Graphics, or Page from the Display Mode section of the Screen dialog box. (This is the fastest technique.)

Choosing a Display Mode

Whether you use Text, Graphics, or Page mode depends on your equipment, what you're doing at the moment, and your personal taste. Text mode looks just like earlier versions of WordPerfect, so you might like it just because it's familiar. Text mode is also noticeably faster than Graphics or Page mode.

The Graphics and Page modes, though slower, do have the advantage of letting you see, as you work, what your document will look like when printed. But to use Graphics or Page mode, you need about 520 KB of RAM available, and at least an EGA or VGA graphics adapter and monitor.

Getting Along with Dialog Boxes

In addition to showing you menus, WordPerfect will present dialog boxes from time-to-time. In a dialog box, you "complete the dialog" by making choices and then choosing OK. Figure 2.4 shows a sample dialog box with some of the types of *controls* pointed out.

Moving within a Dialog Box

If you're accustomed to DOS, you'll probably be tempted to use the ↵ key and the arrow keys to move from item to item in a dialog box. However, the ↵ key usually completes the dialog and then *closes* the dialog box!

T I P

In general, it's easier to get along with dialog boxes if you use a mouse rather than the keyboard.

FIGURE 2.4

A sample dialog box in Graphics mode

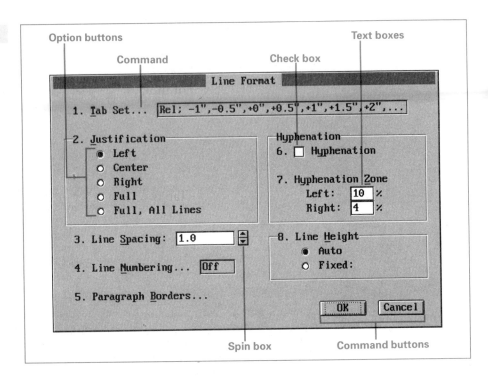

Here's a rundown of the keys you can use to navigate within a dialog box:

Tab, Shift+Tab	Moves from one command (control) to the next
→, ↓, ↑, ↓	Moves through options within a group (if the highlight is within a group)
Spacebar	Toggles a check box on and off
↵	Selects the currently highlighted option—usually the OK command button, which saves current settings and closes the dialog box

The following sections explain how to use each type of control in more detail. Some examples of the controls appear in the margin.

Text Boxes

A text box in a dialog box accepts text. Typically, you need to type in text (or a number). Use one of the methods below to change the contents of a text box:

- Click the text box. To *replace* the entire contents, type new text. To change the current contents, click where you want to make changes, then type.

- Press Tab or Shift+Tab until the text box is highlighted. Then, to replace the contents of the text box, just type. To change the contents, position the cursor using ← or → keys, then type.

N O T E   In Text mode, a text box looks like a large empty box that you type into.

Many of the general editing techniques described in Chapter 3—such as selecting (blocking), inserting, deleting, and overwriting text—work when you're in a text box, as do keys like Home and End. If in doubt, try it out.

Entering Measurements

Though we often say that measurements are in *inches,* you can choose a different unit of measurement by typing the number followed by one of the letters or symbols below:

LETTER OR SYMBOL	MEANING
"	inches
i	inches
c	centimeters
m	millimeters
p	points

LETTER OR SYMBOL	MEANING
w	1200ths of an inch
u	WordPerfect 4.2 units (line and column number)

For example, to enter a measurement of 10 points, you'd type **10p**.

If you omit the letter or symbol following the measurement, WordPerfect will use the default unit of measurement (which is usually " for inches). You can use the File ➤ Setup ➤ Environment command to change the default unit of measurement (Chapter 19).

Option Buttons

Option buttons represent mutually exclusive options. You can select only one of the options in a group. Option buttons are sometimes called "radio buttons" because, as in a car radio, selecting one of the buttons automatically deselects the previously selected button. Use one of these methods to choose an option button:

- Click the option you want.

- Type the highlighted or underlined letter that identifies the option group, or press Tab or Shift+Tab until that group name is highlighted. Then use the arrow keys to highlight the option you want. Press the spacebar or Tab to move out of the group.

Alternatively, you can press ↵ to select the highlighted option and close the dialog box.

N O T E

In Text mode, option buttons are represented by a pair of parentheses. They look like this ( ) when deselected, like this (■) when selected.

Check Boxes

A check box can have one of two possible values: *selected* (the check box contains an ×) or *deselected* (the check box does not contain an ×). Unlike option buttons, check boxes are *not* mutually exclusive, even when they're grouped together. Here's how to select or deselect a check box:

- Click the check box.
- Or, press Tab or Shift+Tab until the check box option is highlighted, then press the spacebar to select or deselect the option.

N O T E   In Text mode, a deselected check box looks like this [ ] and a selected check box looks like [X].

Spin Boxes

A spin box is similar to a text box that contains a number. However, the spin box has two small arrows next to it. There are two ways to work a spin box:

- Click the ▲ button to increase the value in the box; click the ▼ button to decrease the value.
- Press Tab or Shift+Tab until the spin box is highlighted, then type in a new number.

N O T E   In Text mode, a spin box has these ▲ and ▼ characters just to the right of the number. You can click on either small arrow.

Drop-Down Lists

Some text boxes will have a drop-down list button to one side, as in the example shown at left. With these text buttons, you can either type an entry into the text box or choose an option from the drop-down list. Use either of these methods to open the drop-down list:

- Click the drop-down list button.

- Click in the text box or press Tab or Shift+Tab until the cursor lands in the text box or the text box is highlighted, then press ↓.

In Text mode, a drop-down list button looks like this: ↓.

Once the list appears, you can use the PgUp, PgDn, ↑, and ↓ keys to scroll through the list and highlight an item in the list. Then you can click that option or press ↵ to select that item from the list. (You can also scroll through the list using the *scroll bars*, which I'll describe in a moment.)

In some lists, you can type the first letter(s) of an item in the list to highlight that item quickly.

Pop-Up Lists

You'll notice that some command buttons have up- and down-pointing triangles on them. (In Text mode, the character looks like this ↕.) These are pop-up lists. To activate a pop-up, use one of the following methods:

- Click the pop-up list button, *keep the mouse button depressed*, drag the highlight to the option you want, then release the mouse button.

- Press Tab or Shift+Tab until the option is highlighted, then press ↵ to open the list. Or, click on the option or type its underlined or highlighted letter. Then click on the option you want, or use the ↑ and ↓ keys to highlight an item and press ↵ to select the item.

Scroll Bars

Scroll bars let you scroll to areas that aren't currently visible on the screen. They work only when there's more information available than can

fit on the screen at one time. To use the scroll bars, pick one of the following techniques:

- Click the ↑ button at the top of the scroll bar to scroll up one line at a time; click the ↓ button at the bottom of the scroll bar to scroll down.

- Drag the scroll box (the lighter portion) up or down the bar to wherever you want the scroll box to move.

- Click the darker portion of the scroll bar to scroll one "boxfull" at a time.

N O T E If you're using the keyboard, use the PgUp, PgDn, arrow, and other cursor-movement keys described in Chapter 3 to move around the list or document.

Scroll bars within dialog boxes are displayed automatically. But scroll bars for the entire document appear only if you've selected the Horizontal Scroll Bar and Vertical Scroll Bar commands from the View menu (see Chapters 3 and 4).

N O T E In Text mode, vertical scroll bars have ↑ and ↓ symbols on the ends; horizontal scroll bars have ← and → symbols.

Commands...

Any command in a dialog box that's followed by ... leads to another dialog box. To select that command, you can

- Click the command

- Type the highlighted number next to the command

- Press the highlighted or underlined letter

- Press Tab or Shift+Tab until the option you want is highlighted, then press ↵.

Command Buttons

Command buttons usually appear along the bottom of a dialog box:

These are simple to operate:

- Click the command button you want.

- Or, press Tab or Shift+Tab until the button you want is highlighted, then press ↵ to select the button.

- You can typically press Escape as a shortcut to selecting the Cancel key, or press ↵ to select the OK key.

- If the command button has a shortcut key name on it, you can press the shortcut key.

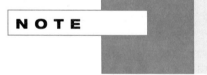

NOTE   In Text mode, command buttons appear as colored or highlighted rectangles without the raised 3-D appearance.

Saving and Abandoning Dialog Box Selections

Most dialog boxes have an OK command button and/or a Cancel command button, usually located somewhere near the bottom. Here's the difference between these buttons:

OK   If you choose OK, choices you made in the dialog box will be activated, and WordPerfect will proceed with the initial command.

Cancel The Cancel button lets you "bail out" of a dialog box without activating any changes.

T I P

If you ever get confused while using a dialog box (or you get to a dialog box that you don't understand), use the Cancel button (or Escape key) to back out gracefully. You can exit any dialog box and save your changes by pressing F7.

Getting Instant Help

Thanks to WordPerfect's online Help system, this book isn't your only source of information about the application. In fact, you have access to *tons* of information right on your screen. The trick is knowing where to find the information you're looking for.

Getting Context-Sensitive Help

A good starting point for getting quick information is to press the F1 key. This will bring up *context-sensitive* help. Context-sensitive help provides help with whatever you happen to be doing at the time you press F1. If you have a document open but you're not actually doing anything with it, you'll be taken to the Help Contents, which is a Table of Contents for the WordPerfect Help system.

N O T E

If your copy of WordPerfect is configured for WordPerfect 5.1 keystrokes, pressing F1 will do nothing. You need to press F3 instead. See "Defining F1, F3, and Escape," later in this chapter, for more information.

When you've gotten the information you need from the Help screen, and you're ready to return to whatever you were doing before you pressed F1,

- Click the Cancel button near the lower-right corner of the screen...
- Or, press the Escape key (once).

Getting More General Help

If the context-sensitive Help screen doesn't give you the information you're looking for, or you're not even sure how to begin getting help, you can go to the Help Contents using either of these techniques:

- If you haven't already entered the Help system, press F1 or choose Help ➤ Contents from the menu bar.
- If you're already in a Help window, choose the Contents command button near the bottom of the Help window.

You'll be taken to the Help Contents window shown in Figure 2.5. Notice that this window contains certain boldfaced (or brightened) words and a number of command buttons.

The words in bold are called *jump words* because they lead to other topics. There are several ways to choose a jump word:

- Double-click the jump word.
- Click the jump word, then click the Look command button.
- Use the arrow keys to highlight the jump word you want, then press ↵.

After choosing a jump word, you'll be taken to the next Help screen. From there, you can

- Choose another jump word to keep going.
- Choose the Previous command button to return to the previous screen.
- Press Escape or choose the Cancel command button to leave the Help system and return to your work.

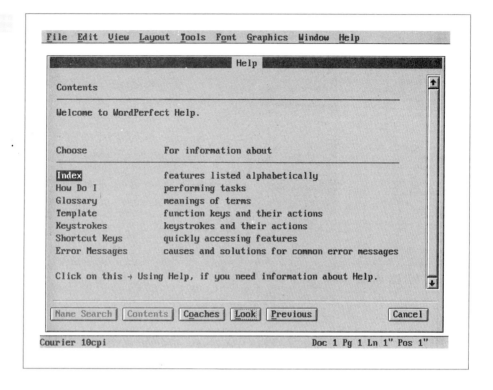

Here's a quick summary of the other options available from the Help Contents screen:

Index   Provides an index, similar to one you might find at the back of a book. Scroll or use the Name Search command button to look up a word.

How Do I   Lists topics by the type and name of common tasks.

Glossary   Defines terms. (When you see an underlined word in any Help screen, you can double-click that word, or highlight it and press ↵ or the spacebar, to view its glossary definition.)

Template   Presents a function key template indicating the roles of the various function keys.

Keystrokes   Lists the functions of various special keys and control-key combinations.

Shortcut Keys   Lists common shortcut keys.

Error Messages   Lists causes and solutions for common error messages.

Using Help   Teaches you how to use the Help system.

Exiting Help

In order to continue working on your document, you'll need to exit Help. Just press Escape, or choose the Cancel button at the bottom of any Help window, to exit Help and return to your document.

Built-In Coaches

You'll notice a button titled Coaches at the bottom of the Help window. Coaches guide you through every step of an operation—just like an infinitely patient flesh-and-blood teacher. They'll even demonstrate an operation (just choose the *Show Me* button when it's available) and then let you do it. To use a coach, click the Coach button, or choose Help ➤ Coaches from the pull-down menus. Select the coach you want from the list that appears and follow the instructions. You'll be an expert in no time flat.

Checking the Version Number

Keep in mind that this book is specifically about Version 6 of WordPerfect for DOS. If you use several different computers and you want to make sure that you're using Version 6 of WordPerfect at any given time, just follow these steps:

1. Starting at the menu bar, choose Help ➤ WP Info.

2. The first entry, next to Version, should be (at least) WP 6.0. (If it's not, you're using an earlier version of WordPerfect, and features described in Appendix C will not be available to you. You can purchase an upgrade to Version 6.0 through your local computer dealer or WordPerfect Corporation.)

3. Click the OK button, or press ↵, to leave the WP Info dialog box.

Fine-Tuning WordPerfect

Figure 2.6 shows some optional tools that you can turn on and off as you wish. All these tools will be discussed in more detail in Chapter 4. For now, here's how you can turn them on and off.

- If you want the menu bar to be visible always, so you don't have to right-click or press Alt+= to display it, choose <u>V</u>iew ➤ <u>P</u>ull-Down Menus.

- The Ribbon offers mouse shortcuts for many common tasks. To turn the Ribbon on or off, choose <u>V</u>iew ➤ <u>R</u>ibbon.

FIGURE 2.6

You can turn these optional tools on and off using commands on the View menu.

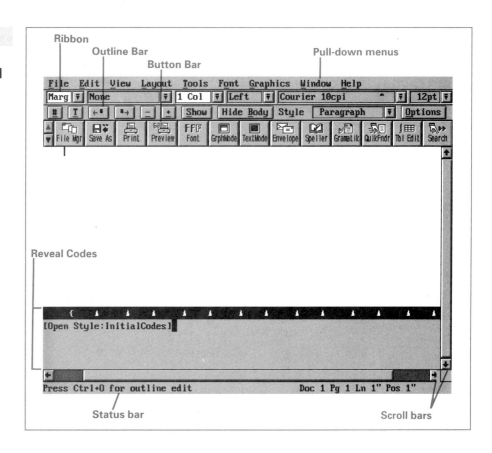

- The Outline Bar offers handy tools for working with outlines. Choose <u>V</u>iew ➤ <u>O</u>utline Bar to turn it on or off.

- To hide or display the Button Bar, choose <u>V</u>iew ➤ <u>B</u>utton Bar. You can click buttons on the Button Bar instead of choosing menu options.

- To turn the Reveal Codes window on or off, choose <u>V</u>iew ➤ Reveal <u>C</u>odes, or press Alt+F3.

- To turn scroll bars on or off, choose <u>V</u>iew ➤ <u>H</u>orizontal Scroll Bar and/or <u>V</u>iew ➤ <u>V</u>ertical Scroll Bar.

You can change the magnification by choosing <u>V</u>iew ➤ <u>Z</u>oom, then selecting a magnification, or by choosing a magnification from the Ribbon. I'll talk more about these tools in Chapter 4 (except for the Outline Bar, which I'll cover in Chapter 14).

Fine-Tuning the Menus

Here are two tips that might help you reach the menu bar more easily:

- You can choose <u>V</u>iew ➤ <u>P</u>ull-Down Menus to leave the menu visible on the screen at all times. From then on, you can just click whatever option you want, or hold down the Alt key and type the highlighted letter to open a menu. For example, pressing Alt+F will open the File menu.

- If you want to activate the menu bar simply by pressing Alt, rather than Alt+=, choose <u>V</u>iew ➤ Scree<u>n</u> Setup. Then select the Alt Key Activates Menus check box. From then on you can just press and release the Alt key when you want to activate or deactivate the menu bar.

Defining F1, F3, and Escape

In most DOS and Windows programs, the F1 key calls up the Help system. Early versions of WordPerfect, however, used the F3 key to access Help. They also used the F1 key for Cancel and the Escape key for Repeat. All this can become rather confusing, particularly if you use several different programs.

You can indicate which standard you want your copy of WordPerfect to use by following these steps:

1. Choose File ➤ Setup ➤ Environment.

2. To use the older WordPerfect standard, select WordPerfect 5.1 Keyboard (see Table 2.1). Otherwise, deselect that option.

3. Choose OK.

TABLE 2.1: Old and New WordPerfect Standards for F1, F3, and Escape

KEY	NEW STANDARD	OLD STANDARD
F1	Help	Cancel
F3	Switch to Document	Help
Escape	Cancel	Repeat

Before Shutting Down...

You should always remember to exit WordPerfect and, if necessary, save your work before turning off your computer. If you forget to do this, you'll probably keep losing your documents, which means that you'll waste a lot of time duplicating work you've already done. To exit WordPerfect, follow the steps below:

1. Choose File ➤ Exit WP, or press Home, then F7.

2. If WordPerfect prompts you, select which document(s) you want to save (see Chapter 3 for more information on saving documents and assigning valid file names).

3. Choose Exit or, if you're saving, choose Save And Exit.

You'll be returned to the DOS command prompt (or wherever you were when you first started WordPerfect).

Logging Off from a Network

If your computer is connected to a network, your network administrator might request that you always log off before turning off your computer. Ask the administrator for the logging off command.

One Last Tiny Bit of Insurance

The safest time to turn off your computer is after you've tested to make sure you haven't temporarily exited (shelled out) to DOS. If you enter the EXIT command and see only the DOS prompt again after pressing ↵, then you know it's a safe time to turn off your machine.

In this chapter I've covered some of the absolute basics of getting along with WordPerfect, and with your computer in general. For a quick overview of important techniques covered here, refer to the Fast Track at the beginning of the chapter.

CHAPTER

3

Opening, Editing, Printing, and Saving Documents

fast TRACK

IN Chapter 1's guided tour of WordPerfect 6.0, you learned the basics of creating, printing, and saving a document. In this chapter, we're going to look first at how to open a previously saved document so you can work on it some more or print it again. Then we'll take a closer look at techniques for typing, editing, and saving documents.

Opening (Retrieving) a Document

When you want to work on a document that you've previously saved and closed, the first thing you need to do is to open that document. Start WordPerfect, then follow these steps:

1. Choose File ➤ Open (or press Shift+F10). You'll see a dialog box similar to this one:

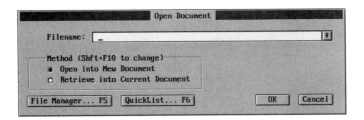

2. Type the name of the file exactly as you typed it when you first saved it (for example, type **myfirst.wp**). Then press ↵ or choose OK. (If you prefer, you can click the drop-down list button or press ↓ for a list of recently saved files. If you see the name of the file you want to open, double-click it, or highlight it and press ↵.)

Assuming you've spelled the file name correctly (don't worry about upper- and lowercase letters), and nobody has deleted or moved the file, the document should appear on your screen, ready for editing.

N O T E   If you have any problems opening a file, or you get a "Read Only" message, see "File Problems" in Appendix C.

Picking Up Where You Left Off

If you want to move the cursor back to wherever you left off when you last saved the file, just press Ctrl+F (Find QuickMark). For more information about this command, refer to the section on bookmarks in Chapter 9.

Differences among New, Open, and Retrieve

You may notice that the File menu includes three options that appear to have something to do with opening and creating files: New, Open, and Retrieve. Here are the basic differences among those three commands:

File ➤ New   Opens a new, blank *document window* for creating a new document from scratch. By default, this new document is named "(Untitled)".

File ➤ Open   Copies a previously saved document from disk into a new document window on the screen. The file is not combined with any other open documents.

File ➤ Retrieve   Copies a previously saved document from the disk into the *current* document, at the place where the cursor was positioned when you chose the command. Use File ➤ Retrieve to combine the two documents.

Actually, the only difference between Open and Retrieve is that Open preselects Open Into A New Document and Retrieve preselects Retrieve Into Current Document in the dialog box that appears after the selection.

You can change your mind while you're in that dialog box by pressing Shift+F10 or clicking the option you want.

If you start to lose track of which documents are open and which are closed, you can choose Window ➤ Cascade to cascade, or stagger, the windows and see all their titles. I'll talk more about managing document windows in Chapter 4.

Typing with WordPerfect

Typing with WordPerfect is almost identical to typing with a typewriter. There are four main differences:

- In WordPerfect, avoid using the letter *l* in place of the number *1*, and avoid using the letter *O* in place of the number *0*. These characters are not the same to a computer, nor do they look the same when displayed by most printers.

- In WordPerfect's Text mode, you cannot see the left and right margins on your screen. However, they'll be there when you print the document. You need not indent text at the start of each line to create a margin.

- When you want to indent a line, paragraph, title, or anything else in WordPerfect, *don't* use the spacebar. If you do, your printed text might come out incorrectly aligned. Instead use Tab, Center (Shift+F6), Flush Right (Alt+F6), or other indenting commands (these are described in Chapter 5).

- As you type past the right margin on your screen, WordPerfect automatically *word-wraps* text to the next line. You should press the ↵ key only to end a short line that does not reach the right margin, to end a paragraph, or to add a blank line.

This last point is perhaps the hardest one for experienced typists to get used to. It's important to let WordPerfect handle the right margins automatically, and not press ↵ until you've finished typing a paragraph. This gives you maximum flexibility to add, change, or delete words or sentences in the middle of the paragraph later.

If you want to add a blank line between paragraphs, press ↵ *twice* at the end of each paragraph. If you press the ↵ key accidentally and catch the mistake right away, just press the Backspace key once for each ↵ you typed.

To illustrate, Figure 3.1 shows a sample printed business letter typed with WordPerfect. Figure 3.2 shows the same letter, with symbols indicating where you would press ↵ while typing that document. (The ↵ symbols normally won't show up on your screen or on the printed copy.)

FIGURE 3.1

A sample business letter

```
August 7, 1993


Sidney R. Jackson, M.D.
Bayside Medical Group
5231 East Statton Drive, Suite 106
Los Angeles, CA 92312


Dear Dr. Jackson:

The update on your insurance policy is as follows. I am including
a letter from the Regional Manager of Farmstead regarding the
information specific to your occupational and medical concerns.
Pending receipt of a referral letter from your previous doctor,
this letter serves as an important part of your policy and should
be safeguarded with your other documents.

I have turned over your policy to a full-time insurance agent,
Bastien Cole. He will be able to serve you more adequately and
provide the detailed information you may need for your specific
problems. This will also allow me to relinquish my commissions in
order to better serve you in a consultant capacity. In the
meantime, however, you do have coverage in effect.

As indicated earlier by phone, I will be out of town for the next
three weeks. Should you have any questions, please feel free to
leave a message for me at my Florida office. I will be in contact
with them daily for messages. Rest assured that I hope to
continue to be of service to you.

Sincerely,



Edna R. Jones, M.D.

ERJ:ess

cc: Bastien Cole
```

FIGURE 3.2

↵ symbols show when you would press Enter while typing the letter—at the ends of short lines, at the ends of paragraphs, and wherever you want a blank line to appear.

```
August 7, 1993 ↵
↵
↵
Sidney R. Jackson, M.D. ↵
Bayside Medical Group ↵
5231 East Statton Drive, Suite 106 ↵
Los Angeles, CA 92312 ↵
↵
↵
Dear Dr. Jackson: ↵
↵
The update on your insurance policy is as follows. I am including
a letter from the Regional Manager of Farmstead regarding the
information specific to your occupational and medical concerns.
Pending receipt of a referral letter from your previous doctor,
this letter serves as an important part of your policy and should
be safeguarded with your other documents. ↵
↵
I have turned over your policy to a full-time insurance agent,
Bastien Cole. He will be able to serve you more adequately and
provide the detailed information you may need for your specific
problems. This will also allow me to relinquish my commissions in
order to better serve you in a consultant capacity. In the
meantime, however, you do have coverage in effect. ↵
↵
As indicated earlier by phone, I will be out of town for the next
three weeks. Should you have any questions, please feel free to
leave a message for me at my Florida office. I will be in contact
with them daily for messages. Rest assured that I hope to
continue to be of service to you. ↵
↵
Sincerely, ↵
↵
↵
↵
↵
Edna R. Jones, M.D. ↵
↵
ERJ:ess ↵
↵
cc: Bastien Cole ↵
```

TIP

If you accidentally press ↵ at the end of a line, or you import a non-WordPerfect file that's formatted with ↵ characters at the end of each line, you may be able to use WordPerfect's Search and Replace feature to fix things up in a matter of seconds (see Chapter 9).

How Big Can My Document Be?

Don't let the size of the WordPerfect document window fool you into thinking that you can create only small documents. This entire book was created with WordPerfect, and it's far from being small! WordPerfect automatically *scrolls* text to give you more room when you need it.

You can easily review and change text that is scrolled out of view by using the mouse or the various scrolling keys, such as ↑, ↓, Page Up (PgUp), and Page Down (PgDn). I'll describe these and other scrolling keys in a moment.

Large, but Not *Too* Large...

One word of advice—the larger a document is, the longer it will take WordPerfect to perform basic operations like printing, saving, checking spelling, and so forth. Therefore, if you plan to create a *really* big document, like a book, it's best to treat each individual chapter or portion as a separate document. You can then use WordPerfect's Master Document feature (explained in Chapter 32) to combine the documents temporarily for page numbering, indexing, and so forth.

Moving the Cursor

When you type new text into a document, WordPerfect places that new text at the *cursor*, or *insertion point*—the small, blinking line that appears in the document. The first step to learning how to edit existing text is learning how to place the cursor at the point where you want to make changes. You can use the mouse, the keyboard, or both to position the cursor.

NOTE Before I explain how to move the cursor, keep in mind that I'm talking about working within a document that already contains text. In addition, be aware that the mouse and the cursor-positioning keys cannot move the cursor beyond the end of a document. If you need to move the cursor past the end of the text in a document, you can use the spacebar, Tab, and ↵ keys to insert spaces, tabs, and blank lines into the document.

Mouse Typing takes place at the position of the cursor, not at the position of the mouse pointer. Therefore, you must position the mouse pointer and *click* to move the cursor to a particular place in the document.

Use the scroll bars at the edge of the document window to move your mouse pointer beyond the visible portion of the document. (If the scroll bars aren't visible, choose View ➤ Vertical Scroll Bar and/or View ➤ Horizontal Scroll Bar.)

Keyboard You can also use the cursor-positioning keys listed in Table 3.1 to move the cursor within text. If you want to use the keys on the numeric keypad, Num Lock must be turned off (see Chapter 2).

NOTE If you press ← or → and the cursor does not move, or moves erratically, don't worry. It's not a malfunction: WordPerfect is moving the cursor through hidden codes that aren't currently visible. I'll discuss these codes in Chapter 4. Just press or hold down the arrow key until the cursor moves where you want it.

TABLE 3.1: Keys for Positioning the Cursor (Standard Configuration)

TO MOVE...	USE THIS KEY...
Right one character	→
Left one character	←
Up one line	↑
Down one line	↓
Next word	Ctrl+→
Previous word	Ctrl+←
Start of line	Home Home ←
End of line	Home Home → or End
Next paragraph	Ctrl+↓
Previous paragraph	Ctrl+↑
Top of screen	Home ↑ or Gray - key on numeric keypad
Bottom of screen	Home ↓ or Gray + key on numeric keypad
Next page	PgDn
Previous page	PgUp
Top of document (under codes)	Home Home ↑
Top of document (above codes)	Home Home Home ↑
End of document	Home Home ↓
To a specific character or page	Go To (Ctrl+Home)
To a specific word or phrase	Edit ➤ Search (F2) (see Chapter 9)
To a QuickMark bookmark	Ctrl+F (see Chapter 9)

N O T E

If you have any problems with the keys listed in Table 3.1, first make sure that you're not using the old-style cursor-positioning keys. Choose File ➤ Setup ➤ Environment, and make sure that WordPerfect 5.1 Cursor Movement, is deselected.

Repeating a Keystroke

You can repeat any keystroke simply by holding the key down for a while. To repeat a keystroke a specific number of times, follow the steps below:

1. Choose Edit ➤ Repeat, or press Ctrl+R (or Escape if you've selected WordPerfect 5.1 Keyboard (F1=Cancel) in the Environment dialog box. You'll see this dialog box:

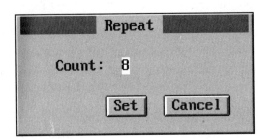

2. Type a number indicating how many times you want to repeat the next keystroke.

3. Press any cursor-positioning key.

For example, suppose that you're in a large document, and you want to move the cursor down 20 pages. Rather than pressing PgDn 20 times, you could just press Ctrl+R, type 20, then press PgDn.

Using Go To

Another way to move the cursor in your document is to use the Go To dialog box:

1. Choose Edit ➤ Go To, or press Ctrl+Home.

2. Type any one of the following:

- Type a character to move to that character (for example, type a period to move to the end of the current sentence).
- Type a number and then press ↵ to go to a specific page (for example, type **25** and then press ↵ to go to page 25 of the current document).
- Press ↑ to go to the top of the current page.
- Press ↓ to go to the bottom of the current page.

Returning the Cursor to Its Previous Position

If you want to move the cursor back to wherever you just came from, press Ctrl+Home+Home. (That is, hold down the Ctrl key, press Home twice, then release the Ctrl key.) This is handy for getting right back to where you were if you press a cursor-positioning key accidentally.

Fancy Ways to Position the Cursor

You can also use the following techniques to position the cursor:

- To mark your place with an invisible bookmark, press Ctrl+Q. To return to that bookmark later, press Ctrl+F. See Chapter 9 for more information on bookmarks.
- To move the cursor to a particular word, phrase, or code within your document, use the Search feature (described in Chapter 9).

What the Status Bar Shows

As you move the cursor around in your document, the *status bar* at the bottom of the document window provides you with information about the document. The status bar displays the following:

Doc (Document)   Tells which document you're in (always **1** if you have only one document open).

Pg (Page)   Tells which page you're on.

Ln (Line)   Tells how far down from the top of the page the cursor is.

Pos (Position)   Tells how far the cursor is from the left edge of the page.

By default, WordPerfect leaves a one-inch margin around your document. So when you're at the very top of a new document, the status bar will usually show **Ln 1″ Pos 1″**. You can change the margin widths at any time (see Chapter 5).

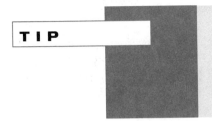

TIP

Pos in the status bar also informs you when certain keys or features are on (active). For instance, when Caps Lock is on, the indicator appears as *POS*. When underlining is on, the number following *Pos* appears underlined or highlighted.

Inserting and Replacing Text

When editing a document, you can choose between two modes of adding text: *Insert mode* and *Typeover mode*. In Insert mode, new text is inserted between existing characters. For example, suppose you move the cursor to the letter *P* in the word *WordPerfect*. Then, in Insert mode, you type *XXX*. Those three letters would be inserted into the text, like this:

WordXXXPerfect

If you put the cursor on the letter *P* and typed *XXX* in Typeover mode, those three letters would *type over* (overwrite) three existing letters, like this:

WordXXXfect

Switching between Insert and Typeover Modes

Normally, WordPerfect is in Insert mode. To switch to Typeover mode, press the Insert (Ins) key once. The message "Typeover" will appear in the status bar near the lower-left corner of the screen, where the name of the font (or the file name if you've saved the file) usually appears. The Insert key acts as a *toggle*: To switch from Typeover mode back to Insert mode, just press Insert (or Ins) again.

Inserting Text, Spaces, and Lines

To insert text, spaces, or lines in a document, follow these steps:

1. Move the cursor to the place where you want to insert text, spaces, or lines.

2. Make sure you're in Insert mode. (If "Typeover" appears in the status bar, press the Insert key.)

3. Type as you normally would:

   - To insert a blank space, press the spacebar.
   - To insert text, just type it.
   - To insert a blank line or to break a line into two pieces, press ↵.

When you insert new text, be aware that some existing text may scroll off the right edge of the screen and seem to disappear. Don't worry about that. When you've finished typing your new text, just press ↓ or ↑, and WordPerfect will readjust all the text to fit within the margins.

If you make mistakes while inserting new text, you can correct them using Backspace, Delete, or Undo (which is described later in this chapter).

NOTE There's a slight difference between the way the Backspace key operates in Insert mode and in Typeover mode. In Insert mode, pressing Backspace deletes the character to the left of the cursor and drags all characters to the right of the cursor along with it, filling in any "holes" that would otherwise be left by the deleted text. In Typeover mode, the Backspace key deletes the character to the left of the cursor, but does not drag any characters with it.

Splitting and Joining Lines and Paragraphs

Occasionally you might accidentally press ↵ in the middle of a line, causing the line to split in two, like two separate paragraphs. If this happens, just move the cursor to the beginning of the lower line and press Backspace. Or, move the cursor to the end of the top line and press Delete. This deletes the *hard return* ([HRt]) code that's splitting the line. (You'll learn more about hidden codes in Chapter 4.)

To split one paragraph into two, move the cursor to the place where you want to make the split. Then press ↵ once or twice, and, if you wish, press Tab to indent. If you go too far, just use the Backspace key to back up.

Selecting (Blocking) Text

Before you work with text in a document, you need to *select* (or "block") the text. You can select any amount of text: a single character, an entire document, or any quantity in between. For example, you can select a group of words, a sentence, a page, or a paragraph.

N O T E

Earlier versions of WordPerfect used the term *block* to refer to the act of choosing a chunk of text to work with. However, in most programs, this operation is called *selecting*. In this book I'll stick with the newer terminology.

Selected text appears in reverse colors on your screen, as in the example shown in Figure 3.3. Once you've selected a chunk of text, you can move it, copy it, delete it, print it, save it to a separate file... whatever! I'll summarize the things you can do with selected text later on in this chapter.

FIGURE 3.3

Selected text appears in reverse colors on your monitor.

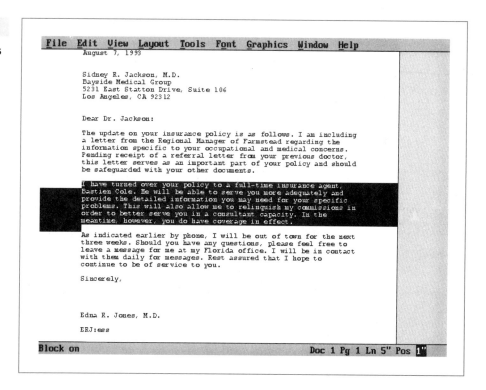

Selecting Text with a Mouse

To select text using a mouse, follow the steps below:

1. Move the mouse pointer to the first character of text that you want to select.

2. Hold down the mouse button and drag the pointer to the last character that you want to select.

3. When the text you want to work with is selected, release the mouse button.

Here are some shortcuts for selecting text with a mouse:

- To select a word, double-click anywhere in that word.

- To select a sentence, triple-click anywhere in that sentence.

- To select a paragraph, quadruple-click anywhere in that paragraph.

Selecting Text with the Keyboard

Here's how to select text from the keyboard:

1. Move the cursor to the first character that you want to select.

2. Choose Edit ➤ Block, press Alt+F4, or press F12. "Block on" appears in the status bar near the lower-left corner of the screen.

3. Extend the selection using any of these methods:

- Press any of the cursor movement key(s) listed in Table 3.1.

- Type a character or letter you want to extend the selection to. (For example, type a period to extend the selection to the end of the current sentence.)

- If you previously placed a Ctrl+Q bookmark in your document, you can press Ctrl+F to extend the selection to that bookmark.

- You can extend the selection to a specific word, phrase, or formatting code using the Search key (F2), described in Chapter 9.

Regardless of whether you use the mouse or the keyboard to select text, the text will appear highlighted on the screen, and the status bar will display the message "Block on" in the lower-left corner of the screen.

News for Windows Users

If you're a Windows fanatic, you'll be happy to know that you can use the Shift key with cursor positioning keys to select text. But first, you'll need to switch to WordPerfect's *CUA* (Common User Access) keyboard. To do this, choose File ➤ Setup ➤ Keyboard Layout, highlight CUA, and choose Select.

The CUA keyboard follows the same conventions that all Windows applications use for moving the cursor and selecting text with the keyboard. For example, pressing Home moves the cursor to the start of a line, while pressing Shift+Home selects text from the cursor position to the start of the line. In this book, however, I'll assume that you're using the standard WordPerfect 6.0 keyboard layout and positioning keys described in Table 3.1. (If you've chosen the CUA keyboard and want to switch back to the standard keyboard, just choose File ➤ Setup ➤ Keyboard Layout, highlight [ORIGINAL], and choose Select.)

Selecting Large Blocks

Here are some tips to keep in mind when you're selecting a large block of text:

- If you're using the mouse and the selection gets to the edge of the screen, just drag the pointer off the edge of the screen. Text will scroll into the selection area until you release the mouse button or move the mouse pointer back onto the display.

- If you run out of desk space while rolling the mouse, keep the mouse button depressed, lift the mouse and reposition it, then resume rolling the mouse.

- If you get tired of dragging the mouse around, you can always mix mouse techniques with keyboard cursor-movements. For instance, you can start selecting a block by dragging with the mouse, then use the cursor-movement keys to finish blocking the text.

TIP   If you start selecting text, then make a mess of things, you can deselect the text by clicking anywhere within the document, pressing Escape, Alt+F4, or F12, or by choosing Edit ➤ Block.

Reselecting the Same Block

If you deselect some selected text accidentally, and you want to reselect the same text, follow these steps:

1. Select Edit ➤ Block or press Alt+F4 or F12 again.

2. Press Ctrl+Home+Home (hold down the Ctrl key and press the Home key twice).

Shortcuts for Selecting a Sentence, Paragraph, or Page

If you want to select the sentence, paragraph, or page that the cursor is in at the moment, WordPerfect has some shortcuts for you:

1. Choose Edit ➤ Select.

2. Choose Sentence, Paragraph, or Page depending on how much text you want to select.

If the Sentence, Paragraph, and Page options are dimmed and unavailable, most likely some text is already selected. Press Escape until the *Block on* indicator in the status bar goes off, then try again.

Things You Can Do with Selected Text

Once you've selected a block of text, and the Block On message appears in the status bar, you can do all kinds of things with that text. In this chapter I'll discuss moving, copying, deleting, and changing the case of blocked text. For future reference, Table 3.2 lists all the operations you can perform on selected text, together with cross-references to where these operations are covered in more detail.

TABLE 3.2: Things You Can Do with Selected Text

ACTION	MENU CHOICES	SHORTCUT	CHAPTER
Add to another file	Edit ➤ Append ➤ To File		3
Add to Clipboard	Edit ➤ Append ➤ To Clipboard		3
Alphabetize/sort	Tools ➤ Sort	Ctrl+F9	22
Boldface	Font ➤ Bold	F6 or Ctrl+B	6
Center	Layout ➤ Alignment ➤ Center	Shift+F6	5
Change appearance	Font	Ctrl+F8	6
Change case	Edit ➤ Convert Case	Shift+F3	2
Change size	Font	Ctrl+F8	6
Comment	Layout ➤ Comment ➤ Create	Ctrl+F7 CC	4
Copy to Clipboard	Edit ➤ Copy	Ctrl+C	3

TABLE 3.2: Things You Can Do with Selected Text (continued)

ACTION	MENU CHOICES	SHORTCUT	CHAPTER
Copy within the document	Edit ➤ Copy and Paste	Ctrl+Ins or press Ctrl while dragging	3
Delete	Edit ➤ Cut	Delete or Backspace	3
Flush right	Layout ➤ Alignment ➤ Flush Right	Alt+F6	5
Italicize	Font ➤ Italics	Ctrl+I	6
Move to Clipboard	Edit ➤ Cut	Ctrl+X	3
Move within current document	Edit ➤ Cut and Paste	Ctrl+Del or drag with mouse	3
Print	File ➤ Print/Fax	Shift+F7	10
Protect	Layout ➤ Other ➤ Block Protect	Shift+F8 B	8
Save	File ➤ Save As	F10	3
Search/replace	Edit ➤ Search Edit ➤ Replace	F2 (or Alt+F2)	9
Spell check	Tools ➤ Writing Tools ➤ Speller	Ctrl+F2	11
Style	Layout ➤ Styles	Alt+F8	17
Table (Convert To)	Layout ➤ Tables ➤ Create	Alt+F7 TC	7
Underline	Font ➤ Underline	F8 or Ctrl+U	6

Moving and Copying Text (Cut-and-Paste)

One of the most common editing operations is reorganizing text by moving it around. Another common task is copying. For example, if you were typing a list of names and addresses of people who lived in the same neighborhood, you might want to copy the street address, city, state, and zip code from one person to the next to avoid having to retype the same information. Or, you might want to copy certain passages of text, such as standardized paragraphs, from one document to another.

The basic steps for moving and copying are practically identical. The only difference between the two operations is that *moving* text takes it from one place and puts it in another, as illustrated in Figures 3.4 and 3.5, while *copying* leaves the text in its original position and places a copy of that text

FIGURE 3.4

Before moving text, you must select it.

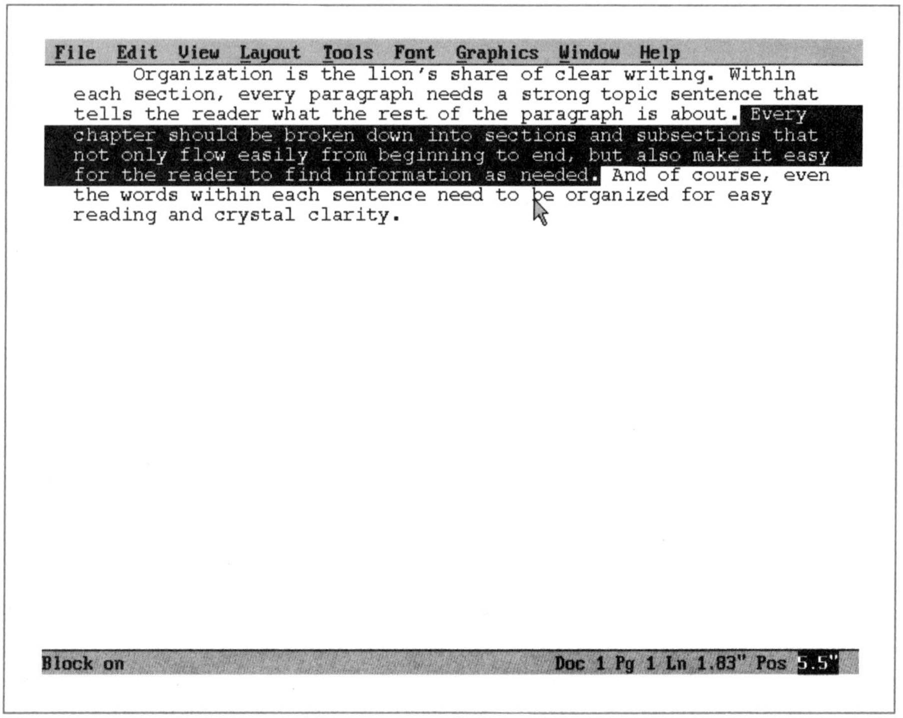

```
File  Edit  View  Layout  Tools  Font  Graphics  Window  Help
      Organization is the lion's share of clear writing. Within
each section, every paragraph needs a strong topic sentence that
tells the reader what the rest of the paragraph is about. Every
chapter should be broken down into sections and subsections that
not only flow easily from beginning to end, but also make it easy
for the reader to find information as needed. And of course, even
the words within each sentence need to be organized for easy
reading and crystal clarity.



Block on                                    Doc 1 Pg 1 Ln 1.83" Pos 5.5"
```

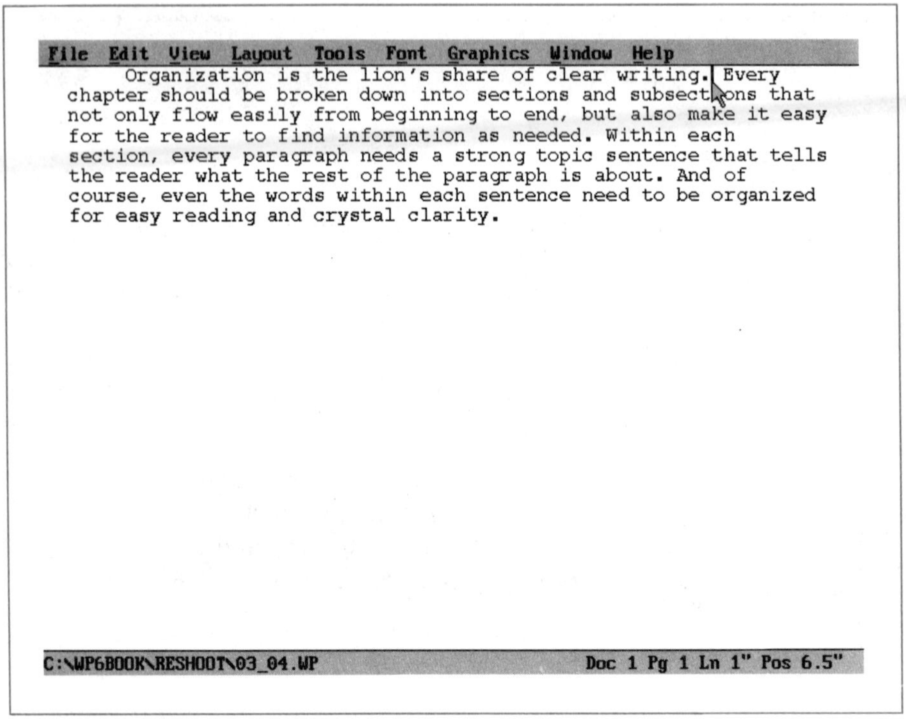

FIGURE 3.5

The selected block of text from Figure 3.4 has been moved up. It's now the second sentence in the paragraph.

```
 File  Edit  View  Layout  Tools  Font  Graphics  Window  Help
      Organization is the lion's share of clear writing. Every
 chapter should be broken down into sections and subsections that
 not only flow easily from beginning to end, but also make it easy
 for the reader to find information as needed. Within each
 section, every paragraph needs a strong topic sentence that tells
 the reader what the rest of the paragraph is about. And of
 course, even the words within each sentence need to be organized
 for easy reading and crystal clarity.




 C:\WP6BOOK\RESHOOT\03_04.WP                  Doc 1 Pg 1 Ln 1" Pos 6.5"
```

in a new location. This is demonstrated in Figures 3.6 and 3.7.

To move or copy text, follow these steps:

1. Select the text you want to move or copy, as described previously in this chapter.

   - If you want to *move* the text, choose Edit ➤ Cut or press Ctrl+X.
   - If you want to *copy* the text, choose Edit ➤ Copy or press Ctrl+C.

2. Move the insertion point to where you want to place the cut or copied text.

3. Choose Edit ➤ Paste or press Ctrl+V.

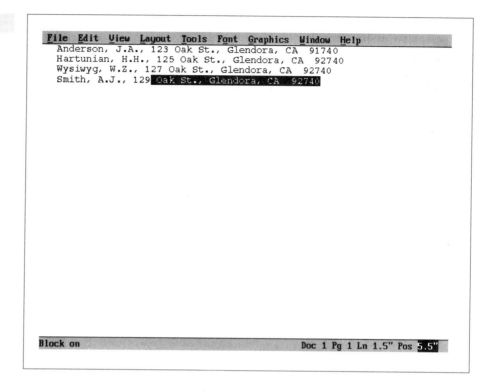

That's the most common technique for copying or moving text. In fact, it's the method most programs use. Of course, there are some alternatives and shortcuts…

Moving and Copying with Drag-and-Drop

WordPerfect has a nifty feature known as *drag-and-drop*, so called because you can simply drag selected text where you want it and drop it into place. Here's how to use this method:

1. Select the text you want to move or copy.

2. Click anywhere on the selected text, and, while holding down the mouse button, move the cursor to the new position for the text. (Don't release the mouse button until you finish step 4 below!)

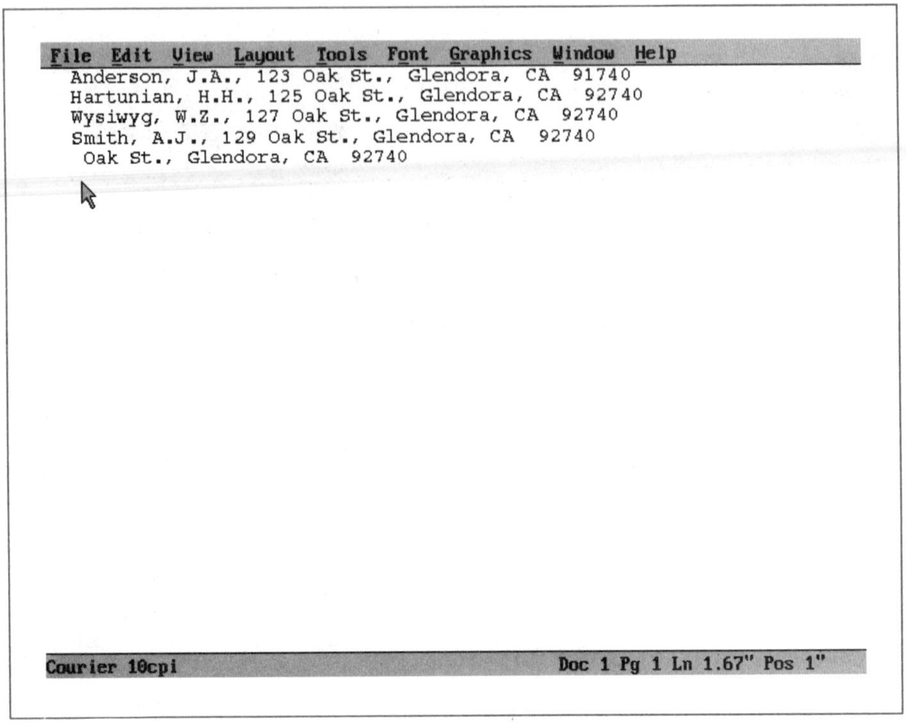

FIGURE 3.7

The selected text in Figure 3.6 has been copied to the next line down.

```
 File  Edit  View  Layout  Tools  Font  Graphics  Window  Help
 Anderson, J.A., 123 Oak St., Glendora, CA  91740
 Hartunian, H.H., 125 Oak St., Glendora, CA  92740
 Wysiwyg, W.Z., 127 Oak St., Glendora, CA  92740
 Smith, A.J., 129 Oak St., Glendora, CA  92740
  Oak St., Glendora, CA  92740









 Courier 10cpi                              Doc 1 Pg 1 Ln 1.67" Pos 1"
```

3. If you want the text to remain selected after you move or copy it, hold down the Alt key (leave it down until you finish step 4).

4. Complete the move or copy as follows:

   - If you want to *move* the text, release the mouse button.
   - If you want to *copy* the text, hold down the Ctrl key while you release the mouse button.

Moving and Copying the "Old Way"

If you're used to older versions of WordPerfect, where you move the cursor then press ↵ to move or copy selected text, you may prefer this method:

1. Select the text you want to move or copy.

- If you want to *move* the text, choose <u>E</u>dit ➤ Cut And Past<u>e</u> or press Ctrl+Del.

- If you want to *copy* the text, choose <u>E</u>dit ➤ Cop<u>y</u> And Paste or press Ctrl+Ins.

3. The message "Move cursor; press **Enter** to retrieve" appears in the status bar. Move the cursor to the place you want to paste the text, and then press ↵.

Moving and Copying across Documents

As soon as you select Cut or Copy from the Edit menu, a copy of the selected text is placed in the *Clipboard*. The Clipboard is a chunk of memory that holds the text until you cut or copy some *other* chunk of text or you exit WordPerfect. Even though you can't see the Clipboard, it's good to remember that it's there and it contains a copy of whatever you last cut or copied.

Why is this good to know? Well, you might just want to move text from one place in the current document to another. But there are other things you can do with the contents of the Clipboard

- Choose <u>F</u>ile ➤ <u>N</u>ew to create a new empty document, then choose <u>E</u>dit ➤ <u>P</u>aste to copy the text into that new document.

- Choose <u>F</u>ile ➤ <u>O</u>pen to open a previously saved document, position the cursor in that document, then use <u>E</u>dit ➤ <u>P</u>aste to paste in the text.

- Use the Windows menu, Shift+F3, or F3 (explained in Chapter 4) to switch to a different open document, then choose <u>E</u>dit ➤ <u>P</u>aste to paste in the text.

So you see, once you've cut or copied text using <u>E</u>dit ➤ Cu<u>t</u> or <u>E</u>dit ➤ <u>C</u>opy, you can position the cursor anywhere you want and choose <u>E</u>dit ➤ <u>P</u>aste (or press Ctrl+V) to paste in the text. You can even select <u>E</u>dit ➤ <u>P</u>aste a bunch of times to keep pasting in multiple copies of the same text. Just remember that if you exit WordPerfect, the Clipboard will be emptied.

TIP

Normally, text that you move or copy to the Clipboard *replaces* whatever was there before. If you're running WordPerfect from the Shell, you can *add* more text to the Clipboard without deleting what's already there. Just select the text you want to add, then choose Edit ➤ Append ➤ To Clipboard. Although you won't see anything happen, WordPerfect will copy the selected text to the Clipboard, below whatever you placed there previously. See Chapter 24 for more information on the Shell.

Making the Clipboard Last to Another Session

If you want to save a copy of the Clipboard contents for future sessions in WordPerfect, you must write it out to a file:

1. Select the text you want to store. (If that text is in the Clipboard, but not on your screen, choose Edit ➤ Paste, then select the text to store.)

2. Choose File ➤ Save As or press F10.

3. Enter the name for this file (for example, CLIPBRD.WP), and choose OK.

If a file with the name you specified already exists, and you don't mind overwriting (replacing) that file, choose Yes. If you don't want to replace an existing file, choose No and enter a different file name. If you want to *add* the currently selected text to the existing file, choose Cancel and then use Edit ➤ Append ➤ To File to copy the selected text to the file.

NOTE

If you want to copy the text for use with a different program, see the section on exporting text in Chapter 33.

At any time (even in a later text-editing session), you can open the CLIPBRD.WP file (or whatever file contains the Clipboard contents) using File ➤ Open. Select all of its text, and recopy that text into the Clipboard. Or, you can position the cursor where you want the contents of the CLIPBRD.WP file to appear, then choose File ➤ Retrieve to retrieve the contents of that file.

Undoing a Recent Change

You can usually undo your most recent action, including moving or copying text, provided that you do so right away, and provided the Undo feature is active (that is, the File ➤ Setup ➤ Environment ➤ Allow Undo box is checked).

To undo your most recent action, simply choose Edit ➤ Undo or press Ctrl+Z.

TIP

If Undo gives you a hard time, see "Problems with Undo" in Appendix C.

Deleting Text

Deleting text is easy—in fact, so easy you might do it by accident from time to time. Fortunately, WordPerfect also makes it easy to *undelete* text. You can delete and undelete as small or as large a chunk of text as you wish. See Table 3.3 for a summary of ways to delete text.

TABLE 3.3: Different Ways to Delete Text

TO DELETE	POSITION CURSOR AT	AND PRESS
Break at end of a line	End of upper line	Delete
Character/space at cursor	Character	Delete
Character/space left of cursor	Next character	Backspace
Word	Word	Ctrl+Backspace or Ctrl+Del
Blank line	Start of blank line	Delete or Backspace
Rest of line	Start of deletion point	Ctrl+End
Rest of page	Start of deletion point	Ctrl+PgDn
Rest of document	Start of deletion	Alt+F4 Home Home ↓ Delete
Selected text	Selected text	Delete or Backspace

Undeleting Text

If you delete a chunk of text by accident (or you change your mind after the fact), follow these steps:

1. Choose Edit ➤ Undelete or press Escape. (Press F1 if you're using the older-style WP 5.1 keyboard.)

2. The deleted text reappears, highlighted on the screen.

    *   If the highlighted text is what you want to undelete, choose Restore.

- If the highlighted text isn't what you want to undelete, choose <u>P</u>revious Deletion. Then, when the text you want to undelete appears on the screen, choose <u>R</u>estore.

- If you don't find the text you want to delete within three tries, choose Cancel or press Escape to give up.

Undelete can "remember" no more than your last three deletions. So if you don't find the text you want to undelete after choosing <u>P</u>revious Deletion twice, you're out of luck (unless you recently saved the file, as I'll explain later in this chapter).

Undo vs. Undelete

In case you're wondering why WordPerfect has an Undelete feature as well as Undo, here are the differences between the two commands:

- Undelete "remembers" up to your last three deletions. Undo only remembers your (one) most recent action.

- Undelete puts recovered text at the current cursor position. Undo puts recovered text back in its original spot.

TIP An alternative way of moving text and hidden codes is to delete whatever you want to move, then move the cursor to the new location and undelete it.

- Undelete can only "undo" a deletion. Undo can undo almost any action, including move, copy, change case, etc.

- Undelete is always available. Undo is only available if the feature is turned on via <u>F</u>ile ➤ Se<u>t</u>up ➤ <u>E</u>nvironment ➤ <u>A</u>llow Undo. (See Chapter 19.)

Switching Upper/Lowercase

WordPerfect lets you change the case of a section of text (from upper- to lowercase, or vice versa). Here's how:

1. Select the text you want to change.

2. Choose Edit ➤ Convert Case (or press Shift+F3).

3. Choose Uppercase, Lowercase, or Initial Caps, depending on how you want the results to be formatted:

   THIS IS UPPERCASE
   this is lowercase
   And This Is Initial Caps

> **NOTE**
>
> Initial Caps uses all lowercase for some words that people typically leave as lowercase when typing headings (especially articles, prepositions, and most pronouns).

Choose Edit ➤ Undo if you change your mind and want to revert to the initial case.

Printing Your Document

You can print the document that you're currently working on by following these simple steps:

1. Choose File ➤ Print/Fax, or press Shift+F7.

2. Choose P<u>r</u>int (or just press ↵).

3. Wait a few seconds.

After a brief delay, the printer should kick in. (If the printer refuses to co-operate, please refer to Chapter 10, as well as to "Printer Problems" in Appendix C.)

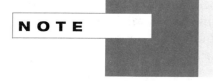

NOTE   You'll learn how to print multiple copies, choose from several installed properties, and use other printing options in Chapter 10.

You'll notice that your printed document has one-inch margins all the way around, which do not appear on the document window. These are the *default* margins, which WordPerfect uses for every printed document. The term *default* refers to any setting that you do not intentionally alter. You can change those margins if you wish (see Chapter 8).

Your printed document will also have a smooth right margin, which can cause some extra space between words in each line. The smooth right margin is another default setting (called *full justification*). You'll learn how to switch to a ragged right margin (*left justification*) in Chapter 5.

WARNING   When printing is complete, don't be in too big a hurry to turn off your computer! You'll probably want to save your document for future use, and you should always *exit* WordPerfect properly before turning off your computer. (Saving and exiting are discussed later in this chapter.)

Saving Your Work

It's important to understand that any recent work you've done on open documents is stored in memory (RAM) only. If you turn off your computer without saving those documents, you'll lose all the work you've done.

When you save a WordPerfect document, it is stored as a file on your disk. Individual files are often stored in groups, called *directories*. Every file in a given *directory* must have a unique name. In other words, no two files in the same directory can have the same name.

If you're not familiar with drives, directories, and files, don't sweat it right now. You can learn the details at your leisure by referring to Chapter 20 and/or to any good introductory DOS book.

Naming Documents

Before saving a document for the first time, you need to think up a file name that conforms to these rules:

- The name can be up to eight characters long and may contain letters, numbers, or a mixture of both.

- You can follow the file name with a period and an *extension* up to three characters long. The period that separates the file name from the extension is the only period allowed in the file name.

- Neither the name nor the extension can contain blank spaces.

- A file name can contain underscore characters (_) or hyphens (-). However, you cannot use the following characters in a file name:

  * ? + = [ ] : ; " / \ | > <

- File names are not *case-sensitive*. Therefore, SMITH.WP, Smith.Wp, and smith.wp are actually all the same file name.

Table 3.4 gives some examples of valid and invalid file names.

TABLE 3.4: Examples of Valid and Invalid File Names

FILE NAME	VALID/INVALID
LETTER	Valid
LETTER.1	Valid
SMITH.LET	Valid
1991TAX.QT1	Valid
QTR_1.WP	Valid
QTR-1.WP	Valid
MyLetter.wp	Valid
QTR 1.WP	Invalid (contains a blank space)
QTR1.W P	Invalid (extension contains a blank space)
12.1.91.WP	Invalid (too many periods)
MYFIRSTLETTER.TXT	Invalid (too long, will be converted to MYFIRSTL.TXT)
WON'T.WP	Invalid (contains a punctuation mark)

Use File Names You'll Remember

When deciding on a file name, try to use a descriptive name that will make it easy to find the file again in the future. For example, the file name XXX tells you nothing about the contents of that file. But the file name SMITH gives you a clue that the file contains something about somebody named Smith—perhaps a letter to that person.

While the extension to a file name is optional, it can be handy for remembering the type of information stored in the file. For example, you might want to use the file name extension .WP when saving WordPerfect documents. That way, you can tell which files on your disk are WordPerfect documents simply by looking at the file name extension.

Using consistent file name extensions also makes it easier to select a group of files based on their extensions with the File Manager feature discussed in Chapter 20.

Saving a File for the First Time

A new document that's never been saved has no name. Its document window, if framed, will display the name (Untitled). To save a previously unsaved document, follow the steps below:

1. Choose File ➤ Save.

2. Type a valid file name, then choose OK. (Include or choose a path, as discussed in Chapter 20, if you wish.)

A copy of the document will remain on your screen for editing, and the document will also be copied to disk.

Quick-Saving Recent Changes

Once you've saved a file and given it a name, it's easy to save your changes as you go along. In particular, you might find it useful to save your file...

- Just after doing something that was tough.
- Just before trying something you think is risky.
- Every five minutes or so, regardless of what you're doing.

To save the file, just choose File ➤ Save. You'll see a brief message as WordPerfect updates the copy of your file on disk to match the current copy in memory.

Saving a File with a Different Name

If you want to keep the previously saved copy of your document on disk, and save the current document in a new, separate file, proceed as follows:

1. Choose File ➤ Save As, or press F10.

2. Type in a new (different) file name for the copy that's currently on your screen.

3. Choose OK.

Any additional changes you make to the document and save will be saved under this new file name only. The previous version of the document will remain unchanged under its original file name.

Closing a Document without Exiting WordPerfect

To close the document you're working on (and save it if you wish), without leaving WordPerfect, just follow these steps:

1. Choose File ➤ Close.

2. You'll be asked if you want to save the current version. Choose Yes (unless you've made a mess of this copy and would prefer to keep the last copy you saved).

Creating a New Document without Closing the Current One

If you want to create a new document without closing the one that's currently open on your screen, choose File ➤ New. Then you can use commands and shortcuts on the Window menu to switch among open documents. (There's more about this in Chapter 4.)

Preventing and Undoing Major Boo-Boos

Earlier I mentioned that you should save your work just before trying something risky. I say this because if that action involves several steps and really makes a mess of things, the Undo feature won't be much help in getting your document back to its earlier pristine state.

But if you quick-save the document using File ➤ Save just before you foul up, you can always "undo" by replacing the messed-up copy on your screen with the good copy you saved just before the screw-up. Here's how:

1. Remember to use File ➤ Save to save the file just *before* trying the procedure you feel nervous about.

2. Do the procedure. If you end up doing more harm than good, choose File ➤ Close to close this copy of the file.

3. When asked about saving, choose No.

4. Use File ➤ Open to reopen the copy of the file you saved just before the foul-up.

The trick, of course, is remembering *always* to save your work just *after* you complete a job successfully and just *before* you try something that might mess things up royally.

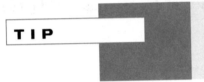

TIP If you press Ctrl+Q to place a QuickMark just before you save and close the file, you can then use Ctrl+F to return to that place after you reopen the file.

Saving and/or Exiting in One Fell Swoop

Remember that you always want to exit WordPerfect before you turn off your computer, just to make sure that you haven't left any work behind in memory (RAM). To exit WordPerfect, follow these easy steps:

1. Choose File ➤ Exit WP, or press Home then F7.

2. If there's any unsaved work in memory, WordPerfect will give you a chance to save that work. A dialog box containing check boxes will appear, as shown below:

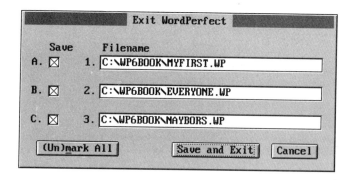

- If you want to save all of your unsaved work, make sure each check box in the Exit WordPerfect dialog box contains an X.
- If you don't want to save your work, make sure each check box is empty. You can choose the (Un)mark All button to select and deselect the check boxes.
- You can choose which files you do and don't want to save by selecting and deselecting individual check boxes next to file names.

3. Choose Save And Exit (or Exit, if you're not saving any work), and follow the prompts that appear on the screen. You'll be returned to DOS, or wherever you were when you started WordPerfect.

This chapter covered stuff you really have to know to use WordPerfect reasonably well. In the next chapter, you'll learn ways to get the most out of WordPerfect.

Getting the Most from WordPerfect

fast TRACK

To make it easier to switch among various open documents   125

choose Window, then Cascade, Tile, or Minimize.

To reveal the hidden codes within your document   131

choose View ➤ Reveal Codes, or press Alt+F3.

Auto Code Placement repositions hidden codes   139

to prevent "code clutter" and competing codes. Use File ➤ Setup ➤ Environment to activate or deactivate Auto Code Placement.

Use document comments   142

(Layout ➤ Comment) to include notes to yourself or others within a document.

To insert the current date into a document   146

without actually typing the date, choose Tools ➤ Date, then choose either Text for a date that never changes or Code for a date that always reflects the current system date.

To preview your document before printing it   148

choose File ➤ Print Preview, or press Shift+F7 V. Use options on the View and Page menus to move around and change your point of view. Choose File ➤ Close or press F7 to return to the editing window.

NOW THAT you've had a chance to learn the basics of creating, editing, printing, and saving a document, you may want to start exploring some of WordPerfect's more powerful features. As the sheer size and weight of this book attests, there are lots of these features. In this chapter we'll look at optional time-saving general-purpose tools and techniques that will help you be more productive when you use WordPerfect.

Instant Screen Setup

In this chapter I'll focus on optional tools that you can turn on and off at will. Before you search through the chapter looking for specific techniques, however, I should point out that there's a quick way to decide which tools you want on or off:

1. Choose View ➤ Screen Setup. You'll see the dialog box shown in Figure 4.1.

2. Select the tools or features you want to turn on, then choose OK.

The appearance of each tool on your screen depends on whether you're in Text mode or Graphics/Page mode. (Pull down the View menu or press Ctrl+F3 to switch from mode to mode.) Figures 4.2 and 4.3 illustrate how the tools look in Graphics and Text modes. In Page mode, the tools look basically the same as in Graphics mode.

```
                          Screen Setup
┌─1. Screen Options───────────┐  ┌─4. Window Options───────────┐
│  ☒ Pull-Down Menus          │  │  ☐ Framed Window            │
│  ☐ Alt key activates menus  │  │  ☐ Hor. Scroll Bar (Graphics)│
│  ☐ Ribbon (Graphics)        │  │  ☐ Hor. Scroll Bar (Text)   │
│  ☐ Ribbon (Text)            │  │  ☐ Vert. Scroll Bar (Graphics)│
│  ☐ Outline Bar              │  │  ☐ Vert. Scroll Bar (Text)  │
│  ☐ Button Bar (Graphics)    │  │  ☒ Display Comments         │
│  ☐ Button Bar (Text)        │  │  Status Line [Filename ⬍]   │
│  Select Button Bar...       │  └─────────────────────────────┘
│  Button Bar Options...      │  ┌─5. Reveal Codes─────────────┐
└─────────────────────────────┘  │  ☐ Display Details          │
┌─2. Display Characters───────┐  │  Window Percentage: [25 ⬍]  │
│  Hard Return Character: [ ]  │  └─────────────────────────────┘
│  Space Character: [ ]        │  ┌─6. Zoom─────────────────────┐
└─────────────────────────────┘  │  ○ Percentage:    [138 ⬍]   │
┌─3. Display of Merge Codes───┐  │  ● Margin Width             │
│  ● Show Full Codes           │  │  ○ Page Width               │
│  ○ Show Codes as Icons       │  │  ○ Full Page                │
│  ○ Hide Codes                │  └─────────────────────────────┘
└─────────────────────────────┘
                                     [  OK  ]   [Cancel]

Courier 10cpi                        Doc 1 Pg 1 Ln 1" Pos 1"
```

Turning the Ribbon On and Off

The Ribbon is a handy tool that allows you to change the zoom lens, justification, font, and other features in a jiffy. The Ribbon is of value only if you have a mouse, since there is no way to use it via the keyboard. To turn the Ribbon on or off, choose View ➤ Ribbon.

FIGURE 4.2

Various tools as they appear in Graphics and Page modes

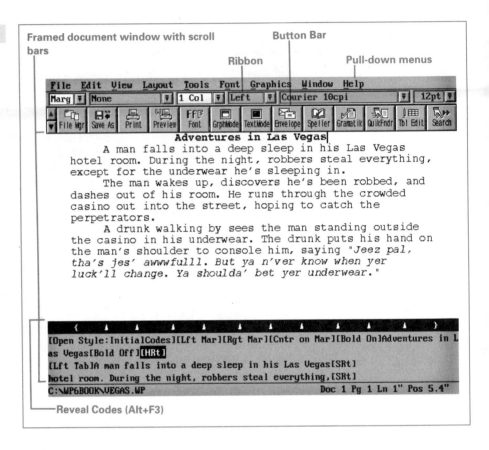

Various tools as they appear in Graphics and Page modes

Turning the Button Bar On and Off

The Button Bar is another handy tool that you can use as an alternative to selecting a series of commands from the menus. Like the Ribbon, the Button Bar is useful only if you have a mouse. You cannot select buttons with the keyboard.

To turn the Button Bar on or off, choose <u>V</u>iew ➤ <u>B</u>utton Bar.

FIGURE 4.3

The same tools shown in Figure 4.2, in Text mode. Not quite so pretty!

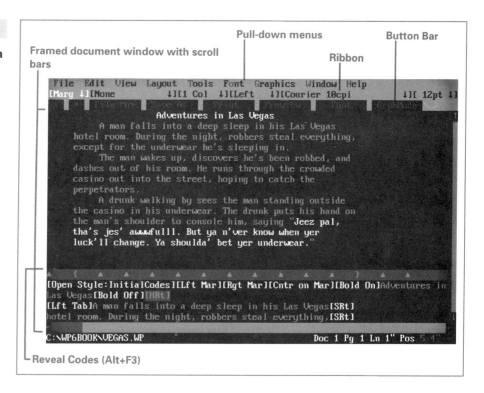

Using the Button Bar

To use the Button Bar, simply click the button for the feature you want. For example, if the current Button Bar has GrphMode and TextMode buttons, you can click these buttons to switch from one mode to the other. As you'll see in a moment, you can add your own buttons to the Button Bar and you can even create entirely new Button Bars.

If the Button Bar has more buttons than can fit on the screen at the moment, it will include a ▲ or ▼ button (or both). You can scroll the hidden buttons into view by clicking the ▲ or ▼ button until you find the one you want.

Repositioning the Button Bar

You can move the Button Bar to wherever you think it would be most convenient:

1. Choose <u>V</u>iew ➤ Button Bar <u>S</u>etup ➤ Options. You'll see this dialog box:

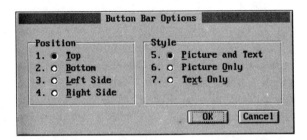

2. Choose any one of the available positions in the Button Bar Options dialog box: T<u>o</u>p, <u>B</u>ottom, <u>L</u>eft Side, or <u>R</u>ight Side.

3. Choose any available style: <u>P</u>icture And Text (the default; both text and the icon will appear on each button), Picture <u>O</u>nly (only the icons will appear on the buttons—no text), or Te<u>x</u>t Only (no icons will appear on the buttons).

4. Choose OK to exit the Button Bar Options dialog box.

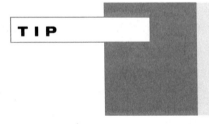

TIP

Any given Button Bar might contain more buttons than can fit across or down the screen. To display the maximum number of buttons, choose either <u>L</u>eft Side or <u>R</u>ight Side, and choose Te<u>x</u>t Only. Button pictures never appear in Text mode.

Selecting a Button Bar

You can create and maintain as many Button Bars as you wish. To choose which Button Bar you want to use at any time, follow the steps below:

1. Choose <u>V</u>iew ➤ Button Bar <u>S</u>etup ➤ Select (or choose <u>V</u>iew ➤ Scree<u>n</u> Setup ➤ <u>S</u>creen Options ➤ <u>S</u>elect Button Bar). The Select Button Bar dialog box will appear on your screen:

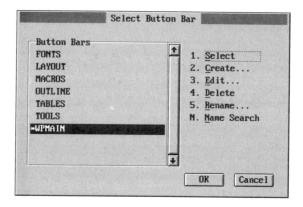

2. Choose one of the names in the Button Bar list by double-clicking on it, or by highlighting it with the ↑ and ↓ arrow keys then pressing ↵.

The Button Bar you chose will appear on the screen, replacing any Button Bar that was previously displayed.

Creating Your Own Button Bar

With WordPerfect, you can create your own custom Button Bar from scratch:

1. Choose <u>V</u>iew ➤ Button Bar <u>S</u>etup ➤ <u>S</u>elect.

2. Choose <u>C</u>reate.

3. Give the Button Bar a file name without an extension. (The name can be up to eight characters long, and it cannot contain blank spaces, a period, or other invalid punctuation marks.)

4. Choose OK.

5. Add buttons to your custom Button Bar, as described in the next section. When you're done adding buttons, choose OK.

You can view your custom Button Bar by selecting its name from the Select Button Bar dialog box, as described earlier in this chapter. (To get to the Select Button Bar dialog box, choose View ➤ Button Bar Setup ➤ Select.)

Adding Your Own Buttons to a Button Bar

You can add your own buttons to any Button Bar. First, select the Button Bar that you want to add a button to. Then follow these steps:

1. Choose View ➤ Button Bar Setup ➤ Edit. The Edit Button Bar dialog box will appear on your screen:

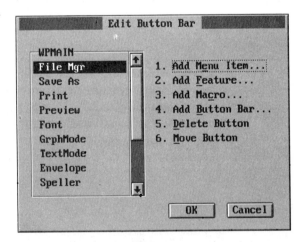

- If you know the menu sequence for the command you want to automate, choose Add Menu Item, then use your mouse to select the menu commands you want to automate. For example, you could choose File ➤ New to make a button that creates a new document.

- If you wish, you can choose Add Feature, then select an option from the alphabetized Feature Button List that appears. (You can usually guess the meaning of a feature from its abbreviation. If in doubt, just try it out.

- If you'd like to run a *macro* from the Button Bar, choose Add Macro, then choose the name of a macro. (See Chapter 18 for more about macros.)

- If you want to create a button that will switch you to a different Button Bar, choose Add Button Bar, then choose the name of the Button Bar you want the button to display.

2. Create as many buttons as you wish, then choose OK to close the Edit Button Bar dialog box.

Moving and Deleting Buttons

If you want to rearrange or delete buttons on the current Button Bar, select the Button Bar you want to change, and then follow these steps:

1. Choose View ➤ Button Bar Setup ➤ Edit.

- To delete a button, click the name of the button you want to delete in the list in the Edit Button Bar dialog box. Then choose Delete Button or press the Delete key. Choose Yes when prompted for confirmation.

- To move a button, click the name of the button you want to move (in the list inside the Edit Button Bar dialog box) then choose Move Button. Move the highlight to the name of the button that should be below the moved button (again, using the list within the dialog box), and choose Paste Button.

2. Choose OK when you're ready to return to your document.

What Buttons Should I Create?

The reason that WordPerfect's Button Bars are so flexible is that you're likely to use some features more than others. If you find yourself using a certain feature often, or you frequently select the same series of commands, consider creating a button for that operation. You'll probably find that your work goes faster when you reduce frequent tasks to a single mouse click on the Button Bar.

Managing Button Bars

You can work with entire Button Bars (as opposed to buttons within them) by following these steps:

1. Choose View ➤ Button Bar Setup ➤ Select.

2. Choose one of the following options:

   Select   Select and use an existing Button Bar.

   Create   Create a new Button Bar.

   Edit   Alter the current Button Bar.

   Delete   Delete the entire Button Bar whose name is high-lighted in the Button Bars list.

   Rename   Change the name of the Button Bar file that's highlighted in the list.

   Name Search   Search the list of Button Bar files for a particular name.

3. Follow the prompt on the screen.

You can also work with Button Bars through the File Manager or through DOS. Each Button Bar is stored with the file name you assign, followed by a .WPB extension, on the directory defined in File ➤ Setup ➤ Location of Files ➤ Macros/Keyboards/Button Bar.

Zooming In for a Closer Look

If you're editing in Graphics mode or Page mode, you can zoom in for a close-up of your document or zoom out for a bird's-eye view. Figure 4.4 shows a sample document at 50% magnification. Figure 4.5 shows the same document at 200%. You can set the magnification on your own screen to whatever you like.

FIGURE 4.4

A sample document
at 50% magnification

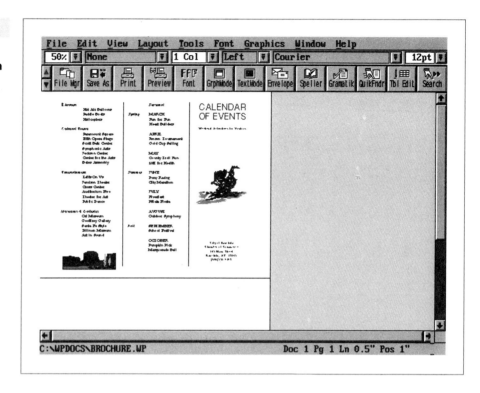

If the Ribbon is turned on, you can just click the first button in the Ribbon and click on whichever magnification you want. Or, you can choose <u>V</u>iew ➤ <u>Z</u>oom and select one of the options listed below:

<u>5</u>0 and <u>7</u>5%   Text is shown at a reduced size to give you an arm's-length view.

<u>1</u>00%   Text is shown at its approximate printed size.

1<u>2</u>5%, 15<u>0</u>%, and <u>2</u>00%   Text is magnified for a closer look.

<u>Margin Width</u>   Shows the text between the left and right margins.

Page <u>W</u>idth   Shows the full width of the page from one edge of the page to the other.

<u>F</u>ull Page   Shows a view of the entire page.

You can also press Ctrl+F3 and choose <u>Z</u>oom then <u>P</u>ercentage to set a more exact zoom percentage.

FIGURE 4.5

The document shown in Figure 4.4 at 200% magnification

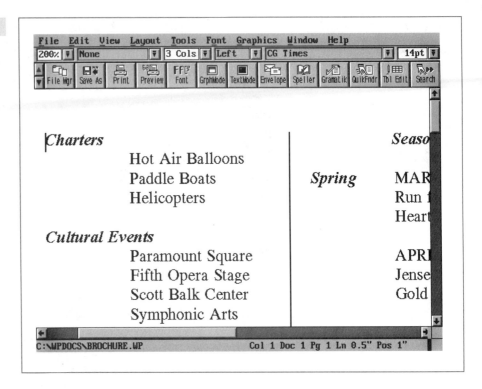

TIP

If you find yourself switching between certain magnifications often, consider creating buttons on the Button Bar for them.

Editing Multiple Documents

WordPerfect 6.0 lets you edit up to nine documents at a time. This is particularly handy when you need to move and copy text across several documents.

Each open document is placed in its own *document window*. A document window can be the full size of the editing portion of your screen, or you can reduce it to a small *window* that occupies only part of your screen.

NOTE Most of the commands on the Window menu don't do much unless you have several documents open at once. As mentioned in Chapter 3, you use File ➤ Open to open existing documents. Use File ➤ New to create a new document in its own document window.

It's easy to control the arrangement of document windows:

1. Choose <u>W</u>indow from the menu bar to open the Window menu.

2. Choose one of these options from the Window menu:

M<u>i</u>nimize   Reduces the window to its smallest size (about all you'll see is a tiny chunk of text and the document number in the title bar).

<u>F</u>rame   Allows you to move, size, and exit the window using the displayed tools (described in a moment).

Maximize   If the window isn't full-sized, this option expands the window so it fills in the entire editing area and removes the window frame.

<u>T</u>ile   If multiple documents are open, this option arranges all the documents in the window in a tiled format (where none of the windows overlap).

<u>C</u>ascade   If multiple documents are open, this option arranges document windows in an overlapping format, where one window is on top, and the titles of the other windows are visible (see Figure 4.6).

<u>N</u>ext   Takes you to the next document window (if there is one).

<u>P</u>revious   Takes you to the previous document window (if there is one).

<u>S</u>witch (same as pressing Shift+F3)   Switches back and forth between the most recently used document windows.

S<u>w</u>itch To (same as pressing F3)   Displays a list of all open documents, where you can choose which document you want to switch to by typing the window's document number, by clicking, or by highlighting and pressing ↵.

FIGURE 4.6

Multiple docu-
ments, named
BROCHURE.WP,
LETTER.WP, and
VEGAS.WP, in a
cascaded ar-
rangement like
stacked sheets
of paper

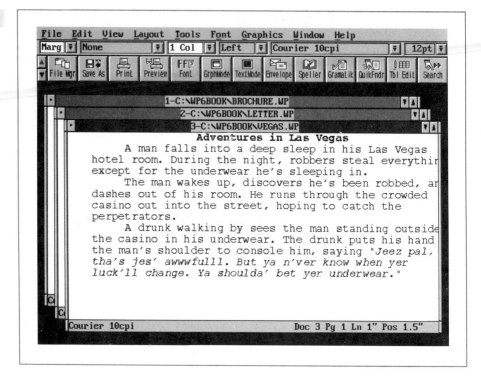

Managing Document Windows

When you reduce a document window to its framed size, various tools appear in the frame. You can use those tools (illustrated in Figure 4.7) to move, size, and close the document windows:

Control Box Lets you close the current window. If you've changed the document recently, you'll be given a chance to save your work before the window closes. (Pay attention to any prompts that follow to make sure you save your work before closing the window.)

Minimize Reduces the document window to its smallest size.

Maximize Expands the window to full size and removes the tools (choose Window ➤ Frame to restore the tools).

FIGURE 4.7

These tools, which appear in any framed document window, let you size, move, and close the window.

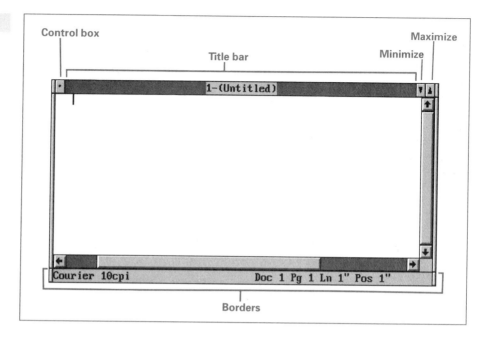

The scroll bars along the right and bottom edges of the document window appear only if you select the scroll bar options from the View menu or from <u>V</u>iew ➤ Scree<u>n</u> Setup.

Title Bar   You can move the window by dragging its title bar with your mouse pointer. You can also bring a window to the front, so that it's not covered by other windows, simply by clicking its title bar. The title bar displays "(Untitled)" until you name the document by saving it.

Borders   You can size the window by dragging its left, right, or lower border. Use the lower corners to size the window diagonally.

The scroll bars along the right and bottom edges of the document window appear only if you select the scroll bar options from the View menu or from <u>V</u>iew ➤ Scree<u>n</u> Setup.

About the Active Window

Even though you can have several documents open at once, you can actually edit only one at a time. That is, the cursor can be in only one document at a time. The document that the cursor is in is called the *active window*.

You can tell at a glance which window on your screen is active by looking for the following clues:

- The title bar of the active window is colored or shaded differently from the other windows.
- The active window is never covered by other windows: It always overlaps any other open windows.
- The cursor appears only in the active window.

Uncovering Hidden Windows

When you have lots of document windows open, there's a good chance that the windows will stack up and cover one another. Don't worry about it. You can easily get them into shape using any of these techniques:

- If at least part of the window that you want to use is visible, you can click anywhere on that window to bring it to the top.
- You can choose the Window ➤ Cascade command to stack all the open windows neatly.
- To switch to a different window, press F3 and click the name of the window or type its document window number.
- You can choose Window ➤ Tile to view all of the windows at once.

There's no need to feel overwhelmed with lots of documents open because it's so easy to reshuffle the documents. But don't forget that all those open documents are in memory, not necessarily on disk. Therefore, you must be sure to save *all* your work when you exit WordPerfect and turn off your computer. When you choose File ➤ Exit WP (or Home F7), WordPerfect will prompt you to save everything.

Moving and Copying Text between Multiple Document Windows

You can easily move and copy text from one open document to another. Just use the cut-and-paste technique described in Chapter 3. That is, select the text you want to move or copy and choose Edit ➤ Copy or Edit

➤ Cut. Then, switch to the document you want to put the text into, move the cursor to the place where you want the text to appear, and choose Edit ➤ Paste.

Minimizing Window and File Confusion

Remember that each document window represents one file. To avoid confusion about how commands on the File menu relate to document windows, keep in mind the following points:

- File ➤ New creates a new, empty document window (think of it as a clean sheet of paper). Other windows remain open but are behind this new window.

- File ➤ Open opens a previously saved document in its own document window. This new window will probably cover other document windows.

- File ➤ Retrieve pulls a copy of a previously saved file into the *current* document window at the cursor position, combining the two documents into one.

- File ➤ Save saves the document in the active window with its existing file name (if it has one).

- File ➤ Save As lets you save the document in the active window with a different file name.

- File ➤ Exit (F7) lets you save and close the active document window without closing other document windows and without exiting WordPerfect.

- File ➤ Exit WP gives you a chance to save any changes in all open, modified document windows, then exits WordPerfect.

Viewing Several Parts of a Document at Once

Suppose you're working in a large document and you want to view page 5 and page 20 at the same time. Maybe you'd even like to move or copy text from one page to the other.

With WordPerfect 6.0 you can easily open two or more copies of the same document at once. Just use File ➤ Open (up to nine times!) to open additional copies of the active document. (Choose Window ➤ Tile or Window ➤ Cascade to arrange the windows, if you like.)

Be aware that you should edit and save changes to only *one* copy of the document, because only the last saved version "wins." For example, suppose you've changed both document 1 and document 2 of a file named FERD.WP, and then you save document 2 (but not document 1). Now the copy of FERD.WP on disk will match document 2 only. However, if you saved document 1 last, the disk copy will match document 1 only. Remember that the opened documents are just a snapshot of what was on disk when you chose File ➤ Open. Therefore, only the most recently saved version on screen will match the copy on disk.

For greatest safety, only make changes to the lowest-numbered document when you've opened multiple copies of the same file. (Look for the document number in the document's title bar and status bar.)

Cut-and-Paste with Multiple Views of a Single Document

If you have two or more copies of a single document open, and you want to move or copy text within that document, first go to the copy with the number 2 or greater in the title bar (in other words, make the higher-numbered copy the active document window). Select the text you want to move or copy, then choose Edit ➤ Cut (to move text) or Edit ➤ Copy.

Next, switch to the lowest-numbered document window (most likely the window with the number 1 in the title bar and status bar). Scroll to the place where you want to put the text and choose Edit ➤ Paste. Works like a charm!

Just be careful to keep track of which copy of the document is in which window. To avoid confusion, always cut or copy *from* a large-numbered document window (2 or greater) *to* document number 1. That way you'll know that window number 1 contains the latest version of the document.

Revealing the Hidden Codes

All the formatting features that you use in a WordPerfect document, including hard returns (when you press ↵), page breaks, and the many formatting features you'll learn about in future chapters, are controlled by hidden *codes* within the document. The reason these codes are hidden initially is that WordPerfect wants your document to look normal as you type and make changes. If your screen were cluttered with a bunch of strange-looking codes, your work would be much more complicated.

However, you can use these hidden codes to your advantage, particularly when you start using WordPerfect's more advanced features. For this reason, WordPerfect lets you view the codes so that you can see what's going on behind the scenes.

To display the hidden codes, you need to open the Reveal Codes window. To do so, choose <u>V</u>iew ➤ Reveal <u>C</u>odes or press Alt+F3. (F11 also works.)

When you open the Reveal Codes window, your document window will split into two sections: The upper part shows the regular text, and the lower part shows the same text but with the codes revealed. Figures 4.2 and 4.3 near the beginning of this chapter show some examples.

Codes in the Reveal Codes window are enclosed in square brackets ([ ]). Usually the codes are highlighted or colored differently. In Figures 4.2 and 4.3, a hard return code, [HRt], is highlighted. The cursor is in the same position in the Reveal Codes window and in the upper portion of the document window—at the end of the centered title in the first line.

NOTE   To close the Reveal Codes window, choose <u>V</u>iew ➤ Reveal <u>C</u>odes or press Alt+F3 (the same thing you do to open it).

Practical Uses of Hidden Codes

Every code plays some role in WordPerfect. For example, a hard-return code, [HRt], tells WordPerfect and your printer to end the line and go to a new line. In the normal text portion of the screen (the upper portion of the split window), you see only the short line of text; but in the Reveal Codes window you actually see the [HRt] code. If you were to move the highlight to that hidden code and press Delete, the [HRt] code would disappear, and the line would be joined to the line below it in the regular text window.

It's possible to edit and format a document without *ever* looking at hidden codes. However, as you start doing more refined work, you'll probably find Reveal Codes is an indispensable aid in formatting and troubleshooting your documents. Future chapters provide more specific information, but for now I'll give you some general guidelines for using WordPerfect's Reveal Codes feature effectively.

About Single and Paired Codes

Most features in WordPerfect are controlled by a single code, such as [HRt] or [SRt] (hard return and soft return). However, some features are controlled by *paired codes*. For example, suppose you boldface a block of text (as discussed in Chapter 5), so that the text appears in boldface on the normal (upper) screen. On the Reveal Codes (lower) screen, the hidden codes that cause the text to appear boldfaced would look like this:

[Bold On]This text is boldfaced**[Bold Off]**, and this is not.

Here WordPerfect is using paired codes to activate and deactivate a specific feature, boldface type. In paired codes, the starting code, which turns the feature on, usually contains the word "On," as in **[Bold On]**. The ending code, which turns the feature off, usually contains the word "Off" as in **[Bold Off]**. When you print the sentence shown above, or view it in a graphical mode (as opposed to Text mode), it appears partly boldface, partly normal, like this:

This text is boldfaced, and this is not.

About Paired Single Codes

As mentioned, most formatting features insert single codes into your document. Examples include line spacing and justification (Chapter 5), but there are dozens more. Single codes affect text from the cursor position to the end of your document, or until you change the formatting feature again. For example, if you change the line spacing from 1 to 2 in the middle of your document, WordPerfect inserts a [Ln Spacing:2.0] code at the cursor position. That new line spacing will be effective to the end of the document, unless WordPerfect encounters a different line spacing code later.

Suppose you only want to change the line spacing in a chunk of text. You could set the line spacing at the beginning of the chunk, then reset it to another value at the end of the chunk. But here's an easier way:

1. Select (block) the text you want to format.

2. Set the formatting feature you want. (For example, choose Layout ➤ Line ➤ Line Spacing, type 2, and choose OK.)

Assuming that your document started out single spaced, and you double-spaced the selected text, WordPerfect would insert two codes in your document—one at the beginning of the block and one at the end of the block—something like this:

[+Ln Spacing:2.0]double-spaced text would be here...**[HRt][-Ln Spacing:1.0]**single-spaced text would be here...

The first code says "start this formatting feature here." The second code says "return to the original formatting here." I call these *paired single codes* because they are paired versions of a code that usually appears as a single code.

About Hard and Soft Codes

In most cases, codes are inserted in a document when you press some key (such as ↵) or choose a formatting feature (such as boldface). In other cases, codes are inserted automatically, behind the scenes. For example, when you're typing a paragraph, and you type past the right margin, WordPerfect inserts a soft-return code ([SRt]) at the end of the upper-most line. This code tells WordPerfect and your printer to end the line there and resume text on the next line.

In general, codes that you insert yourself are referred to as *hard codes*, and codes that WordPerfect inserts for you are referred to as *soft codes*. (The distinction between hard and soft codes varies slightly, but is sufficient for our purposes right now.)

Positioning the Cursor in Reveal Codes

When Reveal Codes is on, you can use the mouse and cursor-movement keys to move the cursor about in either the upper or lower window. When the cursor lands on a hidden code rather than on some character, the entire code is highlighted in the Reveal Codes window. In some cases, the code will actually expand to show you more information. For example, when the cursor is directly on a [Bold On] code, that code might expand like this:

[Bold On:Courier Bold; 12pt]

This expanded code tells you exactly which font is in use. This extra information can be very helpful when you're doing advanced designing and editing.

As far as placing the cursor on a particular character or code, I generally find that it's easiest to use the upper, normal, text window to get the cursor into the right ballpark. Then you can zero in on a particular code on the lower screen using the arrow keys or mouse.

T I P

You can also use the Search feature to locate a specific code in Reveal Codes (see Chapter 9).

You can delete, move, or insert codes in the Reveal Codes window using the same techniques that you use with regular text. As you gain experience with WordPerfect, you'll really appreciate this convenience. In the next few sections, I'll describe the general techniques for editing codes.

Deleting Codes

If you're having a problem with the format of your document, sometimes simply removing the code that's activating a particular feature that you no longer want to use will fix the problem.

Deleting a code is the same as deleting any other character on the screen:

1. If you haven't already done so, turn on Reveal Codes.

2. Move the cursor to the code you want to delete so that the entire code is highlighted in the Reveal Codes window.

3. Press Delete.

Of course, you might delete a code by accident. No big deal. Typically you can just use Edit ➤ Undo to undo the change.

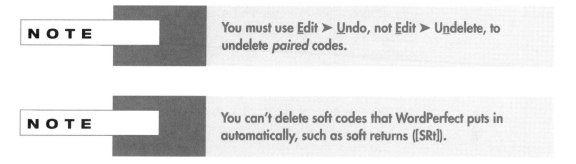

NOTE You must use Edit ➤ Undo, not Edit ➤ Undelete, to undelete *paired* codes.

NOTE You can't delete soft codes that WordPerfect puts in automatically, such as soft returns ([SRt]).

Deleting one code in a paired-code set, such as [Bold On]…[Bold Off] or [+Ln Spacing]…[-Ln Spacing], automatically deletes the other code. To undo a paired-code deletion, you must use Edit ➤ Undo (not Undelete).

Deleting Codes without Reveal Codes

When Reveal Codes is turned off, you can still delete many codes with the standard text deletion techniques. For example, if you move the cursor to a blank line and press Delete, the hard-return code that's causing the blank line, [HRt], will be deleted. Similarly, if you select a section of text and then delete it, any codes that were in that selected text will also be deleted, regardless of whether or not Reveal Codes is on.

On the other hand, WordPerfect won't delete certain codes when Reveal Codes is off. For example, if you're deleting individual characters with the Delete or Backspace key and you get to boldfaced text, WordPerfect won't delete the [Bold On] code. It's as though WordPerfect thinks, "Since you can't see the hidden codes right now, I'll assume you want to delete the text, not the codes." But when Reveal Codes is on, WordPerfect seems to think, "Since you *can* see the codes now, and you pressed Delete or Backspace while a code was highlighted, I'll assume you do want to delete that code."

Deleting Codes the "Old Way"

The fact that WordPerfect won't delete certain codes when Reveal Codes is turned off is a "6.0 thing." In earlier versions, WordPerfect would ask for permission before deleting a code with Reveal Codes turned off. If you'd like Version 6.0 to behave this way, follow the steps below:

1. Choose File ➤ Setup ➤ Environment.

2. Select WordPerfect 5.1 Cursor Movement, so it's marked with an X.

3. Choose OK.

Once you've done these steps, if the cursor happens to be on a code when you press Backspace or Delete, you'll see a prompt similar to this one:

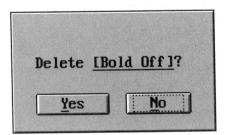

Choose Yes to delete the code. Otherwise, choose No, and the code will be retained. Remember, the above message will appear only if Reveal Codes is turned off. When Reveal Codes is on, WordPerfect assumes that you want to delete the code.

Deleting Selected Text and Codes

I think I should mention that if you *select* a chunk of text, then delete it, WordPerfect will delete all the selected text and codes, regardless of whether Reveal Codes is on or off. The assumption is that since you went to the trouble of selecting a large chunk of text to delete, you apparently wanted to get rid of the whole kit and caboodle.

Deleting Codes throughout the Document

If you want to delete all the codes in a document *globally* (for example, delete all the codes for boldface), you can use the Replace feature, which is discussed in Chapter 9.

Moving and Copying Codes

When you move or copy selected text that contains codes, the codes within the selection are moved or copied with the text. So, rarely will you need to move or copy a single code or set of codes.

But then again, there's always that once-in-a-while situation where it would be really handy just to move or copy a bunch of existing codes, rather than going through all the menu commands to put them into the document from scratch. This is especially true for pictures, lines, and other graphic elements that are stored as codes in your document (you'll learn about these later on).

Moving a Single Code

The easiest way to move a single (unpaired) code is to delete it, then un-delete it in some new place:

1. If you haven't done so already, activate Reveal Codes.

2. Move the cursor to the code you want to move, so that the entire code becomes highlighted.

3. Press Delete to delete the code.

4. Move the cursor to the new location for the code.

5. Choose <u>E</u>dit ➤ U<u>n</u>delete (or press Escape).

6. Choose <u>R</u>estore. The code is inserted at the new cursor position.

Note that you cannot move or copy only one code in a set of paired codes.

Moving or Copying Several Codes

If you want to copy a single code, or move or copy several codes, you can select them and then use cut-and-paste:

1. If you haven't done so already, turn on Reveal Codes.

2. Move the cursor to the first code that you want to move or copy, so that the code becomes highlighted.

3. Press Alt+F4 or F12, then use the arrow keys to extend the selection so that all the codes you want to move or copy are highlighted. Be sure to move the cursor one character or code *past* the last code that you want to include in the selection.

4. If you want to move the codes, choose <u>E</u>dit ➤ Cu<u>t</u>. To copy the code(s), choose <u>E</u>dit ➤ <u>C</u>opy.

5. Move the cursor to the new position for the codes and choose <u>E</u>dit ➤ <u>P</u>aste.

There are four things to keep in mind here:

• The paragraph may be reformatted immediately after you paste the codes, so don't be surprised if text moves right away.

• If Auto Code Placement (discussed later in this chapter) is turned on, WordPerfect might also rearrange the codes after you paste them in.

• It's impossible to move or copy only one of a paired code or to move a pair of codes without the text that's between them. It's easier to insert or delete text between the codes. (Or just delete the codes and start over.)

• It takes a little time to master the art of juggling text and codes. Be patient, and give yourself time.

Summary of Hidden Codes

In most cases, you can guess what a code does simply by looking at its name within the square brackets. However, it's by no means necessary to memorize, or even understand, the role of every code to use WordPerfect successfully. Nonetheless, I've included descriptions in Appendix D of some of the more mysterious codes that WordPerfect puts into your document.

Using Auto Code Placement

Some codes are specifically designed to format an entire page. Others are designed to format just a paragraph or line. If you don't place these codes at the beginning of the appropriate page or paragraph, the end result might not be what you expected.

In their never-ending quest to make life at the keyboard a bit easier, WordPerfect Corporation has added an Auto Code Placement feature to WordPerfect 6.0.

N O T E

If you're a new or casual WordPerfect user, you might want to skip this discussion of AutoCode placement. WordPerfect will usually do the right thing with your codes, so you needn't worry about what's going on behind the scenes.

Auto Code Placement automatically places a code at the place that's "most likely" the correct place. For example, it might shoot the code over to the beginning of a paragraph, or even to the top of a page. In addition, Auto Code Placement reduces "code clutter" by deleting any nearby codes that would compete with and cancel out the new one.

For example, let's say you're using an older version of WordPerfect, without Auto Code Placement. There's a [Ln Spacing:2] code for double-spacing at the start of a paragraph. You move the cursor to the beginning of that paragraph, change the line spacing to three, and *voilà*—nothing happens. Why? Probably because the old [Ln Spacing:2] code comes *after* the new [Ln Spacing:3] code, so the old code cancels out the new one. This phenomenon drove many WordPerfect users absolutely bonkers (until they learned about Reveal Codes).

Now let's play out the same scenario with Auto Code Placement. If you change the line spacing to three *anywhere* in that paragraph, WordPerfect not only puts the [Ln Spacing:3.0] code at its (most likely) proper position—at the start of the paragraph—it also *deletes* the old [Ln Spacing:2.0] code from the beginning of the paragraph.

Codes Affected by Auto Code Placement

Auto Code Placement affects only those codes that apply specifically to paragraphs and pages. Table 4.1 summarizes those features and tells where Auto Code Placement shifts the codes.

TABLE 4.1:   Where Formatting Codes Are Placed When Auto Code Placement Is On

FEATURE	CODE PLACED AT START OF	FEATURE ACTIVATED BY
Baseline Placement	Page	Layout ➤ Document
Borders (page)	Page	Layout ➤ Page
Borders (paragraph)	Paragraph	Layout ➤ Line
Center Page	Page	Layout ➤ Page
Columns	Paragraph	Layout ➤ Columns
Footer	Paragraph	Layout ➤ Header/Footer/Watermark

TABLE 4.1: Where Formatting Codes Are Placed When Auto Code Placement Is On (continued)

FEATURE	CODE PLACED AT START OF	FEATURE ACTIVATED BY
Header	Paragraph	Layout ➤ Header/Footer/Watermark
Justification	Paragraph	Layout ➤ Justification
Hyphenation Zone	Paragraph	Layout ➤ Line
Left and Right Margins	Paragraph	Layout ➤ Margins
Letterspacing	Paragraph	Layout ➤ Other ➤ Printer Functions
Line Height	Paragraph	Layout ➤ Line
Line Height (Leading) Adjustment	Paragraph	Layout ➤ Other ➤ Printer Functions
Line Numbering	Paragraph	Layout ➤ Line
Line Spacing	Paragraph	Layout ➤ Line
Outline On	Paragraph	Tools ➤ Outline
Page Numbering	Page	Layout ➤ Page
Paper Size	Page	Layout ➤ Page
Suppress	Page	Layout ➤ Page
Tab Set	Paragraph	Layout ➤ Line
Top and Bottom Margins	Page	Layout ➤ Margins
Watermark	Paragraph	Layout ➤ Header/Footer/Watermark
Word Spacing	Paragraph	Layout ➤ Other ➤ Printer Functions
Word Spacing Justification Limits	Paragraph	Layout ➤ Other ➤ Printer Functions

If you want a simple rule-of-thumb to go by, remember that Layout ➤ Line codes generally move to the start of the paragraph, whereas Layout ➤ Page codes move to the top of the page.

Turning Auto Code Placement On and Off

If you're an experienced WordPerfect user who does fancy things with codes, you may find Auto Code Placement to be annoying at times. Fortunately, you can just follow these steps to disable it:

1. Choose File ➤ Setup ➤ Environment.

2. Deselect the Auto Code Placement setting.

3. Choose OK.

You can repeat these steps to turn Auto Code Placement back on, selecting its check box in step 2 so it contains an X.

Using Document Comments

Occasionally you may want to write notes to yourself in a document. If you work in a group, you might want to write notes to the editor, writer, or other group members. You can use *document comments* to put such notes in your documents.

Document comments are framed so that they stand out from the rest of your text. Document comments are visible only in the Text and Graphics modes (Ctrl+F3). Figure 4.8 shows an example: a note to the author of an article (AU) from the editor (ED). Document comments never appear on the printed copy of the document, so you can always review a clean copy of the text without being distracted by the comments.

FIGURE 4.8

A document comment within a document. In Reveal Codes, only the [Comment] code appears.

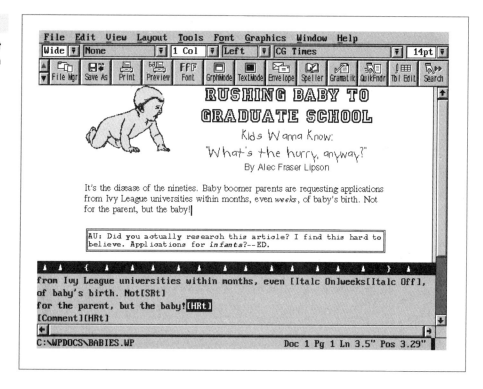

To add a comment to a document, follow these steps:

1. Position the cursor where you want the comment to appear.

2. Choose Layout ➤ Comment ➤ Create. What appears to be a new, clean document will open on your screen.

3. Type your comment using the standard editing keys to make changes and corrections. Keep the comment short—half a page or so at most.

4. Press F7 or click the "Press F7 when done" prompt at the bottom of the screen when you've finished typing the comment.

The comment appears within a box in your document. (If it doesn't, see "Hiding and Displaying Document Comments," later in this chapter.)

Changing a Document Comment

If you need to change the text within a document comment, follow these steps:

1. Move the cursor to just below the comment you want to change. You can use Search (F2) to locate the [Comment] code. (See Chapter 9.)

2. Choose Layout ➤ Comment ➤ Edit. This returns you to the screen for editing the comment.

3. Make whatever changes you wish, then press F7.

Moving, Copying, and Deleting a Comment

Each document comment you create is placed in a hidden [Comment] code at the cursor. Like all codes, the [Comment] code is visible only when Reveal Codes is turned on. To move, copy, or delete a [Comment] code (and the comment itself), use the techniques described in the Reveal Codes section earlier in this chapter.

TIP

You can delete all the comments in a document in one step by using the Replace feature to replace all the [Comment] codes with "nothing" (see Chapter 9).

Converting Text to a Comment

You can convert any text in a document to a comment. This might come in handy if, say, you can't decide whether or not to leave a particular passage in text, but you don't want to delete it altogether. Just follow these steps:

1. Select the text that you want to convert to a comment.

2. Choose Layout ➤ Comment ➤ Create.

The selected text is removed from the regular text and displayed within a comment.

Converting a Comment to Text

If you want to convert a comment to normal text within the document, follow these steps:

1. Move the cursor just below the comment you want to convert to text.

2. Choose Layout ➤ Comment ➤ Convert To Text.

The text within the comment is converted to normal text, and the [Comment] code is removed. If necessary, add spaces or hard returns (press ↵) to blend the text with existing text.

Hiding and Displaying Document Comments

If you want to hide document comments on the screen so that you can focus on the regular text, follow these steps:

1. Choose View ➤ Screen Setup ➤Window Options.

2. Deselect Display Comments to hide the comments and choose OK.

To take the comments back out of hiding, choose View ➤ Screen Setup ➤ Window Options and reselect Display Comments.

Printing Document Comments

There is no way to print document comments within their boxes or to display them on the Print Preview screen: You must convert them to text first. Or, you can use graphics boxes, rather than document comments, to write notes to yourself and others (see Chapter 26).

You can create a macro that converts all the document comments to text boxes, so that they'll be printed, framed, and shaded for easy recognition. A similar macro can go though the document and convert all those text boxes back to document comments when convenient. (See Chapter 18.)

TIP

WordPerfect also lets you create hidden text which you can either show or hide (Font ➤ Hidden Text). If the hidden text is showing, you can print it. (See Chapter 6.)

Shortcuts for Typing the Date

A simple, though handy, feature of WordPerfect is its ability to *date-stamp* a document. You might put the date at the top of a business letter or a memo, or perhaps you would include a date to indicate the current revision or printing of a document. There are two types of dates you can include in your document automatically:

Date Text   Types the current date; the date never changes.

Date Code   Places a [Date] code that appears as the current system date; the date automatically changes when the system date changes.

TIP

The *system date* is determined by your computer's system clock. If necessary, you can correct the date and time using the DOS DATE and TIME commands. Refer to your DOS manual.

Each of the date options is useful in its own way. You might want to use Date Text when typing a letter, since you don't really want the date in the letter to change. But, you might want to insert the Date Code in a page footer (Chapter 8) in your document. That way, when you print the document, the bottom of each page will show when that copy was printed. (This is very handy if you print several drafts of a document, and you want the date of each version to appear on each printed copy.)

T I P

When you save your work in WordPerfect, the current date and time are recorded with the file name. You can use DOS or the File Manager (Chapter 20) to check the date of the document.

Inserting the Date

To use WordPerfect's shortcut for typing a date, follow the steps below:

1. Move the cursor to wherever you want the date to appear.

2. Choose Tools ➤ Date (or press Shift+F5), then choose either Text or Code, depending on which type of date you want to insert.

The date will appear at the cursor position.

Changing the Date Format

If you want to display the date in a format other than the one WordPerfect uses, follow these steps:

1. Choose Tools ➤ Date ➤ Format.

2. Choose the format you want (or the one that most closely matches the format you want) from the options shown below:

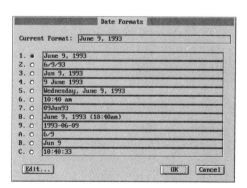

3. If you want to customize the format you selected to suit your needs, choose Edit, and then use the Edit Date Format dialog box to make changes. (If you need help with this, just press F1.)

4. Choose OK to return to the document.

Only dates that you put into the document *after* changing the format and *past* the hidden [Date Fmt] code will appear in the new format. Use Reveal Codes, if necessary, to locate the [Date Fmt] code and to delete (or move) any previous [Date] codes.

Previewing Your Printed Document

The Print Preview screen lets you see your document pretty much as it will look when printed. You can also zoom out for an arm's-length view or zoom in for a close-up view. The Print Preview screen even lets you view facing pages, thumbnail sketches, and more. Be forewarned that Print Preview can be painfully s-l-o-w when displaying a document with lots of graphics. If you lose your patience, press Escape.

To see your document in Print Preview, choose File ➤ Print Preview, or press Shift+F7 V. You'll be taken to the Print Preview screen (see Figure 4.9). Be aware that you cannot make any changes to a document in Print Preview mode.

NOTE

Menu sequences are often shown as a function key or combination keystroke followed by a space and another letter or a series of letters (as in Shift+F V). That just shows you the keyboard shortcut and the hotkey(s) to press. (Don't type the plus sign or the space!)

FIGURE 4.9

A sample document
in Print Preview mode
after choosing the
Facing Pages view

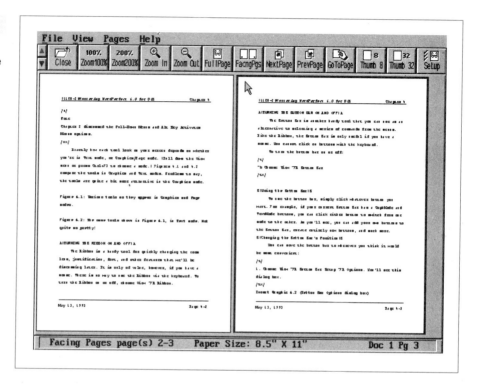

Print Preview Button Bar

The Print Preview screen has its own Button Bar, which offers shortcuts for menu commands. To turn the Button Bar on or off, choose View ➤ Button Bar. To reposition the Button Bar, choose View ➤ Button Bar Setup ➤ Options. You can add, move, and delete buttons using View ➤ Button Bar Setup ➤ Edit, as described earlier in this chapter.

Color, or Black and White?

If you're using a black-and-white printer, you might prefer to see your text and any graphics you might have in black and white. To switch between color and black-and-white, follow these steps:

1. Choose File ➤ Setup.

2. Select (or deselect) <u>V</u>iew Text & Graphics in Black & White.

3. Choose OK.

Using Zoom with Print Preview

Print Preview has more sophisticated "zooming" capabilities than the document window. To try these out, click any button in the Button Bar or choose an option from the <u>V</u>iew menu. Your options are as follows:

<u>100</u>% View   Approximately the printed size.

<u>2</u>00% View   Double the printed size.

Zoom <u>I</u>n   Zooms in on the currently selected page (the page that's highlighted or bordered).

Zoom <u>O</u>ut   Zooms out to a more distant view.

Zoom <u>A</u>rea   After selecting this option, the mouse pointer changes to a magnifying glass. Click the magnifying glass on whichever portion of the document you want to zoom in on, or use your arrow keys to move the glass and press ↵.

S<u>e</u>lect Area   A rectangle appears after you select this option. Use your mouse to drag the rectangle to the area you want to zoom in on, or press the arrow keys to move the rectangle and then press ↵.

TIP

You can also use your mouse to zoom in on an area of any size, without choosing any menu options or Button Bar buttons. First, move the mouse pointer to one corner of the area, then drag diagonally to outline the area you want to view close up. When you release the mouse button, WordPerfect will zoom in on that area.

<u>R</u>eset   Restore view to the initial view.

<u>F</u>ull Page   Zoom to view the entire page.

Facing Pages View even-numbered pages on the left, odd-numbered pages on the right.

Thumbnails Choose from various thumbnail-sized views, ranging from a single page to 255 pages.

Moving in Print Preview

You can move around your document in Print Preview using these options on the Pages menu (or equivalent buttons on the Button Bar):

Go To Page Lets you enter the number of the page you want to go to.

Previous Page Skips to the previous page (if there is one).

Next Page Skips to the next page (if there is one).

The current page number appears next to Pg in the status bar, near the lower-right corner of the screen.

Scrolling in Print Preview

While you're viewing a document at 100% magnification or greater, you can use the arrow, PgUp, and PgDn keys to scroll through the document. Use ← and → to scroll left and right when the page is magnified wider than the screen. You can also use the scroll bars to scroll with your mouse.

Closing Print Preview

When you're finished previewing the document, choose File ➤ Close, or press F7 or Escape. Or, if the Button Bar is displayed and there's a Close button on it, just click that button.

Instant Document Statistics

If you want to get quick statistics on your document, such as the number of words, lines, sentences, or whatever:

1. Choose Tools ➤ Writing Tools ➤ Document Information. (I'll assume that this particular dialog box speaks for itself.)

2. After reviewing the information, choose OK or press ↵ to return to your document.

In this chapter we've looked at some handy general-purpose tools that can make your time at the keyboard easier and more productive. Next, we'll look at ways to control spacing, alignment, and indenting in your documents.

PART TWO

...And the Start of Everything Else

Spacing, Aligning, and Indenting Text

fast TRACK

type the number or special character that identifies the item in the list. Next press F4 or Shift+F4. Type the text of that item. Finally, press ⏎ once or twice to start the next item in the list. Repeat these steps for the remaining list items.

position the cursor or select a block of text. Choose Layout ➤ Tab Set, and adjust the tab stops on the tab ruler. You'll be able to see changes to tabbed text below the cursor as you adjust the tabs.

press Ctrl+F6 instead of Tab before typing the text or number you want to align.

position the cursor or select a block of text. Choose Layout ➤ Character ➤ Decimal/Align Character (or press Shift+F8 CD), then type the decimal-align character you want. To change the thousands separator, choose Thousands Separator and type the character you want.

press Alt+F6 twice where you want the dot leaders to start. You can also press Shift+F6 twice to insert dot leaders in front of centered text.

MANY typing and writing projects require you to space, justify, indent, and align text. As you'll discover in this chapter, Word-Perfect offers much more flexibility for these tasks than even the most sophisticated typewriter. Here's just one small example: On a typewriter, you must set your tab stops before you start to type. But with WordPerfect, you can change the tab stops *after* you've typed your text, and your text will adjust instantly to the new settings. And that's just the beginning!

N O T E

The Line Format dialog box provides an alternative way to use several of the formatting features discussed in this chapter. To reach this dialog box, choose Layout ➤ Line. Then choose Tab Set, Justification, or Line Spacing, as you wish.

All the formatting features discussed in this chapter insert hidden codes into your document. For most features, you can position the cursor at a specific place in your document, or you can select text before choosing a formatting option. If you selected the text before formatting it, your changes will affect the selected text only and will insert hidden codes at the beginning and end of the selected text. If you don't select text first, the hidden codes will appear at the cursor position and your changes will affect text to the right of and below the cursor. To watch these codes appear as you format your text, simply turn on Reveal Codes (press Alt+F3 or F11) before you choose a formatting option.

If the formatting doesn't seem to work as you want it to, your document may contain some conflicting codes. Please see "Revealing the Hidden Codes," and "Using Auto Code Placement" in Chapter 4, and Appendix D, if you need more information about codes.

Changing Line Spacing

Suppose you use a typewriter to type a single-spaced document, only to discover that you should have doublespaced it. You have no choice but to retype the entire document.

In WordPerfect, retyping isn't necessary. You can just click on a few menu options or press a shortcut key to change the line spacing to any measurement you wish. Here's how it works:

1. Move the cursor to the first character of the line where you want to change the line spacing (or where you're about to type new text). Or, select the text that should have the new line spacing.

2. Choose Layout ➤ Line ➤ Line Spacing (or press Shift+F8 LS).

3. Type the new line spacing amount.

4. Choose OK.

In step 3 above, you can even enter fractions (up to two decimal places). For example, *1* is single spacing, *2* is double spacing, *1.25* is one-and-a-quarter spacing, and *1.5* is one-and-a-half spacing. Figure 5.1 illustrates these four types of line spacing. You can enter just about any value for line spacing (*3* for triple spacing, *4* for quadruple spacing, and so on).

N O T E

In Text mode, the document window may not exactly reflect the line spacing you choose. For a more accurate picture, switch to Graphics or Page mode, or check the Print Preview screen.

Sometimes a printer will print at double the spacing you requested (perhaps you want single spacing, but the printer prints double). This can happen when the Auto LineFeed or Auto LF setting on your printer is turned on. Consult your printer manual to learn how to turn this switch off.

FIGURE 5.1

Text set with single (1), double (2), one-and-a-quarter (1.25), and one-and-a-half (1.5) line spacing

---

Single spacing

Here is a paragraph that uses the default single spacing. To change the line spacing, position the cursor wherever you want to change the spacing (either before or after typing the text), and select Layout ▸ Line ▸ Line Spacing. Then type a number and press ↵ twice.

Double spacing

Here is a paragraph that uses the double spacing (2). To select double spacing,

position the cursor wherever you want to start double spacing (either before or

after typing the text), and select Layout ▸ Line ▸ Line Spacing. Then type **2**

and press ↵ twice.

One-and-a-quarter spacing

You can enter fractions when you define the line spacing. For example, this text uses one-and-a-quarter (1.25) spacing. WordPerfect lets you set the line spacing to just about any number — you're not at all limited to 1, 1.5, and 2.

One-and-a-half spacing

In this example, the text uses one-and-a-half (1.5) spacing. As you can see,

WordPerfect line spacing can be as flexible (and varied) as you want it to be.

Adjusting the Space between Paragraphs

Many people like to type text so that a blank line appears between paragraphs. One way to accomplish this is to press ↵ twice after each paragraph. But if you're lazy, or you want to separate paragraphs by fractions of lines, follow these steps instead:

1. Move the cursor to where you want the spacing changes to begin, or select the paragraphs you want to adjust.

2. Choose <u>L</u>ayout ➤ <u>M</u>argins ➤ <u>P</u>aragraph Spacing (or press Shift+F8 MP).

3. Type the number of lines that should appear between paragraphs. For example, type **2** to place a blank line between paragraphs. Type **2.5** to add a blank line, plus half a line, between paragraphs.

4. Choose OK.

Changing the Margins

WordPerfect places a default 1-inch margin around every printed page of your document. This is illustrated in Figure 5.2. However, you can change the margins at any time, either before or after typing the document.

TIP

You don't need to change the margins to indent a block of text. You can use the Indent keys instead, as discussed a little later in this chapter.

To change the margins in a document, follow these steps:

1. Position the cursor where you want the new margins to start. (press Home Home ↑ to change margins for the entire document). Or, select a block of text to change margins in that block only.

2. Select <u>L</u>ayout ➤ <u>M</u>argins (or press Shift+F8 M). You'll see the Margin Format dialog box, shown in Figure 5.3.

3. Select the margin you want to change.

4. Type a measurement for the margin, such as **2** for 2 inches or **1.5** for 1$^1/_2$ inches, then press ↵. You can specify up to two decimal places (for example, 1.25, 2.75).

5. Repeat steps 3 and 4 until you've changed all the settings you want.

FIGURE 5.2

By default, WordPerfect uses 1-inch margins.

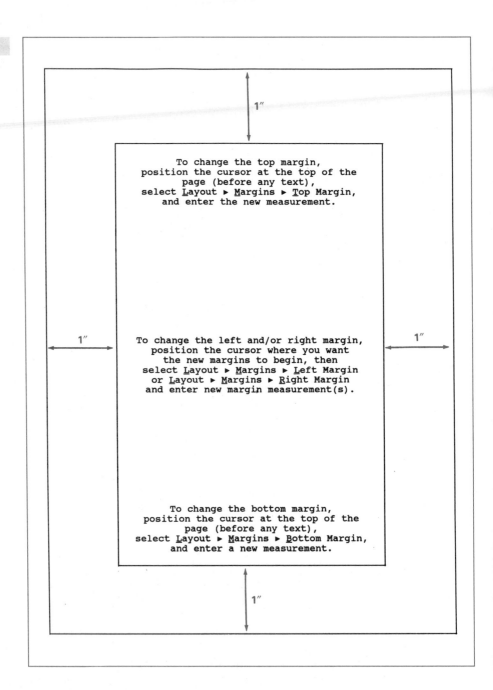

FIGURE 5.3

The Margin Format
dialog box

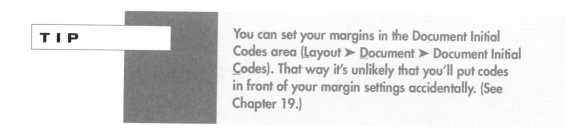

```
                    Margin Format
 ┌─Document Margins──────────────────────────┐
 │ 1. Left Margin:              [1"        ]  │
 │ 2. Right Margin:             [1"        ]  │
 │                                           │
 │ 3. Top Margin:               [1"        ]  │
 │ 4. Bottom Margin:            [1"        ]  │
 └───────────────────────────────────────────┘
 ┌─Paragraph Margins─────────────────────────┐
 │ 5. Left Margin Adjustment:   [0"        ]  │
 │ 6. Right Margin Adjustment:  [0"        ]  │
 │                                           │
 │ 7. First Line Indent:        [0"        ]  │
 │ 8. Paragraph Spacing:        [1.0      ]⬍ │
 └───────────────────────────────────────────┘
                        [  OK  ]  [Cancel]
```

6. Choose OK.

WordPerfect will automatically reformat all text below the cursor (or the text you selected) to fit in the new margins. You may want to use the Page mode screen (Ctrl+F3 P) or the Print Preview screen (File ➤ Print Preview) at Full Page or 100% view to verify your new settings.

TIP

You can set your margins in the Document Initial Codes area (Layout ➤ Document ➤ Document Initial Codes). That way it's unlikely that you'll put codes in front of your margin settings accidentally. (See Chapter 19.)

Minimum Margin Widths

Laser printers and other printers that feed paper from a tray do so with small wheels that pull the paper by its edges through the printer. The outer edges of the page are called the "dead zone" because the printer cannot print there. (If text were printed within the dead zone, the small wheels would probably smudge the printed text.)

You can't set the margins to a value that falls within the dead zone. For example, if you try to set the margins to 0″, WordPerfect will automatically increase your margin measurement to compensate for the dead zone. Typically the minimum value falls between 0.20 and 0.30 inches.

TIP

If you have problems printing text within the margins, the paper may simply be misaligned in your printer. See Chapter 10 for some tips.

Aligning and Justifying Text

WordPerfect offers five ways to align (or *justify*) written text. These are Left, Full, Center, Right, and Full, All Lines. Figure 5.4 illustrates and describes each type of justification.

NOTE

WordPerfect can also center text vertically between the top and bottom margins. You'll learn about this type of centering in Chapter 8.

Justifying text is a lot easier than justifying your expense account. Here's how to do it:

1. Move the cursor to the place where the new justification should take effect. This can be the first character of existing text or the point where you're about to type new text. Or, select a block of text to limit your changes to that block only.

Full Justification ————————————————————

Unless you tell it otherwise, WordPerfect will print paragraphs with full justification, where both the left and right margins are smooth. Full justification is one of the hallmarks of documents created with a word processor instead of a typewriter. To smooth out the the left and right margins, WordPerfect must add space between words and letters. This can make the text look "gappy," and even produce rivers of white space running down the page in large documents.

Full Justification (All Lines) ————————————————

Full justification (All Lines) is a lot like full justification, where both the left and right margins are smooth. However, unlike plain old full justification, the all lines flavor tries to spread out short lines as well. This can look very strange, but it m u s t   b e   t h e r e   f o r   a   r e a s o n .

Left Justification ————————————————————

Left justification produces a ragged-right margin, as in this example. This method creates a more personalized "hand-typed" look. Because left justification doesn't add extra spaces just to make text reach the right margin, words and letters appear without extra gaps, and rivers of white space are never a problem. Many people prefer left-justified documents because they tend to be easier on the eyes.

Center Justification ——————————————————————

Self-Centered Text in a Cockeyed World
by
Ann E. Buddee

August 18, 1994

Right Justification ————————————————————

Rightly Justified, Inc.
1234 Walla Walla Lane
P.O. Box 1234
Cucamonga, CA 91234

2. Choose Layout ➤ Justification (or press Shift+F8 LJ). You'll see the various justification options.

3. Select a justification style (Left, Center, Right, Full, or Full, All Lines).

If you change your mind and want to use another kind of justification, you can do any of the following:

- Go into Reveal Codes and delete the [Just] code that you inserted earlier.
- Change the newly added justification to another kind of justification.
- Switch to another kind of justification later in your document.

Centering or Right Justifying One Short Line

You can center or right-align a single short line of text by following these steps:

1. Position the cursor where you're about to type the short line or at the start of the short line if you've already typed it.

2. Do one of the following:
   - To center the line, press Shift+F6 or choose Layout ➤ Alignment ➤ Center.
   - To right-align the line, press Alt+F6 or choose Layout ➤ Alignment ➤ Flush Right.

3. If you haven't done so yet, type the short text and press ↵.

4. If you've already typed a short line, press the End key, then press ↓ or ↵.

To center or right justify several lines at once, simply select those lines in step 1 above.

Indenting Paragraphs

As Figure 5.5 illustrates, there are almost as many ways to indent paragraphs as there are to cheat on your income tax. All of these indentations are easy to achieve with WordPerfect.

Indenting with Tab

    To indent the first line of a paragraph, just press Tab before typing the first line. That's how you'd do it on a typewriter, and that's how I did it at the beginning of this paragraph. Of course, if you've already typed the entire paragraph, *then* decide to indent the first line, just move the cursor to the start of that line and press Tab.

Indenting with Indent→ (F4)

    To indent the entire left margin of a paragraph, move the cursor to the beginning of the paragraph you want to indent (or where you're about to type a paragraph). Now press Indent→ (F4) as many times as you need to get the indentation level you want. WordPerfect will indent the entire left margin of that paragraph, like it did for this one. (Here, I pressed →Indent twice and then typed the paragraph.)

Indenting with Indent→← (Shift + F4)

    To indent both the left and right margins, move the cursor to the beginning of the paragraph you want to indent (or where you're about to type a paragraph). Now press Indent→← (Shift + F4) as many times as you need to get the indentation level you want. This technique is great for long passages of quoted text.

Outdenting the First Line

To indent all the lines *beneath* the first line in a paragraph, move the cursor to the beginning of that paragraph (or where you're about to start typing that paragraph). Next, press Indent→ (F4) then Back Tab (Shift + Tab).

Hanging (outdenting) into the Left Margin

To hang the first line of a paragraph out into the margin, move the cursor to the beginning of that paragraph (or where you're about to start typing that paragraph), then press Back Tab (Shift + Tab).

Indenting One Paragraph

Here are the general steps to follow for indenting a single paragraph:

1. Move the cursor to the place where you'll start typing your paragraph. If you've already typed the paragraph, move the cursor to the first character in the paragraph.

2. Depending on what you want, do one of the following:

   • To indent the first line of the paragraph, press Tab.

- To indent the entire left side of the paragraph, press F4 or choose <u>L</u>ayout ➤ <u>A</u>lignment ➤ <u>I</u>ndent →.

- To indent both the left and right sides of the paragraph by equal amounts, press Shift+F4 or choose <u>L</u>ayout ➤ <u>A</u>lignment ➤ I<u>n</u>dent→←.

- To "outdent" the first line of the paragraph, press F4 and then press Shift+Tab. Or select <u>L</u>ayout ➤ <u>A</u>lignment ➤ <u>H</u>anging Indent. (An outdented paragraph is sometimes called a *hanging indent* because the first line hangs out, and the remaining lines are indented.)

- To hang the first line of a paragraph into the left margin, press Shift+Tab or choose <u>L</u>ayout ➤ <u>A</u>lignment ➤ <u>B</u>ack Tab at the beginning of the line.

3. Repeat step 2 as often as you wish to deepen the indent or outdent.

4. If you haven't typed the paragraph yet, go ahead and do so now. Then press ↵.

Regardless of how you indent or outdent a paragraph, you can change your mind and un-indent or un-outdent the text later by removing the hidden codes. If you want to change the *amount* of indentation (or outdentation), you'll need to change the tab stops, as described later in this chapter.

N O T E   The indenting described above applies only to the current paragraph. When you end the paragraph (press ↵), the indenting ends as well.

Indenting Many Paragraphs

The indent features discussed in the previous section affect one paragraph only. If you'd like to indent several paragraphs at once, follow these steps:

1. Move the cursor to where you want paragraph indenting to start, or select the paragraphs you want to indent.

2. Choose <u>L</u>ayout ➤ <u>M</u>argins or press Shift+F8 M. You'll see the Margin Format dialog box shown earlier in Figure 5.3.

3. Now, select any of the options listed below:

> **L<u>e</u>ft Margin Adjustment**   Indents the left margin for subsequent paragraphs or the selected paragraphs.
>
> **R<u>i</u>ght Margin Adjustment**   Indents the right margin for subsequent paragraphs or the selected paragraphs.
>
> **First Line Indent**   Indents the first line of subsequent paragraphs or the selected paragraphs.

4. Specify a new setting and press ↵. You can type the exact measurement you want or use a relative measurement. For example, to indent by 1 inch, just type **1**. To increase the measurement by 1 inch more than the current measurement, type **+1**. To decrease the measurement by 1 inch less than the current measurement, type **-1**.

5. Repeat steps 3 and 4 until you're done, then choose OK.

Typing Lists

Figure 5.6 shows several examples of short lists. These are easy to type if you follow the steps below:

1. To indent the item number or letter (or bullet, pointing hand, or check box) from the left margin, press Tab until you've indented as far as you want.

2. Type the item number, letter, bullet, pointing hand, or check box.

3. Press F4 or Shift+F4 if you want to indent the text from both sides.

4. Type the text of the item and press ↵ (press ↵ twice if you want to place a blank line between items).

That takes care of the first list item. Now simply repeat these steps for the remaining items in your list.

FIGURE 5.6

Several types of lists

Numbered List

1. To type a numbered list, type the number (and perhaps a period) that identifies the item (e.g., **1.** next to this item).

2. Press Indent→ (F4) or Indent→← (Shift+F4) if you want to indent text from both sides.

3. Type the text (this part).

4. Press ↵ (once or twice) and repeat steps 1-3 for the next item in the list.

Indenting the Entire List

1. If you want to indent the entire list like this...

2. Press Tab as often as necessary to move the cursor to the tab stop that you want to align the numbers on, then type the number (e.g., **2.**).

3. Press F4 or Shift+F4 and type the text next to the number, as usual.

Changing the Tab Stops

1. I typed this list exactly like the one above...

2. But then I changed the tab stops to narrow the gap between the left margin, each number, and its text. You'll learn about tab stops later in this chapter.

Bulleted List

*   A bulleted list is the same as a numbered list...

*   Except that you type a bullet (a special character) instead of a number to identify each item in the list.

Check List
☐ A check list is like any other list...
☐ Except that each item starts with a large hollow square (another special character).
☐ I single-spaced this example pressing ↵ only once after typing each item.

Pointing List
☞ This list is just like any of those above...
☞ Except it uses a different special character to the left.

NOTE   Bullets, pointing hands, check boxes, and other special characters are discussed in more detail in Chapter 6.

Here are some ways to refine your lists:

- Typing each number, letter, or bullet in a list can be a crashing bore, especially if you rearrange your lists often. Happily, WordPerfect has a remedy in the form of *automatic numbering* or *outlining*, which I'll cover in Chapter 14. These features offer a real advantage because they automatically adjust all numbers (or letters, bullets, or special characters) whenever you rearrange or delete items in your list.

- Styles, covered in Chapter 17, can also help you type lists, particularly those that use special characters.

- The gaps between the number (bullet, letter, etc.) in each list item and the item's text are controlled by *tab stops*. To narrow or widen the gap, simply change the tab stops, as described in the next section.

Setting Tab Stops

WordPerfect automatically sets tab stops at every half inch, starting at the left edge of the page. That's why all indents and outdents created with the Tab, Shift+Tab, F4, and Shift+F4 keys are initially in half-inch increments: The first indent level is one-half inch from the left margin, the next level is 1 inch from the left margin, and so forth.

NOTE   Just in case you're not a typist, a *tab stop* is the place where the cursor stops when you press the Tab or indent. That is, the tab stops here.

Viewing the Tab Ruler

The *tab ruler* shows the current tab settings. To view the tab ruler, simply turn on Reveal Codes. (Press Alt+F3, or choose View ➤ Reveal Codes.) The tab ruler will appear between the editing area at the top of the screen and the Reveal Codes section at the bottom. Turning the tab ruler off is as easy as turning it on: Simply turn off Reveal Codes.

NOTE You can't change the tab stops when you're viewing the tab ruler in Reveal Codes. I'll explain how to change the tab stops later.

In Figure 5.7 you can see the tab ruler between the editing window and the Reveal Codes window. The triangles represent current tab stops. A left curly brace ({) or left bracket ([) shows the left margin setting, and a right curly brace (})

FIGURE 5.7

The tab ruler at the bottom of the Edit screen

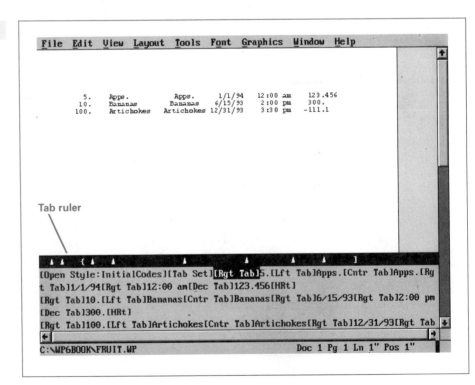

or right bracket (]) shows the right margin setting. (You'll see braces if the margin falls on a tab setting and brackets if it doesn't.)

You can change the tab stops used for indenting before or after you've typed your text, or you can change them in a selected block of text. Word-Perfect lets you change tab stops in as many places as you need. You'll learn how in the next few sections.

Types of Tab Alignment

At each tab stop, you can change both the position and alignment of text. Your alignment options are as follows:

Left   Text typed at the tab setting is left-aligned at the tab stop (the default method).

Center   Text is centered at the tab stop.

Right   Text is right-aligned at the tab stop.

Decimal   Text is aligned on a decimal point or some other character.

Dot Leader   Empty space to the left of the tab stop is filled with dots. (You can use dot leaders with any of the tab settings above.) The next section explains how to change the dot leader and the spacing between the dot leader characters.

Figures 5.8 through 5.10 show various tab alignments and dot leaders. In the figures, you can see the ruler, which is used to set tab stops. I'll explain how to display and use this ruler in a moment.

Changing the Dot Leader

Period (.) is the default repeating character in a dot leader. Each period is usually separated by one space. However, you can choose any dot leader character and spacing you wish, by following these steps:

1. Place the cursor wherever you want the changes to take effect, or select a block of text to limit your changes to that block.

2. Choose Layout ➤ Character ➤ Dot Leader Character (or press Shift+F8 CL).

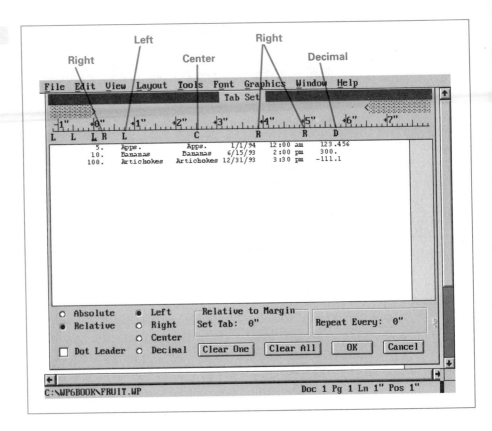

3. In the Character text box, type any keyboard character. Or, press Ctrl+W, choose a character Set, then select any WordPerfect character, and choose Insert. (Chapter 6 explains how to enter WordPerfect Characters.)

4. In the Spaces Between Dots text box, type the number of spaces that should appear between each dot leader character.

5. Choose OK.

The new dot leader character will affect dot-leader tab stops, text that you center by pressing Shift+F6 twice, and text that you right-align by pressing Alt+F6 twice.

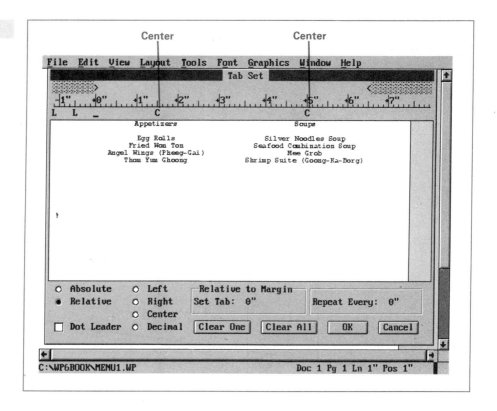

FIGURE 5.9

Two center-aligned
tab stops

Alternatives to Tabs

In all fairness, I should tell you that tab stops provide just one way to arrange text in tabular columns. Other—often much easier—methods include using tables (Chapter 7) and columns (Chapter 27). These alternate techniques are best when you need to have text wrap around in two or more columns, or you want to do fancier formatting than tabs allow.

But don't stop reading here! You still need to understand the basics of using tab stops to control the amount of indenting and outdenting, or the "gaps" in lists.

FIGURE 5.10

Dot leaders

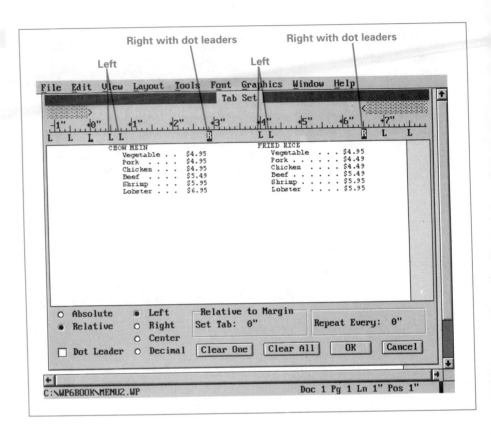

Setting and Changing Tab Stops

Here are the basic steps for setting or changing tab stops:

1. Move the cursor to where you want the tab settings to begin, or select a block of text if you want to change tabs in that block only.

2. Select <u>L</u>ayout ➤ Ta<u>b</u> Set (or press Shift+F8 LT). The Tab Set dialog box will appear (see Figure 5.11).

3. Adjust the tab stops as described in the sections below.

4. Choose OK.

Figure 5.11 shows WordPerfect's default tab stops and tab ruler. The ruler is marked in inches, just like a desk ruler or yardstick.

FIGURE 5.11

The Tab Set dialog box. The text is the same as the text in Figure 5.10.

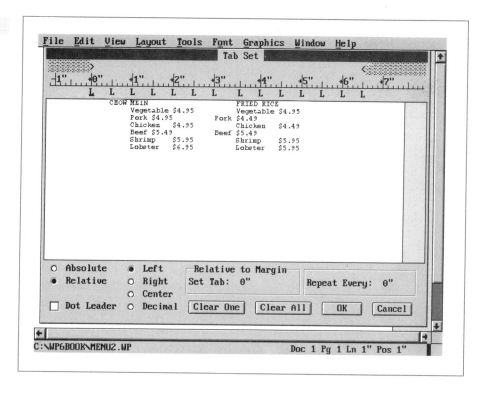

Notice that the text in Figure 5.11 is the same as the text in Figure 5.10, but it's aligned differently and has a different tab line. Figure 5.11 is the *before* shot, using the default tab settings of $1/2$ inch, while Figure 5.10 shows the text alignment and tab ruler *after* I set the tab stops.

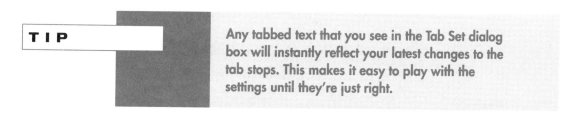

TIP

Any tabbed text that you see in the Tab Set dialog box will instantly reflect your latest changes to the tab stops. This makes it easy to play with the settings until they're just right.

There are many ways to change settings on the tab ruler, and you can do most of the steps in any order you wish.

Moving the Cursor along the Ruler

Before you can do anything useful, you need to move the cursor to a tab stop position or existing tab stop. Here's how:

- To move the cursor along the ruler, click on any position in the ruler or press the ← and → keys.

- To move the cursor to the edges of the tab ruler quickly, use these cursor-movement keys:

  Home ←   Left edge of the ruler

  Home Home ←   Extreme left edge of the ruler

  End   Extreme right edge of the ruler

  Home →   Right edge of the ruler

- To move the cursor from tab stop to tab stop, press the ↑ key (next tab stop) or ↓ key (previous tab stop).

Deleting Tab Stops

After you position the cursor on a tab stop, you can delete the tab stop, if you wish:

- To delete the current tab stop, press the Delete key or click the Clear <u>O</u>ne button (shown at left).

- To delete all the tab stops to the right of the cursor, press Ctrl+End.

- To delete all the tab stops on the ruler, click the Clear <u>A</u>ll button (the cursor position doesn't matter).

Choosing the Type of Tab Stop

You can change the type of any tab stop (left, right, center, or decimal). If you're changing an existing tab stop, move your cursor to it first. If you're creating a new tab stop, move your cursor to the place where you want the tab stop to appear. Then type the first letter of the tab type you want (**L**, **R**, **C**, or **D**), or click the <u>L</u>eft, <u>R</u>ight, <u>C</u>enter, or <u>D</u>ecimal option button near the bottom of the Tab Set dialog box.

Adding or Changing a Tab Stop

To add a new tab at the cursor position, simply select the tab type as described above.

If you know the exact location for the tab stop, you can set it this way: Choose Set Tab, type the exact position where you want the tab to appear, and press ↵. Then choose the tab type. Your setting can have up to two decimal places. For example, you would type **5.25** in the Set Tab box to set a tab stop at $5\frac{1}{4}$ inches.

T I P

To set a left tab stop quickly, double-click on the ruler at the spot where you want the tab stop to appear.

Adding Several Tab Stops at Once

It's easy to set up equally spaced tabs. First, clear the tab ruler. Next, use the Set Tab box to set the position for the first tab stop. Then select Repeat Every, type in the tab interval (using up to two decimal places), and press ↵. For example, you would type **0** in the Set Tab box and **.5** in the Repeat Every box to set tabs $\frac{1}{2}$ inch apart.

Moving a Tab Stop

You can move an existing tab stop to a new place on the ruler line by deleting it and setting it again. Or, you can move the cursor to the tab stop, then press Ctrl+← or Ctrl+→ until the tab stop is where you want it (much easier!).

Adding a Dot Leader

To add a dot leader, move the cursor to an existing tab stop and press the period (.) or check the Dot Leader box at the bottom of the Tab Set dialog box. The tab stop will appear in reverse video, or a different color. To turn off the dot leader, simply repeat the steps you used to turn it on. (Remember that you can change the dot leader character that appears in your document, as explained earlier under "Changing the Dot Leader.")

NOTE   If you turn on the dot leader in an empty area of the tab ruler, WordPerfect will place a right tab with dot leader in that spot.

Changing the Relative or Absolute Measurements

You can choose the Absolute or Relative option button in the dialog box to specify absolute or relative tab stops.

With *relative* measurement (the default setting), WordPerfect always measures tab stops from the left margin. In other words, the tab stops "float" with the left margin. Suppose that you've set relative tab stops every $1/2$ inch and then you move the left margin $1/4$ inch to the right. All tab stops will automatically move $1/4$ inch to the right. This way, the first tab stop remains 1 inch from the left margin.

When you use *absolute* measurement, WordPerfect measures tab stops from the left edge of the *page*, independent of the left margin. Unlike relative tabs, absolute tab stops don't float with the left margin. To illustrate, imagine that you've set *absolute* tab stops every $1/2$ inch and then you move the left margin $1/4$ inch to the right. This time, the tab stops remain unchanged. The first tab stop is $1/4$ inch from the left margin, the second is $3/4$ inch from the left margin, and so forth.

Generally speaking, *relative* tab stops are the easiest to get along with because the indent keys always have the same effect, no matter where you've set the left margin. However, if you're working with graphics and multicolumn layouts (see Part 7 in this book), absolute tab measurements may be better, since they let you control exactly where each tab stop is.

Using Tab Stops

When you're ready to use the tab stops you've set, return to the document window. Then press the Tab, Shift+Tab, F4, or Shift+F4 keys to make the cursor jump to the next tab stop. Until you press one of those keys, the tab stop does nothing.

For example, to create the two-column menu shown in Figure 5.9, you'd need to move the cursor to the next tab stop by pressing Tab. Then you'd type the name of an appetizer or soup. In Figure 5.12, I didn't get dot leaders unless I pressed Tab after typing a Chow Mein or Fried Rice entry. Also, to *prevent* dot leaders from appearing between the "CHOW MEIN" and "FRIED RICE" headings, I typed **CHOW MEIN**, pressed the spacebar until the cursor was past the right tab stop, then pressed Tab to move to the proper tab stop for the "FRIED RICE" heading. You can see these extra spaces before the [Lft Tab] code in the Reveal Codes screen shown in Figure 5.12.

FIGURE 5.12

The menu with its final tab settings

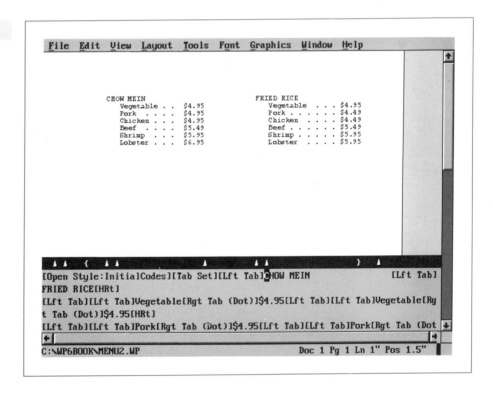

When Pressing Tab Doesn't Insert Tabs

When you work with text that's already tabbed into place, remember these two important points:

- When you're in Insert mode, pressing Tab inserts another tab code in the text.

- When you're in Typeover mode, pressing Tab simply moves the cursor to the next tab stop, without inserting a tab code.

Therefore, when you edit text that's already aligned on tab stops, you might want to press the Insert key to switch to Typeover mode. Then you can press Tab or Shift+Tab to move from column to column without inserting extra tabs and back tabs (which would move the text out of alignment). Of course, you can also use the mouse or the arrow keys to position the cursor without inserting unwanted tabs.

Fixing Alignment Errors

Beware of these three tab-alignment bugaboos:

- Lines between the columns are wavy instead of straight.

- Columns are misaligned because of missing or extra tab-alignment codes.

- Columns are misaligned because the text is wider than the columns themselves.

In the next few sections, we'll look at ways to avoid these pitfalls.

TIP Use the Tables feature (Chapter 7) or Columns feature (Chapter 27) to avoid alignment maladies.

Fixing Wavy Columns

Figure 5.13 shows an example of printed text that should be evenly spaced in columns but is wavy instead. This problem often occurs when you use blank spaces to separate columns instead of tabs. Wavy columns look especially bad when you use proportionally-spaced fonts (Chapter 6), such as the CG Times font in Figure 5.13.

To fix the problem, replace each group of blank spaces with a tab, and then set proper tab stops. (Or start all over and use the Tables or Columns feature.)

FIGURE 5.13

Wavy columns caused by using spaces instead of tabs to separate columns

Number	Date	Description	Deposit	Withdrawal
	8/1/93	Deposit	$1,000	
1001	8/1/93	Rent		$500.00
1002	8/1/93	Utilities		$75.00
1003	8/5/93	Water		$19
1004	8/14/93	Credit Card		$75.00
	8/15/93	Deposit	$1,000	
1005	8/16/93	Ray Co. (clothes)	$167.77	
1006	8/17/93	Dr. Dolittle	$88.00	
1007	8/20/93	WP Seminar	$250.00	

Fixing Misaligned Columns

Another common problem occurs when most of the text lines up neatly into columns but occasionally goes out of whack. This is illustrated by Strappman's street address and phone number in Figure 5.14.

If you look at the Reveal Codes screen in Figure 5.14, you'll notice two [Lft Tab] codes in front of Strappman's address. The extra code pushes the address out to the second tab stop. The simplest solution is to remove one of the tabs in front of the address.

The alignment problem in Figure 5.15 looks a lot like the extra tab problem in Figure 5.14. However, if you look at the Reveal Codes screen, you'll see that *every* address has only one tab code in front of it. So, if there aren't any extra tab codes, what's causing some addresses to shoot over to the third column?

FIGURE 5.14

Columns are misaligned because I added an extra tab.

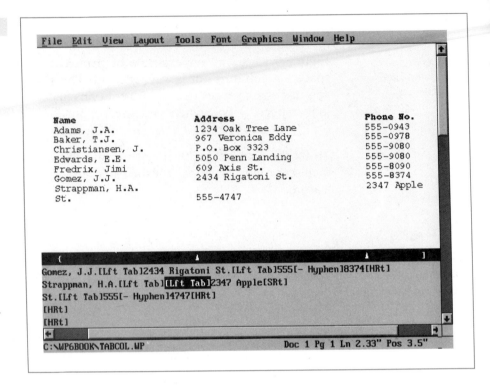

The answer is that some names in the first column are simply too wide for that column. Because the name in the first column extends past the first tab stop, the next tab code in that column forces the address out to the third column.

To clear up this mess, you'll need to change the tab stops at the start of the list so that the first column is wide enough to hold the longest name. (See the section on "Refining Tab Stops" later in this chapter.)

Checking the Tab-Stop Codes

When you change the tab ruler, be sure to position the cursor immediately to the *right* of the existing [Tab Set] code you want to change (just after the] character). That way WordPerfect will adjust the existing [Tab Set] code rather than creating a new one.

Beware! When two or more [Tab Set] codes (or other "same type" formatting codes) occur in succession, WordPerfect ignores all but the *last* code.

FIGURE 5.15

In this example, the first column spills into the second.

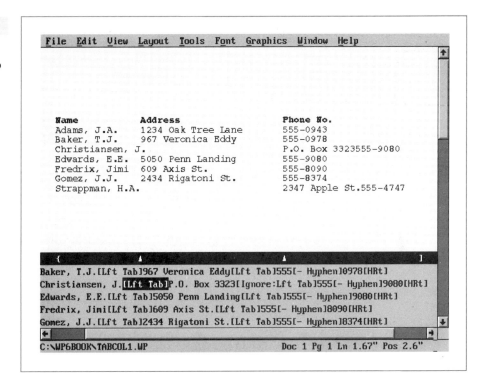

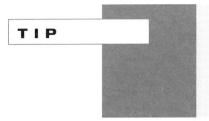

TIP If you're having trouble with tab stops, use Reveal Codes to see if multiple [Tab Set] codes appear anywhere before the problem area. Then delete the extra codes that follow the one you want to use. See Chapter 4 for more on using Reveal Codes.

Fixing Back Tab Errors

If you press Shift+Tab when the cursor is in the middle of a line of text, your text may disappear. This happens because the back-tabbed text overwrites existing text. To remedy the problem, go to the Reveal Codes screen and delete the [Back Tab] code in the sentence.

Similarly, if you move text into the left margin inadvertently or you change your mind about typing text in the left margin, use Reveal Codes to delete the [Back Tab] code that's pushing the text into the margin.

Refining Tab Stops

Unless you're a genius or just plain lucky, you probably won't get your tab stops right the first time every time. But that's OK. You can easily refine existing tab stops, like this:

1. Turn on Reveal Codes (press Alt+F3), then move the code highlight to the first character or code *after* the [Tab Set] code you want to change.

2. Choose Layout ➤ Tab Set from the menus (or press Shift+F8 LT). The Tab Set dialog box will appear, with the current settings on the tab ruler.

3. Use the techniques explained earlier in this chapter to adjust the tabs. The text in the Tab Set dialog box will reflect your changes immediately.

4. Choose OK.

Hard Tabs vs. Soft Tabs

Maybe you've wondered about soft tabs and hard tabs (or maybe not). *Soft tabs* are the "natural" tabs you get when you press the Tab key. Their hidden codes appear in mixed case on the Reveal Codes screen ([Lft Tab], [Cntr Tab], [Rgt Tab], and [Dec Tab]). They are called "soft tabs" because they will change automatically if you change the alignment on the tab ruler. For example, if you change a center-aligned tab stop to a right-aligned tab stop, WordPerfect will automatically convert any [Cntr Tab] codes at that tab stop (and below the tab ruler) to [Rgt Tab] codes.

You can prevent a tab code from changing when the tab ruler changes (though there's rarely a need to do so). When you type your document, just press Home Tab, instead of Tab. This makes the code a *hard tab*. Hard tabs appear in uppercase on the Reveal Codes screen ([LFT TAB], [CNTR TAB], [RGT TAB], and [DEC TAB]).

Here's the bottom line: Soft tabs immediately adjust to any changes in the tab ruler, but hard tabs never adjust to changes in the tab ruler. On the Reveal Codes screen, soft tab codes appear in upper- and lowercase letters, while hard tab codes appear in uppercase letters only.

Aligning Text on the Fly

In this section I'll tell you some quick ways to use a normal tab stop as a decimal-aligned, right-aligned, or dot-leader tab stop. These shortcuts let you align text on the fly without changing the tab settings (oh, that poor fly!)

Quick Decimal and Right Alignment

Follow these steps if you want to decimal-align or right-align text in a jiffy—without changing the tab settings:

1. Press Ctrl+F6 or select <u>L</u>ayout ➤ <u>A</u>lignment ➤ <u>D</u>ecimal Tab (instead of Tab) to move the cursor to the tab stop where you want to align text.

2. Type the text. The text will be decimal-aligned if it includes a period (as in *123.45*). If it doesn't include a period (as in *the cat in the hat fell flat*), the text will be right-aligned.

3. Press Tab or Ctrl+F6 to move to the next tab stop, or press ↵ to end the line.

By default, the period (decimal point) will line up on the tab stop. If you want, you can choose a different alignment character, as explained in the next section.

N O T E   Decimal Align inserts a hard tab code in the document (see "Hard Tabs vs. Soft Tabs," above).

Changing the Decimal Alignment Character

In general, dates, times, and numbers with equal decimal places (or no decimal places) look fine when you right-align them (see Figure 5.16).

FIGURE 5.16

Examples of right-aligned and decimal-aligned text

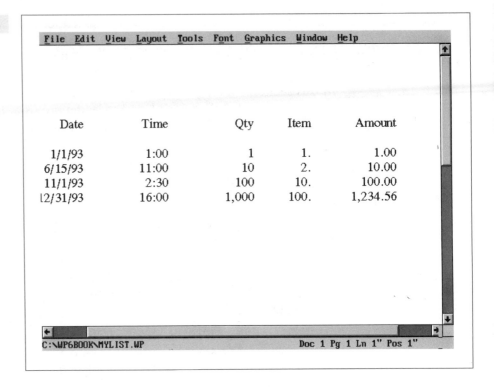

Date	Time	Qty	Item	Amount
1/1/93	1:00	1	1.	1.00
6/15/93	11:00	10	2.	10.00
11/1/93	2:30	100	10.	100.00
12/31/93	16:00	1,000	100.	1,234.56

However, if you right-align numbers with unequal decimal places, the decimal points won't line up vertically (see the left column in Figure 5.17).

To fix that problem, you need to align the numbers on their decimal points, instead of right-aligning them. I used decimal-alignment to line up the numbers in the second column of Figure 5.17.

Notice that I've aligned the numbers in Figure 5.17 on the comma instead of on the decimal point. Here's how to change the alignment character and thousands separator to handle European-style (or any other style) numbers.

1. Position the cursor where the new decimal alignment character should take effect, or select text to limit your changes to the selected block.

2. Choose Layout ➤ Character ➤ Decimal/Align Character (or press Shift+F8 CD).

FIGURE 5.17

Right-aligned
numbers,
American-style
numbers aligned
on decimal points,
and European-style
numbers aligned
on commas

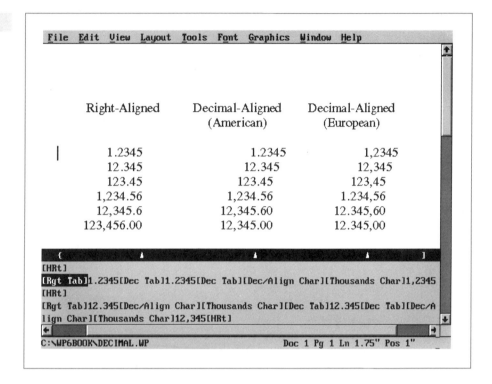

3. In the Decimal/Align Character text box, type the character you want to use for aligning the numbers. For example, type a comma to use the European way.

4. Select Thousands Separator and type the character that should separate thousands in the number. For example, type a period if you're using the European system.

5. Choose OK.

TIP

You can use any character, including special characters described in Chapter 6, for decimal alignment and thousands separation.

You can use this technique for numbers that you've decimal-aligned with tab stops on the tab ruler or on the fly with Ctrl+F6. To return to American-style decimal alignment, repeat steps 1–5 wherever you want to resume that alignment style.

If you want to use two different decimal-alignment characters in side-by-side columns, you'll need to change the decimal-alignment character before each number. In the Reveal Codes part of the screen in Figure 5.17, you can see that the first tab stop is right-aligned [Rgt Tab] and the next two are decimal-aligned [Dec Tab].

To switch between aligning on a period and a comma in the two right-hand columns, I had to redefine the decimal-alignment character several times (notice the many [Dec/Align Char] and [Thousands Char] codes in the Reveal Codes window). If you need to use many unusual alignments like this, you're better off using the Tables feature (see Chapter 7).

Creating Dot Leaders on the Fly

You can also add dot leaders to a column of text without changing the tab settings. This is very handy when you need a simple two-column list of items, like the menu shown in Figure 5.10.

To use this shortcut, simply type the text in the first column, press Alt+F6 twice, or select Layout ➤ Alignment ➤ Flush Right twice. Then type the text in the second column. WordPerfect will right-align the text at the right margin. (To narrow the gap between the two columns, just adjust the left and right margins.)

> **TIP**
>
> To remove the dot leaders, delete the [Flsh Rgt (Dot)] code on the Reveal Codes screen, then press Alt+F6 once.

Why Does My Text Look Weird in Text Mode?

In this section, I'll describe something that only applies when you're working in Text mode (choose View ➤ Text Mode or press Ctrl+F3 T). So if you never bother with Text mode, you can skip this section.

In Text mode, WordPerfect always displays characters at the same size (typically 0.1 inch) on the document window, even if you're using fonts of different sizes. (Chapter 6 explains how to change fonts.)

Normally this works just fine, since WordPerfect automatically calculates the proper place to wrap the text from line to line, whether you're using small fonts or larger ones. But if you're working with columns separated by tabs, you may see some weird stuff. For example,

- WordPerfect moves the text display far off the right edge of the screen to handle the many text characters and tab spaces on a line.

- Text typed immediately before a tab stop disappears from the display.

NOTE

Your printed document and the Graphics mode, Page mode, and Print Preview screens will display text exactly as it will look when printed—proper font sizes and all—regardless of the display pitch you've set.

The display pitch setting controls how many character widths something will occupy on the screen. If text disappears under tab stops as you edit, you can switch off the Automatic Display Pitch feature and *decrease* the display pitch enough to uncover hidden text. Here's how:

1. Place the cursor anywhere in the document, then choose Layout ➤ Document ➤ Display Pitch (or press Shift+F8 DD).

2. In the Display Pitch text box, type a smaller measurement and press ↵. Remember that a *smaller* pitch setting spreads out the text columns; a larger number moves columns closer together.

3. Select Manual.

4. Choose OK.

The new display pitch takes effect immediately (although the characters will still appear the same size). If some text remains hidden, repeat the steps above, but enter an even smaller Display Pitch setting. The display pitch does not insert any codes in the document, so you can reset it as often as you like without worrying about cursor placement or old codes. WordPerfect saves the settings with your document.

Moving, Copying, and Deleting Tabular Columns

At the risk of sounding like a commercial for WordPerfect tables...the tables feature really is the easiest way to create multicolumn tables.

But suppose you've used tabs instead. Now you decide to move, copy, or delete a particular column. Do you have to type everything over again? Of course not! You can do this by blocking. Unfortunately, blocking columns can be tricky, so I recommend that you save your document before attempting this. Here are the general steps:

1. Save your document by choosing File ➤ Save (or pressing F10) just in case you do more harm than good.

2. Move the cursor to the top left character in the column you want to move, copy, or delete.

3. Select text up to and including the last character in the column. Initially, the selection covers text in adjacent columns, as shown in Figure 5.18.

Text from the top to the bottom of the second column is selected, but the selected area initially includes text in adjacent columns.

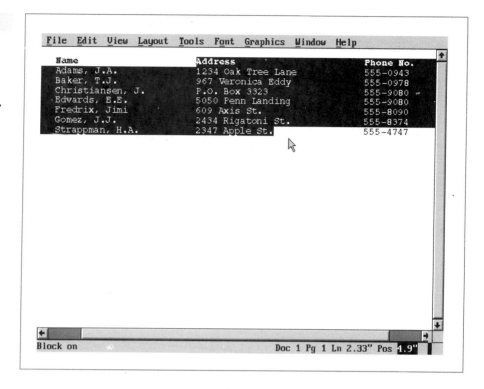

4. Select Edit ➤ Select ➤ Tabular Column. Now only one column is selected, and the Move Block dialog box appears (see Figure 5.19).

5. To delete this column, choose Delete. Choose Cut And Paste if you want to move the column or Copy And Paste if you want to copy the column.

6. If you chose Cut And Paste or Copy And Paste, place the cursor where you want the top left corner of the moved or copied column to appear. Press ⏎.

You may need to adjust the tab ruler to get exactly the effect you want after you delete or rearrange a column. Just use the general technique described earlier in "Refining Tab Stops."

FIGURE 5.19

Here a single column of text is selected (blocked).

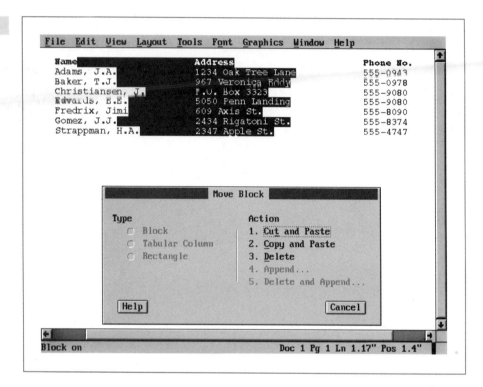

TIP

You can use the Sort feature (Chapter 22) to sort text in tabular columns into alphabetical, numerical, or chronological (date) order.

Undoing a Botched Move, Copy, or Delete

If you make more of a mess than an improvement, and you'd like to undo the whole operation, just choose Edit ➤ Undo or press Ctrl+Z. If you chose Cut And Paste, you'll also need to place the cursor where the top left corner of that column belongs and choose Edit ➤ Paste (or press Ctrl+V).

Here's another way to recover if you saved your file first: Choose File ➤ Close ➤ No. Then choose File ➤ Open (or press Shift+F10), type the file name, and press ↵ to retrieve the file in the state it was in before you made your changes.

WordPerfect's justification, indentation, and alignment techniques range from simple tabs to fancy indentations and every possible kind of text alignment. In the next chapter, you'll find out how to spruce up your documents with fonts, lines, and special characters.

Fonts, Lines, Borders, and Special Characters

fast TRACK

To type a special character   228

choose F<u>o</u>nt ➤ <u>W</u>P Characters (or press Ctrl+W), choose a
character set and character, and choose Insert.

To draw a graphic line   237

position the cursor and choose <u>G</u>raphics ➤ Graphics <u>L</u>ines ➤
<u>C</u>reate. Then choose either a Horizontal or Vertical orienta-
tion, and set other line characteristics. Choose OK when
you're done.

To draw borders around paragraphs   243

move the cursor to the first paragraph to be bordered. Or, select a small amount of text (perhaps one character) within a
single paragraph or select several paragraphs. Choose <u>G</u>raph-
ics ➤ B<u>o</u>rders ➤ <u>P</u>aragraph (Alt+F9 OP). Choose the border
style options you want, and then choose OK.

To draw a border around the current page   246

choose <u>G</u>raphics ➤ B<u>o</u>rders ➤ P<u>a</u>ge (Alt+F9 OA). Choose
the border styles you want, and then choose OK.

To change the print color of text   250

choose F<u>o</u>nt ➤ <u>P</u>rint Color, and select the color you want.

To redraw (refresh) your screen   252

when it's cluttered up or out of whack, press Ctrl+F3 and
choose <u>R</u>ewrite, or press Ctrl+F3 twice.

WORDPERFECT lets you change the size, appearance, and typeface of printed text. You can also add lines, borders, boxes, and special characters to your document to really jazz things up. These capabilities can make your printed documents more attractive and visually interesting. For example, Figure 6.1 shows a sample document using plain text. Figure 6.2 shows the same document spruced up a bit with the kinds of features I'll be covering in this chapter.

If It Doesn't Work...

Up to this point, every WordPerfect feature that I've described will work like a charm regardless of what type of printer you're using. But now we've come to a point where certain features I'll talk about aren't really WordPerfect features at all. Instead, they're printer-specific features that WordPerfect can use if (and only if) your printer can produce them.

If you try to use a special feature that isn't available with your printer, WordPerfect will ignore your request, making you feel as though *you've* done something wrong. If you cannot find a particular font that you'd like to use, most likely that font isn't built into your printer or it's not available in the current font collection.

So if you start feeling confused about fonts, remember...

- In *this* chapter, I'll talk about fonts that have already been installed and are ready for use in WordPerfect.

- In Chapter 10, "Mastering Your Printer and Fonts," I'll discuss ways to expand your collection of fonts and install them for use with WordPerfect.

```
                        Angela T. Joseph

        18424 Mountain View Court Lake Meyer, Co.  93415    (319) 555-0938

        OBJECTIVE           Produce word processing and desktop
                            publishing documents on a freelance basis.

        EDUCATION           Bachelor of Arts, Business Administration,
                            State University of Colorado, Denver, 1980.

        EXPERIENCE          Sole Proprietor, Angela T. Joseph Word
                            Processing, Sturgeon Pond, Colorado.
                                                    1985 to Present

                              Freelance secretary and home-based word
                              processing services.

                                Secretary for small office of architects
                                Freelance secretary for various offices
                                as temporary help

                            Clerk Typist II, Morgan T. Williams
                            Corporation, River Bend, Colorado
                                                    1974 to 1985

                              Clerk typist and receptionist for the
                              general business office of a consulting
                              firm.

                                Process and type forms and reports from
                                outside consultants
                                Compile and ensure accuracy of monthly
                                statistical reports
                                Perform general duties including heavy
                                typing and filing

        PROFESSIONAL        Chamber of Commerce, Denver, Colorado
        ORGANIZATIONS       Business & Professional Association of Lake
                            Meyer, Colorado

        REFERENCES          Available upon request
```

About Fonts

Unless you're already familiar with computers or typesetting, the term *font* may be new to you. A font is basically a combination of three things:

- A *typeface* (sometimes called a *typestyle* or a *face*)

Angela T. Joseph

18424 Mountain View Court   *Lake Meyer, Colorado 93415*   *(319) 555-0938*

OBJECTIVE   Produce word processing and desktop publishing documents on a freelance basis.

EDUCATION   Bachelor of Arts, Business Administration, State University of Colorado, Denver, 1980.

EXPERIENCE   **Sole Proprietor**, *Angela T. Joseph Word Processing*, Sturgeon Pond, Colorado.   1985 to Present

Freelance secretary and home-based word processing services.

- Secretary for small office of architects
- Freelance secretary for various offices as temporary help

Clerk Typist II, *Morgan T. Williams Corporation*, River Bend, Colorado   1974 to 1985

Clerk typist and receptionist for the general business office of a consulting firm.

- Process and type forms and reports from outside consultants
- Compile and ensure accuracy of monthly statistical reports
- Perform general duties including heavy typing and filing

PROFESSIONAL ORGANIZATIONS   Chamber of Commerce, Denver, Colorado
Business & Professional Association of Lake Meyer, Colorado

REFERENCES   Available upon request

- A *weight,* such as **boldface**, *italic,* or roman
- A size, measured in *points* or characters per inch (*cpi*)

Typefaces

Figure 6.3 shows examples of various typefaces. Different occasions call for different typefaces. For example, Courier, a typewriter font, is good for printing documents that you want to look typewritten.

FIGURE 6.3

Examples of different typefaces

Courier
Times
Helvetica
ASTAIRE
Barron
Billboard
Bodoni
Burlesque
Capelli Ultra
CARGO
Cathedral
Center City
Chainlink
Chestnut
COMIC STRIP
Coronet
Cyclone
Domenic
Elegance Italic

Empire Script
EXOTICA
Felicia
Freehand
FREEPORT
HOT AIR
Industrial Heavy
IVY LEAGUE
Kidstuff
Opera
Optimum
PERSEUS
Samuri
Stagecoach
Stimpson
Victorian Bold
Weissach
Wright
ZORBA

Wingdings (below)

Weights

Figure 6.4 shows a single typeface, Times, in a variety of weights. Boldface (or bold) is thicker than the regular roman weight. Italic (also called *oblique*) is generally lighter and slanted. (Many decorative fonts, such as Dingbats, are only available in a single weight—there is no bold or italic version.)

FIGURE 6.4

Examples of various weights

Times Roman
Times Bold
Times Italic
Times Bold Italic

Sizes

Figure 6.5 shows a single typeface and style (Times Roman) in a variety of sizes. A point is roughly $1/72$ of an inch, so 72 points is about 1 inch tall, 36 points is about $1/2$ inch, and so on.

Proportional vs. Monospaced Fonts

Although some fonts are measured in points, others are measured in characters per inch. (The term *pitch* is sometimes used in place of cpi.) The reason for this is that there are two different ways to space characters horizontally along a line:

Monospacing   Every character takes up the same amount of space (for example, an *i* is just as wide as a *w)*.

Proportional spacing   Every character takes up only the space it needs (an *i* takes up less space than a *w*).

Figure 6.6 illustrates this with a string of the letters *i* and *w* in a mono-spaced font (Courier) and a proportionally spaced font (Times). The letters

FIGURE 6.5

Examples of various type sizes

6 points
8 points
10 points
12 points
14 points
18 points
24 points
36 points
48 points
72 points
144 p

FIGURE 6.6

Monospaced and proportionally spaced fonts compared

`iwiwiwiwiwiw`	In a monospaced font, like Courier, every letter is the same width.
iwiwiwiwiwiw	In a proportionally spaced font, like Times, each letter uses only the space it needs.

are the same width in the monospaced font, but the *i* is narrower than the *w* in the proportional font. This packs the letters together more tightly.

Because each character in a monospaced font takes up the same amount of space, its size can be measured in characters per inch (cpi). Two common Courier sizes are *pica* (10 cpi) and *elite* (12 cpi). Proportionally spaced fonts cannot really be measured in characters per inch because the characters are different widths. These fonts are measured in terms of *height*, in points, instead. (The point size of a character usually includes a little blank space, called *leading*, at the top.)

N O T E   A 10-cpi monospaced font is about the same size as a 12-point proportional font.

Serif vs. Sans-Serif Fonts

Times is a *serif* font. A serif is the little curlicue, or tail, at the top and bottom of each letter. Serif fonts are often used for small- to medium-size print because the serifs help your eyes move through the text and read more easily.

Helvetica is a *sans-serif* font (the letters have no tails). Sans-serif fonts are mainly used for large text—from the headlines in newspapers to the messages on street signs (as a glance at any road sign will prove).

Decorative Fonts

Decorative fonts are strictly for decoration. They aren't particularly easy to read (especially in smaller sizes), but they look nice and are often used to draw attention or create a mood. Examples abound, from the elegance of a wedding invitation to the zaniness of a humorous greeting card. Figures 6.7 and 6.8 show some examples using decorative fonts. In general, it's best to reserve decorative fonts for special occasions and use them sparingly.

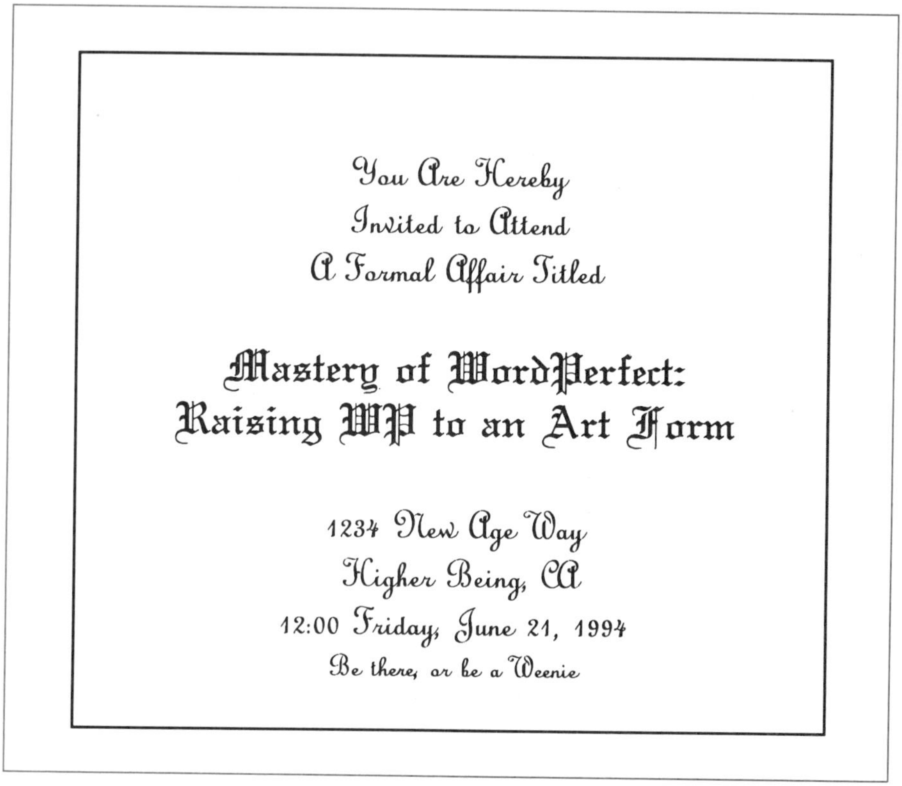

FIGURE 6.7

An elegant decorative font adds to the formality of this document. (To center each line, I chose Layout ➤ Justification ➤ Center at the top of the document and ended each line by pressing the ↵ key.)

You Are Hereby
Invited to Attend
A Formal Affair Titled

**Mastery of WordPerfect:
Raising WP to an Art Form**

1234 New Age Way
Higher Being, CA
12:00 Friday, June 21, 1994
Be there, or be a Weenie

WORDPERFECT FOR WEENIES

Getting Started

Start your computer (yikes!), get to the DOS command prompt (huh?), type **wp** and press ←. No, you can't just type **wordperfect** instead. Yes, you do have to press ← after you type the wp.

Getting A Clue

Pick up the phone, hook it between your neck and shoulder, and call someone who has a clue. If that person is too busy / expensive / cranky / malodorous / nonexistent for you, hang up. Then press F1. Fumble around. Ignore everything on your screen. Then press Escape until nothing else happens.

Giving Up

When you've had enough, choose File ▸ Exit WP, or press Home then press F7. Ignore all the rest of the stuff on your screen. Turn off your computer as soon as possible. Do something else.

Scalable vs. Nonscalable Fonts

Some fonts are *scalable*, which means that you can choose a size, such as 10.5 points, on the fly. Most modern graphic fonts, including the popular TrueType and PostScript fonts, are scalable. WordPerfect can tell whether a font is scalable, and it lets you choose a size for the font as soon as you've chosen the typeface. (I'll talk about modern graphic fonts in more detail in Chapter 10.)

Non-scalable fonts cannot be sized on the fly. They are available in predetermined sizes only: 10 point, 12 point, etc. When using a non-scalable font, you choose the size and typeface in a single step. WordPerfect will not allow you to set an in-between size, such as 11 points, for a non-scalable font.

Choosing a Font

Fortunately, using fonts in WordPerfect is much simpler than learning all the terminology. The steps you need to follow are given below.

NOTE If you have several printers attached to your computer, keep in mind that each printer might have its own unique fonts. See Chapter 10 if you need more information.

1. Move the cursor to wherever you want to switch to the new font. This can be either before existing text or at the point where you want to start typing new text. To change the font for a portion of existing text, select that text (as discussed in Chapter 3).

2. Choose Font ➤ Font (or press Ctrl+F8). A dialog box like the one shown in Figure 6.9 will appear. Notice that the name of the

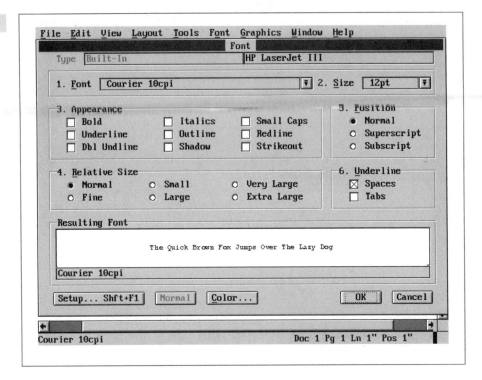

currently selected printer appears near the upper-right corner of the dialog box (HP LaserJet III in the example shown here) and the currently selected font appears in the Font text box (Courier 10cpi in the example). The Resulting Font box shows you how the font, size, appearance, and relative size look.

3. If you want to change the typeface, choose the Font option. A partial list of available typefaces will appear, as shown in the example below. Select the typeface you want by scrolling then double-clicking or by highlighting the name of a typeface and pressing ↵. You can also type the first few letters of the font name to highlight or select a font.

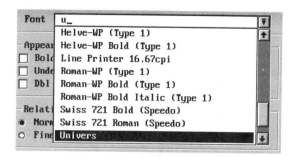

4. If the highlighted font is *scalable,* and you want to change its size, choose Size and type in a new size. Alternatively, you can use the Size drop-down list to select a size by double-clicking or by highlighting and pressing ↵.

5. If you want to change the appearance, position, relative size, underline method, or print color, you can do so by choosing appropriate options in this dialog box.

6. When you're done making your selections, choose OK to return to your document.

If you're in Graphics mode or Page mode and you selected text or positioned the cursor in front of existing text in step 1, the font change will be readily apparent on your screen when you return to the document window. If you put the cursor after all existing text, any new text you type will be in the new font you chose.

NOTE

Fonts appear in WYSIWYG format in Graphics mode and Page mode (Ctrl+F3) and in Print Preview (Shift+F7 V). However, they do not appear in WYSIWYG in Text mode. The status bar displays the name of the current font.

When you change the font in a document, WordPerfect inserts a hidden [Font] code and, if you change the size of a scalable font, a [Font Size] code. These codes are visible only in the Reveal Codes window (Alt+F3).

If you change the font in a document and nothing seems to happen, there's probably a competing [Font] code right after the code you just inserted. To fix this problem, you need to highlight the old [Font] code and press Delete to delete it. (See Chapter 4.)

Using the Ribbon to Choose a Font

The Ribbon offers a shortcut way to change the font:

1. Make sure the Ribbon tool is on (choose <u>V</u>iew ➤ <u>R</u>ibbon if it's not).

2. Move the cursor to wherever you want to change the font. Or, select the text you want to change.

3. In the Ribbon, click the drop-down list button next to the name of the currently selected font. A list will appear, as in the example shown below.

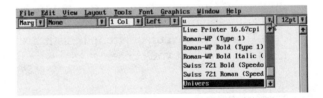

4. Choose the font you want by double-clicking its name, or type the first few letters in the name (or use the ↓ and ↑ keys to highlight a name) and press ↵.

5. If you want to change the point size, choose the Size option on the Ribbon and double-click a point size in the list, or type a new size into the text box and press ↵.

TIP

If you want to use fonts consistently with the various design elements in your document (heads, subheads, body text, etc.) you should definitely know about *styles* (see Chapter 17). Styles let you change the font of a design element throughout the entire document in one simple action.

Using Relative Font Sizes

If you want to change only the size of the current font, it's not necessary to choose a different font. You can just choose a new size in relation to the current size. Here's one advantage to using a relative size: If you change the point size of the current font, the text that is sized relatively will be resized relative to the new point size automatically.

For example, WordPerfect's "fine" font is a relative size that's usually 60% of the *base font* size (the current size). Thus, when the base font is 10 points, fine text will be 6 points in size. If you double the base font size to 20 points, WordPerfect will automatically double the fine text as well, to 12 points.

On the other hand, suppose you decided to create your fine text manually. First you set your base font to 10 points. Then you selected the fine text and set it to 6 points. Now, suppose you change the base font size to 20 points. Text in the base font changes without any problems. However, the 6-point text that you set manually stays at 6 points. You'd need to select the small text and adjust it manually (to 12 points) if you wanted the appearance of WordPerfect's fine font.

Figure 6.10 shows examples of the relative sizes available to you. Each size is a percentage of the current base-font size.

If your printer has scalable fonts, WordPerfect will calculate the relative type size mathematically, since anything goes with scalable fonts. If your printer does not offer scalable fonts, WordPerfect will select the font that best approximates the size you've requested. Therefore, if your printer has

FIGURE 6.10

Examples of sizes in relation to a 16-point font

Base Font: Times Roman 16pt

This ends with a ^{superscript}

This ends with a _{subscript}

This is Fine Size

This is Small Size

This is Large Size

This is Very Large Size

This is Extra Large Size

a limited selection of fonts, the sizes available may not match WordPerfect's predefined percentages. (Figure 6.11, shown later in this chapter, shows the default percentages for each of WordPerfect's relative font sizes.)

Changing the Relative Size and Position of Text

To change the relative size of text, follow the steps below:

1. Select the text that you want to change. Or, if you haven't typed the text yet, place the cursor where you want to start typing in the new size. Then use either of the techniques below to select a new font size or position:

   - Choose Font ➤ Size/Position, then choose an option from the menu that appears. You can select relative size options (normal, fine, small, very large, or extra large), or position options (normal, superscript, or subscript).

   - Choose Font ➤ Font (or press Ctrl+F8), then choose a Position and/or Relative Size. Choose OK when you're done.

2. If you didn't select text in step 1, type the new text now. Press →
   when you're ready to start typing normal-sized text again.

NOTE Pressing → in step 2 above moves the cursor past the hidden code that turns the size or position setting off. You can see the cursor move when Reveal Codes is on.

Relative font sizes are controlled by paired codes. The code that starts the size change contains the word "On." The code that ends the size change contains the word "Off." For example, all text between a [Large On] code and a [Large Off] code would be printed at the Large size.

Changing the Size Ratios

The ratios of relative text sizes aren't etched in granite; they are simply the defaults that WordPerfect uses for convenience. You may want to specify a different ratio—for example, to make your superscripts and subscripts a little smaller or to make your extra-large sizes a little larger. You can change the relative-size ratios by following these steps:

1. Choose Font ➤ Font or press Ctrl+F8.

2. Choose Setup (or press Shift+F1).

3. Change the ratios near the bottom of the dialog box however you wish (see Figure 6.11).

4. Choose OK twice to return to your document.

WARNING Be aware that changing the size ratio affects the entire current document, as well as any other documents that use relative sizing.

FIGURE 6.11

To change the ratios of relatively-sized fonts, press Ctrl+F8, then press Shift+F1, and change the % values in the Font Setup dialog box.

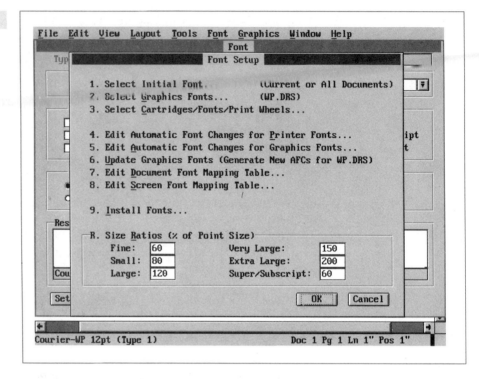

Troubleshooting Relative Sizing Problems

If you open a document and the relative font sizes look out of whack, you may need to troubleshoot the situation. Here's how:

- If you use multiple printers, be sure to select the correct printer for that document (File ➤ Print/Fax ➤ Select).

- Repeat the steps given above ("Changing the Size Ratios") to check the relative size ratios. If necessary, change the ratios.

- Use Reveal Codes to check the positions of font and size codes. (Only the text between the starting and ending codes will appear in the specified size.)

- Remember that if the currently selected printer doesn't have scalable fonts, WordPerfect will do the best it can to size the text to the proportions you've defined.

Changing the Document Initial Font

Normally, the starting font for a document is the default font for the currently selected printer (see Chapter 10). If you want to use a different starting font (also called the *base font*), follow these steps:

1. Choose Layout ➤ Document ➤ Initial Font (or press Shift+F8 DF). The Initial Font dialog box appears.

2. Choose Font and select a font from the drop-down list of available fonts.

3. Indicate whether you want this new selection to affect the current document only or the current document plus all new documents you create. (The default is the current document only.)

4. Choose OK (or Close) until you return to your document.

NOTE   Any font defined at the top of the document or in the document initial codes (Chapter 19), will override the initial font for the printer.

Changing the Appearance of Text

You don't have to choose a new font to change the appearance of text. You can change the *appearance attributes* of text to get boldfaced, italicized, and underlined text. Figure 6.12 shows some of the appearances available in WordPerfect.

Not all printers and fonts support the full range of appearances, however. For example, Outline is available only on PostScript, LaserJet III, LaserJet 4, and compatible printers. Redline and Shadow tend to look different

FIGURE 6.12

Examples of
appearance attributes

Normal
Bold
<u>Underline</u>
<u>Double Underline</u>
Italic
Outline
Shadow
SMALL CAP
Redline
~~Strikeout~~

different on different printers. You may need to experiment to find out how the various appearances will look when you print them.

The steps for changing the appearance of text are nearly identical to those for changing the relative size:

1. Select the text you want to change the appearance of, or, if you haven't typed that text yet, place the cursor where you plan to type the text.

   - Choose F<u>o</u>nt and then select an attribute from the Font pull-down menu.

   - Or, choose F<u>o</u>nt ➤ F<u>o</u>nt (or press Ctrl+F8) and choose one or more <u>A</u>ppearance options from the Font dialog box. Then choose OK.

2. If you selected text in step 1, you're done. Otherwise, type the new text, and press → when you want to start typing normal text without the attributes again.

If you're using Graphics mode or Page mode, the appearance change will be apparent on your screen immediately (or when you start typing). But remember that not all appearances are available on all printers. WordPerfect may ignore your request for a particular appearance if it's not available on your printer, or it may substitute a different font for the appearance you requested.

Hidden Codes for Appearances

Font attributes are controlled by hidden codes. For example, if you choose Bold and Italics, the text that has both those attributes will be surrounded by two pairs of codes, like this:

[Bold On][Italc On]*'Tis Bold and Italic*[Bold Off][Italc Off]

Remember that only text within both pairs of codes will have both characteristics. When typing new text between multiple codes, you need to press → to move past each [... Off] code. Or, you can press End or Home Home Home → to move past all the [... Off] codes. As mentioned in Chapter 4, you can see the position of the cursor in relation to the codes only when Reveal Codes (Alt+F3) is on.

Appearance Shortcuts

Because bold, underline, and italic are such common font appearances, each one has a shortcut key. To make selected text bold, just press F6 or Ctrl+B. To underline, press F8 or Ctrl+U. To italicize, press Ctrl+I. You can create your own shortcuts for other appearances using Button Bar buttons (Chapter 4), macros (Chapter 18), or both.

Combining Sizes and Appearances

You can combine relative size, position, and appearances in any way you want. Figure 6.13 shows some examples.

A look behind-the-scenes at a couple of the examples in Figure 6.13 will demonstrate how these effects were achieved. The "$e = mc^2$" example looks like this in Reveal Codes:

> [Italc On]Italic sentence with [Bold On]e=mc[Suprscpt On]2[Suprscpt Off][Bold Off] in bold with superscript[Italc Off]

Notice that the starting and ending codes for each size and appearance correspond exactly to how the example looks when printed.

FIGURE 6.13

Examples of combined sizes and appearances

Extra Large, Outline Title

Call me Ishmael...

Chapter

1 *GETTING STARTED*

Sale!
Sale!
Sale!

Italic sentence with $e=mc^2$ in bold with superscript.

♪Hoyd♪ ♪it♪ ♪thru♪ ♪da♪ ♪grape♪-♪vahn♪♪

The "Chapter 1" example looks like this in Reveal Codes:

[Small On]Chapter[Small Off][HRt]
[Ext Large On][RedIn On] 1 [RedIn Off][Ext Large Off][Und On][Sm
Cap On][Font: Univers Bold Italic]Getting Started[Sm Cap Off][Und
Off]

T I P

If you're interested in creating more dramatic special effects with your text, see Chapter 28.

Undoing Size and Appearance Changes

To undo a size or appearance change immediately, just choose Edit ➤ Undo or press Ctrl+Z. Or, if you've made more changes since the size/appearance change, move the cursor to where you want to undo the change, turn on Reveal Codes, and delete either the On or Off code for the appearance you want to eliminate.

You can also remove a size or appearance change by selecting the text, then pulling down the Font menu or opening up the Font dialog box (Font ➤ Font). The sizes and appearances for the text will already be selected in the menu or shaded in the dialog box. Just choose whichever options you want to turn off.

T I P

A quick and easy way to remove all the size and appearance codes from a chunk of text is to select all the text that you want to remove the codes from, then choose Font ➤ Normal.

Spaces and Tabs: To Underline or Not to Underline?

The Underline and Double Underline appearances normally underline words and blank spaces between words. But you can choose whether or not to have WordPerfect underline spaces and tabs. Figure 6.14 shows examples of your options, where tabs are used to separate Name, Address, and City, and spaces separate City, State, and Zip.

To choose an underlining method, follow these steps:

1. Move the cursor to the first character or blank space where you want to change the underlining method or select the text where you want to change the underlining.

2. Choose Font ➤ Font or press Ctrl+F8.

3. Choose Underline, then select or deselect the check boxes for Spaces or Tabs (deselect both check boxes if you don't want to underline either spaces or tabs).

4. Choose OK to return to your document.

All underlined and double-underlined text past the cursor will adhere to the new underlining method.

FIGURE 6.14

Underlining methods, available for both single underlining and double-underlining.

Spaces
<u>**Name**</u>   <u>**Address City, State Zip**</u>

Spaces and Tabs
<u>**Name**</u>   <u>**Address City, State Zip**</u>

Neither Spaces nor Tabs
<u>**Name**</u>   <u>**Address City, State Zip**</u>

Using Redline Markings and Strikeout Text

Redline and strikeout are often used to denote changes in contracts and other legal documents. Redline indicates suggested additions to the original document; strikeout marks suggested deletions. Figure 6.15 shows an example.

N O T E

You can use the File ➤ Compare Documents command to compare two copies of a document and automatically add redline and strikeout based on the differences between each document. See Chapter 31.

On some printers, WordPerfect prints redline text as a grayed shade. On other printers, redline text appears with a shaded background or with dots beneath the characters. On color printers, redline text is printed in red.

FIGURE 6.15

Redline and strikeout in a sample document

> **THE PURCHASE PRICE INCLUDES:** All tacked down carpeting, ~~all existing window treatments,~~ all existing window and door screens, all built-in appliances, all ~~fixtures,~~ shrubs, trees and items permanently attached to the real property, all window treatments excluding the wooden louvers in the dining room, and all fixtures excluding chandelier in the dining room. Pool and spa equipment, if any, is also to be included.

Special Techniques for Redline and Strikeout

You can change the appearance of redline text if you wish. To do so, choose File ➤ Print/Fax ➤ Setup. This will take you to the Print Setup dialog box. Choose Redline Method and select the option you want:

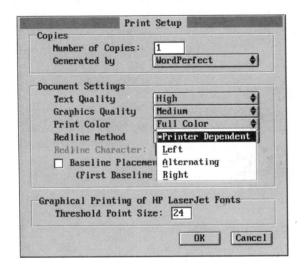

Here's a summary of the redline options available to you:

Printer Dependent Redline is printed as specified by your printer.

Left Redline text is marked by a character in the left margin.

Alternating Redline text is marked by a character in the left margin on even-numbered pages and a character in the right margin on odd-numbered pages.

Right Redline text is marked by a character in the right margin.

If you choose Left, Right, or Alternating, you can also select a character to use as the redline mark. Normally, WordPerfect uses a vertical bar (|).

To change that character, choose Redline Character. Type any single character to display in the margin as the redline mark. Or press Ctrl+W and choose a special character from the available character sets (special characters are described later in this chapter).

When you've finished defining your redline method, choose OK, then choose Close to return to your document.

Removing Redline Markings and Strikeout Text

WordPerfect lets you remove all the redline markings and strikeout text from a document with a single command. This is useful when you want to print a final draft of a document, after you're certain that you no longer need the redline markings or the text that has been struck out. Follow these steps:

1. Choose File ➤ Compare Documents ➤ Remove Markings.

2. Choose whether you want to remove both redline and strikeout (option 1) or strikeout only (option 2).

If you want to save the original copy of the document with redlines and strikeout still intact, save this copy of the document with a new file name using the File ➤ Save As command.

Using Hidden Text

Chapter 4 explained how you could use document comments (Layout ➤ Comment) to write notes to yourself or to someone else who might be reviewing your document. Document comments appear in framed boxes within your document. However, they don't print unless you convert them to text.

Hidden text offers a flexible alternative to document comments. Like document comments, hidden text is useful for questions, messages, and comments. However, hidden text offers these advantages over document comments:

- You can show or hide hidden text. When you show the text, it appears both on-screen and in your printed document. When you hide the text, it's invisible on the screen and in printouts.

- You can include text, fonts, attributes, lines, graphics—*anything*—between the hidden text codes.

- When hidden text is visible, WordPerfect treats it like any other information in your document. When it's invisible, it's just that—completely invisible.

Turning on the Hidden Text Attribute

Here's how to turn on hidden text attributes:

1. Place the cursor where you want hidden text to start, or select the text (including any graphics or lines) that you want to hide.

2. Choose F<u>o</u>nt ➤ <u>H</u>idden Text. You'll see the Hidden Text dialog box shown below:

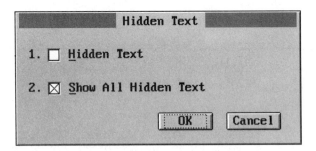

3. Select <u>S</u>how All Hidden Text if that box isn't checked already.

4. Select <u>H</u>idden Text to turn on hidden text.

5. Choose OK.

WordPerfect uses paired codes for hidden text, as it does for bold, italics, and other font attributes described in this chapter. Any information that you place between the [Hidden On] and [Hidden Off] codes will have the hidden text attribute.

Displaying and Hiding Hidden Text

To control whether hidden text appears on your screen and in your printed document, choose F<u>o</u>nt ➤ <u>H</u>idden Text. Then, to display the hidden text in your document, select <u>S</u>how All Hidden text in the Hidden Text dialog box. To hide the hidden text, deselect that option. You can toggle between showing the hidden text and hiding it at any time.

TIP

When you've turned off the hidden text display, only the [Hidden On] code is visible in Reveal Codes (the [Hidden Off] code disappears temporarily). You can take a quick look at the hidden text in the Reveal Codes screen by highlighting the [Hidden On] code. The [Hidden On] code will expand to show all the text and codes hidden within it.

Turning Off the Hidden Text Attribute

You turn off hidden text attributes the same way that you turn off bold, underline, and other paired attributes. That is, you can do any of the following:

- Turn on Reveal Codes and delete the [Hidden On] or [Hidden Off] code.

- When you're done typing new hidden text, press → until your cursor moves past (to the right of) the [Hidden Off] code.

- Repeat the five steps given under "Turning on the Hidden Text Attribute," above, except *deselect* Hidden Text in step 4, above.

Typing Special Characters

You can type all the letters, numbers, and punctuation marks needed for most documents right from your keyboard. However, many situations call for special characters, such as bullets, copyright symbols (for example, © and ™), foreign currency signs, and the ↑, ↓, →, ←, and ↵ characters used in this book.

WordPerfect offers over 1400 special characters, including foreign-language characters, mathematical equations, and scientific symbols. The Greek alphabet is available to you, as well as Hebrew, Russian, and Japanese characters.

If you have a graphics printer, you'll be able to print all the special characters that WordPerfect offers. If you don't have a graphics printer, you'll probably be able to print quite a few of these symbols anyway.

To insert a special character into your document, follow these steps:

1. Move the cursor to the place where you want to type the special character.

2. Choose F<u>o</u>nt ➤ <u>W</u>P Characters, or press Ctrl+W. The WordPerfect Characters dialog box appears:

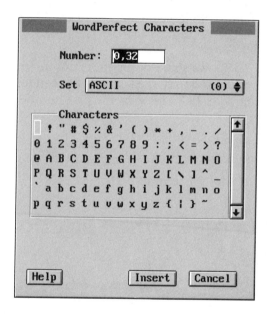

TIP

If you know the two-letter shortcut or the number code of the character you want, you can type that two-letter shortcut or number (including the comma) under <u>N</u>umber in the dialog box, then press ↵.

3. To choose a different character set, choose <u>S</u>et and then select one of the set names in the list.

4. Click on a character or choose <u>C</u>haracters, then use the arrow keys to highlight a character.

5. Choose Insert or press ↵ to insert the character into your document.

The special character you selected will appear in the document window. When you move the cursor to that character, you can see the character and its code in the Reveal Codes window, like this:

[©:4,23]

Figure 6.16 shows some of the more commonly used special characters and the codes used to type each one. You can tell which character set each special character belongs to by the first number in the code, as follows:

4   Typographic Symbols

5   Iconic Symbols

6   Math/Scientific

Dingbats and Other Special Characters

If you've chosen a Dingbat font or other symbol font, you might be able to type the special characters using the regular typing keys. If that's not the case, try to locate the characters in the User-Defined character set in the WordPerfect Characters dialog box.

To view the entire character set for any font, you can open the CHAR-MAP.TST or CHARACTR.DOC file that came with your WordPerfect program. Near the top of that document, choose the font you're interested in. Then print the document with Graphics Quality set to High. It might take a while! You can speed things along by using your mouse or Alt+F4to select character set 12 (or whatever) before you print.

Shortcuts for Commonly Used Special Characters

WordPerfect offers yet another shortcut for typing some special characters. You can use a two-letter code in place of the two-number code.

FIGURE 6.16

Examples of special characters not found on the keyboard, but available through Font ➤ WP Characters or by pressing Ctrl+W

Bullets	
●	4,0
○	4,1
■	4,2
•	4,3
○	4,37
□	4,38
●	4,44
○	4,45
■	4,46
■	4,47
□	4,48
□	4,49
☞	5,21
☜	5,22
✓	5,23
□	5,24
⊠	5,25

Currency	
£	4,11
¥	4,12
Pt	4,13
ƒ	4,14
¢	4,19
¤	4,24
$	4,57
₣	4,58
₢	4,59
₠	4,60
₤	4,61

Fractions	
½	4,17
¼	4,18
¾	4,25
⅓	4,64
⅔	4,65
⅛	4,66
⅜	4,67
⅝	4,68
⅞	4,69

Graphics	
♥	5,0
♦	5,1
♣	5,2
♠	5,3
♂	5,4
♀	5,5
☼	5,6
☺	5,7
☻	5,8
☹	5,26
☎	5,30
⊘	5,31
⌛	5,32

General	
¶	4,5
§	4,6
®	4,22
©	4,23

General	
'	4,27
'	4,28
'	4,29
"	4,30
"	4,31
"	4,32
–	4,33
—	4,34
†	4,39
‡	4,40
™	4,41
SM	4,42
℞	4,43
…	4,56
c/o	4,73
‰	4,75
№	4,76
°	6,36
★	6,112
►	6,27
◄	6,28
▲	6,29
▼	6,30

Keyboard	
↵	5,20
→	6,21
←	6,22
↑	6,23
↓	6,24

To use a two-letter shortcut, choose Font ➤ WP Characters (or press Ctrl+W). Then, rather than searching for the appropriate character, just type the two-character combination shown in the middle column under each heading of Figure 6.17 and press ↵. For example, to type a small bullet, you can press Ctrl+W, then type *. and press ↵.

Sizing Special Characters

The size of the current font determines the size of special characters. For example, the first list in Figure 6.18 uses special character 5,21 from the Iconic Symbols set. In the first list, the pointing hands in front of each item are the same size as the current font. In the remaining lists, each pointing hand was increased to the Very Large size.

NOTE   You can also change the size of a special character by changing the font (Font ➤ Font) just to the left of the character. For example, the happy face in Figure 6.18 is special character 5,7 from the Iconic Symbols set, printed in a 140-point font.

In the third example of pointing hands in Figure 6.18, the hands line up better with the text to the right. That's because I used the Advance feature to lower each hand by eight points. I also knocked four points (-4p) out of the leading in the second two examples. As you'll learn in Chapter 28, you can get to the Advance and Leading options via the Layout ➤ Other command.

TIP   The best way to define a bullet (like the pointing hands in Figure 6.18) is to use a *style* (Chapter 17) that includes the font and character you need. That way, should you later decide to change the size or character used for the bullet, you could do so throughout the entire document simply by changing the style definition.

Char	Shortcut	Code
Char	*Shortcut*	*Code*

Bullets and Fractions

●	*.	[4,3]
●	**	[4,0]
○	*o	[4,45]
○	*O	[4,1]
½	/2	[4,17]
¼	/4	[4,18]

Currency Symbols

¢	c/	[4,19]
ƒ	f-	[4,14]
£	L-	[4,11]
¤	ox	[4,24]
Pt	Pt	[4,13]
¥	Y=	[4,12]

Math/Scientific Symbols

±	+-	[6,1]
≤	<=	[6,2]
≠	/=	[6,99]
≡	==	[6,14]
≥	>=	[6,3]
≈	~~	[6,13]

Foreign Language

¡	!!	[4,7]
¿	??	[4,8]
æ	ae	[1,37]
Æ	AE	[1,36]
å	ao	[1,35]
ij	ij	[1,139]
IJ	IJ	[1,138]
œ	oe	[1,167]
Œ	OE	[1,166]
ß	ss	[1,23]

Other Typographic

«	<<	[4,9]
»	>>	[4,10]
©	co	[4,23]
—	m-	[4,34]
—	--	[4,34]
–	n-	[4,33]
¶	P¦	[4,5]
®	ro	[4,22]
℞	rx	[4,43]
SM	sm	[4,42]
TM	tm	[4,41]

Printing Two Characters in One Space

If you can't find a special character or symbol that you need, you may be able to create it by typing two or more characters in a single space using

FIGURE 6.18

Examples of special characters in different sizes

☞ *Complete the order form*
☞ *Include your check or money order*
☞ *And mail it today!*

☞ *Complete the order form*
☞ *Include your check or money order*
☞ *And mail it today!*

☞ *Complete the order form*
☞ *Include your check or money order*
☞ *And mail it today!*

the Overstrike feature. Here's how:

1. Move the cursor to the spot where you want to type multiple characters.

2. Choose Layout ➤ Character ➤ Create Overstrike. The dialog box below will appear on your screen:

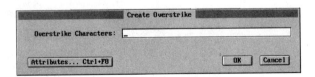

3. If you want to choose a size and/or appearance attribute(s) for the characters, choose Attributes (or press Ctrl+F8) and make a selection. (Repeat this step if you want to assign multiple attributes to the overstruck characters.)

4. Type the characters that you want to overstrike. For example, typing **O/** will produce Ø in the document.

5. Choose OK when you're done.

The characters appear in the same space in the document window. In Reveal Codes, the characters are displayed in an [Ovrstk] code.

If you need to change an overstrike character, position the cursor just past the overstrike characters you want to change, choose Layout ➤ Character ➤ Edit Overstrike, and use the standard editing keys to make changes. When you're done, choose OK to return to your document. To delete an overstrike character altogether, turn on Reveal Codes and delete the [Ovrstk] code.

Adding Lines and Borders

Lines and borders provide a great way to spruce up a document, as illustrated in Figure 6.19. You'll learn to create complex documents like the one shown here in Part VII of this book. For now, just notice that I've used various types of lines in the document.

There are actually several ways to add lines to a document:

- The Underline and Double Underline appearances can be used to underline text and/or spaces and tabs, as described earlier in this chapter.

- Graphic lines, such as the vertical lines separating the columns in Figure 6.19, work only with graphics printers. You can control the thickness, shading, and exact position of graphic lines.

- To draw lines *around* text and graphics, you can use the Graphic Borders feature described later in this chapter. The *Tables* feature (Chapter 7) also lets you place lines around text and graphics.

The Vacationer

Vol. 1 No. 1   Travel fun for everyone   January 1994

Newsletter Debut

by Joan Smith
We're pleased to bring this first
issue of our newsletter, *The
Vacationer*, to our many loyal
customers. The newsletter was
inspired by your ideas and
questions. You've asked us where to
find the best
travel fares,
where to go for
the person who
has been
everywhere, what
to eat and how to
eat it when
visiting faraway
countries. We've
responded by creating this
newsletter.

Here we'll bring you the latest news
about great deals on vacations in
exotic corners of our planet, fun
places for inexpensive weekend
getaways, and out-of-the-way spots
you might never have thought to ask
us about. We'll include handy
vacation planning tips and introduce
you to exciting foods, puzzling
customs, and important laws you'll

encounter during sojourns to foreign
lands. So relax, enjoy, and travel
with us as we bring you a new issue
every quarter of the year...   ✿

Celebrate With Us

by Jill Evans
In honor of our newsletter's maiden
voyage, we'd like
to invite you to
an Open House at
7:00pm on
January 11,
1994, at our
offices. Feel free
to dress casually,
or make an
appearance in
your most fashionable travel togs. ✿

*Join us at our
Open House
January 11, 1994
7:00 PM*

Tropical Travel

by Elizabeth Olson
Travel to tropical islands is on the
increase. Just look at the graph
showing our clients' recent tropical
trips and you'll see how dramatic
the numbers really are. There's a
good reason for these increases --
tropical vacations are great fun,
especially when the wind and snow
are swirling at your doorstep in the

- You can also use Line Draw (Ctrl+F3) to draw lines (Line Draw
  is described later in this chapter). Though awkward to use, Line
  Draw has the advantage of working with *any* printer.

Drawing Graphic Lines

Graphic lines require that your printer be able to print graphics (most printers can do this). To put a graphic line in your document, follow the steps below:

1. Move the cursor to the place that you want to put the line.

2. Choose Graphics ➤ Graphics Lines (or press Alt+F9).

3. Choose Create. You'll see the Create Graphics Line dialog box shown in Figure 6.20.

4. Choose a Line Orientation—either Horizontal or Vertical—then choose other options as described in the sections that follow.

5. Choose OK to return to your document.

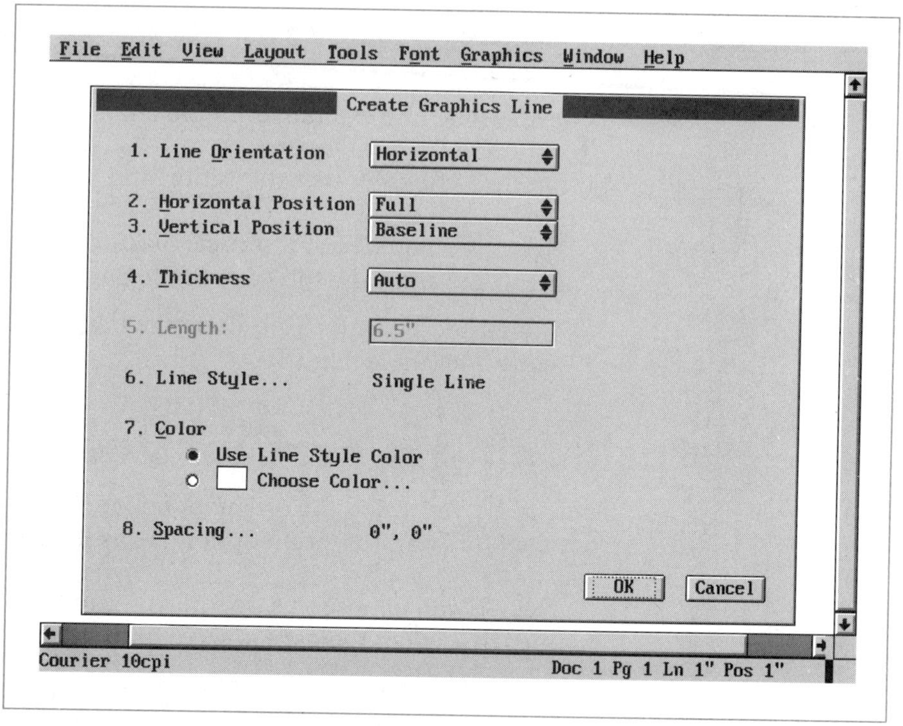

FIGURE 6.20

The Create Graphics Line Dialog box lets you add graphic lines to your document.

| File | Edit | View | Layout | Tools | Font | Graphics | Window | Help |

Create Graphics Line

1. Line Orientation   Horizontal

2. Horizontal Position   Full
3. Vertical Position   Baseline

4. Thickness   Auto

5. Length: 6.5"

6. Line Style...   Single Line

7. Color
   ● Use Line Style Color
   ○ ☐ Choose Color...

8. Spacing...   0", 0"

OK   Cancel

Courier 10cpi   Doc 1 Pg 1 Ln 1" Pos 1"

The graphic line will appear on your screen in Graphics and Page modes, as well as on the Print Preview screen. The hidden code for a graphic line appears as [Graph Line...] in Reveal Codes, and it expands to display additional information when you move the cursor to it.

Positioning a Horizontal Line

If you chose Horizontal as the line orientation, you can then choose Horizontal Position and select these options:

Set   If you choose Set, you can then enter the starting point in the text box to the right. The measurement is expressed in inches from the left side of the page (not the left margin). The default is the current cursor position.

Left   The line extends from the left margin to the current cursor position.

Right   The line extends from the current cursor position to the right margin.

Centered   The line is centered between the left and right margins.

Full   The line extends from the left margin to the right margin.

You can then choose Vertical Position and select these options:

Set   Lets you define a vertical position on the page, in inches, as measured from the top edge of the paper (not the top margin).

Baseline   Runs the line along the bottom of the letters on this same line (the default).

Positioning a Vertical Line

If you chose Vertical as the orientation for your graphic line, your choices from the Horizontal Position option are as follows:

Set   If you choose this option, you can type in the distance from the left edge of the page where you want to place the line.

Left   The line is printed along the left margin.

Right   The line is printed along the right margin.

Centered   The line is centered between the left and right margins.

Between Columns   Lets you place the line between two columns. After choosing this option, enter numbers indicating which columns the line goes between (for example, **1** and **2** to put the line between the first two columns). If you haven't divided the page into columns, choosing this option places the line at the right margin.(For more information, please see Chapter 27.)

Next, you can choose **V**ertical Position and choose any of the options below:

Set   If you choose this option, you can then enter a measurement indicating where the line should start, as measured from the top edge of the page.

Top   Starts the line at the top margin.

Bottom   Starts the line at the bottom margin.

Centered   Centers the line between the top and bottom margins.

Full   The line runs the full length of the page, from top margin to bottom margin.

Other Line Settings

While you're in the Create Graphics Line dialog box, you can also use these options to define your line:

Thickness   **A**uto automatically sets the thickness of the line. **S**et lets you define your own thickness (in inches). See Figure 6.21 for examples.

Length   If you don't choose Full as your line position, enter a length (in inches) here.

Line Style   Lets you choose a line style (such as Double Line or Dashed Line) from a predefined list. You can also create your own style (see Chapter 17).

FIGURE 6.21

Examples of various
graphic line widths

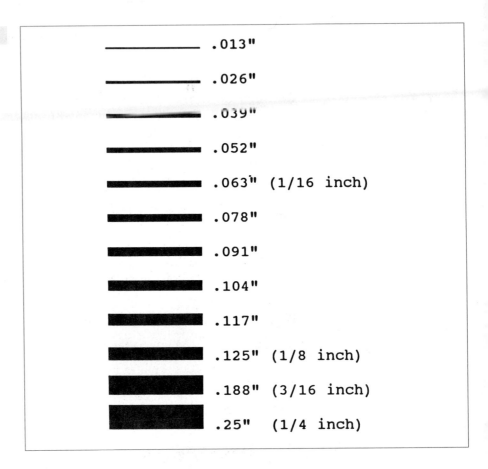

.013"

.026"

.039"

.052"

.063" (1/16 inch)

.078"

.091"

.104"

.117"

.125" (1/8 inch)

.188" (3/16 inch)

.25" (1/4 inch)

Color   You can use the color that's currently defined in the style, or you can select the Choose Color option, then pick a color and/or %Shading from the Color Selection palette. (There's more on colors later in this chapter.)

Spacing   Lets you determine how much space you want between the line and neighboring text. Zero inches (0″) leaves no excess spacing.

The line appears in the document window if you're in Graphics mode or Page mode. You can also view the line in Print Preview.

Changing a Graphic Line

To change the size, position, or any other aspect of a graphic line in your document, just follow these steps:

1. Move the cursor to just after (or just below) the graphic line. You might want to turn on Reveal Codes so you can see the [Graph Line...] code.

2. Choose Graphics ➤ Graphics Lines ➤ Edit. Then...

   - If you can see the number of the line you want to change (in Reveal Codes) choose Graphics Line Number and type in the number.
   - Or, choose Next Graphics Line to edit the next line beyond the cursor.
   - Or, choose Previous Graphics Line to edit the first line above, or to the left of, the cursor.

3. Choose Edit Line.

You'll be taken to the Edit Graphics Line dialog box, where you can change any of the settings you previously assigned to the line.

Deleting a Graphic Line

To delete a graphic line, turn on Reveal Codes (Alt+F3) and delete the [Graph Line] code for the line. If the line doesn't disappear right away, press Ctrl+F3 and choose the Rewrite button or press Ctrl+F3 twice.

Using Your Mouse to Edit Lines

If you have a mouse, you can use it to move graphic lines around on the screen, change their thickness and length, delete them, or open the Edit Graphics Line dialog box.

Here are some techniques you can use:

- To see the entire line on your screen before making changes, reduce the view of your document. For example, choose View ➤ Zoom ➤ 50% or choose the 50% option from the Ribbon.

- To go directly to the Edit Graphics Line dialog box, move the mouse pointer to the middle of the line (approximately), then double-click. The Edit Graphics Line dialog box will appear on your screen.

- To change the line length or thickness or move the line elsewhere, select the line by clicking on it. Figure 6.22 shows the selection handles that appear when you click on a horizontal line. The labels in that figure correspond to the explanations below:

1. Drag this selection handle diagonally to change the line length and thickness.

2. Drag this selection handle to change the line length only.

3. Drag this selection handle to change the line thickness only.

4. Drag the line (but not a selection handle) to move it to a new position in your document.

FIGURE 6.22

A graphics line after clicking on it with the mouse. The numbers correspond to the discussion of moving and resizing lines.

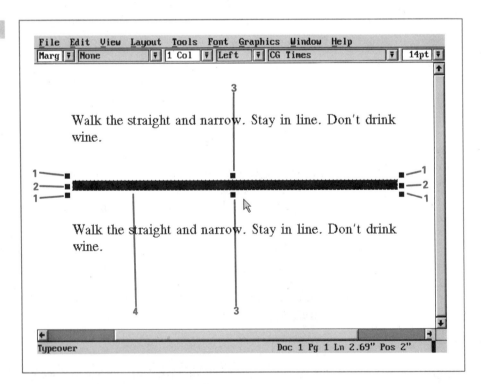

To delete the line, move the mouse pointer to the line and click. Selection handles will appear. Now press the Delete key and choose Yes when WordPerfect asks if you're sure you want to delete the graphics line.

Changing a vertical line is almost the same, except that the selection handles will be rotated by ninety degrees. Thus, three selection handles appear at the top and bottom of the selected line, and two appear at the left and right of the line.

TIP To deselect a line, simply click on some text in your document or press Escape. To undo changes immediately, choose Edit ➤ Undo or press Ctrl+Z.

Drawing Graphic Borders and Boxes

Another way to add lines to a document is by drawing borders around text. You can draw lines around the entire page, around all paragraphs, or around specific paragraphs.

Drawing Borders around Paragraphs

To draw borders around paragraphs, follow the steps below:

1. Type the paragraph(s) that you want to draw borders around. Then...

   - If you want to put a border around several paragraphs, select those paragraphs.

- If you want to put borders around a paragraph and all subsequent paragraphs, move the cursor to anywhere within the first paragraph you want bordered.
- If you want to put a border around one paragraph only, select a small amount of text within that paragraph (you can select as little as a single character).

2. Choose Graphics ➤ Borders ➤ Paragraph (or press Alt+F9 OP). You'll see the Create Paragraph Border dialog box:

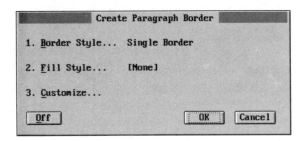

- If you wish, choose Border Style and select one of the available styles.
- If you want to shade the paragraph(s), choose Fill Style, then select one of the available fill styles.
- If you wish, choose Customize and customize the border to your liking.

3. When you've finished defining your border, choose OK to return to your document.

If you don't use any of the customization features, your paragraph will appear with a simple single-line border around it. As you can see in Figure 6.23, you can customize borders in various ways, as I'll explain later in this chapter. Feel free to experiment while defining your paragraph borders.

FIGURE 6.23

Examples of various
paragraph border
styles and a simple
single-line page
border

> This paragraph is bordered by the standard single-line border. After typing all the paragraphs on this page, I selected a small chunk of text within this paragraph. Then I chose Graphics ▸ Borders ▸Paragraph. Then I chose OK to use all the default options.

> This paragraph is bordered by the thin and thick lines. After typing all the paragraphs on this page, I selected a small chunk of text within this paragraph. Then I chose Graphics ▸ Borders ▸Paragraph. Then I chose Border Styles, and Thin Thick border before choosing OK.

> *I should also mention that you can put text in graphics boxes. If you do, you can then use your mouse to size and position the box anywhere on the page, wrap text around the box, turn the text sideways or upside down... do all kinds of things. See Chapters 26 and 28, when convenient, for examples and info.*

To put the border around the page, I chose Graphics ▸ Borders ▸ Page, and then just chose OK to use the standard single-line border. By the way, that arrow to the left is a piece of clip art. You'll learn about graphics in Chapter 26.

T I P

If you find that you need to add text below a bordered paragraph, but you can't get the cursor out of the borders, choose Graphics ➤ Borders ➤ Paragraph, then choose Off. Later, you can repeat the steps given above to put borders around whichever paragraphs you wish.

Deleting Paragraph Borders

You can easily disable paragraph bordering at certain paragraphs. Like most things in WordPerfect, paragraph borders are controlled by hidden codes. This means you can delete a paragraph border by deleting the [Para Border] code at the beginning of the bordered paragraph. You can also select several bordered paragraphs and choose Graphics ➤ Borders ➤ Paragraph ➤ Off.

Drawing Page Borders

To draw a border around the current page, follow these three steps:

1. Place the cursor anywhere on the page that you want to put a border around.

2. Choose Graphics ➤ Borders ➤ Page (or press Alt+F9 OA).

3. If you wish, choose Border Style, Fill Style, or Customize.

4. Choose OK.

If you don't choose any customization features, the page (and all subsequent pages) will have a single-line border around the page margins.

Turning Off a Page Border

To stop page bordering in your document, place the cursor anywhere on the first page where you want to stop the page borders, and choose

Graphics ➤ Borders ➤ Page ➤ Off. That page, and all subsequent pages, will no longer have page borders.

To resume page bordering, go to the page where you want the bordering to start again, and repeat the steps given in the preceding section.

Customizing Borders

When you're creating borders, feel free to experiment with a variety of designs. The easiest way is to choose Graphics ➤ Borders, then select the type of border you want to experiment with. Next choose Customize to get to a dialog box like the one shown in Figure 6.24.

As you try out options 1 through 7, your current selections are instantly reflected in the sample border displayed in the Customize dialog box. Remember that you can always press F1 for help if necessary.

FIGURE 6.24

The Customize dialog boxes let you experiment with various combinations of border styles.

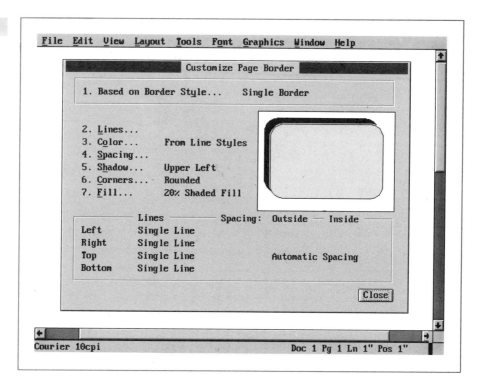

Using Line Draw

Line Draw lets you draw character-based lines, which you can then print with a non-graphics printer. Line Draw is also useful for drawing lines in documents that you might later export to a word processor or text editor that does not support graphic lines.

For Line Draw to work properly, you should use a monospaced font that includes line-drawing characters, such as Courier Line Draw. Proportional fonts make line drawing difficult. Also, use left justification to prevent characters in the lines from spreading across the margins. Here are the steps:

1. Move the cursor to wherever you want to start drawing a line or box.

2. Choose your monospaced font for drawing lines (choose F<u>o</u>nt ➤ F<u>o</u>nt).

3. Choose <u>G</u>raphics ➤ Line <u>D</u>raw, or press Ctrl+F3 and choose Line Draw. You'll see a dialog box like the one shown below near the bottom of your screen:

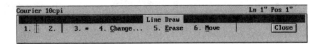

4. Choose a line-drawing character (option 1, 2, or 3). Or, if you want to change the line-drawing character, choose <u>C</u>hange (option 4). Then, when the Change Line Draw Character dialog box appears, do one of the following:

   • Click on the line-drawing character you want to use (or type its number).

   • Or, choose <u>U</u>ser-defined. Then, *either* type a character (such as ★), *or* press **Ctrl+2,** type the code or shortcut for the character you want. (For example, you could enter **4,3** or ★. to choose a bullet as the User-defined character.) Figures 6.16 and 6.17 show codes and shortcuts for many special characters.

5. Use the ↑, ↓, ←, and → keys to draw lines using the selected character. (You can't use a mouse to position the cursor or draw in Line Draw.) You can also use the keystrokes below to draw lines quickly:

- Home ← (draw to left margin, or to first character to the left of cursor)
- Home → (draw to right margin, or to first character to the right of cursor)
- Home ↑ (draw to top margin, or to first character above cursor)
- Home ↓ (draw to bottom margin, or to first character below cursor)
- Home Home ← (draw to left margin)
- Home Home → (draw to right margin)
- Home Home ↑ (draw to top margin)
- Home Home ↓ (draw to bottom margin)

6. If you need to move the cursor without drawing, choose <u>M</u>ove from the Line Draw dialog box and position the cursor. If you need to erase lines, choose <u>E</u>rase from the Line Draw dialog box and move the cursor over existing lines.

7. Repeat steps 4–6 as necessary to complete your drawing.

8. When you've finished drawing, choose Close (or press Esc).

NOTE

When a character created with Line Draw is highlighted in Reveal Codes, that character's code appears (for example, [3,48]).

The lines created with Line Draw will appear in any display mode. Depending on which character you use to draw the line, you may notice a small arrow at the beginning and end of the line in Text mode. That arrow will not appear in the printed document. It simply indicates the direction that you're going and marks the end of a line. Nonetheless, you can get rid of the arrow by moving the cursor to the arrow and pressing Delete.

Coloring Your Text

If you're one of the fortunate few who own color printers, you can easily add color to your printed text. But even if you don't own a color printer, your local print shop or service bureau can probably print your documents in color for you.

Choosing a Print Color

Chapter 19 explains how to select color palettes and customize print colors in detail. However, if you're eager to get started with color printing, you can follow the steps below:

1. Place the cursor where you want the color to start, or select the text you want to color.

2. Choose F<u>o</u>nt ➤ <u>P</u>rint Color, or press Ctrl+F8 C. The Color Selection dialog appears, as shown in Figure 6.25.

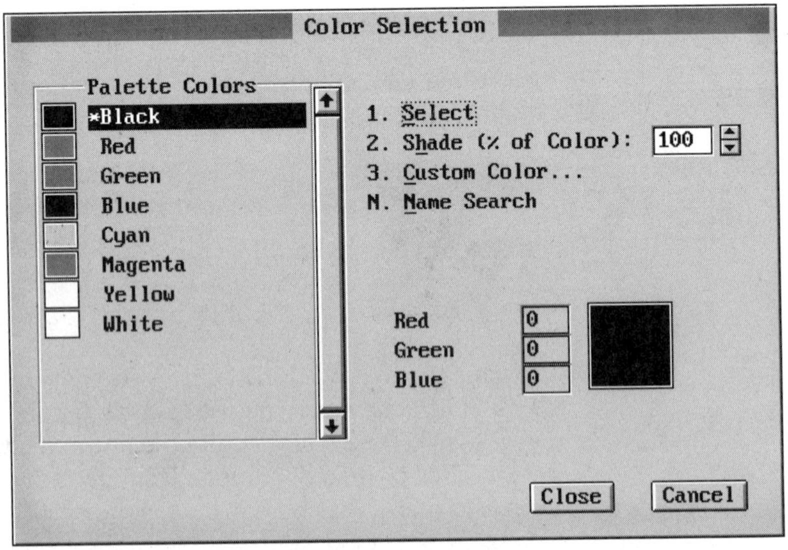

FIGURE 6.25

The Color Selection dialog box appears when you choose <u>F</u>ont ➤ Print <u>C</u>olor.

Color Selection

Palette Colors
- ✱Black
- Red
- Green
- Blue
- Cyan
- Magenta
- Yellow
- White

1. <u>S</u>elect
2. <u>S</u>hade (% of Color): 100
3. <u>C</u>ustom Color...
N. <u>N</u>ame Search

Red   0
Green 0
Blue   0

Close   Cancel

3. Highlight the print color you want in the Palette Colors list.

4. If you want to change the shade, choose Shade (% of Color) and type in a percentage, in the range of 0 to 100. (The smaller the number, the paler your color will be.)

5. Choose Select to return to your document.

Text colors are controlled by [Color] codes, which you can see in Reveal Codes. Shading is controlled by [Char Shade Change] codes. You can move or delete these codes like any other codes (see Chapter 4).

NOTE If your screen only shows grays, you may not be using a color monitor, or you may need to switch to a color graphics driver. Try choosing File ➤ Setup ➤ Display ➤ Graphics Mode Screen Type/Colors ➤ Screen Type ➤ Auto Select. See Chapter 19.

Printing in Color

When you're ready to print your document in color, make sure that you've selected the Full Color option by choosing File ➤ Print/Fax. Then choose Setup or press Shift+F1 and set the Print Color option to Full Color. (To print the document in black and shades of gray on a color printer, set the Print Color option to Black.)

If you don't have a color printer, you can still print text in shades of gray, using the techniques described above. You can either choose Black as your color and then adjust the shading or choose the color from the Palette Colors list that is closest to the shade you want.

Different printers will interpret different gray shades and colors differently. Therefore, you may need to experiment to find just the right shades for your printer. Figure 6.26 shows gray shades and colors printed by the Hewlett-Packard LaserJet. The percentage values indicate the Shade (% of Color) setting with Black as the selected Palette Color.

FIGURE 6.26

Examples printed with a non-color printer using the Shade (% of Color) setting and the Palette Color set to Black

100%	**Black**
90%	**Red**
80%	Green
70%	**Blue**
60%	Cyan
50%	**Magenta**
40%	Yellow
30%	

Redrawing Your Screen

As your document becomes more complex, there's always a chance that things will start looking a little crazy because your monitor can't keep up with the changes. Similarly, if you share documents on a network, another user's mail or message might cover part of your document.

Before you panic, rewrite the screen to see if it's current with the data in memory: Press Ctrl+F3, then choose Rewrite or, press Ctrl+F3 twice.

If things still look out of whack, they probably really are. You can use Print Preview for a closer look, and use Reveal Codes to help you locate and fix any faulty codes.

In this chapter you've learned about a number of techniques for sprucing up the appearance of a document. In the next chapter, you'll learn about one of WordPerfect's most powerful (yet also one of the easiest) tools for organizing text in columns—the Tables feature.

Creating Dazzling Tables

fast TRACK

To insert or delete rows and columns   271

> press Ctrl+Ins to insert a row or Ctrl+Del to delete a row. Alternatively, switch to Table Edit mode and use the Ins and Del buttons (or Insert and Delete keys) to insert multiple rows or columns.

To join two or more cells   278

> go into Table Edit mode, select the cells you want to join, then choose Join.

To add, change, or remove table lines   281

> go to Table Edit mode, select the cells you want to change the lines on, and choose Lines/Fill. Choose line styles for the Entire Table or just the Current Cell or Block.

To shade one or more cells   284

> go into Table Edit mode, select the cell(s) you want to shade and choose Lines/Fill, then Fill. Next, choose a Fill Style.

To delete, copy, or move an entire table   304

> use the normal document window, but turn on Reveal Codes (Alt+F3) so you can see the hidden codes. Then select the entire table including the [Tbl Def] at the top and [Tbl Off] at the bottom of the table. To delete, press Delete. Otherwise, use standard cut-and-paste techniques to move or copy the table to a new location or document.

WORDPERFECT'S Tables feature lets you type text into columns that you can later widen, narrow, or rearrange without ever changing a tab stop. As the name implies, the Tables feature is very helpful when it comes to typing up small tables, like the example shown in Figure 7.1.

Destination	Arrives	Ticket Price
Oceanside	8:30 am	$12.50
San Clemente	9:00 am	$17.50
Santa Ana	10:00 am	$37.50
Anaheim	10:30 am	$40.00
Los Angeles	11:45 am	$55.00
Malibu	1:00 pm	$70.00

What most people don't realize, however, is that the Tables feature is good for much more than "obvious" tables. As you'll see in this chapter, it's a good tool for just about any document that's formatted into columns, uses printed lines, or both.

About the only kinds of multicolumn documents that the Tables feature isn't particularly good for are multiple-page documents and documents with newspaper-style columns. For those kinds of documents, you'll probably prefer the Columns feature discussed in Chapter 27.

Hidden Advantages of Tables

As an example of how you might use the Tables feature to create a multi-column document, Figures 7.2 through 7.4 show a sample itinerary with parallel columns. In Figure 7.2 you can see the first draft of the itinerary, in which the Tables feature was used to organize some of the text into columns.

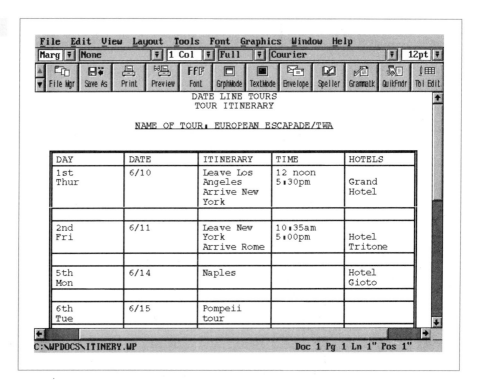

FIGURE 7.3

The second draft of
the itinerary, after
changing some
column widths

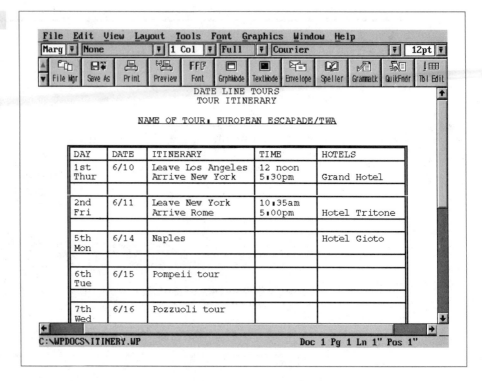

You can widen or narrow columns and join and split cells at any time to get the appearance you want. Text within each cell will automatically wrap to fit the cell, and you can see your changes right on the screen as you make them. Figure 7.3 shows the sample itinerary after column widths within the table have been adjusted to accommodate the text inside the cells.

When you're done adjusting column widths and cells, you can easily change or remove any of the lines in the table. For example, Figure 7.4 shows the completed itinerary after removing most of the lines from the table. Text is placed neatly into columns, without an abundance of lines appearing.

FIGURE 7.4

The sample itinerary
with most of the lines
removed

```
                           DATE LINE TOURS
                            TOUR ITINERARY

                 NAME OF TOUR: EUROPEAN ESCAPADE/TWA


        DAY      DATE    ITINERARY          TIME       HOTELS
        1st      6/10    Leave Los Angeles  12 noon
        Thur             Arrive New York    5:30pm     Grand Hotel


        2nd      6/11    Leave New York     10:35am
        Fri              Arrive Rome        5:00pm     Hotel Tritone


        5th      6/14    Naples                        Hotel Gioto
        Mon


        6th      6/15    Pompeii tour
        Tue


        7th      6/16    Pozzuoli tour
        Wed


        8th      6/17    Island of Ischia             Isla Hotel
        Thu              (Boat Tour)


        9th      6/18    Sorrento
        Fri


        10th     6/19    Leave Rome         1:15pm
        Sat              Arrive New York    4:20pm


        11th     6/20    Leave New York     7:30pm
        Sun      6/27    Arrive Los Angeles 10:30pm
```

Tables Terminology

The Tables feature has some terminology of its own. Basically, a table consists of *rows* and *columns*. The place where a row and a column meet is a
cell. Each cell has an *address* that indicates its position in the table. Whenever the cursor is inside the table, the address of the current cell appears
on the status line as you move the cursor from cell to cell (see Figure 7.5).

Table columns are named alphabetically from left to right, and the rows
are numbered from top to bottom. So the cell in the upper-left corner is
always cell A1, the cell to the right of that is cell B1, and so forth. Beneath

FIGURE 7.5

Columns, rows, and a
cell in a table

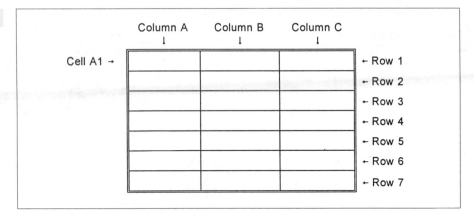

cell A1 are cells A2, A3, etc. As you'll see, when you're creating or editing
a table, the column names and row numbers are clearly visible outside the
borders of the table.

Creating a Table

To create a table, follow these steps:

1. Move the cursor to wherever you want the table to begin.

2. Choose <u>L</u>ayout ➤ <u>T</u>ables ➤ <u>C</u>reate (or press Alt+F7 TC). You'll
    see the dialog box shown below:

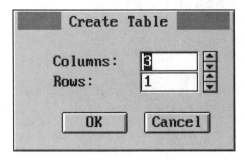

3. Type or use the spin box arrows to indicate the number of columns (across) and rows (down) you want in the table. The largest possible table size is 32 columns by 32,756 rows. (You can easily change the dimensions later, so don't be too concerned about getting it exactly right just now.)

4. Choose OK. You'll see the Table Edit screen, as shown in Figure 7.6.

FIGURE 7.6

Screen for creating and editing a table

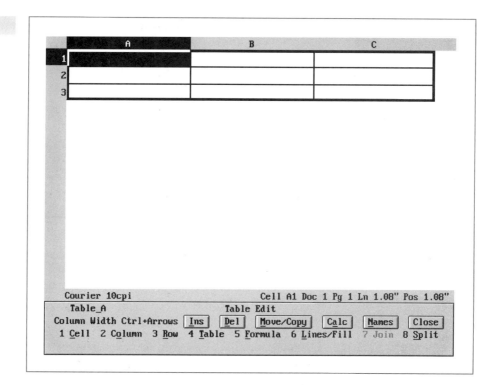

Working with a Table

Once you create a table, you can work with it in either of the following modes:

Table Edit Mode   When you first create a table, you're in Table Edit mode (Figure 7.6). Here you can change the overall appearance of the table but *not* the contents of individual cells. Notice that column letters and row numbers are plainly visible, the cursor is expanded to the full size of a cell, and Table Edit options appear near the bottom of the screen.

Document Window When you want to work on the *contents* of cells within the table, you work in the normal document window. Here you can see other text (if there is any). The column letters and row numbers are hidden (though the status line indicates the current cell), and the cursor is generally small, except when you're selecting text.

Switching to and from Table Edit Mode

It's easy to switch from one mode to the other:

- If you're in Table Edit mode and you want to return to normal editing, click the Close button or press F7 (Exit).

- If you're in the regular document window, move the cursor anywhere within the table and choose <u>L</u>ayout ➤ <u>T</u>ables ➤ <u>E</u>dit (or press Alt+F11) to switch to Table Edit mode.

- If you're in the regular document window, you can also just click the table, then click the Tbl Edit button on the Button Bar to switch to Table Edit mode. If the current Button Bar doesn't have a Tbl Edit button, you can easily add such a button, using techniques discussed in Chapter 4.

NOTE If you try to switch to Table Edit mode, but the Edit option is dimmed and unavailable (or the Tbl Edit button in the Button Bar does nothing), you probably have text selected. Click any single cell, or press Escape, until the *Block on* indicator disappears from the lower-left corner of the screen. Then try again.

Moving through a Table

Regardless of whether you're in the document window or Table Edit mode, you can move the cursor to any cell within the table simply by using your mouse to click the cell you want to move the cursor to. You can also use the keys listed in Table 7.1 to move around the table. Notice that there are some differences between the way some keys work in Table Edit mode and in the normal document window.

TABLE 7.1: Keys Used to Move through a Table

TO MOVE...	IN TABLE EDIT	IN NORMAL EDIT
One cell right	→ *or* Tab	Alt+→ *or* Tab
One cell left	← *or* Shift+Tab	Alt+← *or* Shift+Tab
Up one cell	↑	↑
Down one cell	↓	↓
Start of row	Home ←	Home Home Home ← *or* Alt+Home ←
End of row	End *or* Home →	Home Home Home → *or* Alt+Home →
Top of column	Home ↑	Alt+Home ↑ *or* Ctrl+Home Home ↑
Bottom of column	Home ↓	Alt+Home ↓ *or* Ctrl+Home Home ↓
First cell	Home Home ↑	Alt+Home Home ↑ *or* Ctrl+Home Home Home ↑
Last cell	Home Home ↓	Alt+Home Home ↓ *or* Ctrl+Home Home Home ↓
Any cell	Ctrl+Home *cell address*	
To normal Edit	F7 *or* Close button	
To Table Edit		Layout ➤ Tables ➤ Edit *or* Alt+F11 *or* Tbl Edit button

NOTE: In the normal editing mode, the ↑, ↓, →, and ← keys move through existing text, if any, before moving to another cell.

Typing and Editing Table Text

Once you've created an empty table, it's easy to type and edit text in it. If you're in Table Edit mode, return to the document window first (click the Close button or press F7). Next, move the cursor to whichever cell you want to type in or change. Now type or edit your text normally.

You can also use WordPerfect's formatting features when typing or changing text in a cell. For example, you can center, bold, and underline text, and you can change fonts (see Chapters 5 and 6).

Word-Wrap in a Table

If the text you type is too wide for the cell, WordPerfect will word-wrap the text as though the cell were a page. The height of the entire row will expand to accommodate the text in that cell. (You can later widen or narrow the cell to change the word-wrap within the cell.)

Tabbing and Indenting within a Table

When the cursor is in a table, the Tab and Shift+Tab keys move you around the table. If you want to indent, you can use the various options on the Layout ➤ Alignment menu or the shortcut keys listed in Table 7.2. (See Chapters 5 and 6 for more information about alignment, tabs, and dot leaders.)

Removing Extra Blanks in a Row

One common, pesky mishap occurs when you inadvertently press ↵ after typing text in a table. There's no harm in doing this, but it does cause the current row to double in height. You probably won't want this extra blank space across the row. So to get rid of it, press Backspace. Or, if you've

TABLE 7.2: *Shortcut Keys for Tabbing and Aligning within a Table Cell*

TAB TYPE	KEYSTROKE	WITH DOT LEADERS
Left tab	Home Tab	Home Home Tab
Right tab	Home Alt+F6	Home Home Alt+F6
Center tab	Home Shift+F6	Home Home Shift+F6
Decimal tab	Home Ctrl+F6	Home Home Ctrl+F6
Flush right	Alt+F6	Alt+F6 Alt+F6

already moved the cursor elsewhere, go back to the offending cell, turn on Reveal Codes, and delete the [HRt] code at the end of the cell's text.

Emptying Cells

You can delete the contents of cells during normal editing or in Table Edit mode. Select the cells you want to empty (as discussed in the next section), then press Delete. If you're in Table Edit mode, select the cells, choose <u>D</u>el or press Delete, and choose OK. If you change your mind, press Ctrl+Z to bring back the selected text.

Selecting Cells

You can select a group of cells that you want to reformat or change. The basic techniques for selecting cells are the same as for selecting text outside of a table:

- Move the mouse pointer to the first cell you want to select, hold down the mouse button, and drag until the cells you want to select are highlighted.

- Or, move the cursor to the first cell you want to select, press Alt+F4 or F12, then use the cursor-movement keys (shown in Table 7.1) to extend the selection to the cells you want to select.

If you need to start over, just click any cell or press Escape (or Alt+F4 or F12) until the *Block on* indicator in the lower-left corner disappears.

Resizing Columns

Perhaps the most important advantage that the Tables feature has over tab stops is that it lets you change column widths interactively. Your text instantly word-wraps to fit within the column. To change the width of a column, follow the steps below:

1. Move the cursor to the column you want to resize and (if you haven't already done so) switch to Table Edit mode.

2. Hold down the Ctrl key and press → to widen or ← to narrow the column to your liking.

Figure 7.7 shows a small sample table before and after resizing the columns. As you can see, widening and narrowing columns helps you control the row height, the word-wrap within each column, and the distance between the text in the columns.

This convenient feature takes the guesswork out of calculating tab stops and column widths before typing text into columns. Instead, you can just figure out how many columns you need, type text into each column, then adjust the column widths so that the text fits within each column. And, as the bottom example in Figure 7.7 shows, you can also align text within columns, use shading and text appearances, and change lines to further improve the appearance of your tables (you'll find out how later in this chapter).

Sizing Columns to a Specific Width

If you want to set a column or group of columns to a known width, such as 2.5 inches, follow these steps:

1. Switch to Table Edit mode (if you aren't there already).

2. Move the cursor to the column you want to resize. If you want to set several adjacent columns to the same size, select those columns as described earlier in this chapter.

FIGURE 7.7

A sample table
before and after
changing column
widths

Original table, before sizing columns...

Item No.	Description	Size	Qty	Price
BW-111	Boy's Bermuda Short	22	1	$29.95
BW-204	Boy's Tank Top	12	1	$19.95
BW-607	Boy's Polo Shirt	12	1	$24.95

The same table after sizing the columns to better fit the text...

Item No.	Description	Size	Qty	Price
BW-111	Boy's Bermuda Short	22	1	$29.95
BW-204	Boy's Tank Top	12	1	$19.95
BW-607	Boy's Polo Shirt	12	1	$24.95

And finally, the same table after realigning columns and shading some cells.

Item No.	Description	Size	Qty	Price
BW-111	Boy's Bermuda Short	22	1	$29.95
BW-204	Boy's Tank Top	12	1	$19.95
BW-607	Boy's Polo Shirt	12	1	$24.95

3. Choose Column from the Table Edit options at the bottom of the screen.

4. Choose Width and type a width measurement, in inches (for example, *2.5*), points (*72p*), or your preferred unit of measure. Then choose OK.

Be aware that you cannot widen the table beyond the width that the current margins allow. For instance, if you're using 1-inch margins on paper that's $8\frac{1}{2}$ inches wide, the combined widths of all the columns in your table cannot exceed $6\frac{1}{2}$ inches.

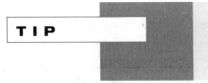

TIP   See "Making More Room in a Table," later in this chapter, for tips on squeezing more information into a table.

Maintaining a Fixed Width in a Column

As you widen a column in the table, WordPerfect will automatically narrow other columns, as necessary, to make room. This can be a bother if you've already set the width of a particular column precisely to your needs. To prevent WordPerfect from changing the width of a column, proceed as follows:

1. If you aren't already there, go to Table Edit mode.

2. Move the cursor to the column or select the columns to which you want to assign a fixed width.

3. Choose Column, then choose Fixed Width (so the checkbox is marked with an ×).

4. Choose OK.

Changing the Size of a Table

WordPerfect also lets you change the size of any table, even if you've already filled in many of the cells. The next few sections explain how to insert and delete rows and columns.

Inserting Rows and Columns

To insert a single row into a table, first move the cursor to wherever you want to insert the row. Then press Ctrl+Ins. (If you're in the document window, you can also choose Layout ➤ Tables ➤ Insert Row.)

To insert columns or multiple rows, follow these steps:

1. Switch to Table Edit mode (if you're not there already).

2. Move the cursor to wherever you need to add rows or columns.

3. Press Insert (Ins) or click the Ins button. You'll see this dialog box:

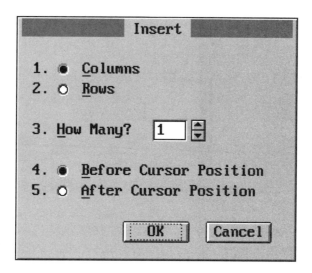

4. Choose either Rows (to insert rows) or Columns (to insert columns). Then, if you want to insert more than one, set the How Many? value accordingly.

5. Choose whether you want to insert the new row or column Before (above or to the left of) or After (below or to the right of) the current cursor position.

6. Choose OK.

TIP

You can quickly add a new row to the bottom of the table. First, move past the text in the last cell in the table (press Ctrl+Home Home Home ↓ End), then press the Tab key.

You can use blank rows and columns to add space between rows and columns, if you wish. For example, Figure 7.8 shows a document with a blank column separating the two columns of text and a blank row separating each section of text. Figure 7.9 shows the same document with the lines removed. The blank column and blank rows become extra blank space in the finished document.

Deleting Rows and Columns

You can delete entire rows or columns as easily as you can insert them. If you just want to delete the current row, press Ctrl+Delete and choose Yes. (If you're in the document window, you can choose Layout ➤ Tables ➤ Delete Row instead.)

To delete columns or multiple rows, follow the steps below:

1. Make sure you're in Table Edit mode.

2. Move the cursor to the row or column you want to delete, or select the rows or columns you want to delete.

3. Press Delete (Del) or click the Del button. Then...

   - If you want to delete the column(s), choose Columns.
   - If you want to delete the row(s), choose Rows.
   - If you only want to delete the text within the rows or columns, choose Cell Contents (or Block).
   - If you want to delete more than the current row or column, indicate the number you want to delete in How Many?

4. Choose OK.

As usual, you can press Ctrl+Z if you change your mind.

FIGURE 7.8

A blank column and blank rows used for extra spacing in a table

MINUTES OF SCHEDULED REGULAR MEETING

Conservation Commission
San Fernando, California

7:00 p.m.   Conference Room 5
Monday, February 25, 1994   Community Building

CALL MEETING TO ORDER/ROLL CALL		Meeting was called to order at 7:00 p.m. by President Jones. Present: Commissioners Abbott, Bates, Carter, Smith. Absent: Dory, Edwards. Excused: Fox.
APPROVAL OF MINUTES		It was MSP (Bates/Carter) to approve the minutes of February 12, 1994.
NEW BUSINESS		Guest speaker Dave Garcia, City of Los Angeles Park and Recreation Dept., updated the Commission on the proposed renovation of Swift Park. The estimated cost for the first phase of the project is $2.9 million, to include enhancement of the existing parking lot.

COMMITTEE REPORTS		See attached reports.
		    Abbott - Parks and Recreation
		    Bates - Road Repair
		    Carter - Environmental Task Force

OLD BUSINESS		Abbott handed out sample letters to elected officials for the letter-writing campaign. Bates reported on the meeting he attended with the Condo Association.
STAFF REPORT		Mr. Smith reported that the next meeting of the Planning Group will include a public hearing on the proposed freeway.
ADJOURNMENT		The meeting was adjourned at 8:00 p.m. to the next meeting of Monday, March 25, 1994.

FIGURE 7.9

The table shown in
Figure 7.8 with the
lines removed

MINUTES OF SCHEDULED REGULAR MEETING

Conservation Commission
San Fernando, California

7:00 p.m.   Conference Room 5
Monday, February 25, 1994   Community Building

CALL MEETING TO ORDER/ROLL CALL	Meeting was called to order at 7:00 p.m. by President Jones. Present: Commissioners Abbott, Bates, Carter, Smith. Absent: Dory, Edwards. Excused: Fox.
APPROVAL OF MINUTES	It was MSP (Bates/Carter) to approve the minutes of February 12, 1994.
NEW BUSINESS	Guest speaker Dave Garcia, City of Los Angeles Park and Recreation Dept., updated the Commission on the proposed renovation of Swift Park. The estimated cost for the first phase of the project is $2.9 million, to include enhancement of the existing parking lot.

COMMITTEE REPORTS	See attached reports.
	    Abbott - Parks and Recreation
	    Bates - Road Repair
	    Carter - Environmental Task Force

OLD BUSINESS	Abbott handed out sample letters to elected officials for the letter-writing campaign. Bates reported on the meeting he attended with the Condo Association.
STAFF REPORT	Mr. Smith reported that the next meeting of the Planning Group will include a public hearing on the proposed freeway.
ADJOURNMENT	The meeting was adjourned at 8:00 p.m. to the next meeting of Monday, March 25, 1994.

Positioning the Table on the Page

By default, WordPerfect makes the table as wide as your margins will allow. If you make the table narrower than that, you can pick a position on the page by following these steps:

1. Move the cursor into the table and switch to Table Edit mode (if you haven't already done so).

2. Choose <u>T</u>able.

3. Choose <u>P</u>osition, and then select one of the following options:

> **Left**   Aligns the table with the left margin.
>
> **<u>R</u>ight**   Aligns the table with the right margin.
>
> **<u>C</u>enter**   Centers the table between margins.
>
> **<u>F</u>ull**   Extends the table from the left margin to the right margin.
>
> **<u>S</u>et**   Lets you type a measurement in inches into the Distance setting to indicate how far from the left side of the page (not the margin) you want the table to be.

4. Choose OK.

You can check your work by returning to the document window (press F7) then viewing the table in Page mode (<u>V</u>iew ➤ P<u>a</u>ge Mode) or Print Preview (<u>F</u>ile ➤ Print Pre<u>v</u>iew). Use Zoom, as necessary, to expand your view.

Wrapping Text around a Table

If you want text to wrap around a table, you need to cut and paste the table into a graphics box, such as a Table box. Then you can work with the table inside the graphics editor, and size and position the graphics box. See Chapter 26 for more information on graphics boxes.

Using Tables in a Multicolumn Layout

If you create a table, then later you decide to switch to a multicolumn layout with two or more columns, the table probably won't fit into the column correctly. If you activate the columns before you create the table, WordPerfect will automatically size the table to fit within the column. However, that might be too narrow for your needs.

As for wrapping text around a table, the solution here is to put the table into a graphics box (such as a Table box). Then you can size and position the graphics box.

Figure 7.10 shows some examples of text wrapping around tables within a multicolumn document and describes briefly how each example was created. Please see Chapters 26 and 27 for more information on graphics boxes and multicolumn layouts.

TIP

The white text on a black background in Figure 7.10 is a one-cell table with shading set to 100% and the print color (Font ➤ Print Color) set to white. See "Printing White on Black," near the end of this chapter, for more information.

Preventing Page Breaks

If you want to ensure that a small table is never split across two pages in your document, your best bet is to place the table in a graphics box (see Chapter 26) and reference the table by its number. This method is commonly used in larger documents. For example, the text would refer the reader to Table 2.1, and Table 2.1 would be placed as close to the reference as possible, without being split across two pages.

Another advantage of placing tables in graphics boxes is that you can use *automatic referencing* (Chapter 31). With automatic referencing, if you add or delete a table, all the table numbers will adjust automatically, as will the textual references to those tables. This means that you won't need to renumber all the tables and the references to them manually.

FIGURE 7.10

An example using graphics boxes to wrap text around tables and span two or more columns

ON THE VERGE

FREE — **A Newsletter For The Overworked and Underpaid**

Welcome

This newsletter isn't really about being on the verge of anything. Rather, it's just an example of three different ways to put a table in a multicolumn document.

Get In Line

If you just want the table to fit into the column, you should create the columns before you create the table. Then, put the cursor to wherever you want to place the table, and choose Layout ▸ Tables ▸ Create, as usual. When WordPerfect sizes the table, it'll fit it right into the column, like this.

This table is in a graphics box that's anchored to the center of the page.

CAN'T REALLY PUT A CAPTION ON THIS TABLE, BECAUSE IT'S NOT IN A GRAPHICS BOX.

Front and Center

The table right smack in the middle of this document is in a graphics box. I created the box with the cursor *in front of* (above) the codes

that start the columns. Then I anchored that box to the Page, with a vertical position of Center, and a Horizontal Position of Margin, Center. Text in both columns just flows around the box.

Get To The Bottom of This

The table in the lower-right corner of this page is also in a graphics box. That one is anchored to the bottom of the page, right margin. Like the table in the middle, the hidden code for that graphics box is way up at the top of the document, *before* the codes that start the columns.

And About That White-On-Black

That little black bar with white text in it, just under the headline, is also a table. More on that at the end of this chapter. Okee Dokee?

This table is also in a graphics box, anchored to the bottom, right-hand margin of the page.

Managing Lines and Cells

You can format a table in almost any way imaginable, even if you've already entered text in the table. Some of the first things you should learn are how to join and split cells and how to change lines. These topics are discussed in the next few sections.

Joining Cells

To *join* cells means to remove the boundaries (lines) between them. You can join any number of adjacent cells into a single cell. Just follow these steps:

1. If you aren't already there, switch to Table Edit mode.

2. Select the cells you want to join.

3. Choose Join, then choose Yes when asked for confirmation.

If you're not happy with the results, press Ctrl+Z. Remember, Undo only works if Allow Undo is selected in File ➤ Setup ➤ Environment ➤ Allow Undo.

Figure 7.11 shows an example of cells in the top row of a table before, during, and after joining cells and centering text within the cell. In this figure, shading indicates selected (highlighted) cells. Of course, this is just one example; you can join *any* group of adjacent cells in a table. You'll see additional examples later in this chapter.

If you join cells that already contain text, the text will be separated by [Tbl Tab] codes. If you don't want the text to be separate, go back to the normal document editing mode and use Reveal Codes to delete the unwanted codes.

Splitting Cells

Splitting cells is the opposite of joining them. Rather than removing the boundaries between cells, splitting adds boundaries. You can use this feature to resplit cells you've joined or to split a cell so that you can type text

Train Schedule		
Destination	**Arrives**	**Price**
Oceanside	8:30 am	$12.50
San Clemente	9:00 am	$17.50
Santa Ana	10:00 am	$37.50

Step 1: In Table Edit mode, move highlight to one of the cells to be joined (cell A1 in this example.)

Train Schedule		
Destination	**Arrives**	**Price**
Oceanside	8:30 am	$12.50
San Clemente	9:00 am	$17.50
Santa Ana	10:00 am	$37.50

Step 2: Select the cells to join using your mouse or Block (Alt+F4 or F12). Here, I've selected all the cells across row 1.

Train Schedule		
Destination	**Arrives**	**Price**
Oceanside	8:30 am	$12.50
San Clemente	9:00 am	$17.50
Santa Ana	10:00 am	$37.50

Step 3: From the Table Edit menu, choose Join. Then choose Yes when asked for confirmation.

Train Schedule		
Destination	**Arrives**	**Price**
Oceanside	8:30 am	$12.50
San Clemente	9:00 am	$17.50
Santa Ana	10:00 am	$37.50

Step 4: Optionally, select Cell and then set the Alignment Justification to Center, to center the title like this.

in two or more rows or columns within the cell. The basic steps for splitting cells are almost the same as for joining them:

1. Make sure you're in Table Edit mode.

2. If you want to split several cells, select those cells. Otherwise, just move the cursor to the cell you want to split.

3. Choose <u>S</u>plit. You'll see this dialog box:

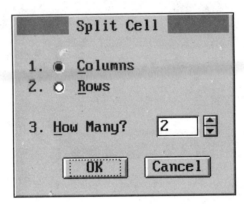

4. Choose <u>C</u>olumns or <u>R</u>ows, depending on whether you want to split the cell into columns or rows.

5. Use the <u>H</u>ow Many option to indicate the number of rows or columns you want to split the cell into.

6. Choose OK.

If you're not happy with the results, press Ctrl+Z.

If you're using the Split option to undo the effects of a previous join, Word-Perfect will place the cell boundaries so that they line up with existing boundaries. If you split a single cell into two or more cells, WordPerfect will create equal-size rows or columns within the cell. The new columns or rows will have the same formatting as the original cell. Figure 7.12 shows a single cell before and after it was split into three columns.

A table with three columns, and two rows...

Results of splitting cell B1 into three columns...

Changing the Lines in a Table

To change, add, or remove table lines, follow these steps:

1. Make sure you're in Table Edit mode.

2. If you want to change the lines for a single cell, move the cursor to that cell. If you want to change the lines for several cells, select those cells.

3. Choose Lines/Fill. You'll see this dialog box:

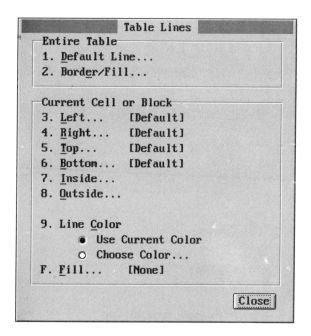

4. Choose appropriate options from the Entire Table section of the dialog box. Your options are as follows:

Default Line   Lets you choose the style and color of all the lines in the table.

Border/Fill   Lets you choose a border and fill style for the entire table. (You can choose Customize from the dialog box that follows and experiment with the possibilities.)

In the Current Cell or Block section, these are your options:

Left   Affects only the line at the left of the current cell or selected area.

Right   Affects only the line to the right of the current cell or selected area.

Top   Affects only the line above the current cell or selected area.

Bottom   Affects only the line under the current cell or selected area.

Inside   Affects only lines inside the selected area.

Outside   Affects only lines outside the current cell or selected area.

Line Color   Lets you choose a color for the selected line(s).

Fill   Lets you choose a fill color and style for the selected cell(s).

5. Choose Close (or OK) as appropriate to work your way back to the Table Edit screen.

Figure 7.13 shows some examples of the line styles. To create the button, I set the top and left lines to the Button Top/Left and the bottom and right lines to the Button Bottom/Right line styles. Then I added a 30% shaded fill.

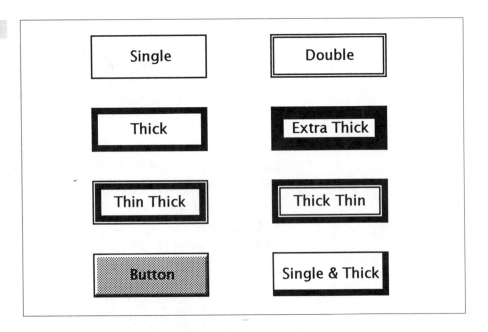

Figure 7.14 shows a sample scenario in which lines are removed from a table, then some outside border lines and a drop shadow are added.

One potential little "gotcha" in all of this occurs when you inadvertently "double up" on a line. For example, if the bottom of row 1 is a single line, and the top of row 2 is a single line, those lines combine to make a line that's somewhat darker than the rest. Figure 7.15 shows an example.

FIGURE 7.14

Changing lines in a table

Table of Contents	
Introduction	1
Experimental Design .	3
Results	4
Conclusion	6

Step 1: We create a table with two columns and five rows. In Table Edit, we select the first two columns, and choose Join ▸ Yes. Then we choose Cell ▸ Justification ▸ Center. We can also narrow column B using Ctrl+←. Then Close table edit mode. In the document window, type in the text. (Press Alt+F6 wherever you want to insert a dot leader.)

```
            Table of Contents

Introduction . . . . .       1
Experimental Design. .       3
Results. . . . . . .         4
Conclusion . . . . . .       6
```

Step 2: Now let's go back and fiddle with the lines. Press Alt+F11 to get back to Table Edit. Then choose Lines/Fill. Under Entire Table choose Default Line ▸ Line Style ▸ [None] ▸ Select ▸ Close. Then choose Border/Fill ▸ Border Style ▸ [None] ▸ Select ▸ OK ▸ Close.

```
            Table of Contents

Introduction . . . . . .     1
Experimental Design . . .    3
Results . . . . . . . .      4
Conclusion . . . . . . .     6
```

Step 3: Maybe we can bring those dot leaders in a little closer to the page numbers. Choose Table ▸ Column Margins and reduce the Left and Right margins each to about 0.04". Then choose OK. Now you can use Ctrl+← and Ctrl+→ to fine tune the widths of columns A and B.

Table of Contents	
Introduction	1
Experimental Design . . .	3
Results	4
Conclusion	6

Step 4: Hmmmm. I suppose that some lines would look better than none at all. Let's choose Lines/Fill ▸ Border/Fill ▸ Border Style ▸ Single Border ▸ Select. Then choose Customize ▸ Shadow ▸ Shadow Type ▸ Upper Left. Then perhaps Shadow Color and set the Shade (% of Color) number to 50 (%). Choose Close and OK as necessary to get back to the document window. Voila—I like it!

FIGURE 7.15

Doubling of lines
at the bottom of the
top cell

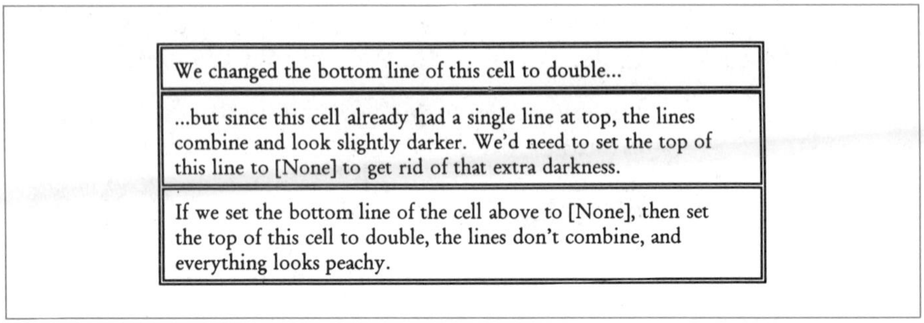

| We changed the bottom line of this cell to double... |
| ...but since this cell already had a single line at top, the lines combine and look slightly darker. We'd need to set the top of this line to [None] to get rid of that extra darkness. |
| If we set the bottom line of the cell above to [None], then set the top of this cell to double, the lines don't combine, and everything looks peachy. |

To fix that problem, you'd need to change the line at the bottom of row 1, or at the top of row 2, to [None]. To avoid the problem in the first place, it helps to keep in mind how WordPerfect defines lines when you first create the table. This is summarized below:

Top line	Single Line
Left line	Single Line
Right line	None
Bottom line	None
Table line	Double Border

In other words, you can change the top or left line on an interior cell without worrying about doubling up the lines.

Shading Cells

Shading is a really great way to add pizzazz to a table (provided, of course, that your printer can print shades of gray!) Shading can be a nice alternative to lines as well, as illustrated in Figure 7.16.

To shade a cell, or group of cells, follow these steps:

1. Make sure you're in Table Edit mode.

2. Move the cursor to the cell you want to shade, or select the cells you want to shade.

3. Choose Lines/Fill, then choose Fill.

FIGURE 7.16

Shading used as an
alternative to lines

Milk	A	B$_1$	B$_2$	B$_6$	B$_{12}$
			Vitamin (mg)		
Whole	307	.093	.395	.102	.871
Lowfat (2%)	500	.095	.403	.105	.888
Skim	500	.088	.343	.098	.926
Buttermilk	81	.083	.377	.083	.537
Condensed	1004	.275	1.27	.156	1.36
Evaporated	306	.059	.398	.063	.205
Chocolate	302	.092	.405	.1	.835

4. Choose Fill Style and double-click a fill style, or highlight the fill style and choose Select. The % ratings are shades of black, where 10% is a very light gray and 100% is completely black.

5. If you wish, choose foreground and background colors from the options provided. (Leave them set to Foreground Color: Black and Background Color: White for normal gray shading.)

6. Choose OK, then Close, to return to the table.

In Figure 7.16, I selected a 20% Shaded Fill style with black as the Foreground Color and white as the Background Color.

Formatting the Table's Contents

Formatting helps you improve the appearance of text within the table. You can format a single cell, a group of cells, a column, or several columns in a single operation. The table shown in Figure 7.17 was created using several formatting techniques.

Figure 7.18 shows how the table in Figure 7.17 looked before splitting some cells and removing the default inside and outside lines. But there's more to it than just playing with the lines. I've used quite a few special

FIGURE 7.17

A nicely formatted table

	Eastern	*Central*	*Mountain*	*Pacific*
		FEB 25 1994		
Registration	10:00 am	9:00 am	8:00 am	7:00 am
Conference Starts	10:30 am	9:30 am	8:30 am	7:30 am
Conference Ends	6:30 am	5:30 am	4:30 am	3:30 am

FIGURE 7.18

The table in Figure 7.17 with the original inside single lines and outside double lines

			FEB 25 1994			
	Eastern	*Central*		*Mountain*	*Pacific*	
Registration	10:00 am	9:00 am		8:00 am	7:00 am	
Conference Starts	10:30 am	9:30 am		8:30 am	7:30 am	
Conference Ends	6:30 am	5:30 am		4:30 am	3:30 am	

techniques for adjusting column widths, changing row heights, and so forth. Many of these formatting features are available in Table Edit mode.

The first thing to understand about formatting is how your selections take precedence:

- Formatting options assigned at the Cell level override those assigned at the Table and Column levels.

- Formatting options assigned at the Column level override options assigned at the Table level; however, they do *not* override options assigned at the Cell level.

- Formatting options assigned at the Table level affect only those cells that haven't already been formatted at the Column or Cell levels.

In other words, when you're formatting a table, you might want to get the general format at the Table level first. Then, you may wish to align text at the Column level. Finally, do your more specific cell-by-cell formatting last. In any event, here's how to format a table:

1. Move the cursor into the table and switch to Table Edit mode (if you aren't already there).

2. If you want to assign attributes to the table as a whole, choose Table. Or, if you want to format one or more columns, select those columns, then choose Column. If you want to format a single cell or group of cells, select those cells and choose Cell.

It may sound complicated, but it makes perfect sense. For instance, in general, you might want to left-align all the text in your *table*. However, perhaps you want just one *column* to be right-aligned. Choosing an option for that column would affect only that column. Then again, maybe you want a centered title at the top of that right-aligned column. Choosing Center alignment for just that *cell* would center only the column heading, not the entire column or table. Make sense? (It will after you've done it a few times.)

Whether you choose Table, Column, or Cell, you'll be taken to a Format dialog box that looks something like Figure 7.19. We'll look at the general formatting options available in the sections that follow.

Changing the Appearance of Text

The Appearance options are described in Chapter 6. Be aware that these options are cumulative. For example, if you assign the Outline appearance to some cells and then assign the Bold appearance to any of the same cells, the result is Bold and Outline combined.

To undo the appearance attributes of a cell or column, you must deselect the box in front of the option by clicking on the box once. If you want a particular cell or a group of selected cells to take on the appearance of other cells in the same column, you can choose Attributes from the Use Column group (this will be available only if you chose Cell in the previous steps).

FIGURE 7.19

General formatting
attributes for table
contents

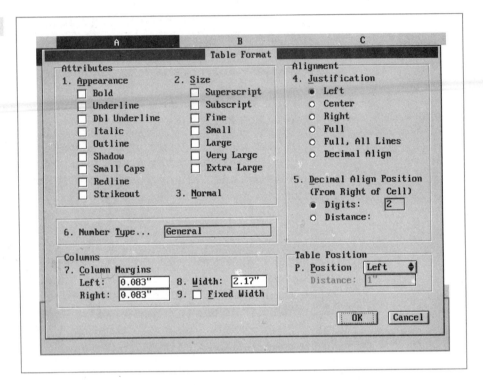

Changing the Text Size

You can choose a size from the table formatting dialog boxes as well. If you choose a large size, the height of the entire row in the table will be expanded to accommodate the large size. If you choose a small size for all the cells across a row, the height of the row will *not* be decreased. (However, you can use the Row feature, discussed later in this chapter, to change the height of the row, if you wish.)

Changing the Horizontal Alignment

Alignment determines how text and numbers are aligned within the column. Figure 7.20 shows examples of the various types of alignment.

FIGURE 7.20

Examples of various types of alignment in columns

Left	Center	Right	Full	Full, All Lines	Decimal
ABC Corp.	ABC Corp.	ABC Corp.	ABC Corp.	ABC Corp.	ABC Corp.
Ann Nye Chiropractic	Ann Nye Chiropractic	Ann Nye Chiropractic	Ann Nye Chiropractic	Ann Nye Chiropractic	Ann Nye Chiropractic
100	100	100	100	1 0 0	100
123.45	123.45	123.45	123.45	1 2 3 . 4 5	123.45
(123.45)	(123.45)	(123.45)	(123.45)	(1 2 3 . 4 5)	(123.45)
12/31/93	12/31/93	12/31/93	12/31/93	1 2 / 3 1 / 9 3	12/31/93

TIP

With Full alignment, only word-wrapped lines (lines that end in a [SRt] code) are fully justified. With Full, All Lines alignment, every line in the cell is fully justified (see Chapter 5).

NOTE

If you use decimal alignment and display negative numbers in parentheses, you might get that peculiar wrapping of the closing parenthesis, as in the last column of Figure 7.20. See "Tips for Using Parentheses for Negative Numbers," later in this chapter, for the cure.

Remember the order of precedence here. For instance, if you want to right-align all the numbers in a column, choose C̲olumn from the Table Edit screen, and choose R̲ight under the J̲ustification options. Then, if you want to center the heading at the top of that column, move the cursor to that cell, choose C̲ell from the Table Edit screen, and then choose C̲enter from the J̲ustification options.

NOTE If you want to change the appearance of only part of the text in a cell (for example, double-underline a single word), don't use Table Edit mode. Instead, go to the normal document window, select the text you want to reformat, then choose appearance options from the regular Font pull-down menu, as described in Chapter 6.

Changing the Appearance of Numbers

Before we dive into number formatting, keep this point in mind: Numbers that you type into a cell *never* change appearance, no matter how or when you change the number format. Rather, the number format you specify works only on numbers calculated with the Formula option on the Table Edit screen, as discussed in Chapter 25. If you want the numbers that you're typing into the table to have the same appearance as the format for the column, just type the numbers in with the correct format to begin with. (I know it sounds strange, particularly if you're accustomed to using spreadsheets, but don't blame me. I don't write these programs—I just write about them.)

Here's how to select an appearance for calculated numbers:

1. Go to Table Edit mode (if you're not already there).

2. Move the cursor to the cell or column you want to format, or select specific cells and columns to format. Then choose Cell, Column, or Table, depending on how much you want to format.

3. Choose the Number Type option. You'll be taken to a dialog box like the one in Figure 7.21.

4. Now you have free rein in choosing a format for numbers. You can choose any one of the standard formats illustrated in Figure 7.22. Depending on which standard format you choose, you may also be able to choose Options and change the other appearance options summarized below.

FIGURE 7.21

The Number Type Formats dialog box lets you define the appearance of numbers. To get here, start in Table Edit mode, choose Cell, Column, or Table, and then choose the Number Type option.

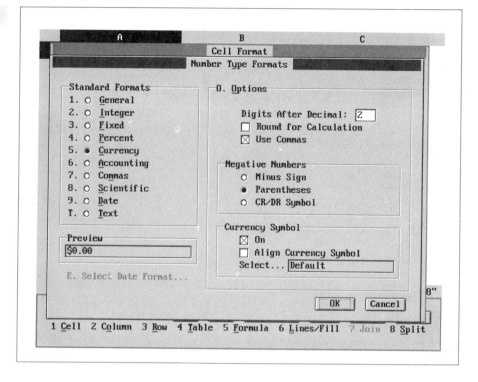

FIGURE 7.22

Examples of the standard number formats

General	12345.67	-12345.67	-12345.678
Integer	12346	-12346	2
Fixed	12345.67	-12345.67	-12345.68
Percent	1234567.00%	-1234567.00%	-1234567.80%
Currency	$12,345.67	($12,345.67)	($12,345.68)
Accounting	$ 12,345.67	$ (12,345.67)	$ (12,345.68)
Commas	12,345.67	(12,345.67)	(12,345.68)
Scientific	1.23e+04	-1.23e+04	-1.23e+04
Date	October 19, 1933	January 1, 1900	January 1, 1900
Text	12345.67	-12345.67	-12345.678

TIP

Look to the Preview box for a sample number displayed in your currently selected format.

Digits after Decimal　Determines how many digits you want to appear to the right of the decimal point (unless you chose General or Integer format).

Round for Calculation　If you're using table math, selecting this option will round numbers before calculating, so you don't get rounding errors that can cause totals and other calculations to be "a penny off."

Use Commas　If you choose this option, your numbers will have commas between thousands (12,345.67, rather than 12345.67).

Negative Numbers　Lets you choose whether to have negative numbers preceded by a minus sign (*-123.45*), displayed within parentheses (*(123.45)*), or displayed with credit (CR) and debit (DR) symbols (*123.45 CR* and *123.45 DR*).

Currency Symbol　Depending on the standard format you've chosen, you have the option of displaying the currency symbol (by selecting <u>O</u>n) or not displaying it (by deselecting <u>O</u>n).

Align Currency Symbol　If your number format displays currency symbols and the <u>O</u>n box is checked, you can select <u>A</u>lign Currency Symbol to put space between the symbol and its number so they align. If you deselect <u>A</u>lign Currency Symbol, the currency symbols will attach to the number, as in the examples below:

Aligned Currency Sign	Not Aligned
$ 123.45	$123.45
$ (123.45)	($123.45)
$ 12,345.00	$12,345.00
$ (12,345.00)	($12,345.00)

Select   Lets you choose a currency symbol.

Select Date Format   If you chose Date as your number format, this option lets you choose from predefined date format options.

5. Choose OK after defining your number format.

Tips for Using Parentheses for Negative Numbers

If you're displaying negative numbers in parentheses, and those numbers have a fixed number of decimals (for example, the number type is Fixed, Currency, or some other format that displays two pennies), you'll probably get the best results if you decimal-align the numbers with an extra digit. To do this, start in Table Edit mode, move the cursor into the column (or select the columns) you want to realign. Choose Column, and under Justification, choose Decimal Align.

Next, under Decimal Align Position, choose Digits and set the value to one greater than the number of digits you're actually showing. For example, if you're using the Currency or Accounting format, which display two decimal places, set the Digits option to 3.

If you've previously typed in negative numbers with leading minus signs (hyphens), WordPerfect *won't* convert them to the parentheses format. You need to edit the existing negative numbers to put them in parentheses. When typing in new negative numbers, use parentheses rather than the leading hyphen (minus sign).

If you use a non-American numbering system that aligns numbers on something other than a period (such as the comma in the European format *123.456,78*), change the alignment character anywhere above and to the left of (or even above and outside of) the decimal-aligned column. Do so by choosing Layout ➤ Character ➤ Decimal/Align Character.

NOTE   If you want to align part of the text within the cell, don't use Table Edit mode. Instead, move into the cell in the normal document window and use the options in the Layout menu, or use the shortcut keys listed in Table 7.2.

Why Some Attributes Won't Go Away

Suppose you assign certain attributes to a cell, then later you assign different attributes to the column as a whole. The cell attributes you assigned earlier will still take precedence over the new column attributes because cell formatting is more specific than column formatting. Those former cell attributes just won't go away!

If you want to undo those previous cell attributes, so that the cells will have the same characteristics as other cells in the column, follow the steps below:

1. Make sure you're in Table Edit mode.

2. Move the cursor to the cell you want to remove attributes from, or select the cells you want to remove attributes from.

3. Choose Cell.

4. Choose Use Column, and then choose one of these options:

   Attributes   Select (check) this to remove the cell appearance attributes.

   Justification   Select this to remove the cell justification attributes.

   Number Type   Select this to remove Number Type cell attributes.

5. Choose OK when you're done.

If that doesn't work, chances are that the attributes were assigned in the regular edit mode rather than in Table Edit. To find out, leave Table Edit, move into the problem cell, and turn on Reveal Codes. You'll probably discover the codes that are causing the problem right there, and you can then just delete any unwanted codes.

Using Fonts in a Table

Changes to the font in a table act like changes to the font in any other text. You change fonts while you're in the normal document window, *not* in Table Edit mode.

- If you move the cursor to a cell then change fonts using the Font menu, all text and numbers beyond the current cursor position will appear with the new font.

- If you select text first then choose a font, only the selected text will appear in the new selected font.

The [Font] codes that control the font appearance are stored within their cells; they are readily visible when Reveal Codes is on.

Changing the Spacing within a Table

By default, WordPerfect leaves a little blank space of .083″ at the left, top, and right edges of each cell and about .033″ at the bottom edge of each cell. You can change the spacing within the table by changing the column and/or row margins. For example, you might want to reduce the space between columns if you plan to remove the lines in the finished table. Or, you might want to tighten the space between rows, as illustrated in Figure 7.23.

FIGURE 7.23

You can adjust
the space between
columns and rows by
adjusting the margins
within columns
and rows.

Examples of Spacing Between Text and Lines (Left-justified text)	Examples of Spacing Between Text and Lines (Right-justified text)
Default spacing between text and lines	Default spacing between text and lines
Spacing: Left=0, Right=0, Top=0, Bottom=0	Spacing: Left=0, Right=0, Top=0, Bottom=0
Spacing: Left=.1, Right=.1, Top=.07, Bottom=.03	Spacing: Left=.1, Right=.1, Top=.07, Bottom=.03
Spacing: Left=.25, Right=.25, Top=.25, Bottom=.25	Spacing: Left=.25, Right=.25, Top=.25, Bottom=.25

Table with default column and row margins, and all lines removed.

Wanda Carneros	(123)555-0123
Tersha d'Elgin	(818)555-0987
Victoria Dumplin	(313)555-0385
Ambrose Pushnik	(714)555-5739
Frankly Unctuous	(414)555-0312

Same table as above after changing the top margin space across rows to 0.025.

Wanda Carneros	(123)555-0123
Tersha d'Elgin	(818)555-0987
Victoria Dumplin	(313)555-0385
Ambrose Pushnik	(714)555-5739
Frankly Unctuous	(414)555-0312

Adjusting the Column Margins

Here's how to adjust the column margins:

1. Switch to Table Edit mode (if you're not already there).

2. If you want to change the margins for the entire table, choose Table. If you want to change the margins for one or more columns, move the cursor to the column, or select the columns you want to change, then choose Column.

3. Choose <u>C</u>olumn Margins and type in the new widths for the Left and Right margins in inches (*.25* for one quarter inch) or points (2p for two points).

4. Choose OK.

Changing the Space between Rows

You can also set the top and bottom margins for rows. This will affect the distance between each row. Here are the steps:

1. Make sure you're in Table Edit mode.

2. Move the cursor to the row, or select the rows, that you want to change margins in.

3. Choose <u>R</u>ow. You'll see the Row Format dialog box shown below:

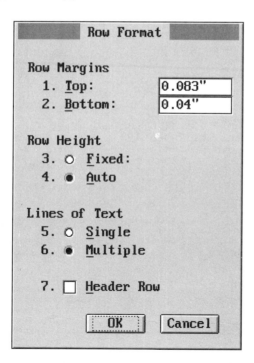

4. Under Row Margins, type in a new measurement for the <u>T</u>op and <u>B</u>ottom settings in inches or points.

5. Choose OK.

Locking In the Row Height

You can also decide how tall you want a row to be, and whether or not you want it to wrap into multiple lines when there's more text than can fit into the cell. To do so, complete steps 1–3 from the previous section to get to the Row Format dialog box. Then...

- To assign a fixed row height, choose <u>F</u>ixed and type in a value in inches or points.

- If you want the row height to adjust to the cell's contents automatically, choose <u>A</u>uto.

- To prevent the row from wrapping text and increasing the row height, choose <u>S</u>ingle. Any text that doesn't fit into the cell will be hidden from view when you print the table. (If you switch back to <u>M</u>ultiple, or reduce the size of the font, the hidden text will come out of hiding.)

- If you want WordPerfect to word-wrap in your table, choose <u>M</u>ultiple.

Choose OK to return to the Table Edit menu.

TIP

The narrow rows in the Progress Chart in Figures 7.34 and 7.35 (near the end of this chapter) have a small, fixed row height, and serve as blank lines between other rows.

Aligning Cell Contents Vertically

You can also decide how you want WordPerfect to align the text vertically within each row. Figure 7.24 shows how you could use these options to format your table.

FIGURE 7.24

Examples of vertical
alignments in cells

Top Vertical Alignment	This cell contains enough text to extend through three lines
Center Vertical Alignment	This cell contains enough text to extend through three lines
Bottom Vertical Alignment	This cell contains enough text to extend through three lines

To change the vertical alignment of text and numbers, follow these simple steps:

1. If you haven't already done so, switch to Table Edit mode.

2. Move to the cell, or select the cells, you want to realign.

3. Choose Cell.

4. Under Vertical Alignment, choose Top, Bottom, or Center.

5. Choose OK.

Note that the cell's contents will be aligned with respect to the top and bottom margins defined in the cell. If the alignment seems off, you might need to change the cell margins as described under "Adjusting the Column Margins," earlier in this chapter.

Repeating a Table Header on Multiple Pages

A *table header* is a row or group of rows in a table that is repeated on each page where the table is printed. This is very useful when your table spans several pages of text and you want a table title or column titles to appear at the top of the table on each printed page. You can use any number of rows at the top of the table for a header. Here's how to do it:

1. Go into Table Edit mode (if you aren't already there) and move the cursor to the row you want to be the header. If you want to use several rows on the table as the header, select those rows.

2. Choose Row.

3. Choose the Header Row option (so it's marked with an X), then choose OK.

TIP Once you define a header row in a table, WordPerfect won't rearrange that row when you sort or alphabetize the table (see Chapter 22). Very handy little bonus!

Normally, the header rows won't appear on the screen after every page break (however, they *will* appear in Page Mode or Print Preview). You can identify which rows are headers by moving the cursor into any row and glancing at the status bar. If the cursor is in a header row, the current cell's address will be marked with an asterisk, like this:

Cell A1* Doc 1 Pg 1 Ln 1.14" Pos 1.12"

Moving and Copying within a Table

There are two ways to move or copy table columns and rows—both require that you be in Table Edit mode. First, you can move or copy entire rows or columns (this often changes the actual structure of the table). For example, when you copy an entire row, the copied row is *added* to the table, and the table becomes one row larger.

Second, you can move or copy text (the contents of cells) only. This type of move is called a *block move*, and it doesn't change the structure of the table. When you block copy the contents of one row to another, the contents of these rows will match; however, WordPerfect does not add a new row to the table. Figure 7.25 illustrates the difference between these two copy procedures.

If you want to move/copy table text, go into Table Edit mode (Alt+F11). Select that text using your mouse, Alt+F4, or F12. Then choose Move/Copy ▸ Block ▸ Copy or Move ▸ OK.

Apples	Bananas	Cherries

Move the cursor to wherever you want to put the first item of text, (cell A2 in this example) and press ↵. The text is copied into the current row, like this:

Apples	Bananas	Cherries
Apples	Bananas	Cherries

If, in the first step, you choose Move/Copy ▸ Row, rather than Block, when you position the cursor and press ↵, WordPerfect will insert an exact duplicate of the row into the table, as below. Notice that the table now has four, rather than three rows.

Apples	Bananas	Cherries
Apples	Bananas	Cherries

If you use cut-and-paste in the regular document window, without going into Table Edit, the moved/copied text will end up in one cell, like this:

Apples	Bananas	Cherries
Apples Bananas Cherries		

Moving or Copying a Row or Column

To move or copy a row or column, proceed as follows:

1. If you haven't already done so, switch to Table Edit mode.

2. Move the cursor to the row or column you want to move or copy. Or select the rows/columns that you want to copy.

3. Choose the Move/Copy command button.

4. Choose either Row, or Column, depending on which you want to move, then choose either Move or Copy. (If you choose Move, the row or column will disappear.)

5. As instructed near the bottom of the screen, move the cursor to where you want to insert the moved or copied row or column. Press ⏎.

The row is inserted above the row you put the cursor in. Or, if you're moving a column, it's moved to the left of the column that the cursor is in.

TIP To move the second-to-last row or column in your table to the end of the table, move the cursor to the last row or column in your table. Choose Move/ Copy, then choose either Row or Column. Choose Move, then press ⏎.

Moving or Copying Cell Contents in Table Edit Mode

You can also move or copy text in Table Edit mode. Make sure there are sufficient blank rows or columns to accept the text you're moving or copying. Then...

1. Select the text you want to move or copy and click the Move/Copy command button.

2. Choose Block, then choose either Move or Copy, depending on which you want to do.

3. Move the cursor to the new location for the text (or the upper-left corner of the group of cells you'll be pasting in).

4. Press ↵ to complete the move or copy.

Moving or Copying Cells in the Document Window

Moving or copying a single cell's text to another cell from the document window is easy because it uses standard cut-and-paste techniques. First, select the cell's text using your mouse, Alt+F4, or the F12 key. Then, choose Edit ➤ Cut (Ctrl+X) if you want to move the text, or Edit ➤ Copy (Ctrl+C) if you want to copy it. Move the cursor to an empty cell, or to wherever you want the new text to appear in a cell that already contains text. Choose Edit ➤ Paste (Ctrl+V) to finish the job.

TIP   As a shortcut, you can select the cell's text and then drag and drop it into its destination cell (Chapter 3).

You can also select several rows or columns in a table and use cut-and-paste to copy those cells to another cell in the table. However, be aware that the *entire block* will be placed within a single cell, which might not be what you want.

The same thing will happen if you select a block of text outside the table and move or copy that block into a table cell. If that's not what you had in mind, first convert that block of text to a table (see "Converting Text to a Table," later in this chapter). Then join that new table to the existing table (see "Joining Two Separate Tables into One").

Managing Tables

The remainder of this chapter discusses general topics concerning tables and how you use tables in combination with other features of WordPerfect. Chapter references to these related features are provided.

Hidden Codes for Tables

When you create a table, WordPerfect stores several hidden codes in the document, starting with [Tbl Def] and ending with [Tbl Off]. Between these, the [Row] codes mark the beginning of a new row in the table, and the [Cell] codes precede the contents of each cell. All these codes, of course, are visible on the Reveal Codes screen.

A cell cannot contain another table. That is, it can't contain [Tbl Def] and [Tbl Off] codes. It can, however, contain a code to display a graphic box that contains a table. So technically, it is possible to display a table within a table (though you may be hard-pressed to think of a practical reason for doing so).

Moving and Copying Entire Tables

Moving or copying an entire table is like moving or copying anything else. Just be sure to include the [Tbl Def] and [Tbl Off] codes in the selection: Open Reveal Codes (Alt+F3) and select everything from [Tbl Def] to just past [Tbl Off] before you choose Edit ➤ Copy or Edit ➤ Paste. That way, the entire table will be copied to the Clipboard. Then, you can just position the cursor anywhere in any document and choose Edit ➤ Paste to bring the table in at that position. (You can also select the entire table and use drag and drop to move or copy it, as described in Chapter 3.)

Deleting a Table

To delete an entire table, including all of its contents, select the whole table. Be sure to include the [Tbl Def] code at the top and the [Tbl Off] code at the bottom of the table in the selection. Then press Del.

Converting a Table to Text

If you wish, you can use the Tables feature to organize your text and then convert the table to standard text. This is sometimes handy for exporting a document to a typesetting machine or another word processor that cannot interpret WordPerfect codes.

To convert a table to text, move the highlight to the table's [Tbl Def] code in Reveal Codes. Then press Del to delete the table. WordPerfect immediately converts [Cell] codes to [Lft Tab] codes. The spacing of the table depends on the current tab settings. Most likely, you will need to change the tab settings above the text to get it properly aligned and to get exactly the spacing you want (see Chapter 5).

Figure 7.26 shows an example in which text was initially entered in a table. The middle example shows the table just after the [Tbl Def] code was removed. The phone numbers are out of alignment because the current tab stops weren't set properly. The bottom example shows the table after the tab stops were changed to better align the text.

FIGURE 7.26

Converting a table to text

A sample table...

Wanda Carneros	(123)555-0123
Tersha d'Elgin	(818)555-0987
Victoria Dumplin	(313)555-0385
Ambrose Pushnik	(714)555-5739
Frankly Unctuous	(414)555-0312

Same table as above after removing the [Tbl Def] code...

```
Wanda Carneros    (123)555-0123
Tersha d'Elgin (818)555-0987
Victoria Dumplin   (313)555-0385
Ambrose Pushnik    (714)555-5739
Frankly Unctuous   (414)555-0312
```

Same as above after changing the tab stops...

```
Wanda Carneros    (123)555-0123
Tersha d'Elgin    (818)555-0987
Victoria Dumplin  (313)555-0385
Ambrose Pushnik   (714)555-5739
Frankly Unctuous  (414)555-0312
```

Converting Text to a Table

If you currently have text that is organized into columns with tabs and you want to convert it to a table, follow these steps:

1. Move the cursor to the first character of text that you want to put into a table.

2. Select the text you want to convert to a table, making sure to extend the selection area past the last [HRt] code at the bottom of the text you want to convert.

3. Choose Layout ➤ Tables ➤ Create (Alt+F7 TC). You'll see this dialog box:

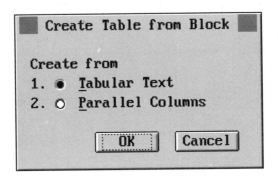

4. If you're creating the table from text organized with tabs, choose Tabular Text. If you formatted the text with parallel columns (discussed in Chapter 27), choose Parallel Columns.

5. Choose OK.

The table will appear, and you can use the techniques described in this chapter to make changes, if you wish. If the table comes out looking something like Figure 7.27, it's because you didn't set tab stops properly.

Figure 7.28 shows text on the document window neatly arranged into columns. However, the original tab ruler was used, so in some cases it requires two or more Tab codes, as in the [Lft Tab][Lft Tab] sequence in the figure, to move text over to the appropriate tab stop. If you used two Tab codes in any place to get over to the next tab stop, you will get two cells, rather than one, in the table.

FIGURE 7.27

The results of
converting text to a
table without regard
to tab stops

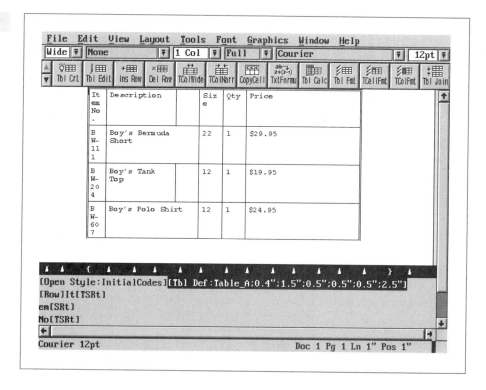

Fixing the table can be a pain. It's much easier to convert the table back to text using Edit ➤ Undo or by deleting the new [Tbl Def] code at the top of the text. Then, move the cursor to the top of the columns and remove any double tab codes. Next, adjust the tab ruler, as discussed in Chapter 5, so that only one Tab code is necessary to separate each column (see Figure 7.29).

Finally, return to the normal document window, select the text you want to move into a table, and create a table. The result is much neater and easier to format into properly sized columns, as Figure 7.30 shows.

Moving and Copying Rows and Columns between Tables

To move or copy rows or columns from one table to another, follow these steps:

1. Put the cursor into the table you want to move or copy *from,* and go into Table Edit mode.

FIGURE 7.28

Columns typed using the initial ½-inch tab stops caused occasional double tabs. This leads to double cells when the text is converted to a table.

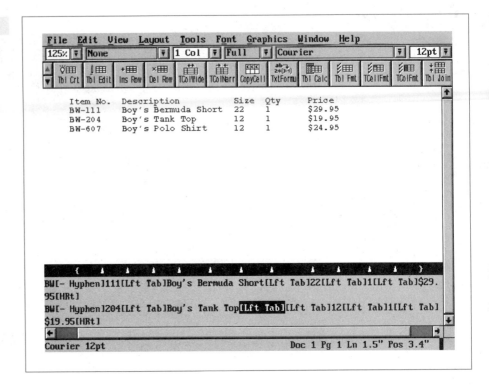

2. Select the rows or columns you want to move or copy.

3. Choose the Move/Copy button, then choose Row if you're moving rows or Column if you're moving columns.

4. Choose Copy. (You could choose Move, but Copy is a little safer, in case you don't get it right the first time.)

5. Choose Close to return to the document window.

6. Move the cursor into the table you want to move or copy *to,* and go into Table Edit mode.

7. Move the cursor to where you want the incoming rows to appear. For example, move to the last cell in the leftmost column to add rows to the bottom, or move to the topmost cell in the last column to add columns to the right.

8. Choose the Move/Copy button again.

FIGURE 7.29

The text shown in
Figure 7.28 after
removing multiple
Tab codes and
adjusting the tab ruler

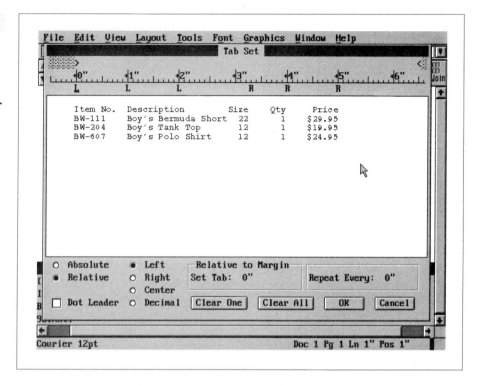

9. Choose whichever option you chose back in step 3, either Row or Column.

10. Choose the Retrieve button.

If you moved columns, chances are you'll need to narrow some of the original columns (using Ctrl+←), then widen the new columns, which are barely visible, using Ctrl+→.

If the two tables didn't have equal numbers of rows or columns, the text might not be placed exactly as you intended. You may have to try to equalize the number of rows and columns in the two tables to get a better match. Delete the rows or columns you just moved or copied, try to increase or decrease the number of rows and columns in the two tables so that they match, then try again.

FIGURE 7.30

The results of
converting the text
shown in Figure 7.29
to a table

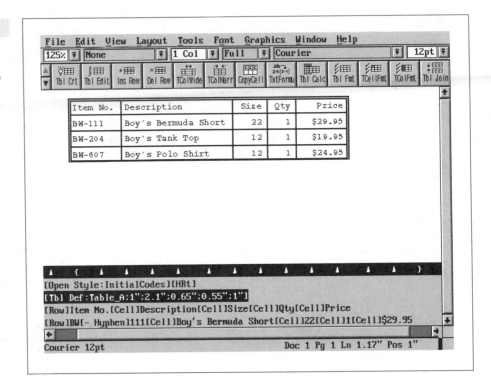

If your text came in properly but not exactly in the correct sort order, you can use the standard techniques to move the rows or columns within this table to new locations. Or, you can sort (or alphabetize) the entries using techniques described in Chapter 22.

If your copy was successful, but you really wanted to move the rows or columns, just go back to the original table in Table Edit mode and delete the text that you no longer need there using Ctrl+Del or the Del button to delete rows.

Joining Two Separate Tables into One

If the tables you want to join have an equal number of columns, you can use this quick technique to join them:

1. In the regular document window, move the cursor to the end of the first table and turn on Reveal Codes (Alt+F3).

2. If there are any codes or text between the [Tbl Off] code that marks the end of the first table and the [Tbl Def] code that marks the beginning of the second table, move or delete them.

3. Move the cursor into the last cell of the table on top, and choose Layout ➤ Tables ➤ Join.

If the tables you want to join do not have an equal number of columns, just use the techniques described in the previous section to copy all the rows from one table to the other. If the copy is successful, you can delete the original table.

Splitting One Table into Two

To break a large table into two smaller ones, follow these steps:

1. In the regular document window, move the cursor into whatever row you want to be the first row of the new, separate table.

2. Choose Layout ➤ Tables ➤ Split (or press Alt+F7 TS).

You can add some space between the tables by moving the cursor to just after the [Tbl Off] code that marks the end of the table on the top (use Reveal Codes to help with this). Then press ↵ to insert as many blank lines as you wish.

Making More Room in a Table

One of the most common problems with tables is simply not having enough space on the page to get all the information you need into the table. There are several ways to solve this problem, and you can use any one or any combination of these methods:

• Change the font to a smaller point size (see Chapter 6) just to the left of the [Tbl Def] code. The entire table will use the font, so more characters will fit into each cell.

• Reduce the left and right margins just above the table so that you can widen the table.

• If your printer can do it, print the table sideways on the page by changing the paper size/type to landscape format (see Chapter 8).

After you've changed the paper size, you can add more columns to the new page width or widen existing columns.

- Reduce the spacing within the table by changing cell margins, as described earlier in this chapter.

- Use the various printer functions described in Chapter 28 to reduce leading and word/letter spacing, as appropriate.

Taking It to Extremes

The Tables feature is a great tool for typing text into tables. But as you've seen, it's also a great tool for typing any kind of multicolumn text, such as the sample itinerary shown earlier in this chapter. With a little ingenuity, you can use the Tables feature to create some extraordinary documents, rivaling those produced by graphic artists. The next few sections present some examples that you can use as food for thought, if you're so motivated, in creating your own advanced documents.

Calendar

Figure 7.31 shows a sample calendar that I created with WordPerfect. The picture at the top is in a graphics box, as discussed in Chapter 26. (That particular picture is from the Presentation Task Force clip art collection.)

To stretch AUGUST 1994 across the width of the page, I created a one-cell table, with the Cell justification set to Full, All Lines, and the vertical alignment set to Center. I also reduced the left and right margins within the cell and removed all the lines from the one-cell table. After leaving Table Edit mode, I set the font to Bodoni 48pt and typed **AUGUST 1994** into the one-cell table.

The days of the month are in a table consisting of seven columns and six rows. The day names are in shaded cells with 20% shading. Each row below the day names has a fixed height of 1″. Each number is right-aligned within its cell using Flush Right (Alt+F6) and is followed by a hard return. This allows you to type text below the number if you want. (You'll probably want to use a smaller font if you type text within each day.)

FIGURE 7.31

A sample calendar
created with the
Tables feature

AUGUST 1994

Sun	Mon	Tue	Wed	Thu	Fri	Sat
	1	2	3	4	5	6
7	8	9	10	11	12	13
14	15	16	17	18	19	20
21	22	23	24	25	26	27
28	29	30	31			

The cells after day 31 are joined using the Join technique described earlier in this chapter. And that's about all there is to that one.

Org Chart

Tables are a great way to create organizational charts, like the one shown in Figure 7.32. Figure 7.33 shows the org chart after joining and filling cells but before removing any lines.

FIGURE 7.32

A sample org chart

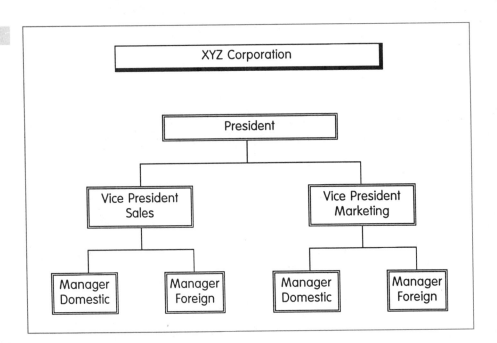

Notice in the bottom row of the org chart that you need to join a pair of cells to create one box. This is necessary to get the centered vertical line to come out of the top of the box. You also need at least one blank cell to separate each box. The drop-shadow appearance of the topmost cell was created by setting the top and left lines to Single and the right and bottom lines to Thick.

FIGURE 7.33

The org chart before removing table lines

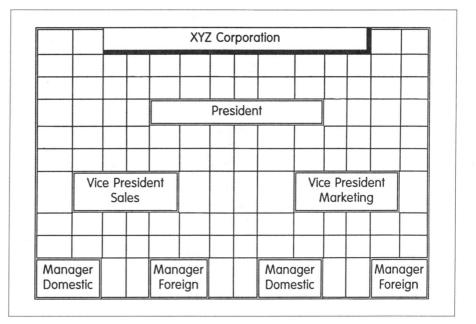

Progress Chart

Figure 7.34 shows a progress chart created with the Tables feature. The chart is printed sideways on the page (landscape format), as discussed in Chapter 8. Figure 7.35 shows the chart before removing any lines from the table.

Two basic tricks were used to create the progress chart. First, I used the Row option in Table Edit mode to narrow every other row, starting at the second row, to 0.1″. This reduced the gap between the bars in the chart.

To draw the bars, I went into Table Edit mode and selected the cells I wanted to shade in one row. Then I used the Line/Fill options and Fill to set the fill style to 100% Shaded Fill (black). For row 1 and column A, I used a gray (20%) shaded fill.

Next, I removed most of the table lines, except for the outermost lines and the ones below row 1 and to the right of column A.

FIGURE 7.34

A sample progress chart created with Tables

FIGURE 7.35

The progress chart before removing table lines

	Write	Submit	Copy edit	Resubmit	Tech edit	Resubmit	Galleys	Beta test	Pages	
Front matter										
Chapter 1										
Chapter 2										
Chapter 3										
Chapter 4										
Chapter 5										
Chapter 6										
Chapter 7										
Chapter 8										
Chapter 9										
Chapter 10										
Chapter 11										
Chapter 12										
Chapter 13										
Chapter 14										
Index										

Play-off Chart

Figure 7.36 shows a sample play-off chart created with the Tables feature. The chart is printed sideways on the page (landscape format), as discussed in Chapter 8. Figure 7.37 shows the chart before removing any table lines.

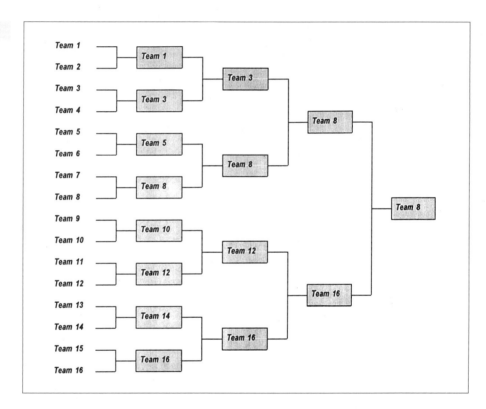

The general design of the play-off chart is fairly simple. Each box is actually two cells (one atop the other) joined by choosing Join in the Table Edit mode. This makes the centered line come out of the right side of the box. You need two empty columns to the right of a box to get the lines needed to join the boxes.

Fill-in Forms

Tables are also great for creating your own company fill-in forms, like the invoice shown in Figure 7.38. This invoice is actually a collection of three tables on a single page, as you can see in Figure 7.39. This latter figure shows the invoice after joining cells and filling them with text but before shading cells and removing table lines.

Actually, one of the trickiest parts of creating this form was getting the company name and address to align next to the table. To accomplish that, I put the text in a User box (see Chapter 26) that was anchored to the upper-right corner of the page with Text Flows set to Through Box.

FIGURE 7.38

A sample fill-in form
created with Tables

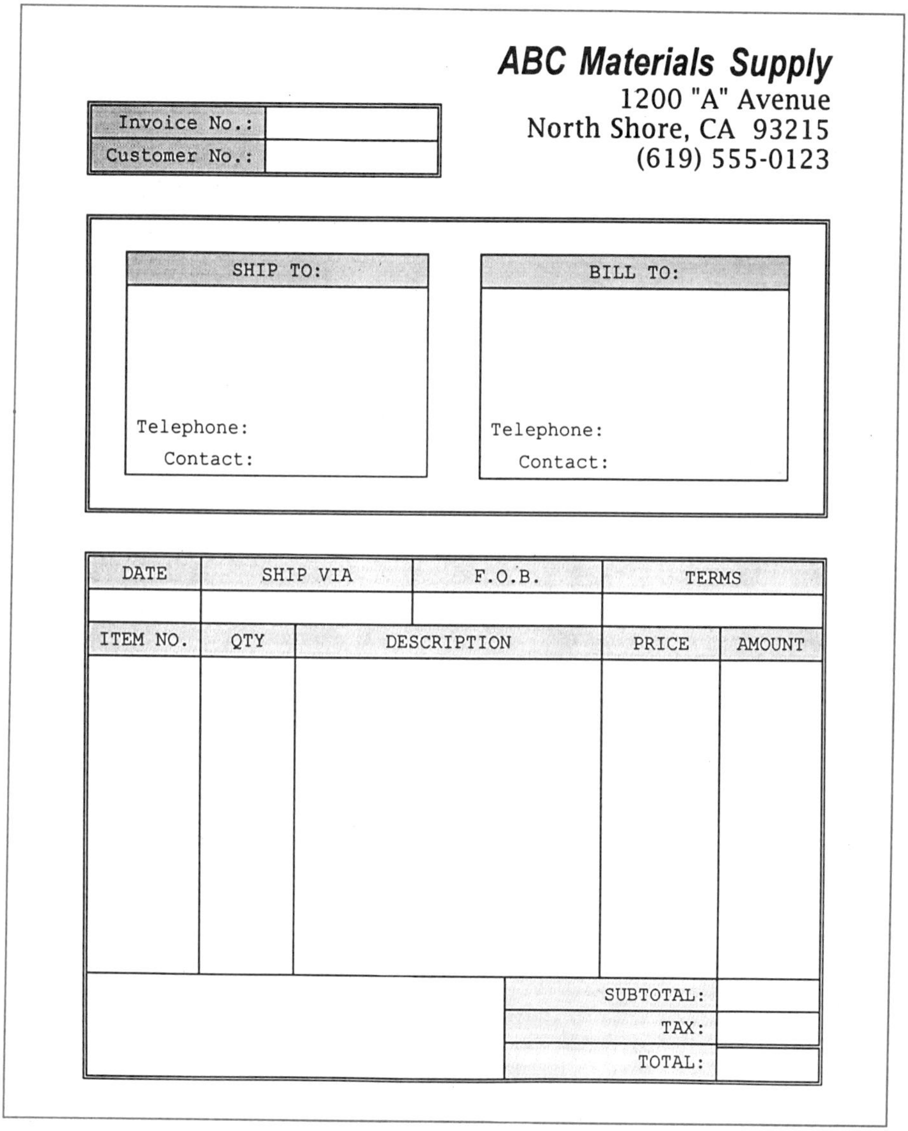

ABC Materials Supply
1200 "A" Avenue
North Shore, CA 93215
(619) 555-0123

| Invoice No.: | |
| Customer No.: | |

SHIP TO:	BILL TO:
Telephone:	Telephone:
Contact:	Contact:

DATE	SHIP VIA	F.O.B.	TERMS

ITEM NO.	QTY	DESCRIPTION	PRICE	AMOUNT
			SUBTOTAL:	
			TAX:	
			TOTAL:	

If you create a form that someone will fill out on the screen, you might want to lock all the cells *except* those that need text typed into them. Pressing Tab and Shift+Tab will then move the cursor only to cells that should contain new text. To lock cells, go to Table Edit mode, select the cells you want to lock, choose Cell, then select Lock from the dialog box that appears.

FIGURE 7.39

The fill-in form before removing lines from the three tables

FIGURE 7.39

The fill-in form before removing lines from the three tables

You could also write-protect the blank form, using the DOS ATTRIB command. That way, you could call up a blank form at any time and complete it in WordPerfect. But you'd be forced to save the filled-in copy under a different file name, so you wouldn't lose the original, blank form.

Vertical Column Headings

Now, for the truly hard-core users who have laser printers capable of rotating fonts, Figure 7.40 shows an example with the column headings rotated 90 degrees.

FIGURE 7.40

A sample table with column headings rotated 90 degrees in the top row

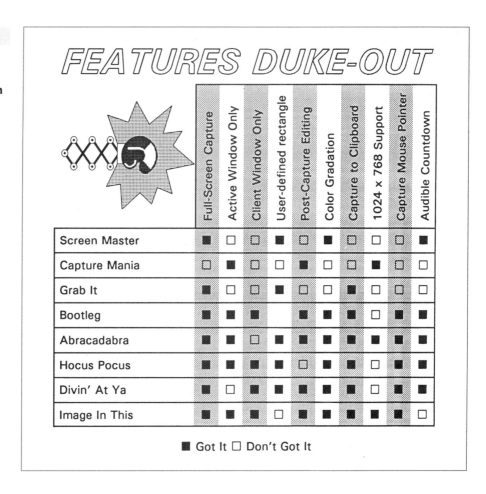

FEATURES DUKE-OUT

	Full-Screen Capture	Active Window Only	Client Window Only	User-defined rectangle	Post-Capture Editing	Color Gradation	Capture to Clipboard	1024 x 768 Support	Capture Mouse Pointer	Audible Countdown
Screen Master	■	□	□	■	□	■	□	□	□	■
Capture Mania	□	■	□	□	■	□	□	■	□	□
Grab It	■	□	□	■	□	□	■	□	□	□
Bootleg	■	■	■		■	■	■	□	■	■
Abracadabra	■	■	□	■	■	■	■	■	■	■
Hocus Pocus	■	■	■	■	□	■	■	□	■	■
Divin' At Ya	■	□	■	■	■	■	■	□	■	■
Image In This	■	■	■	□	■	■	■	■	■	□

■ Got It □ Don't Got It

To create this one, I started with an empty table with nine rows and eleven columns. I gave columns B through K a fixed height and width of 0.347″. Then, to put in the first sideways title, I moved the cursor to cell A2 (in the normal document window) and created a graphics box. In that box,

I set the font to about 10 points, typed the text for the first title (*Full-Screen Capture* in this example), and used Alt+F9 to rotate that text 90 degrees. I anchored the graphic to the paragraph, gave it a horizontal position of Centered, and a fixed size of 2 inches, and made it into a borderless User box. You'll learn to do all this in Chapter 26.

Next, I went back and actually printed the document with just that first title. I did so mainly because I discovered that what you see on the screen here doesn't necessarily match up with printed reality. Anyhow, after tweaking the cell margins and User box spacing options until the sideways text was just the way I wanted it, I copied that User box to each of the remaining cells. Then, I just edited the text in each box (that's easier than creating each box from scratch).

I removed most of the vertical lines from the table, and I used 20% shading in every other column starting with Column B. The solid and empty squares inside each cell are special characters 38 and 46 from the Word-Perfect Typographic Symbols character set, printed at a size slightly larger than the text in the table.

The graphic in cell A1 is in a graphics box. Like many examples in this book, that graphic comes from the Presentation Task Force clip art collection.

Mini-Tables

Figure 7.41 shows some examples of small tables used to create special desktop publishing effects. Figure 7.42 shows these same figures with the original inside, single and outside, double lines.

Here's a quick run-down on features used in these examples:

- The *WOW!* example is just a large font in cell A1 and a smaller font in cell B1. After I removed the lines, the text in cell B1 wrapped to only three lines.

- In *So What Do You Think,* cell A1 contains small text that's centered vertically and right-aligned. Cell B1 contains large text that's bottom-aligned and fully justified. Cell C1 contains small text that's centered vertically and left-aligned.

WOW! *I never thought to use a table to align small text next to large.*

So what **DO YOU THINK** of that?

FUN TO WEAR *UNDERWEAR*

POWER TRIP

WESTERN REGIONAL
GLASS
RECYCLING CENTER
UNIVERSITY SQUARE

S T R E T C H

FIGURE 7.42

Examples from
Figure 7.41 before
removing lines

- *Fun To Wear* started out as a table with three columns and two rows. After joining cells A1 and A2, then joining cells C1 and C2, I put large letters in the end cells and smaller letters in between. The horizontal and vertical alignment are similar to the example above. I then narrowed and widened the cells for a best fit.

- *Power Trip* started out as a table with three columns and three rows. After joining the cells in the bottom row, I put a picture into the cell using the graphics box tools. Then I joined cells B1 and B2, put in the title, and changed and removed lines to form the frame. I also centered the title vertically and horizontally within the cell.

- *Western Regional Glass* started out as five rows and one column. After typing the text into each cell, I manually fixed the height of each row. Then I shaded cells A1, A3, and A4 and set the print color of A3 and A4 to white (I'll describe how to do this in a moment). I controlled the spacing between letters using the letterspacing commands described in Chapter 28.

- *Stretch* is just a single-cell table with the word STRETCH typed into it, with cell justification set to Full, All Lines. Zeroing-out the left and right column margins then removing the table lines, ensures that the text stretches the full width of the margins.

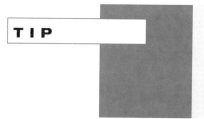

TIP

If your stretched text contains more than one word, most of the spacing will be placed between the words rather than the letters. But you can use the word- and letterspacing features (Chapter 28) to change that.

Printing White on Black

Many examples in this chapter show white text printed on a black background. Not all printers can do this, and not all screens can display it correctly. The only way to know whether your equipment can print white text on black is to try it. The basic procedure is as follows:

1. Create your table, choose your fonts, type your text, and set your alignments normally.

2. Select the text that should print in white.

3. Choose Font ➤ Print Color, and then choose White from the Palette Colors. The text will seem to disappear for now.

4. In Table Edit mode, select the cells that should have a black background, and then choose Lines/Fill and then Fill to fill the cell(s) with a 100% shaded Fill style (black).

5. Choose OK and Close until you get back to the normal document window.

6. Now use File ➤ Print/Fax ➤ Print to print the document and see if your printer can do the white-on-black trick.

Of course, you needn't use just white and black. You can use shades of gray for the fill, the text, or both.

The Tables feature is so powerful and so useful that it's practically a product in itself. And we haven't even touched on its math capabilities, which are perfect for typing financial reports, invoices, and more (we'll get to that in Chapter 25). In the next chapter, we'll take a look at ways to format your pages.

Formatting Your Pages

fast TRACK

To keep a block of text together on a page 353

select the text you want to protect, then choose Layout ➤ Other ➤ Block Protect (or press Shift+F8 OB).

To keep a certain number of lines together on a page 353

move the cursor above the first line in the group you want to keep together. Then choose Layout ➤ Other ➤ Conditional End Of Page (or press Shift+F8 OC), type in the number of lines to keep together, and press ↵.

To keep words together on a line 355

insert a hard space (Home Space), instead of a regular space, between the words.

To select paper sizes other than 8.5″ × 11″ 357

choose Layout ➤ Page (or press Shift+F8 P). Choose Paper Size/Type for standard papers or Labels for labels. Highlight the paper size you want to use and choose Select.

To create an envelope interactively 361

choose Layout ➤ Envelope, or press Alt+F12, and fill in the Envelope dialog box. Then, to print the envelope, choose Print. To insert the envelope contents into the current document, choose Insert.

To type text on labels 368

enter your text as usual. Press Ctrl+↵ when you want to start a new label.

N THIS chapter you'll learn many ways to format documents that are longer than a single page. Among other things, you'll learn how to create title pages, number your pages, and use non-standard paper sizes such as envelopes and mailing labels.

You'll find most features discussed in this chapter in the Page Format dialog box shown in Figure 8.1. To open this dialog box, choose Layout ➤ Page from the pull-down menus or press Shift+F8 P.

FIGURE 8.1

The Page Format
dialog box

```
┌─────────────────────────────────────────────────────────────┐
│                          Page Format                         │
│                                                              │
│   1. Page Numbering...  │None                              │ │
│                                                              │
│  ┌Center Page (Top to Bottom)─┐ ┌F. Force Page──────────┐   │
│   2. ☐  Center Current Page    │   ○ Odd      ○ New       │   │
│   3. ☐  Center Pages           │   ○ Even     ● None      │   │
│  └────────────────────────────┘ └─────────────────────────┘   │
│                                                              │
│  ┌Paper Sizes──────────────────────────────────────────┐    │
│   4. Paper Size/Type... │Letter (Portrait)            │ │    │
│   5. Labels...          │                             │ │    │
│   6. Subdivide Page...  │                             │ │    │
│   7. Envelope...                                       │    │
│  └─────────────────────────────────────────────────────┘    │
│                                                              │
│   8. Double-sided Printing │None        ⬍│               │
│   9. Suppress... (Page Numbering, Headers, etc.)             │
│   D. Delay Codes...                                          │
│   B. Page Borders...                    ┌────────┐ ┌────────┐ │
│                                         │   OK   │ │ Cancel │ │
│                                         └────────┘ └────────┘ │
└─────────────────────────────────────────────────────────────┘
```

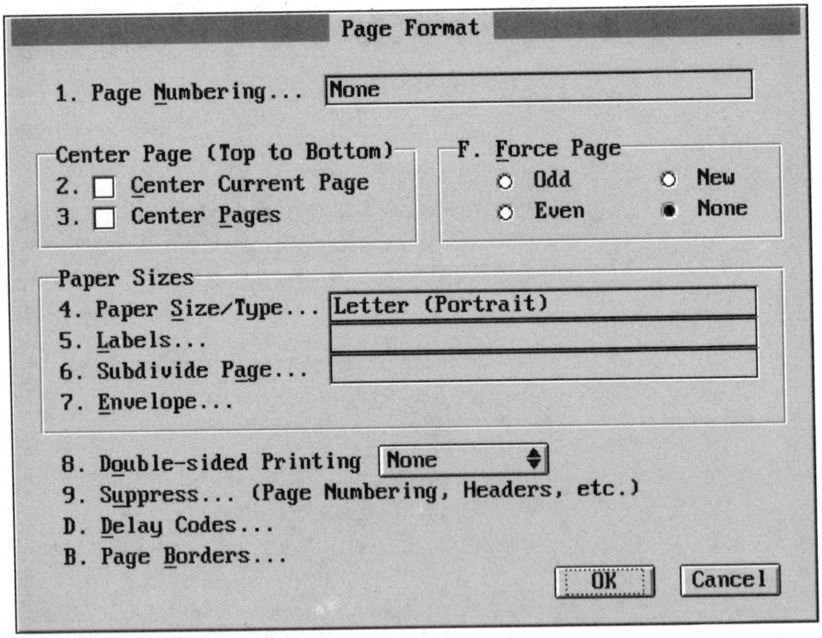

To use just about any page formatting feature, follow these basic steps:

1. Move the cursor to the page where you want the formatting feature to take effect. (Usually, it's easiest to start at the *top* of the page, before any text. To start numbering at the top of the document, press Home Home ↑.)

2. Choose Layout ➤ Page (or press Shift+F8 P).

3. Select the feature or features you want.

4. Choose OK until you return to the document window.

Here are some additional tips that will help you get the most out of page formatting:

- Most page formatting changes are visible in Page mode (Ctrl+F3 P), on the Print Preview screen (Shift+F7 V), in Reveal Codes (Alt+F3), and when you print your document. They generally won't appear in Graphics mode or Text mode.

- For best results, leave Auto Code Placement on (checked) in the File ➤ Setup ➤ Environment options.

- To see which hidden code is inserted when you activate a page formatting feature, turn on Reveal Codes *before* you activate the feature. See Chapter 4 and Appendix D for more information on hidden codes.

- To delete a page formatting feature, you can simply delete its code in Reveal Codes. (I'll mention other methods as appropriate.)

- To add a border around your pages, position the cursor to the page where borders should start, and choose Layout ➤ Page ➤ Page Borders or press Shift+F8 PB. (See Chapter 6.)

- When you write documents that have long sections, consider placing each chapter or section in a separate file. The Styles (Chapter 17) and Master Document (Chapter 32) features can help you manage large documents.

- Chapter 10 delves into printing techniques, including how to format pages for binding and double-sided printing.

- Often, it's nice to set up the codes for an entire document, or all future documents, without having to worry about other text pushing them out of the way. To do this, choose Layout ➤ Document ➤ Document Initial Codes (or press Shift+F8 D). (See Chapter 19 for more information.)

Vertical Centering

Vertical centering is handy for centering all the text on title pages, brief letters or memos, and invitations. Figure 8.2, shows a sample title page that I've centered both horizontally and vertically. (Chapter 5 explains horizontal centering.)

Here's how to add or remove vertical centering on the page:

1. Position the cursor on the page where vertical centering should start.

2. Choose Layout ➤ Page (or press Shift+F8 P).

FIGURE 8.2

A sample page with text centered horizontally and vertically

```
                        ALL-AMERICAN LIFE

             A Flexible Premium Life Insurance Policy




                            Issued by:


                   PREMIUM INSURANCE COMPANY
                  1234 Avenue of the Americas
                     New York, NY  10019
                      (800)555-1234




              Supplement Dated August 30, 1993

                              to

              Prospectus Dated June 1, 1993
```

3. Now, do one of the following:

- To center just the current page, select (check) Center Current Page. To "uncenter" the current page, deselect Center Current Page.
- To center the current page and all future pages until you turn off centering, select Center Pages. To turn off centering for this and subsequent pages, deselect Center Pages.

4. Choose OK until you return to the document window.

Starting Text on a New Page

WordPerfect automatically breaks a long document into separate pages. That is, as you type beyond the length of a page, WordPerfect inserts a soft page break, which appears as a long horizontal line across the document window. It's called a soft page break because WordPerfect will adjust it automatically as you add and delete text in your document. (You can't delete soft page breaks.)

You generally should let WordPerfect break pages for you. Sometimes, however, you may want to force a new page at a certain point in your document. For example, if your document starts with a title page, you could break the page after the last title line so that later text would start on a new page.

WordPerfect offers several ways to force new pages. The simplest way is to insert a *hard page break*, like this:

1. Position the cursor where you want to end the current page.

2. Press Ctrl+↵.

WordPerfect will insert a [HPg] code, and you'll see a long, double horizontal line where the page will break, as in Figure 8.3. As you move the cursor above or below the hard page break, the status line will show which page the cursor is on.

FIGURE 8.3

**A hard page break
at the bottom of a
title page**

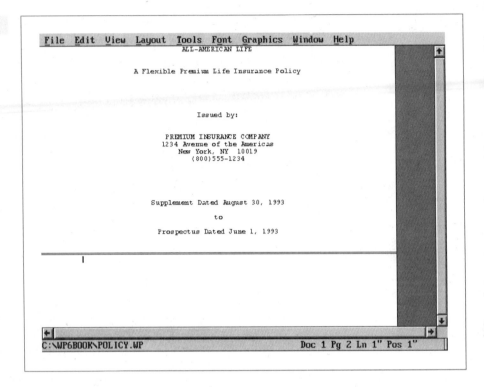

You can also use the Force Page options to make sure that a certain page
in a document always has an odd or even page number or starts on a new
page. Unlike a hard page break, a forced page won't start a new page if a
soft page break occurs immediately before it. Here's how to force a page:

1. Place the cursor where you want the page to break.

2. If you want to guarantee that the following text starts on a new
   page, regardless of whether a soft page break precedes it, press
   Ctrl+↵.

3. Choose <u>L</u>ayout ➤ <u>P</u>age ➤ <u>F</u>orce Page (or press Shift+F8 PF).

4. Choose one of the following options:

   <u>O</u>dd   Inserts a page break (if necessary) to start the following text on an odd page. This is especially useful for
   starting book chapters on an odd-numbered (right-hand)
   page or printing mail-in coupons on an odd-numbered
   page, so they won't appear on the back of another page.

Even   Inserts a page break (if necessary) to start the following text on an even page.

New   Inserts a page break (if necessary) to start the following text on a new page.

None   Turns off the force page feature (this is the default setting).

5. Choose OK until you return to the document window.

Automatic Page Numbering

You never need to type page numbers in a WordPerfect document because WordPerfect can number the pages for you automatically. The page numbers will always be in proper sequence and in the right place on each page no matter how much text you add, change, or delete.

All the page-numbering features are stashed in the Page Numbering dialog box, which appears when you choose Layout ➤ Page ➤ Page Numbering (or press Shift+F8 PN), as shown in Figure 8.4. We'll look at these features next.

Turning On the Page Numbers

There are two ways to number your pages in WordPerfect. You can use the automatic page numbering features described in this section, or you can place page number codes in page headers and footers (I'll describe this method later in the chapter).

Here's how to turn on automatic page numbering:

1. Place the cursor where page numbering should begin.

2. Select Layout ➤ Page ➤ Page Numbering ➤ Page Number Position (or press Shift+F8 PNP). You'll see the Page Number Position dialog box shown in Figure 8.5.

FIGURE 8.4

The Page Numbering
dialog box

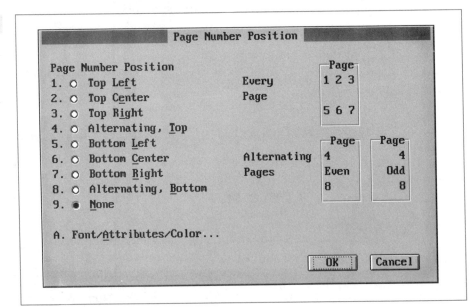

FIGURE 8.5

The Page Number
Position dialog box

3. Select one of the eight page number positions to indicate where you want page numbers to appear. (Choose <u>N</u>one to turn off automatic page numbering.)

4. If you want to change the page number's font, select Font/<u>A</u>ttributes/Color, then make your choices from the Font dialog box that appears (see Chapter 6). When you're done, choose OK.

5. Choose OK until you return to the document window.

Numbering Method and Starting Number

WordPerfect usually keeps track of page numbers in sequence, starting with page 1, and displays the numbers in Arabic numerals (*1, 2, 3...*). Sometimes, however, a different numbering method or starting page number might be better. This might be handy in a book or report that begins with a title page and other front matter that should be numbered with roman numerals (*i, ii, iii...*).

Here's how to set the page-numbering method and starting page number:

1. Move the cursor to the page where you want to make the change.

2. Select <u>L</u>ayout ➤ <u>P</u>age ➤ Page <u>N</u>umbering ➤ Page <u>N</u>umber (or press Shift+F8 PNN). You'll see the Set Page Number dialog box, shown below.

```
┌─────────────────────────────────────────────┐
│          Set Page Number                      │
│                                               │
│  1. New Number:        ┌─────────────────┐   │
│                        │1                │   │
│                        └─────────────────┘   │
│  2. Numbering Method   ┌─────────────┬──┐   │
│                        │Numbers      │ ◆│   │
│                        └─────────────┴──┘   │
│  3. ☐ Increment Number                       │
│                                               │
│  4. ☐ Decrement Number                       │
│                                               │
│  5. ☐ Display in Document                     │
│                                               │
│              ┌──────┐  ┌────────┐            │
│              │  OK  │  │ Cancel │            │
│              └──────┘  └────────┘            │
└─────────────────────────────────────────────┘
```

3. Choose any of the options described below, then choose OK. Your options are as follows:

New <u>N</u>umber   Lets you type in a new starting page number.

Numbering <u>M</u>ethod   Lets you choose numbers, letters, or roman numerals for page numbering.

<u>I</u>ncrement Number   When selected, adds 1 to the current page number.

De<u>c</u>rement Number   When selected, subtracts 1 from the current page number.

<u>D</u>isplay in Document   When selected, displays the current number at the cursor position.

NOTE

Changing the page-numbering method or starting page number doesn't turn on numbering automatically. You still need to turn on page numbering either by choosing Page Number Position in the Page Numbering dialog box or by setting up a header or footer that includes the page number.

Secondary, Chapter, and Volume Page Numbers

WordPerfect provides lots of flexibility for your page-numbering scheme. In fact, you can use up to four numbering levels, including page number, secondary page number, chapter, and volume. WordPerfect increments the page and secondary page numbers automatically, while the chapter and volume page numbers stay the same unless you change them manually.

You can also use *counters* to count or number anything in your document manually. Like page numbers, counters can have several levels and can display numbers, letters, or Roman numerals. See Chapter 15 for details.

Suppose you're working on Volume II of your life story, and you've finally made it to Chapter 5 (*My Life with Joe*). You might want the first page of this chapter to look like this:

Volume II ➤ Chapter 5 ➤ Page 1

Notice that I've used a volume number, chapter number, and page number in this example. (I didn't bother with the secondary page number this time.) The first step is to set up a multilevel numbering scheme, like this:

1. Position the cursor where you want the numbering scheme to begin.

2. Choose <u>L</u>ayout ➤ <u>P</u>age ➤ Page <u>N</u>umbering (or press Shift+F8 PN). You'll see the Page Numbering dialog box shown earlier.

3. Choose the numbering level you want to change (options 2–5). Pick a starting page number and numbering method, as described earlier, then choose OK.

4. Repeat step 3 for each numbering option you want to change.

5. Choose OK until you return to the document window.

Next you need to define a page number format that uses your new scheme.

Formatting a Page Number

Normally, WordPerfect numbers your pages by placing a plain page number, such as *1* or *A* or *I*, at the position you've specified. You can jazz this up to include text, special characters, and the chapter, volume, and secondary page numbers.

Here's how to define a fancy page number format:

1. Position the cursor on the page where you want the format to start.

2. Choose Layout ➤ Page ➤ Page Numbering ➤ Page Number Format.

3. Fill in the text box, as described below. (Normally, a [page #] code will already appear in the text box. You can delete it if you wish, by pressing the Del key.)

4. Choose OK until you return to the document window.

In step 3 above, you can type text, blanks, or WordPerfect Characters (Ctrl+W) wherever you want them to appear. When you're ready to insert a page numbering code, choose Number Codes or press F5. Then choose Page Number, Secondary Page Number, Chapter Number, or Volume Number. You can only insert each type of numbering code once. If you need to move a code, simply delete it from the text box (using the Del or Backspace key), move the cursor where you want the code to appear, and insert the code again.

Displaying a Page Number in Text

You can display the current formatted page number, or any individual component of the page number, anywhere in your text (including headers and footers, as explained later in this chapter). Here are the steps to follow:

1. Position the cursor where you want the number to appear.

2. Choose Layout ➤ Page ➤ Page Numbering (Shift+F8 PN).

3. Now, do one of the following:

    - To insert a single component, choose Page Number, Secondary Page Number, Chapter, or Volume. Then, select (check) Display In Document.
    - To insert the entire formatted page number, choose Insert Formatted Page Number.

4. Choose OK until you return to the document window.

Displaying a Running Total of Pages

You can easily show a running total of how many pages are in the entire document, and also display the current page number within a chapter or section. To see how this works, let's assume you have a 100-page document that's divided into ten chapters of ten pages each. Now switch to Page Mode (Ctrl + F3 P) so that you can see your changes, and follow these steps:

1. Move the cursor to page 1 of Chapter 1.

2. Choose Layout ➤ Page ➤ Page Numbering, and make sure that all numbers start at 1.

3. Choose Chapter, change the Numbering Method to Upper Roman, and choose OK.

4. Choose Page Number Format and set the format to something like *Page [chpt #]-[scndy pg #] of [page #]*. Be sure to choose Number Codes or press F5 to fill in the codes shown within brackets.

5. Choose Page Number Position, select a location for your page numbers, and choose OK. (Or, create a header or footer that contains the formatted page number, if you prefer.)

6. Choose OK until you get back to your document.

Now, for each chapter, move the cursor to the first page of the chapter and choose Layout ➤ Page ➤ Page Numbering. Next, set the Secondary Page Number to 1 and set the Chapter page number to whatever chapter you're working on. Choose OK until you return to your document.

When you're done, you'll see page numbers like these:

Page I-1 of 1 (on page 1 of Chapter 1)

Page II-10 of 20 (on page 10 of Chapter 2)

Page VIII-5 of 75 (on page 5 of Chapter 8)

Page X-10 of 100 (on page 10 of Chapter 10)

See Chapter 31 for another way to create dual page numbers, such as *Page 2 of 20*. Refer to Chapter 32 for information about managing large documents that are stored in several files.

Page Headers, Footers, and Watermarks

If you've ever had to type a document that needed headers or footers repeated on every page, you're sure to love WordPerfect's page headers and page footers feature. And if you'd like to display a drawing, logo, graphic, or pale gray text behind the printed document text on every page, the watermark feature is definitely worth a try. Note that, unlike most other page formatting features, WordPerfect's watermarks show up only on the Print Preview screen and the printed document, *not* in page mode.

NOTE   Rather than repeating the terms *header, footer,* and *watermark* throughout this chapter, I'll usually refer to these as *repeating elements*.

Here are some other useful things to remember about repeating elements:

- You only have to create the repeating elements once. From that point on, WordPerfect will print them on every page (or alternating pages, if you request it), regardless of whether you add or delete paragraphs.

- *Page headers* and *watermarks* normally start just below the top margin. *Page footers* normally start just above the bottom margin.

- Normally, WordPerfect leaves 0.167″ of space between the header or footer and the body text. You can adjust this default spacing if you wish.

- Repeating elements can include up to a page of text and WordPerfect Characters (Ctrl+W), page numbers, the current date/time and file name, graphic lines and boxes, boldface, italics, centering, and other formatting features. Figure 8.6 illustrates many of these features.

FIGURE 8.6

A sample document with page header, footer, and watermark

WordPerfect Questions and Answers   First Draft

Help! How Do I...

Most questions that WordPerfect users ask start with those three little words, *How do I...* That is, you know exactly how you want your finished document to look, but you don't know which of WordPerfect's features to use.

Books...

One solution is to find a book that shows you sample pictures of what you want to do, and then lists the keystrokes for achieving that goal. Essentially, you just look at the picture and the book tells you how to do it.

Online Help & Lessons...

You can also look up your task in WordPerfect's online help. For instance, try Help ▸ How Do I, or let Help ▸ Coaches take you through the paces. If you're new to WordPerfect, try out the hands-on lessons in *Mastering WordPerfect*, or go through WordPerfect's online tutorial (Help ▸ Tutorial).

Questions & Answers...

Here are some questions that nearly every beginner has, along with some smart-alecky answers:

ANSWERS TO COOL QUESTIONS

- As Figure 8.7 illustrates, you can display different repeating elements on alternating pages. For example, you could show Header A on even-numbered pages and Header B on odd-numbered pages.

FIGURE 8.7

Two different headers, one for even-numbered pages and one for odd-numbered pages

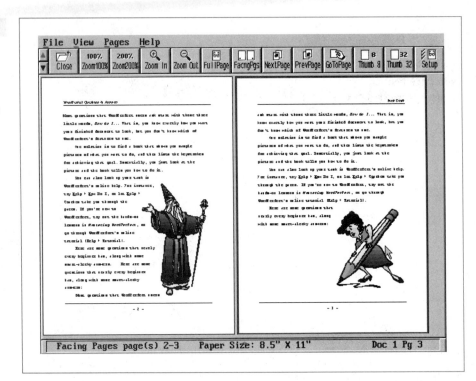

Creating and Editing a Repeating Element

Follow these steps to create a repeating element:

1. Place the cursor on the page where the feature should start.

2. Select <u>L</u>ayout ➤ <u>H</u>eader/Footer/Watermark, or press Shift+F8 H. You'll see the Header/Footer/Watermark dialog box, shown below:

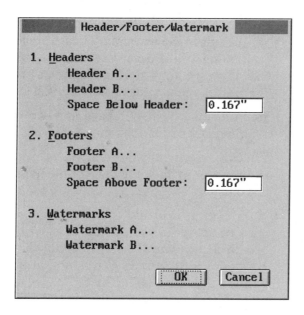

3. Select <u>H</u>eaders, <u>F</u>ooters, or <u>W</u>atermarks, as appropriate.

4. Select <u>A</u> or <u>B</u>.(Remember, you can define two different "flavors"— A and B—for each repeating element, as in the Header A and Header B example above.)

5. Now, select <u>A</u>ll Pages (to print the feature on every page), E<u>v</u>en Pages (to print the feature on even-numbered pages only), or <u>O</u>dd Pages (to print the feature on odd-numbered pages only).

6. Choose <u>C</u>reate. A blank editing window will appear.

7. Enter the text, graphics, lines, and characters for the repeating element using standard WordPerfect techniques.

8. Press F7 or click the "Press F7 when done" message at the bottom of the screen when you're done editing. Then choose OK until you return to the document window.

Here are some other things you can do in step 7 above:

- To position the watermark on the page, press ↵ as many times as necessary, or center the watermark vertically on the page.

- You can place the watermark in a graphics box for more precise positioning on the page, or if you want to rotate the watermark text. If you've put watermark text in a graphics box, you may wish to adjust the text color or shading (Chapter 26).

- You can add a formatted page number or individual numbering component, as described in "Displaying a Page Number in Text."

- You can date-stamp your document by adding the current date and time, or include the current file name, as discussed later in this chapter.

- You can press ↵ to add extra space below the header or watermark or above the footer. However, for headers and footers, it's best to change WordPerfect's default spacing via the Space Below Header or Space Above Footer options in the Header/Footer/Watermark dialog box. The Space Below Header option adjusts only the default header spacing (it doesn't affect watermark spacing).

It's easy to change an existing repeating element without retyping it:

1. Position the cursor just to the right of the repeating element you want to change (turning on Reveal Codes will help).

2. Choose Layout ➤ Header/Footer/Watermark, or press Shift+F8 H.

3. Select the repeating element you want to change. For instance, to edit Header A, choose Headers, then Header A.

4. Choose Edit.

5. Edit the repeating element as desired. When you're done, press F7, then choose OK until you return to the document window.

NOTE

When you edit a repeating element, WordPerfect searches backward from the current cursor position and lets you edit whichever code it finds first.

The section "Turning Off the Page Formatting," later in this chapter, explains how to suppress, or turn off, repeating elements.

Getting Perfect Repeating Elements

Here are some tips and tricks that will help you create perfect repeating elements.

- To display a repeating element within the top and bottom margins, simply reduce the top and bottom margin settings (Chapter 5). You can then increase the default spacing below the header or above the footer by changing the Space Below Header or Space Above settings in the Header/Footer/Watermark dialog box. Make sure that the [Top Mar] and [Bot Mar] margin codes are on the same page as the codes for the repeating elements.

- If your repeating elements don't appear on the proper page, you can use Reveal Codes to move the codes to the page where you want the repeating elements to begin (see Chapter 4).

- If your repeating elements print on top of one another, simply align text in each repeating element so that printing won't overlap. For example, left align the text in one header and right-align text in another. Or, press ↵ several times at the beginning of a watermark to prevent it from printing in the same place as the header.

- Remember that headers, footers, watermarks, and automatic page numbering use the same areas of the page. For instance, if you set up automatic page numbering at the top center of the page, the page number may appear on the same spot as your headers and watermarks. Again, simply align all the text so that your repeating elements and page numbers don't cancel each other out.

- If you've put page numbers in the headers or footers, you should turn off automatic page numbering for all pages that display that header or footer. Otherwise, the page number will appear twice on each page: once in the position set by the automatic page numbering and again in the header or footer.

Displaying the Current Date, Time, or File Name

It's a good idea to *date-stamp* each printed copy of a document that you'll be revising many times. That way, you can see at a glance how recent it is. Here are the steps:

1. Position the cursor where you want the date stamp to appear (usually this will be in the header, footer, or watermark).

2. Press Shift+F5 to get to the Date dialog box.

3. If you want to change the date or time format, choose Date Format, define the format you want, and choose OK. (See Chapter 4.)

4. To display the current date/time whenever you retrieve the document, choose Insert Date Code. To display a date/time stamp that doesn't change again, choose Insert Date Text.

If you've ever printed a document and forgotten which file you stored it in, your troubles are over. WordPerfect lets you insert the file name right in the document text or repeating element. If you rename your file later, WordPerfect will automatically update the file name displayed in your document. Very convenient! Here are the steps:

1. Place the cursor where you want the file name to appear.

2. Choose Layout ➤ Other ➤ Insert Filename (or press Shift+F8 OF). Then choose Insert Filename (to show the file name only) or Insert Path And Filename (to include the disk drive and directory location as well as the file name).

3. Choose OK until you return to the document window.

Turning Off the Page Formatting

WordPerfect offers two ways to hide page formatting on a single page or on future pages, without disrupting the page-numbering sequence or deleting the formatting code. This can be helpful on pages that display a full-page illustration or graph, or when you want to print an intentionally blank page.

For This Page Only...

You can turn off (suppress) automatic page numbering or repeating elements on the current page only. Here's how:

1. Move your cursor to the page where you want to suppress the feature.

2. Choose <u>L</u>ayout ➤ <u>P</u>age ➤ S<u>u</u>ppress, or press Shift+F8 PU (what an unfortunate shortcut!). You'll see the Suppress (This Page Only) dialog box, shown below.

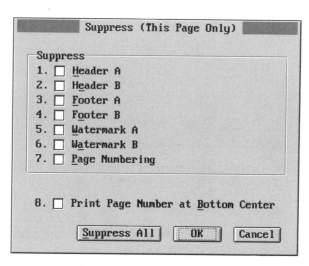

3. Select (check) whatever feature or features you want to suppress. Or, choose Suppress All to suppress all features at once.

4. If you've turned on automatic page numbering and want to print a page number at the bottom center of the page, select the Print Page Number At Bottom Center box. (This option isn't available if you've suppressed Page Numbering.)

5. Choose OK until you return to the document window.

WordPerfect will hide the selected page-formatting feature or features on the current page only. To turn the suppressed features back on, deselect the appropriate check boxes, or remove the appropriate [Suppress] code in Reveal Codes.

For Current and Future Pages...

To turn off automatic page numbering on the current page and all pages that follow, just follow the steps below:

1. Place the cursor on the page where you want to discontinue automatic numbering.

2. Choose Layout ➤ Page ➤ Page Numbering ➤ Page Number Position ➤ None (or press Shift+F8 NPN).

3. Choose OK until you return to the document window.

Turning off repeating elements is just as easy:

1. Move the cursor to where you want to discontinue the feature.

2. Choose Layout ➤ Header/Footer/Watermark (or press Shift+F8 H).

3. Select the feature that you want to discontinue (for example, choose Headers, then Header A).

4. Choose Off.

5. Choose OK until you return to the document window.

If you change your mind about discontinuing the feature, simply delete the appropriate "Off" code (such as [Header A:Off]) in Reveal Codes.

Note that, if you turn off a repeating element on the same page where you defined it, WordPerfect will delete the code for the repeating element instead of inserting an "off" code.

Starting a Code a Specified Number of Pages from Now

You can insert formatting codes that won't take effect until a certain number of pages after the current page. This is like saying "make this new code take effect *n* pages after this one." This "Delay Codes" feature works with any open formatting code, including paper size/type, justification, line numbering, font, margins, headers, footers, watermarks, and so forth.

NOTE   *Open codes affect the document from the cursor position to the end of the document, or until another code of the same type changes the format again.*

Delay Codes might come in handy if you're using letterhead stationery with a custom logo for your first page, and ordinary paper for the remaining pages. You could set the paper size/type for both kinds of paper at the start of your document (as described later in this chapter). First, you'd set the paper size/type for the letterhead paper. Then you'd use Delay Codes to make the paper size/type for normal paper take effect "one page from now"—that is, starting on the second page.

Just follow these steps to delay a formatting code for a certain number of pages:

1. Place the cursor at the start of the document (or on the page where you want to start delaying codes).

2. Choose <u>L</u>ayout ➤ <u>P</u>age ➤ <u>D</u>elay Codes (or press Shift+F8 PD).

3. Type the number of pages (from the current page) to delay the new codes that you'll be adding, and choose OK. For example, type **2** if you're on page 3 and you want the new codes to start taking effect on page 5. A Delay Codes editing window will appear.

4. Select the features you want to delay, just as you normally would when you're editing a document. For example, go through all the steps for creating Header A. When you get to the Header A editing window, type the new header that should appear *n* pages from now, and press F7. Each time you finish selecting a feature, WordPerfect will add that feature's code to the Delay Codes editing window.

5. When you're done entering codes to delay, press F7 or click the "Press F7 when done" message. Choose OK until you return to your document.

WordPerfect will insert a [Delay:*n*] code, where *n* is the number you entered in step 3. When Auto Code Placement is on, all Delay Codes will appear at the top of your document (or right under the hard page break that's above the cursor if your document contains hard page breaks).

To edit the [Delay] codes later, move the cursor to the top of your document, or to the hard page break where you entered the original codes that you now want to change. Now, simply repeat the steps above. When you get to the Delay Codes editing window, you'll see the codes you entered earlier and can change or delete them just as if you were editing a normal document.

Here are some points to remember about Delay Codes:

- For best results, always leave Auto Code Placement on (checked) when using Delay Codes. To verify the current Auto Code Placement setting, choose File ➤ Setup ➤ Environment.

- If Auto Code Placement is off, the [Delay] code will appear at the cursor position instead of the top of the document or below the hard page break. This can lead to conflicting [Delay] codes that might cause you some trouble (simply delete the conflicting codes in Reveal Codes to solve the problem). Also, be aware that you can't edit a [Delay] code *unless* Auto Code Placement is on.

Keeping Text Together

WordPerfect provides several ways to keep text together on a page or line. These include block protect, conditional end of page, widow and orphan protection, and hard spaces. We'll take a look at these features next.

Keeping Text Together on a Page

There are two ways to keep blocks of text together on one page: Block Protect and Conditional End of Page. Block Protect prevents passages of text, such as a quotation, sidebar, or columnar table, from splitting across two pages. Conditional End of Page keeps a certain number of lines together on a page (for example, a section heading and some of the following text).

To use Block Protect, follow these steps:

1. Select (block) the text you want to keep together.

2. Choose <u>L</u>ayout ➤ <u>O</u>ther ➤ <u>B</u>lock Protect (or press Shift+F8 OB).

3. Choose OK until you return to the document window.

TIP   It's often easiest to place text or tables in graphics boxes to prevent them from splitting across a page.

Conditional End of Page is a great way to keep a paragraph title from ending up at the bottom of one page, with its related paragraph at the top of the next page. Here's how to use the feature:

1. Count the number of lines to keep together, including any blank lines. For instance, in the example below, you'd probably want to keep the heading, blank line, and at least two lines in the paragraph together at the bottom of a page.

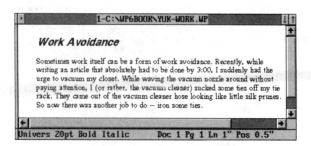

2. Move the cursor to the first line of text that you want to keep together with the lines below it.

3. Choose Layout ➤ Other ➤ Conditional End Of Page (or press Shift+F8 OC).

4. Type the number of lines you want to keep together.

5. Choose OK until you return to the document window.

Perhaps you're wondering why WordPerfect has both Block Protect and Conditional End of Page. After all, they seem to serve the same purpose. But, there *is* a subtle difference.

Block Protect places paired codes—[Block Prot:On] and [Block Prot:Off]—around a protected block. Any changes that you make to the protected block, including new or deleted lines, will still keep the entire block protected.

On the other hand, Conditional End of Page inserts only one hidden code, [Condl EOP:n]. This tells WordPerfect to skip to the next page if it doesn't have enough space to display at least n lines. Whether the text beneath the [Cndl EOP] code grows or shrinks is irrelevant, because the idea is simply to keep a few lines from being split, not a whole body of text.

To turn off the Block Protect or Conditional End of Page feature, simply delete the appropriate code in Reveal Codes.

Preventing Widows and Orphans

All those rumors about widow and orphan protection being the latest government social program are totally false. In word processing lingo, a *widow* occurs when the first line of a paragraph appears on the last line of a page. An *orphan* occurs when the last line of a paragraph appears on the first line of a new page. Either situation can offend a person's aesthetic sense (just ask any proofreader!)

When widow and orphan protection is on, WordPerfect avoids widows by moving the first line of a paragraph to the top of the next page. It avoids orphans by moving the next-to-last line of a paragraph to the top of the next page.

Here's how *you* can avoid widows and orphans:

1. Move the cursor to where widow and orphan protection should start (usually, the beginning of the document).

2. Choose <u>L</u>ayout ➤ <u>O</u>ther ➤ <u>W</u>idow/Orphan Protect (or press Shift+F8 OW).

3. Choose OK until you return to the document window.

To disable widow/orphan protection anywhere in your document (so that later pages aren't protected), move the cursor to where you want to turn off widow/orphan protection, and repeat steps 2 and 3 above.

Keeping Words Together on a Line

You can prevent two words from being separated onto two lines by placing a *hard space* between the words. Suppose you're printing phone numbers with area codes, like *(415) 555-8233*. You could use a hard space to keep WordPerfect from placing the area code on one line and the rest of the phone number on the next line or page.

Inserting a hard space is easy. When typing new text, just press Home and then the spacebar (Home Space), instead of pressing the spacebar by itself. If you've already typed the words, delete the space between them, then press Home Space. Although the hard space looks like any other blank space in the document window, a look at the Reveal Codes screen will show the hidden [HSpace] code.

Printing on Nonstandard Page Sizes

WordPerfect assumes that you'll print documents on the *standard* page size, which is 8.5" × 11" in the United States. But some documents use pages of other sizes. Legal documents, for example, require 8.5" × 14" paper. Labels are only a few inches wide and high. And many preprinted forms, such as invoices and packing slips, use unusual paper sizes as well.

Whether you can print text on nonstandard page sizes depends largely on your printer. For instance, most laser printers require a special sheet feeder for legal-size paper. Many dot-matrix and other tractor-fed printers can only print sideways on the page if the platen (the paper roller) is wide enough to accommodate 11-inch wide paper. Laser printers can print sideways on a page even though the paper is fed normally.

N O T E If you have trouble with techniques in this section, you should study printing in general (see Chapter 10) and perhaps consult your printer's manual to learn more about your printer.

Selecting a Paper Size

WordPerfect's printer installation program creates a *printer resource file* of information and options for whatever printer you installed (see Appendix A). This file, which has a .PRS extension, includes some commonly used paper sizes and types for that printer.

To use any predefined paper size, follow the steps below:

1. If you've installed multiple printers for WordPerfect, select the one you want to use (choose File ➤ Print/Fax ➤ Select).

2. Move the cursor to the page that should use the new size.

3. Choose Layout ➤ Page ➤ Paper Size/Type, or press Shift+F8 PS.

4. You'll see the Paper Size/Type dialog box shown in Figure 8.8. (However, the paper sizes displayed depend on your printer and the paper sizes you've created.)

5. Highlight the paper name you want. (As you scroll through the list with your arrow keys, WordPerfect will display the specifications of the highlighted paper name.) If you don't see the paper size you need, you can add it as described later in this chapter.

6. Choose Select, or double-click the desired paper name.

7. Choose OK until you return to your document.

FIGURE 8.8

The Paper Size/Type
dialog box

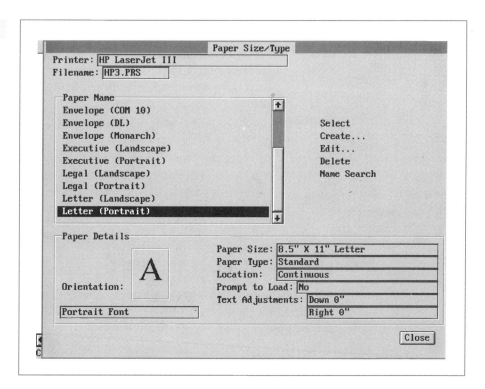

Printing Sideways on the Page

Most documents use *portrait* printing, so-called because the text appears vertically (the way artists usually paint portraits). Sometimes, however, you'll want to print a document sideways. Sideways printing is often called *landscape* printing, because the text or graphic appears horizontally across the page (the way artists usually paint landscapes).

Landscape printing is handy for many types of documents, particularly large, lengthy tables. Figure 8.9 shows a table at arm's length in portrait mode and in landscape mode. Notice that landscape mode makes much better use of the available space on the page.

How you print sideways on a standard-size page depends on what kind of printer you have. Here are the basic steps:

1. Select the 11″ × 8.5″ landscape paper size, as described earlier. This is usually named *Letter (Landscape)*.

2. Now, insert the paper as follows:

    *   If you're using a *laser printer*, insert the paper normally. The laser printer will print sideways on the page, even though you feed the page into the printer normally.
    *   If you're using a regular (nonlaser) printer, you'll probably need to feed the paper into the printer sideways, as shown in Figure 8.10. The platen must be wide enough to accommodate the page. Thus, you can only print sideways on an 8.5″ × 11″ page if your printer can accept paper that's 11 inches wide.

3. Choose File ➤ Print/Fax ➤ Print to print your document.

Printing on Letterhead

Most businesses use letterhead stock to print letters. Typically, you'll print only the first page of a multipage letter on letterhead; the remaining pages are printed on plain sheets.

FIGURE 8.9

A large table shown
in portrait and
landscape modes

If you need to...	Choose	Notes
Change the margins	Layout ▸ Margins	If Auto Code placement isn't on, be sure to move the cursor to the top of the page where you want to change the margins.
Center text on the page	Layout ▸ Page ▸ Center Current Page or Layout ▸ Page ▸ Center Pages	If you've centered the current page only, insert a hard page break (Ctrl+↵) after your title page text.
Number pages	Layout ▸ Page ▸ Page Numbering	You can define the position, numbering method, starting number, and style of the page number.
Choose a paper size	Layout ▸ Page ▸ Paper Size/Type	If you can't find the paper size you want, you can create it. Just make sure your printer can handle the settings you specify.

portrait

If you need to...	Choose	Notes
Change the margins	Layout ▸ Margins	If Auto Code placement isn't on, be sure to move the cursor to the top of the page where you want to change the margins.
Center text on the page	Layout ▸ Page ▸ Center Current Page or Layout ▸ Page ▸ Center Pages	If you've centered the current page only, insert a hard page break (Ctrl+↵) after your title page text.
Number pages	Layout ▸ Page ▸ Page Numbering	You can define the position, numbering method, starting number, and style of the page number.
Choose a paper size	Layout ▸ Page ▸ Paper Size/Type	If you can't find the paper size you want, you can create it. Just make sure your printer can handle the settings you specify.

landscape

Assuming your letterhead appears at the top of the paper, you don't need to adjust the margins to print beneath the letterhead. You just have to make sure the first line of your letter starts below the letterhead.

The easiest way to do that is to measure the distance from the top of the page to where you want the first line of your letter to appear (see Figure 8.11). Next, move the cursor to the top of your document, and press ↵ until the Ln (line) measurement in the lower-right corner of the document

FIGURE 8.10

Landscape printing
with laser and
nonlaser printers

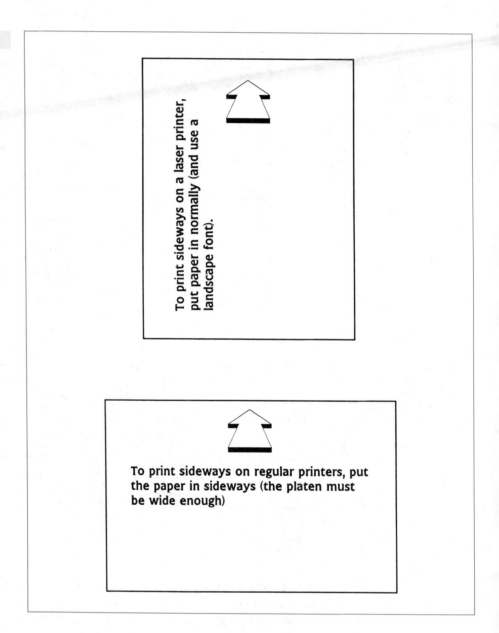

To print sideways on a laser printer, put paper in normally (and use a landscape font).

To print sideways on regular printers, put the paper in sideways (the platen must be wide enough)

window is about where you want to print the first line. Finally, type your letter, save it, and prepare the printer so that you can print it.

If your printer is fed from a tray, put as many blank letterhead bond pages into the tray as you need to print all pages after the first one. Then put the

FIGURE 8.11

Measure the distance from the top of the page to where you want the first line of your letter to appear.

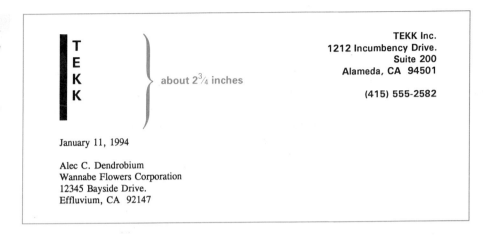

letterhead page on top of those pages. If you have a tractor-fed printer, put the letterhead page into the printer, and place the top of the page just slightly above the print head. (You may need to remove the tractor first.) Finally, go ahead and print as you normally would.

NOTE If your tractor-fed printer doesn't give you enough time to load new pages after it prints the first one, simply use (or create) a paper size that pauses and waits for you to load each sheet. To do this, you'll need to set the paper location to Manual, as explained in "Adding a Paper Size," later in this chapter.

Printing on Envelopes

Printing envelopes in older versions of WordPerfect was a clunky job. But not any more, thanks to the nifty envelope feature. Here's how it works:

1. Grab your envelopes. You'll need to know the size of the envelope, which usually is written on the box (of course, you can also measure it with a ruler).

2. If you wish, open the letter for the current envelope. If you'd like WordPerfect to use text from your letter as the mailing address for your envelope, just select the text that you want to include.

3. Choose Layout ➤ Envelope, or press Alt+F12. Or, just click the Envelope button on the Button Bar. You'll see the Envelope dialog box shown in Figure 8.12. If you selected text in Step 2, WordPerfect will retrieve the mailing address from your current document automatically.

4. Fill in the dialog box as described below.

5. If you want to print your envelope immediately, choose Print. If you want to save the envelope information in the current document (without printing), choose Insert.

If you chose to print your envelope, simply insert the envelope into the printer (according to your printer manual's instructions) and let

FIGURE 8.12

The Envelope
dialog box

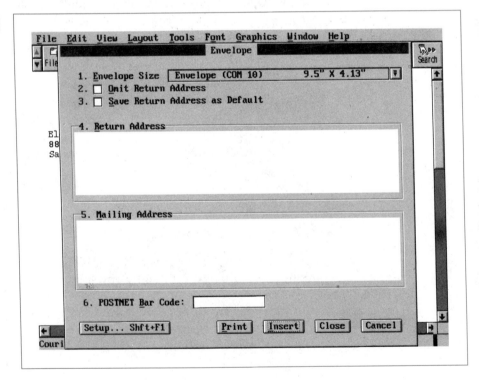

WordPerfect do the rest. Figure 8.13 shows a sample printed envelope that includes fancy fonts, special characters, and POSTNET bar codes for the zip code 92024-4747.

Here's a summary of options you can choose in the Envelope dialog box:

Envelope Size Lets you select an envelope size from a drop-down list.

Omit Return Address Select (check) this option if you don't want to print a return address (useful with envelopes that already include the return address).

Save Return Address as Default Select (check) this option if you want this return address to display whenever you create envelopes in the future.

Return Address Lets you type in a return address. Press F7 when you're done typing.

Mailing Address Lets you type in a mailing address. Press F7 when you're done typing.

FIGURE 8.13

An envelope printed with WordPerfect's envelope feature

Wanda B. Granolabar
1234 Calle Fuerte
Rancho Santa Fe, CA 92067
Wilson Dendrobium
Attaboy, Inc.
P.O. Box 7784
Encinitas, CA 92024-4747

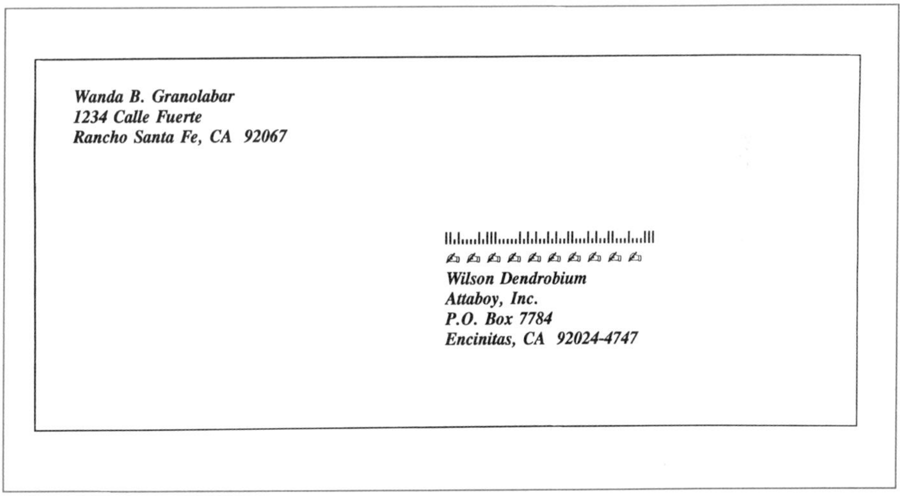

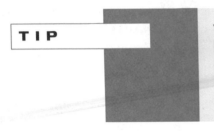

TIP You can use the pull-down menus and shortcut keys to add fonts, graphics, lines, WordPerfect Characters (Ctrl+W), and other good stuff to the addresses. (Be sure to press ↵ after typing each address line.)

POSTNET Bar Code   Lets you enter a standardized postal (zip) code. Contrary to popular belief, those weird little vertical lines on your mail aren't Martian (or postal clerk) scribbles. Instead, they're machine-readable postal codes, called *POSTNET Bar Codes*, which speed up mail delivery. POSTNET codes must contain 5, 9, or 11 digits (for example, *92123* or *91234-1234*).

Setup   Lets you select or create envelope sizes, change the default positions for the addresses, and control how the POSTNET Bar Code is created. (You can also press Shift+F1 for this option.)

TIP You can add the POSTNET code later if you used Insert to put envelope text into a document but forgot the POSTNET code. Simply position the cursor where you want the code to appear, then choose Layout ➤ Other ➤ Bar Code (Shift+F8 OR). Type in the POSTNET code (5,9, or 11 digits) and choose OK. WordPerfect will display the bar code you typed.

Creating information for several envelopes at once is a snap if you follow these steps:

1. Start from a clear document window.

2. Press Alt+F12, fill in the address information you want, and then choose **I**nsert (instead of **P**rint).

3. Repeat step 2 for each envelope you want to print. WordPerfect will automatically add a hard page break between each envelope.

4. Save your file (just in case), then print it.

If you want to print more than two or three envelopes or labels, you may want to look into the Merge feature (Chapter 21).

Printing on Labels

Most printers can print directly on labels, though you'll need to buy special sheet-fed labels that can tolerate high heat if you're using a laser printer. (Avery offers many laser printer labels.) Figure 8.14 shows some printed sheet labels, though the sheets are generally 11 inches long and can accommodate six or seven rows of labels.

Dot-matrix and similar printers use tractor-fed labels. These are usually single-column labels, on long, continuous rolls (or connected sheets) of paper, with holes on both edges for feeding through the printer tractor. Figure 8.15 shows some printed tractor-fed labels. You can find both types of labels at most office supply or computer supply stores.

To print on labels, you must first select the appropriate label size. Word-Perfect makes this easy:

1. Place the cursor where you want the labels to start (usually at the top of the document).

2. Choose Layout ➤ Page ➤ Labels, or press Shift+F8 PL. You'll see the Labels dialog box, shown in Figure 8.16.

FIGURE 8.14

Some printed sheet-fed labels

```
Mr. David E. Kenney
Attorney at Law
Crane and Fabian
123 Wilshire Blvd.
Los Angeles, CA  91234


Occupant
P.O. Box 123
123 A St.
Glendora, CA  91740


XYZ Corporation
P.O. Box 345
123 C. St.
Glendora, CA  91740
```

```
Shirleen Isagawa
123 Okinawa
Pindowa, Minowa   OUR2CL
Fiji


Miss Anna Jones
Design Consultant
P.O. Box 1234
17047 Sobre Los Cerros
Rancho Santa Fe, CA  92067


Dr. Wilma Rubble
Senior Staff Scientist
Rocket Propulsion Laboratories
P.O. Box 12345
7143 Technology Rd.
Pasadena, CA  91432
```

FIGURE 8.15

Some printed
tractor-fed labels

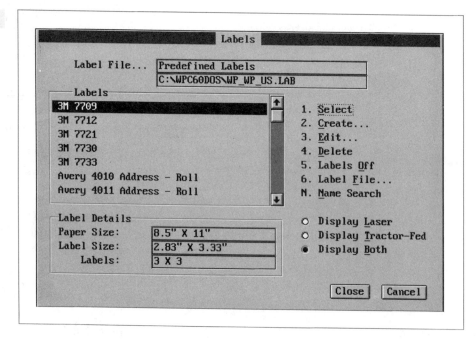

FIGURE 8.16

The Labels dialog box

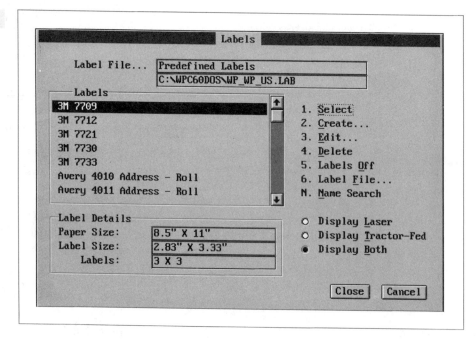

3. If you wish to limit which labels appear in the list, choose Display Laser (to show laser labels only) or Display Tractor-Fed (to show tractor-fed labels only). To display both laser and tractor-fed labels, choose Display Both.

4. Highlight the label you want from the list, then choose Select (or double-click the label name). If the label size you want isn't listed, you'll need to create it first (see "Creating a Paper Size for Labels," later in this chapter), then select the label name.

TIP

You can zoom quickly to a name in a list whenever the Name Search option is available. Simply choose that option and start typing the name you want. WordPerfect will look for the closest match and highlight it in the list.

5. Depending on the label you chose, another dialog box might ask whether you want to adjust the labels. Pick the options you want (if any), then choose OK.

6. Choose OK or Close until you return to the document window.

You've probably noticed that the Labels dialog box (Figure 8.16) has many options. Don't let that scare you off; most of them are harmless. Here are some points to help you work your way through the label maze:

- The option buttons in the lower right-hand corner let you select which types of labels appear in the Labels list.

- The names in the Labels list correspond to the "official" label names that manufacturers use for their labels. You'll find those names on the box of labels. This list will also display the names of label formats that you've created.

- As you scroll through the Labels list, the details about the highlighted label will appear in the Label Details area.

- The options along the right side of the dialog box let you create, edit, and delete labels (options 2–4), turn the label format off (option 5), switch to a different file of label formats (option 6), and search for a label name (option N).

Once you've selected the paper size for printing on labels, you can think of each label as a "page" of text. Typing on individual labels is almost like typing on individual pages. Here are some tips:

- To center text *horizontally* on all the labels, choose Layout ➤ Justification ➤ Center (or press Shift+F8 LJC) before you type the first label. To center a single line of text, press Shift+F6 at the beginning of the line.

- To center text *vertically* on all the labels, choose Layout ➤ Page ➤ Center Pages (or press Shift+F8 PP) before you type the first label.

- When you're done typing a label, you can press Ctrl+↵ to start a new "page" (label).

- To see how your labels will look when printed, switch to Page mode (Ctrl+F3 P) or the Print Preview screen (choose File ➤ Print Preview or press Shift+F7 V).

Figure 8.17 shows some sample labels typed in the document window in Page mode. The [Paper Sz/Type] and [Labels Form] codes in Reveal Codes set the label format, and the [Cntr Pgs] code centers each label vertically. Although you can't see the [HPg] code, each label ends with a hard page break (Ctrl+↵).

When you're ready to print, load your labels into the printer. For a dot-matrix printer, position the paper so that the print head is where you want the first label to print. For a laser printer, simply load in the sheet labels. Then print normally.

If the text doesn't line up properly on each label, you may have misaligned the labels in your dot-matrix printer, or you may need to edit the label's paper size, as described later in this chapter.

FIGURE 8.17

Sample labels in the document window, with Reveal Codes on

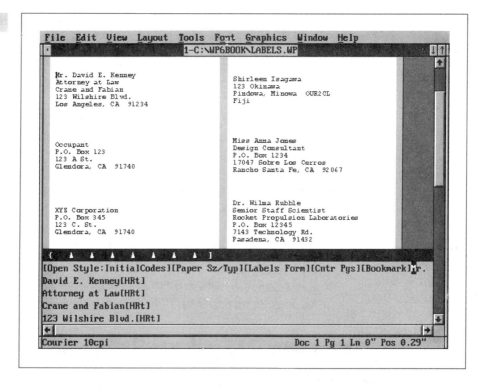

Adding a Paper Size

WordPerfect comes with a zillion predefined formats for just about every printer imaginable. But if that's not enough, you can define your own paper size for envelopes, labels, and other nonstandard papers. You only need to define a new paper size once. In the future, that size will appear in the list automatically, and you can choose it just as you would choose any predefined size.

The first step, of course, is to break out your trusty ruler and measure the paper, or each label on the paper. The next few steps are the same for all types of paper, including labels:

1. If you've installed multiple printers for WordPerfect, select the printer first by choosing File ➤ Print/Fax ➤ Select.

2. Choose Layout ➤ Page (or press Shift+F8 P), then do one of the following:

   • To define **any paper size** (labels, envelopes, legal, standard, and so forth), choose Paper Size/Type. If you'd like to base your new definition on one that already exists, highlight the existing definition.

   • To define **label formats** only, choose Labels. Highlight an existing label definition if you wish.

   • To define **envelope formats** only, choose Envelope, then press Shift+F1. Next choose Envelope Size, and highlight an existing envelope size if you wish. Choose Create.

3. Choose Create.

From here, the steps depend on whether you're creating regular paper and envelopes, or labels. I'll talk about labels later. For now, let's concentrate on regular paper and envelopes.

Creating Non-Label Paper Sizes

Assuming you've chosen regular paper or envelopes, you'll see the Create Paper Size/Type dialog box, shown in Figure 8.18.

Now, simply follow these steps:

1. Type a paper name (such as **Fancy Shmancy Paper**) in the Paper Name text box and press ↵. This name will appear later in the list of available paper sizes. The name must be unique.

2. Now choose any options you need to customize the paper size and type, as described below.

3. When you're done, choose OK to return to the Paper Size/Type dialog box. Select your new paper size, if you wish.

4. Choose OK or Close until you return to the document window.

FIGURE 8.18

The Create Paper Size/Type dialog box after I entered a paper name

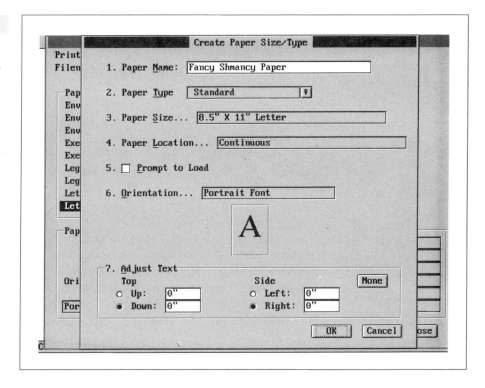

Here's a quick rundown of options available in the Create Paper Size/Type dialog box:

Paper Type   Lets you choose a basic *paper type*, which is purely a descriptive name. This name will appear in the Paper Details area of the Paper Size/Type dialog box.

Paper Size   Lets you select the size of paper you'll be using. If you don't see the paper size you want, choose Other and enter your own width and height measurements.

Paper Location   Lets you define where and how paper is loaded into the printer. The available options depend on your printer, but usually they include Continuous and Manual Feed. Choose *Continuous* if your printer can feed paper through a tractor or from the standard bin (sheet feeder) on a laser printer. Choose *Manual* if you want to feed sheets one at a time and have WordPerfect pause after printing each page.

Prompt to Load　Select (check) this option to have WordPerfect beep, display a message, and wait before it prints a document. This is useful if you want WordPerfect to remind you to load new paper into the printer before printing.

NOTE　You don't need to select both Manual Location and Prompt To Load, since the Manual Location waits for you to feed each sheet.

Orientation　Lets you specify how text should print across the page. Again, the available options depend on your printer, but usually they include Portrait Font and Landscape Font. *Portrait Font* prints text across the page, top to bottom. *Landscape Font* prints sideways on the page, even though you insert the page normally into the printer. (As you scroll through the orientation options, the big "A" in the dialog box will change to reflect your current selection.)

Adjust Text　Lets you adjust where text prints on the page, without having to change the margins. You can move the text up or down, and to the left or right. If you change your mind about the text adjustment, return to the <u>A</u>djust Text option and choose <u>N</u>one.

TIP　Don't use Adjust Text to *create* margins on your pages. Use it only to *adjust* the text when WordPerfect's margin measurements don't come out right on your printed pages.

Creating a Paper Size for Labels

If your label size doesn't appear in the labels list, you'll have to create it manually. Your first task is to get the exact measurements of your labels.

Typically, these measurements are printed on the box containing the labels. (Some manufacturers even include instructions for creating label paper sizes in WordPerfect.)

If the measurements aren't handy, break out your trusty ruler and measure the labels yourself. Most important, you need to know the label height and width. Figure 8.19 shows the measurements that WordPerfect will ask you about.

The procedures for defining *sheet* labels (those on separate sheets) and *tractor-fed* labels (those on a continuous roll, for nonlaser printers), vary slightly. You may need to make some adjustments to print properly on tractor-fed labels.

Here's a tip that can save you some money. Since labels can be expensive, it's good practice to print sample labels on plain paper until you've refined the label definition. After printing, place the printed plain-paper labels on top of a blank sheet of labels. Then hold them up to a strong light so that you can see the label outlines behind the paper. If the text appears neatly aligned within the label borders, your label definition should work the next time you print "real" labels.

Here are the basic steps for creating a label definition:

1. Select the appropriate printer for your labels.

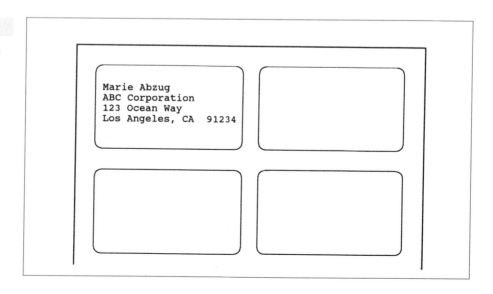

2. Place the cursor where you want the new label size to take effect, if you wish.

3. Choose Layout ➤ Page ➤ Labels. If you'd like to base your new labels on an existing definition, highlight that definition.

4. Choose Create. You'll see the Create Label dialog box, shown in Figure 8.20.

5. Complete the dialog box, as described below.

6. Choose OK to return to the Labels dialog box.

7. Select your new label size, if you wish.

8. Choose OK or Close until you return to the document window.

Here are the options available in the Create Label dialog box:

Label Description   The description that will appear in the Labels list. Each label name must be unique.

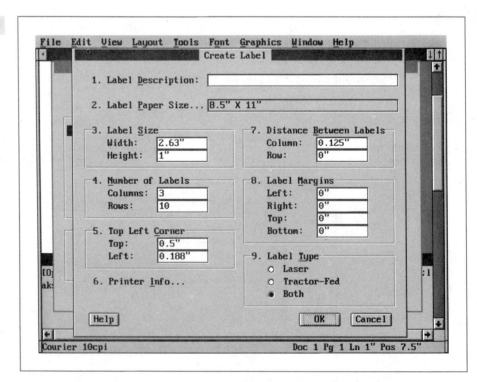

Label Paper Size Lets you select a paper size.

- If you're defining sheet labels for your *laser printer*, select Letter (8.5 × 11). This is the size of the entire sheet of labels.
- If you're defining *tractor-fed* labels, select Other. Now, enter the combined width of the labels (and any space between them) as the Width, and the height of a single label as the Height. Let's suppose you're using two-across labels for a dot-matrix printer, and each label is 4″ wide and 1.938″ ($1^{15}/_{16}$″) tall, with 0.063″ ($^{1}/_{16}$″) space between each row of labels. For this example, you'd enter **8** (or **8.5″**) as the page width and **2** as the page height.

Label Size Lets you specify the Width and Height of a single label. For tractor-fed labels, include the distance between labels in the label width and height. For example, if labels are 2.938″ ($2^{15}/_{16}$″) tall with 0.063″ ($^{1}/_{16}$″) in between each row, define the label height as 3″.

NOTE You can enter measurements as decimal numbers (for example, .063) or as fractions (for example, $^{1}/_{16}$). WordPerfect will round them off if necessary.

Number of Labels Lets you specify the number of columns and rows in each sheet of labels.

- For Columns, enter the number of labels across the page.
- For Rows, the number depends on the type of labels you're defining. If you're defining sheet labels, enter the number of labels down one column on a sheet. If you're defining continuous (tractor-fed) labels, enter **1**.

Top Left Corner Lets you define the location of the top left corner of the first label. (If you're defining tractor-fed labels, you can set both measurements to 0 inches. However, before printing you'll need to align the first label so that the print head is exactly where you want to print the first character of the label.)

- For <u>T</u>op, enter the measurement from the top of the page to the top of the first label.
- For <u>L</u>eft, enter the distance from the left edge of the page to the first label.

Printer <u>I</u>nfo   Lets you control various printing options. For example, you can choose the location of labels (for example, continuous or manual), prompt-to-load message, landscape mode, and text adjustment.

Distance <u>B</u>etween Labels   The distance between labels isn't easy to measure exactly. Typically, it's 0 inches (no space), 0.063" ($\frac{1}{16}$"), 0.125" ($\frac{1}{8}$"), or perhaps 0.25" ($\frac{1}{4}$").

- For <u>C</u>olumn, type the distance between columns (the physical space between adjacent labels). If you're defining tractor-fed labels, enter this distance as 0, regardless of the actual distance between two or more labels.
- For <u>R</u>ows, type in the distance between two rows. Again, just type 0 for tractor-fed labels, since you've already included the distance between labels in your height measurement.

Label <u>M</u>argins   Lets you specify the margins for a single label. Typically, you don't want WordPerfect to word-wrap the mailing label text, so you can leave these settings at zero. However, you might want to adjust margins if:

- You think the text will be too close to the left edge of the label. Specify a small left margin (about 0.25" or so).
- Your company's labels already include the company logo and return address.
- You're using $3\frac{1}{2}$" disk labels. It's nice to leave a top margin of about 0.68". This prevents WordPerfect from printing on the part of the label that wraps to the back of the disk and helps you center text vertically on the front of the label.

Label <u>T</u>ype   Determines which list or lists will display your new format in the Labels dialog box.

N O T E The left-right position of the tractors and vertical position of the print head on the first label affect where text appears on tractor-fed labels. WordPerfect doesn't know (or care) how you've aligned the labels in your printer; it just starts printing at the current print-head position. See Chapter 21 for more information.

Changing or Deleting a Paper Size

Changing or deleting a paper (or label) size is easy. Just follow the steps below:

1. Select the printer you want to use (Shift+F7 S).

2. If your document uses the paper size you're about to change, place the cursor just after the existing [Paper Sz/Typ] code on the Reveal Codes screen, or just delete the old code.

3. Choose Layout ➤ Page (or Shift+F8 P), then select Paper Size/Type or Labels.

4. Highlight the paper or label size you want to change or delete. Then, do one of the following:

   - If you want to *change* the highlighted definition, choose Edit. From here, the steps are the same as for creating a new paper definition.

   - If you want to *delete* the highlighted definition, choose Delete or press the Del key, then choose Yes when prompted.

5. Choose OK until you return to the document window.

WARNING It's best not to delete the predefined paper and label definitions. After all, you never know when you'll need them again. You can't undo a deleted definition. If you do delete a predefined definition, you can reinstall the printer driver to get it back (see Chapter 10 and Appendix A).

The [All Others] Paper Size

You may have noticed the [ALL OTHERS] paper size, which appears at the bottom of the Paper Name list in the Paper Size/Type dialog box. Basically, it's just a catch-all category for invalid paper sizes.

Suppose a friend creates some disk labels using a paper size for Avery 5197 ($5\frac{1}{4}$" disk) labels. He gives you a copy of the document, and you open the file. If you haven't defined the Avery 5197 label size for your printer, WordPerfect will automatically assign the [ALL OTHERS] paper size to that document.

Typically, WordPerfect assigns standard 8.5" × 11" paper to the [ALL OTHERS] size. If necessary, you can define a new paper size for the document, delete the [Paper Sz/Typ code], or choose an existing size that closely matches the one used for the original document.

You can change the [ALL OTHERS] size if you want (though offhand I can't think of any practical reasons for doing so, since it's just a catch-all for invalid paper sizes).

You've now explored dozens of ways to format your pages using centering, page numbering, headers, footers, watermarks, custom paper sizes, and other features. In the next chapter, we'll switch gears and talk about how to search for and replace text and codes in your document, and how to mark your place so that you can return to it quickly and effortlessly.

Searching, Replacing, and Marking Text

fast TRACK

HAVE you ever typed a long report only to discover consistent mistakes throughout? Maybe you used the word *Co.* instead of *Corp.* in a company name or you typed *Dewey Cheatem and Howe* instead of *Dewey Cheatem and Nowe*. Perhaps you used 14-point Bodoni-WP Bold instead of 12-point CG Times. WordPerfect can make quick work of fixing problems like these by searching rapidly through a document to locate specific text and codes. And it lets you replace the text and codes it finds with other text and codes.

Suppose you're working on a long document, but you don't have all the information you need to complete it. Wouldn't it be nice if you could mark your place with a "bookmark"? This, too, is easy in WordPerfect.

So, if you find yourself asking questions like

- Where did that text or code go?
- How can I fix this mess throughout my document?
- Where am I?

you've come to the right place.

Searching for Text and Codes

The Search feature lets you locate a specific sequence of characters anywhere in your document. You tell WordPerfect what you're looking for, and WordPerfect finds it for you.

To do a search in the document you're currently viewing on the screen, follow the steps below:

1. Move the cursor where you want the search to start (for example, move it to the top of the document (Home Home ↑) if you want to search the entire document). If you want to search a specific portion of your document, select that portion using the mouse, Alt+F4, or the F12 key.

2. Choose Edit ➤ Search, or press F2 (Search). You'll see the Search dialog box:

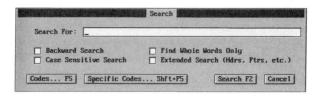

3. In the Search dialog box, you have several options:

- If you want to search for a **word** or **phrase**, type that word or phrase in the Search For text box (preferably in lowercase letters, as discussed in a moment).

- If you want to search for a **hidden code**, like [Lft Tab], choose Codes or press F5. Choose the code you want to search for by double-clicking it or by highlighting it and pressing ↵. (To get to the general vicinity of a code in the list, type the first few letters of the code you want, for example **lft**.)

- If you want to search for a **specific code**, such as a specific font, style, or justification, choose Specific Codes or press Shift+F5. Select the code you want to search for, then choose or fill in the specific information from the dialog box(es) that follow. Choose OK to get back to the Search dialog box.

- If you want to include a **WordPerfect special character** in your search, press Ctrl+W and choose the character you want.

- To search for a **pattern of text**, you can substitute ★ for any number of characters, and **?** for any single character. For example, a search for **ABC CO★** would find *ABC Company*, *ABC Co.*, *ABC Corp.*, and so forth. A search for **A?C** would find *AAC, ABC, AXC,* etc. (however, it would not find *AXXC*, because there are two letters, rather than one, between the A and the C).

4. After typing your *search string* (the text and/or codes you want to find) in the Search For text box, you have some more choices:

   - If you want to search **backwards** from the cursor position, choose Backward Search.

   - If you want to search for words that match the exact **upper- and lowercase** letters in the search string, choose Case Sensitive Search.

   - If you want to find **whole words only** (for example, you're looking for *cat* and don't want to come across *catalog* or *scat* along the way), choose Find Whole Words Only.

   - If you want to include in the search **headers, footers, and other elements** that aren't part of the main body of your document, choose Extended Search (Hdrs, Ftrs, etc).

5. To begin the search, choose Search, press F2, or press ↵ (twice, if you're still in the Search For text box).

You might see a message near the lower-left corner of the screen indicating that WordPerfect is searching your document. If it finds what you asked for, it will place the cursor just after the matching text or code. You can start editing right there at the cursor position if you like.

If Search Finds the Wrong Thing...

There's always the chance that the first thing that Search finds won't be exactly what you're looking for. For instance, suppose you were trying to move down to the word *dog*, but Search stopped at *dogmatic*. No problem. You can repeat the search to find the next match. Just press F2 twice, or, to search backwards for the previous occurrence, press Shift+F2 twice.

Returning to Where You Were

Suppose you used Search to take a look at something in your document, but you don't need to make any changes there. Just press Ctrl+Home twice (or hold down the Ctrl key and press Home twice) to move the cursor back to where it was before you started the search.

What to Do If the Search Fails

If the Search feature doesn't find what you're looking for, it will report "Not found." If this happens, choose OK to clear the message from your screen. If you're sure the text you're searching for is somewhere in the document, start the search again, and make sure you typed whatever it is you're looking for correctly.

If the search string is correct, it may be that the text you're searching for is in a header, footer, or some other formatting code. Position the cursor at the top of the document (Home Home ↑), then repeat the search, choosing Extended Search (Hdrs, Ftrs, etc.) when you get to the Search dialog box.

If you're searching a block of text, it's possible that you accidentally searched in the wrong direction. Try searching the other way. For example, if you searched forward, press Shift+F2 twice to search backward through the document.

Replacing Text and Codes throughout a Document

WordPerfect's Replace feature lets you choose any sequence of characters or codes and globally change it to something else. With one command you can change every *aunt* in your document to *uncle*, every *red* to *blue*, every *night* to *day*. Suppose you used Helvetica 18pt font to format all the headings in your document, then you change your mind and decide to go with Helvetica Bold 16pt. With Replace, all you need to do is search and replace the specific Helvetica 18pt code with a code for Helvetica Bold 16pt.

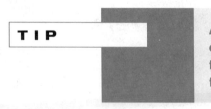

TIP Actually, a more reliable way to control the font appearance and elements that are repeated through your document, such as headings, is to use the Styles feature, discussed in Chapter 17.

You can also use Replace to make changes selectively rather than globally. The term *global* refers to any operation that affects an entire document or an entire block of text within a document.

Replacing is almost identical to searching. However, because it involves making significant changes to the document, you'd be wise to save your document *just before* performing the replace operation. That way, if you end up making a mess of things, you can just close the current copy of the document (using File ➤ Close) *without* saving it, then reopen the good copy with the File ➤ Open command.

TIP If you forget to save, Edit ➤ Undo (Ctrl+Z) can still bail you out *if* you don't make any other changes before you notice the damage that Replace has done.

Here's the smart way to do a Replace:

1. Use File ➤ Save to save the document in its current state.

2. Move the cursor where you want the replacement to start (the top of the document if you want to replace throughout the entire document). Or, select the text first to search and replace in the selected text only.

3. Choose <u>E</u>dit ➤ Re<u>p</u>lace, or press Alt+F2. You'll see the Search And Replace dialog box:

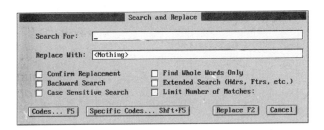

4. Type the text you want to replace in the <u>S</u>earch For text box, or choose the codes or specific codes you want to replace just as you would for a standard Search. (See "Searching for Text and Codes," above, if you're unsure of the steps.)

5. Choose <u>R</u>eplace With. Now type the text or insert the codes or specific codes with which you want to replace the text or codes you specified in step 4. (Choose Codes (F5) or Specific Codes (Shift+F5) if you want to replace with a code or a specific code.)

6. When you've filled in the Search For and Replace With text boxes, you can choose from the following options:

Con<u>f</u>irm Replacement   Select this option to have Word-Perfect prompt you before making each change. This is a good idea if you're not feeling confident enough to let WordPerfect make the decision on its own.

<u>B</u>ackward Search   Select this if you want to search backwards.

<u>C</u>ase Sensitive Search   Select this option to match your search string with exact upper- and lowercase letters (for example, your search string is *smith* and you want to re-place *smith*, but not *Smith* or *SMITH*).

Find <u>W</u>hole Words Only   Check to match whole words only. This option is very important when you're replacing a single word. For example, if you're searching for *cat* and replacing with *dog*, and you *don't* choose Find Whole Words Only, WordPerfect will replace words like *catalog* and *scat* with *dogalog* and *sdog*.

Extended Search (Hdrs, Ftrs, etc.) Check this option to extend the replacement to text inside headers, footers, and other formatting codes.

Limit Number of Matches If you want to replace only the next few occurrences of the Search For text with the Replace With text, choose this option and indicate how many replacements you want to make.

7. When you've finished choosing Replace options, choose Replace or press F2.

TIP To stop the replacement operation, press Esc or choose Cancel at any time *before* choosing Replace from the Search And Replace dialog box.

What happens next depends on whether you selected Confirm Replacement in the Search And Replace dialog box:

- If you left Confirm Replacement unchecked, WordPerfect will replace all matching occurrences of the search string without further comment.

- If you checked Confirm Replacement, WordPerfect will prompt you for permission before making a replacement. You can choose Yes to change the current text, No to skip the current text (leaving it unchanged), Replace All to replace this occurrence and all the rest of the matches in the document, or Cancel (Esc) to terminate the search-and-replace operation.

Next, WordPerfect will display a message telling you how many occurrences it found and how many replacements it made. If it couldn't find the search string, you'll see the message "Not found." Choose OK or press ↵ to clear the message.

TIP

To save time and typing, you might want to use abbreviations, like *ABC*, for longer names, like *ABC Corporation*, throughout your document. Then you can go back and replace all the *ABCs* with *ABC Corporation* using the Replace feature.

Replacing Specific Codes

You can use Replace to replace specific codes, like a particular font, with another code. Just use the Specific Codes button (Shift+F5) while you're defining your Search For and Replace With codes.

Replacing Paired Codes

Paired codes have an "on" code and an "off" code. For instance, when you turn on boldface, you get a [Bold On] code before the boldfaced text and a [Bold Off] code after it. You can use the Replace feature's Codes button to swap one pair of codes for another.

When you're in the Search And Replace dialog box, just use the Codes button (F5) to choose the "On" code for the attribute you want to change (for example, [Italc On] to change italics). Next, select Replace With and use the Codes button (F5) to choose the "On" code for the new attribute (for example, [Und On] to change italics to underline). Then proceed with the replacement, as described under "Replacing Text and Codes throughout a Document."

Deleting Text and Codes throughout a Document

WordPerfect's Replace feature offers a handy way to delete text and codes throughout your document. For example, you could strip out all the underlining in your document simply by replacing the underline code, [Und On] or [Und Off], with nothing.

NOTE When you delete the starting or ending code of a paired code, WordPerfect deletes the other code automatically. Thus, replacing all the [Und On] codes with nothing deletes all the [Und Off] codes as well.

The basic procedure is simple: Follow the steps for replacing codes throughout a document (given earlier in this chapter) but don't supply a replacement string. That is, when you get to the Replace With text box, delete any existing text and codes in that text box and press ↵. WordPerfect will insert the word <Nothing> in the Replace With dialog box to remind you that you're replacing the Search For text with "nothing."

Be sure to check any other options that seem appropriate, such as Confirm Replacement and Find Whole Words only. Then choose Replace, or press F2, as usual.

Finding Your Place with Bookmarks

When WordPerfect loads a document, it places the cursor at the top of the first page. You may recall that you can press Home Home ↓ to get to the end of the document quickly.

But what if it's a long document that's taken days or weeks to create, and you were last working on text in the middle of the document? How can you find where you left off? Or, what if you want to go back to a few juicy spots that you didn't quite finish during your last key-pounding session? How can you get to those spots without scrolling through page after page?

The answer is to insert a *bookmark* as a placeholder in the text. Then, when you need to locate your place again, simply use WordPerfect's bookmark feature to zoom back to that spot in a flash.

Here's the quick and easy way to create a bookmark:

1. Before you move the cursor, press Ctrl+Q (as in *QuickMark*) or choose Edit ➤ Bookmark ➤ Set QuickMark (or press Shift+F12 then Ctrl+Q). WordPerfect places a [Bookmark] code in the document (the code is visible only in Reveal Codes).

2. Scroll through your document to your heart's content, or use Search if you like. When you're done looking around, press Ctrl+F (as in *Find*) to return to your bookmark. It's that easy!

Setting a Bookmark Automatically

You can tell WordPerfect to set a bookmark in your document automatically whenever you close the document. That way, whenever you open a document you can just press Ctrl+F to get right back where you left off.

To turn on the automatic bookmark feature, follow the steps below:

1. Choose Edit ➤ Bookmark (or press Shift+F12).

2. Select the Set QuickMark In Document On Save check box (if it isn't already selected).

3. Choose OK.

The feature will stay on for all future documents unless you repeat the steps above and clear the × from the Set QuickMark In Document On Save check box.

Putting Several Bookmarks in a Document

The QuickMark is not the only bookmark you can add to your document (though it's the only one that Ctrl+F will find). You can put as many bookmarks in your document as you wish. And you can move, delete, and rename existing bookmarks. Here's how to work with bookmarks in WordPerfect:

1. If you're adding a new bookmark or you want to move an existing bookmark, move the cursor to where you want to put the bookmark. (Otherwise, skip to step 3.)

2. If you wish, you can have the bookmark select text when you move back to it later by creating a *blocked bookmark*. To do this, just select the text that you'll want to jump back to later. If you don't want a blocked bookmark, skip this step.

3. Choose Edit ➤ Bookmark (Shift+F12). The Bookmark dialog box, shown in Figure 9.1, will appear.

4. Now you have several choices:

   • To **create a new bookmark**, choose Create and type a unique name for your bookmark (something that will be easy to remember later). Choose OK.

FIGURE 9.1

The Bookmark dialog box lets you create, find, delete, and move multiple bookmarks in a document. To get here, choose Edit ➤ Bookmark.

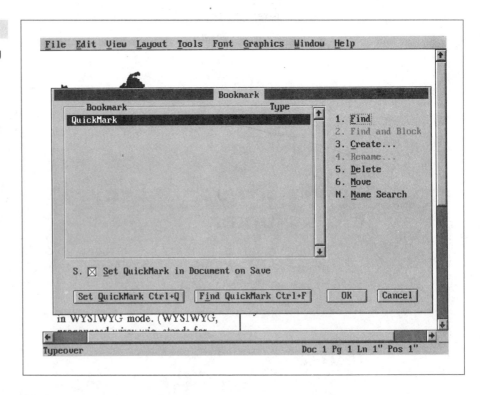

- To **return to a bookmark** that you created earlier, double-click its name or highlight its name and choose Find. To return to a bookmark that you created with **selected text**, highlight the bookmark's name and choose Find And Block.

- To **delete a bookmark** that you're not using any more, highlight its name, press Delete (Del) or choose Delete and answer Yes when prompted for verification. (You can also delete a bookmark by deleting its code in Reveal Codes.)

- To **move a bookmark** to the current cursor location in your document, highlight the bookmark's name and choose Move.

- To **rename a bookmark,** highlight the bookmark, choose Rename, and type in (or edit) the name.

- If you have lots of bookmarks and you want to **look up a name in the bookmark list,** choose Name Search and type the first few characters of the bookmark you want to find. When you get on or near the bookmark you want, press ↵ to leave the Name Search text box.

5. Choose OK, if necessary, to return to the document window.

In Reveal Codes, the [Bookmark] code expands to show the bookmark name when you put the highlight right on it. Blocked bookmarks are marked with a [+Bookmark] code at the start and a [-Bookmark] code at the end.

In this chapter you've learned about three of WordPerfect's most indispensable workhorse tools: Search, Replace, and Bookmarks. In Chapter 10 we'll switch gears and talk about how to master your printer and fonts. This is an important topic for anyone who wants to take full advantage of the printer's capabilities.

CHAPTER

10

Mastering Your Printer and Fonts

fast TRACK

To print multiple copies of a document   **405**

> choose File ➤ Print/Fax ➤ Number Of Copies (Shift+F7 N). Enter the number of copies you want. Under Generated By, choose WordPerfect if you want the copies to be collated, or choose Printer for faster printing with uncollated pages. Then choose Print.

To control print jobs and maximize their speed   **414**

> choose File ➤ Print/Fax ➤ Control Printer (Shift+F7 C).

To install graphics fonts   **420**

> install the fonts to your hard disk according to the manufacturer's instructions. Use one directory for all your TrueType fonts, another directory for all your Speedo fonts, and so forth. To install the fonts for use in WordPerfect, start WordPerfect and choose Font ➤ Font ➤ Setup (Shift+F1). Then choose Install Fonts, and choose the type of graphics font you want to install. Choose Directories For Files, and indicate your directories. Then mark with an asterisk all the fonts you want to have access to, and choose Install Marked Fonts. Follow the instructions on the screen, then choose Exit and Close as appropriate to work your way back to the document window.

To install cartridge fonts, soft fonts, and other printer fonts   **427**

> choose Font ➤ Font ➤ Setup (or Shift+F1). Choose Select Cartridges/Fonts/Print Wheels. Choose the category and type of font you want, then mark fonts to install with an asterisk.

AS I mentioned in Chapters 1 and 3, you can print a copy of the document on your screen simply by going to the Print/Fax dialog box and choosing the Print button (Shift+F7 R). But as you'll see in this chapter, there are many things you can do to control your printer and maximize its speed. And you can expand your font collection in lots of ways to create ever more dazzling documents.

TIP

If you have problems with your printer or fonts, refer to Appendix C for quick tips on diagnosing and solving problems.

How to Print Documents

WordPerfect offers many ways to control the appearance of your printed document and the speed at which it prints. Let's take it from the top, step by step.

Step 1: Get Your Document(s) Ready

If you have multiple documents open on your screen but want to print only one of them, make that document's window the active window. Use Window ▶ Switch To (F3) to do so.

Printing a Portion of Your Document

If you want to print only a portion of the document that's currently on your screen, select the portion you want to print (see Chapter 3). Or, if you want to print a single page, just move the cursor to the page you want to print.

Printing Several Documents

If you want to print several documents, including several documents that are currently open, your best bet is to save and close all the documents you want to print so that the copies on disk are up-to-date. Then, start the File Manager (F5), mark the files you want to print with an asterisk (*), choose Print, and respond to the prompts. See Chapter 20 for more information on the File Manager.

TIP

To avoid having to reprint the document to fix simple spelling mistakes, run the document through the Speller (Alt+F1 S) just before printing it. (See Chapter 11.)

Step 2: Get Your Printer Ready

Before you get started, take a quick glance at the printer and make sure it's turned on and online. (See your printer manual if you need help).

Tractor-Fed (Dot-Matrix) Printer

If you're using a tractor-fed (dot-matrix) printer, take a look at the position of the print head in relation to the page that's in the platen. (The *print head* does the actual printing. The *platen* is the roller that moves the paper through the printer.) If the print head isn't lined up near the top of a new page (or wherever you want to start printing on that page), *turn the printer off, manually crank the paper into position, then turn the printer back on.* Make sure the printer is online.

Sheet-Fed (Laser) Printer

If you're using a sheet-fed (laser) printer, chances are that you don't need to do anything at this point. But, if there's a partially printed page in the printer (and the form feed button is lit), you may want to eject that page from the printer. Use your printer's form feed button (according to the instructions in the manual), or just print a blank page in WordPerfect (File ➤ New, Shift+F7 R, File ➤ Close).

Step 3: Go to the Print/Fax Dialog Box

Next, you want to get to the Print/Fax dialog box. To do so, choose File ➤ Print/Fax or press Shift+F7. You'll be taken to the Print/Fax dialog box, shown in Figure 10.1. This dialog box is sort of like "command central" for telling WordPerfect exactly what you want to print and how to print it.

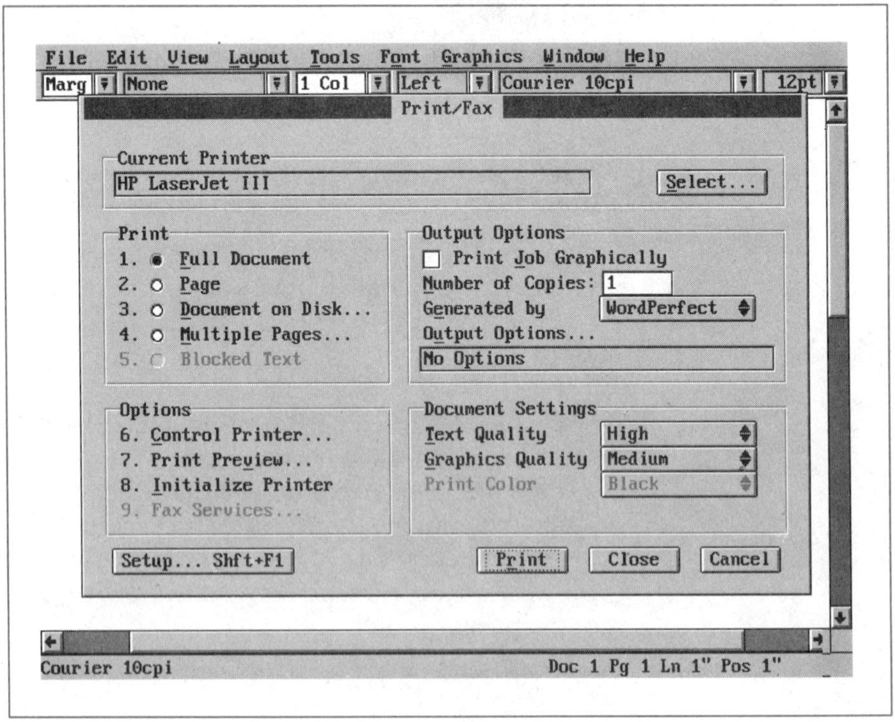

FIGURE 10.1

The Print/Fax dialog box lets you tell WordPerfect what to print and how to print it. To get here, choose File ➤ Print/Fax or press Shift+F7.

In the remaining steps, I'll assume you're in the Print/Fax dialog box.

Step 4: Select Your Printer

If you've installed multiple printers for use in WordPerfect, take a look at the printer name under Current Printer. If that's not the printer you want to use, choose Select, then choose the name of the printer you want to use by double-clicking, or by highlighting and pressing ↵.

Step 5: Tell WordPerfect What to Print

Next, you want to tell WordPerfect exactly what you want to print using options in the Print group of the Print/Fax dialog box. Your options are

Full Document   Prints the entire document that's in the currently active document window.

Page   Prints only the page that the cursor is on.

Document on Disk   Lets you print a document that's not open at the moment. After choosing this option, specify the file name of the document you wish to print.

Multiple Pages   Choose this option if you want to print only certain pages from the document, or if you want to use other special features described under "Printing Part of a Document," below. Choose OK after making your selections to return to the Print/Fax dialog box.

Blocked Text   This option will already be chosen if you selected text before coming to the Print/Fax dialog box. (Otherwise it will be dimmed and unavailable.)

Step 6: Tell WordPerfect How to Print

There's a general rule of thumb that applies to most printers. The lower the print quality you use, the worse the document looks, but the faster it prints.

For quick drafts of a document, you might want to try printing at a low print quality:

1. Choose Text Quality, then select a quality for printing the text from the pop-up list.

2. Choose Graphics Quality, then select a quality for printing graphics from the pop-up list.

3. If you have a color printer, choose Print Color to specify whether you want the document printed in Full Color or in Black ink.

T I P

If your computer runs out of memory while trying to print a complex document, you can choose Text Quality or Graphics Quality and then select Do Not Print to print just text or graphics. See "If Your Printer Runs Out of Memory..." in Chapter 26.

Step 7: Start Printing

At this point, you can select other options described later in this chapter. But if you're ready to print right now, just choose the Print button. There may be a delay as WordPerfect gets ready to print. Then you'll be returned to the document window, and the printer will start doing its thing.

Step 8: In a Hurry?

If you just completed "Step 7: Start Printing," and you don't need to work on any documents at the moment, you can maximize the speed of the print job by going to Control Printer (Shift+F7 C). Then just stay there until the print job is done. When the Control Printer dialog box is on the screen, WordPerfect "knows" you won't be editing any text. Therefore, it doesn't bother to check to see if you've done anything with the mouse or keyboard recently. And that, in turn, makes the whole print job go a little faster.

If there are other print jobs ahead of yours, and you want to "take cuts" in line, you can highlight your print job and choose Rush Job, as discussed under "Controlling Print Jobs," later in this chapter. But be forewarned: If you share a printer with other users, taking cuts is not likely to win you any popularity contests.

Printing Part of a Document

As mentioned under "Step 5: Tell WordPerfect What to Print," you can use the Multiple Pages option in the Print/Fax dialog box to print a portion of the document. Once you've selected that option, you will be taken to the Print Multiple Pages dialog box, shown below:

```
┌─────────────────────────────────────────────────┐
│ ████████████  Print Multiple Pages  ███████████ │
│                                                  │
│  1. Page/Label Range: │(all)                  │  │
│  2. Secondary Page(s): │                       │  │
│  3. Chapter(s):        │                       │  │
│  4. Volume(s):         │                       │  │
│                                                  │
│  5. Odd/Even Pages  │Both ▲▼│                    │
│                                                  │
│  6. ☐  Document Summary                          │
│  7. ☐  Print as Booklet                          │
│  8. ☐  Descending Order (Last Page First)        │
│                                                  │
│                       ┌──────┐  ┌────────┐       │
│                       │  OK  │  │ Cancel │       │
│                       └──────┘  └────────┘       │
└─────────────────────────────────────────────────┘
```

Here, you can define the following:

- Choose Page/Label Range, then choose specific pages or ranges of pages to print. (If you're using a label paper size, each label is considered a page.)

● If you've defined secondary page numbers, chapters, or volumes (as described in Chapter 8), you can select one of those options and specify the page(s) to print.

● You can choose Odd/Even Pages, then the pages you want to print. For example, to print back-to-back on a nonduplex printer, you can first print all the odd pages. Then, put those printed pages back in the printer and print the even-numbered pages on the back.

● You can choose Document Summary to print the document summary (if the document has one).

When specifying the pages to print, use a comma (,) to separate individual page numbers, and a hyphen (−) to specify a range. *Always start with the earliest page number, and work your way toward the end.* For example, entering **3,5,15-20, 25-30** prints pages, 3, 5, 15 through 20, and 25 through 30. (Press F1 if you need additional help.)

After defining your pages, choose OK. Then choose Print from the Print/Fax dialog box if you're ready to start printing.

What to Do if Your Printer Puts the Last Page on Top

Some laser printers eject pages face-up. So, when your print job is done, the last page will be on the top, and the first page will be on the bottom.

To fix that, go to the Print/Fax dialog box, choose Multiple Pages, then choose Descending Order (Last Page First). Next, choose OK to get back to the Print/Fax dialog box, and print your document.

Printing Multiple Copies

Here's how to print several copies of a document:

1. In the Print/Fax dialog box, choose Number Of Copies.

2. Type in the number of copies you want to print (for example, **3** for triplicate).

3. Choose Generated By and specify how you want the copies printed. Your options are as follows:

   WordPerfect   Though usually a little slower than the Printer option, this option has the advantage of collating the copies. For example, you'd get a complete copy of the document, then a second complete copy of the document, and so forth.

   Printer   If your printer can make the copies on its own, this is usually the fastest way to print multiple copies. However, the pages won't be collated. For example, you'd get three copies of page 1, then three copies of page 2, and so forth.

   Network   The network will send the copies to the printer one job at a time, and collate the copies. (This option is available only if you're linked to a network printer.)

Printing on Both Sides of the Page

If you have a duplex printer (one that can print on both sides of the page), like the LaserJet IID or LaserJet IIID, here's how you can get WordPerfect to print on both sides of the page:

Open the document that you want to print.

2. Choose Layout ➤ Page ➤ Double-Sided Printing.

3. Choose the type of binding you want: Long Edge or Short Edge (see your printer manual for examples, if necessary). Choose OK.

4. Choose File ➤ Print/Fax (Shift+F7) to print the document.

TIP To print back-to-back with a non-duplex printer, print the odd-numbered pages first. Then print the even-numbered pages on the backs of those pages. (See "Printing Part of a Document," above.)

Using Fancy Output Bins

Depending on the capabilities of your printer, you can use commands under the Output Options in the Print/Fax dialog box to control how pages come out of the printer.

1. Get to the Print/Fax dialog box (File ➤ Print/Fax or Shift+F7).

2. Choose Output Options, then select the option(s) you want (options that aren't relevant to your printer will be dimmed and unavailable):

Sort Use Sort with the Output Bins option to print several copies of a document, each collated and fed to a separate bin.

Group Use Group with the Output Bins option to print documents grouped by page, where each page is stacked in a separate output bin (copies are not collated).

None Deselects all currently selected options.

Output Bins If your printer has multiple output bins, use this option to specify where to send the print job. Once you've selected this option, you can use Name Search to locate the bins.

Offset Jogger   If your printer can jog (offset) the output pages left or right, select this option to have each copy printed in a separate stack.

3. Choose OK to return to the Print/Fax dialog box. Then choose other options as appropriate, or P̲rint to start printing.

Using Fancy Sheet Feeders

If your printer uses an oversized or multiple bin paper feeder (excluding the regular paper bin or sheet feeder that came with your printer), you may need to tell WordPerfect to use that feeder before you can take advantage of its capabilities.

To do so, select F̲ile ➤ P̲rint/Fax (or press Shift+F7). Then choose S̲elect Printer and highlight the printer you want to define new bins for. Then choose E̲dit ➤ S̲heet Feeder from the dialog boxes. Select a sheet feeder from the list of available options (or N̲one to use your regular, original sheet feeder). You can also choose I̲nformation to get more information about a particular feeder. After choosing your sheet feeder, choose Close, then choose OK as necessary to return to the document window.

Now, if you like, you can go back and define different sizes of papers for different feeders using L̲ayout ➤ P̲age ➤ Paper S̲ize/Type. Choose a paper size, then choose E̲dit. Choose Paper L̲ocation, then Sheet F̲eeder, and choose the sheet feeder you want to use to print that paper size.

TIP   You can press F7 as many times as necessary to return from one or more dialog boxes to the document window.

Printing One Page at a Time

If you want to print one page at a time, move the cursor to the top of the document, and choose Layout ➤ Page ➤ Paper Size/Type. Change the current paper size, or create another with the same dimensions but a different name. Then choose Edit and set the Paper Location to Manual Feed. You can also choose Prompt To Load if you want to be prompted to load each page. (See Chapter 8 for more information on creating and using paper sizes.)

Save the paper size and return to the document window. Whenever you want to print one page at a time, move to the top of the document you're about to print, choose that Manual Feed paper size, and print normally (Shift+F7 R). You can then feed one page at a time. If necessary, go to the Control Printer dialog box (Shift+F7 C), and look for instructions in the Message and Action prompts.

NOTE

If WordPerfect expects you to take an action in the Control Printer dialog box, you'll see the message "Press Shft F7, 6 to resume printing" in the status bar.

Printing a Job Graphically

If you try to print light text over a dark background without using a graphic font, WordPerfect will probably do the opposite: print the dark background over the light text. But, if you choose File ➤ Print/Fax ➤ Print Job Graphically before you print, and you have at least one graphic font in your font list, WordPerfect will switch to the graphic font, and then (in most cases) print the light text over the dark background.

As an example, Figure 10.2 shows a (slightly retouched) photo in a graphics Figure box, with <u>T</u>ext Flows set to <u>T</u>hrough Box. The word INCOGNITO is typed right into the document, with a print color of white. I selected Print <u>J</u>ob Graphically before printing the document and you can see the result. See Chapter 26 for information on creating graphics boxes and Chapter 6 for information on choosing a print color.

T I P

If you print photos often, be aware that you can also choose the *dithering* method that your printer uses for a graphic image. See "Image Print Parameters" in Chapter 26.

FIGURE 10.2

Results of printing white text across a graphic image, with Print <u>J</u>ob Graphically selected in the Print/ Fax dialog box

I should point out that the Print Job Graphically option can affect the appearance of graphics as well. You might want to try printing any document that has graphics both with and without that option selected to see which looks best.

Printing a Booklet

The booklet feature is one of WordPerfect 6.0's best features. It lets you print subdivided pages (or labels) in booklet format for binding. Here's how to use it:

1. Start with a new document window, and use Layout ➤ Page to get to the Page Format dialog box.

2. Choose Paper Size/Type and a paper size. For example, if you want to print a 5.5″ × 8.5″ booklet (letter-sized paper folded in half), choose Letter (Landscape). For a 4.25″ × 11″ pamphlet or brochure, choose Letter (Portrait). Choose Select to return to the Page Format dialog box.

3. Choose Subdivide Page and specify 2 columns, 1 row. Choose OK to return to the Page Format dialog box.

4. If you want to put a border around each page, choose Page Borders, then select a Border Style and/or other options you want. Choose OK as necessary to return to the document window.

To make life easy, you might want to switch to Page view here (choose View ➤ Page Mode, or press Ctrl+F3 P) and zoom in or out a bit (View ➤ Zoom).

Now you can type your document normally. Start by typing the cover, then leave a blank page after that for inside the back cover. (Or, if you want text inside the back cover, type it on page 2.) If you want the table of contents or chapter title to start on an odd-numbered (right-hand side) page, you may need to press Ctrl+↵ to insert a hard page break or put a Force Odd code at the top of that page (Layout ➤ Page ➤ Force Page ➤ Odd). You can force the back cover to be an even-numbered page as well.

TIP

See Chapter 8 for more information on page formatting and Chapter 27 for more on subdividing pages.

If you want to number the pages, move the cursor to the top of the first numbered page and use Layout ➤ Page ➤ Page Numbering to set the starting page number and style (see Chapter 8). To turn off page numbering, move to the top of the page where page numbering should stop. Now choose Layout ➤ Page ➤ Page Numbering ➤ Page Number Position ➤ None and return to the document window.

You can get a quick preview of your pages using a thumbnail sketch in Print Preview (Shift+F7 V). Figure 10.3 shows an example. Notice how I've inserted blank pages after the cover and table of contents. If you have an electron microscope handy, maybe you can even see where the alternating page numbers at the bottom of the numbered pages begin and end.

FIGURE 10.3

A document prepared for printing as a booklet using letter landscape paper, subdivided into two columns and one row

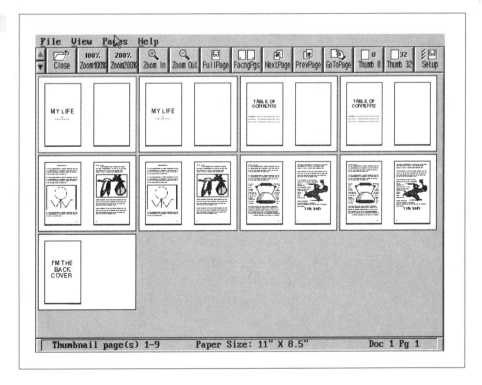

Unfortunately, the thumbnail sketch displays each page twice when the pages are subdivided. But you get the basic idea.

When you're ready to print your document, leave Print Preview, then follow these steps:

1. Choose File ➤ Print/Fax (Shift+F7) as usual.

2. Choose Multiple Pages ➤ Print As Booklet, then choose OK.

3. Choose any other options you might want, such as text and graphics qualities, then choose Print to start the print job.

4. Switch to Control Printer (Shift+F7 C) and wait for the first set of pages to finish printing.

5. Now (on most printers) slide the printed pages out of the bin, but don't rotate them or flip them over.

6. Put the top printed page back into the manual feed of the printer (or just put the whole stack in the bin with the back of the last page facing up).

7. As instructed on the screen, press **g** to print the next page. Keep following instructions to print the back side of each page by pressing **g** until the print job is done. (Then you can choose Close to get back to your document.)

Now you should be able to remove the stack from the printer, fold it in half, and *voilà*—you've got a booklet! To bind the pages, you just need a stapler with a long enough reach to get to the middle of the page.

Printing for Binding

If your document will be printed (or copied) back to back and then bound like a book, you might want to leave some extra space for the right margin of even-numbered pages and the left margin of odd-numbered pages. To do this…

1. Move the cursor to the top of the document and choose Layout ➤ Other ➤ Printer Functions ➤ Binding Offset.

2. Choose either Binding Offset (Add To Margin) to define the binding offset in relation to the left margin, or choose From Edge to define the offset relative to the Left, Right, Top, or Bottom of the page.

3. Type in the amount of space you want to allot for binding (for example, **1/2** or **.5** to leave a half-inch of space).

4. Choose OK as necessary to return to the document window.

Changing the binding offset alone may not be sufficient for printing your document because it may decrease the right margin too much. You can make the margins look more symmetrical by reducing the binding offset by half, and adding that value to both the left and right margins (or top and bottom margins) of the document.

For example, suppose you want a 0.5″ binding offset and 1″ margins on both sides of each printed page. The magic number you need to even out the margins is half of the binding offset. In this case the binding offset is .5″, so the magic number would be .25″. Return to the document window, move to the top of the document, choose Layout ➤ Margins and set the document margins. Increase both the left and right margin settings by the magic number. For example, if you're currently printing with 1″ left and right margins, change those both to 1.25″.

Undocumented Printer Secrets

Your printer documentation contains all the information about your particular printer. But WordPerfect Corporation might have some things to say about that particular printer as well. To find out what these are…

1. Choose File ➤ Print/Fax ➤ Select (Shift+F7 S).

2. Highlight the name of any printer, and choose Information.

3. Scroll through any text, or choose Sheet Feeder Information.

When you're done, choose Close to return to the document window.

Controlling Print Jobs

Whenever you tell WordPerfect to print a document, it treats your request as a *print job*. Rather than making you wait for your entire document to be printed, it sends a quick printed copy to disk, then prints that copy "in the background," so you can go back to editing documents.

You can "stack up" printer jobs simply by printing the next document as soon as the keyboard is available. You can also use a variety of techniques to control those print jobs, via the Control Printer dialog box. To get there, choose File ➤ Print/Fax ➤ Control Printer (Shift+F7 C). Figure 10.4 shows the Control Printer screen with some hypothetical documents stacked up for printing.

FIGURE 10.4

The Control Printer screen

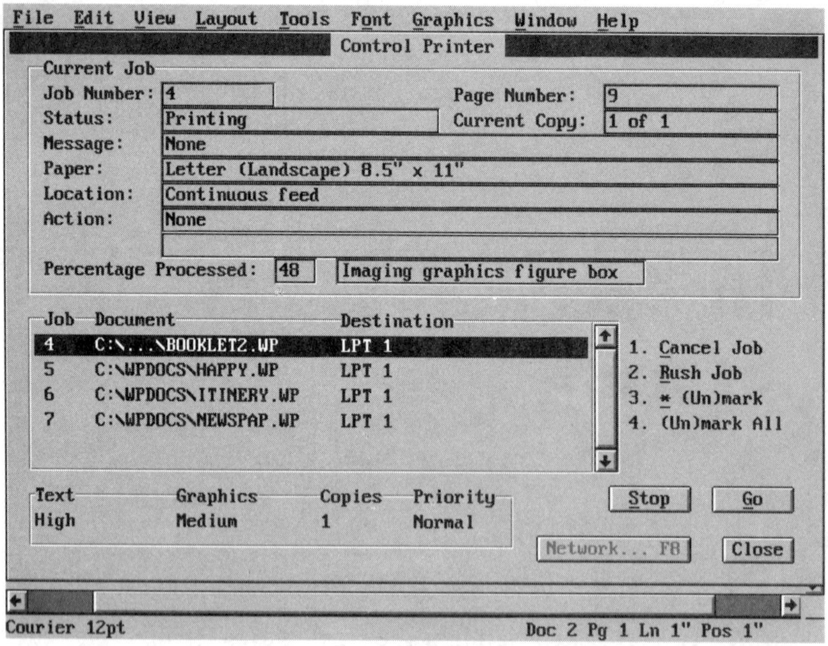

TIP As I mentioned earlier, you can also stack up print jobs by marking files in the File Manager and choosing Print. See Chapter 20 if you need more information.

The Control Printer screen is divided into two main sections. The *Current Job* portion of the screen provides information about the document that's being printed at the moment, including any *Messages* that you need to be aware of, as well as the *Action* you might want to take to fix a problem. The *Job List* lists all the print jobs that are awaiting their turn at the printer. (This list is also called the *print queue.*)

Here's what you can do to control the print jobs once you're in the Control Printer screen:

- To **stop the current job** temporarily, choose Stop. You can then do whatever it is you need to do (for example, change the ribbon).

- To **resume a job** that you stopped, choose Go. (Look to the Message and Action prompts for additional instructions and options.)

- If you're on a Novell network, you can choose Network to view the **network print queue**.

- To **cancel a print job**, highlight the job you want to cancel, choose Cancel Job, and then choose Yes. If the job is currently printing, you can either wait for the last page to finish printing or type i to cancel immediately. (Read the instructions in the Message and Action text boxes on the screen.)

- To **move a job up** in the line, highlight that job, choose Rush Job, then choose Yes.

- To **cancel or rush several jobs**, mark the jobs with an asterisk (★) before selecting Cancel Job or Rush Job.

Follow any additional instructions that appear in the Message and Action areas of the screen until no more instructions appear. Then, if you want, you can choose Close to return to the document window. Or stay in the Control Printer screen to print as quickly as possible.

"How Do I Stop This Thing?!?"

Suppose a label peels off and sticks to the platen, and the printer keeps trying to print. Or your printer starts printing a few goofy-looking characters on each page, spewing out page after page of garbage. Often, these types of things happens after WordPerfect has sent the entire print job to the printer, so canceling the print job from within WordPerfect doesn't help.

> **WARNING**
>
> Before you read on, be aware that I'm not recommending that *you* yank the paper tray out of your printer. I suspect that if I told the printer engineers I do that, they'd roll their eyes or inhale sharply through clenched teeth.

Here are some things you can do to bring the printer back to its senses:

- On my laser printers, I usually yank the paper tray out of the printer and let the last page finish printing, so that no pages get stuck in the print path. Then I turn off the printer.

- If you're using a dot-matrix printer, or you're using a laser printer and don't want to yank the paper tray, simply turn off the printer.

- After the printer stops, go back to the Control Printer dialog box (Shift+F7 C) and cancel all the remaining print jobs. Choose Go when you're done to clear any Messages and Action prompts, then close the dialog box.

- If you're using a dot-matrix printer, roll the paper up or down so that the print head is at the top of a new page. If you're using a laser printer and you turned it off while there was a page in the print path, you might need to open the printer and remove that page. See your printer manual for instructions on clearing paper jams.

Turn the printer back on and wait for it to warm up. Now you're back to square one. If you want to pick up a print job where you left off, use Multiple

Pages in the Print/Fax dialog box to start printing after the last successful page. For example, entering **15-** as the page range prints everything from page 15 on.

Choosing a Printer Port/Destination

To change the port that a printer is assigned to, follow these steps:

1. From the document window, choose File ➤ Print/Fax ➤ Select (Shift+F7 S).

2. Highlight the printer whose port assignment you want to change, then choose Edit.

3. Choose Port.

4. Choose your port and/or other options, as appropriate. (Press F1 if you need help.)

5. Choose OK and Close, as necessary, to return to the document window.

Printing to Disk

If you want to print a document to a disk file, follow the first three steps above. In step 4, choose Filename and press ↵. This leaves the Filename text box empty and automatically selects Prompt For Filename. When you print the document, WordPerfect will ask for a file name just before it starts printing.

You can print that document later on any computer that has the appropriate printer attached, even if that computer doesn't have WordPerfect stored on it. To do that, you just copy the file to the printer port from the

DOS prompt. For example, suppose you use the HP LaserJet 4 printer to create a document, and then you print that document to disk. When you get to the computer that has the LaserJet 4 connected to the LPT1 port, you can start at the DOS command prompt and enter the command

copy *filename* lpt1

where *filename* is the location and name of the file you want to print. For example, the command **copy a:\mydoc.lj4 Lpt1:** tells DOS to print the document named MYDOC.LJ4 on the disk in drive A. For more information on copying files to a printer, please see your DOS documentation.

T I P

Chapter 33 explains how to transfer documents from one word processor to another, particularly for editing purposes.

You can use a similar technique to prepare a document for high-end typesetting equipment. Please see "Preparing a Document for Typesetting" in Chapter 28.

Exiting while Printing

If you attempt to exit WordPerfect while it's still printing, you'll see a message asking if you want to "Cancel All Print Jobs." If you choose <u>Y</u>es, you'll exit WordPerfect and the print job will be canceled. (You *can* exit WordPerfect while the printer is running if WordPerfect has already sent all its text to the printer buffer. The Control Printer screen can help you see whether all the documents have been sent.)

If you need to get to DOS (or some other program) while you have one or more print jobs going, choose <u>F</u>ile ➤ <u>G</u>o To Shell (or press Ctrl+F1). Then choose <u>G</u>o To DOS (or whatever command seems appropriate). The print job will continue to run until the print buffer is empty.

WARNING	Do not load any memory-resident (TSR) programs while temporarily exited to DOS. If you do, you may not be able to return to WordPerfect.

To return to WordPerfect and resume printing (and to save your work before turning off the computer) go back to the Shell (Ctrl+F1) and switch to WordPerfect. Or if you temporarily exited to the DOS command prompt, type **exit** and press ↵.

Expanding Your Font Collection

Back when I wrote the first edition of *Mastering WordPerfect 5.1 for DOS*, fonts were a confusing and overwhelming topic. Since that time, we've been introduced to *graphics fonts*. Now fonts are an *extremely* confusing and overwhelming topic. In the sections that follow, I'll try to demystify it for you.

About Graphics and Printer Fonts

Actually, fonts are simpler than they've ever been *if* you remember that there are basically two kinds of fonts in the world today:

- **Printer Fonts,** the fonts of the 80s, were created for individual printers, mainly PostScript and LaserJet (PCL) printers. Built-in fonts, soft fonts, and cartridge fonts all fall into this category. (Any fonts you used in versions 5.1 and earlier of WordPerfect for DOS can generally be included in the category of printer fonts.)

- **Graphics fonts** are the fonts of the 90s. They work with any dot-matrix or laser printer that can print graphics. They work with both DOS and Windows versions of WordPerfect, they're scalable (they can be printed at any size), great-looking, fast, and (perhaps best of all) remarkably inexpensive. TrueType, Type 1, Bitstream Speedo, AutoFont, and Intellifont are all examples of modern graphics fonts.

The main difference between printer and graphics fonts is that with printer fonts, the *printer* handles all the behind-the-scenes jobs required to print the font. With graphics fonts, the *computer* handles those jobs. In general, graphics fonts are much easier to use than printer fonts.

Installing Graphics Fonts

When you installed WordPerfect 6.0, along with a printer that supports graphics, several sample graphics fonts were probably added to your font list. You can identify those sample graphics fonts by the words *Type 1* and *Speedo* that appear next to the font names in the font list. (To select a font, or just to see which fonts are installed, choose F<u>o</u>nt ➤ F<u>o</u>nt ➤ <u>F</u>ont, or press Ctrl+F8 F, and proceed as discussed under "Choosing a Font" in Chapter 6.) Any graphics fonts that you install later will also be followed by a similar name. Figure 10.5 shows a partial font list that includes TrueType, Speedo, and Type 1 fonts.

Probably the best and cheapest way to expand your font collection is to buy additional graphics fonts. But be aware that many graphics fonts are specifically designed for Windows. While you can certainly *use* Windows graphics fonts in WordPerfect 6.0 for DOS, you'll often need to have Windows 3.1 (or later) to *install* those fonts to your hard disk. So if you don't have Windows, be sure to purchase only graphics fonts that don't require Windows for installation.

Once you've purchased your graphics fonts (from your local computer store, computer magazine ad, or mail-order house), getting them to work in WordPerfect 6.0 is basically a two-step process:

- Copy the fonts to your hard disk.
- Tell WordPerfect how to find the fonts.

In the fonts list (Ctrl+F8 F), graphics fonts, such as TrueType, Speedo, and Type 1, are identified by font type in parentheses.

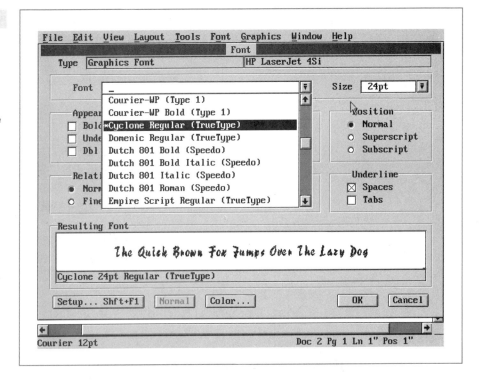

I'll discuss each step in the sections that follow.

Copying Graphics Fonts to Your Hard Disk

Before you can use any graphics fonts, you must install them on your hard disk or on a shared network drive. You'll probably need to run an Install or Setup program from DOS or Windows to do this. See the instructions that came with your font package for details.

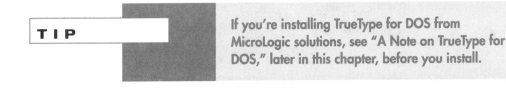

TIP

If you're installing TrueType for DOS from MicroLogic solutions, see "A Note on TrueType for DOS," later in this chapter, before you install.

It's especially important to keep track of *where* you've installed the fonts, and to keep all the fonts of a particular type together in one directory. For example, Speedo, Type 1, and TrueType fonts are often stored on these directories:

FONT TYPE	DIRECTORY
Bitstream Speedo	C:\BTFONTS
Type 1	C:\PSFONTS
TrueType	C:\WINDOWS\SYSTEM

The TrueType font assumes you've already installed Windows 3.1 on your system. But you can use any directory you want for any fonts so long as

- You put all the same type of fonts on one directory (all the Speedo fonts on one directory, all the TrueType fonts on another directory, and so forth), and

- You tell programs (including WordPerfect) where those fonts are, as I'll discuss shortly.

Telling WordPerfect Where to Find the Fonts

Assuming that your graphics fonts are now on your hard disk, and you know which drive and directory they're on, you can follow the steps below to install the fonts for use in WordPerfect:

1. Run WordPerfect in the usual manner, and choose File ➤ Print/Fax ➤ Select.

2. Highlight the name of the printer you want to install the fonts for, and choose Select.

3. Choose Select from the Print/Fax dialog box again, then choose Edit.

4. Choose Font Setup.

5. Choose Install Fonts. You'll see the Font Installer, which looks something like this:

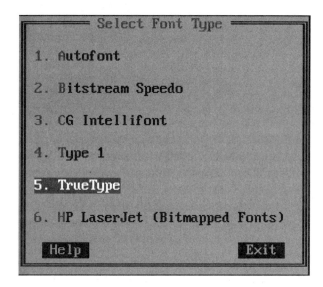

6. Choose the type of font you want to install.

7. If prompted, enter the location of your graphics fonts. For example, enter **c:\windows\system** if you're installing Windows TrueType (.TTF) fonts. Also enter the path to your WP.DRS file (typically **c:\wp60dos**) if prompted. Then choose OK.

8. Mark all the fonts that you want to install by highlighting them and typing an asterisk (*) or a space. (They may already be selected.) Or press Home then * to mark or unmark all the fonts.

9. Choose Install Marked Fonts.

10. Wait while the Font Installer does its job.

When you see a message that the font installation is complete, choose Continue (or press ↵) and then press F7 until you return to the Font Setup dialog box. There, you may need to wait a few moments for the Font Installer to update the fonts.

When the updating is done, return to the document window. To verify the installation, choose Font ➤ Font ➤ Font. You should see the newly installed fonts listed with the rest of your fonts.

"But I Don't See My Newly Installed Graphics Fonts"

If you don't see your newly installed fonts in the font list, first make sure you've selected the printer to which you installed the fonts (File ➤ Print/Fax ➤ Select). Then return to the document window and try this:

1. Choose File ➤ Setup ➤ Location Of Files.

2. Choose Graphics Fonts Data Files.

3. Highlight whichever type of font is giving you trouble (for example, TrueType).

4. Choose Edit Path.

5. Type the drive and directory where your fonts are stored (for example, **c:\windows\system** for TrueType), and choose OK.

6. If that font type isn't marked with an asterisk, type an asterisk next to the name. (This tells WordPerfect that you want to see all the fonts in that category whenever you view the font list.)

7. Choose OK until you get back to the document window.

Choose Font ➤ Font ➤ Font again to view your list of available fonts. Scroll through the list, and you should see the fonts you've installed. If it still doesn't work, use File ➤ Print/Fax ➤ Select to make sure that the correct printer is selected. Then check the font list again.

If you're *still* having problems, do what I always do in these situations. Try a little magic and superstition:

1. Save all your work, exit WordPerfect all the way back to DOS, turn off the computer, wait a few moments for your hard disk to stop spinning, then turn the computer back on.

2. Run WordPerfect in the usual manner.

3. Choose Font ➤ Font ➤ Setup (or press Ctrl+F8 Shift+F1).

4. Choose Select Graphics Fonts.

5. Mark all the fonts that you want to use with an asterisk (★) (if they're not already marked).

6. Choose OK, then wait until you're returned to the Font Setup dialog box.

7. Choose Update Graphics Fonts (Generate New AFCs For WP.DRS).

8. When the updating is finished, choose OK.

9. Choose Font, and scroll through the list of installed fonts.

Your installed fonts should definitely be included in the font list now.

Speeding Up the Font List

If you have hundreds of fonts installed, you might get tired of waiting around for WordPerfect to generate the font list every time you choose a new font. You can speed up the list by hiding fonts you aren't using in the current document:

1. Choose File ➤ Setup ➤ Location Of Files.

2. Choose Graphics Fonts Data Files.

3. Press * to add or remove the asterisk to the left of a font category. Only font categories that are marked with an asterisk are included in the font list.

4. Choose OK and Close as necessary to return to the document window.

When you open the font list again, only fonts in those categories that you marked with an asterisk will appear in the font list.

If you want to hide individual fonts in the font list, follow these steps:

1. Choose Font ➤ Font ➤ Setup ➤ Select Graphics Fonts.

2. Use the asterisk (*) to mark fonts that you want to appear in the list. Unmark fonts that you don't want to appear in the list. (Remember that the font is just hidden, not deleted from your disk.)

3. Return to the document window.

A Note on TrueType for DOS

MicroLogic Software's *TrueType for DOS* is one of the few TrueType font packages that you can install without Windows. (MicroLogic Software is in Emeryville, CA; their phone number is (510) 652-5404.) If you buy that product, be aware that you do *not* need to go through the rigmarole required to install the fonts for WordPerfect 5.0/5.1.

Instead, run the *TrueType for DOS* installation as instructed in the manual—typically by entering **a:\hello** at the DOS command prompt. If you already have other TrueType fonts on your system, specify the same directory as the directory for the TrueType fonts you'll be adding now. (You can use the suggested C:\TT directory for the *TrueType for DOS* program files.)

Complete the installation, swapping disks as instructed, so that all the fonts are copied to your hard disk and expanded. When you get to the Configuration dialog, where it asks you to select your application, you can simply choose OK, press Esc, and choose Exit To DOS. (You don't need to install to a particular application, such as WordPerfect 5.0/5.1.)

Then start WordPerfect in the usual manner, and install the TrueType fonts as graphics fonts, as described under "Telling WordPerfect Where to Find the Fonts," earlier in this chapter.

Using Your Graphics Fonts in Windows 3.x

If you have Windows 3.1 (or later), and have just completed the steps required to install graphics fonts for your WordPerfect program, you can also install those fonts for use in Windows. Start Windows and open the Main group in the Program Manager. Open Control Panel, and choose the Fonts icon. Then select fonts to install, as discussed in your Windows documentation or in the help screens (F1).

Installing Printer Fonts

Printer fonts are destined to become a thing of the past. But you may have some favorite cartridges and/or printer soft fonts that you don't want to trash just because you've upgraded to WordPerfect 6.0.

There are basically three types of printer fonts:

- **Built-in (resident) fonts** are built into your printer and require no installation whatsoever. When you install the printer for use in WordPerfect, the built-in fonts are readily available in the font list.

- **Cartridge fonts** are stored in a cartridge that you can plug into a slot on the front of your printer, as per instructions in your printer manual. (Usually you need to turn the printer off before you insert the cartridge.)

- **Printer (non-graphics) soft fonts** are stored on your hard disk and *downloaded* (sent) to your printer as needed. Like cartridge fonts, soft fonts must be purchased separately.

In most cases, the font package will include specific instructions for installing the font with WordPerfect. Your best bet is to follow those specific instructions to a tee. Alternatively, you can follow the more general instructions in the sections that follow.

Copying Printer Soft Fonts to Your Hard Disk

If you're installing printer soft fonts, your first step will be to copy the soft fonts to your hard disk. You'll need to refer to the font manufacturer's instructions to find out how to do that. Typically, you'll run an installation program from DOS.

Also, be sure to follow any instructions for using the fonts with WordPerfect, particularly any instructions that refer to updating the WordPerfect printer .ALL file. The font names must be copied into the .ALL file before you can install them to your font list.

Keep track of which directory you copied the soft fonts to. If you've copied printer soft fonts to your hard disk in the past, use the same directory for any new soft fonts you install.

Installing a Cartridge, Print Wheel, or Printer Soft Font

Once you have your cartridge in hand, or your printer soft fonts copied to your hard disk, you can follow the steps below to update a WordPerfect printer driver to use those fonts.

> **WARNING**
>
> If you're installing graphics fonts, such as TrueType, Speedo, Type 1, Autofont, or Intellifont, follow the instructions under "Installing Graphics Fonts," above, and ignore the steps below.

1. Run WordPerfect in the usual manner, and choose File ➤ Print/Fax ➤ Select.

2. Highlight the name of the printer for which you are installing fonts, and then select Edit.

3. If you're installing printer soft fonts, choose Directory For Soft Fonts, and enter the name of the directory that your soft fonts are stored on. You can use the Directory Tree (F8) and/or QuickList (F6) to help locate the directory (see Chapter 20).

4. Choose Font Setup, then select Cartridges/Fonts/Print Wheels.

5. In the next dialog box, highlight the type of font you're installing (for example, Cartridge or Soft Font).

6. Notice the *Quantity* and *Available* settings for your printer. For example, there may be 2 cartridge slots, with 2 available. Or there may be 700 KB of memory for soft fonts, with the full 700 KB available.

7. If (and *only* if) your printer has more memory available for soft fonts than is shown under Quantity, choose Quantity. Then type in the number of kilobytes of printer memory available for soft fonts. (The number shown will be correct already, unless you've opted to install additional memory into your printer.)

8. Choose Edit.

9. If a Font Groups dialog box appears, highlight the font group you want and choose Edit, or double-click the group. You'll see a Select Fonts dialog box like the example shown in Figure 10.6.

Now you can mark the fonts that should appear in your font list using any of the following methods:

- Mark with an asterisk any cartridge that will be in the printer when a particular print job begins.

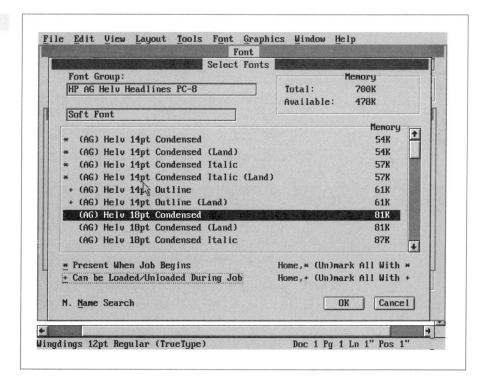

- If you're installing soft fonts, mark with an * any font that you'll be using regularly and will download to the printer before starting a print job. (See "Downloading Soft Fonts You Marked with *" for more information.)

WARNING

You can only mark with an asterisk as many fonts as will fit into memory. Once the available memory runs out, you'll need to mark any remaining fonts with a plus sign. Never, ever, mark fonts that you don't own. WordPerfect can only *use* the fonts you've purchased and installed. It cannot *create* those fonts for you!

- Mark with a plus sign (+) any soft font that you want to use on the fly. Most likely you'd use the + for decorative fonts that you use occasionally or when there isn't enough memory left next to Available, near the top of the dialog box.

- On some printers, you can mark a font with both an asterisk and a plus sign. Doing so allows WordPerfect to "swap out" the font, if necessary, to make room for another incoming font. At the end of the printer job, the original font will be "swapped" back into the printer.

- Leave unmarked any font that you don't want to appear in the font list.

- Choose OK after marking your fonts.

There may be a brief delay as WordPerfect updates the font .PRS file. After that, you can press F7 until you return to the document window. To verify that your selected fonts are now in the font list, choose F<u>o</u>nt ➤ F<u>o</u>nt ➤ <u>F</u>ont, and scroll through the list.

If you have problems, please refer to the documentation that came with your soft fonts or font cartridge.

Downloading Soft Fonts You Marked with *

If you marked any soft fonts with only an asterisk (*), you must download them to your printer before using them to print a document. Otherwise, WordPerfect will substitute a font that has already been downloaded, or some built-in font. Here's how to download those fonts:

1. Start at the document window and choose File ➤ Print/Fax ➤ Initialize Printer.

2. Follow the instructions on the screen.

WARNING

If you forget to initialize the printer before printing a document that expects certain fonts to be in the printer, WordPerfect will substitute other fonts. You can cancel the print job (if it's a lengthy one), initialize the printer, then reprint the document to correct the problem.

Downloading is treated like any other print job, so you can watch its progress using File ➤ Print/Fax ➤ Control Printer. Once the downloading is complete, the fonts will reside in the printer until you turn off the printer.

Choosing a Default Font for the Printer

Typically, WordPerfect uses a basic "typewriter" font (typically 10 cpi) if you choose to print a document without specifically selecting a different font within that document. If you'd like to change this default font...

1. Start from the document window, and choose File ➤ Print/Fax ➤ Select (Shift+F7 S).

2. Highlight the printer whose initial font you want to change, then choose Edit.

3. Choose Font Setup ➤ Select Initial Font.

4. Choose a font and size from the Font and Size drop-down-lists.

5. If you want this change to affect all future documents that you create, choose All New Documents (Created With Current Printer).

6. Choose OK and Close, as necessary, to return to the document window.

Keep in mind that your selection will not affect any documents that you've created and saved in the past.

Understanding the Printer .ALL, .PRS, and .DRS Files

WordPerfect stores most of the information about your printer(s) and fonts in three files, the .ALL file, the .PRS file, and the .DRS file. Understanding the roles played by these various files can make getting along with printers and fonts a little easier.

The .ALL File

Information about all the printers in a particular category, and all the printer fonts available for those printers, is stored in a file with the .ALL extension, typically in your C:\WPC60DOS directory. For example, information about Hewlett Packard printers is stored in WP60HP01.ALL.

When you install third-party soft fonts (*excluding* graphics fonts), the installation procedure will usually require that you update the printer's .ALL file. Otherwise, there'd be no way to select those fonts for inclusion on your font list.

If you install third-party fonts to your .ALL file, then later replace the printer .ALL file (by reinstalling the printer from floppies), the new copy of the .ALL file won't include those third-party fonts. You'll need to reinstall those fonts to the .ALL file, as per the font manufacturer's instructions, before you can make them available in WordPerfect.

The .PRS File

For each printer you install, WordPerfect creates a printer resource (.PRS) file and stores it on your WordPerfect Corporation shared directory (typically C:\WPC60DOS). That file is automatically created from the .ALL file when you install the printer. Any additional fonts (excluding graphics fonts) that you add to that printer, as well as any custom paper sizes you create, are stored in the .PRS file for that particular printer.

If you reinstall the same printer driver from floppy disks, you'll lose any fonts and/or paper sizes that you created for that printer driver. You'll need to go through the steps described in your fonts manual or earlier in this chapter to reinstall fonts. You'll also need to recreate any paper sizes using Layout ➤ Page, as discussed in Chapter 8.

The .DRS File

The WordPerfect .DRS file contains all the graphics font information for both the screen and printer. The graphics fonts are not stored in the .PRS file because they're not specific to a given type of printer. Any graphics printer and graphics monitor can use the graphics fonts that are listed in the .DRS file.

If you inadvertently delete or overwrite the .DRS file, you'll need to reinstall your graphics fonts for use in WordPerfect, as described under "Telling WordPerfect Where to Find the Fonts."

Understanding Font Substitution Codes

Let's suppose you create a document using numerous fonts from your font list. You save and close that document. Later, you select some other printer via File ➤ Print/Fax ➤ Select. Then, you reopen the original file with this different printer selected.

The first thing you might notice is the message "Formatting for" followed by the name of the currently selected printer. Since different printers will likely have different printer fonts, WordPerfect has to do something about fonts that are in your document, but not available in the currently selected printer. That is, it must pick whichever printer font in the current printer best matches the font you chose while creating the document in the original printer.

When WordPerfect substitutes a font, it puts an asterisk in front of the font name in the code. Thus, if you turn on Reveal Codes you might see a font code that looks something like this:

[Font:*Arial Italic]

This code means that you used some other printer to create this document and chose some font that isn't available to the currently selected printer. WordPerfect has substituted your original font choice with Arial Italic in this example.

The same thing happens if you select a different printer midway through creating a document. That is, if you have a document on the screen, and switch to another printer, WordPerfect will automatically change the fonts right there on the spot. The substituted printer fonts will be indicated with the asterisk (*) in the [Font:*...] code in Reveal Codes.

Instant * Removal

Now, before we go any further, let me say that if you now choose File ➤ Print/Fax ➤ Select and select the original printer, WordPerfect will instantly restore your original fonts. That is, the asterisk (*) will disappear from all the [Font:...] codes, and everything will return to the way it was.

Preventing Font Substitution at Document Opening

Formatting a document to match the currently selected printer is a default setting. If you don't want WordPerfect to change the fonts in a document when you open it, follow these steps:

1. From the document window, choose File ➤ Setup ➤ Environment (Shift+F1 E).

2. Either select or deselect Format Document For Default Printer On Open, depending on whether or not you want WordPerfect to format the document for the currently selected printer.

3. Choose OK and Close, as necessary, to return to the document window.

Assuming you cleared (deselected) the Format Document For Default Printer On Open option above, WordPerfect will do the opposite of what it usually does. That is, when you open a document, WordPerfect will select the printer that was selected when you saved that document, and not mess with the font codes at all.

This only works if you're using one computer with several different printers installed. If someone sends you a copy of a document that was created using, say, an Epson MX printer, and you don't have a driver for that printer installed, then WordPerfect has no choice but to format that document for the currently selected printer.

Getting Control over Font Substitutions

Let's suppose that you switch printers fairly often, and you're not particularly thrilled with the fact that every time you switch from Printer A to Printer B, WordPerfect converts your beautiful Swiss Sans Souci Culotte 11pt font to an awful Monospace Line Draw 16.67 cpi font. Can you do anything about that, short of manually changing the font each time you switch printers? Yes, you can.

To simplify the following discussion, I'll refer to the printer that contains the "good font" (Swiss Sans Souci...) as Printer A and the printer that does the bad substitution (Monospace Line Draw...) as Printer B.

The document's *font mapping table* decides which font will be substituted for another when you switch documents. To control font substitutions, you need to change that mapping table. Here's how:

1. Choose File ➤ Print/Fax ➤ Select, and select Printer A (the "good font" printer).

2. Open or create a document that contains the fonts you want to gain control over.

3. Now select Printer B (the one that's doing the bad substitutions).

4. Choose Font ➤ Font ➤ Setup (Ctrl+F8 Shift+F1) to reach the Font Setup dialog box.

5. Choose Edit Document Font Mapping Table. You'll see a list of fonts in the current document, with their original Printer A names.

6. Highlight the font you want to control, then choose Select Font For Printing.

7. Pick the font you want WordPerfect to substitute in the future. Your selection appears in the Font and Screen text boxes near the bottom of the dialog box.

8. Choose OK as necessary to return to the document window.

In the future, whenever you switch from Printer A to Printer B, WordPerfect will substitute the font you specified in step 7 for the font you chose in step 6.

TIP   If you want to go back to the original font substitution method at any time, choose Auto Map Font in step 6.

Understanding Automatic Font Changes (AFCs)

Let me clarify one thing: Automatic Font Changes (dubbed *AFCs* by WordPerfect Corporation) have nothing to do with font substitution. Font substitution involves multiple printers. AFCs involve font changes that WordPerfect makes within a document when you *don't* switch printers. WordPerfect would do that, for instance, if you assigned some *attribute*, such as boldface, italic, extra large, or subscript, and the currently selected font couldn't really display that attribute.

Suppose you have one Courier font, Courier 12 cpi. You tell WordPerfect to print some text in that font at Extra Large size. But WordPerfect can't make Courier 12 cpi any larger, because it's a nonscalable printer font that can only be displayed at 12 cpi. What does WordPerfect do? It checks to see if there is a similar font that *can* be displayed at an extra large size. If it finds such a font, it automatically changes to that font, so it can show your text in extra large size.

If you were to highlight the [Extra Large On] code in Reveal Codes, you might see something like this:

[Extra Large On:Letter Gothic; 17pt]

This says, "In order to show the text that follows in extra large size, I automatically switched to a Letter Gothic 17-point font."

I'd be tempted not to even bother you with that tidbit of information, were it not for the following fact: You can control exactly which font WordPerfect chooses when making these automatic font changes. Here's how:

1. Start at the document window, choose File ➤ Print/Fax ➤ Select (Shift+F7 S), and highlight the name of the printer that should make "better" font change decisions.

2. Choose Edit, then Font Setup.

3. If you want to change AFC for printer fonts, choose Edit Automatic Font Changes For Printer Fonts. If you want to change AFC for graphics fonts, choose Edit Automatic Font Changes For Graphics Fonts.

> **NOTE**
>
> WordPerfect can't switch from a printer font to a graphics font, or vice versa, during an automatic font change. Both fonts must be either printer fonts or graphics fonts.

4. Highlight the font that you want to control (Courier 12 cpi in my example). Then choose Edit.

5. Highlight the attribute that you want to control (for example, Extra Large Print), then choose Edit. You'll see the Select New Automatic Font Change dialog box.

6. Highlight the name of the font that you want WordPerfect to use during this automatic font change. (For example, highlight CG Times if you want WordPerfect to use that instead of Letter Gothic.)

7. Choose Select.

You'll return to the Edit Font Attribute dialog box. Using my example, that dialog box might now look something like Figure 10.7, which indicates that when the font Courier 12 cpi is in use, and you assign the Extra Large Print attribute to that font, WordPerfect will switch to CG Times.

You can repeat steps 5 through 7 for as many attributes as you wish. You can also use Next Font and Previous Font to work with other fonts. When you're done, choose OK and Close as necessary to return to the document window. WordPerfect will use the font you specified in step 6 whenever you choose the font and attribute you chose in steps 4 and 5.

Generating AFCs for New Fonts

One more thing on those AFCs. If you use the WordPerfect Font Installer to install graphics fonts from the DOS command prompt, the AFCs for those new fonts won't be generated. To bring your AFCs up to date, run WordPerfect. Choose Font ➤ Font ➤ Setup ➤ Update Graphics Fonts (Generate New AFCs for WP.DRS). Choose OK until you get back to the document window.

FIGURE 10.7

According to the Edit Font Attribute dialog box shown here, WordPerfect will automatically switch to CG Times font when you use Courier and specify the Extra Large size.

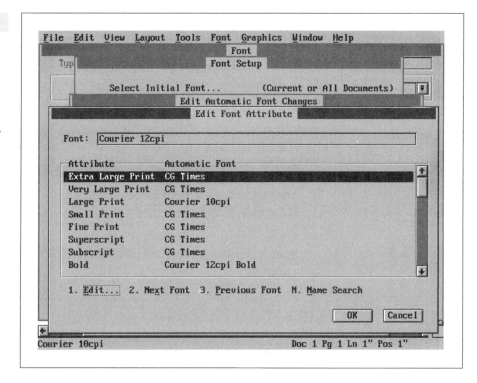

Defining How Printer Fonts Are Represented on the Screen

Suppose you choose a printer font like Albertus Extra and type some text, but it looks more like Aquiline Black on your screen. If you happen to notice the difference, you might say to yourself, "Hey! That's not the font I chose!" Yet when you look at the [Font:...] code in Reveal Codes, it certainly indicates that you chose Albertus. So what gives?

Well, when you choose a *printer font* in your document, WordPerfect goes out to the .DRS file, and locates the *graphics font* that most closely matches that printer font. Because it can't "draw" a printer font on the screen, WordPerfect uses the nearest graphics font to represent the printer font on the screen. (It *will* use the correct printer font when you print the document.)

Suppose you don't like the graphics font that WordPerfect chose, and you know of a font that would better represent that printer font. No problem. Just proceed as follows:

1. Start at the document window and choose Font ➤ Font ➤ Setup (Ctrl+F8 Shift+F1).

2. Choose Edit Screen Font Mapping Table. You'll see a list of all the printer fonts for the currently selected printer.

3. Highlight the font you want to represent differently on the screen, and choose Select Screen Font.

4. From the drop-down list that appears, choose the graphics font that best represents the font you chose in step 3, either by double-clicking or by highlighting and pressing ↵. That name now appears in the Screen text box.

5. Choose OK and Close as necessary to return to the document window.

The change will affect all documents that contain the printer font that you chose in step 3.

TIP   If you ever want to return to WordPerfect's original screen font, choose Auto Map Font in step 3.

My Fonts, Clip Art, and Photos

Sometimes people call or write about a sample document in one of my books and ask "Where did you get *that* font?" So I'll tell you a little about my personal font collection.

Many of the examples shown in this book use the built-in fonts for the LaserJet III, the LaserJet 4Si MX, and the Apple LaserWriter (PostScript)—the printers I used to create the sample documents. The samples also use many of the graphics fonts that come with WordPerfect 6.0 for DOS.

All the rest are TrueType fonts, which I've collected since TrueType was first released. The fonts are from MicroLogic's TrueType for DOS package (mentioned earlier in this chapter), Microsoft's TrueType Font Pack (for Windows), and Typecase and Typecase II (also for Windows) from Swfte (Rockland, DE). Remember, you need Windows in order to install Windows graphics fonts. But once they're installed, you can use those graphics fonts in WordPerfect 6.0 for DOS.

Most of the clip art used in my examples comes from WordPerfect, WordPerfect Presentations (both from WordPerfect Corporation), and the Presentation Task Force clip art collection mentioned in Chapter 26. I have about 8500 pieces of clip art on a hard disk, hogging about 50 MB, as well as some other clip art on CD-ROM. I used only a smattering of that collection in this book (mostly from Presentation Task Force).

I scanned the photos, logos, and signatures, using the Hewlett-Packard ScanJet IIc and the software that comes with that scanner. Actually, the scanned images that I print and send to the publisher are often photographed by the publisher's production department. So what you see in my sample documents is often a photograph-of-a-scan-of-a-photograph.

In this chapter I've covered virtually everything you need to know about mastering your printer and fonts. This concludes Part Two of the book. In Part Three, we'll look at some tools you can use to improve your typing and writing.

PART THREE

Tools to Improve Your Writing

CHAPTER

11

Auto-Checking Your Spelling

fast TRACK

● **When adding a word to a supplemental dictionary   460**

you can have the Speller skip the word during spell checks, replace it with another word, or set up a list of alternate words to choose from.

● **To choose different or additional main and supplemental dictionaries   460**

press Ctrl+F2, then click the Setup button or press Shift+F1. Next, choose one of the Chain options, select a language, and add, delete, or edit the file names of dictionary files you want to use.

● **To create supplemental dictionaries   467**

first set up your chain of supplemental dictionaries. Then press Ctrl+F2 and choose Edit Supplemental Dictionary from the Speller dialog box. Double-click the dictionary you want to edit, or use the Create New Sup button to create a new dictionary. Next, Add, Edit, Or Delete words in the supplemental dictionary.

UNLESS you happen to be the local spelling bee champ, you'll probably need to use the dictionary to check your spelling from time to time. But you can put away your old paper dictionary once and for all. WordPerfect has a built-in dictionary that's much, much quicker.

About the Speller

Before learning how to use the Speller, you should understand a little bit about how it works. It's not smart. (As we like to keep in mind, computers in general are not smart, and rate with turnips on the IQ scale.) The Speller works by comparison only. That is, it checks words in your document against its own dictionary of about 115,000 words. If it can't find a word in its dictionary, it offers a list of alternative word choices.

It's important to understand that the Speller knows nothing of context. For example, the Speller wouldn't find anything wrong with this sentence:

Due u c what eye mien?

Because the words *Due*, *eye*, and *mien* are in the dictionary, along with single letters, like *u* and *c*, the Speller finds no misspellings in the sentence. (I should point out, however, that the grammar checker discussed in Chapter 12 can help with these kinds of errors.)

Another thing that can throw the Speller off is the fact that there are many technical terms that don't appear in the dictionary, with new ones being added daily. For example, the Speller will assume that a technical term like *adrenocorticotroph* (a pituitary hormone), or its acronym ACTH, is a misspelling. A foreign word like *lilangeni* (a native word in Swaziland) will also rate as a misspelling. And, many proper names, like Simpson, are categorized as misspelled words.

None of these last examples poses any problems though. If the Speller locates a word that isn't in its dictionary, but is, nonetheless, spelled correctly, you can add that word to the dictionary on the spot. That way, it will never again be considered a misspelling when you spell-check your document.

It Checks More than Spelling

While the Speller is looking up words in its dictionary, it will also check for these other common errors:

- Typing the same word twice (*Look at the the moon*).

- Peculiar capitalization caused by pressing the Shift key too late, or for too long. For example, the Speller would notice and help you correct all the capitalization errors in *LIghten Up on tHE sHIFt kEy.*

- Typing numbers instead of letters. For example, *L1ke, I d0n't see the pr0blem* uses the number 1 for the letter L, and the number 0 for the letter O. (Computers hate it when you do that.)

When to Use the Speller

You should use the Speller just before you're ready to print a document or hand it over to someone else. After all, spell-checking takes only a few moments, and it's easy to do. What's more, it saves you the embarrassment of sending out a document that's loaded with misspellings, and it reduces the paper waste that occurs when you don't notice a mistake until the document is printed.

Using the Speller

Using the Speller is a breeze:

1. If you *don't* want to spell-check the entire document, move the cursor wherever you want to start checking your spelling. If you wish, you can select a specific block of text to check.

2. Choose <u>T</u>ools ➤ <u>W</u>riting Tools ➤ <u>S</u>peller, or use one of these shortcuts: Press Ctrl+F2, or press Alt+F1 S, or click the Speller button in the Button Bar.

3. If you selected text in step 1, the Speller just starts doing its thing. If you didn't select text first, you can tell the Speller how much material you want to check by choosing from among the following options:

   <u>**Word**</u>   Checks the spelling of the word at the cursor position.

   <u>**P**</u>**age**   Checks spelling on the current page only.

   <u>**Document**</u>   Checks spelling in the entire document.

   <u>**F**</u>**rom Cursor**   Checks spelling from the cursor position to the end of the document.

   <u>**L**</u>**ook Up Word**   Looks up the word at the cursor position. Also lets you type a word or word pattern so you can look up a word that you're not sure how to spell. (More on this under "Looking Up a Word.")

   <u>**E**</u>**dit Supplemental Dictionary**   Doesn't spell check, but rather, lets you change a supplemental dictionary. I'll explain how a little later in this chapter.

4. Once the Speller gets going, what you do next depends on what the Speller finds (if anything). The various possibilities are covered in the next few sections.

Correcting or Ignoring a "Misspelled" Word

When the Speller comes across a word that isn't in its dictionary, it displays the Word Not Found dialog box, shown in Figure 11.1. Your options at this point are described below.

Skip Once   Ignores the misspelling, this time only.

Skip in this Document   Skips the word here, and throughout the rest of the current document. The word is added to a supplemental dictionary that's stored with the document.

Add to Dictionary   Adds the misspelled word to the dictionary, so that it's never counted as a misspelling again.

FIGURE 11.1

When the Speller finds a word that's not in the dictionary, it displays this Word Not Found dialog box.

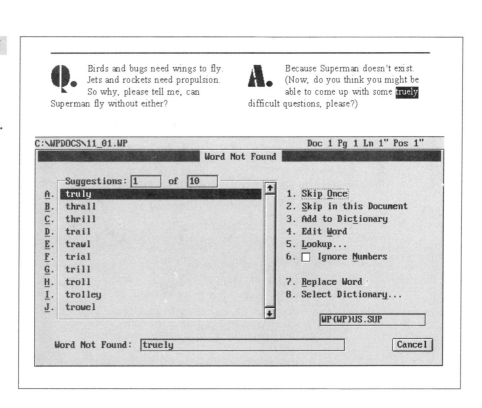

Edit Word   Lets you switch to the document and edit the misspelled word. Use the ← and → keys to move the cursor within the same line as the misspelled word, and then type your corrections. (This option is handy for inserting and deleting spaces, as when two words are run together.) Press F7 or ↵ when you're ready to continue spell-checking.

Lookup   Lets you look up another word. Type in the word or word pattern you want to look up and press ↵. You can then replace the misspelled word with one of the suggestions presented.

Ignore Numbers   If WordPerfect finds an embedded number, as in Part Code *ABJ3-01NS*, and you don't want it to count such "words" as misspellings in this document, select this option.

Replace Word   If WordPerfect lists suggestions for the misspelled word (these would be words from the dictionary that resemble what you typed), you can choose any one of the suggested words by double-clicking, or by highlighting and choosing Replace Word. The misspelled word will be replaced with the word you choose.

Select Dictionary   Lets you choose a different supplemental dictionary for words that you add using Add To Dictionary. There's more on supplemental dictionaries later in this chapter.

Correcting Double Words

If the speller finds the same word twice in a row, like *the the*, it highlights the second word and displays a dialog box like this:

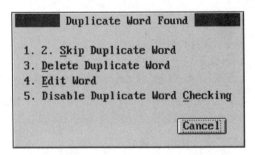

Your choices here are as follows:

Skip Duplicate Word   If the duplicate word is intentional, choose option 1 or 2 to skip it in this instance.

Delete Duplicate Word   Choose this option if you want to delete one of the duplicate words.

Edit Word   Choose this option to edit the text in your document. When you're done editing, press F7 or ↵ to return to the Speller.

Disable Duplicate Word Checking   Choose this option if you want the Speller to skip these duplicate words and stop checking for duplicate words throughout the rest of the document.

Correcting Irregular Capitalization

If the Speller finds irregular capitalization in a word, as in *THe*, it displays a dialog box like the one below.

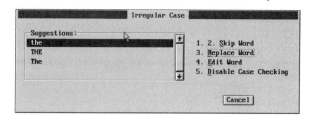

The options available are as follows:

Skip Word   Leaves the word as is.

Replace Word   You can double-click one of the suggestions in the Suggestions list (if any). Or, highlight any suggestion and choose Replace Word. The word in the text will be replaced with the one you choose.

Edit Word Choose this option to move the cursor into the document and correct the word yourself. Press F7 or ↵ when you're done.

Disable Case Checking Ignores this irregular case and stops checking for irregular case in the current document.

I should mention that sometimes this dialog box will be titled Capitalization Difference, rather than Irregular Case. The difference is that Irregular Case is triggered by any peculiar use of upper- and lowercase letters. Capitalization Difference is triggered when a word uses capitalization that's different from the capitalization of a custom word you added to the dictionary. (More on case-sensitivity in supplemental dictionaries in a moment.)

Canceling and Exiting the Speller

When the Speller has finished its job, it displays the message "Spell Check Completed." Choose OK or press ↵ to clear the message.

If you want to cancel the Speller before it has finished its job, press Escape or choose Cancel from the dialog box. Any words that have been changed so far will remain changed.

Choosing Speller Features

You can decide up front how you want the Speller to behave in this and future WordPerfect sessions. You can also change the options *before* you spell-check a document.

1. Press Ctrl+F2.

2. Choose the Setup button or press Shift+F1. You'll see the Speller Setup dialog box, with the options described below:

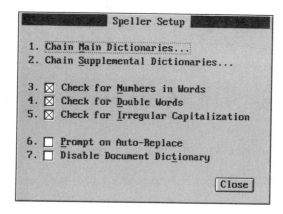

Chain... I'll explain these first two chaining options in just a bit.

Check for <u>N</u>umbers in Words Enables or disables checking for embedded numbers in words.

Check for <u>D</u>ouble Words Enables or disables checking for double words.

Check for <u>I</u>rregular Capitalization Enables or disables checking for irregular capitalization.

<u>P</u>rompt on Auto-Replace If you select this option, the Speller will prompt you before changing a word that you've previously designated as "auto-replace" (this is described under "Changing a Supplemental Dictionary," later in this chapter). If you clear this option, the Speller will auto-replace without prompting first.

Disable Document Dic<u>t</u>ionary If you select this option, the Speller will stop at misspelled words that you previously ignored in the current document only. If you leave this option cleared, the Speller will continue to skip those words in the current document.

3. Choose Close or press F7 twice to return to your document.

Remember that the selections you make in the Speller Setup dialog box stay in effect through the current session and through all future WordPerfect sessions, that is, up until the time you change the options again.

Looking Up a Word

You can use WordPerfect's Speller to look up a word's spelling before you type it. To do so, just follow these steps:

1. Choose Tools ➤ Writing Tools ➤ Speller, or press Ctrl+F2.

2. Choose Look Up Word. The Look Up Word dialog box will appear, the Speller will highlight the word the cursor is on (if any), and that word will appear in the Word or Word Pattern text box.

3. Type a new word or word pattern, or edit the existing word in the text box. Then press Tab or ↵. You'll see a list of words that are similar in pronunciation or construction to the word you typed. (The word you typed will appear in the list if it's in the Speller's dictionary.)

NOTE   The Speller looks up words in the main dictionaries only. It ignores the supplemental dictionaries.

4. From here, you can take any of the following steps:

- Choose the Word or Word Pattern option to look up another word (return to step 3).
- Choose Cancel to exit the dialog box.
- Add one of the words to your document. To do this, double-click the word you want, highlight the word, and press ↵, or type the underlined letter next to the word.

5. WordPerfect may ask if you want to add the word to your text or replace the currently selected word (if any). Choose <u>Y</u>es or <u>N</u>o, as appropriate.

Using Wildcards with Lookup

When you type a word to look up, you can use the question mark (?) and asterisk (*) wildcards to stand for letters you're not sure about. These wildcards replace a single letter or group of letters within a word. The Speller will scan the dictionary and look for any words that match the letters and wildcards you've specified.

The ? wildcard stands for a single character in a word. For example, if you type **?ing**, the Speller will show all four-letter words in its dictionary that end in *ing*.

The * wildcard stands for a group of any number of letters (from no letters to all the letters in the word). Typing ***ing** displays all words (of any length) that end in *ing*. This can be a real boon to poets searching for the perfect rhyme. But watch out! You can end up with a long, long list if you do this.

N O T E   WordPerfect Corporation also offers a product called Rhymer, which is specifically designed to find rhyming words.

The * and ? wildcards can appear anywhere in a word, and you can use ? and * together to create a search. For example, the combination **i?p*** will find any word that starts with *i*, has a *p* in its third position, and ends with any combination of characters. As the example below shows, there are over 500 such words!

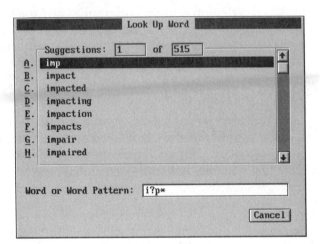

Disabling the Speller

You can temporarily disable the Speller and the grammar checker in any part of your document. This is particularly useful in passages that contain foreign words or technical terms that *you* know are correct, but that will give your writing tools fits. To disable the writing tools temporarily, follow these steps:

1. Move the cursor to where you want to disable spell-checking and grammar-checking. To disable checking in the entire document, place the cursor at the beginning of the document (press Home Home ↑).

2. Choose Tools ➤ Writing tools, or press Writing Tools (Alt+F1).

3. Check the Disable Speller/Grammatik box.

WordPerfect will insert a hidden [Speller/Grammatik:Off] code at the cursor location. You can delete this code if you change your mind later.

To enable the tools in another part of the document, move the cursor to where you want spell-checking and grammar-checking to resume. Then repeat step 2, and clear (deselect) the Disable Speller/Grammatik option.

Understanding the Speller Dictionaries

When the Speller is doing its job, it generally looks up words in three separate dictionaries in this order: the document's supplemental dictionary, the general supplemental dictionary, and the main dictionary. Each of these dictionaries is described below.

The Document's Supplemental Dictionary

The document's supplemental dictionary (also called the *document-specific* dictionary) is stored with the document. Initially, it's empty. However, each time you choose Skip In This Document during a spell check, WordPerfect stores the highlighted word in the document's supplemental dictionary. That's how the Speller knows to skip future occurrences of that word in the current document (only).

The General Supplemental Dictionary

WordPerfect's general supplemental dictionary file has the file name WP{WP}xx.SUP, where xx is the abbreviation for the dictionary's language. For example, the default supplemental dictionary in the United States is WP{WP}US.SUP.

Whenever you choose Add To Dictionary during a spell check, WordPerfect adds the highlighted word to this general supplemental dictionary.

WordPerfect always opens this dictionary when you do a spell check, so any word that's included in this dictionary is not counted as a misspelling—in *any* document.

The Main Dictionary

The main dictionary is the one that contains the 115,000 or so words most often used in everyday English. This dictionary is stored on the WordPerfect shared programs directory—typically C:\WPCDOS60—in a file named WP*xx*.LEX. Again, *xx* is the abbreviation for the dictionary's language. For example, the main dictionary file is called WPUS.LEX in the United States.

Because the main dictionary is by far the largest of the three dictionaries, WordPerfect always checks this dictionary last. You can speed up spell-checking by customizing your supplemental dictionaries to ward off spelling errors that you make often. We'll talk about that next.

Personalizing the Speller

If you understand the roles of the various dictionaries WordPerfect uses, you can further customize the Speller. For example if, like many people, you have a habit of typing *hte* instead of *the* you can tell WordPerfect not to bother prompting you to correct this misspelling. Instead, when it finds *hte* it will automatically change it to *the*. It doesn't bother looking up *hte* in the main dictionary and presenting umpteen different suggestions. This simplifies and speeds up the spell-checking process.

Changing a Supplemental Dictionary

The best way to personalize the Speller is to modify the supplemental dictionaries. As I mentioned earlier, during a spell check, the document-specific dictionary is automatically updated whenever you choose Skip In This Document. The general supplemental dictionary is updated whenever you choose Add To Dictionary.

This technique of updating the supplemental dictionaries can't solve every problem, however. For example, if you tend to type things like *don;t* instead of *don't* the Speller will always pester you to correct that mistake. There is no way to tell the Speller to change *don;t* to *don't* except by editing the supplemental dictionary yourself.

To get started, you first need to follow the steps below.

WARNING

If you want to include several supplemental dictionaries in this procedure, be sure to add those dictionaries to the *chain* first, as discussed later in this chapter.

1. Press Ctrl+F2 (Speller), then choose Edit Supplemental Dictionary.

2. Choose which dictionary you'd like to customize by double-clicking or by highlighting and choosing Edit (or pressing ↵). You can choose the dictionary that's specific to the document you're working on at the moment, or (more likely) the general supplemental dictionary WP{WP}US.SUP (in the United States).

3. The Edit Supplemental Dictionary dialog box appears, as shown in Figure 11.2.

We'll take a look at the various things you can do in this dialog box in the sections that follow. But first, you should understand some basic concepts about how the supplemental dictionary works.

- When you add words to the supplemental dictionary, lowercase is considered to be the same as uppercase, but not vice versa. For example, if you add *dBASE* to your supplemental dictionary, the Speller will accept it (without pointing out the irregular case). It will also accept DBASE, because the lowercase *d* "matches" the uppercase *D*. However, the Speller will still point out other capitalization differences, such as *Dbase*, which has a lowercase *b*, and *dBaSe*, which is just plain funky.

FIGURE 11.2

Use the Edit Supplemental Dictionary dialog box to auto-replace certain words, and to add, edit, and delete words from your supplemental dictionary.

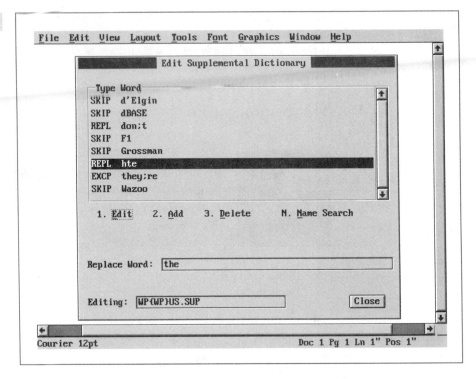

- WordPerfect will alphabetize your supplemental dictionary automatically, so you don't need to enter new words in any particular order.

- The automatic hyphenation feature (Chapter 16) uses the same *main* dictionaries as the Speller. It does not look at any supplemental dictionaries. When adding words to your supplemental dictionaries, be sure that you *don't* type in hyphens, because they're treated as spaces during a spell-check. For example, if you mistakenly add the word *Den-dro-bium* to your supplemental dictionary instead of *Dendrobium*, WordPerfect will treat your entry as three different words: *Den*, *dro*, and *bium*. The only way to add a hyphenated word to the Speller's dictionary is to fire up the Spell utility (described later in this chapter), select a main dictionary, and use the Add Word(s) to Dictionary option.

- If you want to add a hyphenated name, like *Grossman-Wazoo*, to the dictionary, just make two separate entries: one for Grossman and another for Wazoo. (You can do this by choosing Add To Dictionary during a normal spell check.)

Auto-Replacing, Skipping, and Listing Suggestions

While you're in the Edit Supplemental Dictionary dialog box, you can choose <u>A</u>dd to add a new word to the dictionary. You'll see these options in the Add To Supplemental dialog box:

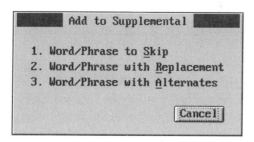

```
╔══════════ Add to Supplemental ══════════╗

  1. Word/Phrase to Skip
  2. Word/Phrase with Replacement
  3. Word/Phrase with Alternates

                              ┌────────┐
                              │ Cancel │
                              └────────┘
```

Word/Phrase to <u>S</u>kip   If you simply want the Speller to skip a word, choose this option.

Word/Phrase with <u>R</u>eplacement   If you want the Speller to replace a word automatically (for example, replace *don;t* with *don't*), choose this option.

Word/Phrase with <u>A</u>lternates   If you want the Speller to give you some choices when it finds the word, choose this option.

What happens next depends on which option you chose. If you chose the Word/Phrase to <u>S</u>kip option, you'll see this dialog box:

```
╔══════════ Add Word/Phrase To Skip ══════════╗

  Word: ▁_____

                        ┌──────┐  ┌────────┐
                        │  OK  │  │ Cancel │
                        └──────┘  └────────┘
```

Here, you can type in a word or phrase for the Speller to ignore, and then choose OK. The word will appear next to SKIP in the list of words.

If you chose the second option, Word/Phrase With Replacement, you'll see a dialog box like this:

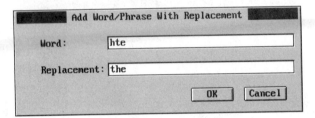

Type in the erroneous word you want to replace and the word you want to replace it with. In the example above, I've told the Speller to replace *hte* with *the*. Choose OK after typing the words. The erroneous word will appear next to REPL (replace) in the list.

If you chose the Word/Phrase with Alternates option, you'll be taken to the dialog box shown in Figure 11.3. There you can fill in the erroneous

FIGURE 11.3

The Add Word/Phrase With Alternates dialog box lets you identify an erroneous word and come up with a list of suggestions for correcting it.

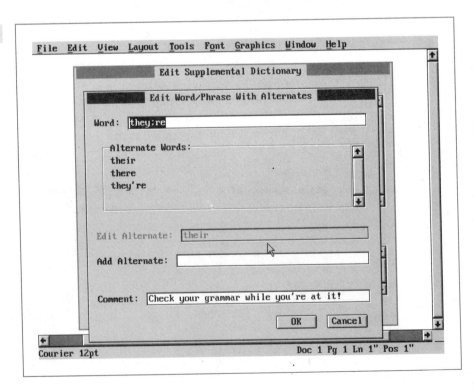

word and use the Add Alternate button to create a list of alternatives. You can also add a comment of your own.

In my example, I've told the Speller that when it finds *they;re*, it's to give me the following choices: *they're*, *their*, and *there*. I've also added a little note to myself in the Comment text box. Later, when I run a spell check and the Speller finds *they;re* in my document, it will display the dialog box below (note that the alternatives are always listed in alphabetical order—not necessarily the order you typed them in).

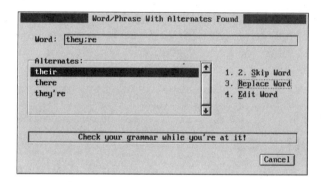

The erroneous word (*they;re* in my example) appears next to EXCP in the list.

Deleting a Word from the Supplemental Dictionary

What happens if the Speller finds a misspelled word in your document and you choose Add To Dictionary, but later, you realize that the word really *was* misspelled. In that case, you don't want the Speller to skip that word after all.

No problem. Just get to the Edit Supplemental Dictionary dialog box and, if necessary, use Name Search to look up the word that you want to get rid of. When the highlight is on that word, just choose <u>D</u>elete or press the Delete key, and then choose <u>Y</u>es when prompted for permission.

Editing a Word in the Supplemental Dictionary

If you want to improve any changes you've made to the supplemental dictionary, just go to the Edit Supplemental Dictionary dialog box, as discussed earlier. Then highlight the word you want to change and choose Edit. You'll be taken back to the dialog box you used to add that word, where you can make whatever changes you like.

The one thing you can't do with Edit is change a SKIP, REPL, or EXCP type to another type. Instead, you'll need to delete the entry in your supplementary dictionary, then add it again using the Add command, followed by the type of entry you want to make.

Closing the Edit Supplemental Dialog Box

To save the changes you made in the Edit Supplemental Dictionary dialog box, just choose Close or OK (or press F7) as necessary to work your way back to the document window. All your changes will be saved automatically.

Using Foreign Language Dictionaries

If you write in a foreign language, or regularly use foreign language words in your English documents, you might want to consider purchasing a separate foreign language dictionary from WordPerfect Corporation. The documentation that comes with it will explain how to install the dictionary.

There are several ways to use the foreign language dictionary. If you are working *solely* in the foreign language, you can just use that dictionary by itself. To do so, choose File ➤ Setup ➤ Environment ➤ Language (or press Shift+F1 EL) and select a language from the list. From that point on, WordPerfect will use only the dictionary you specified. (To return to English, you'll need to repeat the procedure and choose the English-U.S. dictionary.)

A second alternative is to switch from one language dictionary to another within the document. Move the cursor to wherever you want to begin using a different language dictionary. Then choose Layout ➤ Other ➤ Language. Choose the language dictionary you want and choose OK. WordPerfect inserts a hidden [Lang:...] code at the cursor position. During a spell check, WordPerfect will switch to that other dictionary the moment it comes across this code. You can add as many [Lang:...] codes to your document as you wish.

A third alternative is to *chain* the dictionaries (chaining dictionaries is discussed a little later on in the chapter). That way, you can use the English language dictionary and a foreign language dictionary simultaneously. This would come in handy, say, if you're writing a tutorial on a particular language, and both English words and foreign words are dispersed throughout the document.

Creating Your Own Supplemental Dictionaries

If you do a lot of word processing for a variety of professions, you might want to consider creating your own independent supplemental dictionaries. For example, you might create a supplemental dictionary of medical terms (and perhaps name it MEDICAL.SUP). If you work with an orchidist, you might create a supplemental dictionary containing orchid names and terminology.

The value of having these separate, specialized dictionaries is that it keeps each dictionary small. That, in turn, makes each one easier to manage. Also, the spell-checking process goes faster when you use a particular supplemental dictionary, as opposed to *all* your supplemental dictionaries.

To create a specialized supplemental dictionary, follow the steps below:

1. Press Ctrl+F2, then choose Edit Supplemental Dictionary.

2. Choose Create New Sup.

3. Enter a file name, with the .SUP extension, for this new dictionary, and choose OK.

4. Type the word to add. You might want to add just a couple of words for starters, using the Add command and Word/Phrase To Skip (or one of the other options described earlier).

5. Repeat steps 1–5 to add as many terms as you wish. Then choose Close or press F7 twice to get back to the document window.

Chaining Dictionaries

If you want to use more than one dictionary during a spell check, or you want to use specialized supplemental dictionaries that you've created, you need to *chain* those dictionaries. A chain is simply a list of dictionary files that the Speller will search for words.

Suppose, for example, that you write articles for medical journals in both English and Spanish. You've purchased English and Spanish main dictionaries from WordPerfect Corporation, and you've set up some English and Spanish supplemental dictionaries that contain specialized medical terminology. Figure 11.4 illustrates this scenario.

Here, the main dictionaries are WPES.LEX (Spanish) and WPUS.LEX (English). I've chained two supplemental Spanish dictionaries, named WP{WP}ES.SUP and MEDICAL.SUP, and two supplemental English dictionaries, named WP{WP}US.SUP and MEDICAL.SUP.

When the Speller sees the [Lang:] code for Spanish, it will use the document's supplemental dictionary, the two Spanish supplemental dictionaries, and the Spanish main dictionary. When it finds the [Lang:] code for English, it will switch to the two English supplemental dictionaries and the English main dictionary (while continuing to use the document's supplemental dictionary).

FIGURE 11.4

How the Speller uses dictionary chains to spell check a document in multiple languages

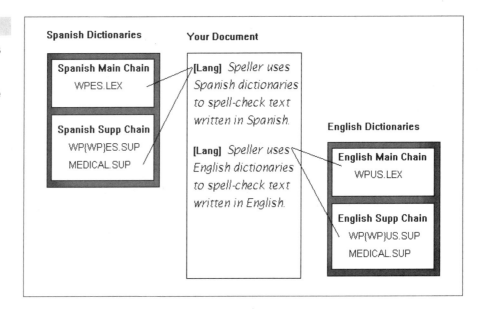

TIP You can reuse supplemental dictionaries in different chains, as I've done here with MEDICAL.SUP.

Setting up a Dictionary Chain

Here's how to set up a dictionary chain and add dictionaries to it:

1. Press Ctrl+F2.

2. Click the Setup button or press Shift+F1. You'll see the Speller Setup dialog box shown earlier.

3. Now choose one of the two Chain options presented.

   • To set up or edit a main dictionary (.LEX) chain, select Chain Main Dictionaries. Remember that the Speller looks through main dictionaries *after* it checks the document supplemental and general supplemental dictionaries.

   • To set up or edit a supplemental dictionary (.SUP) chain, select Chain Supplemental Dictionaries.

4. You'll see the Dictionary Chains dialog box shown here.

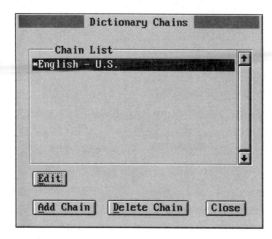

5. Choose one of the options below, depending on what you want to do:

- If you want set up a *new* language chain (for example, the Spanish chain), choose <u>A</u>dd Chain. Next, select the language you want to use, by highlighting it and choosing OK (or by double-clicking the language name). Make sure you choose a language for which you've already purchased and installed a dictionary.

- If you want to add a dictionary to an *existing* chain, highlight the language chain you want to use in the Chain List, and choose <u>E</u>dit.

NOTE You can create up to six supplemental chains and six main language chains, and each chain can include up to six dictionaries. Whenever you create a new language chain, the default dictionary for that language is added to the chain automatically.

6. If the dictionary you want to add to the chain isn't already in the list, choose <u>A</u>dd To Chain.

7. Type the name of the dictionary you want to add to the chain, or press F5 and use the file list to choose the file by name. In the example below, I've included WP{WP}US.SUP (the general supplemental dictionary), as well as MEDICAL.SUP, in the chain.

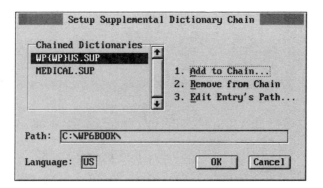

WARNING   The chains for a given language should include dictionaries for that language only. Also, be careful not to mix main dictionaries in with supplemental dictionary chains and vice versa, or the Speller won't work correctly.

8. Repeat steps 6 and 7 if you wish to add more dictionaries to the chain.

9. Choose OK and Close as necessary to return to your document.

When you spell-check a document, the Speller will use all the dictionaries you've chained for the language that's currently selected. Keep in mind that if you're using multiple language dictionaries, spell checking will take longer.

Changing a Dictionary Chain

You can change dictionary chains in three ways:

- If you're no longer using a particular language to spell-check documents, you can delete the entire chain for that language.

- If you no longer want WordPerfect to look through a particular dictionary for misspelled words, you can delete that dictionary from the chain. This speeds up spell-checking considerably.

- If you've moved a dictionary to another directory on the disk, you can tell WordPerfect the new location of that dictionary.

Here's how to update a dictionary chain.

1. Press Ctrl+F2.

2. Choose Setup or press Shift+F1.

3. In the Speller Setup dialog box, choose Chain Main Dictionaries (if you want to update a main dictionary chain), or Chain Supplemental Dictionaries (if you want to update a supplemental dictionary chain). You'll see the Dictionary Chains dialog box.

4. If you want to delete an entire chain, highlight the language chain you want to delete and choose Delete Chain.

5. If you want to delete an individual dictionary from a chain, or tell WordPerfect to look for a dictionary in a different directory, highlight the language chain for that dictionary and choose Edit. Next, highlight the dictionary you want to work with, and choose one of these options:

   - If you want to delete the dictionary from the chain, choose Remove From Chain.

   - If you want WordPerfect to look for the dictionary in a different directory, choose Edit Entry's Path, type in the new directory location, and choose OK.

   - If you've changed the name of a dictionary, first delete it from the chain (choose Remove From Chain), and then add it to the chain (choose Add To Chain).

6. Choose OK and Close, as necessary, to return to the document window.

Keep in mind that none of the changes above deletes or moves the dictionary files themselves. They only tell WordPerfect how to find the dictionaries (or whether to look for them at all).

Which Supplemental Dictionary Gets Updated?

The next time you spell-check a document, the Speller will use the supplemental dictionaries you specified in the supplemental dictionary chain. When it finds a word that's not in *any* of the dictionaries, it will present the usual options to Skip, Ignore, and so forth.

If you want to *add* the currently highlighted word to one of your supplemental dictionaries, you can choose Select Dictionary near the bottom of the Word Not Found dialog box. Choose whichever dictionary you want to add the word to by double-clicking, or by highlighting and pressing ↵. Then choose Add To Dictionary.

Using the SPELL.EXE Utility

As in previous versions of WordPerfect, Version 6.0 comes with an optional Spell utility. With all the flexibility built into the new Speller, it seems unlikely that you'll ever need to use this utility, except perhaps to convert some existing WordPerfect 5.*x* supplemental files to 6.0 format. So here I'll just tell you how to get the Spell utility started. Then, you can choose whichever options seem appropriate from the menus that appear:

1. Exit WordPerfect (choose File ➤ Exit WP or press Home F7). Save your work, if prompted.

2. When you get to the DOS command prompt, switch to the WordPerfect 6.0 shared directory, typically C:\WPC60DOS. (You would type **cd \wpc60dos** and press ↵ at the command prompt.)

3. Type **spell** and press ⏎. You'll see the Speller And Hyphenation Utility menu, shown in Figure 11.5.

N O T E   If DOS can't find or load the Spell utility, you may need to install it from the WordPerfect 6.0 for DOS Utilities disk. Please refer to the documentation that came with your WordPerfect package for installation instructions.

The name of the currently selected dictionary (the one your actions will affect) appears near the top of the list. Here's a brief explanation of each option:

Change\Create Dictionary   Lets you choose a different main dictionary to work with in the Spell utility

Add Word(s) to Dictionary   Lets you add words to the main dictionary. You can add words from the keyboard or a file, and you can add hyphenated words if you wish.

FIGURE 11.5

The Speller and Hyphenation Utility menu

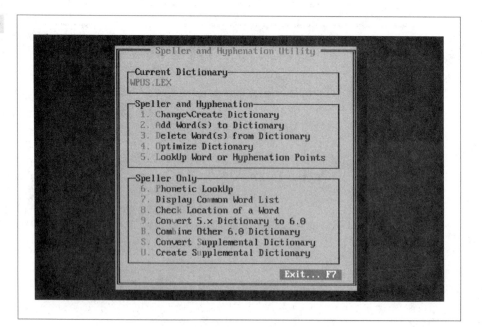

Delete Word(s) from Dictionary   Lets you delete words from the main dictionary. You can delete words from the keyboard or a file.

Optimize Dictionary   After adding words to or deleting words from the main dictionary, you can use this option to compress the file and speed up spell-checking later. (This can take a *long* time— perhaps several hours with a large main dictionary.)

Look Up Word or Hyphenation Points   Lets you take a quick look at a word in the main dictionary and view its hyphenation points.

Phonetic Look Up   As in the Speller, lets you look up a word in the main dictionary by sound or patterns (for example, you can look up words that sound like "kwik").

Display Common Word List   Displays the main dictionary's common word list (the words it checks first because of their frequent use).

Check Location of a Word   Displays which main dictionary word list contains a word that you type in. (The result will be "Not Found in Dictionary," "Found in Common Word Area," or "Found in Main Word Area.")

Convert 5.x Dictionary to 6.0   Lets you convert a WordPerfect 5.x dictionary to 6.0 format.

Combine Other 6.0 Dictionary   Lets you combine another main dictionary into the current main dictionary, as an alternative to chaining the dictionaries.

Convert Supplemental Dictionary   Lets you convert a supplemental dictionary to a simple list of words in WordPerfect 6.0 format. You can edit the list as you would any normal WordPerfect file, or convert it to ASCII Text format (see Chapters 20 and 33) for export to a different program's Speller. Of course, you'll have to check that program's documentation to be sure that it accepts exported dictionaries.

Create Supplemental Dictionary   Lets you create a new supplemental dictionary from a pre-typed list of words stored in a WordPerfect 6.0 document file.

If you want to create a supplemental dictionary from a WordPerfect 6.0 document file, make sure that you type each word on a separate line, by pressing ↵ at the end of each word. Choose File ➤ Close ➤ Yes when you're done typing the list. Give the file a name like ORCHIDS.TXT, keep track of which directory it's in, then exit WordPerfect and return to DOS.

Next, run the Spell utility, and choose Create Supplemental Dictionary. When prompted, type the name of your WordPerfect file in the 6.0 Filename text box (for example, C:\WPDOCS\ORCHIDS.TXT) and press ↵. Then type the name for your new supplemental dictionary in the Supplemental Filename text box (e.g., C:\WPC60DOS\ORCHIDS.SUP) and press ↵. Choose OK to create the dictionary. You can then go back to WordPerfect and use options described earlier in this chapter to chain, or modify, that new supplemental dictionary.

If you exported another program's dictionary to an ASCII text file, you can use it to create a supplemental dictionary. First, however, you need to convert the ASCII file to a WordPerfect 6.0 file. That's easy. Just start up WordPerfect and open the text file (File ➤ Open). When WordPerfect asks you to select the file's format, choose Select or press ↵ to accept the suggested ASCII text format. Now, choose File ➤ Save As, type a *different* file name (so that you don't replace the original text file), and choose Format. From the drop-down list, select *WordPerfect 6.0* and then choose OK. Finally, choose File ➤ Exit WP and return to the DOS prompt. Now run the Spell utility to create your new supplemental dictionary, as described above.

In this chapter, you've learned about the Speller, a powerful tool that helps you make every document "word perfect." You've also learned how to customize the Speller and create your own dictionaries of specialized terms.

Next we'll look at Grammatik, a writing tool that checks your grammar and writing style. Grammatik may not turn you into an Abraham Lincoln or an Ernest Hemingway, but at least you'll be able to avoid writing documents that read like the fine print in an insurance policy.

CHAPTER

12

Auto-Checking Your Grammar

fast TRACK

PROOFREADING a document involves more than just checking your spelling and confirming that you've dotted all your *i*'s and crossed all your *t*'s. It also involves reading your writing to make sure that it is appropriate for your intended audience, it gets the message across, and it uses the mother tongue properly and with style.

Of course, there's no substitute for careful editing and rewriting to hone your work to a rapier edge. However, WordPerfect's built-in grammar checker—appropriately named *Grammatik*—can do some of the work for you. Moreover, it can increase your awareness of how you write, and it can even help you break sloppy writing habits.

What Grammatik Can Do for You

Grammatik (rhymes with *dramatic*) is a writing tool that checks your spelling, identifies grammatical errors, points out poor writing style, and suggests corrections or revisions.

But as effective as Grammatik is, it cannot take the place of a critical human eye. As you know, few people ever agree completely about what makes writing "good" or "bad." Therefore, you certainly shouldn't rely solely on a computer program that's just following a bunch of predefined rules to come up with its suggestions. Some of those suggestions will make a lot of sense; others will be downright silly. The idea is to use Grammatik as a *tool*, not as a substitute for your own common sense and creativity. One thing is certain, though: If you work with Grammatik for a while, your prose probably *won't* read like the fine print in an insurance policy.

T I P

Like WordPerfect's Speller, Grammatik's spell checker can identify misspelled words, duplicate words, and capitalization errors. However, you can save yourself some time and frustration by running your document through WordPerfect's Speller first—it's faster, smarter, and more flexible. With misspelled words out of the way, you can then use Grammatik to focus on your *writing* problems.

Using Grammatik

Here's the quickest way to get up and running with Grammatik:

1. Open the file you want to work with in WordPerfect. (This step is optional; you can open a file directly in Grammatik, as explained in step 3.)

2. Choose Tools ➤ Writing Tools ➤ Grammatik, press Alt+F1 G, or click the Grammatik button in the Button Bar. You'll see the opening screen shown in Figure 12.1.

3. If the file you want to check is not open, type **O** or choose File ➤ Open from the menu bar and select the file you want to check. The screen provides complete instructions for selecting files.

4. Type **I** to begin checking your document interactively or **T** to get statistical information about the document.

5. Follow the prompts on the screen.

To exit the program and return to WordPerfect, press Esc until you return to the main menu. Then press **Q**, choose File ➤ Quit, or press Esc and choose Yes.

Of course, there's a lot more to using Grammatik than the steps above might suggest. Let's take a closer look.

FIGURE 12.1

Grammatik's opening screen

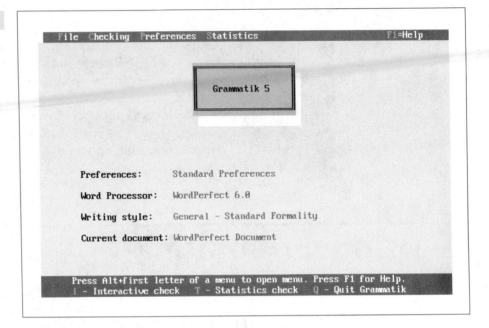

Getting Around in Grammatik

Grammatik is an easy program to get around in. The screen provides helpful prompts and shortcuts at all times. In addition, most of what you already know about getting around in WordPerfect applies here as well.

TIP

The Escape (Esc) key says, "let me out." Just press or click Esc to back out of any screen or operation.

Choosing Options from Menus

To open a menu, simply click on its name in the menu bar at the top of the screen. You can also press the Alt key plus the colored or highlighted letter to open a menu.

Once you've opened a menu, you can select options from it. Click the option you want with your mouse, or use the arrow keys to highlight an option and then press ↵.

Instead of choosing options from the menus, you can often press shortcut keys or function keys to get to work right away. Available shortcut keys appear at the bottom of the opening screen (see Figure 12.1) and at other positions on other Grammatik screens. You'll also see shortcut keys next to some options when you open a menu. (I'll show these as underlined hotkeys in this chapter.)

The example below shows the opened Checking menu from Grammatik's main screen:

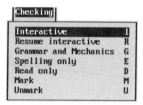

From here, you could select an option by clicking on the option or by pressing the shortcut letter that appears next to the option. If you look back at Figure 12.1, where the menu isn't pulled down, you'll see other ways to select options:

- Click on or press the letter **I**, **T**, or **Q** (each is highlighted at the bottom of the screen).

- Type any shortcut key that Grammatik recognizes for the current screen. On the main screen, the shortcut keys include I, T, and Q, as well as R, G, E, D, M, and U (shown in the Checking menu above). Other shortcut keys are available on the File, Preferences, and Statistics menus.

Getting Help

Grammatik's online help is really quite remarkable. Not only does it offer complete guidance on how to use the program at every step, but it also can give you a great education on grammar and good writing. There are three ways to get help from Grammatik:

- If you'd like help with whatever you're doing at the moment, simply press F1.

- If you'd like help with a particular menu option, open the menu you're interested in, then use the arrow keys to highlight the option you want. Finally, press F1 and then ↵.

- If you'd like to learn more about general help topics, return to Grammatik's main screen, then press F1. Now, click on the topic you're interested in, or highlight the topic and press ↵. The general topic options are Opening Screen, Opening Menu Bar, Rule Classes, Commands, Word Processor, Writing, and Glossary.

When you're done reading a Help screen, simply press Esc until you return to the screen you came from.

A Dramatic Grammatik Sample Session

Now that you know your way around Grammatik, let's look at a quick interactive session with the program. Figure 12.2 shows a sample business letter named TOUR.DOC, which I'll use to demonstrate Grammatik. As you can see, this document has many problems.

FIGURE 12.2

A business letter that
could really use
Grammatik's help

November 9, 1993
Wanda Granolabar, Vice President
WANDOLA ENGINEERING CORPORATION
2230 Strappman Avenue
Strappman, CA 92147

Dear Ms. Granolabar:

Thank you for giving Hanley and I the opportunity to submit the attached proposal. It
is always a pleazure doing business with your firm.

Quality and excellence is reflected in every office facility htat we design. All ready
this year we have won three awards. We pride ourselves on our ability to deliver
well-engineered designs within budget constraints. We have yet to miss a deadline in
our many years of operation, our ten-year anniversary was celebrated last year. We
are familiar with your staff's needs due to the fact that we worked with you two years
ago on the parking garage project. As you may recall, that interior, designed by
Hanley, was given an award.

Our Human Factors study report shows that the best use of office space is to divide
the room into nine cubicles, 4 private offices, and 2 shared offices. Statistics indicate
that most workers prefer private spaces that are in close proximity to the people they
work with. The same principle applies to managers and chief executives. According
to our research, the number of Worker Compensation claims among employees who
suffer from a from of repetitive motion syndrome or other similar problems, such as
neck or back pain, greatly decreases when employees use high-quality, adjustable
chairs and desks..

We have forwarded a copy of this proposal to your Operations Manager, W. B.
Hickox, as requested. Thank you for taking the time to review this proposal.

Sincerely,

M. Kim Cozee, Human Factors Consultant
Hanley Blake, Inferior Designer
PROFESSIONAL OFFICE DESIGNS

Checking the Document for Problems

Suppose you've just typed and saved the sample TOUR.DOC file and
now you want to check it for spelling, grammar, and writing style. (You
might want to go ahead and type this file. That way, you'll be able to follow
the sample session on your own computer.)

To start checking this document, press Alt+F1 G, and then press or click **I**.

1. The first problem Grammatik finds is the "misspelled" word *Granolabar* (see Figure 12.3). This word is OK, so we can do any of the following:

   - Choose F10 to skip this problem and go on to the next one.
   - Choose F7 to have Grammatik add this word to its spelling dictionary.
   - Choose F5 to ignore this word in the document and go on to the next problem. Let's choose this option.

N O T E

After you press F5 to ignore a word, Grammatik will continue to ignore the word until you exit the program and open it again.

FIGURE 12.3

Grammatik thinks "Granolabar" is a misspelled word.

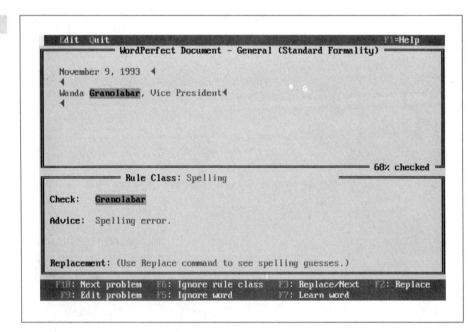

```
  Edit  Quit                                                    F1=Help
 ┌──────────────── WordPerfect Document - General (Standard Formality) ─────┐
 │                                                                          │
 │ November 9, 1993 ◄                                                       │
 │ ◄                                                                        │
 │ Wanda Granolabar, Vice President◄                                        │
 │ ◄                                                                        │
 │                                                                          │
 │                                                                          │
 │                                                                          │
 │                                                          68% checked ────│
 ├──────────────── Rule Class: Spelling ────────────────────────────────────┤
 │ Check:   Granolabar                                                      │
 │                                                                          │
 │ Advice:  Spelling error.                                                 │
 │                                                                          │
 │ Replacement: (Use Replace command to see spelling guesses.)             │
 └──────────────────────────────────────────────────────────────────────────┘
   F10: Next problem   F6: Ignore rule class   F3: Replace/Next   F2: Replace
   F9: Edit problem    F5: Ignore word         F7: Learn word
```

2. Next, Grammatik stops at *WANDOLA*, which it also thinks is misspelled. Press F5 again.

3. Another stop at *Strappman*. Press F5 to ignore this "misspelling."

4. Now Grammatik finds the grammar problem shown in Figure 12.4 and suggests replacing *I* with *me*. That's the right thing to do, so choose F3 to replace the word and go on to the next problem.

TIP   To cancel proofreading at any time and discard any changes you've made, press Ctrl+C, then choose Yes.

5. The next problem is the misspelled word *pleazure*. Press or click F3 to see a list of suggested replacements. Choose *pleasure* by double-clicking it or highlighting the word and pressing ↵. Grammatik moves on to the next problem.

6. Grammatik finds another spelling error, *htat*. This word is obviously wrong, so press or click F3, choose *that* from the list, and move on to the next problem.

FIGURE 12.4

Grammatik notices incorrect use of the object pronoun "I" and suggests replacing it with "me."

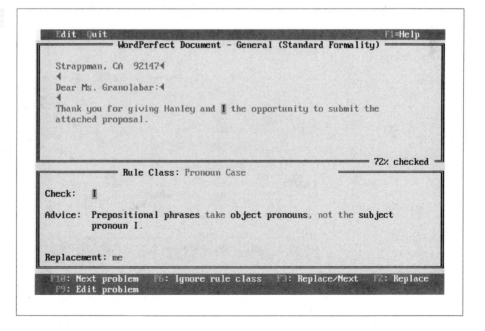

7. Now Grammatik catches the incorrect use of *is* in the first sentence of the second paragraph ("Quality and excellence is reflected…"). Again, press F3 to replace *is* with *are* and move on.

8. Our next stop is the problem shown in Figure 12.5—that dreaded bugaboo *passive voice*. That's going to take a rewrite, so press or click F9 and use your mouse, arrow keys, and other editing keys to change the sentence as shown below. When you're done making changes, press F10 to continue to the next problem.

Every office facility that we design reflects our commitment to quality and excellence.

TIP

You can press the Insert key to toggle between Insert mode and Typeover mode, just as in WordPerfect. Press Home to move the cursor to the start of a line, or press End to move it to the end of a line.

FIGURE 12.5

Grammatik doesn't like passive voice and suggests that we revise the sentence.

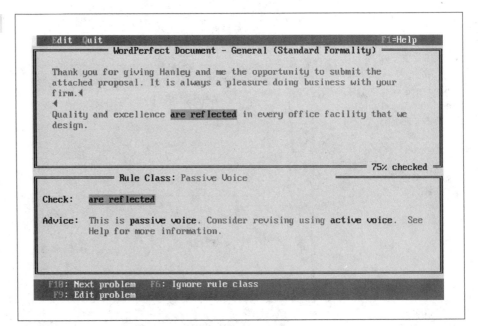

9. Next, Grammatik chokes on *All ready* and suggests replacing it with *already*. Choose F3 to accept the suggestion and move on.

10. Figure 12.6 shows problems with run-on sentences. Press F9, rewrite the sentences as shown below, and press F10.

   We celebrated our ten-year anniversary last year, and haven't missed a single deadline yet.

11. Next, Grammatik complains that our correction in step 10 introduced the word *haven't*, which might be too informal. That word seems fine (to me, anyway), so press F10 to move on to the next problem.

12. At the next stop, Grammatik states that we've started the last three sentences with *We* (see Figure 12.7). That last sentence is pretty bad anyway, so let's rewrite it. Press F9, edit the sentence as shown below, and press F10 to continue.

   The parking garage project we worked on with you two years ago acquainted us with your staff's needs.

FIGURE 12.6

Oops! Problems with run-on sentences

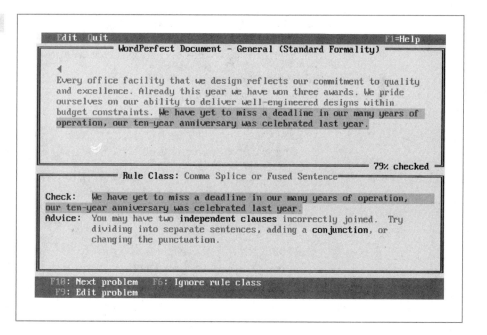

FIGURE 12.7

Grammatik tells us
that we've started too
many sentences in the
same way and urges
us to be more
creative.

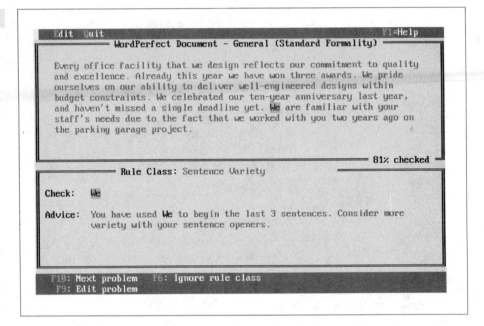

```
 Edit  Quit                                                    F1=Help
 ┌─ WordPerfect Document - General (Standard Formality) ─────────┐
 │                                                                │
 │ Every office facility that we design reflects our commitment   │
 │ to quality and excellence. Already this year we have won three │
 │ awards. We pride ourselves on our ability to deliver well-     │
 │ engineered designs within budget constraints. We celebrated    │
 │ our ten-year anniversary last year, and haven't missed a       │
 │ single deadline yet. We are familiar with your staff's needs   │
 │ due to the fact that we worked with you two years ago on the   │
 │ parking garage project.                                        │
 │                                                                │
 │                                                  81% checked   │
 ├─ Rule Class: Sentence Variety ─────────────────────────────────┤
 │                                                                │
 │ Check:    We                                                   │
 │                                                                │
 │ Advice:   You have used We to begin the last 3 sentences.      │
 │           Consider more variety with your sentence openers.    │
 │                                                                │
 ├────────────────────────────────────────────────────────────────┤
 │ F10: Next problem     F6: Ignore rule class                    │
 │ F9: Edit problem                                               │
 └────────────────────────────────────────────────────────────────┘
```

13. Grammatik flags passive voice again in the last sentence of the second paragraph in our original letter. Go ahead and press F9, rewrite the sentence as shown below, and press F10 to continue.

    (You may recall that Hanley Blake designed the garage's award-winning interior.)

14. Our next stops are at the numbers *4* and *2*, which Grammatik suggests replacing with *four* and *two*. Press F3 (twice) to accept each suggestion and continue.

15. Grammatik now objects to the wordiness of "Statistics indicate...in close proximity to..." in the third paragraph. It suggests replacing *in close proximity to* with *near* or *close to*. Press F3 and choose *close to*.

16. Now Grammatik asks us to simplify the word *indicate* in the same sentence (notice that we've gone back a step here). It suggests that we change *indicate* to *show, say,* or *suggest*. Press F3 and choose *suggest*.

17. Our next stop, shown in Figure 12.8, illustrates an important point: Grammatik isn't foolproof! Here it criticizes *principle* and suggests that we replace it with *principal*. That's clearly wrong, so press F10 to ignore the suggestion and move on.

18. Grammatik has now recovered its smarts (and quite well). It noticed the misuse of *from* when we meant *form* in the sentence "According to our research...who suffer from a **from** of...." Press F3 to replace *from* with *form* and move on.

19. Next, Grammatik detects the double period (..) after the third paragraph. Press F3 to replace it with one period and continue.

20. In Figure 12.9, we've taken another step backward in the document; however, Grammatik's protest is right on! That convoluted Worker Compensation sentence really is long and difficult to understand. Press F9, revise the sentence as shown below, and press F10 to continue.

Our research shows that high-quality adjustable chairs and desks greatly reduce Worker Compensation claims for repetitive motion syndrome and similar problems, such as neck or back pain.

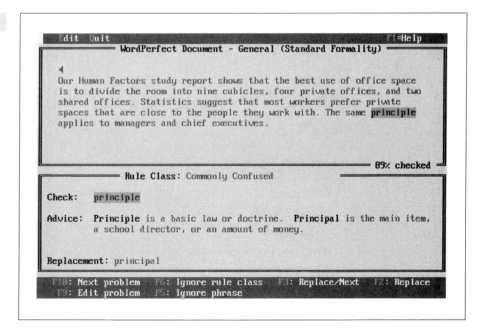

FIGURE 12.8

Grammatik complains that we've used the word "principle" incorrectly. In this case, Grammatik is wrong and we're right.

FIGURE 12.9

Grammatik hates
long, complex
sentences. So do
SYBEX editors.

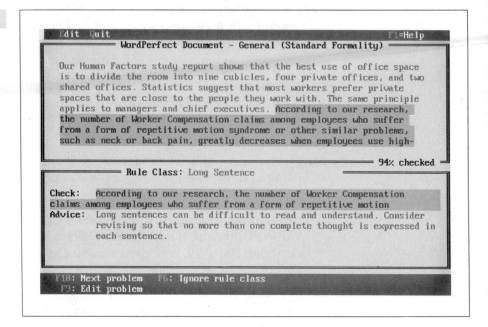

21. Finally, Grammatik trips over the names *Hickox* and *Cozee*, which are spelled correctly. Press F5 to ignore each error.

Grammatik is now finished checking the document and returns to the main screen.

Getting Statistics about the Document

Let's look at some interesting statistics for the revised document. Type or click **T** at the main Grammatik screen to display various readability statistics for the document. Figure 12.10 shows the first screen of statistics. Press ↵ to see the explanation of those statistics shown in Figure 12.11. Press Esc when you're ready to return to Grammatik's main screen.

To compare your document against the Gettysburg Address, a Hemingway short story, and a life insurance policy, choose Statistics ➤ Comparison Charts from the menus, or press **N** when you're at the main screen.

FIGURE 12.10

Statistics for the revised business letter

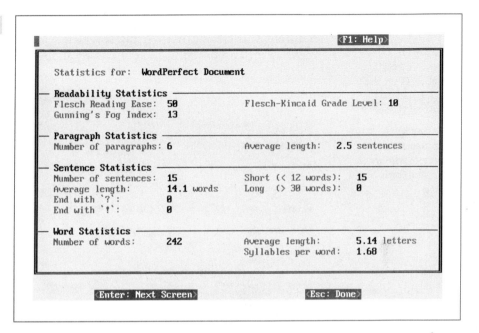

FIGURE 12.11

An explanation of the statistics in Figure 12.10

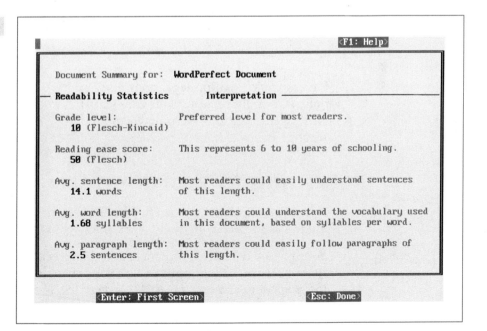

Figure 12.12 shows the first screen of comparative charts for our sample document and three other writing standards. Your document will always appear as the top bar in each set of comparison charts.

FIGURE 12.12

Grammatik compares our document with three other standards of writing

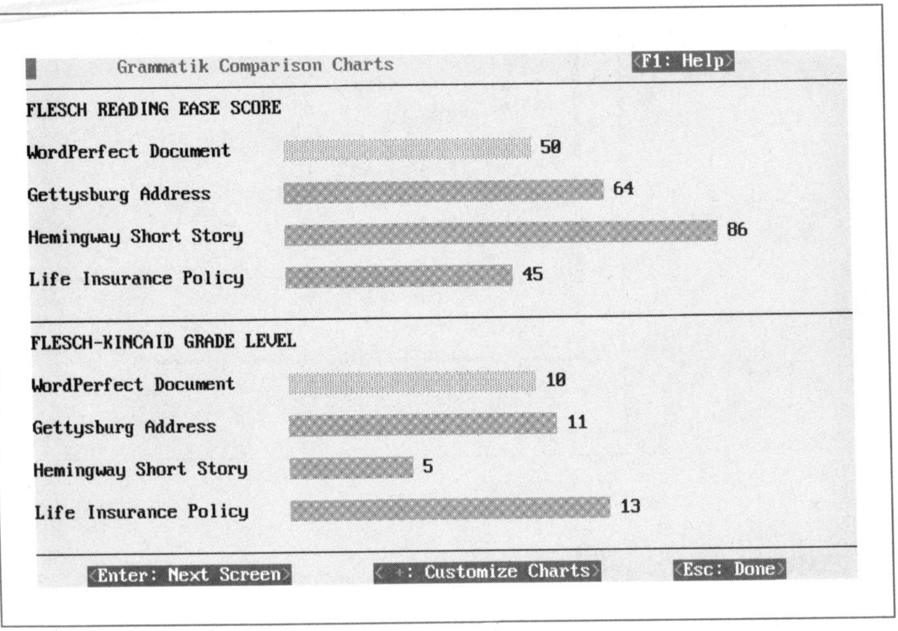

```
┌─────────────────────────────────────────────────────────────┐
│ ■      Grammatik Comparison Charts              <F1: Help>    │
│                                                              │
│ FLESCH READING EASE SCORE                                    │
│                                                              │
│ WordPerfect Document      ▓▓▓▓▓▓▓▓▓ 50                        │
│                                                              │
│ Gettysburg Address        ▓▓▓▓▓▓▓▓▓▓▓ 64                      │
│                                                              │
│ Hemingway Short Story     ▓▓▓▓▓▓▓▓▓▓▓▓▓▓ 86                   │
│                                                              │
│ Life Insurance Policy     ▓▓▓▓▓▓▓▓ 45                         │
│                                                              │
│ FLESCH-KINCAID GRADE LEVEL                                   │
│                                                              │
│ WordPerfect Document      ▓▓▓▓▓▓▓▓▓ 10                        │
│                                                              │
│ Gettysburg Address        ▓▓▓▓▓▓▓▓▓▓ 11                       │
│                                                              │
│ Hemingway Short Story     ▓▓▓▓ 5                             │
│                                                              │
│ Life Insurance Policy     ▓▓▓▓▓▓▓▓▓▓▓ 13                      │
│                                                              │
│ <Enter: Next Screen>    <←: Customize Charts>  <Esc: Done>   │
└─────────────────────────────────────────────────────────────┘
```

Unless you're writing legal contracts, military documents, or insurance policies, you'll probably want your statistics to lean more toward the Gettysburg Address and Hemingway Short Story numbers than the Life Insurance Policy numbers.

Returning to WordPerfect

When you're ready to return to WordPerfect, press Esc to return to Grammatik's main screen (if necessary), then press **Q**.

Your revised document will appear on the screen. Now choose File ➤ Save As or press F10 if you want to save your changes. You can either overwrite the original document (press ↵ to accept the suggested name) or type in a new name so that you'll have a copy of both the old and new versions.

N O T E   If you used Grammatik's File ➤ Open command or O shortcut key to retrieve a document, Grammatik will update the retrieved file automatically. You won't see it on the screen when you return to WordPerfect.

Figure 12.13 shows the revised letter. Some people might argue that the letter is still terrible. However, they'd probably agree that it's an improvement over the version shown in Figure 12.1.

FIGURE 12.13

The letter after revising it with Grammatik's help. Compare this version with the one in Figure 12.2.

November 9, 1993
Wanda Granolabar, Vice President
WANDOLA ENGINEERING CORPORATION
2230 Strappman Avenue
Strappman, CA 92147

Dear Ms. Granolabar:

Thank you for giving Hanley and me the opportunity to submit the attached proposal. It is always a pleasure doing business with your firm.

Every office facility that we design reflects our commitment to quality and excellence. Already this year we have won three awards. We pride ourselves on our ability to deliver well-engineered designs within budget constraints. We celebrated our ten-year anniversary last year, and haven't missed a single deadline yet. The parking garage project we worked on with you two years ago acquainted us with your staff's needs. (You may recall that Hanley Blake designed the garage's award-winning interior.)

Our Human Factors study report shows that the best use of office space is to divide the room into nine cubicles, four private offices, and two shared offices. Statistics suggest that most workers prefer private spaces that are close to the people they work with. The same principle applies to managers and chief executives. Our research shows that high-quality adjustable chairs and desks greatly reduce Worker Compensation claims for repetitive motion syndrome and similar problems, such as neck or back pain.

We have forwarded a copy of this proposal to your Operations Manager, W. B. Hickox, as requested. Thank you for taking the time to review this proposal.

Sincerely,

M. Kim Cozee, Human Factors Consultant
Hanley Blake, Inferior Designer
PROFESSIONAL OFFICE DESIGNS

Now that you've seen Grammatik in action, you should have little trouble using its other features. The remaining sections in this chapter summarize many of the program's capabilities.

Checking Out Your File

Grammatik's Checking menu offers several ways to check your document. These are summarized below:

Interactive Lets you view Grammatik's analysis on-screen and use its suggestions to revise your writing. You saw the interactive method in the sample session above.

Resume Interactive Lets you begin interactive checking at a bookmark instead of at the beginning of the document. To set a bookmark at the cursor location while you're doing an interactive check, choose Quit ➤ Place Bookmark or type **B.**

Grammar and Mechanics Starts interactive checking but flags grammar and mechanics errors only. Grammatik will ignore style errors, including cliches, jargon, and wordiness. *Mechanics* include capitalization, punctuation, spelling, and form (abbreviations, numbers, word division, etc.).

Spelling Only Starts interactive spell checking.

Read Only Proofreads the document and displays each problem, but doesn't let you make any changes.

Mark Proofreads the document non-interactively, marks each problem with special marking characters, and displays advice next to the problem text. You can return to WordPerfect to view the marked areas, which will look like this:

|--(ADVICE WILL BE HERE)--|your text is here|--(MORE ADVICE HERE)--|more text here

Unmark Removes all advice and marking characters from a document that was marked via the Checking ➤ Mark option.

Interactive Checking

You've already seen a detailed example of how interactive checking works. Perhaps you noticed the Edit and Quit menus that appeared in the menu bars of Figures 12.3–12.9. Those menus give you added flexibility during any interactive checking session.

Table 12.1 summarizes the Edit menu options. Most of these options also appear as function keys at the bottom of the interactive screen. The options available depend on the type of problem Grammatik has found. For instance, the Learn Misspelled Word option (F7) won't be available when Grammatik is asking you to fix a doubled-word problem.

TABLE 12.1: Edit Options Available during Interactive Checking

FUNCTION KEY	EDIT MENU OPTION	PURPOSE
F2	Replace Problem	Lets you replace this problem word or phrase with one that Grammatik suggests
F3	Replace Problem, Skip to Next	Same as F2, but continues to the next problem
F4	Show Parts of Speech Info	Diagrams the current sentence, showing its parts of speech
F5	Ignore Phrase from Now On	Ignores the phrase for this proofreading session
F6	Ignore Class from Now On	Turns off the rule class for this proofreading session
F7	Learn Misspelled Word	Adds the word to Grammatik's spelling dictionary
F8	Mark This Problem	Marks this problem for now and goes on to the next one
F9	Edit This Problem	Lets you edit this problem (press Esc when done)

TABLE 12.1: Edit Options Available during Interactive Checking (continued)

FUNCTION KEY	EDIT MENU OPTION	PURPOSE
F10	Skip to Next Problem	Doesn't make any changes and goes on to the next problem
	Restore Rule Classes	Restores ignored rule classes

As interactive checking progresses, Grammatik saves your changes to a temporary file. You can interrupt the check at any time by choosing options on the Quit menu or by pressing the corresponding shortcut keys. Those options let you quit and save your work, put in a bookmark, mark the rest of the document non-interactively, or cancel all changes made so far. Table 12.2 summarizes the Quit options that you can use.

TABLE 12.2: Quit Options Available during Interactive Checking

KEYBOARD SHORTCUT	QUIT MENU OPTION	PURPOSE
S	Quit, Save Work So Far	Stops proofreading, but saves work done so far
B	Quit, Place Bookmark	Stops proofreading and places a bookmark here so you can resume interactive editing later
	Quit, Mark Rest of Document	Stops proofreading and marks problems in the rest of the document
Ctrl+C	Cancel, Ignore Work So Far	Stops proofreading and discards work done so far

Disabling Grammatik in Part of a Document

You can temporarily disable the grammar checker (and WordPerfect's Speller) in any part of your document, as explained in Chapter 11. In case you missed that chapter, the steps are summarized below.

1. If you're using Grammatik at the moment, return to WordPerfect (press **Q** from the main Grammatik screen).

2. Move the cursor to where you want to disable the grammar checker and speller, or press Home Home ↑ to start at the top.

3. Choose <u>T</u>ools ➤ <u>W</u>riting Tools, or press Alt+F1.

4. Select (check) D<u>i</u>sable Speller/Grammatik. WordPerfect will insert a hidden [Speller/Grammatik:Off] code at the cursor location. You can delete this code if you later change your mind about disabling the tools.

To resume grammar and spell checking in another part of the document, move the cursor to that location, press Alt+F1, and deselect D<u>i</u>sable Speller/Grammatik. WordPerfect will insert a hidden [Speller/Grammatik:On] code at the cursor location.

Customizing Grammatik

Grammatik's Preferences menu lets you customize the program in several ways. The sections below explain the customization options available to you.

Customizing the Writing Style and Formality Level

As you know, different types of writing call for different styles and levels of formality. For instance, one writing style might work wonderfully in a pulp novel, but it wouldn't be at all appropriate for a technical report.

You can choose Preferences ➤ Writing Style (or press **W** when you're at the main Grammatik screen) to select a different writing style to use while proofreading a document.

Figure 12.14 shows Grammatik's ten built-in writing styles. Each style has a default formality level of Informal, Standard, or Formal. Notice that the screen provides complete instructions for choosing a new style and formality level, and it explains how to create a custom writing style of your own. Grammatik will use the writing style you select for all future sessions, until you change the style again.

You might want to create a customized writing style (F2) if Grammatik's complaints about certain types of errors become annoying. Grammatik lets you create up to three custom writing styles, and it lets you change the formality levels of built-in styles. In general, the less formal styles are more forgiving.

FIGURE 12.14

This screen lets you change the writing style that Grammatik uses when it proofreads your documents.

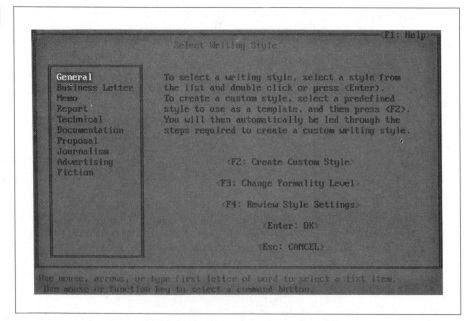

Options for Checking Documents

The Preferences ➤ Options command in Grammatik's main menu lets you change the settings shown below. For instance, you can swap the left and right mouse buttons without changing the mouse driver.

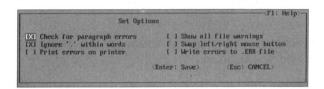

Customizing the Screen Colors

If Grammatik's default screen colors offend you or just don't look great on your monitor, you can change them by choosing Preferences ➤ Screen Attributes from Grammatik's main menu. There are six built-in color schemes (Utah, California, New Mexico, Wyoming, Black and White, and Reverse Black and White).

Choosing a Word Processor

Most of the time, you'll use Grammatik with WordPerfect 6.0. However, Grammatik can also proofread documents created in many other word processors.

Simply choose Preferences ➤ Word Processor to tell Grammatik which word processor created your documents. You can also use this option to set a default document path and extension and have Grammatik ignore embedded formatting codes used by Ventura Publisher.

After you change the word processor option, you can use Grammatik's File ➤ Open or **O** command to open documents that you want to check.

Getting and Saving Preferences

Grammatik saves your preferences for the default writing style, word processor, and other information in its preferences file (usually C:\WPC60DOS\GK51GK.INI). You can save the current preferences to another Preferences file and then restore those preferences whenever you want to use them.

For example, suppose you've just customized Grammatik to use cool California colors, an informal memo writing style, and the Word-Perfect 5.1 word processor. To save your new preferences, start from Grammatik's main screen, then choose File ➤ Save Preferences File and enter a file name (such as C:\WPC60DOS\GK51COOL.INI). Whenever you want to use your new preferences, simply choose File ➤ Get Preferences File and select the preferences file you want (for example, GK51COOL.INI) from the list that appears.

Keep in mind that Grammatik will return to its *original* preferences file after you go back to WordPerfect. Therefore, you'll need to remember to choose File ➤ Get Preferences File whenever you want to use your own preferences, instead of Grammatik's default preferences.

NOTE   When you exit Grammatik, the program automatically saves your preferences in the currently selected preferences file. Therefore, you need to choose File ➤ Save Preferences File only when you want to store your preferences in a *different* preferences file.

More Grammatik Statistics

You can run your document through a variety of statistical analyses by choosing options from Grammatik's Statistics pull-down menu. Figures 12.10–12.12 illustrated several examples of Grammatik's statistical prowess.

The statistical options are as follows:

Show Statistics   Displays readability, paragraph, sentence, and word statistics and interprets their meaning (see Figures 12.10 and 12.11).

Historical Profile   Provides an alphabetical list of all the words you've used during the past several Grammatik sessions and the number of times you've used them. Use it to explore your vocabulary (especially words you tend to overuse).

Single-Document Profile   Same as the Historical Profile option, except that it lists words for the current document only.

Comparison Charts   Displays bar charts that compare your document's readability with those of three old standbys—Abraham Lincoln's Gettysburg Address, an Ernest Hemingway short story, and a life insurance policy (see Figure 12.12). You can use Grammatik's customizing features to add your own comparison standards, if you wish.

Restore Default Comparisons   Restores the default comparison statistics used in comparison charts.

Save Statistics in File   Saves the statistics for the current document in a text (ASCII) file with the extension .SUM. The statistics are the same ones that you'll see in the first screen that appears after you choose Statistics ➤ Show Statistics. You can open and print the .SUM file in WordPerfect or any text editor.

This chapter covered the Grammatik application, which can check your document's spelling, grammar, and writing style. After you've used Grammatik a few times, you'll view your writing with a much more critical eye.

Next, we'll move on to the Thesaurus, a tool that can help you find just the right *word* (term, expression, statement, or utterance) for any *occasion* (affair, circumstance, episode, happening, incident, or occurrence).

CHAPTER 13

Finding Just the Right Word with the Thesaurus

fast **TRACK**

HAVE YOU ever found yourself smack-dab in the middle of writing a sentence, only to discover that you're suddenly at a loss for words? Maybe you've already overused a word like *exciting* and want to try something spicier like *delightful, electrifying, exhilarating, inspiring,* or *thrilling.* Even if you have the vocabulary of a verbal genius, you'll appreciate the convenience of having an online thesaurus that not only suggests the right word to use but types it in for you as well.

Using the Thesaurus

WordPerfect's Thesaurus can help you out when you're at a loss for words. It can help you find a more precise or expressive synonym for a word, such as *enormous* instead of *big.* It can also find antonyms. For example, if you need a word that means the opposite of *arrogant,* but you just can't think of the right word, you can look up *arrogant* in the Thesaurus and discover antonyms like *polite* and *humble.*

To use the Thesaurus, just follow these steps:

1. Place the cursor on the word that needs a synonym or antonym.

2. Choose <u>T</u>ools ➤ <u>W</u>riting Tools ➤ <u>T</u>hesaurus, or press Alt+F1 T. You'll see a list of suggested synonyms and antonyms, as shown in Figure 13.1.

FIGURE 13.1

The Thesaurus screen
for the word *big*

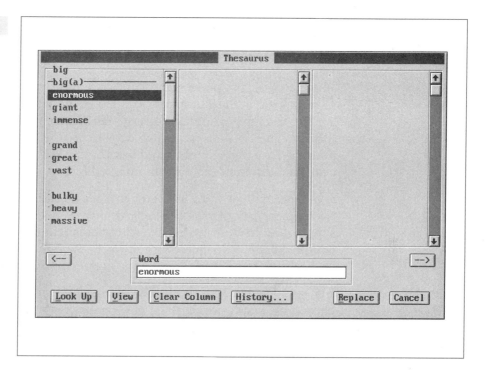

NOTE

If WordPerfect can't find a synonym or antonym for
the word the cursor is on, the Thesaurus columns
will be empty. You can type in another word to look
up and press ↵, or choose Cancel or press Esc to
return to your document.

3. To replace the highlighted word in your document with a word
   from the Thesaurus, select the word from the list (by clicking on it
   or highlighting it) and choose Replace. If you decide not to replace the word, simply click Cancel or press Esc to return to the
   document window without making any changes.

There are many other ways to look up more synonyms and antonyms.
You'll learn about these next.

Looking Up More Synonyms and Antonyms

You can look up other synonyms and antonyms whenever suggested words appear in the Thesaurus dialog box. Notice that the Thesaurus dialog box has three columns, each of which can contain synonyms and antonyms. The columns may show ways to use the word as an adjective (*a*), noun (*n*), or verb (*v*). If the word has any opposites, that group will appear near the bottom of the column, marked by (*ant*).

A bullet next to a word indicates that it's a *headword*, for which the Thesaurus has a synonym list. To view synonyms or antonyms for a headword, simply double-click the headword (or highlight it and press ↵). The new words will appear in their own column to the right, with the headword you chose at the top of the column, above the word list.

Figure 13.2 presents the screen shown in Figure 13.1 after I double-clicked the headword *vast*.

FIGURE 13.2

The synonyms for the headword *vast*

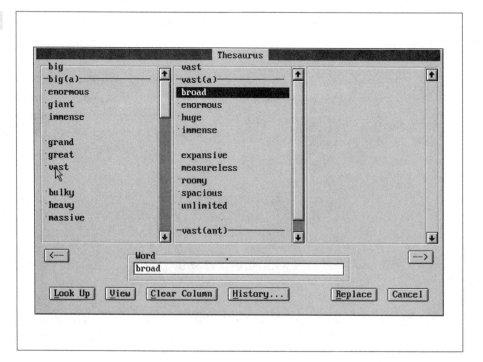

You can use the columns to refine your search for the right word. Simply double-click any headword in any column, until you find exactly the word you want. When you find the word you want, highlight it in its column (by clicking it once or using the ↑ and ↓ keys), then choose the Replace button.

NOTE   To clear a column, highlight any word in that column and choose Clear Column. You may need to choose Clear Column again if the column contained many words.

Moving through the Columns

Moving through the columns is easy. You can scroll up and down by clicking the scroll arrows or dragging the scroll boxes, pressing the ↑ and ↓ keys, or pressing the PgUp and PgDn keys. To move the highlight from column to column, press the → (or Tab) and ← (or Shift+Tab) keys, click in the column you want, or click the <-- and --> buttons in the dialog box.

Viewing the Document from the Thesaurus

Sometimes it's handy to switch to your document so that you can see the words and sentences surrounding the word you're looking up. You can do that without leaving the Thesaurus simply by choosing View. WordPerfect will let you scroll through the document to your heart's content (though you won't be able to make any changes). When you're ready to return to the Thesaurus, press F7 or Esc, or double-click anywhere in the Thesaurus dialog box.

Using the Thesaurus to Look Up a Word

You can use the Thesaurus to look up any word you want—whether you've already typed it into your document or not. Just run the Thesaurus as you normally would, then click the Look Up button (if necessary) to move the cursor to the Word text box. Type in the word you want to look up and press ↵. You can then use the Thesaurus columns to look up more synonyms or antonyms for the word you typed in. When you find the word you want, highlight it and choose <u>R</u>eplace.

Reviewing the Lookup History

WordPerfect keeps a history of the last several headwords that you've looked up during the current Thesaurus session (the list is erased each time you open the Thesaurus). To view the Thesaurus History List, choose <u>H</u>istory. You can then select a word from the History List to make that word the new headword. This provides a convenient way to back up and start over at an earlier headword choice.

Choosing a Different Thesaurus

The default Thesaurus is named WPUS.THS. It resides in the WordPerfect shared programs directory (C:\WPCDOS60). As with the Speller, you can buy and install foreign-language modules from WordPerfect Corporation.

When you want to use some other installed Thesaurus, choose <u>F</u>ile ➤ Se<u>t</u>up ➤ <u>E</u>nvironment ➤ <u>L</u>anguage (Shift+F1 EL) and select the language you want.

NOTE To locate or change the default directory for the Speller, Thesaurus, and Hyphenation files, choose <u>F</u>ile ➤ Se<u>t</u>up ➤ <u>L</u>ocation Of Files ➤ <u>W</u>riting Tools (Shift+F1 LW).

You now know how to use the Thesaurus to help you find the right word for any occasion. In the next chapter, you'll learn how to use WordPerfect's automatic outlining and paragraph-numbering features.

PART FOUR

Automating Your Work

Automatic Outlining

fast TRACK

● **To create a new outline** 520

> move the cursor to where you want to begin the outline, choose Tools ➤ Outline ➤ Begin New Outline (or press Ctrl+F5 B), choose a style, then type the text for the first item. To enter another item, press ↵ one or more times. You can then demote the outline level (press Tab) or promote it (press Shift+Tab), if you wish, and type the text. Enter as many items as you wish. When you're finished typing the last item, choose Tools ➤ Outline ➤ End Outline (or press Ctrl+F5 E).

● **To display the Outline Bar** 525

> choose View ➤ Outline Bar.

● **To move through the outline** 533

> click your mouse, press the arrow keys, or press the Alt+arrow keys to move through outline families.

● **To remove an item from an outline** 533

> move to the beginning of the item and press Backspace followed by the usual keys for deleting text. Or highlight the item in Outline Edit mode (Ctrl+O), press Delete, then press F7.

● **To switch text between an outline level and body text** 534

> move the cursor to the text you want to change and press Ctrl+T to toggle back and forth.

To change an outline level   535

move the cursor to the beginning of the item. To demote the item, press Tab or click the Next Level button in the Outline Bar. To promote the item, press Shift+Tab or click the Previous Level button in the Outline Bar.

To change an outline style   536

move the cursor into the outline and choose a style from the Style drop-down list in the Outline Bar.

To hide or show an outline family   541

move to the topmost item in the family, then click the Hide Family (–) or Show Family (+) button in the Outline Bar.

To hide or show an outline level or all levels   541

move to any item in the outline and click the Show button in the Outline Bar. Select the level you want, or choose All to restore all levels to view. To hide the outline altogether, press Ctrl+F5 HO.

To hide or show body text   542

move to any item in the outline and click the Hide Body or Show Body button in the Outline Bar.

**UTOMATIC** outlining and numbering are powerful and versatile tools that you can use for any type of numbering—items in numbered lists, sections in a legal contract, outlines, and so forth.

What's great about numbering things automatically (as opposed to manually) is this: If you add, change, or delete a numbered item, WordPerfect will update all the other numbered items instantly to reflect the change. For many people, this one feature alone is worth the price of WordPerfect. Even better, automatic outlining is easy to use.

Outlining in a Nutshell

Your outline can be as simple as a numbered list (1, 2, 3, 4, 5, and so on), or it can involve a hierarchical scheme with up to eight levels (for example 1, 1.1, 1.1.1, 1.1.1.1, and so on). WordPerfect offers seven built-in numbering styles. If those aren't enough, you can create your own numbering scheme.

The basic procedure for using the outlining feature is simple:

- Move the cursor to where you want to begin the outline.
- Begin the outline and select a numbering scheme (Tools ➤ Outline ➤ Begin New Outline, or Ctrl+F5 B).

- Type in your outline items, as described later in this chapter.
- End the outline (<u>T</u>ools ➤ <u>O</u>utline ➤ <u>E</u>nd Outline, or Ctrl+F5 E).

It's easy to change numbered items to a different numbering scheme with just a few keystrokes, and you can reorganize the outline just as easily. Each document can have as many different outlines and numbering schemes as you want.

What Is a Numbering Scheme?

A numbering scheme (or *style*) is simply a way to number items. Figure 14.1 shows two different numbering styles: two levels used in a simple list and a more complex numbering scheme with three levels used in a contract.

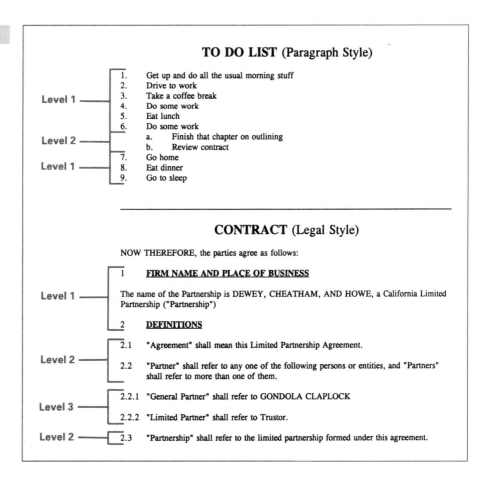

The automatic number or style change that appears in your document depends on the number of times you indent before inserting the numbered item. (You can also assign a specific level number to an item.)

In some numbering styles, each new level actually moves inward (indents) by a tab stop, as the "to do" list in Figure 14.1 shows. In other styles, the numbering changes to reflect the current indent level, but WordPerfect doesn't actually indent the numbered item. The contract in Figure 14.1 shows an example of "unindented" levels. Here, the numbers 1 and 2 are at the first indent level. The numbers 2.1, 2.2, and 2.3 are at the second level, and 2.2.1 and 2.2.2 are at the third level.

N O T E   Many outline styles display numbers in front of the text at each level. Others use bullets, and still others use letters, roman numerals, boldface, large type, and so forth. We'll keep things simple here by referring to the outline-level marker as the "number."

Automatic and Manual Numbering Styles

WordPerfect offers two basic types of outline styles: automatic and manual. In the *automatic* style, WordPerfect inserts the next item number automatically, as soon as you turn outlining on and whenever you press the ↵ key at the end of a numbered line or paragraph. All the built-in styles, except the *Headings* and *Numbers* styles, are automatic. In the *manual* style, you need to tell WordPerfect explicitly when you want to enter another numbered item. (*Counters*, discussed in Chapter 15, offer another way to number, or count, anything in your document.)

The built-in numbering styles are listed below. Figure 14.2 shows samples of each one.

Bullets   Perfect for bulleted lists.

Headings   Useful for headings in books, memos, and reports.

Legal   A popular style for legal documents.

FIGURE 14.2

Examples of
WordPerfect's built-in
numbering styles

BULLETS STYLE

● This is level 1
    ○ This is level 2
        - This is level 3
            ■ This is level 4
                * This is level 5
                    + This is level 6
                        ● This is level 7
                            x This is level 8

HEADINGS STYLE

This is level 1

This is level 2
This is level 3
    This is level 4
    This is level 5
1.   This is level 6
    a.   This is level 7
        1)   This is level 8

LEGAL STYLE

1   This is level 1
1.1   This is level 2
1.1.1 This is level 3
1.1.1.1   This is level 4
1.1.1.1.1   This is level 5
1.1.1.1.1.1 This is level 6
1.1.1.1.1.1.1 This is level 7
1.1.1.1.1.1.1.1   This is level 8

Legal2   Another legal style.

Numbers   Useful for numbered paragraphs and lists.

Outline   The most popular numbering style for outlines.

FIGURE 14.2

Examples of
WordPerfect's built-in
numbering styles
(continued)

LEGAL2 STYLE

```
1       This is level 1
1.01    This is level 2
1.01.01         This is level 3
1.01.01.01      This is level 4
1.01.01.01.01           This is level 5
1.01.01.01.01.01        This is level 6
1.01.01.01.01.01.01     This is level 7
1.01.01.01.01.01.01.01          This is level 8
```

NUMBERS STYLE

```
1.This is level 1
      a.This is level 2
            i.This is level 3
                  (1)This is level 4
                        (a)This is level 5
                              (i)This is level 6
                                    1)This is level 7
                                          a)This is level 8
```

OUTLINE STYLE

```
I.      This is level 1
      A.      This is level 2
            1.      This is level 3
                  a.      This is level 4
                        (1)     This is level 5
                              (a)     This is level 6
                                    i)      This is level 7
                                          a)      This is level 8
```

PARAGRAPH STYLE

```
1.      This is level 1
      a.      This is level 2
            i.      This is level 3
                  (1)     This is level 4
                        (a)     This is level 5
                              (i)     This is level 6
                                    1)      This is level 7
                                          a)      This is level 8
```

Paragraph Handy for numbering paragraphs and lists. Unlike the Numbers style, this one's automatic.

The numbering style you choose is completely up to you. It's easy to switch between different styles until you get the look you want. If the seven built-in styles don't suit your fancy, you can define new styles of your own. (Chapter 17 is devoted completely to matters of style, so look there to find out how to create your own outline styles.)

Using the Outline Bar

WordPerfect's Outline Bar is a handy tool that will speed up any outlining or automatic numbering task. The Outline Bar includes buttons and a drop-down list that you can click with your mouse. These provide a quick alternative to pressing keys or choosing options from menus.

To display the Outline Bar, choose <u>V</u>iew ➤ <u>O</u>utline Bar. When you want to hide the Outline Bar, simply choose <u>V</u>iew ➤ <u>O</u>utline Bar again. Figure 14.3 shows the Outline Bar in Graphics or Page mode. In Text mode, the Outline Bar is rather difficult to work with and certainly less attractive to look at. Therefore, I suggest that you stick with Graphics or Page mode when using the Outline Bar.

You'll learn more about how to use each button in the Outline Bar as you read through this chapter. But for now, you might want to take a quick look at Table 14.1, which summarizes each feature on the Outline Bar.

FIGURE 14.3

The Outline Bar in Graphics and Page mode

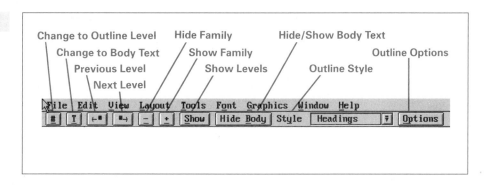

TABLE 14.1: A Quick Guide to the Outline Bar's Buttons and Features

BUTTON OR FEATURE	WHAT IT DOES
Change to Outline Level (#)	Converts body text to an outline item
Change to Body Text (T)	Converts an outline item to body text
Previous Level (←)	Promotes an outline item to a higher level
Next Level (→)	Demotes an outline item to a lower level
Hide Family (–)	Hides an outline family
Show Family (+)	Shows a previously hidden outline family
Show Levels (Show)	Shows specific outline levels or all levels
Hide/Show Body Text (Hide Body)	Toggles between hiding body text within the outline and showing it
Outline Style (Style)	Lets you choose a different outline numbering style from a pull-down list
Outline Options (Options)	Opens the Outline dialog box (same as choosing Tools ➤ Outline ➤ Outline Options, or pressing Ctrl+F5)

Using the Outline Menus and Outline Dialog Box

You probably won't be surprised to learn that WordPerfect offers several ways to select outline options. You've already learned about the Outline

Bar (Figure 14.3 and Table 14.1), which offers just about everything you'll need. The other methods are described below:

- The Tools ➤ Outline menu, shown in Figure 14.4, has nearly every option you need for automatic numbering and outlining.

- For a complete list of outlining features, you can turn to the Outline dialog box (see Figure 14.5). To display the Outline dialog box, click the Options button in the Outline Bar, press Ctrl+F5, or choose Tools ➤ Outline ➤ Outline Options.

- WordPerfect provides several keyboard shortcuts for certain outlining tasks. Table 14.2 lists those shortcuts.

You can decide which method of selecting outline options works best for you. In this chapter, I'll focus on the simplest keyboard and mouse methods that accomplish a task.

FIGURE 14.4

The Tools ➤ Outline
pull-down menu

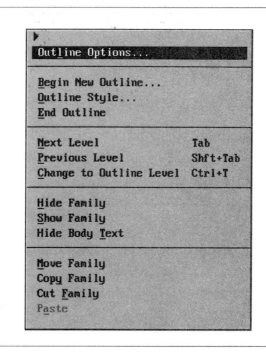

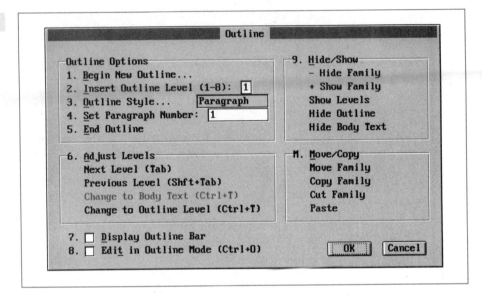

TABLE 14.2: Handy Keyboard Shortcuts for Outlining

KEYBOARD SHORTCUT	MEANING
Tab	Moves item to the next level (demotes)
Shift+Tab	Moves item to the previous level (promotes)
Ctrl+T	Changes item to body text (if it's numbered) or to an outline level (if it's unnumbered body text); also adds a new outline item
Ctrl+O	Edits in Outline mode
Alt+→	Moves cursor to next outline item
Alt+↓	Moves cursor to next outline item at same or higher level
Alt+←	Moves cursor to previous outline item
Alt+↑	Moves cursor to previous outline item at same or higher level

Creating an Outline

We all learned in school that an outline is a great way to get started with any large document. But we also learned (perhaps the hard way) that developing an outline is often a trial-and-error effort. We start with a basic list, add topics and subtopics, then often delete, change, and move ideas as we revise. As we refine our thoughts, we erase, cut, paste, and rewrite the outline to match our latest view of the subject.

Developing and refining an outline manually can be a messy job. But WordPerfect's Outline feature makes it easy to modify and even reorganize your outline to match your latest whim. Moreover, it renumbers every item in the outline automatically as you make changes, so you never have to do that job yourself.

NOTE   I'm using the term *outline* here to refer to anything that WordPerfect should number automatically. As mentioned previously, I'm using the term *numbers* to refer to numbers, bullets, heading styles, roman numerals, letters, or any other character or appearance change that WordPerfect can display.

Creating a New Outline

To create a new outline, follow these steps:

1. Move the cursor to where the outline should begin.

2. Choose <u>T</u>ools ➤ <u>O</u>utline ➤ <u>B</u>egin New Outline (or press Ctrl+F5 B). The Outline Style List dialog box, shown in Figure 14.6, will appear.

3. Double-click the outline style you want, or highlight the style and choose <u>S</u>elect (or press ↵). Remember that the built-in Headings and Numbers styles are manual, while the other styles listed are automatic. Custom styles that you've defined may be manual or automatic.

FIGURE 14.6

The Outline Style List dialog box

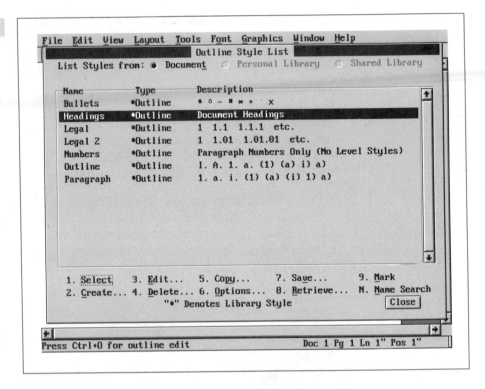

4. An outline numbering character or other style change will appear on your screen.

5. To enter your text, do one of the following:

- To keep the item at the current level, type the text for the item. You can let the text wrap to as many lines as you wish. That is, the text can be one line or an entire paragraph.

- To move the item down to a lower level (*demote* the item), press the Tab key or click the Next Level button in the Outline Bar once for each level you want to move down. (You can have up to eight levels.) Now type your line or paragraph of text.

- To move the item up to a higher level (*promote* the item), press the Shift+Tab key or click the Previous Level button in the Outline Bar once for each level you want to move up, and then type your text.

- To move the item to a specific level number (between 1 and 8), open the Options dialog box (press Ctrl+F5 or click the Options button in the Outline Bar). Select Insert Outline Level (1–8), and type the level number you want. Now type in your text. If you are already on a line of text, WordPerfect will move that text to the level you choose.

6. After you've finished typing the item, you can enter another numbered item by following one of the steps below:

   - If you're using an *automatic style,* press ↵ to move to the next item. WordPerfect will insert the next number (or style) at the current outline level. You can press ↵ more than once if you want to add blank lines between items and move the outline number down.

   - If you're using a *manual style,* press ↵ (as many times as you want), then press Ctrl+T or click the # button in the Outline Bar. An outline numbering character (or style) will appear.

TIP To turn off automatic numbering temporarily, press Ctrl+T or click the T button in the Outline Bar. To turn the numbering on again, press Ctrl+T again or click the # button in the Outline Bar.

7. Repeat steps 5 and 6 as many times as you wish.

8. When you're ready to switch back to normal, unnumbered paragraph text, end the outline by choosing Tools ➤ Outline ➤ End Outline (or press Ctrl+F5 E). (If a leftover outline number appears above the cursor, press Backspace as many times as needed to remove it.)

NOTE WordPerfect will end any previous outline automatically when you start a new outline.

You don't need to reactivate the Outline feature if you want to change your outline later. Simply move the cursor anywhere within the existing outline and make your changes. I'll talk about how to change the outline in just a moment. But first, you should know about a potential "gotcha."

Avoiding Number Style Pitfalls

If you chose the Number style for your outline, you might have noticed that WordPerfect doesn't insert an indent or tab after displaying the automatic number. You can still indent the text yourself. However, your first instinct—pressing the Tab key—wouldn't be right. That's because the Tab key demotes the numbering level; it doesn't indent. Here's what to do instead:

- Press F4 to indent the text (see Chapter 5). This is the easiest method.

- Or, press the spacebar and then press the Tab key.

Changing an Outline

Changing text that you've numbered automatically is a cinch. Just follow these steps:

1. Move the cursor to the item you want to change. Or, if you want to change some feature that affects the entire outline (such as the outline style), move the cursor anywhere in the outline. I'll discuss ways to move through the outline in a moment.

2. To make your change, you can click a button in the Outline Bar, press a shortcut key, or select an option from the Tools ➤ Outline menu or the Outline dialog box (Ctrl+F5).

That's basically all there is to it! If you're in an adventurous mood, you can experiment with the Outline Bar now (see Table 14.1 for a reminder about its buttons and features). If you're not feeling adventurous, or you're working with a document that you want to be cautious with, please read on.

Moving through the Outline

Updating an outline is like making any other change in WordPerfect: Position the cursor, then make your change. You can position the cursor by clicking the mouse or pressing the arrow keys. Or, to move through the outline families quickly, press the Alt+↑, Alt+↓, Alt+←, and Alt+→ keys listed in Table 14.2. (An outline *family* consists of a topic and any subtopics below it.)

To position the cursor at the beginning of an outline item, click on the item's outline number, or move to the first line in the item and press Home ←. To position the cursor on the Outline numbering character (which is actually a hidden code), press Home Home Home←.

Adding Outline Items

Adding a new outline item is a lot like creating an outline item in the first place. Start by moving the cursor to the end of the line that will be *above* the new item. For instance, to add an item after section 2.2 of the contract shown in Figure 14.1, move the cursor after the period at the end of the sentence.

Next, do one of the following:

- If you're using an *automatic* style, press ↵ (as many times as you want), then type your text.

- If you're using a *manual* style, press ↵ (as many times as you want), then press Ctrl+T or click the # button in the Outline Bar. Now type your text.

The new item will have the same numbering level as the one above it, and WordPerfect will automatically adjust any numbers below the item.

Deleting Outline Items

There are two ways to delete outline items: Use the usual methods for deleting any text, or use the special Outline Edit mode to delete outline items or families.

The first method is best when you want to delete a topic that contains subtopics, but you *don't* want to delete the subtopics. Move your cursor to the beginning of the first line in the topic you want to delete (press Home ← or click at the beginning of the line). Then press Backspace to delete the outline number. Now delete the rest of the text for the item in the usual way (for instance, press Delete repeatedly or select the text and press Delete).

Outline Edit mode is best for deleting the lowest level item under a topic or for deleting a topic and its subtopics. (See "Using Outline Edit Mode," later in this chapter, for more details.)

Switching between Outline Levels and Body Text

In WordPerfect parlance, the numbered items in an outline are called *outline levels* and the "normal" unnumbered text is *body text.* You can freely mix outline levels with body text in any outline. This combination style is common in contracts like the one shown in Figure 14.7, and will come in handy for any documents where you need to suspend numbering temporarily. In Figure 14.7, the paragraph that begins "The name of the Partnership" is body text; the remaining numbered items are outline levels.

With just a few keystrokes, you can instantly switch any text in your document between an outline level and body text. To begin, position the cursor in the text you want to transform. (If you want to convert several outline level items to body text, select all the items you want to convert.) Then...

- Press Ctrl+T to toggle between outline level and body text. If the current item is body text, WordPerfect will change it to outline level text. If the item is an outline level, WordPerfect will change it to body text. This is the quickest way to turn outline numbering off or on.

- Click the # button in the Outline Bar to change body text to an outline level.

- Click the T button in the Outline Bar to change outline level text to body text.

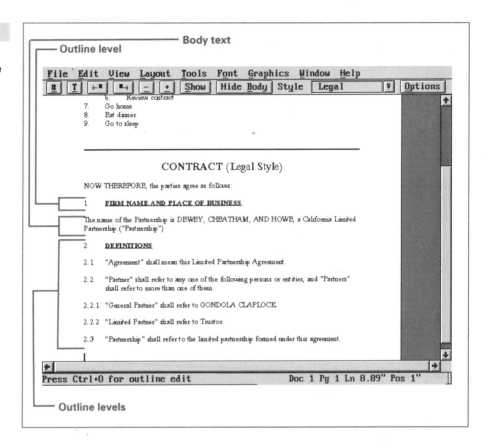

A sample contract that combines outline levels with body text

TIP   You can also use these methods to suspend or resume automatic outline numbering when you're typing a new outline item.

Changing an Outline Level

It's not always easy to organize your thoughts in a logical manner the first time you try (or even after many tries). As the outline unfolds, you may decide that ideas you once thought were part of a broader topic actually should stand on their own. Or perhaps a free-standing idea really is part of one of the higher-level concepts. Then, you may decide to change the level of a topic.

To change the level of an outline item, move the cursor to the *beginning* of the outline item (press Home ← or click your mouse on the outline number). Now change the outline level as follows:

- To move the item down to a lower level (*demote* the item), press the Tab key or click the Next Level button in the Outline Bar once for each level.

- To move the item up to a higher level (*promote* the item), press the Shift+Tab key or click the Previous Level button in the Outline Bar once for each level.

- To move the item to a specific level number (between 1 and 8), open the Options dialog box (Ctrl+F5), select Insert Outline Level (1–8), and type the level number you want.

WordPerfect will adjust the level number of the item you changed and will renumber the remaining items automatically.

T I P

You can place the cursor anywhere in the item if you aren't using Tab or Shift+Tab to demote or promote an item.

Changing the Outline Style

If you don't like the outline style, you can change it to another style with just a few keystrokes. Here are the steps:

1. Place the cursor anywhere in the outline.

2. Click the Style drop-down list in the Outline Bar, or press Ctrl+F5 O.

3. Highlight the style name you want and press ↵, or double-click the style name. You can choose any built-in style (see Figure 14.2) or any custom outline style that you've defined.

The outline style will change instantly. (This is almost too easy, isn't it?)

NOTE   The outline style change will affect only the outline that your cursor is in; it won't affect the style of other outlines in your document.

Changing the Starting Outline Number

Suppose your outline begins with number 1 and you want it to start with number 5 instead. You can change the starting outline number for any numbered level in your outline by following these steps:

1. Position the cursor on the item you want to change. Usually this will be the first item in the outline.

2. Open the Outline dialog box (Ctrl+F5) and choose <u>S</u>et Paragraph Number.

3. Type the starting number you want. You must type Arabic numerals separated by commas, spaces, or periods. For instance, to start numbering at VI.C.7, type **6.3.7**.

4. Press ↵ or choose OK.

WordPerfect will change the starting number and renumber the remaining items in the outline. (You won't notice any change if you've chosen a non-numeric numbering scheme such as bullets. However, if you switch to a numbered outline style, your new starting number will appear.)

TIP   If your outline numbering seems "off" (perhaps some numbers are repeated), a stray [Para Num Set] code may be running loose. To solve this problem, turn on Reveal Codes (press Alt+F3) and delete the offending codes.

Using Outline Families

Most outlines consist of groups of related ideas, with each idea or topic placed on a level by itself. Ideas related to the topic appear one level below the topic as subtopics, or *daughters*, of the original topic. Topics at the same organizational level are called *sisters*. A topic and all of its subtopics are known as a *family*, as illustrated in Figure 14.8.

WordPerfect provides several options for working with entire families of topics in an outline: These are Move Family, Copy Family, Cut Family, and Paste. To use one of these options, proceed as follows:

1. Move the cursor to the topmost item in the family that you want to work with.

2. Open the Outline dialog box (Ctrl+F5).

FIGURE 14.8

Sample outline with daughter, sister, and family defined

Words of Wisdom Book Outline

I. Introduction
   A. What *Words Of Wisdom* can do for you
   B. How to use this book
      1. Guided tour
      2. Reference
      3. Icons
   Keep it short and snappy. Get the reader excited about WOW's capabilities and show lots of examples.

Sister topics, all daughters to topic B, above

II. Getting Started
   A. A guided tour
   Keep the guided tour to 30 fun-filled pages.

   B. The WOW on-line tutorial

III. The LEAST you need to know
   A. Getting around in WOW
   B. Opening documents
   C. Closing documents
   D. Printing documents
   E. Saving documents
   F. Getting help

Family

IV. Becoming a WOW Guru
   TBD (We don't even know how yet!)

V. Appendices

VI. Index

3. Choose Move/Copy, then Move Family, or Cut Family, depending on what you want to do.

4. If you chose Cut Family or Move Family, the family will disappear immediately. You can paste the family elsewhere if you wish.

5. Now use the arrow keys or your mouse to select a new position for the family.

6. If you chose Move Family or Copy Family, press ↵ to complete the move or copy. If you chose Cut Family, you can paste the cut family by choosing Tools ➤ Outline ➤ Paste.

Choose Edit ➤ Undo or press Ctrl+Z if you immediately regret your decision to move, copy, or delete the family. The outline will return to its previous state, with the family members intact.

You can also work with outline families in Outline Edit mode, which I'll discuss in the later section "Using Outline Edit Mode."

Hiding and Showing Parts of the Outline

Until now, only dedicated outlining programs allowed you to collapse (hide) or expand (show) different levels in an outline. One of Word-Perfect 6.0's hottest new outlining features lets you collapse and expand the outline, so you can focus on any level(s) of detail. You can...

- Hide or show selected families
- Hide outline levels below a certain level
- Hide the body text and show only the outline
- Hide the outline and show only the body text

Figure 14.9 shows the effects of using these features on the outline in Figure 14.8. In the top example, I hid the family for items I, II.A and III. The middle example shows only the items at level 1. In the third example, I've shown only level 1 items and hidden all the body text.

FIGURE 14.9

The sample outline from Figure 14.8 in various stages of collapse

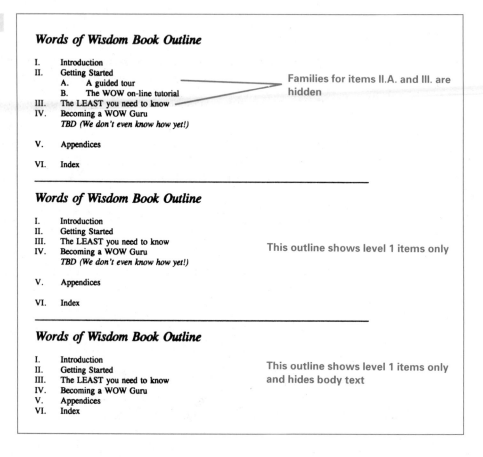

The next few sections explain how to collapse and expand your outlines.

The outline collapse and expand features affect only the outline that your cursor is in; they have no effect on other outlines in your document.

Hiding and Showing Families

You can hide or show the daughters of any outline family. First, move the cursor into the topmost item in the family that you want to work with. Then...

- To hide (collapse) the family, click the – button in the Outline Bar (or press Ctrl+F5 H-). The daughter topics will disappear from view. (If you're using Outline Edit mode, a + character will also appear next to the outline item that you collapsed.)

- To show (expand) the family, click the + button in the Outline Bar (or press Ctrl+F5 H+). The daughter topics will reappear. (If you're using Outline Edit mode, a – character will appear next to outline items that are fully expanded.)

- To show all families in the outline, click the Show button in the Outline Bar (or press Ctrl+F5 HS). Then choose All from the pop-up buttons that appear. This option instantly expands all families in the outline. It's especially handy when you're not sure whether or not you've collapsed parts of the outline.

Hiding and Showing Outline Levels

The Show Family and Hide Family options are useful for expanding or collapsing one family at a time. But suppose you want to view only the outline items at level 5 or above (that is, levels 5, 4, 3, 2, and 1). Or maybe you want to see just the items at level 1.

Start by moving the cursor to anywhere in the outline. Then click the Show button in the Outline Bar (or press Ctrl+F5 HS). Choose a level number from the pop-up buttons that appear. WordPerfect will instantly display only items with a level number equal to or lower than the one you chose. That is, you'll only see items at or above the level you selected.

Hiding and Showing Body Text

You can temporarily hide the body text in an outline, which helps you focus on the major ideas in the outline and makes the outline shorter when you print it or view it on the screen. As usual, you begin by placing the cursor in the outline. Then...

- To hide the body text (including blank lines) from view, click the Hide Body button in the Outline Bar (or press Ctrl+F5 HB).

- To make the body text visible again, click the Show Body button in the Outline Bar (or press Ctrl+F5 HB).

By the way, the name of the button in the Outline Bar toggles between Hide Body and Show Body, depending on the current state of body text. Thus, if body text is visible, the button name is Hide Body; if it's invisible, the button name is Show Body. Similar name changes—Hide Body Text or Show Body Text—occur in the Outline dialog box (Ctrl+F5).

Hiding and Showing the Outline

In addition to hiding or showing the body text, you can hide or show the outline itself. When the outline is hidden, only the body text is visible. To hide the outline, move the cursor into the outline, and press Ctrl+F5 HO.

To make your hidden outline reappear, move the cursor to where you think the outline is (just past the [Outline] code in Reveal Codes). Now, click the Show button in the Outline Bar (or press Ctrl+F5 HS) and select All from the buttons that appear.

Using Outline Edit Mode

Outline Edit mode offers another way to work with an outline. It's most useful for restructuring outlines quickly and working with outline families.

As you move through the outline with the Alt+arrow keys, or by clicking your mouse, WordPerfect selects (highlights) a family. You can't change any text or use the menus while in Outline Edit mode. However, all the Outline Bar features (including the Options button) are available, and you can use many of the keyboard shortcut keys.

To activate Outline Edit mode, press Ctrl+O. When you're finished using Outline Edit mode, do one of the following:

- Press F7 or click the "Press F7 when done" message.

- Or, press Ctrl+O.

- Or, press Esc.

Figure 14.10 shows the outlines from Figure 14.9 in Outline Edit mode. Notice that + signs appear next to hidden families and – signs indicate fully expanded families.

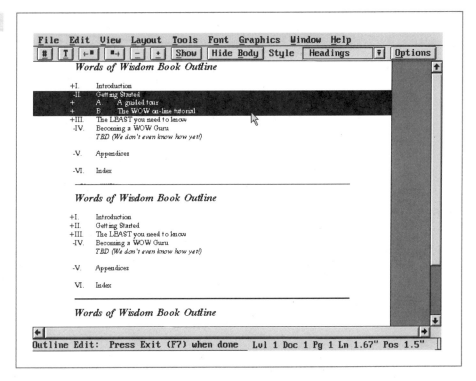

After you highlight a family in Outline Edit mode, you can use the following techniques to work with it:

- Use any feature on the Outline Bar, as discussed throughout this chapter. As an alternative to clicking the buttons in the Outline Bar, you can also press the highlighted or underlined character on those buttons.

- Use shortcut keys to do something to the selected text. Table 14.3 shows the most useful shortcut keys for Outline Edit mode.

TABLE 14.3: Shortcut Keys You Can Use in Outline Edit Mode

TO DO THIS…	PRESS THIS KEY
Copy text to Clipboard	Ctrl+Ins
Cut text to Clipboard	Shift+Del
Delete text	Del
Demote text to lower level	Ctrl+→
Exit Outline Edit mode	Esc, Ctrl+O, or F7
Open Outline dialog box	Ctrl+F5
Paste text from Clipboard	Shift+Ins
Promote text to higher level	Ctrl+←
Turn Reveal Codes on/off	Alt+F3
Undo changes	Ctrl+Z

Creating Your Own Outline Style

Chapter 17 discusses WordPerfect styles, which are a great tool for using design elements easily and consistently throughout a document. Outline styles are just a special case of WordPerfect's general style features. You can define a new outline style for a single document, or you can store it in a library that will be available to any document you create. Once you've defined the style, you can use it as you would any of WordPerfect's built-in outline styles.

If you're curious, here's how to start creating your own outline style: Choose Tools ➤ Outline ➤ Outline Style ➤ Create, or press Ctrl+F5 OC. Now define the new style as explained in Chapter 17.

You've seen how convenient it is to create outlines, bulleted lists, numbered paragraphs, and other types of documents that present ideas in a hierarchical manner. In the next chapter, you'll find out how to number the lines in your document and how to set up counters.

Automatic Line Numbers and Counters

fast TRACK

You can use counters to number or count

anything in your document. To reach the Counters dialog box, choose <u>L</u>ayout ➤ Cha<u>r</u>acter ➤ <u>C</u>ounters (or press Shift+F8 CC). Or, choose <u>G</u>raphics ➤ Graphics <u>B</u>oxes ➤ <u>N</u>umbering (or press Alt+F9 BN). Select List <u>S</u>ystem Counters if you want to view counters for Equation, Figure, Table, Text, and User Boxes.

To create a counter

position the cursor where you want to create the counter, and go to the Counters dialog box. Choose <u>C</u>reate and then specify the counter name, number of levels, and numbering method.

To change a counter's value

position the cursor where you want the counter to appear, then go to the Counters dialog box. Highlight the item you want to change, then choose <u>I</u>ncrement, Dec<u>r</u>ement, or Set <u>V</u>alue.

To display a counter in your document

position the cursor where you want the counter to appear, then go to the Counters dialog box. Choose Dis<u>p</u>lay In Document, and then choose OK. Or, to increment the counter and display it in one step, choose Increment & Display or press F8.

CHAPTER 14 covered WordPerfect's powerful outlining features, which let you organize your text into simple lists or hierarchical outlines. In this chapter, I'll cover two more numbering features: line numbers and counters.

Numbering the lines in your document takes only a few keystrokes. The line numbering can be continuous, or it can restart anywhere in the document. You can choose exactly where the line numbers will print and how they will look.

Counters provide a "semi-automatic" way to count or number anything in your document. They're sort of a compromise between the automatic numbering features discussed in Chapter 14 and the page numbering features covered in Chapter 8.

Line Numbering, Quick and Easy

WordPerfect can number every line in your document or just certain sections. Such formats are common in the legal profession, and in other situations where it's necessary to reference information by line number.

It's most common to print the numbers in the left margin of the document, as shown in Figure 15.1. However, WordPerfect lets you print the numbers anywhere on the page, even between columns in newspaper-style documents.

FIGURE 15.1

**Sample document
with line numbers**

```
 1   STEVEN C. SMITH
 2   53505 Orange Avenue
 3   Los Angeles, CA  90025
 4
 5   Telephone:  (123) 435-1200
 6
 7
 8   STEVEN C. SMITH, Complainant
 9
10
11
12
13                  UNITED STATES OF AMERICA
14
15                       BEFORE THE
16
17        COMMODITY FUTURES TRADING COMMISSION
18
19
20
21   In the Matter of the Reparations   )   CFTC DOCKET NO. 90-S205
22   Proceeding Between:                 )
23                                       )   COMPLAINANT'S APPEAL
24   STEVEN C. SMITH                     )   INFORMAL DOCUMENT
25                                       )
26        Complainant,                   )
27                                       )
28   and                                 )
29                                       )
30   LEVER BROTHERS, INC.                )
31   and JOHN JONES                      )
32                                       )
33        Respondents.                   )
34   _____
35
36
37                      INTRODUCTION
```

38   My Work Priority Policy - A prerequisite to other outside

39   involvement activities. My work requires that I have no outside

40   interruption of any kind, except in an emergency.

41   As an introduction to any discussion of my undertaking with

42   others, including financial investments that could disturb me at my

43   work, except for emergencies, that the above policy be carefully

-1-

> **NOTE**
>
> The vertical line separating the line numbers from the text in Figure 15.1 is a graphic line. I'll show you how to add separator lines a later in this chapter (see "Adding a Separator Line)".

Adding Line Numbers to a Document

Adding line numbers to a document takes just a few steps:

1. Place the cursor where you want to start the line numbering.

2. Choose <u>L</u>ayout ➤ <u>Line</u> ➤ Line <u>N</u>umbering (or press Shift+F8 LN). The Line Numbering Format dialog box, shown in Figure 15.2, will appear.

FIGURE 15.2

The Line Numbering Format dialog box

```
┌─────────────────────────────────────────────────────────────┐
│                    Line Numbering Format                      │
│                                                               │
│  1. ☐ Line Numbering On                      ┌Sample Numbering│
│                                              │        1        │
│  2. Starting Line Number:      [1  ] [▲▼]   │        2        │
│  3. First Line Number Printed: [1  ] [▲▼]   │        3        │
│  4. Numbering Interval:        [1  ] [▲▼]   │        4        │
│  5. Numbering Method [Number          ▼]     │        5        │
│                                              │        6        │
│  6. Position of Number:        [0.6"  ]      │        7        │
│     ● From Left Edge of Page                 │        8        │
│     ○ Left of Margin                         │        9        │
│                                              │       10        │
│  7. ☒ Restart Numbering on Each Page         │       11        │
│  8. ☒ Count Blank Lines                      │       12        │
│  9. ☐ Number all Newspaper Columns           │                 │
│                                              └─────────────────│
│  A. Font/Attributes/Color...                                  │
│                                     [  OK  ]  [ Cancel ]       │
└─────────────────────────────────────────────────────────────┘
```

3. Select (check) Line Numbering On. Don't forget to check this box if you ever want to see any line numbers!

4. Select other options if you wish. Look to the Sample Numbering area of the dialog box for a preview of the numbering options you've chosen so far. (I'll describe these options later.)

5. Choose OK (or Close) until you return to your document.

As you type, you'll be able to see the line numbers at most magnifications in Graphics mode (Ctrl+F3 G), Page mode (Ctrl+F3 P), in Print Preview (Shift+F7 V), and when you print the document.

Turning Line Numbers Off

Turning line numbering off is almost the same as turning it on. Only this time, you first must position the cursor where you want line numbering to *stop*. Next, choose Layout ➤ Line ➤ Line Numbering (Shift F8 LN) and deselect Line Numbering On. Choose OK (or Close) until you return to the document window.

What Counts as a Line Number?

WordPerfect usually counts blank lines when it numbers your document's lines. However, it doesn't count or number the following items:

- Lines in footnotes and endnotes (see Chapter 31)
- Page headers and footers (see Chapter 8)
- Lines that are left blank by your line-spacing setting

WordPerfect also won't count blank lines if you've deselected Count Blank Lines in the Line Numbering Format dialog box.

Changing the Line Numbering Format

You can change the appearance of line numbers when you turn on line numbering, or any time later, simply by choosing options from the Line Numbering Format dialog box (see Figure 15.2).

If you're changing the line numbers after the fact, here's how to begin:

1. Move the cursor to where you want the line number format to change. Usually this will be the first line-numbered paragraph in the document, but it can be anywhere that you want another format to appear.

2. Choose Layout ➤ Line ➤ Line Numbering (or press Shift+F8 LN).

3. Make your changes in the Line Numbering Format dialog box, as described below.

4. Choose OK (or Close) until you return to the document window.

Now, let's look at how each Line Numbering Format option shown in Figure 15.2 affects line numbering.

Starting Line Number   Lets you start numbering at any line number you wish. Even if you've chosen a different numbering method, you still must type the starting line number as a number (not as a letter or roman numeral). This option is handy if you've stopped numbering lines in the middle of a page or document and want to resume numbering later.

T I P

The Sample Numbering area will reflect your formatting changes after you make a selection and move to another option. This feature makes it easy to preview your changes before you leave the dialog box.

First Line Number Printed   WordPerfect usually starts printing line numbers at the spot where you turn line numbering on. This option lets you start printing numbers at a different line number. In the example below, I turned on line numbering at the beginning of the document and changed the first line number printed to 4. So, although line counting starts at the top, with line 1, WordPerfect doesn't actually begin printing line numbers until line 4:

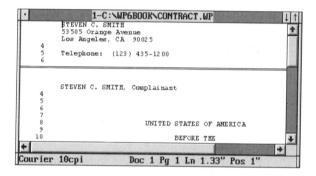

Numbering Interval   Sets the increment for the *printed* line number. When you set the option to 1 (the default), WordPerfect prints every line number. When you set it to 2, WordPerfect prints every other line number, and so on. Remember that this option does *not* change how the line numbers are calculated; it only changes how often WordPerfect prints the numbers. As usual, the Sample Numbering area of the dialog box will show the line number skips, so you can get a good idea of how the numbering will look in your document.

Numbering Method   You can use this option to select another numbering method. Your choices are Number (1, 2, 3), Lower Letter (a, b, c,), Upper Letter (A, B, C), Lower Roman (i, ii, iii), or Upper Roman (I, II, III).

Position of Number   Lets you change the distance between the line numbers and the left edge of the page or left margin (the default distance is 0.6″). Type the distance you want and press ↵. You can then choose one of these positioning options:

> **From Left Edge of Page**   WordPerfect starts measuring at the left edge of the page and then moves the line numbers right by the specified distance.

Left Edge of Margin WordPerfect starts measuring at the left edge of the text and then moves the line numbers left by the specified distance. This option is especially handy for numbering all newspaper columns (discussed below).

WARNING Don't place the line numbers between the page or column margins. If you do, WordPerfect is likely to clobber the text by printing line numbers on top of it (*not* good). Thus, if you have a 1″ left margin and the line number position is relative to the left edge of the page, your Position Of Number entry should be less than 1″.

Restart Numbering on Each Page Determines whether line numbering will start anew on each page. When selected (checked), numbering for each page restarts at the number specified in the Starting Line Number option (usually 1), as shown below:

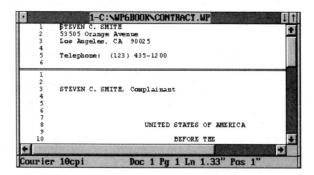

You can deselect this option if you want WordPerfect to number consecutively from the previous page, like this:

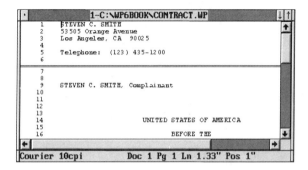

Count Blank Lines   When selected (checked), WordPerfect counts and numbers the blank lines created by multiple hard returns. When deselected, WordPerfect only counts and numbers lines that contain text. (WordPerfect never numbers lines that are left blank by your line-spacing setting, as the numbering for lines 37–43 of Figure 15.1 clearly shows.)

Number All <u>N</u>ewspaper Columns   Select (check) this option if you want to number the lines in each newspaper column. To display the two-column newsletter in Figure 15.3, I turned on line numbering at the top of the document, checked Number All <u>N</u>ewspaper Columns, set <u>P</u>osition Of Number to 0.25″, and changed the position to L<u>e</u>ft Of Margin. (See Chapter 27 for information on designing multicolumn formats.)

T I P

If you number all newspaper columns, it's best to reduce the <u>P</u>osition Of Number setting and select L<u>e</u>ft Of Margin to prevent WordPerfect from printing numbers over the text.

FIGURE 15.3

A two-column newspaper format document with line numbering on for all newspaper columns

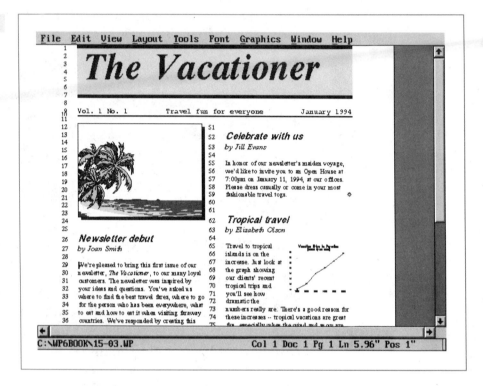

Font/Attributes/Color   Lets you choose a different font for line numbering. When the Font dialog box appears, select the font, size, appearance, and other options, as discussed in Chapter 6.

Adding a Separator Line

In Figure 15.1 I added a vertical line to separate the line numbers from the text on every page. This actually is quite easy if you know the secret (which won't be a secret much longer). Simply place a vertical graphic line in a header that's printed on every page, like this:

1. Move the cursor to the top of the document (press Home Home ↑).

2. Choose Layout ➤ Header/Footer/Watermark. Then choose Headers, followed by Header A or Header B. Now select All Pages (the default), and choose Create or press ↵.

3. From the pull-down menus, choose <u>G</u>raphics ➤ Graphics <u>L</u>ines ➤ <u>C</u>reate (or press Alt+F9 LC).

4. Change the Line <u>O</u>rientation to <u>V</u>ertical. You can also change the line options if you wish (I used all the default options in Figure 15.1). Choose OK when you're done.

5. Press F7 to return to the document window.

To verify your new header, go to the View Document window, or print a page (you can print graphics lines only if you have a graphics printer). See Chapter 8 for more information on using headers and footers.

Counters

WordPerfect offers many ways to automatically number things, including

- Page numbering (Chapter 8)
- Footnote and endnote numbering (Chapter 31)
- Graphics box numbering (Chapter 26)
- Outline numbering (Chapter 14)
- Line numbering (Chapter 15)

You can also create and use *counters* to count or number anything in your document, including paragraphs, chapters, sections, graphics boxes, widget names—whatever! Counters can display numbers, letters, and roman numerals, and they can appear anywhere in your document. Each counter can have as many levels as you want.

The main point to remember about counters is that they don't work automatically (except for system counters, described below). Therefore, you must tell WordPerfect exactly what values they should have and where to display them. I'll describe the specific steps in a moment.

System Counters

WordPerfect uses these five built-in system counters to number your graphic boxes: Equation Box, Figure Box, Table Box, Text Box, and User Box. You can use system counters just as you would any other counter that you create. However, you should keep in mind that the system counters have the special properties listed below:

- System counters initially have only one level, though you can change this if you wish.

- WordPerfect automatically increments the *lowest level* of the appropriate system counter when you create a graphics box. For example, when you add a second figure box to your document, WordPerfect will increment the Figure Box counter to 2 automatically.

- The *highest level* of each type of system counter is automatically included when you add a caption to a graphics box.

- Graphics box captions (and the counters they display) are marked automatically for inclusion in lists. You just need to define the location and format of whatever graphics box list you want to generate, as described in Chapter 31.

Some Counter Examples

The example in Figure 15.4 shows several counters in action. The relevant counter techniques used in this figure are listed below:

- I changed the default Figure Box counter to include two levels, and then I set the first level to 15.

- I displayed both levels of Figure Box counters in the paragraph titles (for example, *15-1 Work Avoidance*) and figure captions (*Figure 15.1 Poor PC*).

- I changed the default figure caption style to include the second-level counters. (See "Using Counters with Graphics Boxes," later in this chapter, for more information on doing this.)

- I set up two counters of my own—one for Fruits and one for Vegetables. Each counter had a single level.

15-1 Work Avoidance

Sometimes work avoidance is necessary to keep everyone on an even keel. For example, when your computer's mind is blown from working too hard, you're probably better off going to a movie. Let your PC play a video game for entertainment.

Figure 15.1 Poor PC

15-2 Work Enjoyment

When you return, you'll feel refreshed, and your computer will have had some time to cool off. Now you can go back to whatever you were doing with new zest and unstoppable enthusiasm.

Figure 15.2 Cool Fellow

15-3 More Counter Examples

Fruits	*Vegetables*
Apples	Carrots
Oranges	Celery
Pineapples	Tomatoes
Papayas	Lettuce

There are 4 <u>fruits</u> and 5 <u>vegetables</u> in this document (don't forget that mushrooms are a vegetable).

- I incremented the Fruits counter before typing **Oranges, Pineapples**, and **Papayas**. I incremented the Vegetables counter before typing **Carrots, Celery, Tomatoes**, and **Lettuce**. I displayed each counter in the last paragraph on the page, without incrementing the counters first.

Getting to the Counters Dialog Box

You'll find all the counter features in the Counters dialog box, shown in Figure 15.5. There are two ways to reach this dialog box. You can use whichever method is most convenient:

- Choose <u>L</u>ayout ➤ Cha<u>r</u>acter ➤ <u>C</u>ounters (or press Shift+F8 CC).

- Choose <u>G</u>raphics ➤ Graphics <u>B</u>oxes ➤ <u>N</u>umbering (or press Alt+F9 BN).

In Figure 15.5 you can see the five built-in system counters and the Fruits and Vegetables counters that I used in Figure 15.4. Notice that I added a second level to the Figure Box counter. This allowed me to create a two-level numbering scheme like the one used to mark figures in this book (for example, Figure 15.3).

FIGURE 15.5

The Counters
dialog box

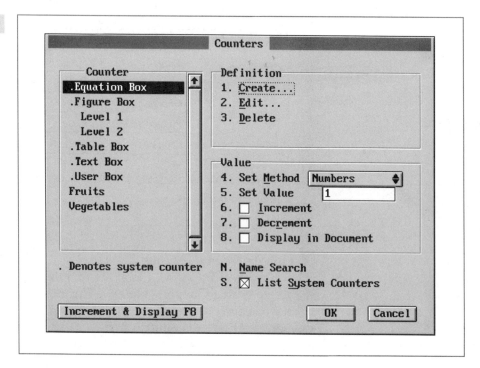

Defining a Counter

When you're ready to create a counter, follow these steps:

1. Get to the Counters dialog box as explained earlier.

2. Choose Create. You'll see the Create Counter Definition dialog box shown below:

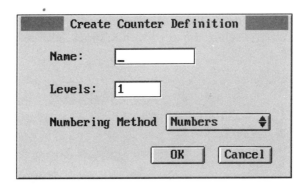

3. In the Name text box, type a name of your choosing.

4. If you want this counter to have more than one level, enter the number of levels in the Levels text box and press ⏎. For example, the number *1.1.1* has three levels. You can define as many levels as you need.

5. If you want to change the numbering method, choose Numbering Method, and then select Numbers, Lower Letter, Upper Letter, Lower Roman, or Upper Roman. WordPerfect will use this method for each level.

6. Choose OK until you return to the document window.

Displaying and Changing a Counter

Once you've defined a counter, it's easy to change, delete, or display it in your document. Just follow these steps:

1. If you want to display or change a counter, position the cursor to where you want the change to take effect or the counter to appear. Or, if you want to change only a portion of the document's counters, select the appropriate block of text.

TIP

If you need to get to the Counters dialog box often, consider adding an appropriate button to the Button Bar. Use <u>V</u>iew ➤ Button Bar <u>S</u>etup ➤ <u>E</u>dit ➤ Add Feature to add the Counters feature. See Chapter 4 if you need more information.

2. Go to the Counters dialog box, as explained earlier.

3. If you want to work with system counters, select (check) List <u>Sys</u>tem Counters. To hide system counters, deselect this option. (By default, system counters appear when you go through the <u>G</u>raphics ➤ Graphics <u>B</u>oxes ➤ <u>N</u>umbering options; they don't appear when you choose <u>L</u>ayout ➤ Cha<u>r</u>acter ➤ <u>C</u>ounters.)

4. Highlight the counter or counter level you want to work with.

5. Choose as many of the options described below as you wish.

6. Repeat steps 4 and 5 for as many counters as you want to change (or display) at this spot in your document.

7. Choose OK until you return to your document.

Here are the options you can use to change, delete, or display counters in your document:

Edit Lets you change the highlighted counter's name, number of levels, and numbering method, as needed. (For multilevel counters, you can only change the number of levels if you highlight the counter *name*, not one of its levels.)

Delete Lets you delete a counter. You can only use this option to delete the counter itself, not an individual level. (Use Edit if you want to reduce the number of levels in a counter.) This option won't let you delete a built-in system counter, but you *can* use it to reset a system counter to its default value.

Set Method Lets you change the numbering method for the highlighted counter.

Set Value Lets you set the highlighted counter to a specific value.

Increment Select (check) this option if you want to increment the highlighted counter by 1.

Decrement Select (check) this option if you want to decrement the highlighted counter by 1.

Display in Document Select this option if you want to display the highlighted counter at the cursor position when you return to your document.

Increment & Display Click this button or press F8 if you want to increment the highlighted counter and display it in your document in a single step. You'll be returned to the document window.

When you define, display, and set counter values, WordPerfect inserts hidden codes in the document. You can see these in Reveal Codes, and can use the techniques discussed in Chapter 4 to delete or move the codes as necessary. Table 15.1 summarizes the codes that will appear.

TABLE 15.1: Counter Codes

CODE	COUNTERS DIALOG BOX OPTION	DESCRIPTION
[Count Meth]	Set Method or Numbering Method (in Create or Edit Counter Definition)	Defines the numbering method (numbers, letters, or roman numerals)
[Count Disp]	Display in Document or Increment & Display (or F8)	Displays the counter number in your document
[Count Inc]	Increment or Increment & Display (or F8)	Increases the counter number by 1
[Count Dec]	Decrement	Decreases the counter number by 1
[Count Set]	Set Value	Sets the counter to a new value

Counter Tips

Here are some tips for using counters effectively:

- Each counter begins life with an initial value of 1. Therefore, you should display at least one counter number before you increment or decrement it.

- When you increment a higher level of a multilevel counter, Word-Perfect will automatically reset the lower levels to 1. For example, suppose you're using a three-level counter that currently has the values *3, 4,* and *5.* If you increment the first level to 4, the counter values will be *4, 1,* and *1* the next time you return to the Counters dialog box.

- If you just want to count something, increment the counter, but don't display it. Then, when you want to show the final total, display the counter but don't increment it. The fruits and vegetables example in Figure 15.4 illustrates this use of counters.

Here's the quickest way to display all levels of a multilevel counter in your document:

1. Move the cursor to where you want the counter to appear, then go to the Counters dialog box.

2. Highlight the first level for the counter that you want to display.

3. Select (check) Display In Document.

4. Select (check) Increment or Decrement, if you wish.

5. Highlight the next level for the counter that you want to display.

6. Repeat steps 3–5 until you've gone through all the levels.

7. Choose OK until you return to your document.

The counters will appear in your document one after the other, in order from the highest level to the lowest level selected. For example, if you selected levels 1, 2, and 3 of a counter with the values *3*, *4*, and *5*, respectively, you'll see *345* at the cursor location. Now, use standard editing techniques (in Insert mode) to add text and punctuation that will make your multilevel counter more readable. For example, you could change the bare-bones *345* to *Widget 3.4.5* or *Map Number 3-4-5*.

Using Counters with Graphics Boxes

As I mentioned earlier, system counters play a role in graphics box numbering. WordPerfect automatically increments the *lowest level* of the appropriate system counter when you create an Equation, Figure, Table, Text, or User Box. Moreover, the *highest level* counter for the box style will appear automatically when you add a caption to a graphics box.

When you change a system counter to use more than one level, WordPerfect doesn't insert those extra levels into captions automatically. However, it's easy to do this yourself. Just follow these steps:

1. Move the cursor before the first graphics box where you want the caption style change to take effect.

2. Create or edit your graphics box as described in Chapter 26. For example, press Alt+F9 BC (to create a box) or Alt+F9 BE (to edit a box).

3. If necessary, choose Based On Box Style, highlight the type of style you want to change, and choose Select.

4. Choose Create Caption or Edit Caption.

5. Press Alt+F9 CE to edit the caption style. You'll see the Caption Number Style dialog box shown below:

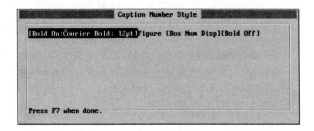

6. Move the cursor after the [Box Num Disp] code. Type any punctuation that you want to use as a separator between the counter levels (for example, a period or hyphen).

7. Press Alt+F9 BN to open the Counters dialog box. Highlight the counter level you want to insert in the caption style (for example, Level 2), select Display In Document, and choose OK.

8. For each additional counter level you want to display, type another punctuation character and repeat step 7.

9. When you're done, press F7, choose Close, press F7 again, and choose OK until you return to your document.

Repeat the steps above for each type of graphics box that has a multilevel counter.

T I P

When you edit a graphics box (Alt+F9 BE), you can select the box you want to edit by choosing Document Box Number and typing in a number. Alternatively, you can choose Counter Number, select the type of counter you want, and type in the counter number of the box you want to change.

Using Counters with Lists

As I mentioned earlier, WordPerfect automatically marks captioned graphic boxes for inclusion in the appropriate Equation Box, Figure Box, Table Box, Text Box, or User Box list. However, counters that you create *aren't* marked automatically. To mark a counter (and any surrounding text), select the text and counter code that you want to include in the list (use Reveal Codes to help you see the code, if necessary). Choose Tools ➤ List ➤ Mark (or press Alt+F5 L), type (or accept) the list name, and choose OK. After marking your counters, define the list and generate it, as explained in Chapter 31.

That about wraps it up for automatic line numbering and counters. In the next chapter, you'll learn about automatic hyphenation, a tool that lets you tighten loose lines that contain too much white space.

Auto-Hyphenating
Your Text

fast TRACK

- **To insert a hard hyphen** 579

    press Home –. This prevents WordPerfect from breaking the word at the hyphen.

- **To insert a soft return** 581

    press Home ↵. WordPerfect will simply break the word at the location of the soft return (without adding a hyphen) if the entire word won't fit at the end of the line.

- **If a long word refuses to be hyphenated** 582

    remove the [Cancel Hyph] code in front of that word in Reveal Codes.

- **To change the hyphenation zones** 588

    choose Layout ➤ Line (Shift+F8 L) ➤ Hyphenation Zone (Shift+F8 LZ) and type in the new Left and Right zone settings (in percentages). You can decrease the zones for more hyphens and tighter text, or increase them for fewer hyphens and looser text.

HYPHENATION adds a smoother, more professional look to your documents by tightening loose lines that contain too much white space. The first fully-justified paragraph in Figure 16.1 illustrates how a long word can cause a very loose line. That same paragraph looks much tighter with a hyphen added to the long word, as the second paragraph in Figure 16.1 shows.

You can hyphenate words in two ways: by inserting your own hyphens or by letting WordPerfect do it for you. You'll learn both ways in this chapter.

FIGURE 16.1

A fully-justified
paragraph with and
without hyphenation

Very long words like supercalifragilisticexpialidocious, of Mary Poppins fame, cause very loose lines (too much white space) if you leave them unhyphenated, especially when you squeeze them into tight margins.

Very long words like supercalifragilis- ticexpialidocious, of Mary Poppins fame, cause very loose lines (too much white space) if you leave them unhyphenated, especially when you squeeze them into tight margins.

Hyphenating Text Automatically

Here's how to turn on automatic hyphenation:

1. Move the cursor to where you want automatic hyphenation to begin, or to the start of the document (Home Home ↑). Or, select one or more paragraphs of text that you want to hyphenate.

2. Choose Layout ➤ Line or press Shift+F8 L.

3. Select (check) Hyphenation.

4. Choose OK until you return to your document.

Helping WordPerfect Hyphenate a Word

Once you've turned automatic hyphenation on, WordPerfect will check for long words at the end of lines as you type new text or move the cursor through existing text below the cursor. When it finds a line where it can improve the spacing with a hyphen, one of two things will happen:

- WordPerfect will hyphenate the word without asking for your help.

- Sometimes, WordPerfect won't know how to hyphenate the word; you'll hear a beep and see a dialog box asking for your help in hyphenating the word (as discussed below).

WordPerfect uses the Speller dictionary to hyphenate words. If it finds a word that needs hyphenating in the dictionary, WordPerfect will hyphenate it accordingly. If that word isn't in the dictionary, WordPerfect will either leave the word unhyphenated or ask for your help. (See "Refining Automatic Hyphenation," later in this chapter, for information about controlling when WordPerfect asks for help with hyphenation.)

Suppose you type *supercalifragilisticexpialidocious* near the end of a line when auto-hyphenation is on. Since that word isn't in WordPerfect's dictionary, you'll see the Position Hyphen dialog box shown here:

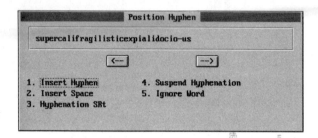

Now you can do any of the following:

- To insert the hyphen where WordPerfect suggests (between the letters *o* and *u* in this example), press ↵ or choose Insert Hyphen. You can also choose Insert Space to separate the letters with a space, or Hyphenation SRt to insert a soft return between the letters.

- To move the suggested hyphen to the left or right, click the mouse where you want the hyphen, or use the ← key (or <-- button) or → key (or --> button) to reposition the hyphen one character at a time. You can only move the hyphen to a location that's within the hyphenation zone. (I'll explain hyphenation zones later.)

- To prevent the word from being hyphenated, choose Ignore Word. The entire word will wrap to the next line, and WordPerfect will insert a [Cancel Hyph] code in front of the word. WordPerfect won't prompt you to hyphenate this word again, even if you change the text. You can also enter the [Cancel Hyph] code at any time. Position the cursor in front of the word that you want WordPerfect to ignore and press Home then /.

- To turn hyphenation off for the moment, choose Suspend Hyphenation. This is especially useful when you don't want WordPerfect to bother you with hyphenation prompts while you're scrolling through a document or spell checking.

Changing an Automatic Hyphen

Suppose WordPerfect automatically hyphenated a word in your document. Then, while scrolling through the document, you discover that you don't like the way WordPerfect hyphenated the word. Here's how to change the hyphen's position when automatic hyphenation is still on:

1. Move the cursor to the hyphen WordPerfect inserted at the end of the line. This appears as a [- Soft Hyphen EOL] hidden code in Reveal Codes.

2. Press the Delete key.

3. You'll hear a beep and see the Position Hyphen dialog box.

Now just choose one of the options discussed above to reposition the hyphen, insert a space or soft return, or prevent WordPerfect from hyphenating the word.

Turning Off Automatic Hyphenation

Turning automatic hyphenation on inserts a [Hyph:On] code into your document. Therefore, automatic hyphenation will be active for all text below that code to the end of the document, or until WordPerfect finds a [Hyph:Off] code, which turns hyphenation off.

As you may have guessed, there are two ways to turn off automatic hyphenation:

- Delete the [Hyph:On] code in Reveal Codes.

- Insert a [Hyph:Off] code where you want automatic hyphenation to stop. To do this, move the cursor to the right spot (or select one or more paragraphs where you want to turn off hyphenation). Choose Layout ➤ Line (Shift+F8 L), and then deselect Hyphenation.

TIP

You can use Search and Replace (discussed in Chapter 9) to locate and remove hyphenation codes discussed in this chapter.

The first method turns off automatic hyphenation below the cursor, but doesn't remove existing hyphens. However, WordPerfect won't hyphenate words again if you add or change text.

The second method leaves hyphenation on above the cursor, but turns it off for text below it. If you selected text before turning off hyphenation, only the selected paragraphs will have hyphenation turned off. This method is best when you want some sections hyphenated but not others. Your document can have as many [Hyph:On] and [Hyph:Off] codes as you want, and any amount of text—from a few lines to many pages—can appear between the [Hyph:On] and [Hyph:Off] codes.

Hyphenating Text Manually

You can hyphenate words manually, without WordPerfect's help, at any time. However, you should understand a few characters—including hyphens, soft hyphens, hard hyphens, and dashes—before you try it.

Hyphen Characters

A *hyphen character* is just a normal hyphen (or minus sign), which you use to divide compound words like *forty-seven*, and compound names like *Claplock-Strappman*. The word will be broken on this character only when the word is too long to fit on the current line and the hyphen falls at the end of the line. In Reveal codes, the hyphen character appears as [- Hyphen].

Soft Hyphens

WordPerfect automatically inserts *soft hyphens* when it needs to break a word at the end of a line. These are called "soft" hyphens because they remain dormant and invisible (except in Reveal Codes) when they're not needed for hyphenation.

You can type in a soft hyphen yourself, to tell WordPerfect where you want it to hyphenate a word if it needs to do so. Here's how:

1. Move the cursor to where you want to insert the soft hyphen.
2. Press Ctrl+- (that is, hold down Ctrl and type the hyphen). You'll only see the hyphen in Reveal Codes, as a [- Soft Hyphen] code.

Hard Hyphens

You can use a *hard hyphen* to keep text on either side of a hyphen together at the end of a line. For example, perhaps you'd prefer to have WordPerfect wrap a long name like *Smythe-Browne* to the next line, instead of breaking it after *Smythe-*. Here's how to add a hard hyphen:

1. Delete any spaces or regular hyphens between the words you want kept together, then position the cursor where you want the hard hyphen to appear.
2. Press Home and type a hyphen (Home -).

TIP

You can also use a *hard space* to keep words together on one line. To enter a hard space, delete any regular spaces between the words, and position the cursor where you want the hard space to appear. Now press Home and type a space (Home Space).

Dashes

People often use a *dash* character to show a sudden break in thought that changes the sentence structure, like this:

Will he—indeed, *can* he—finish the book on time?

There are three types of dashes you can add. A dash, an en dash, or an em dash. The exact appearance of these dashes depends on the currently selected font. In a proportional font, an en dash is the width of the letter *n*. An em dash is the width of the letter *m*. None of the dashes is ever used for automatic hyphenation. They're treated like any other "regular" character.

The en and em dashes are available only from the typographic symbol set in the WordPerfect special characters. Here's an example of each type of dash, and how to type them into your document:

-	Dash	Press Home- (Home then a hyphen)
–	En dash	Press Ctrl+W, type **n-** or **4,33** then ↵
—	Em dash	Press Ctrl+W, type **m-** or **4,34** then ↵

Breaking Words without Hyphens

You can also break words at the ends of lines, without inserting hyphens. This is handy when you want to use a character other than a hyphen to break long words. For instance, the slash (/), the en dash, and the em dash are common. Suppose you create your own compound word, such as *Cattleya/Cymbidium/Dendrobium*, and that word falls at the end of a line. You might want WordPerfect to break the word into two lines at a slash, without adding a hyphen, like this:

...your own compound word like Cattleya/
Cymbidium/Dendrobium...

You can use the *hyphenation soft return* to tell WordPerfect where to break a word at the end of a line without hyphenating. This character is visible only in Reveal Codes, where it looks like this: [Hyph SRt].

Suppose you're typing *Cattleya/Cymbidium/Dendrobium* while hyphenation is turned on and WordPerfect inserts a hyphen, placing *Cattleya/-* on the first line and *Cymbidium/Dendrobium* on the next line. You can delete the hyphen and break the words at the slash as follows:

1. Move the cursor to the hyphen.

2. Press the Delete key to delete the hyphen.

3. When the Position Hyphen dialog box appears, move the cursor to where you want the word to break (after the first / in this example) and choose Hyphenation SRt.

You can also enter a hyphenation soft return when you type the words, even if WordPerfect isn't prompting for hyphenation. This is especially useful with word combinations like *and/or* or the *Cattleya/Cymbidium/Dendrobium* example discussed previously. Inserting the hyphenation soft return is easy:

1. Position the cursor where you want to insert the hyphenation soft return.

2. Press Home, then press ↵ (Home ↵).

As for the soft hyphen, the hyphenation soft return remains dormant until WordPerfect needs it to break the word at the end of a line.

Temporary Soft Returns

The *temporary soft return* is a rather odd code that WordPerfect uses to break long words when automatic hyphenation is turned *off*. The code is invisible in the document window, but appears as a [TSRt] at the end of a line in Reveal Codes.

This code splits the word without hyphenating it. You'll never type this code yourself and don't need to worry about it until you start working with narrow columns of text (see Chapter 27).

Summary of Hyphenation Characters

Table 16.1 shows hyphenation characters and summarizes the roles they play in breaking words at the end of a line. The table also shows the keys you press and the codes that appear in Reveal Codes for each type of hyphen.

What to Do When a Word Refuses to Be Hyphenated

Sometimes a word simply won't hyphenate when you expect it to. This can happen if you previously chose Ignore Word when WordPerfect asked for help during automatic hyphenation. Here's how to solve that problem when you're sure that you *do* want to hyphenate a word that stubbornly refuses to be hyphenated:

1. Move the cursor to the first character in the word that refuses to be hyphenated.

2. In Reveal Codes, delete the [Cancel Hyph] code just before or within the word.

3. WordPerfect may beep and display the Position Hyphen dialog box. Just follow the usual procedure to position the hyphen and select the type of hyphenation you want.

TABLE 16.1: A Summary of Hyphens and Dashes

HYPHEN	DESCRIPTION	KEYSTROKE	CODE
Hyphen character	Permanent hyphen that you can use to break two words at the end of a line	–	[– Hyphen]
Soft hyphen	Temporary hyphen that breaks a word only when necessary (WordPerfect uses this during automatic hyphenation)	Ctrl+–	[– Soft Hyphen] or [–Soft Hyphen EOL]
Dash or hard hyphen	A dash (hyphen) that's never separated at the end of a line	Home -	-
En dash	A dash that's never separated at the end of a line	Ctrl+W **4,33**	–
Em dash	A dash that's never separated at the end of a line	Ctrl+W **4,34**	—
Hyphenation soft return	Breaks words at a certain place without showing a hyphen	Choose Hyphenation SRt in Position Hyphen dialog box, or press Home ↵ when typing a word	[Hyph SRt]
Ignore Word	Wraps the entire word to the next line and prevents future hyphenation	Choose Ignore Word in Position Hyphen dialog box or press Home / when typing a word	[Cancel Hyph]

NOTE: If you can't remember which character produces the hyphenation codes, just choose Layout ➤ Special Codes and select the character you want from the Special Codes dialog box.

Refining Automatic Hyphenation

The Environment dialog box provides options that let you customize how WordPerfect carries out automatic hyphenation. Normally, WordPerfect's default settings will be perfectly adequate for your needs, so feel free to skip the rest of the chapter if you're happily hyphenating your text already. However, the next few sections might be useful if you're simply curious, or you want to refine automatic hyphenation further.

Choosing a Hyphenation Dictionary

The Speller and hyphenation features both use the same dictionary, which is usually named C:\WPCDOS60\WPUS.LEX in the United States. You can also purchase optional foreign-language dictionaries from WordPerfect Corporation and install them.

The two-character language code (US in the United States) tells Word-Perfect which language dictionary you're currently using. You can switch to a different language dictionary for hyphenation and spelling as many times as you want within a single document. To do this, move the cursor to where the new dictionary should take effect (or to the top of the document if that language applies throughout). Now choose File ➤ Setup ➤ Environment ➤ Language (or press Shift+F1 EL), and select a language from the dialog box that appears. Choose OK until you return to your document.

You can also specify a different directory location for your dictionaries. Choose File ➤ Setup ➤ Location Of Files ➤ Writing Tools (or press Shift+F1 LW) and enter the names of directories that contain your main and supplemental dictionaries. If you change this location, be sure to move your dictionaries to that directory. See Chapter 19 for more information on the Setup options.

N O T E

As mentioned above, WordPerfect uses the Speller file that matches the current language code (for example, WPUS.LEX for United States English). You can use the Spell utility, described in Chapter 11, if you want to adjust the way words are hyphenated.

Choosing How Often You're Prompted for Hyphenation

The most convenient way to use automatic hyphenation is the default method, in which WordPerfect asks for help with placing a hyphen only if it can't find a word in its dictionary. That is, WordPerfect prompts you only when it needs your help and is silent otherwise.

However, you can control when and whether WordPerfect prompts you for hyphenation help by following these steps:

1. Choose File ➤ Setup ➤ Environment ➤ Prompt For Hyphenation (or press Shift+F1 EP).

2. Choose one of the Prompt For Hyphenation options described below, then choose OK until you return to your document.

    Never When you select this option, WordPerfect never prompts you to position the hyphen and always hyphenates according to the current hyphenation dictionary. Words that don't appear in the dictionary will be wrapped to the next line (and not hyphenated) if they're too long to fit on a line.

    When Required This is the normal setting. WordPerfect asks for help in placing the hyphen only when it can't find a word in the current dictionary.

    Always If you choose this setting, WordPerfect stops and asks for your help *every time* it needs to hyphenate a word. This can be awfully tedious, but it will give you practice using the hyphenation feature.

Your choice will affect automatic hyphenation in the current document and all future documents, until you repeat the steps above and choose a different prompt option.

Disabling the Beep

If the beep that precedes WordPerfect's hyphenation prompt is driving you nuts, you can turn it off. Choose File ➤ Setup ➤ Environment ➤ Beep Options (or press Shift+F1 EE). Deselect Beep On Hyphenation, then choose OK until you return to your document. This will turn off beeping for the current session and all future sessions, until you check the Beep On Hyphenation box again.

Using Hyphenation Zones

WordPerfect uses *hyphenation zones* to decide when to break a word during automatic hyphenation. You can think of a hyphenation zone as the place on a standard typewriter where the bell sounds to let you know that you're nearing the end of a line as you type. Of course, WordPerfect doesn't sound a bell because it usually hyphenates automatically.

Although you can't see the hyphenation zones on your screen, WordPerfect uses two zones to control hyphenation, one on each side of the right margin. Figure 16.2 shows how these zones would look if they were visible.

WordPerfect follows the rules below to decide whether to hyphenate a word when automatic hyphenation is on, or when you type a hyphen, soft hyphen, or hyphenation soft return character:

- Hyphenate the last word on a line if it starts before the left edge of or within the hyphenation zone and extends past the edge of the hyphenation zone.

- Wrap the last word on a line to the next line without hyphenation if it starts before the left edge of or within the hyphenation zone and is narrower than the zone.

FIGURE 16.2

WordPerfect's
hyphenation zones

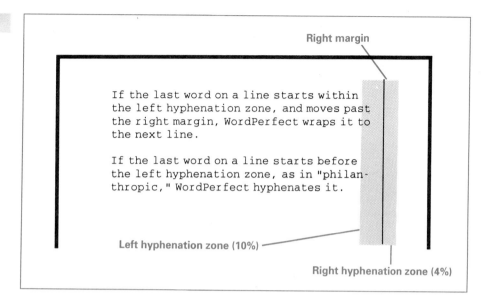

The sample paragraphs in Figure 16.2 show how this works. Notice that the end of the first line in the first paragraph doesn't have enough room for the word *the* before the right margin. Therefore, WordPerfect wraps it to the next line because it's narrower than the hyphenation zones. In the second paragraph, WordPerfect hyphenates the long word *philanthropic* because it starts before the left hyphenation zone and would extend past the right hyphenation zone if it weren't hyphenated.

Figure 16.2 is only for illustration. If you type the paragraphs shown, they may not be wrapped or hyphenated in the same way.

Changing the Hyphenation Zones

The hyphenation zones are measured as percentages of line length. This lets the hyphenation zone adjust to the width of the line and simplifies matters when you create multicolumn documents with narrow columns.

NOTE The distance you're allowed to move the hyphen when WordPerfect prompts you to hyphenate a word is equal to the width of the hyphenation zones.

The default left hyphenation zone is 10%, and the default right hyphenation zone is 4%. Each line is 6.5″ long when you print on standard 8.5″ × 11″ paper, with 1″ left and right margins and 10 characters to the inch. With these facts in hand, some quick mental arithmetic (or a calculator) reveals that the default left hyphenation zone is 0.65″ long, and the default right hyphenation zone is about 0.26″ long.

These preselected hyphenation zones provide a sort of happy medium between how tight the text is in justified paragraphs (or how much space is at the end of ragged-right lines) and the amount of hyphenation required. However, you can change the sizes of the hyphenation zones to tighten the text further or loosen it a bit. Basically, it works like this: Smaller hyphenation zones produce tighter text and many hyphens. Larger hyphenation zones require less hyphenation, but produce looser text.

The decision about whether to use wide or narrow hyphenation zones is completely up to you. You can leave them at their default settings, or change them. If you decide to change them, remember that new hyphenation measurements affect only text that is to the right of and below the cursor (like all formatting codes).

Here's how to change the hyphenation zones:

1. Move the cursor to where you want the new hyphenation zones to start (for example, to the top of the document if you want the entire document to use the new hyphenation zones). Or select one or more paragraphs to change those paragraphs only.

2. Choose <u>L</u>ayout ➤ <u>L</u>ine ➤ Hyphenation <u>Z</u>one (or press Shift+F8 LZ).

3. Type in new settings (in percentages) for either or both the <u>L</u>eft and <u>R</u>ight zones.

4. Choose OK until you return to the document window.

WordPerfect will use the new setting to prompt for hyphenation help when you type new text below the cursor position (or within the paragraphs you selected). Likewise, it will adjust the existing text to comply with new hyphenation zones when you scroll through existing text below the cursor.

If you change your mind about the new settings, you can return to the preset hyphenation zones. Simply go to Reveal Codes and remove the [Lft HZone] and [Rgt HZone] (or [+Lft HZone] and [+Rgt HZone]) codes that you inserted earlier. When you can scroll through existing text below the cursor, WordPerfect will readjust the hyphenation to the original settings, prompting for help when (and if) it needs it.

This chapter covered hyphenation, a feature that smooths out your text by using hyphens to break long words at the end of lines. In the next part of this book, we'll look at ways to manage and simplify your work. We'll begin with *styles*, which make it easy to design a document to precise specifications and then change that design with just a few keystrokes.

PART FIVE

Managing
(and Simplifying)
Your Work

Using Styles
to Simplify Your Work

f a s t TRACK

TO THE uninitiated, styles may seem like a peculiar, confusing topic that's best ignored. But ask anyone in the publishing biz who's been around the block a few times, "What's the best thing about using a word processor?" My bet is that the answer would be "Styles."

Why Use Styles?

A *style* is a predefined format for some design element of your document. A *design element* is anything that's repeated throughout a document. For example, the design elements in the sample newsletter shown in Figure 17.1 include article titles, bylines ("by" followed by the author's name), and the little sunshine character that marks the end of each article.

You might think of a style as your own custom hidden code. For example, WordPerfect has some simple codes, like [Ln Spacing] and [Font], which it inserts for you. It also has some paired codes, like [Bold On] and [Bold Off], which are inserted when you boldface text. Your own hidden codes (styles) can contain any combination of virtually all the codes that Word-Perfect has to offer. For example, a style can define the font *and* the justification *and* the margins *and* whatever else you want in one fell swoop.

In the sample newsletter in Figure 17.1, I created a style to define the basic body text—the column format and font of each article. I also created a style, named Headline, to define the appearance of each article title. Another style, named Byline, formats all the bylines (under the article titles). A third style, End Mark, defines the special character at the end of each article. (The last article continues onto the next page, which isn't shown; that's why it doesn't have an end mark.)

FIGURE 17.1

A sample newsletter that uses styles to define repeating design elements, such as article titles, bylines, and the special character at the end of each article

Vol. 1 No. 1   Travel fun for everyone   January

End Mark style

travel with us as we bring you a new issue every quarter of the year. ☼

CELEBRATE WITH US — Headline style
by Jill Evans
In honor of our newsletter's maiden voyage, we'd like to invite you to an — Byline style Open House at 7:00pm on January 11 at our offices. Please dress casually or come in your most fashionable travel togs. If you miss this event, we'll see to it that your luggage ends up on the Space Shuttle. ☼

End Mark style

TROPICAL TRAVEL — Headline style
by Elizabeth Olson
Travel to tropical islands is on the increase. In just the past four years, our tropical travel sales have tripled. That's really something in a recessionary economy! There's a good reason for these increases -- tropical vacations are — Byline style great fun, especially when the wind and snow are swirling at your doorstep!

Headline style

NEWSLETTER DEBUT
by Joan Smith
We're pleased to bring this first issue of our newsletter, *The Vacationer*, to our many loyal customers. The newsletter was inspired by your ideas and questions. You've asked us where to find the best travel fares, where to go for the person who has been everywhere, what to eat and how to eat it when visiting faraway countries. We've responded by creating this newsletter.

Byline style

Here we'll bring you the latest news about great deals on vacations in exotic corners of our planet, fun places for inexpensive weekend getaways, and out-of-the-way spots you might never have thought to ask us about. We'll include handy vacation planning tips and introduce you to exciting foods, puzzling customs, and important laws you'll encounter during sojourns to foreign lands. So relax, enjoy, and

Body Text style

INSIDE...
Newsletter debut 1
Celebrate with us 1
Tropical travel 1
New employees 2
Travel calendar 3

NOTE

You'll learn to create documents like the one in Figure 17.1 in Part Seven of this book. However, you can start using styles with *any* document right now.

You can create as many different styles as you wish and give them names of your own choosing. Later, when you want to apply a particular style to something in your document, you just "turn on the style." There's no need to go through all the steps required to change the font, the justification, the margins, and so forth, because all those things are already defined within the style.

The Real Beauty of Styles

The real beauty of styles is this: If you change your mind about the appearance of a certain design element, such as the headlines, you don't need to go through the document and change the font for every single headline one at a time. Instead, you just change the Headline style, in one simple action, and *all* the headlines take on the new look instantly. Make sense? You bet it does!

Better still, if you need to come up with another newsletter next month, your work will be much easier because you can use the same set of styles you used in this month's newsletter. No need to recreate all those styles! The consistency applies not only throughout a single document; it actually carries through several documents—be they monthly newsletters, chapters in a book, whatever.

Creating a Style

You create one style at a time, assigning each one a unique name. I'll give you the complete rundown below, including a lot of optional steps you might want to ignore until you get some practice with styles.

Assuming you're at a blank document window or at a window that contains a document you'd like to create some styles for, here's what to do:

1. If you've already created a heading or paragraph that's styled the way you want the rest of them to be styled, move the cursor into the heading or paragraph.

2. Choose Layout ➤ Styles (or press Alt+F8). You'll see the Style List dialog box shown in Figure 17.2. Several styles that WordPerfect Corporation has provided as examples, as well as any styles that you've created and added to the current library, may appear in the list. (Don't worry if your list doesn't look like the example shown.)

FIGURE 17.2

The Style List dialog box. Choose Layout ➤ Styles or press Alt+F8 to get here. Your style list may be different.

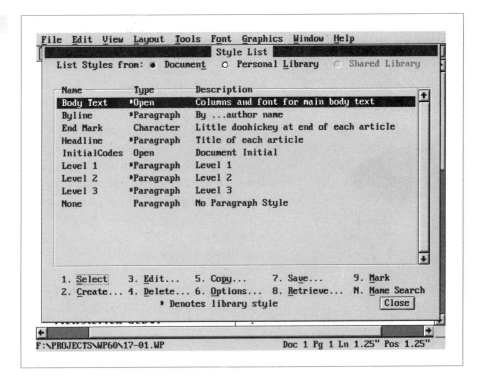

3. Take a peek at the options next to List Styles From (at the top of the dialog box). If Document *isn't* selected, select it now. (I'll explain this later.)

4. Choose Create to start creating your style. You will be taken to this dialog box:

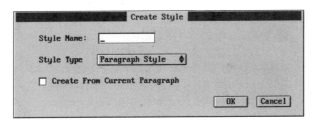

5. In the Style Name box, type a name for the style, up to 12 characters long, including blank spaces if you want them.

6. Choose Style Type and select the type of style you want this to be from the drop-down list. Your options are Paragraph Style, Character Style, and Open Style:

Paragraph Style   As the name implies, this is useful for stylizing individual paragraphs, including single lines in an outline or list. When you activate a paragraph style, it formats text from the cursor position to the first hard return ([HRt] code) that it finds. Examples: headlines that you allow to word-wrap automatically, bylines, single-paragraph quotations that are sprinkled throughout a document.

Character Style   Acts like a paired code in WordPerfect, formatting any number of characters between the [Style On] and [Style Off] codes. Use this style type to format any block of text that's less than or more than a paragraph in length (that is, it contains either no [HRt] codes or several [HRt] codes). If in doubt, use this type rather than the Paragraph type. Examples: single special characters, formats of individual words or phrases, quotations containing hard returns that are sprinkled throughout a document.

Open Style   This has no "ending code." It's like a single code in WordPerfect, such as a code for line spacing, that once turned on, stays on until some other style (or code) takes over. Examples: the codes that set up columns and the font near the start of my sample newsletter (see Figure 17.1).

Table 17.1 summarizes the most important points about the three types of styles.

NOTE   You needn't get the Style Type selection right on the first try. You can always change your mind later. If in doubt, try Character.

7. If you positioned the cursor to formatted text back in step 1, you can choose Create From Current Paragraph to have WordPerfect copy the basic formatting codes from that paragraph into the

TABLE 17.1: Open, Character, and Paragraph Styles Compared

TYPE	DESCRIPTION	START CODE	END CODE	USE TO FORMAT...
Paragraph Style	Starts at cursor position, ends at the nearest hard return (HRt)	[Para Style]	[HRt] ([Para Style End] when highlighted in Reveal Codes)	Short lines such as headings and bylines that end with a [HRt] code
Character Style	Like paired codes, formats everything between the "On" and "Off" codes	[Char Style On]	[Char Style Off]	Any length of text, from a single character to many pages
Open Style	Applies from cursor to end of document, or next overriding code	[Open Style]	(none)	Everything from the cursor down, such as a default font or columns

Style Contents dialog box—a handy shortcut to filling in the codes from scratch. (This option isn't available for Open styles, however.)

8. Choose OK to open the Edit Style dialog box, which appears below:

9. If you wish, choose <u>D</u>escription and type a description for the style, up to 55 characters long, including blank spaces if you like. The description will appear in the Style List later.

10. If you want this style to activate some new format at its end, you can choose Show Style <u>O</u>ff Codes. I'll talk about this option when I show you my sample styles later in this chapter. You needn't select it right now.

11. Choose Style <u>C</u>ontents when you're ready to define your format. Then select formatting features using the menus or the shortcut keys listed above the Style Contents box. As you make your selections, the appropriate codes are added to the Style Contents box. In addition, you can do any of the following to create or change your style as you go:

    - Type in any text or special characters (Ctrl+W) that you want WordPerfect to insert automatically.

    - Delete any codes by highlighting and pressing Delete (Del).

    - Use the pull-down menus to add items that aren't available from the list of shortcut keys. For example, you can choose <u>G</u>raphics ➤ <u>R</u>etrieve to put a graphic figure box in the style (see Chapter 26). Don't worry about choosing an "invalid feature." If you can't use something in a style, its menu option will be dimmed and unavailable.

    - To insert an existing style into the one you're creating (a style within a style, wow!), press Alt+F8 and select a style from the Style List. A message appears indicating that this style is based on some other style. Yes, any changes you make to that "other style" later will carry over into this style—quite convenient.

12. Press F7 when you're done entering the codes and/or text for your style.

13. If you're creating a Paragraph or Character style, you can choose <u>E</u>nter Key Action to change the effect of the ↵ key. Table 17.2 summarizes how you would turn off Character and Paragraph styles when typing new text. That table can help you decide how you want the Enter key to behave. (You may want to ignore this option for the time being, and try it out when you've had some experience with styles and want to fine-tune the role of the ↵ key for a particular style.)

TABLE 17.2: How to Turn Off Character and Paragraph Styles when Typing New Text*

IF ENTER KEY ACTION IS...	FOR CHARACTER STYLE, DO THIS	FOR PARAGRAPH STYLE, DO THIS
Insert a Hard Return	Press → or choose Layout ➤ Styles ➤ Off (or Alt+F8 F)	(not available)
Turn Style Off	Press ↵, →, or choose Layout ➤ Styles ➤ Off (or Alt+F8 F)	Press ↵
Turn Style Off and Back On	Press → or choose Layout ➤ Styles ➤ Off (or Alt+F8 F)	Press ↵ to end the paragraph, then press Backspace
Turn Style Off and Link To	Press ↵ to turn the style off and switch to "linked to" style. Turn off the "linked to" style according to its Enter key requirements. To turn the style off and bypass the linked style, press →.	Press ↵ to turn the style off and switch to the "linked to" style. Turn off the "linked to" style according to its Enter key requirements. To turn off the style and bypass the linked style, press ↵, then press Backspace.

***NOTE:** You can't turn off Open styles, so those aren't included in the table.

14. To return to the Style List dialog box, choose OK or press ↵. The name of your new style appears in the Style List (in alphabetical order).

15. If you want to return to your document, choose Close. If you want to create another style, repeat steps 4–14.

Whew! Finally, you've created a style. Actually, it's a lot easier than these steps might make it seem, especially after you've done it a few times. Next, let's talk about how you can *use* the style you created.

Turning On a Style

You can turn on (activate) any style in your style list at any time by following these steps:

1. First, decide what you want to apply the style to:

   - If you want to turn on a Paragraph or Open style for existing text, move the cursor to where you want to activate the style.
   - If you want to apply a style to a block of text, select that text (by dragging the mouse pointer through it, or by using Alt+F4 or F12 and the cursor-positioning keys).
   - If you want to apply the style to new text, position the cursor where you're about to begin typing.

2. Press Alt+F8 or choose Layout ➤ Styles. Double-click the name of the style you want to activate. Or, highlight the style name and choose Select (or press ↵).

That's all there is to it. You're returned to your document window, and the [Style] codes (visible only in Reveal Codes, of course) are inserted into your document. The selected text, or the text you start typing, will be formatted according to the codes you defined in the style.

If you change your mind right away, you can choose Edit ➤ Undo or press Ctrl+Z to undo the change. If you change your mind later, after making other changes, just flip on Reveal Codes (Alt+F3) and delete the unwanted [Style] code(s).

T I P

You can also turn on Paragraph styles by selecting them from the Ribbon (View ➤ Ribbon).

Turning a Style Off

There are several ways to turn off (deactivate) a style. Here are your options, assuming that you didn't change that Enter Key Action option (which I'll explain later) when creating the style:

- If you selected text before choosing the style, the [Style Off] code will already be at the end of the selected text. Any text you type *between* those codes will have the new style. Any text outside those codes will not have that style.

NOTE   If you use a Paragraph style, the [HRt] code that marks the end of the paragraph will also mark the end of the style. The [Style End] code won't be visible until you move the cursor to that ending [HRt] code in Reveal Codes.

- If you turned on a Character style before typing, you can just press → to move past the [Style Off] code and resume typing.

- If you turned on a Paragraph style without first selecting text, pressing ↵ inserts a hard return and automatically turns off the style.

- If you activated an open style, you really can't turn the style off, because it's a single code (like [Ln Spacing]). However, you can switch to a different style at any point in your document simply by choosing the style you want.

Hidden Codes for Styles

Different types of styles insert different hidden codes, which are visible only in Reveal Codes. For example, an open style starts with an [Open Style:] code that includes the style name. Paragraph styles start with [Para Style:] followed by the style name and end with [Para Style End:] (that code is only visible when the cursor is on the [HRt] code that ends the paragraph).

When you put the cursor directly on the [Style] code in Reveal Codes, the code expands to show the contents of the style. As with everything else in WordPerfect, you can remove styles simply by deleting the hidden codes.

Food for Thought: My Newsletter Styles

Before we go on, let's take a look at the styles I used to format the newsletter back in Figure 17.1. The sections below describe these different styles.

The Body Text Style

The columns and text of articles are defined in an open style named Body Text that contains these codes:

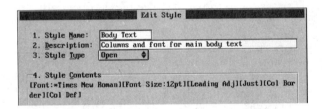

I used the font menu (Ctrl+F8) to define the font. I used Layout (Shift+F8) ➤ Other ➤ Printer Functions (Chapter 28) to reduce the leading between lines by –1p (see Chapter 28). I chose Layout (Shift+F8) ➤ Line to set the Justification to Left. Then I used Layout ➤ Columns to define two newspaper columns, with .35″ in between, and a single separator line (discussed in Chapter 27).

The Headline Style

The article titles are all formatted with a paragraph style named Headline. That style contains the codes shown below:

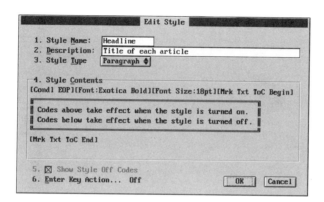

After choosing Create from the Style List dialog box, naming this style Headline, and choosing OK, I selected the Show Style Off Codes check box. Doing so inserted the framed box containing the words "Codes above..." and "Codes below..." that you see in the Style Contents box. I used the Show Style Off Codes check box here because this style uses a "Mark Text" code to identify the article title as a table of contents entry. Next I chose Style Contents to put the codes into the style. Then,

- I used Layout (Shift+F8) ➤ Other ➤ Conditional End Of Page and set the number of lines to keep together to 4. That prevents an article title, byline, and the first couple lines of article text from being split across two columns or two pages.

- I used Ctrl+F8 to define the font and size of the headlines.

- Next is the tricky part: I turned on blocking (Alt+F4 or F12) and pressed ↓ to "select" the comment box. ([Block] appears above the box; the cursor appears below the box.) Then I pressed Alt+F5, selected Table Of Contents, entered 1, and chose OK to mark the table of contents entry.

- Last, I pressed F7, as instructed on the screen, to exit the Style Contents box.

When I apply this style later, each headline will be between a [Mrk Txt ToC Begin] and [Mrk Txt ToC End] code. So when I'm done writing, I can just use the automatic referencing techniques described in Chapter 31 to have WordPerfect whip up a table of contents automatically.

The Byline Style

The codes in my Byline style are shown below. These are just simple [Small On] and [Italc On] codes selected from the Font menu (Ctrl+F8):

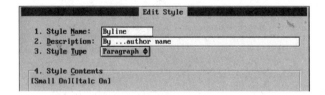

```
                              Edit Style
  1. Style Name:     Byline
  2. Description:    By ...author name
  3. Style Type      Paragraph ◆

  4. Style Contents
[Small On][Italc On]
```

Notice that I *didn't* bother to flip on the Show Style Off Codes option here. That's because in 99% of the cases, when WordPerfect sees the On portion of a paired code it automatically puts the appropriate Off code at the end of the style. Similarly, when a style contains a [Font] code, WordPerfect "knows" to return to the original font at the end of the style. You don't need to put a specific font code at the bottom of the style.

About the only time you *do* need that Show Style Off Codes option is when you're marking text within the style, as in my example of the [Mrk Text ToC] code earlier. In this case, you need to turn that feature on and select the comment box as I did in that example.

You might also want to use the Show Style Off Codes option when you want WordPerfect to do something special at the *end* of the style. For example, suppose you don't want WordPerfect to revert to the original font at the end of a style; rather, you want it to kick in some other font. Then you would want to turn on Show Style Off Codes and put the second font code below the comment box. That way, the new font is activated at the end of the style, rather than at the beginning of the style.

The End Mark Style

The End Mark style is a simple character style that contains just two codes: [Flsh Rgt] (Alt+F6), and the "sun" special character (Ctrl+W, character 5,6 from the Iconic set). The codes are shown below:

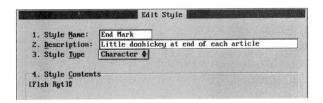

Why bother to put these two simple codes in a style? Because if I decide to use a happy face or some other character, rather than the sunshine one, to end each article, I simply have to change the End Mark style. No need to go searching and replacing through the entire document.

Changing an Existing Style

Let's say you've created some styles and applied them to your document. Now you want to change one of those styles. No problem.

1. Choose <u>L</u>ayout ➤ <u>S</u>tyles, or press Styles (Alt+F8).

2. Highlight the name of the style you want to change.

3. Choose <u>E</u>dit. The Edit Style dialog box for the chosen style appears. You can change the name, description, type, or any other characteristics of the style here.

4. To change the codes in the style, choose Style <u>C</u>ontents and make your changes using the standard editing techniques. Don't forget to press F7 when you're done!

5. Choose OK or press ↵ until you return to your document.

Any text in the document that's currently formatted with the style that you just modified will instantly reflect your changes (though this is only readily apparent in Graphics and Page modes). These styles are a major time saver!

Deleting Styles

Your document's style list might contain numerous sample styles that WordPerfect provides as examples, which you don't really need in the current document. You can save disk space, and speed things along a little, by deleting any styles you don't need in the document:

1. Choose Layout ➤ Styles, or press Alt+F8, to get to the Style List.

2. If you want to be sure you're only deleting styles that are relevant to the current document, make sure Document is selected next to List Styles From near the top of the dialog box. Also, choose Options, make sure that List User Created Styles *is* selected, and List System Styles *isn't* selected. Then choose OK. (I'll explain these options a little later in the chapter.)

3. Highlight the style that you want to delete, and then choose Delete or press the Del key, if it's available. (Some styles cannot be deleted. Some make it look like you can delete them, but will just ask if you want to "Reset to Default State" after you choose Delete. I'll explain this in more detail later. If you're in doubt, choose No.) You'll see this dialog box:

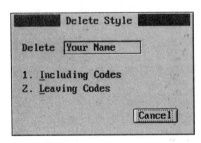

4. Choose one of the following:

Including Codes   Deletes the style from the Style List, removes all style codes for this style from the document, and deletes all hidden codes associated with the style. In other words, it cleans out the style name *and* its codes from the current document.

Leaving Codes   Deletes the style from the Style List, and deletes all style codes for this style from the document. You'd only use this option in the unlikely event that you want to remove a style name from the style list, but leave its codes behind in the current document.

When you're done deleting unwanted styles, you can choose Close to return to the document window.

Saving Styles

Any styles that you create are generally saved with the current document automatically. That is, when you close and save the document, all your styles are saved with it. You don't have to do anything special to save your styles, unless you want to make those styles available in *other* documents. In that case, you need to understand Style Libraries, which I'll explain next.

Understanding Style Libraries

A style library is a collection of styles, stored on disk with its own file name (typically having the .STY extension). For example, I could save my sample collection of newsletter styles to a style library named NEWSLET.STY. When creating future editions of the newsletter, I could just *apply* that style library to the new document I'm about to create. Those styles will then appear in the new document's Style List when I press Alt+F8. So there's no need for me to recreate the styles every time I write a new edition of the newsletter.

Document, Personal, and Shared Style Libraries

Now, there are three different kinds of style libraries you can create:

Document   Styles in a document style library are available in the current document only. This library is stored with the document itself automatically when you save the document. No .STY file is created.

Personal Library   Styles that are stored in a style library on your own (local) hard disk. You can use these styles in any document you create. But they are only accessible from your computer.

Shared Library   Styles that are stored in a style library on a network drive or shared directory. Anyone who's connected to that drive or directory can use the styles in his or her documents.

The last option has far-reaching implications for people who write in teams. Say you've got half a dozen writers and editors working on a large project. They all use the styles in the shared style library in their own documents. You, as grand wazoo of editorial styles, decide to change the font of all chapter titles. No problem. You just open up the shared library and change the style. The change is carried over to everyone else's work instantly, so there's no need to run around changing individual style libraries on each computer.

Where to Store Personal and Shared Libraries

Before you can create a personal or shared library, you need to tell WordPerfect where you want to store them. (Unless, of course, you or somebody else has already done so.) Follow the steps below if you've never defined those locations:

1. Starting from the document window, choose File ➤ Setup ➤ Location Of Files (or Shift+F1 L).

2. Choose Style Files. You'll see the Style Files dialog box.

3. If you wish, choose <u>D</u>irectory For Personal Libraries, and enter a valid DOS drive and directory name to indicate where you want to store personal libraries on your local hard disk.

TIP

You can use the Directory Tree (F8) and QuickList (F6) buttons in these steps to choose existing directory or file names. You can also enter the name of a nonexistent directory and/or file name. WordPerfect will create it for you on the spot.

4. If you think you'll be using a particular set of personal styles regularly, choose Default <u>P</u>ersonal Library and enter a file name. In the future, whenever you create a new document, this library will be readily available to you (though you can, of course, switch to another library at any time).

5. If you want to share styles with other users on a network, choose Di<u>r</u>ectory For Shared Libraries. Then type, or choose, a valid DOS path name from your shared directory or network drive.

6. As in step 4 above, you can choose Default <u>S</u>hared Library to define a shared library that you want to open every time you create a new document.

7. Choose OK and Close as necessary to get back to the document window.

The example below shows how I set up style libraries on my personal system. Personal styles are stored on C:\WP60\STYLES, in a file I decided to name MYSTYLES.STY. My shared libraries are on a network directory, F:\WPSTYLES. I used EVERYONE.STY as the name of the default shared library.

Creating a Personal or Shared Style Library

Once you've told WordPerfect where to store style libraries, it's easy to create them. Anyway, here's how to create a personal or shared library:

1. If it isn't already open, open the document that contains the styles that you created and want to save to a style library.

2. Get to the Style List dialog box (Layout ➤ Styles or Alt+F8).

3. Make sure that the Document option next to List Styles From at the top of the document is selected. You should see all the styles in this document (including Level 1 and other WordPerfect "Library" styles, which I'll explain later).

4. If you can, choose Personal Library or Shared Library (whichever type of library you want to create), then skip to step 10. If you can't select one of those options because it's dimmed, continue with the next step.

5. Choose Options. You'll see the dialog box shown below. (Tip: Use this command when you just need a quick reminder of which style libraries are open at the moment.)

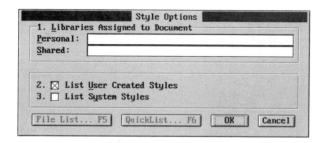

6. Choose Libraries Assigned To Document, then choose either Personal or Shared, depending on which type of library you want to create.

7. Type in a file name (such as NEWSLET.STY). Or, if you want to add some styles to an existing personal or shared library, you can use the File List (F5) and QuickList (F6) to help locate the appropriate file.

8. Make sure List User Created Styles is selected and List System Styles is deselected. (This isn't entirely necessary, but it's convenient when you're doing this kind of thing.)

9. Choose OK to get back to the Style List.

10. Mark the names of the styles that you want to put in a personal or shared library by highlighting and pressing * or choosing Mark.

11. Choose Copy and indicate which library you want to save these styles to, either Personal Library or Shared Library. (These are only available after you've defined a location and file name for the style libraries.) Choose OK.

12. You may see a "Please Wait" message. Then you'll be returned to the Style List.

13. To verify the copy, choose Personal Library or Shared Library, whichever one you just copied styles to, from the top of the Style List dialog box. You should see the names of all the copied files in that library. (If not, choose Options and make sure List User Created Styles is selected, then choose OK.)

14. Now you can choose Save. If you want to save these styles to a style library *other than* the current library, type in a file name.

15. Choose OK.

Your styles are now stored in the library style file under the file name you specified, and on the directory you specified in Location Of Files.

TIP

If you can't remember the name of the currently open personal or shared library, choose Options from the Style List dialog box. You can change to a different shared or personal library here, if you wish.

Now that you've created a personal or shared library, you'll probably want to know how to use its styles in future documents. I'll talk about that next.

Assigning a Style Library to a Document

If you specified default personal and shared style libraries in Location Of Files, those style libraries will already be applied to your document and ready for use every time you create a new document. You can view the styles in those libraries by going to the Style List dialog box (Layout ➤ Styles or Alt+F8), then choosing either Personal Library or Shared Library from the options at the top of the dialog box.

If you didn't specify default personal and shared libraries, or you want to switch to a different personal or shared library, you can follow these steps to do so:

1. Assuming you're in the Style List, choose Options.

2. Choose Libraries Assigned To Document, then specify a file name next to Personal and/or Shared. (You can use the File List (F5) and QuickList (F6) to locate the .STY file you want to open.)

3. One more time, make sure List Under Created Styles is selected; otherwise you won't see the names of the styles you created in the Style List.

4. Choose OK to return to the Style List.

Using Your Personal/Shared Styles

Now you can turn on those styles as you did your document styles. That is, position the cursor or select text, get to the Style List (Alt+F8), and choose Personal Library or Shared Library as appropriate. Double-click the name of the style you want to use, or highlight it and choose Select.

Quicker Access to Personal/Shared Styles

When you want to select a personal or shared style, you have to go through the extra step of choosing the appropriate library from the top of the Style List before you can choose the style you want. As an alternative, you can choose your personal/shared library and mark styles that you want to use in this document with an asterisk (*). Then use the Copy option at the bottom of the Style List to copy those styles into your Document style list. That way, you'll be able to see the style name as soon as you open the Style list.

Order of Precedence among Styles

If your Document, Personal, and Shared Libraries contain styles that have the same name, keep in mind that the style that is most specific to the current document overrides the other styles. For example, if the personal and shared libraries each contain a style named ByLine, then the style in the Personal library takes precedence. But if the Document library also contains a style named Byline, *that* one takes precedence.

If you want the "back" (personal or shared) style to take effect, you can copy it from its current list into your Document or Personal List, using the Mark (*) and Copy technique described earlier. Or, just delete the Document or Personal Style from its list, so it doesn't take precedence over the one that's "farther away."

Assigning versus Retrieving a Style Library

The section titled "Assigning a Style Library to a Document" describes how to choose the personal and/or shared libraries for the current document. But let's suppose that, rather than switching to a different library, you simply want to add the styles from some other library to the library you're already using.

For example, let's say you're using NEWSLET.STY, and you don't want to change that. But you would like to yank a copy of a style you created and named "My Favorite" from some other library into this library. In that case, you don't go through the Options dialog box. Instead, you do the following:

1. Get to the Style List (Layout ➤ Styles or Alt+F8).

2. From the currently available libraries, choose the one into which you want to bring some other style(s): Document, Personal Library, or Shared Library. The latter two are only available if you defined your default libraries or selected a specific library with Options, as described earlier.

3. Choose Retrieve, then use the File List (F5) or QuickList (F6) to specify the name of the style (.STY) file you want to copy styles from. The library can be on either your personal or shared directory of style files.

4. If any of the incoming styles have the same name as styles that are already in this library, you'll be prompted with

   Style(s) already exist. Replace?

5. If you choose No, only styles that don't have the same name as your current styles will be retrieved. If you choose Yes, all the styles from the other library will be retrieved, replacing any styles that have the same name.

6. If necessary, you can now use <u>D</u>elete to delete any styles you don't want in this library. Then choose Close to return to your document window.

What About Those System Styles?

When you use the Styles feature, you can't help but notice that WordPerfect contains some *system styles*. They are only visible after you choose <u>O</u>ptions ➤ List System Styles in the Style List dialog box. They have names like BoxText, Caption, Comment, and so forth, and are indicated by a bullet (•) next to the style type in the Style List.

Those system styles are styles that WordPerfect uses behind the scenes when you create graphics boxes, footnotes, and so forth. While you *can* activate and edit most of those styles by going directly through the style list, you'll probably find it easier to go through the feature that the style is automatically applied to. Table 17.3 lists the various features that use system styles behind the scenes, and the commands you can use to change those styles without going through the Style List.

What's That "• Denotes Library Style" Message?

When you're in the Style List, you may notice this message near the bottom of the dialog box:

• Denotes library style

What that message at the bottom of the Style List dialog box probably *should* say is

• Denotes a style that came with your WordPerfect package that is still in its original state. (You have not changed it.)

TABLE 17.3: Commands That Let You Change System Styles without Going through the Style List

FEATURE	MENU COMMANDS
Column Border	Layout ➤ Columns ➤ Column Borders ➤ Border Style
Column Border (Customize)	Layout ➤ Columns ➤ Column Borders ➤ Customize
Column Fill	Layout ➤ Columns ➤ Column Borders ➤ Fill Style
Footnote Separator Line	Layout ➤ Footnote ➤ Options ➤ Footnote Separator Line ➤ Line Style
Graphics Border	Graphics ➤ Borders ➤ Styles
Graphics Box	Graphics ➤ Graphics Boxes ➤ Styles
Graphics Fill Style	Graphics ➤ Fill Styles
Graphics Line	Graphics ➤ Graphics Lines ➤ Styles
Indexes	Tools ➤ Index ➤ Define ➤ Index Level Styles
Initial Codes	Layout ➤ Document ➤ Document Initial Codes (or Initial Codes Setup)
List	Tools ➤ List ➤ Define
Outline	Tools ➤ Outline ➤ Outline Style
Table Lines and Fill	Layout ➤ Tables ➤ Create (or Edit) ➤ Lines/Fill
Table of Authorities	Tools ➤ Table of Authorities ➤ Define
Table of Contents	Tools ➤ Table of Contents ➤ Define ➤ Table of Contents Styles

But I guess that would crowd the dialog box. If you look at the list of style names, you'll probably see that some are, indeed, marked with a bullet (•) next to the style type.

Even though WordPerfect Corporation gave you those styles (you didn't create them personally), you can still change them if you want. Use the same Edit command and techniques you use to edit your own styles. Once you change one of those styles, it will no longer be identified by a bullet. (Sort of like WordPerfect saying, "You changed it, so it's yours now pal. We're not taking responsibility anymore.")

Reinstating a Default Style

Let's say you change one of those default library styles marked with a bullet, and then later you regret changing it. Not a big problem. Just highlight the style name that has lost its bullet (•) and choose Delete from the bottom of the dialog box. WordPerfect will ask if you want to reset the style to its default state. If you choose Yes, the style takes on its original codes, and the bullet comes back into view.

Styles are much easier to use than they are to explain. I hope this tutorial-oriented chapter has shed some light on the mysteries of styles, libraries, and system styles. But experience is likely to be the best teacher when it comes to styles. (Don't forget, you can always press F1 for help, or refer to your official WordPerfect documentation, if you need reminders or more details.)

Now, on to another time saver—macros!

Saving Time with Macros

fast **TRACK**

To stop a running macro

press the Escape key.

**To convert WordPerfect 5.0 or 5.1 macros
to 6.0 format**

exit to the DOS prompt; type **mcv** *oldmacro newmacro*
and then press ↵. The arguments *oldmacro* and *newmacro* are
the file names of the existing 5.0/5.1 macro and the new
macro you want to create, respectively.

To edit an existing macro

choose <u>T</u>ools ➤ <u>M</u>acro ➤ <u>R</u>ecord or press Ctrl+F10, type in
or select the macro name, choose OK, then choose <u>E</u>dit.

IF YOU'RE tired of choosing the same old sets of menu options or typing the same text over and over, then *macros* are for you. Macros automate mundane, repetitive jobs by letting you record all the keystrokes you need to do those tasks. Once recorded, you can just "play back" those keystrokes with a few mouse clicks or keypresses.

What Is a Macro?

The term *macro* may sound strange if you're new to computers. "Macro" is the opposite of "micro" (small). In a sense, a macro is just a "large keystroke," because by executing a single macro, you can perform the equivalent of many keystrokes.

For example, instead of retyping your company name and address over and over again in different documents, you can simply record the necessary keystrokes in a macro. Then, any time you need to type your company name and address, all you have to do is run the macro, which takes about two seconds flat.

Recording a Macro

Recording a macro is easy. Here are the steps:

1. Choose Tools ➤ Macro ➤ Record, or press Ctrl+F10. You'll see the Record Macro dialog box.

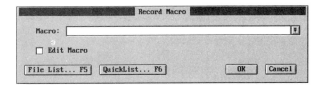

2. Enter a valid DOS file name, from one to eight characters long with no spaces or punctuation, or press Alt plus a letter (for example, press Alt+N). WordPerfect uses the default file extension .WPM for macros, so you don't need to include a file name extension. (You'll learn more about naming macros later in this chapter.)

3. Choose OK.

4. If a macro with the name you've entered already exists, WordPerfect will ask if you want to replace it. Choose Replace to replace the existing macro, or choose Cancel to bail out and return to step 2. WordPerfect displays the message "Recording Macro" near the lower-left corner of the screen, so you know your actions are being recorded.

5. Type the keystrokes you want to record, including any menu choices and shortcut keys. You can select commands and dialog boxes with your mouse, but you *cannot* position the cursor or select text with your mouse. Use the cursor-positioning keys, Alt+F4, F12, or Edit ➤ Select instead.

6. When you're done recording, choose Tools ➤ Macro ➤ Stop, or press Ctrl+F10 again.

Your keystrokes are recorded and stored in the file you specified back in step 2.

Running a Macro

Running a macro is even easier than creating one:

1. If your macro works on a particular section of text (such as italicizing a word), move the cursor to where you want the macro to begin its action or select the text it will act on.

NOTE The terms *run, invoke,* and *execute* all mean the same thing: to "play back" the keystrokes recorded in the macro.

2. Run the macro as follows, depending on how you named it:

   - If it's an Alt+*key* macro, press the Alt+*key* combination (for example, Alt+N), and you're done.

   - If it's a named macro, choose Tools ➤ Macro ➤ Play, or press Alt+F10. You'll see the Play Macro dialog box below:

   Type the name you assigned to the macro when you created it, and choose OK. (You can use the File List (F5) or Quick-List (F6) buttons to help you locate the macro and fill in its file name. See Chapter 20.)

WordPerfect replays all the keys you recorded when you defined the macro, then returns you to the document window. What you'll see at the document window are the *results* of the keys being played back, not the actual keystrokes.

Complex macros might display a "Please Wait" message in the status bar to let you know that they're cranking away. Don't be impatient. Your macro is probably just trying to do its job.

Stopping a Macro

If you've started a macro and want to stop it dead in its tracks (perhaps because you've run the wrong macro or didn't position the cursor properly before running it), press the Escape key (but you'll have to be fast!) This will leave you at whatever point the macro was when you canceled it—maybe in the document window, or perhaps at a dialog box or prompt. Since the macro will probably play back some keystrokes before the cancellation takes effect, you should look at the document and fix any unwanted changes that the macro made.

Let's Try One

If you can't imagine what you might want to record in a macro, try creating one that transposes two letters. In any document window, type a sentence with some transposed letters, like this:

Where si hte cat?

Now move the cursor to between the *s* and the *i* (or, if you're in Text mode, to under the *i*). Then do the following:

1. Press Ctrl+F10 to start recording a macro.

2. Press Alt+X to name the macro ALTX.

3. Choose OK. (If WordPerfect claims that there's already a macro named ALTX, you may want to try a different name. Choose Cancel and try a different name, for example Alt+Z.)

4. Now, you will record your actions. First press Delete (Del) to delete the second character.

5. Press ← once to move the cursor to the left of the letter *s*.

6. Choose Edit ➤ Undelete and then choose Restore when prompted.

7. Stop recording (press Ctrl+F10).

Now that you've recorded the keystrokes to transpose two characters, you can run that macro in any document. For example, move the cursor between the *h* and the *t* in *hte* (or so that it's under the *t* if you're in Text mode). Then press Alt+X (or whatever combination of keystrokes you used to name the macro back in step 2). Bingo—the macro instantly transposes the characters. This macro will work with any pair of characters. Try it!

Details, Options, and Alternatives

At this point you probably know about 95% of what you really need to know about macros. But, as with most WordPerfect features, there are plenty of additional details, options, and alternatives to ponder.

Naming a Macro

The way you name a macro determines how you'll play it back later. You can create three types of macros: Alt+*key* macros, named macros, and temporary (or immediate) macros (discussed in the next section).

Alt+key macros are assigned to various Alt+*key* key combinations on the keyboard, such as Alt+A, Alt+B, and so on. To give a macro an Alt+key name, simply press the Alt+*key* combination when you name the macro after pressing Macro Record (Ctrl+F10). After you stop recording the macro, you can play it any time by pressing the same Alt+*key* combination you used to type the name.

Named macros are macros with file names that follow standard DOS conventions. That is, the names must be from one to eight characters long and cannot include punctuation. Remember that WordPerfect automatically adds the .WPM extension, which identifies the file as a macro. You'll need to press more keys to play back a named macro: Choose Tools ➤ Macro ➤ Play, or press Alt+F10, type the macro name (for example, **heading**), and choose OK.

You can also run a macro from the Button Bar, as I'll explain in a moment.

Recording a Temporary Macro

Some macros are handy for typing repetitive information in the current document, but they're not worth keeping for posterity. You can easily create a temporary macro (also known as an *immediate macro*) that lasts until you replace it with another macro. Any new temporary macro that you record will completely overwrite the old one.

To create a temporary macro, follow the usual steps to record a macro, but rather than giving the macro a name when prompted, just press ↵. After you stop recording the temporary macro (with Ctrl+F10), you can play it back by pressing Alt+F10 and then ↵, or by choosing Tools ➤ Macro ➤ Play and pressing ↵.

Whenever you record a temporary macro, WordPerfect replaces any previous temporary macro, without asking for permission first. Immediate macros are stored in the file WP{WPC}.WPM on the same directory where your macros reside (usually C:\WP60MACROS).

Recording Actions in a Macro

Whenever you're recording a macro, the status bar shows the message "Recording Macro." During that time, nearly everything you do is stored in the macro file as you do it. Specifically,

- Macros record all text you type into the document, and most editing and cursor movement keys you press (like ↵, ↓, ↑, and Backspace).

- Macros record all commands that you can choose via the mouse or keyboard.

When recording a macro, you're free to select text in the document window, but you can do so *only* with the keyboard, not the mouse. You'll need to choose Edit ➤ Block or press Alt+F4 or F12, and then highlight text you want to select (see Chapter 4).

Running Macros from the Button Bar

If you use a mouse, Button Bars (Chapter 4) are one of your best shortcuts available. You can assign any macro you record to a button. Once you've done that, you can simply click the button with the mouse and the macro runs.

When assigning a macro to a button, be sure to select the Button Bar you want (View ➤ Button Bar Setup ➤ Select) if you've created several Button Bars. Work your way back to the document window. Then, with the Button Bar to which you want to add the macro displayed on your screen, follow these steps:

1. Choose View ➤ Button Bar Setup ➤ Edit.

2. Choose Add Macro. The Macro Button List will appear.

3. Double-click the name of the macro you want to add to the Button Bar, or highlight its name and choose Select.

4. If you want, you can choose Move Button. Then, move the highlight to where you want the macro's button to appear in relation to other buttons and choose Paste Button.

5. Repeat steps 2–4 for each button you want to add.

6. Choose OK or press F7 to return to the document window.

Remember, the Button Bar looks best in Graphics or Page mode (Ctrl+F3). If your new button is off the end of the list, you can click the little triangle arrows at the left side of the Button Bar to scroll through the buttons.

Repeating a Macro

If you gave your macro an Alt+*key* name, you can use the Repeat feature to play it as many times as you wish. Just choose <u>E</u>dit ➤ <u>R</u>epeat, or press Ctrl+R. Type in the number of times you want to run the macro. Then press the Alt+*key* combination assigned to the macro.

Running Macros from DOS

You can have WordPerfect run a macro automatically as soon as you start the program. This might come in handy if you share a computer with someone else, and you want to change default format settings, start up Word-Perfect's automatic calculator, play music automatically, or...whatever!

To run a macro when you start WordPerfect, add the /M-*macroname* startup switch to the WP command, where *macroname* is the name of the macro you want to run. For example, to start WordPerfect and run a macro named MyPrefs, type **wp /m-myprefs** and press ⏎ at the DOS prompt.

For DOS Whizzes

If you're a DOS whiz, you can run WordPerfect and a macro automatically at system startup. Just make the WP /M-*macroname* command the very last command in your AUTOEXEC.BAT file.

As an alternative to that, you can add the command **set wp=wp /m-*macroname*** to AUTOEXEC.BAT. WordPerfect won't start up automatically. However, whenever anybody enters the command **wp** to start WordPerfect, the macro represented by *macroname* will be played automatically as soon as WordPerfect is loaded.

Making a Macro Wait for You

In some cases, you might not want your macro to go through *all* the steps in a procedure, but rather to stop and wait for you to do something from time to time. For example, you might want the macro to start running, get to the Font dialog box, and wait for you to pick a font. When you're done making your selection, you might want the macro to proceed and type some text, or go on to some other dialog box.

Waiting at a Dialog Box

To make a macro pause at a dialog box, you need to tell it which dialog box to pause at while you're recording the macro. To do so, record the macro normally, but when you get to the dialog box you want the macro to pause at, select the little check box in the upper-right corner of the dialog box, as in the example below:

Note that this check box is visible *only* if you're recording a macro. (A few dialog boxes don't offer the check box at all.) You can then keep recording keystrokes and commands, go to other dialog boxes and select their check boxes to pause, and so on. When you're done and back in your document window, stop recording the macro using Ctrl+F10.

When you play back the macro, it will stop at every dialog box you checked off along the way. Make your selections in each dialog box, then choose OK or Close, or press F7, to leave the dialog box. The macro will continue with any additional actions you recorded.

Waiting for Text

You might want a macro to pause while it's typing some text, to give you time to type in some text of your own. For example, you might want it to type most of the text in a late payment reminder but pause and let you type in the exact amount owed.

To make a macro stop so you can type in text, follow the steps below:

1. Record the macro normally, and start typing whatever text you want the macro to type. (You can, of course, make any menu selections along the way, pause at dialog boxes, etc.)

2. When you get to a place where you want the macro to wait for you to type something, choose Tools ➤ Macro ➤ Control, or press Ctrl+PgUp.

3. Choose Macro Commands. When the Macro Commands dialog box appears, choose PAUSE. (You can type **p** to move to that command immediately. Then double-click the command, or highlight it and choose Insert.)

4. Go back to typing whatever remaining text you want the macro to type, or choose menu commands as usual.

5. When you're done recording the macro, press Ctrl+F10.

When you play back the macro, it will run up until the point where you inserted that PAUSE command. At that point, you can type anything up to a paragraph in length (that is, you can't press ↵ while typing). When you're done typing, press ↵. The macro will pick up wherever it left off (and it won't put that hard return in your document).

Pausing Macro Recording

If you don't want the macro to pause, but you want to stop recording macro keystrokes temporarily, follow these steps:

1. Assuming you're already recording a macro, choose Tools ➤ Macro ➤ Control, or press Ctrl+PgUp.

2. Select the Macro Record Paused check box and choose OK.

Now you can do anything you want in WordPerfect, without recording the keystrokes (though the "Recording Macro" message will still appear in the status line at the bottom of the screen). When you're ready to resume keystroke recording, just repeat the basic steps above, but clear (uncheck) the Macro Record Paused box in step 2.

Canceling Recording

Suppose you start recording a series of actions—whether they're keystrokes or command selections—then make a mistake and want to start all over. You can't just press Esc, since WordPerfect would record that keystroke like any other.

Instead, you must stop recording keystrokes as though the macro were finished (that is, press Ctrl+F10). Then you can start recording the macro all over from scratch, using the same macro name. WordPerfect will ask for permission before overwriting the faulty macro you just recorded. But in this case, you know it's OK to overwrite the existing macro, so just choose Yes to proceed.

Where Macros Are Stored

The Location Of Files option (File ➤ Setup ➤ Location Of Files ➤ Macros/Keyboards/Button Bar) lets you choose where to store macro files. To prevent cluttering the C:\WP60 directory, you might want to store all your macros (and keyboard files, discussed in Chapter 19) in a separate directory, such as C:\WP60\MACROS.

If you change the location of your keyboard, macro, or Button Bar files, remember to use the WordPerfect File Manager (File ➤ File Manager) immediately to move all those *.WPM, *.WPK, and *.WPB files to the new directory.

Handy Macros That Come with WordPerfect

WordPerfect comes with many handy macros that are ready to run. Table 18.1 lists some of these macros and describes each one briefly. You can run any of these macros with the Tools ➤ Macro ➤ Play commands (Alt+F10). If you have a mouse, you can get at some of the macros by loading the Macros Button Bar (View ➤ Button Bar Setup ➤ Select ➤ MACROS ➤ Select).

TABLE 18.1: Some Handy Macros That You Already Have

MACRO NAME	WHAT IT DOES	NOTES
AllFonts	Creates a document that you can print to see examples of all your installed fonts.	This one can take some time! Run it in Text mode. Don't forget to print the document when the macro is done.
Bullet	Adds (or changes) a bullet character on the current paragraph.	Move the cursor to the start of a paragraph before you run the macro.
Calc	Runs a handy pop-up calculator.	Run only from the main edit screen (see Chapter 25).
EditCode	Lets you edit the code at the cursor.	It's easier to use this macro if you turn on Reveal Codes first (Alt+F3).
ExitAll	Exits from anywhere back to the main editing screen.	Doesn't let you exit WordPerfect.
Glossary	Looks up the current (abbreviated) word in a glossary and automatically expands it to a larger form.	If the current word isn't in the glossary, the macro lets you create new abbreviations and their larger forms.

TABLE 18.1: Some Handy Macros That You Already Have (continued)

MACRO NAME	WHAT IT DOES	NOTES
InitCaps	Capitalizes the first letter of the current word.	Run only from the main editing screen (document window), with no text selected.
Memo	Creates a memo, letter, or FAX cover sheet and positions the cursor for editing.	Try it, you'll like it.
Mod_Atrb	Lets you replace font attributes or add new ones, starting at the cursor position.	Run only from the main editing screen (document window).
NoteCvt	Converts footnotes and endnotes to endnotes and footnotes, starting at the cursor position.	Run only from the main editing screen (document window).
Pleading	Converts the current document to a legal pleading-paper format and inserts a Pleading style into the document's style library.	Run only from the main editing screen. Print the document, or switch to the Print Preview screen to see the pleading format.
SpaceTab	Converts any number of spaces to tabs, starting at the cursor position.	Great for imported documents that use spaces to indent the first line of paragraphs.

Be aware that WordPerfect Corporation often changes its mind and ships different macros with different interim releases of their products. For an accurate, up-to-date list, choose Help ➤ Macros, then highlight List Of Shipping Macros and choose Look.

Converting Macros from WordPerfect 5.x

WordPerfect 6.0 can't directly run macros created under WordPerfect versions 5.0 and 5.1. You must first convert them with the macro conversion program MCV.EXE (also known as *WordPerfect Keystroke to Token Macro Conversion Utility*). This program is copied to your WordPerfect directory (typically C:\WP60) when you install WordPerfect. To use the conversion program, follow the steps below:

1. If you're in WordPerfect or some other program, exit all the way to the DOS command prompt.

2. If necessary, switch to the WordPerfect directory (typically by typing **c:** ↵ then **cd \wp60** and pressing ↵).

3. Enter the **mcv** command followed by a space, the location and name of the macro you want to convert, and a location and name for the converted macro. The basic syntax of the command is

   mcv *oldmacro newmacro*

4. Press ↵ after typing the command.

> **T I P**
>
> At the DOS prompt you can enter the command *mcv /?* for help with the macro converter.

For example, to convert a macro named ALTZ.WPM from your WordPerfect 5.1 macros directory to a 6.0 macro named ALTZ.WPM on your \WP60 directory, you would enter this command:

   mcv c:\wp51\macros\altz c:\wp60\altz

(The .WPM extension is assumed if you omit it.)

The conversion program will do its darndest to make the conversion. If you're converting garden-variety recorded-keystroke type macros, you shouldn't have any problems.

More sophisticated macros, particularly those containing a lot of advanced macro commands, may not be so easy to convert. If any commands didn't convert perfectly, MCV will display messages like these:

Number of conversion problems: 3
Number of conversion warnings: 16

Assuming you're the person who wrote that macro, you'll need to open the converted macro (as I'll describe later), and look around for explanatory comments like these:

//*** Conversion warning ***

or

//*** Warning:

Then you'll have to edit the problem commands to conform to the Word-Perfect 6.0 for DOS macro language.

For Programmers and Power Users

For the rest of this chapter, I'm going to put on my programmer's hat and talk shop with the pros. If you're not a programmer or power user, feel free to skip the rest of this chapter. Everything you need to know about recording and playing back macros has already been covered. If you'd like to get a programmer's hat of your own, I'll talk about some sources of information at the end of this chapter.

What the Macro Really Records

If you're experienced with earlier versions of WordPerfect, you'll be surprised to learn that, unlike previous releases, version 6.0 does not record keystrokes. Instead, it records *events*. That's why you can use the mouse to choose commands from the menus and dialog boxes while recording the macro.

The macro doesn't record anything until you actually complete some task. For example, if you whip through a bunch of menus and dialog boxes, without making any actual selections (or clicking that little pause check box described earlier), the macro records nothing. It only records a completed action, such as opening the Line Format dialog box, changing the line spacing, and choosing OK. That action would be recorded and put in the macro as a command that looks like this (if you set the line spacing to 2):

LineSpacing(2.0)

Opening and Editing a Macro

Another thing that might surprise you if you're accustomed to earlier "keystroke" macros, is that the macros are stored in standard WordPerfect documents. This means that you can create, open, edit, and save a macro using the same techniques you'd use to create, open, edit, and save a letter or memo.

To open any macro, whether it's one you recorded or one that WordPerfect Corporation has supplied, here's what you would do:

1. Choose File ➤ Open.

2. Choose QuickList or press F6, then double-click (or highlight and choose Select) the Macros/Keyboards/Button Bar Personal directory.

3. Optionally, choose Current Dir (or press F5), change the *.* specification to *.WPM, and choose OK to narrow the list down to macro names.

4. Double-click the name of the macro you want to open. (Or highlight its name and choose Open Into New Document.)

NOTE

You can also open a macro by choosing Tools ➤ Macro ➤ Record or pressing Ctrl+F10. Check the Edit Macro box and type the name of the macro (or, if you've edited it recently, just choose its name from the drop-down list). Then choose OK.

Figure 18.1 shows how the document window might look after you open the sample ALLFONTS.WPM macro that came with your WordPerfect package.

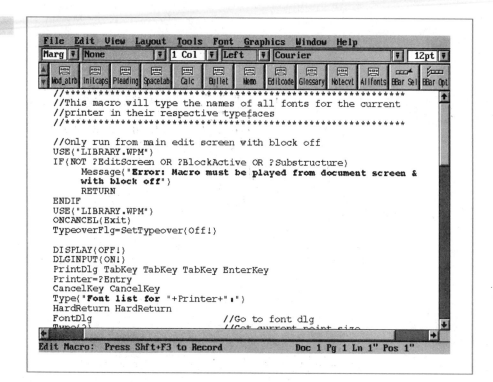

```
File  Edit  View  Layout  Tools  Font  Graphics  Window  Help
Marg  ▼  None              ▼  1 Col  ▼  Left  ▼  Courier                    ▼  12pt ▼
   Mod_atrb InitCaps Pleading SpaceLab  Calc  Bullet  Memo  Editcode Glossary Notecvt Allfonts BBar Sel BBar Opt
//******************************************************************
//This macro will type the names of all fonts for the current
//printer in their respective typefaces
//******************************************************************

//Only run from main edit screen with block off
USE("LIBRARY.WPM")
IF(NOT ?EditScreen OR ?BlockActive OR ?Substructure)
    Message("Error: Macro must be played from document screen &
    with block off")
    RETURN
ENDIF
USE("LIBRARY.WPM")
ONCANCEL(Exit)
TypeoverFlg=SetTypeover(Off!)

DISPLAY(OFF!)
DLGINPUT(ON!)
PrintDlg TabKey TabKey TabKey EnterKey
Printer=?Entry
CancelKey CancelKey
Type("Font list for "+Printer+"▪")
HardReturn HardReturn
FontDlg                              //Go to font dlg
Type(2)                              //Get current point size
Edit Macro:  Press Shft+F3 to Record            Doc 1 Pg 1 Ln 1" Pos 1"
```

What's Inside a Macro?

A WordPerfect macro generally consists of any combination of tokens, keystrokes, comments, and programming commands.

Tokens

A token represents an action. For example, FontDlg is a token that says, "Go to the Font dialog box." Tokens are usually shown in mixed case (for example, FontDlg, PrintDlg, and CancelKey).

Keystrokes

When you're recording a macro, your keystrokes are recorded literally. Text is put in the parentheses of a Type() command. Other keys are recorded as commands. For example, if you record the keystrokes to type *My dog has fleed* followed by a press on the ↵ key, the macro would record this:

```
Type("My dog has fleed.")
HardReturn
```

Comments

Comments are messages and notes typed by programmers into a macro. When WordPerfect compiles the macro (which I'll discuss later), it simply ignores the comments because they're for "human consumption only." Any line that starts with // in a macro is a comment.

Programming Commands

Many of the sample macros provided by WordPerfect also contain programming commands. Programming commands must be inserted into a program "manually," as I'll explain later. The common convention is to show programming commands in all uppercase, as in IF, RETURN, ENDIF, USE, ONCANCEL, and other examples shown in Figure 18.1.

Adding Programming Commands to a Macro

To add a programming command to a macro, you can either just type it in, using exact, proper syntax (as in any programming language), or you can press Ctrl+PgUp or choose Tools ➤ Macro ➤ Control. Then choose the Macro Commands command button. You will be taken to the Macro Commands dialog box as shown on the next page.

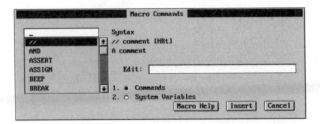

As you scroll through the list of macro commands, the syntax and a brief description of each command appears to the right of the list. You can also switch from the list of commands to the list of system variables by clicking the System Variables option button.

To copy a command or system variable into your macro immediately, press ↵ or double-click the command name. But if the command's syntax requires additional parameters, you'll probably prefer to click the Edit option. The highlighted command will appear in the Edit text box with empty parentheses, like this:

SWITCH()

Use the syntax example above the Edit box to get a basic idea of the syntax, and then type in valid parameters between the parentheses. When you're ready to put the completed command into your macro, choose Insert.

Adding Tokens to a Macro

While you're editing a macro, you can also insert recorded text and tokens without going through the menus. However, you need to open the macro first by going through the Macro menu. That is, if you used File ➤ Open to open the macro, you should close it and save your changes. Then press Ctrl+F10, select the Edit Macro box, and choose the macro's name from the drop-down list (or type it in). Choose OK. When you get to the document window, the status bar will show

Edit Macro: Press Shft+F3 to Record

Now you can put the cursor wherever you want to insert some recorded keystrokes or tokens. Then press Shift+F3, and perform whatever action(s) you want to record. When you're done recording, press Shift+F3 again. The tokens and/or keystrokes required to perform your actions later are inserted into the macro at the current cursor position.

Recording Abbreviated Macro Commands

You can record abbreviated macro language commands, which are easier to edit later because they're shorter. To do this, choose Tools ➤ Macro ➤ Control (or press Ctrl+PgUp), then select the Record Abbreviations check box and return to your macro.

Any commands that you record after that will be abbreviated. For example, rather than something like *AttributeAppearanceOff(Bold!)*, you'd get *AttrAppearOff(Bold!)*. Either the long or the abbreviated version will work in a macro (assuming you don't misspell it). You can use both types of commands in a single macro if you wish.

Saving and Running an Edited Macro

When you've finished editing a macro, just choose File ➤ Close ➤ Yes to save it. After you choose Yes, WordPerfect will compile the macro (if it doesn't contain any errors) and return you to the document window. You can then run the modified macro in the usual manner.

About Macro Compilation

Whenever you create or edit a macro, WordPerfect *compiles* it once before running it. You may see a brief message odometer that shows how long the compilation will take.

The purpose of compilation is two-fold. First, WordPerfect checks the macro for obvious errors and stops compilation when it finds one. Second, during compilation the tokens and programming commands are converted to a language that the computer can interpret quickly. This means that the macro runs much faster than it would otherwise. The compiled commands are in the .WPM file, along with the source code that you created. You never see the compiled commands, however.

Compilation Errors

Whenever you create a macro, there's always a (strong) possibility that you'll make a mistake. If it's a syntax error or some other error that Word-Perfect can detect while it's compiling the macro, you'll see a warning box something like this:

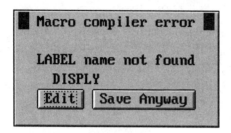

If you want to try to fix the error on the spot, choose Edit. The macro opens with the cursor at or near the offending line. After making your change, just press F7 to save the change and recompile the macro.

If you don't want to try to fix the error on the spot, you can choose Save Anyway instead. Then you can edit the macro at your leisure. (If you try to run the macro after choosing Save Anyway, you'll get the same error message again. The macro won't run until you fix the error.)

Runtime Errors

Sometimes a macro will compile correctly, but then when you try to run it, you'll get a *runtime error*. A runtime error often indicates that the problem isn't so much with the macro, but rather with the context you're trying to run it in. For example, if the macro is supposed to select a particular font, but you've selected a printer that doesn't have that font, the macro can't do its job.

When you get a runtime error, don't go looking inside the macro right away. Rather, think about the job that the macro is supposed to do, then select the appropriate printer and position the cursor at some place in your document where the macro can do its job. Then run the macro again. If the macro still fails, then the problem probably is within the macro itself.

Debugging Aids

If you're having trouble finding the error in a macro, there are a couple of things you can do to make it easier to track it down. First, you can make the actions visible by opening the macro, and changing the DISPLAY(Off!) command to

DISPLAY(On!)

You can also insert a SPEED() command to slow the macro down. You can put the command at the top of the macro, or wherever you think the start of a trouble spot might be. For example, suppose you put this command (on its own line) into the macro:

SPEED(10)

Every command below that line would run at a much slower speed. The larger you make the argument (now 10), the slower the macro will go.

When you're done making these changes, close, save, and run the macro normally to see the results.

Learning More about Advanced Macros

If you want to learn more about advanced programming commands and techniques, the first place to look might be the WordPerfect Online Macros Manual. Just choose Help ➤ Macros, and you're in the online reference manual.

You can also learn by example. Just run any one of the sample macros that came with your WordPerfect package to see what it does. Then you can open that macro file, as discussed earlier under "Opening and Editing a Macro," and use File ➤ Print/Fax to print a copy and see what's inside, and what makes it tick.

If you need more support than the online manual and examples offer, consider checking your local bookstore or inquiring at WordPerfect Corporation for information on getting a book or manual that deals *specifically* with WordPerfect 6.0 for DOS macros.

If you have no programming experience whatsoever and you want some real training, consider taking a programming course. Even an introductory BASIC course would be useful, because you really need to understand fundamental programming concepts (like syntax, looping, subroutines, and variables).

The first half of this chapter has taught you virtually everything you need to know to create and play back just about any macro imaginable. You don't need to be a programmer to create and use macros, but for those who *are* programmers and power users, WordPerfect 6.0 offers a complete macro programming language. You can learn a lot about that language simply by perusing the online macros manual (Help ➤ Macros).

Now I'll doff my programmer's hat, remove my pocket-protector, and tuck them away for the rest of this book. In the next chapter, we'll look at ways any average person with a nontechnical mind can customize WordPerfect to his or her own needs and preferences.

Personalizing
WordPerfect

fast TRACK

To customize the mouse settings or change the mouse driver 677

choose File ➤ Setup ➤ Mouse (Shift+F1 M).

To select or create a color printing and display palette 680

choose File ➤ Setup ➤ Color Printing Palette (Shift+F1 C).

To set the initial codes for the current document 686

choose Layout ➤ Document ➤ Document Initial Codes (or press Shift+F8 DC). Use the pull-down menus or shortcut keys to enter codes, and type any text you want to appear at the start of the document. When you're done, press F7 and then choose OK.

To set the initial codes for new documents that you create 686

choose Layout ➤ Document ➤ Initial Codes Setup (or press Shift+F8 DT). Enter your codes and text as for the Document Initial Codes. When you're done, press F7, then choose OK.

To set the initial font for the current document or new documents 687

choose Layout ➤ Document ➤ Initial Font (or press Shift+F8 DFT). Select the font and size, and decide whether you want to change the font for this document only or for all new documents. Choose OK twice.

The Setup button (in some dialog boxes) and the Styles feature 689

provide other ways to personalize WordPerfect.

WORDPERFECT'S behavior (unlike the weather) is easy to change if you don't like it. In fact, you can personalize just about any WordPerfect setting to match your own tastes, work habits, and office requirements. Any settings you change will stay that way until you change them again.

Remember the trusty F1 key is always ready to provide more information about any customization feature. Also keep in mind that a little experimentation with personalizing WordPerfect goes a long way. Just be sure to jot down the original settings before you make a change, in case you don't like the result.

Using the Setup Options

You can change many of WordPerfect's default settings by choosing File ➤ Setup and then picking an option from the setup menu below:

Alternatively, you can press Shift+F1, which opens the Setup dialog box shown in Figure 19.1.

FIGURE 19.1

The Setup dialog box appears when you press Shift+F1.

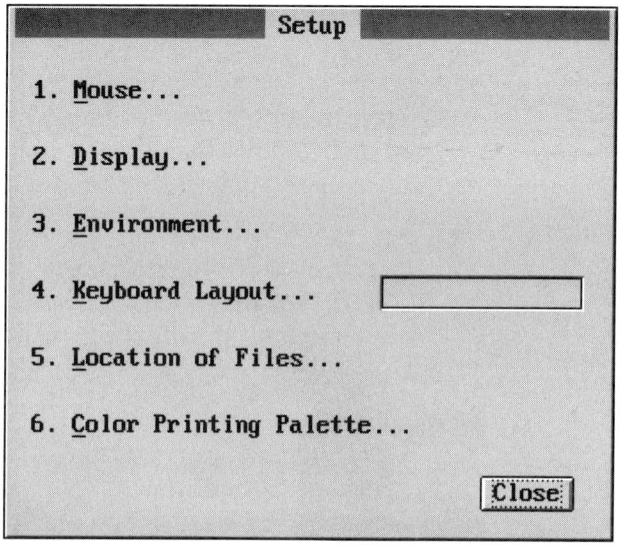

Choosing any option from the Setup menu or dialog box leads to still more dialog boxes, which I'll describe in the sections that follow.

Organizing Your Files

As you know, DOS lets you divide your hard disk into separate drives, directories, and subdirectories. Each directory on a drive is like a separate file cabinet that contains its own set of files. Storing files on separate directories keeps your information organized and prevents individual directories from becoming cluttered with too many file names.

The Location Of Files options let you specify a directory location for various categories of WordPerfect files, so that WordPerfect always knows where to store files as you create them, and where to look for files when you need them.

To set these options, choose File ➤ Setup ➤ Location Of Files, or press Shift+F1 L. When the Location Of Files dialog box appears (see Figure 19.2), follow the steps listed below.

1. Select the option for the category you want to change. For some options, another dialog box will let you set both a personal path and a shared path. I'll talk more about these paths in a moment.

2. Type the drive letter and directory location for that category using proper DOS conventions, then press ↵. For example, type **C:\WP60\MYDOCS** and press ↵ in the Documents text box to set a default directory for your documents.

N O T E

The Style Files option lets you specify a default personal and shared library file name in addition to personal and shared directories. See Chapter 17 for more information on styles.

FIGURE 19.2

Use the Location Of Files dialog box to tell WordPerfect where to look for and store various categories of files.

```
  File  Edit  View  Layout  Tools  Font  Graphics  Window  Help

┌─────────────────────────── Location of Files ───────────────────────────┐
│                                                                          │
│   1. Backup Files:                     C:\WP60                           │
│   2. Macros/Keyboards/Button Bar...    C:\WP60\MACROS                    │
│   3. Writing Tools...                  C:\WPC60DOS                       │
│   4. Printer Files...                  C:\WPC60DOS                       │
│   5. Style Files...                    C:\WP60; C:\WP60                  │
│                                                                          │
│   6. Graphics Files...                 C:\WP60\GRAPHICS                  │
│   7. Documents:                        C:\WP6BOOK                        │
│   8. Spreadsheet Files...                                                │
│   9. QuickFinder Files...                                                │
│                                                                          │
│   R. WP.DRS File and *.WFW Files:      C:\WPC60DOS                       │
│   F. Graphics Fonts Data Files...                                        │
│                                                                          │
│   ☒ Update QuickList                                                     │
│                                                                          │
│   [ Directory Tree... F8 ]  [ QuickList... F6 ]    [  OK  ] [ Cancel ]   │
└──────────────────────────────────────────────────────────────────────────┘

  Courier 10cpi                            Doc 1 Pg 1 Ln 1" Pos 1"
```

3. Repeat steps 1 and 2 as needed. When you're done, choose OK (and Close, if necessary).

Here are some points to keep in mind when you use the Location Of Files options:

- When you can't remember the exact name of a directory, you can use the Directory Tree (F8) or QuickList (F6) buttons and shortcut keys to locate it. Those buttons are discussed in Chapter 20.

- If you specify a nonexistent directory in the Location Of Files dialog box, WordPerfect will offer to create that directory for you.

- After changing a directory location, you'll need to move existing files of that type to the new location if you want WordPerfect to find them in the future. The Move/Rename option in the File Manager dialog box can help you move files (see Chapter 20).

- WordPerfect will generally use the current directory if you leave a Location Of Files option blank. An exception is the backup files, which WordPerfect stores in the same directory as the WordPerfect program (typically C:\WP60) if you leave the Backup Files option blank.

Table 19.1 summarizes the categories and file locations that you can change.

Personal and Shared Paths

WordPerfect lets you specify a personal and shared directory path for many file categories, including printer files, style files, and graphics files. You can set up *personal directories* for files that are just your own and aren't shared with other people. *Shared directories* are for files that you share with other people on a network or workgroup. The shared directory should be one that other users in the network have access to.

TABLE 19.1: Categories of Files Controlled by Location of Files

CATEGORY	FILES INCLUDED	SEE CHAPTER...
Backup Files	Timed and original backup files (.BK?)	19
Macros/ Keyboards/ Button Bar*	Macros (.WPM), keyboards (.WPK), and Button Bars (.WPB)	18 (macros), 19 (keyboard), 4 (Button Bar)
Writing Tools	Speller (.LEX), Thesaurus (.THS), and Grammatik (GK*.*)	11 (Speller), 13 (Thesaurus), 12 (Grammatik)
Printer Files*	Printer files (.ALL and .PRS)	10
Style Files*	Style Libraries (.STY)	17
Graphics Files*	Graphics files (.WPG)	26
Documents	Your documents	20
Spreadsheet Files*	Spreadsheets (e.g., .WK1 for Lotus files)	33
QuickFinder Files*	Index files (.IDX)	20
WP.DRS File and *.WFW Files	Files used with graphics fonts	10
Graphics Fonts Data Files	All graphic fonts	10

*NOTE: You can specify personal and shared directories.

Speeding Up File Searches

WordPerfect searches for files wherever the Location Of Files settings tell it to. If a directory contains hundreds, or thousands, of files, your computer may slow down considerably. Therefore, your computer may work faster if you heed this advice:

- Organize your hard disk into many directories with fewer files, instead of few directories with many files.

- Store WordPerfect's various categories of files in separate directories (see Table 19.1 for a list of categories).

Environmental Settings

You can choose File ➤ Setup ➤ Environment (or press Shift+F1 E) to get to the environmental settings dialog box, shown in Figure 19.3.

Table 19.2 summarizes the Environment options and lists chapters where you can find more information about each feature. In this chapter, we'll focus on the important Backup options.

FIGURE 19.3

The Environment dialog box lets you customize many WordPerfect features.

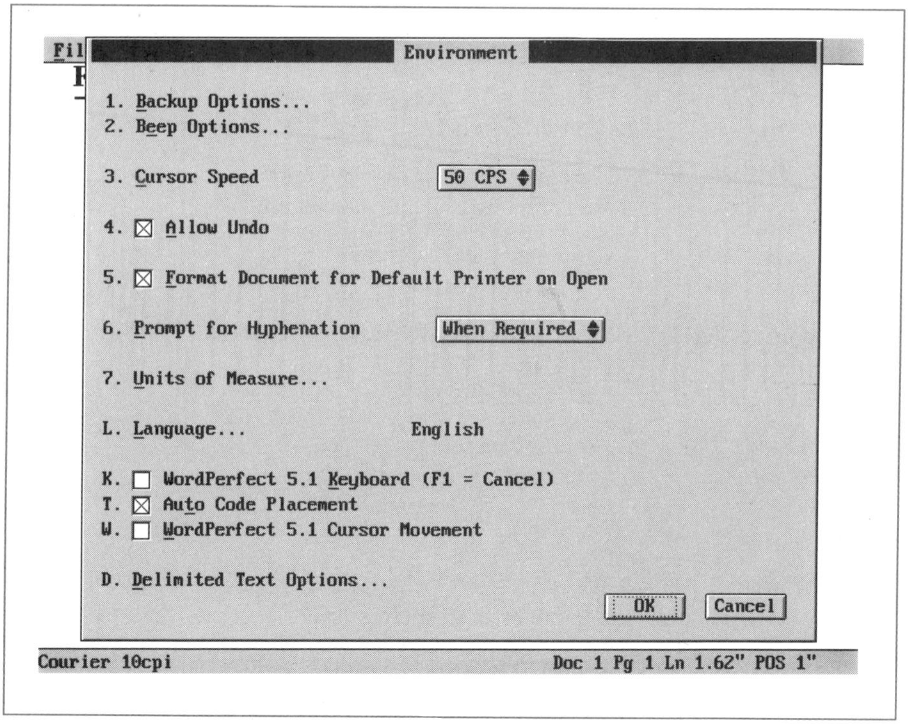

```
Fil                          Environment
H
    1. Backup Options...
    2. Beep Options...

    3. Cursor Speed              50 CPS ⬍

    4. ⊠ Allow Undo

    5. ⊠ Format Document for Default Printer on Open

    6. Prompt for Hyphenation    When Required ⬍

    7. Units of Measure...

    L. Language...               English

    K. ☐ WordPerfect 5.1 Keyboard (F1 = Cancel)
    T. ⊠ Auto Code Placement
    W. ☐ WordPerfect 5.1 Cursor Movement

    D. Delimited Text Options...
                                        OK    Cancel
Courier 10cpi                    Doc 1 Pg 1 Ln 1.62" POS 1"
```

TABLE 19.2: Environment Options and What They Do

OPTION	WHAT IT CONTROLS	SEE CHAPTER...
Backup Options	See "About Automatic Backup Files" in text.	19
Beep Options	Whether WordPerfect beeps at errors, failed searches, and auto-hyphenation.	Appendix C (errors), 16 (hyphenating), 9 (searching)
Cursor Speed	How fast the cursor moves when you hold down an arrow key.	3
Allow Undo	Whether you can undo the last formatting or editing change.	3
Format Documents for Default Printer on Open	Whether WordPerfect adjusts an incoming document to the current printer or reselects the original printer.	10
Prompt for Hyphenation	When WordPerfect prompts for hyphenation help.	16
Units of Measure	How WordPerfect displays and interprets units of measurement.	2
Language	Language used by Speller and Thesaurus.	11, 13
WordPerfect 5.1 Keyboard (F1 = Cancel)	If selected, Esc=Repeat, F1=Cancel, F3=Help. If clear, Esc=Cancel, F1=Help, F3=Switch.	3
Auto Code Placement	Whether certain codes are automatically moved to the beginning of the page or paragraph.	4
WordPerfect 5.1 Cursor Movement	Whether WordPerfect follows 5.1 or 6.0 cursor-movement conventions.	3, 4
Delimited Text Options	Characters used to separate fields and records in imported merge data files.	21, 33

About Automatic Backup Files

The first option in the Environment dialog box lets you activate automatic backup features. Two different types of automatic backups are available: *timed document backups*, and *original document backups*. You can control whether WordPerfect performs automatic backups and how often it makes timed document backups by choosing File ➤ Setup ➤ Environment ➤ Backup Options. These commands take you to the Backup dialog box shown below. From here you can choose the backup options you want.

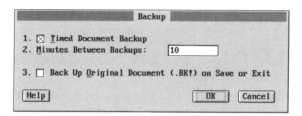

By default WordPerfect makes a *timed document backup* of the active document every ten minutes. This type of backup can prevent you from losing a large amount of work if the equipment or power fails, or you restart the computer accidentally before you've had a chance to exit WordPerfect. When you start WordPerfect again after a failure, you'll have a chance to delete or rename the automatic backup files that were saved prior to the shutdown. If you choose to rename the backup file, you can use it later in case the original version of your file is damaged or isn't as up-to-date as the timed backup.

When the *original document backup* feature is checked (as shown in the Backup dialog box above), and you save changes to a file, WordPerfect will automatically copy the original file to a file with a .BK! extension. For example, suppose the original document backup option is selected and you're editing a file named MYLETTER.WP. When you save that file, WordPerfect will store the original (unedited) file as MYLETTER.BK! and the changed version in MYLETTER.WP.

The original document backup can be helpful in those rare instances when your File ➤ Save trigger finger is a bit too fast and you save some bad changes accidentally. If, for example, you wanted to restore the previous version of MYLETTER.WP, you could close MYLETTER.WP

(File ➤ Close) and open the backup copy in MYLETTER.BK! (File ➤ Open). Assuming that MYLETTER.BK! contains the information that you want to keep, choose File ➤ Save As, specify **myletter.wp** as the file to be saved, and choose Yes when WordPerfect asks if you want to replace the existing MYLETTER.WP file.

Keep in mind that automatic backups are *not* a substitute for saving your work regularly, exiting WordPerfect properly after ending a session, and making backup copies of important documents on separate disks.

Customizing Your Screen

WordPerfect gives you an amazing amount of control over the screen's appearance. For instance, you can choose predefined color schemes or create your own colors. You can also decide whether WordPerfect displays things like the pull-down menu bar, scroll bars, and Button Bar (see Chapter 4). So if you're into customizing your computer's screen, Word-Perfect offers plenty of features to make you happy.

Choosing Screen Colors

You can choose a different monitor type and color scheme for Graphics/ Page mode and for Text mode. For example, in Text mode, you might want to use the predefined Winter Wonderland color scheme, which features stark white colors. In Graphics/Page mode, you might prefer the Clown Town scheme, which uses many bright, fun colors.

NOTE   Even though Graphics mode and Page mode are separate modes, the screen type and color scheme features work the same for both.

Here's how to change your screen type or color scheme:

1. Set your screen to either Graphics/Page mode (press Ctrl+F3 G or Ctrl+F3 P) or Text mode (press Ctrl+F3 T), depending on which mode's features you want to change.

2. Choose File ➤ Setup ➤ Display, or press Shift+F1 D.

3. Depending on your choice in step 1, choose either Graphics Mode Screen Type/Colors (to change the Graphics/Page mode screen) or Text Mode Screen Type/Colors (to change the Text mode screen).

4. Next, choose one of these options:

   • If you want to change the *graphics driver*, choose Screen Type.

   • If you want to select a color scheme, choose Color Schemes.

N O T E

Graphics driver files control how WordPerfect displays the Graphics/Page mode screens and the Graphics Editor, Equation Editor, and Print Preview screens. Graphics drivers, which have a .VRS extension, are stored in the same directory as the WordPerfect program (usually C:\WP60). Appendix A provides more information on installing graphics drivers.

5. Complete the dialog boxes that appear, as explained below.

6. When you're ready to view the results of your changes, choose Close until you return to the document window.

Figure 19.4 shows the Graphics Mode Screen Type/Colors dialog box. (The Text Mode Screen Type/Colors dialog box is the same, except for its title.)

FIGURE 19.4

The Graphics Mode Screen Type/Colors dialog box lets you choose your Graphics mode screen driver and select or create a color scheme.

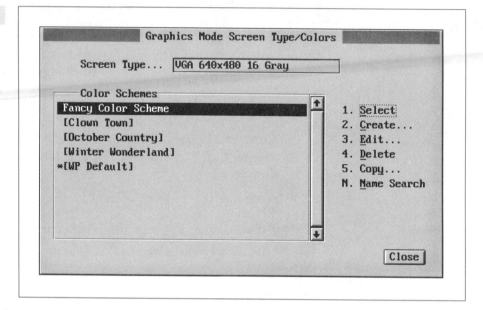

Selecting a Screen Type

The Screen Type option lets you choose which graphics driver WordPerfect will use to communicate with your video display card and monitor. You only need to change the graphics driver if you're having trouble displaying images, you've installed a different monitor, or you want to switch between black-and-white and color on a color monitor.

After choosing Screen Type, you'll see the Setup Graphics Screen Type dialog box, which has these options:

Select   Selects the currently highlighted driver.

Auto Select   Automatically selects the driver that matches your display card and monitor. This is the best option to choose if you're not sure which graphics driver you need.

Directory   Lets you search another directory for graphics drivers, in case the driver files aren't in the default location.

Information   Provides information about the highlighted driver file. This option will be dimmed if no information is available.

Name Search   Lets you search for the driver by name and highlights the closest match to the name (or partial name) that you type.

After you change the screen type, be sure to choose Close until you return to the document window.

Selecting a Color Scheme

The Color Schemes option in the Screen Type/Colors dialog box lets you select, edit, delete, or copy an existing color scheme, or create a new one of your own. The built-in color schemes appear in square brackets, as Figure 19.4 shows. Although you can't change or delete the built-in schemes, you *can* copy them to a new color scheme and edit the copies as described below.

To select the color scheme you want to use, choose Color Schemes. Highlight the color scheme you want, and then choose Select (or double-click its name). Then choose Close until you return to the document window. You can select a different color scheme for Text and Graphics modes.

Copying a Color Scheme

Suppose you want to base a new color scheme on one that already exists. To do that, choose Color Schemes from the dialog box, highlight the scheme you want to copy in the Color Schemes list, and choose Copy. When prompted, type a name for your new color scheme and press ↵. The new name will appear in the Color Schemes list, in alphabetical order above the default color scheme. From here, you can use the Edit option (described next) to customize your new scheme.

Customizing a Color Scheme

The fun really begins when you create or edit a color scheme. The first step is to choose Color Schemes from the Screen Type/Colors dialog box (see Figure 19.4). Then,

- To create a new color scheme, choose Create, type in a name for the new color scheme, and press ↵.

- To edit a scheme, highlight it in the Color Schemes list, and choose Edit.

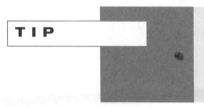

TIP

If you've just selected a different graphics driver, be sure to return to the document window (choose Close as necessary) before you change the screen colors. That way, what you see is what you'll get.

In Graphics mode, the Create and Edit options lead to the Edit Graphics Screen Colors dialog box, shown in Figure 19.5. In Text mode, these options lead to the Edit Text Screen Colors dialog box, which is tailored to the Text mode features, as shown in Figure 19.6.

FIGURE 19.5

Use the Edit Graphics Screen Colors dialog box to customize the colors of the Graphics and Page mode screens.

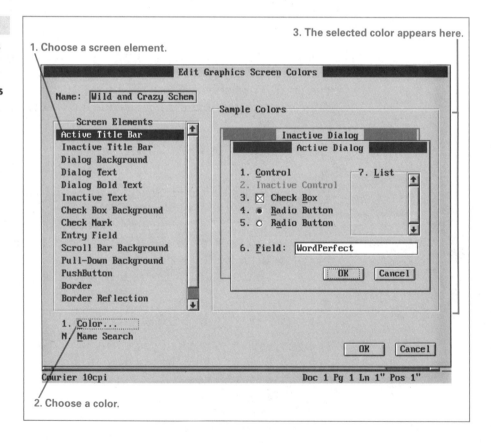

FIGURE 19.6

Use the Edit Text Screen Colors dialog box to customize the colors of the Text mode screen.

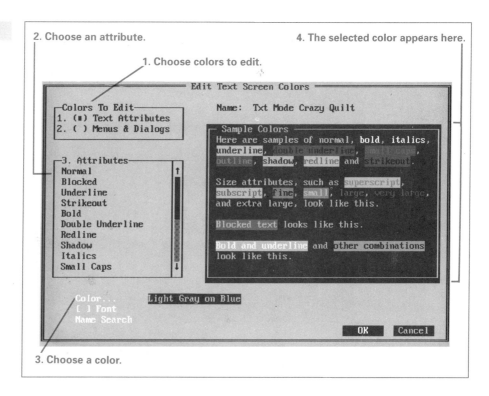

2. Choose an attribute.

1. Choose colors to edit.

4. The selected color appears here.

3. Choose a color.

To change the colors used for an attribute, double-click the attribute you want to change, or move the highlight to that color and choose Color. Then choose the color combination you want to use for that attribute by highlighting and pressing ↵, or, if you're coloring the graphics screen, by double-clicking. When you're done, choose OK and Close as necessary to work your way back to the document window.

Personalizing Your Screen

As you learned in Chapters 2 and 4, the View menu options control which elements appear on your screen. These options include Ribbon, Outline Bar, Pull-Down Menus, Button Bar, Horizontal Scroll Bar, and Vertical Scroll Bar.

The Screen Setup dialog box, shown in Figure 19.7, includes these options, plus many more. To reach this dialog box, choose View ➤ Screen

Setup. Notice how this dialog box is divided into six groups: Screen Options, Display Characters, Display Of Merge Codes, Window Options, Reveal Codes, and Zoom.

FIGURE 19.7

The Screen Setup dialog box lets you choose which elements you want to appear on your screen.

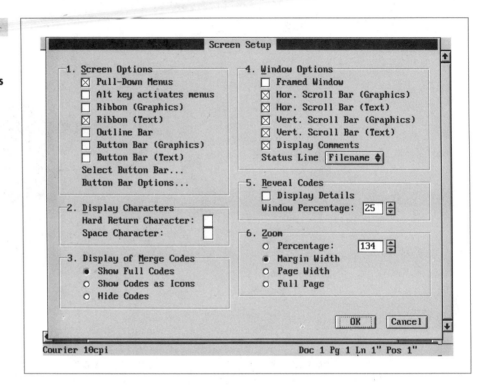

Most of the options on that screen were described in Chapter 4. In this chapter, I'll talk about the Display Characters and Reveal Codes options.

Displaying Spaces and Hard Returns

Normally, spaces appear as just blank spaces, and a hard return just appears as the end of a line in your document window. Some word processors actually display characters for spaces and hard returns. If you're familiar with such a word processor, and would like to add that capability to WordPerfect, choose Display Characters from the Screen Setup dialog box.

Then you can enter a character to display for hard returns and/or spaces. You can even enter a special character by pressing Ctrl+W instead of typing a character from the keyboard. For example, Figure 19.8 shows a sample document after defining special character 5,20 (the ↵ symbol) as the special character for hard returns and character 6,29 (a triangle) for spaces. These special characters appear only on the screen, never in the printed document.

Customizing Reveal Codes

You can choose Display Details under Reveal Codes in the Screen Setup dialog box to expand codes from their normal abbreviated display, such as [Just], to a more detailed display, such as [Just:Full,All]. (Normally, you see that much detail only when the highlight is actually on the code in Reveal Codes.)

The Window Percentage option lets you increase or decrease the size of the Reveal Codes window (when Reveal Codes is active).

FIGURE 19.8

A document with the hard return character set to special character 5,20 and the space character set to 6,29, via the View ➤ Screen Setup commands.

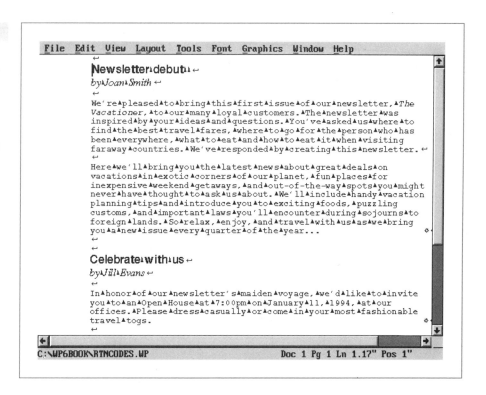

Choosing a Keyboard

WordPerfect comes with several built-in keyboard definitions, which differ from one another mainly in their cursor movement and shortcut keys. You can use any of these definitions, or design custom keyboard definitions of your own.

The predefined keyboard definitions are explained below:

CUAWPW52   Uses the Microsoft Windows Common User Access standards for moving the cursor and selecting text. If you're a confirmed Windows user, you may prefer this keyboard. (See "News for Windows Users" in Chapter 3.)

EQUATION   Makes it easier to type special characters such as θ (theta) and π (pi) into mathematical and scientific documents. This keyboard is particularly handy with the equation features covered in Chapter 29.

MACROS   Includes Alt+*letter* and Ctrl+*letter* shortcut key combinations that will run WordPerfect's built-in macros, which are described in Chapter 18.

[ORIGINAL]   This is the default WordPerfect 6.0 keyboard, and the keyboard I'm assuming that you're using while you read this book. If the keystrokes shown in this book don't work, double-check that you've selected the [ORIGINAL] keyboard layout.

To switch to another keyboard layout, choose File ➤ Setup ➤ Keyboard Layout, or press Shift+F1 K. You'll see the Keyboard Layout dialog box, shown in Figure 19.9. Now, highlight the keyboard definition you want and choose Select.

FIGURE 19.9

The Keyboard Layout dialog box lets you select and change existing keyboard definitions and create new ones.

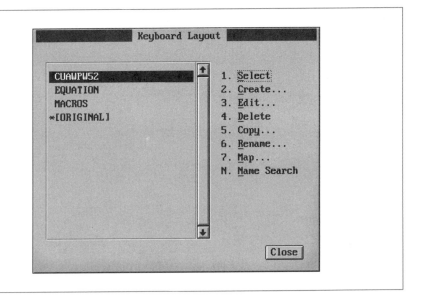

N O T E

Keyboard definitions are stored in files that have a .WPK extension and reside in the personal or shared directory specified in File ➤ Setup ➤ Location Of Files ➤ Macros/Keyboard/Button Bar. The default personal directory for keyboards is usually C:\WP60\MACROS.

The Keyboard Layout dialog box allows you to choose a different keyboard, create new keyboard definitions, and change existing keyboard definitions. Before using the Select, Edit, Delete, Copy, Rename, or Map options, highlight the keyboard definition you want to work with. Then choose the appropriate option. Here's a brief description of each Keyboard Layout option:

Select   Selects the highlighted keyboard definition. WordPerfect will use the definitions for each key in the selected keyboard until you select a different keyboard definition.

Create   Lets you create a new, empty keyboard definition.

Edit   Lets you change the definition of the highlighted keyboard.

Delete   Lets you delete the highlighted keyboard definition. You should avoid deleting the CUAWPW52, EQUATION, and MACROS definitions that come with WordPerfect. If you delete a predefined definition accidentally, you can reinstall it later (see Appendix A).

Copy   Lets you copy the highlighted keyboard definition file to a new file. After selecting Copy, type the new name (up to eight characters) and choose OK. This is handy for creating a new keyboard definition that's similar to an existing one.

Rename   Lets you change the name of an existing keyboard definition file. After selecting Rename, type the new name (up to eight characters) and choose OK.

Map   Provides an alternative way to edit the highlighted keyboard definition.

Name Search   Lets you search for a keyboard definition by name and highlights the closest match to the name (or partial name) that you type.

NOTE   You can change or delete the CUAWPW52, EQUATION, and MACROS keyboards and any custom keyboards that you define. However, WordPerfect will not let you change or delete the [ORIGINAL] keyboard.

Now, let's take a closer look at creating and changing keyboard layouts.

Creating a Keyboard Layout

The four built-in keyboard definitions that WordPerfect offers will satisfy the needs of most people. However, you may want to create new keyboard definitions of your own, or change the existing definitions, if...

- You want to change some WordPerfect keystrokes so that they act like those in other programs you're familiar with.

- You want to type special characters without using the WordPerfect Characters (Ctrl+W) key or having to remember special character codes.

- You want to run macros with your own shortcut keys.

- You'd like to create unique keyboard layouts that organize Word-Perfect features according to the needs of individual projects.

- You like to tinker with things just for the fun of it.

NOTE   Instead of defining custom keyboards, you may prefer to add frequently used features to the Button Bar (see Chapter 4).

You can create a new keyboard definition in one of two ways—by starting from scratch, or by copying the new keyboard definition from an existing file and then changing a few keys here and there. The second method, of course, involves less work for you. To begin, choose File ➤ Setup ➤ Keyboard Layout. You'll see the Keyboard Layout dialog box, shown earlier in Figure 19.9. Then, do one of the following:

- To create a new keyboard definition from scratch, choose Create. When prompted, type a keyboard name and choose OK. You can use any valid DOS file name, up to eight characters long. (Word-Perfect will add the .WPK extension automatically, so don't bother to type it in.)

- To create a new keyboard definition from an existing file, highlight the definition you want to copy from and choose Copy. Type a keyboard name for the new file (up to eight characters long, no extension) and choose OK.

Now that you've created the keyboard definition, you can change it to your liking, as described next.

Changing a Keyboard Layout

When you're ready to customize a keyboard definition, start by highlighting it in the Keyboard Layout dialog box. Then choose either Edit or Map.

The Edit option leads to the Edit Keyboard dialog box, shown in Figure 19.10. Only those keys with definitions that are *different* from the equivalent key in the [ORIGINAL] keyboard definition file will appear here. For example, if you haven't redefined the Ctrl+Q key (which normally sets the QuickMark bookmark discussed in Chapter 9), you won't see it in the dialog box. However, that key *will* appear if you've remapped it.

Choosing Map leads to the Keyboard Map dialog box, shown in Figure 19.11. Notice that this dialog box lists *all* the keys on the keyboard, regardless of whether their definition matches the [ORIGINAL] keyboard. The letters below each key in the map indicate whether the key executes a command (C) or macro (M), or displays text (T).

FIGURE 19.10

The Edit Keyboard dialog box lists only the keys that differ from the [ORIGINAL] keyboard definitions.

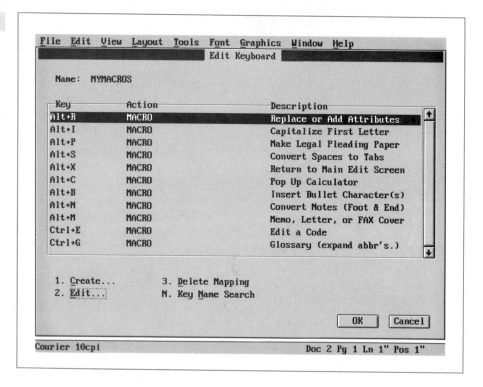

FIGURE 19.11

The Keyboard Map dialog box lists all keys and their definitions.

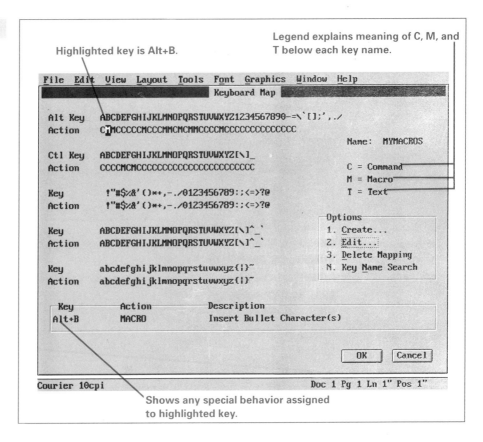

Highlighted key is Alt+B.

Legend explains meaning of C, M, and T below each key name.

```
 File   Edit   View   Layout   Tools   Font   Graphics   Window   Help
                                 Keyboard Map

 Alt Key   ABCDEFGHIJKLMNOPQRSTUVWXYZ1234567890-=\`[];',./
 Action    CMCCCCCMCCCMMCMCMMCCCCMCCCCCCCCCCCCCC
                                                      Name:   MYMACROS
 Ctl Key   ABCDEFGHIJKLMNOPQRSTUVWXYZ[\]_
 Action    CCCCMCMCCCCCCCCCCCCCCCCCCCCCCCCC          C = Command
                                                      M = Macro
 Key       !"#$%&'()*+,-./0123456789:;<=>?@           T = Text
 Action    !"#$%&'()*+,-./0123456789:;<=>?@
                                                     ┌Options──────────
 Key       ABCDEFGHIJKLMNOPQRSTUVWXYZ[\]^_`          │ 1. Create...
 Action    ABCDEFGHIJKLMNOPQRSTUVWXYZ[\]^_`          │ 2. Edit...
                                                      │ 3. Delete Mapping
 Key       abcdefghijklmnopqrstuvwxyz{|}~            │ N. Key Name Search
 Action    abcdefghijklmnopqrstuvwxyz{|}~            └──────────────────

 ┌Key────────Action────────Description────────────────
 │ Alt+B      MACRO         Insert Bullet Character(s)

                                          ┌────┐  ┌──────┐
                                          │ OK │  │Cancel│
                                          └────┘  └──────┘
 Courier 10cpi                       Doc 1 Pg 1 Ln 1" Pos 1"
```

Shows any special behavior assigned to highlighted key.

The Create, Edit, Delete Mapping, and Key Name Search options work exactly the same way in both the Edit Keyboard and Keyboard Map dialog boxes. Choose these options as needed to create, change, and delete your key definitions. When you're finished, choose OK and Close until you're back to the document window.

TIP

Use Key Name Search to quickly locate a key in the Edit Keyboard and Keyboard Map dialog boxes.

Creating or Changing a Key Definition

To create a definition for a new key, follow these steps:

1. Choose Create from the Edit Keyboard or Keyboard Map dialog box. You'll see the Create Key dialog box:

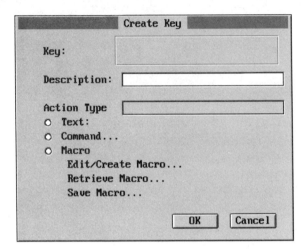

2. Press the key or key combination you want to define. That key name will appear in the Key field. If the key you pressed already has a definition, that definition will be filled in automatically. (If you pressed the wrong key, simply choose Key again and press the key you really wanted.)

3. In the Description text box, type a brief description that explains the action of this key.

4. Choose an action type for the key. I'll describe the action types in a moment. Then Choose OK.

Changing an existing key definition is similar to creating a new one. Here are the steps:

1. Highlight the key name you want to change in the Edit Keyboard or Keyboard Map dialog box.

2. Choose <u>E</u>dit. You'll see the Edit Key dialog box. This is the same as the Create Key dialog box shown above, except that it's filled in with the current definition for the key you selected and it displays a different title.

3. You can change the <u>K</u>ey name, <u>D</u>escription, or Action Type for the key as needed.

4. Choose OK when you're done.

WARNING   To prevent confusion, don't remap WordPerfect shortcut keys, such as Ctrl+I for italics.

Defining the Action Type for a Key

From the Create Key or Edit Key dialog box, you can define the action for any key as <u>T</u>ext, <u>C</u>ommand, or <u>M</u>acro:

Text   Choose <u>T</u>ext, then type the character or characters you want the key to display when you press it. (You can enter up to 27 characters.) To enter WordPerfect Characters, press Ctrl+W and select a character from the WordPerfect Characters dialog box, as explained in Chapter 6.

Command   Choose <u>C</u>ommand, then select the command that should run when you press the key. Each command in the Keyboard Commands list below corresponds to an option on WordPerfect's pull-down menus. For example, assigning the Copy command, shown below, to a keyboard key is the same as selecting <u>E</u>dit ➤ <u>C</u>opy from the pull-down menus or pressing Ctrl+C.

```
┌─────────────────────────────────────┐
│  ▓▓▓   Keyboard Commands   ▓▓▓       │
│  ┌────────────────────────────────┐  │
│  │                                │  │
│  ├────────────────────────────┬───┤  │
│  │ ColumnsOff                 │ ▲ │  │
│  │ ColumnsTablesDlg           ├───┤  │
│  │ CommentConvert             │ ▒ │  │
│  │ CommentCreate              │   │  │
│  │ CommentEdit                │   │  │
│  │ CommentsDisplaySetup       │   │  │
│  │ ComposeDlg                 │   │  │
│  │ ConvertCaseDlg             │   │  │
│  │ ConvertCaseInitialCaps     │   │  │
│  │ ConvertCaseLowercase       │   │  │
│  │ ConvertCaseUppercase       │   │  │
│  │ *Copy                      │   │  │
│  │ CopyAndPaste               │ ▼ │  │
│  └────────────────────────────┴───┘  │
│                                       │
│       ┌────────┐   ┌────────┐         │
│       │ Select │   │ Cancel │         │
│       └────────┘   └────────┘         │
└─────────────────────────────────────┘
```

Macro   Choose Macro and then one of the options below if you want WordPerfect to run a macro when you press this key or you want to save this key's macro definition as a macro file. Your options are as follows:

Edit/Create Macro   Lets you type in new macro programming language commands or edit existing commands for this key. Press F7 when you're done changing the macro. (This option won't help you much unless you're wearing your macro language programmer's hat.)

Retrieve Macro   Type in the name of an existing macro file and choose OK. Use this option if you've recorded a macro and want to assign that macro to a keyboard key.

Save Macro   Type in the name of the macro file you want to save and choose OK. The file name can be up to eight characters long. (Omit the extension, since WordPerfect assigns .WPM automatically.) WordPerfect will save the macro currently associated with this key. You're now free to retrieve this macro for other definitions or run it from the document window.

Chapter 18 explains how to record and run macros and introduces the macro programming language.

Removing a Key Definition

You can easily return a key to its default definition—that is, to the definition it had in the [ORIGINAL] keyboard—at any time. Simply highlight the key definition in the Edit Keyboard or Keyboard Layout dialog box and choose Delete Mapping or press the Del key. Answer Yes when asked to confirm your action.

Customizing the Mouse

WordPerfect will set up your mouse automatically when you install the program if a mouse is connected to your computer. However, you may wish to customize the default settings if you switch to a different mouse, add a new mouse to a computer that didn't have one before, or you simply want to fine-tune your mouse's behavior.

To customize the default settings, choose File ➤ Setup ➤ Mouse, or press Shift+F1 M. You'll see the Mouse dialog box, shown below:

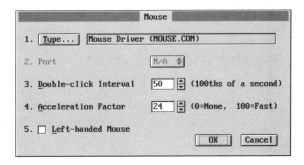

Here's a summary of the Mouse dialog box options:

> **Type**   Opens the Setup Mouse Type dialog box, which lists available mouse drivers. Highlight the name of the mouse driver for your mouse and choose Select. Or, choose Auto Select to have WordPerfect select the driver it thinks will work with your mouse.

NOTE   The mouse driver is a special file of instructions that tells WordPerfect how to communicate with your mouse.

Port For some mice, you'll also need to specify which port your mouse is on (for example, COM1 or COM2). If you don't know this information, don't worry about it—just try a setting. If the mouse works with WordPerfect, you've chosen the correct port. If it doesn't work, try another port setting.

Double-Click Interval Amount of time (in hundredths of a second) between clicks when you double-click. The larger the number, the slower you can double-click the mouse.

Acceleration Factor Determines how responsive the pointer is when you move the mouse. The values range from 0 (no extra boost in speed) to 100 (turbo mode).

Left-Handed Mouse Reverses the normal action of the left and right mouse button, which is great for lefties. With this option selected, the left mouse button cancels an action, displays the menu bar, and scrolls through text; the right button is used to click, double-click, and drag.

Locating the Mouse Driver

Your mouse driver might not be listed in the Setup Mouse Type dialog box. In this case, try looking in your mouse documentation for a compatible driver that *is* listed. If you find a compatible driver, select it.

Unfortunately, some mice are renegades, and for those you'll need to choose the Mouse Driver (MOUSE.COM) option, or try Auto Select. MOUSE.COM is a generic driver that works with most mice. However, it's something of a memory hog. WordPerfect mouse drivers usually take up less memory than MOUSE.COM and are preferred if they work well with your mouse.

Installing a New Mouse

Installing a mouse for use with WordPerfect is easy. First, follow the manufacturer's instructions for installing the mouse hardware and driver program. Then start up WordPerfect and choose File ➤ Setup ➤ Mouse ➤ Type ➤ Auto Select. Finally, choose OK and try out the mouse.

If the mouse works, it's selected properly. If it doesn't work, you'll probably need to select the mouse driver manually by choosing the Type option in the Mouse dialog box shown above. (Your mouse might also be dead or not plugged in properly, in which case changing the WordPerfect settings won't have any effect.)

Choosing a Color Printing Palette

For you lucky dogs who have a color printer or monitor, WordPerfect provides *color printing palettes*. The color printing palettes let you group and name colors so that you can apply them to page elements very quickly, instead of having to select a custom color for every element. For example, you could create a "Cool Man Cool" palette with blues and greens, and a "Hot Chili Peppers" palette with bright reds, oranges, and yellows. Then, you'd just select the palette you want to use and pick colors from that palette for text, borders, shading, lines, and other elements in your document.

Color palettes will display color on your screen only if you've selected a color monitor screen type (choose File ➤ Setup ➤ Display ➤ Graphics Mode Screen Type/Colors ➤ Screen Type, as discussed earlier in this chapter). And, of course, color appears in printed documents only if your printer supports color printing and is currently set to print in color (choose File ➤ Print/Fax, then press Shift+F1 to verify the Print Color setting). If you don't have a color monitor or printer, colors will appear in shades of gray, just like all the figures and graphics in this book.

NOTE Color palettes are stored in files with a .WPP extension, in the directories specified in File ➤ Setup ➤ Location Of Files ➤ Printer Files.

Selecting a Color Palette

Selecting a color palette is easy. Just follow these steps:

1. Choose File ➤ Setup ➤ Color Printing Palette. You'll see the Color Printing Palettes dialog box, shown in Figure 19.12.

2. Highlight the palette you want and choose Select, or double-click the palette name.

3. Choose Close until you return to the document window.

You can choose a different palette whenever you wish. Any elements that you've already colored with another palette will stay the same color in your document, even if you change palettes.

FIGURE 19.12

The Color Printing Palettes dialog box lets you select, create, edit, delete, and rename color printing and display palettes.

```
┌──────────────────────── Color Printing Palettes ────────────────────────┐
│                                                                          │
│  ┌─Color Printing Palettes─────────────────┐ ↑    1. Select             │
│  │ Crayon Palette                           │      2. Create...          │
│  │ *Hot Chili Peppers                       │      3. Edit...            │
│  │ Multi-Colors                             │      4. Delete             │
│  │                                          │      5. Rename...          │
│  │                                          │      N. Name Search        │
│  │                                          │                            │
│  │                                          │ ↓                          │
│  └──────────────────────────────────────────┘                           │
│                                                                          │
│   Color Display Units  RGB (Red Green Blue)            ↕                │
│                                                                          │
│                                                   ┌───────┐             │
│                                                   │ Close │             │
│                                                   └───────┘             │
└──────────────────────────────────────────────────────────────────────────┘
```

The other options in the Color Printing Palettes dialog box are described below. In a moment, I'll show you how to create and edit palettes.

Create   Lets you create a new color printing palette that initially has eight colors.

Edit   Lets you edit the highlighted palette.

Delete   Lets you delete the highlighted palette.

Rename   Lets you change the name of the highlighted palette.

Name Search   Lets you highlight a palette quickly by typing in a few letters of its name.

Color Display Units   Lets you choose one of three systems for defining colors. The color display unit options are listed below:

RGB (Red Green Blue)   Uses the primary colors of light to define colors (this is the default setting).

HLS (Hue Luminosity Saturation)   Defines colors in the context of your monitor, much like the hue, brightness, and contrast knobs adjust colors on a television. In the HLS system, Hue adjusts color, Luminosity adjusts the amount of white and gray, and Saturation adjusts the amount of color.

CMYK (Cyan Magenta Yellow Black)   Uses the same color model that print shops employ for color separations. The maximum settings for all colors produce black, while the zero settings for all colors produce white.

Using Color Palettes

Once you've selected a color palette, you can use it to assign colors to any element in your document. Suppose you want to use a color named Wild Strawberry to display new text that you type. Here are the steps to follow:

1. Select the palette that has the color you want, as described above.

2. Choose F**o**nt ➤ **P**rint Color (or press Ctrl+F8 C).

3. Highlight the color you want in the Color Selection dialog box that appears (see Figure 19.13).

FIGURE 19.13

The Color Selection dialog box lets you color various elements in your document.

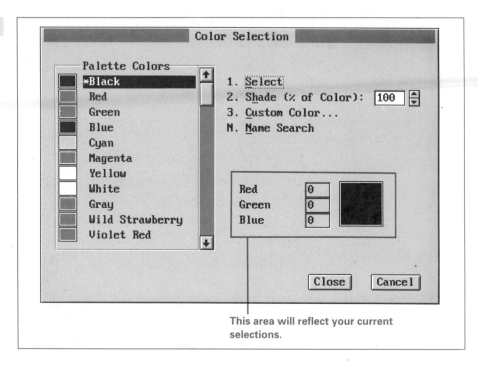

This area will reflect your current selections.

4. Make these additional adjustments if you wish:

• To change the shade, choose Shade (% Of Color), enter a percentage of the selected color, and press ↵. Choose 100 to get the "pure" color shown in the Palette Colors list. Choose a smaller percentage to get a paler version of the selected color.

• To create a custom version of the selected color, and (optionally) add it to the current palette, choose Custom Color. Creating a custom color is similar to creating or changing a color in the palette. (I'll explain how to create and change palettes in a moment.) When you're finished creating the custom color, choose OK. Your custom color will be selected automatically, and you'll be returned to the document window or the Font dialog box.

5. Choose Select when the sample color in the dialog box looks just right. (Skip this step if you created a custom color in step 4.)

The steps for coloring any element in your document are basically the same as those shown above. In step 2, however, you'll need to choose options for the specific element you're coloring. For example, to color the vertical line between columns in a multicolumn document, you could choose Layout ➤ Columns ➤ Column Borders ➤ Customize ➤ Color ➤ Choose One Color For All Lines. This will take you to the Color Selection dialog box, shown in Figure 19.13, above. (See Chapter 27 to learn more about multicolumn layouts.)

Creating and Editing Color Palettes

Creating and customizing color palettes is easy and fun. Start by choosing File ➤ Setup ➤ Color Printing Palette (Shift+F1 C). You'll see the Color Printing Palettes dialog box, shown earlier in Figure 19.12.

If you want to create a new palette, choose Create, type in a name for the palette, and press ↵. WordPerfect will add that palette to the list, in alphabetical order. The new palette will automatically include black, red, green, blue, cyan, magenta, yellow, and white. From here, you can edit the palette as you would any existing palette.

Here's how to edit an existing palette:

1. Choose File ➤ Setup ➤ Color Printing Palette and highlight the palette you want to change in the Color Printing Palettes dialog box.

2. Choose Edit. You'll see the Edit Color Printing Palette dialog box, shown in Figure 19.14.

3. Highlight a color and take one of the following actions:

   • Choose Create to add a new color to the palette. The starting point for the new color is the same as the color you highlighted.

   • Choose Delete and then Yes to delete the highlighted color.

   • Choose Edit to change the highlighted color.

FIGURE 19.14

The Edit Color Printing Palette lets you create, edit, and delete colors in a palette.

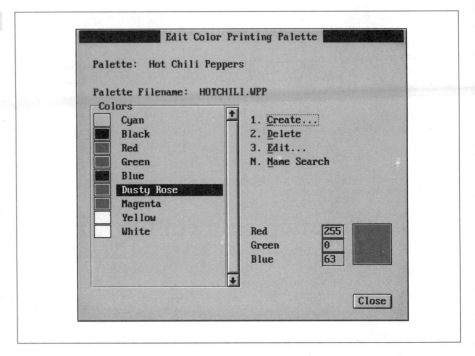

4. Repeat step 3 until your palette is done, then choose Close until you return to the document window.

Changing the Colors

Choosing the Create or Edit options in step 3 above opens the Add Color dialog box (if you chose Create) or Modify Color dialog box (if you chose Edit). They're both the same, except for their titles. Figure 19.15 shows a sample Modify Color dialog box (it's much nicer in color, believe me). The labels in the figure explain how to use the dialog box.

FIGURE 19.15

The Modify Color dialog box (shown here) and Add Color dialog box (not shown) let you assign color names and create custom colors.

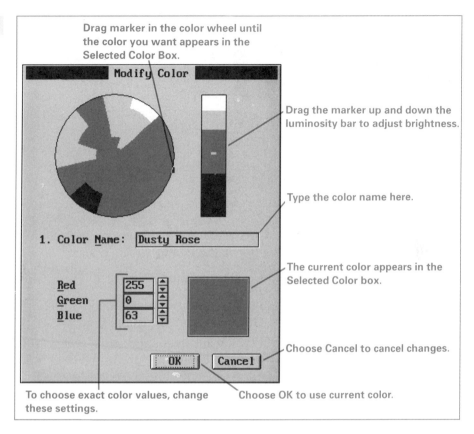

Drag marker in the color wheel until the color you want appears in the Selected Color Box.

Modify Color

Drag the marker up and down the luminosity bar to adjust brightness.

Type the color name here.

1. Color Name: Dusty Rose

The current color appears in the Selected Color box.

Red   255
Green   0
Blue   63

Choose Cancel to cancel changes.

OK   Cancel

To choose exact color values, change these settings.

Choose OK to use current color.

Customizing the Initial Look of Your Documents

Every new document you create starts with an [Open Style:Initial Codes] code, which formats the document with the current Initial Codes settings. You can't delete this code, but you can customize the initial codes settings. For example, you might want to set up different initial margins, spacing, and justification, or choose a different font. You can change the initial settings just for the current document or for all new documents that you create.

NOTE

Like Styles, the initial codes can contain text, graphics, lines, and any formatting features you want. In fact, initial codes are styles, so all the features available in styles are also available in initial codes. Chapter 17 covers styles.

Changing the Initial Codes

Follow these steps to change WordPerfect's initial codes:

1. Choose Layout ➤ Document or press Shift+F8 D. The Document Format dialog box will appear.

2. Choose either of the following options:

    - If you want to change initial codes for this document only, choose Document Initial Codes.

    - If you want to change initial codes for any new documents that you create, choose Initial Codes Setup. WordPerfect will automatically copy the codes in the Initial Codes Setup to the Document Initial Codes of any new document.

3. You'll see an Initial Codes Setup or Document Initial Codes dialog box, which works just like a small Reveal Codes screen. Choose any formatting options you wish, using either the pull-down menus or shortcut keys. You can also add text, graphics boxes, lines, styles, and whatever else WordPerfect offers. Here's an example of a completed dialog box:

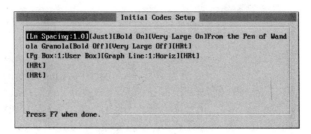

T I P

When you add a graphic to the Document Initial Codes or Initial Codes Setup, it's best to set the Contents option for the graphic to Image On Disk. This will make your documents smaller and will conserve disk space. See Chapter 26 for more information.

4. When you're done, press F7 to return to the Document Format dialog box.

5. Choose OK until you return to your document.

You can change your initial settings by repeating the steps above. To return to WordPerfect's default settings for the current document, simply delete all the codes in the Document Initial Codes dialog box. To return to default settings for future documents that you create, delete the codes in the Initial Codes Setup dialog box.

Figure 19.16 shows the effect on a brand new document of the sample Initial Codes Setup presented above.

Be aware that changing the initial codes has no effect on documents that you've already saved. However, you can open the Document Initial Codes dialog box for a document that has the codes you want to use in another document. Then select all those codes and copy them to the Clipboard. Next, open the Document Initial Codes dialog box of another document (or the Initial Codes Setup dialog box, if you prefer) and paste the codes from the Clipboard. See Chapters 3 and 4 if you need a refresher on cut-and-paste techniques and working with codes.

Changing the Initial Font

You can add font codes to the Document Initial Codes or Initial Codes Setup dialog boxes described above. Alternatively, you can set initial fonts by choosing Layout ➤ Document ➤ Initial Font. When the Initial Font

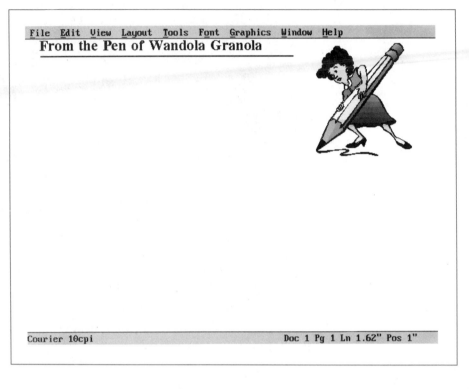

dialog box appears, select a font and font size, and decide whether to change the initial font for the current document only, or for all new documents created with the current printer. When you're done, choose OK until you return to the document window.

Precedence of Initial Codes and Fonts

Now you might be wondering, "What if I change the initial codes setup, the document initial codes, *and* the initial font? Which settings will win the race?" Here are the rules that WordPerfect follows to decide the winners:

- Codes in your *document* override all equivalent codes in the Document Initial Codes, Initial Codes Setup, and Initial Font dialog boxes.

- Codes in Document Initial Codes override all equivalent codes in Initial Codes Setup and Initial Font.

N O T E You can also define initial fonts when you set up fonts for your printer. Please see Chapter 10 for more information on installing fonts.

Other Ways to Change Default Settings

If you think you've learned everything about personalizing WordPerfect, you're in for a little surprise. There are two more ways to personalize the program.

First, many dialog boxes include a *Setup button* (shown below), which you can use to customize settings for certain features:

```
Setup... Shft+F1
```

For example, choosing File ➤ Print/Fax (Shift+F7) and then choosing the Setup button (or pressing Shift+F1) displays the Print Setup dialog box, below. From here, you can customize various printer settings, as explained in Chapter 10.

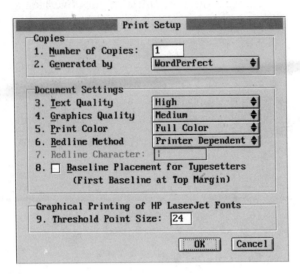

WordPerfect 6.0 also provides scores of built-in *styles* and lets you create styles of your own to control the appearance of nearly everything in a document, including lines, text, graphics, and borders. Chapter 17 is devoted to the topic of styles.

In this chapter, you've discovered many ways to personalize WordPerfect for your own use. Now, let's move on to tools for managing your files.

CHAPTER

20

Managing Your Files

fast TRACK

To use the Directory Tree　　　　　　　　　706

click the Directory Tree button or press F8 in a dialog box that prompts for a directory name. Or, press F5 then F8 from the document window. Highlight the directory you want and choose Select or double-click the directory name.

To use the QuickFinder　　　　　　　　　708

click the Use QuickFinder button or press F4 in a dialog box that prompts for a directory name. Or, from the document window, press F5 and then F4, or click the QuikFndr button in the Button Bar. To search for a file, choose Update Indexes (if any indexed files have changed), type in the word pattern you want to search for, then choose OK. You can use Setup (Shift+F1) to define new QuickFinder index files.

To create a document summary　　　　　　　717

choose File ➤ Summary, or press Shift+F8 DS. Fill in the fields you want and choose OK.

To use the File Manager to locate and manage files　722

choose File ➤ File Manager, press F5, or click the File Mgr button in the Button Bar. Or, choose the File List button or press F5 when those choices are available in a dialog box. Type a directory or wildcard pattern and choose OK. From here, you can move through the directory tree, and open, retrieve, look at, copy, move, delete, or print files. You can also customize the File Manager for your needs.

All programs, databases, spreadsheets, graphics, WordPerfect documents, and other types of information are stored in files on your computer's disk. As you might well imagine, the number of files can quickly mushroom into the thousands. Managing that collection of files can be a job in itself. For example, you might need to delete old files to make room for new ones, copy groups of files to backup disks, or find a file whose name you've forgotten.

These kinds of jobs fall into the category of file management, which is what this chapter is all about. WordPerfect offers a smorgasbord of features for managing files. You'll get the most out of these features if you don't try to learn them all at once. Just experiment with the basics, and then try more sophisticated techniques when you need them. Keep in mind that help for any feature is just an F1 key-press away.

Understanding File Lingo

The first step to mastering file management is to become familiar with basic DOS terminology. You'll find this kind of information in your DOS manuals, or in *Murphy's Laws of DOS* by Charlie Russel, SYBEX, 1993. In particular, you should understand these terms:

Drive   This is where all files are stored. The first floppy drive is named A:, the second (if any) is B:. Hard drives are C:, D:, and so forth. A drive, also called a *disk drive*, is like a file cabinet.

Directory   Each disk drive can be subdivided into numerous directories. Each directory can contain files and other directories (called *subdirectories*). For example, your WordPerfect program and its related files are usually stored on **c:\wp60** and **c:\wpc60dos** (the directories named WP60 and WPC60DOS on hard disk drive C). A directory is like one drawer in a file cabinet.

File This is a single document or program. File names can be up to eight characters long and can be followed by a period and an extension up to three characters long. (A file with the name HANDOUT.WP, for example, would be spoken as "handout dot wp.") A file is like a single manila folder in a file drawer.

Path The combined drive and directory location of a file. The path specifies the exact route to take to find a particular file. For example, the path and file name **c:\wp60\wpdocs\handout.wp** says, "Go to drive C:, then go to the directory named WP60, then to the directory below it named WPDOCS, and then to the file named HANDOUT.WP."

Subdirectory A directory that's below another directory. The terms directory and subdirectory are used interchangeably.

Wildcard A * or ?, used to represent unknown or unspecified characters. The * can match any character or group of characters. The ? matches any single character. Use wildcards in WordPerfect dialog boxes and DOS commands to select groups of files that match a certain pattern, as summarized in Table 20.1.

TABLE 20.1: The DOS Wildcard Characters Used in File Names

WILDCARD	WHAT IT MATCHES	EXAMPLE	DESCRIPTION OF EXAMPLE
?	Any single character	a??.?	Any file name starting with "A" followed by two characters and a one-character extension, e.g. **abc.1**, **axe.z**
*	Zero or more characters	*.exe	All files with an EXE extension
		.	All files
		test*.*	All files that start with the letters "TEST"

Entering File and Directory Names

Many WordPerfect commands lead to dialog boxes that prompt you for file or directory names. Examples include the following options on the File menu: Open, Save, Save As, and Setup ➤ Location Of Files.

If you know the file or directory name, you can simply type it into the dialog box. Here are some techniques you can use:

- If you enter only the file name (for example, **mydoc.wp**), Word-Perfect will store or look for the file on the default drive and directory. (As Chapter 19 explains, the Location Of Files options control the default location for various categories of WordPerfect files.)

- If you enter a subdirectory name and file name (as in **wpfiles\mydoc.wp**), WordPerfect will save the file or retrieve it from the named subdirectory of the current directory. Later in this chapter, you'll learn how to create directories and change the current directory using the File Manager's Change Default Dir option.

- If you enter a complete drive and path, such as **c:\wp60\wpfiles\ mydoc.wp,** WordPerfect will save the file or retrieve it from that drive and directory.

> **NOTE** If you enter a directory name that doesn't exist, you'll usually see the message "Invalid drive/path specification" or "Path Not Found."

When you know a file or directory name, you can simply type it into the appropriate field in a dialog box. However, if you're unsure about the file or directory name, you can choose certain buttons or function keys. These usually lead you to the File Manager, which can help you locate and fill in the name you want. Table 20.2 lists and describes the buttons and function keys available.

TABLE 20.2: File Management Buttons and Shortcut Keys

BUTTON	FUNCTION KEY	DESCRIPTION
`File Manager... F5`	F5	Opens the File Manager, a comprehensive tool for managing files and directories.
File Mgr		You can also reach the File Manager from the document window by choosing File ➤ File Manager, pressing F5, or clicking the File Mgr button in the Button Bar.
`Use QuickFinder... F4`	F4	Lets you quickly search indexed files for words, patterns, or phrases.
QuikFndr		You can also reach the QuickFinder from the document window by pressing F5 and then F4, or by clicking the QuikFndr button in the Button Bar.
`QuickList... F6`	F6	Lets you switch to a frequently used directory, file name, or wildcard pattern.
`Directory Tree... F8`	F8	Lets you select a directory from a directory tree.

Saving Documents

As you work with a document, WordPerfect stores a temporary copy of it in the computer's memory. You must save that copy to disk—by choosing File ➤ Save (Ctrl+F12) or File ➤ Save As (F10)—if you want to keep your changes permanently. The Save Document dialog box for both options appears below:

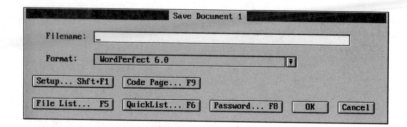

File ➤ Save is useful for saving new documents or quickly replacing the disk copy of an existing file with your on-screen copy. File ➤ Save As lets you save new documents or change an existing document's name, format, password, or code page.

You learned the basic steps for saving files in Chapters 1 and 3. However, you may have wondered about the Format option and the Setup (Shift+F1), Code Page (F9), and Password (F8) buttons that appear in the Save Document dialog box. We'll look at these next.

TIP As added protection against power outages and other mishaps, WordPerfect can save your work automatically at timed intervals. See the sections on automatic backups in Chapter 19.

Exporting to Other Formats

WordPerfect normally saves files under its own WordPerfect 6.0 format. Sometimes, however, you may want to use a different format, such as Microsoft Word for Windows 2.0b or WordPerfect 5.1/5.2, so that you can change the file with a different word processor or text editor. To do this, choose Format from the Save Document dialog box and select the format you want from the drop-down list that appears.

To prevent crucial system files from being damaged accidentally, Word-Perfect automatically saves ASCII Text files in ASCII Text format—*not* in WordPerfect 6.0 format. You can change the format of ASCII Text files if you want to, but don't do this for system files such as CONFIG.SYS or AUTOEXEC.BAT unless you also change the file name. If you save a system file in WordPerfect format accidentally, simply open it and save it again in ASCII Text (Standard) format.

Choosing a Code Page

The *code page* identifies the ASCII character set used in a document. Different ASCII sets are used in different languages. To change the character set used when you save the document, choose Code Page (or press F9) from the Save Document dialog box. When the Code Page dialog box appears, highlight the code page you want and choose Select or double-click the code page name.

Password-Protecting Files

Some documents contain sensitive information. If you're sharing your computer with other people, or if you're using a network, you may wish to prevent others from viewing, printing, or changing that information. You do that by assigning a password of up to 23 characters when you save the file. Only people who know the password can use that document.

There's one catch, though. If *you* forget the password, you'll also be locked out of the document. So once you think up a password, write it down and store it in a safe place. (You might want to use the same password in all your documents to avoid confusion later.)

Follow these steps to add a password to your document:

1. In the Save Document dialog box, choose Password (or press F8).

2. Type the password you want to assign (you won't see any characters as you type), then press ↵ or choose OK.

3. When prompted with "Re-enter Password," type the password again to verify that you typed it correctly the first time, then press ↵ or choose OK.

4. If you typed the same password both times, WordPerfect will accept it. Otherwise, you'll have to start over at step 2.

5. Fill in the rest of the Save Document dialog box and choose OK to save your file with the password.

Opening a Password-Protected File

Whenever you open a password-protected document, you'll see a dialog box like this one:

In the Enter Password text box, type the correct password (your typing will be invisible), and press ↵ or choose OK.

If you type the wrong password, the error message "File is password protected" will appear. Choose OK to clear the message and get back to the Open Document dialog box.

Changing or Removing the Password

You can easily change or remove the password later, as long as you know the original password. First, open the file with File ➤ Open or File ➤ Retrieve and enter the original password. Next, choose File ➤ Save As and click the Password button (or press F8). If you're changing the password, type the new password and press ↵ or choose OK twice. If you prefer to delete the password (so that anyone can open your file), choose Remove or press F6 in the Password dialog box instead of entering a different password. Choose OK to finish saving your document.

Incidentally, password-protecting a file doesn't prevent other users from *deleting* that file from DOS or Windows (though they won't be able to delete it with WordPerfect's File Manager). For that kind of protection, you should always keep an extra copy of your document on a floppy disk in a safe place. Or, refer to the DOS ATTRIB command in your DOS documentation to learn about another way to protect and hide files.

Changing the Save Defaults

You can use the Setup button (Shift+F1) in the Save Document dialog box to get to the Save Setup dialog box shown below. There, you can change the defaults for saving files as follows:

- Select <u>F</u>ast Save (Unformatted) if you want faster saves that don't format the document for printing. Deselect this option if you want slower saves but faster printing.

- If you want WordPerfect to export each document you save to a different file format, instead of using WordPerfect 6.0 format, choose <u>D</u>efault Save Format. Then select a format from the drop-down list that appears.

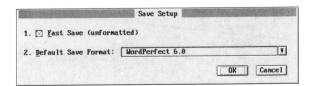

NOTE

Even if you change the Default Save Format, WordPerfect will still save ASCII text files in ASCII format.

Opening "Non-6.0" Documents

Chapter 3 covered the basics of opening files with File ➤ Open (Shift+F10) and combining files with File ➤ Retrieve. If you open or retrieve a document that was saved in any format except WordPerfect 6.0, you'll see this dialog box:

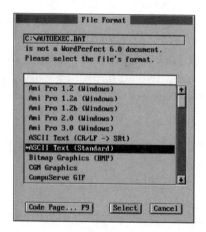

WordPerfect will take its best guess as to the original file format and will highlight that name in the list. If the format is correct, press ↵ or choose Select to retrieve the document, or double-click the format name. Otherwise, scroll through the list and select the proper format. If WordPerfect has no idea what format the file is in, or you've tried to open a file that's in an unsupported format, you'll see an error message. Choose OK to clear the message and return to the Open Document dialog box. Then try opening a different file.

N O T E   After WordPerfect retrieves a file that's in a non-WordPerfect format, future saves will be in WordPerfect format (except for ASCII Text files).

Using the QuickList

The QuickList uses descriptive names for directories, files or wildcards, for easy access and quick recognition. Thus, it provides a handy way to locate directories and files that you use frequently. Many QuickList directory entries are defined automatically when you use File ➤ Setup ➤ Location Of Files and check the Update QuickList box (see Chapter 19). You can also define your own QuickList entries.

For example, if all your personal tax records for 1993 are stored in the directory C:\TAX\YEAR93, you could assign the description *Tax 1993* to the path C:\TAX\YEAR93 and add it to the QuickList. If you're working on your 1993 tax return (stored in the file 1993RTRN.WP), you could set up another QuickList entry for that file. You'd assign the description as *1993 Woe Is Me* and the path as C:\TAX\YEAR93\1993RTRN.WP. Now imagine that you also want a quick way to list Lotus 1-2-3 spreadsheet files stored in that same directory. You could set this description to *1993 Tax Spreadsheets* and the path to C:\TAX\YEAR93*.WK1. (Here, I've used a wildcard to stand for all files that have a .WK1 extension.) Now you don't have to remember convoluted DOS path names to know where your files are stored.

Locating Files and Directories

You can click the QuickList button (shown below) or press F6 in most dialog boxes that prompt for file or directory names.

```
QuickList... F6
```

Doing so displays a QuickList dialog box like the one below. In this example, the highlighted *Documents:* item refers to the directory C:\WP6BOOK, as you can see at the top of the dialog box.

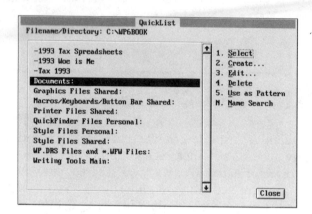

TIP

From the document window, press F5 then F6 to reach the QuickList in a jiffy.

To select an entry, highlight it and choose <u>S</u>elect or double-click the entry you want. After you select an entry, WordPerfect will convert your selection to a path name. Then it will either fill in the dialog box you came from with the path name you chose, or it will open up the File Manager so that you can refine your selection further. The action taken will depend on whether the dialog box was expecting a directory name or file name and whether the QuickList entry you chose refers to a directory name, file name, or wildcard list. (You needn't memorize what happens when. Just go with the flow.)

The QuickList dialog box offers these options, in addition to the Select option I just described:

> **Create** Lets you create a new QuickList entry, as explained in the next section.

Edit   Lets you change the highlighted QuickList entry.

Delete   Lets you delete the highlighted QuickList entry.

Use as Pattern   Inserts this directory name into the dialog box you were using when you chose QuickList.

Name Search   Lets you highlight an entry quickly by typing the first few letters of the name.

TIP

In dialog boxes that offer <u>C</u>reate and <u>D</u>elete options, you can press Ins to choose Create and Del to choose Delete.

Changing the QuickList Entry

When you're ready to create or change a QuickList entry, go to the Quick-List dialog box. Then choose <u>C</u>reate if you want to set up a new entry, or highlight an existing entry and choose <u>E</u>dit. Choosing <u>E</u>dit opens the Edit QuickList dialog box shown below. (The Create QuickList Entry dialog box looks basically the same except that the <u>D</u>escription and <u>F</u>ile-name/Directory boxes will be empty.)

```
                        Edit QuickList Entry

1. Description:        1993 Woe is Me

2. Filename/Directory: C:\WP6BOOK\1993RTRN.WP

  Examples
  Description              Filename/Directory
  Graphics Directory       C:\WP60\GRAPHICS
  Bear Graphic File        C:\WP60\GRAPHICS\BEAR.WPG
  All WPG Files            C:\WP60\GRAPHICS\*.WPG
  All WP---.WPG Files      C:\WP60\GRAPHICS\WP???.WPG


  Directory Tree... F8                    OK    Cancel
```

Now, type in or change the description for this entry in the Description text box and press ↵. Then type in or change the path for this entry in the Filename/Directory text box and press ↵. The path can be a directory or file name and can contain wildcards, as the examples in the dialog box show. When you're done, choose OK.

The description for your entry will appear in the QuickList in alphabetic order. If you want QuickList descriptions to appear at the top of the list, just precede the descriptive text with a punctuation character, such as – (hyphen), * (asterisk), or ; (semicolon). For example, in the sample QuickList shown earlier, I put a hyphen in front of each of the first three names to list those three names first.

Using the Directory Tree

The Directory Tree displays a hierarchy of the directories on a disk drive. When a WordPerfect feature prompts you to enter a directory name, you can use the Directory Tree button (shown below), or press F8, to locate the directory.

| Directory Tree... F8 |

Figure 20.1 shows a sample Directory Tree dialog box. Notice that the current directory is selected initially.

TIP

To reach the Directory Tree from the document window quickly, press F5 and then F8.

You can press the arrow keys or use your mouse to highlight the directory name you want, then choose Select Directory (or double-click the directory name). Depending on which dialog box you came from, WordPerfect will either fill in the dialog box with the directory name you chose, or it will open the File Manager and display files in that directory.

FIGURE 20.1

The Directory Tree dialog box displays your directory tree graphically.

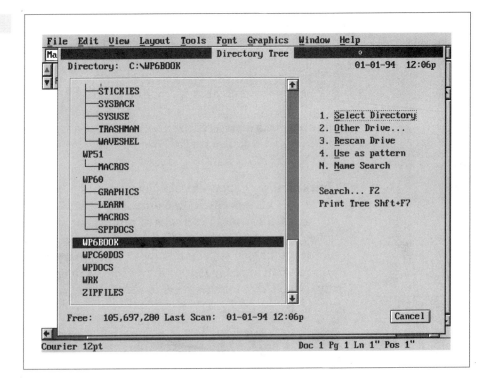

In addition to the Select Directory option, the following choices are available in the Directory Tree dialog box:

Other Drive   Lets you switch to a different disk drive.

Rescan Drive   Forces WordPerfect to rescan the drive and redisplay the directory. This is useful if you've switched floppy disks, or you're using a network.

Use as Pattern   Inserts the path of the directory into the dialog box you were using before you chose Directory Tree.

Name Search   Lets you quickly locate a file by typing the first few letters of its name.

Search   (F2) Lets you search for a directory by name.

Print Tree   (or press Shift+F7) Prints the current directory tree.

Using the QuickFinder

Suppose you've created many documents and need to find all those that mention a woman named *Doris Ajar*. Using the File Manager's Search feature (described later in this chapter) can be slow if she's mentioned in hundreds of documents all over your hard disk. This is clearly a job for the QuickFinder and its indexes.

QuickFinder indexes are alphabetical lists of every word in the files and directories you specify. These indexes are stored in a highly compressed format that QuickFinder can scan almost instantaneously. To find information quickly, you just select the index you want to use and type in the word, phrase, or pattern you want to look for. QuickFinder will scan the index and present matching file names in the File Manager. From there, you can use any of the File Manager tools to search, view, or open the documents.

NOTE

QuickFinder indexes have abolutely nothing to do with the automatic indexing feature described in Chapter 31.

Although QuickFinder indexes contain alphabetical lists of words, they're quite different from conventional indexes like the one at the back of this book. For example, you can't look at a QuickFinder index directly, nor can you print it.

Creating a QuickFinder Index

If you haven't already created a QuickFinder index, you'll need to do that before you can use QuickFinder to search for files. Here's how:

1. Click the QuikFndr button (shown at left) in the Button Bar, if it's available. Or, choose <u>F</u>ile ➤ <u>F</u>ile Manager or press F5, then click the Use QuickFinder button (shown below) or press F4. You'll see the QuickFinder File Indexer dialog box shown in Figure 20.2.

Use QuickFinder... F4

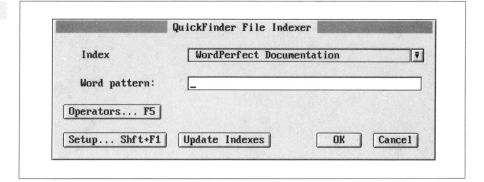

2. Choose the Setup button or press Shift+F1. The QuickFinder File Indexes Setup dialog box, shown in Figure 20.3, will appear next.

3. If you haven't selected a location for your indexes, choose Location Of _F_iles. Then specify a personal path, a shared path, or both for your indexes and choose OK.

NOTE   QuickFinder indexes are stored in files with .IDX extensions. WordPerfect also may use the extensions .LOG and .INC for files associated with QuickFinder indexes.

4. Choose _P_ersonal or _S_hared, depending on which set of indexes you want to update. (These options will be available only if you've defined locations for them in step 3.)

5. In the Index Description list, highlight the entry you want to work with, and then choose from the options listed below. (If you're creating a new index, it doesn't matter which index description you highlight.)

FIGURE 20.3

Use the QuickFinder
File Indexes Setup
dialog box to create,
edit, delete, rename,
and generate
QuickFinder indexes.

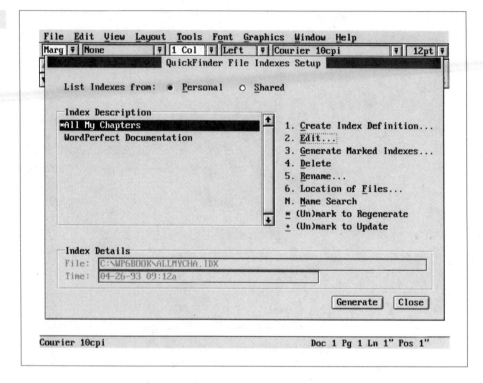

Create Index Definition   Lets you create a new index definition. See the next section, "Creating or Editing an Index Definition," for details.

Edit   Lets you edit the definition that you've highlighted in the Index Description list. (You can also double-click an entry to edit it.)

Delete   Lets you delete the highlighted index file.

Rename   Lets you change the description of the highlighted index file. The new description will appear in the Index Description list in alphabetic order.

Name Search   Lets you highlight an entry quickly by typing the first few letters of the name.

* (Un)Mark to Regenerate   Lets you mark or unmark index entries that you want to regenerate from scratch.

Use this option if you've changed or created an index definition. You can click the option, press *, or press the spacebar to mark or unmark the highlighted Index Description entry. (WordPerfect automatically marks index definitions with a * when you create them.)

± (Un)Mark to Update   Lets you mark or unmark index entries that you want to update. Use this option if you've changed the contents of files or added new files in the highlighted index, but you haven't changed the index definition. You can click the option or press + to mark or unmark the highlighted Index Description entry. (WordPerfect automatically marks index definitions with a + when you change the list of directories and files to include in the index.)

TIP

It's usually faster to update an index than to regenerate one. But updated indexes need more space than regenerated indexes. Therefore, you'll occasionally want to regenerate your indexes.

6. When you're done creating or editing index definitions and marking the ones you want to regenerate or update, choose Generate Marked Indexes or click the Generate button.

7. WordPerfect will update or generate all the marked indexes—be patient, it could take a while—and return to the QuickFinder File Indexes Setup dialog box. Choose Close, then OK to return to your document.

When you choose Generate Marked Indexes or click the Generate button in step 6 above, QuickFinder will index all words found in WordPerfect 4.2, 5.0, 5.1, and 6.0 files. It will also index any ASCII Text words contained in non-WordPerfect files. You can also use the index definition options, discussed in a moment, to exclude certain files from an index.

Creating or Editing an Index Definition

Choosing Create Index Definition or Edit from the QuickFinder File Indexes Setup dialog box leads to another dialog box. An example of the Edit Index Definition dialog box appears in Figure 20.4. (The Create Index Definition dialog box is almost the same, except that its fields will be empty.) Your index definitions can contain as many directories and files as you wish.

FIGURE 20.4

The Edit Index Definition dialog box. The Create Index Definition dialog box is basically the same, though it starts out empty.

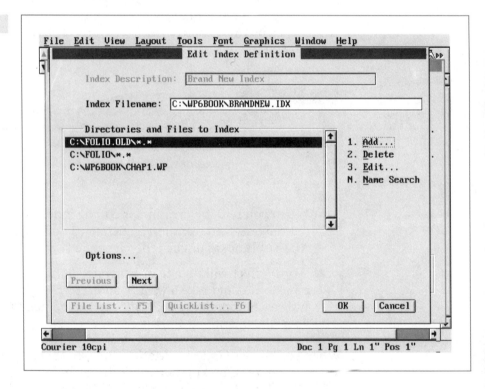

Follow these steps to create (or edit) an index definition:

1. In the Index Description text box, type a description for your index and press ↵. (This option won't be available when you edit an index definition.)

2. In the Index Filename text box, use the suggested file name, or type in one of your own and press ↵. The file name can have up to eight characters. WordPerfect will add the .IDX file extension automatically.

3. If you're creating the first entry in a new index, press ↵ to choose the Add option. Add your new entry, as described under **Add**, just below, then continue with step 5.

4. If necessary, choose Directories and Files To Index, so that the Add, Delete, Edit, and Name Search options will be available (or just click in the Directories and Files To Index list).

5. If you need to change or delete an entry, highlight the entry you want. (You can use the Name Search option to help you highlight an entry quickly.) If you plan to add an entry, the current selection doesn't matter. Now, you can choose any of the following options or buttons:

> **Add**   Lets you add a new entry. Choosing this option leads to the Add QuickFinder Index Directory Pattern dialog box, shown below.

> You can type a file name or pattern in the Filename Pattern text box, or select one from the File List or QuickList. Select the Include Subdirectories check box if you want to include subdirectories of the file name pattern you entered. Choose OK to return to the previous dialog box. You can add as many files, directories, and wildcards to the index as you need.
>
> **Delete**   Lets you delete the highlighted entry.
>
> **Edit**   Lets you change the highlighted entry.

Options Lets you customize the index further. When you choose this option, you'll see the QuickFinder Index Options dialog box, shown in Figure 20.5. The next section, "Speeding Up QuickFinder," provides some tips for using this dialog box effectively. Press F1 if you need additional help.

Next Moves to the next index, if any.

Previous Moves to the previous index, if any.

6. Repeat step 5 until you've defined all the directories and files that you want to include in the index.

7. When you're finished defining the index entries, choose OK. You'll be returned to the QuickFinder File Indexes Setup dialog box. From here you can mark and generate indexes, as explained in the section just above, and then choose Close and OK to return to your document.

QuickFinder Index Options

1. Level   Document ◆

2. Exclude Files: *.exe; *.com

3. ● Index Document Text
4. ○ Index Document Summary
5. ○ Index Both

6. ☐ Index WP Documents Only
7. ☒ Include Numbers
8. ☐ Manual Update Only

OK   Cancel

Speeding Up QuickFinder

The following tips will minimize the amount of time you have to wait around while QuickFinder builds or updates indexes:

- If the files in your indexes seldom change, you can check Manual Update Only in the QuickFinder Index Options dialog box (see Figure 20.5). This prevents WordPerfect from updating the index when you choose the Update Indexes button from the QuickFinder File Indexer dialog box (that button appears in Figure 20.2 and is described later in this chapter).

- If you later need to update an index that you marked for Manual Update Only, go to the QuickFinder File Indexes Setup dialog box, mark the index with a +, and choose Generate Marked Indexes or click Generate.

- Use the QuickFinder Index Options (Figure 20.5) to refine your index for maximum speed. Choose a broad level of detail, such as Document. Index only document text and WordPerfect documents. Exclude any irrelevant file name extensions (*.bat, *.bk!, and so forth), and exclude numbers.

N O T E   QuickFinder always ignores temporary, open, password-protected, other .IDX, and program (.COM and .EXE) files.

Using QuickFinder Indexes

Once you've created a QuickFinder index, using it to search for files is quite easy and lightning fast. Here are the steps:

1. From the document window, click the QuickFinder button (shown at left) in the Button Bar. Or, choose File ➤ File Manager or press F5, then click Use QuickFinder (shown below) or press F4. You'll see the QuickFinder File Indexer dialog box, shown earlier in Figure 20.2.

Use QuickFinder... F4

2. If any files contained in your indexes have changed since the last time you updated the index, or you've added or deleted files in the index's list of directories and files, choose Update Indexes to be sure you're searching the latest information. WordPerfect will update all the indexes, *except* those you've set to Manual Update Only in the QuickFinder Index Options dialog box.

3. Choose the index you want to use from the Index drop-down list.

4. Choose Word Pattern, type the word pattern you want to search, and press ↵. You can type letters in uppercase, lowercase, or any mixture of the two—all are treated the same. If you want to enter fancy word patterns, click the Operators button or press F5 and select an operator, or simply type in the operator you want. Table 20.3 shows the available operators and some sample patterns.

5. Choose OK to start the search.

The QuickFinder will search for all files in the selected index that contain the word pattern you entered, then it will display those file names in the File Manager. You'll be astounded at how fast the search completes!

TABLE 20.3: Word Pattern Operators for QuickFinder[1]

OPERATOR	SAMPLE WORD PATTERN	FINDS
" (Phrase)	"find this phrase"	Files with the phrase *find this phrase*[2]
	"Livingston-Gladstone"	Files with the phrase *Livingston-Gladstone*
& or space (And)	computer&"more productive"	Files with the words *computer* and *more productive*[3]
| (Or)	"New York" | "New Jersey"	Files with the words *New York* or *New Jersey* or both sets of words[3]

TABLE 20.3: Word Pattern Operators for QuickFinder[1] (continued)

OPERATOR	SAMPLE WORD PATTERN	FINDS
- (Not)	"New York"-"New Jersey"	Files with the phrase *New York*, but not the phrase *New Jersey*[3]
? (Match Single Character)	wombat?	Files with the word *wombat* plus a single character. Example: *wombats*
* (Match Multiple Characters)	mort*	Files that have words starting with *mort*. Examples: *mortal, mortally, mortals*

[1]You can type the pattern in uppercase, lowercase, or a mixture of both.

[2]Place double quotation marks around phrases that contain the special operators (space & | - ? *).

[3]The Level option in the QuickFinder Index Options dialog box determines where QuickFinder must find the words. For example, if the level is Line and your pattern is *doris & ajar*, those two words must appear on the same line.

Using Document Summaries

The file name assigned to a document when you save it is limited to the eight-character name, followed by the optional dot and three-character extension. This really limits how descriptive the file name can be.

One way around this problem is to add a *document summary* to your document. The summary provides a general overview of a document and can help you organize and locate your files quickly. Often, you can find out what's in a document simply by taking a quick look at the document summary—no tedious reading required!

WordPerfect stores document summaries as part of your document, but you won't see the summary unless you go to the Document Summary dialog box or the File Manager. Although the document summary doesn't normally print with your document, you can print it if you wish. You can even store a document summary as a separate WordPerfect file.

To create a document summary, follow these steps:

1. Open the document that you want to summarize, or create a new document.

2. Choose File ➤ Summary, or press Shift+F8 DS. You'll see the Document Summary dialog box, shown in Figure 20.6. (See "Document Summary Categories," below, for more information on the document summary fields shown in the figure.)

FIGURE 20.6

An empty Document Summary for a file that has been revised at least once

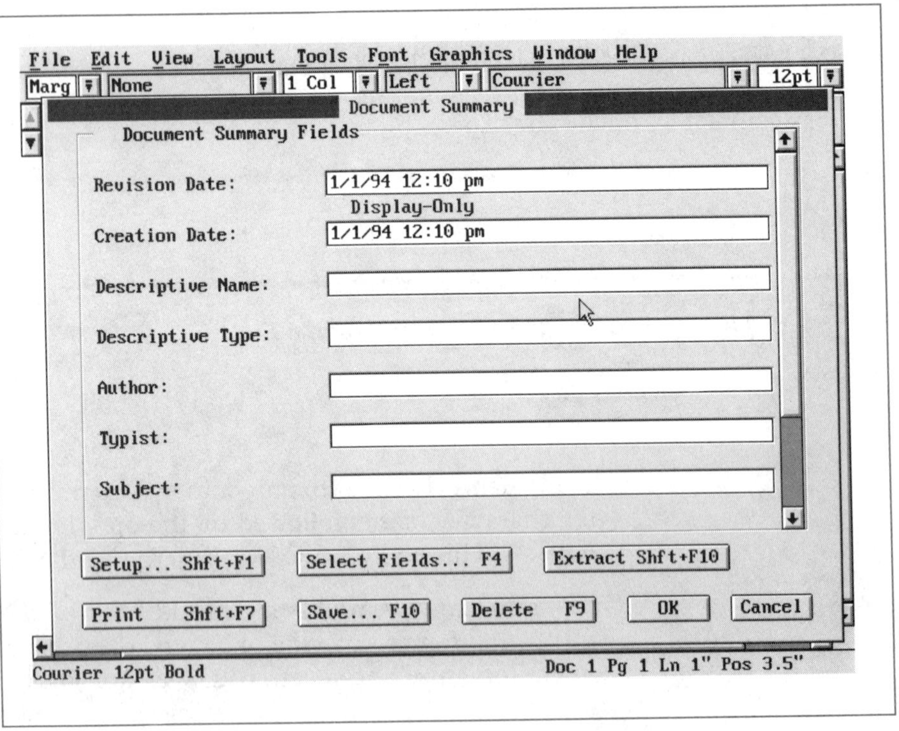

```
 File   Edit   View   Layout   Tools   Font   Graphics   Window   Help
 Marg ▼ None              ▼ 1 Col ▼ Left    ▼ Courier            ▼  12pt ▼
                            Document Summary
    Document Summary Fields                                          ↑

    Revision Date:        1/1/94 12:10 pm
                                Display-Only
    Creation Date:        1/1/94 12:10 pm

    Descriptive Name:

    Descriptive Type:

    Author:

    Typist:

    Subject:
                                                                    ↓
    Setup... Shft+F1    Select Fields... F4    Extract Shft+F10

    Print    Shft+F7    Save... F10    Delete  F9     OK     Cancel

 Courier 12pt Bold                          Doc 1 Pg 1 Ln 1" Pos 3.5"
```

3. If you'd like to fill in some fields automatically, click the Extract button or press Shift+F10, then choose Yes.

4. Fill in the blanks as you like. There are no rules, and you can leave any option blank. However, the Descriptive Name and Descriptive Type options are the most useful, because they're readily visible when you browse through files with the File Manager. The Subject field can also be quite useful. (WordPerfect will fill in the Revision Date and Creation Date fields for you automatically when you save the file.)

5. When you're done changing the summary, choose OK.

WordPerfect will save the document summary the next time you save the document.

Document Summary Categories

Here's a brief description of each category that appears on the default Document Summary screen:

Revision Date   The date and time the document was last changed and saved. WordPerfect updates this entry automatically.

Creation Date   The date and time the document was created; remains constant unless you change the date or time in this field.

NOTE   The revision and creation date and time are based on the system clock, which you can set with the DATE and TIME commands in DOS.

Descriptive Name   Lets you add a longer name to override the eight-character file name limit of DOS. You can search through these longer names with the File Manager (discussed below).

Descriptive Type Lets you describe the type of document using whatever text or numbers you wish (for example, *DRAFT, FINAL, TYPE-47*). You can use the File Manager later to find specific document types. You can use the Setup button (Shift+F1) to change the default description.

Author and **Typist** The author's name and typist's name, respectively. The Extract button (Shift+F10) will copy the Author and Typist entries from the previous document you edited (if any).

Subject A subject of your choosing. If your document contains the abbreviation RE: followed by some text, clicking the Extract button will copy the characters after RE: to the Document Summary. (If you want to change the default subject search text, click the Setup button or press Shift+F1.)

Account An account name of your choosing that will help you identify the document later.

Keywords A list of any keywords (separated by spaces) that might later help you find the document or a group of documents on the same subject. For example, you could later isolate all documents with the keyword *Widget* by searching for that topic in the File Manager.

Abstract Summarizes the contents of the document. Clicking the Extract button copies a portion of the document to the Abstract fields of the document summary.

Document Summary Options

The Document Summary dialog box includes several buttons that let you further customize your document summary. These are listed below:

Setup (Shift+F1) Lets you automate certain summary tasks. Your options after choosing Setup are as follows:

Subject Search Text Lets you define the text that precedes the Subject information in your documents (for example, *RE:*, or *SUBJECT:*, or *WHAT IT'S ALL ABOUT:*). The default setting is *RE:*. When you choose Extract, WordPerfect will extract the line of text that follows the subject search text in the document summary.

<u>D</u>efault Descriptive Type   Lets you define text that should appear automatically in the Descriptive Type summary field.

<u>C</u>reate Summary on Exit/Save   Determines whether or not WordPerfect will display the Document Summary dialog box when you save or exit a document.

Select Fields   (F4) Lets you customize the fields that appear in your document summary. See "Selecting Document Summary Fields" below for more information.

Extract   (Shift+F10) Fills in some of the summary fields automatically by extracting information from the document. Extracted fields include Author, Typist, Subject, and Abstract.

Print   (Shift+F7) Lets you print a text version of the document summary.

Save   (F10) Lets you save the summary as a separate document, with the file name you assign. Be aware that the saved file will contain *only* the document summary (stored as a regular document) and won't contain any text of the document whose summary you are saving. Therefore, be sure to use a unique file name if you decide to save the document summary to disk.

Delete   (F9) Deletes the document summary.

Tailoring the Document Summary

You can add and delete document summary fields, as appropriate for your own work. To do so, starting from the Document Summary dialog box, choose Select Fields (F4) to get to the Select Summary Fields dialog box shown in Figure 20.7.

Fields that are currently included in the document summary are listed under Summary Fields. Other fields to choose from are listed under Available Fields. (Fields that are already selected are marked with an asterisk.) You can use the Tab and Shift+Tab keys to move from one list to the other.

FIGURE 20.7

The Select Summary Fields dialog box lets you choose which fields will appear in the document summary.

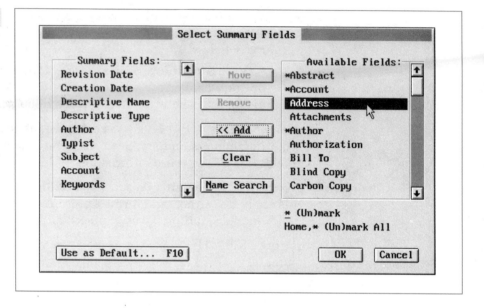

Use the Move, Remove, <<Add, Clear, and Name Search buttons, and * (Un)Mark options to shift fields from one list to the other. When the list on the left includes all the fields you want to use in your document summary, you can choose Use as Default (F10) to apply the fields to all future documents.

When you've finished selecting fields, choose OK to return to the previous dialog box. There, you can use the scroll bar at the right side of the field list to scroll through all your selected fields.

Using the File Manager

The WordPerfect File Manager is a powerful application that lets you locate files and perform many file management tasks including copying, deleting, opening, viewing, and searching. All these features can make it much easier to manage all the files on your computer. With the WordPerfect File Manager at your fingertips, you can forget all those weird DOS commands—any file management task that DOS can do, the File Manager can do more easily. Moreover, the File Manager has some tricks up its sleeve that tired old DOS never even dreamed of.

As mentioned earlier in this chapter, you can also use the File Manager to fill in file names automatically when you're not sure about a file name or location. For example, choosing File ➤ Open leads to the Open Document dialog box, shown below:

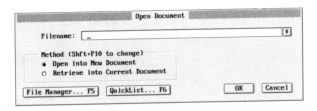

You can click the File Manager button or press F5, and then use the File Manager to select and fill in the file name for you.

There are several ways to open the File Manager, depending on what you're doing at the moment:

- If you're starting from the document window, choose File ➤ File Manager or press F5. Or click the File Mgr button (shown at left) in the Button Bar.

- If you're starting from a dialog box that's expecting you to enter a file or directory name, click the File Manager button (shown below) or press F5.

```
┌─────────────────────────┐
│  File Manager... F5      │
└─────────────────────────┘
```

Regardless of which method you used to get started, you'll see the Specify File Manager List dialog box, shown here:

Now, do whatever your file-managing heart desires:

- To list the contents of the current directory, choose OK.

- To list the contents of a different directory, type in a directory name or wildcard pattern and choose OK. For example, to list all files that have a .WP extension in the directory named C:\WP6BOOK, type **c:\wp6book*.wp** and choose OK.

- To whittle down the list of files displayed, choose QuickList (or press F6), <u>U</u>se QuickFinder (or press F4), or Directory Tree (or press F8). These options were covered earlier in this chapter.

- To redisplay the most recently listed group of file names in the File Manager, choose Redo (or press F5).

The File Manager will appear next, looking something like the example shown in Figure 20.8.

FIGURE 20.8

The File Manager dialog box

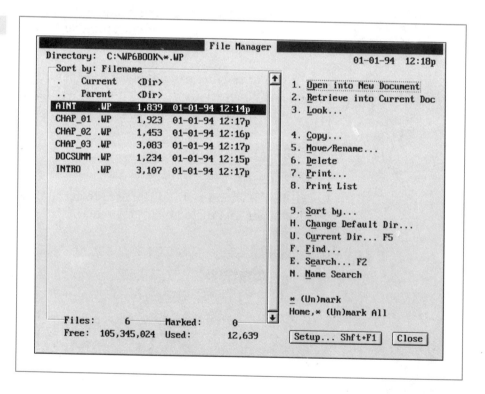

What the File Manager Shows

The File Manager shows lots of useful information, including the name of the current drive and directory, the current date and time, and the name, size, and last modification date of every file on the current drive and directory. Near the bottom of the dialog box, the Files option shows how many files are in the current directory, and Marked shows how many files you've marked with an asterisk (if any). The Free and Used prompts show how much free disk space you have on the drive, and how much you've used.

Quick-Change to Another Directory

The top of the file list often shows directory names indicated by <Dir>. You can switch to any available directory by double-clicking its name. Double-clicking .. Parent moves you up one directory level.

Managing Files

To manage files once you're in the File Manager, first decide whether you want to work with a single file or several files:

- To work with a single file, move the highlight to that file name.
- To work with several files, mark each file you want with an asterisk by highlighting and pressing the asterisk (*) or spacebar.

Once you've chosen one or more files to work with, you can select any of these options:

Open into New Document   Opens file(s) in new document window(s).

Retrieve into Current Doc   Retrieves file(s) into the current document window.

Look   Lets you look at the contents of the currently highlighted file name.

Copy   Lets you copy the file(s) to another drive, directory, and/or file name.

Move/Rename Lets you move the selected file(s) or rename the currently highlighted file.

Delete Deletes the selected file(s).

Print Prints the selected document file(s).

Print List Prints the list of file names.

Sort By Displays the dialog box shown in Figure 20.9, where you can choose a sort order for displaying file names, display lengthier file names from document summaries, reverse the sort order, limit the display to WordPerfect documents, and compress the list to a smaller font for printing (affects only the Print List option above).

Change Default Directory Changes the current directory for the rest of the session. You can also use this option to create a new directory.

Current Dir (F5) Changes the directory and/or file pattern for the current file list only.

Find Lets you search through file contents for specific information (see "Fancy Finds" below).

Search (F2) Lets you search for a particular file name.

Name Search Lets you locate a file name on the current directory by typing the first few characters.

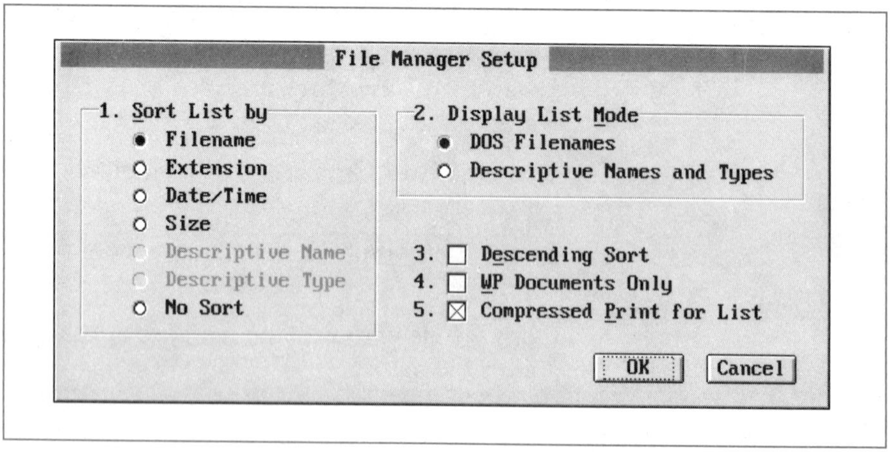

FIGURE 20.9

The File Manager Setup dialog box appears when you choose Sort By or Setup (Shift+F1) in the File Manager.

* (Un)mark   Marks or unmarks the currently highlighted file.

Home,* (Un)mark All   Marks or unmarks every file name in the list.

Setup   (Shift+F1) Takes you to the dialog box shown back in Figure 20.9.

Close   (F7) Leaves the File Manager.

Fancy Finds

If you forget the name of a file but remember something about its name or contents (such as the addressee of a business letter), you can have WordPerfect search the contents of documents for a specific word or phrase. This will narrow down the file list considerably, and if your search is specific enough, it might pinpoint the exact file you're looking for.

To narrow the list of files in this way, choose Find from the File Manager dialog box. The Find dialog box that appears contains the options described below:

Name   Lets you find files by typing the file name or file name pattern. You can use the standard DOS * and ? wildcards described earlier in this chapter to broaden your search, and you can type the name in uppercase, lowercase, or a mixture of both. For example, to search for all files that start with A and have a .WP extension, type **a*.wp** and choose OK.

Document Summary   Lets you find files by typing a word, phrase, or pattern that appears in the document summary.

First Page   Lets you find files by typing a word, phrase, or pattern that's in the first page.

Entire Document   Lets you find files by typing a word, phrase, or pattern that's in the document or document summary.

Conditions   Lets you find files by typing a word, phrase, or pattern that's in selected parts of the file. See "Super Searches" below.

QuickFinder   Lets you use QuickFinder indexes to find files. See "Using the QuickFinder," earlier in this chapter, for details.

Undo Returns the File Manager to the display it had before you chose Find. This is useful if you failed to find the file or files you wanted, or if you just want to return to the previous list of files.

NOTE If you've marked any files, WordPerfect will limit its searches to those files only. To unmark (or mark) all files at once, press Home * or press Alt+F5.

Entering Word Patterns

Most of the options listed above let you enter a word pattern by typing in the pattern you want and pressing ↵ or choosing OK. When entering word patterns, you can type letters in uppercase, lowercase, or any mixture of the two. So, for example, typing **PRIMordial** is the same as typing **Primordial** or **primordial**.

If your search text consists of only one word, just type it in at the *Word pattern:* prompt and press ↵ or choose OK. To search for multiple words, you must enclose them in quotation marks, as in "**Cream of Primordial Soup**" or "**What's Up DOS?**".

As Table 20.4 illustrates, you can also use the ? and * wildcards and several logical operators to perform fancier searches.

Super Searches

The Name, Document Summary, First Page, and Entire Document options in the Find dialog box are great for simple searches. However, the Conditions option is just what you need for more detailed searches that involve various parts of the document or specific document creation dates. Figure 20.10 shows the File Manager Find Conditions dialog box that appears when you choose Find and then Conditions in the File Manager. You can enter words, phrases, or patterns into any of the text boxes. The logical operators and wildcards shown in Table 20.4 apply here as well. Be sure to use double quotation marks (") to enclose multiple words and any words that contain semicolons (;), commas (,), hyphens (-), question marks (?), or asterisks (*).

TABLE 20.4: Word Pattern Operators for the Find Command[1]

OPERATOR	SAMPLE WORD PATTERN	FINDS
" (Phrase)	"find this phrase"	Files with the phrase *find this phrase*[2]
	"Livingston-Gladstone"	Files with the phrase *Livingston-Gladstone*
; or space (And)	computer;"more productive"	Files with the words *computer* and *more productive*
, (Or)	"New York","New Jersey"	Files with the words *New York* or *New Jersey or* both sets of words
- (Not)	"New York"-"New Jersey"	Files with the phrase *New York*, but not the phrase *New Jersey*
? (Match Single Character)	wombat?	Files with the word *wombat* plus a single character. Example: *wombats*
* (Match Multiple Characters)	mort*	Files that have words starting with *mort*. Examples: *mortal, mortally, mortals*

[1]You can type the pattern in uppercase, lowercase, or a mixture of both.

[2]Place double quotation marks around phrases that contain the special operators (space ; , - ? *).

In the example shown in Figure 20.10, I've limited the File Manager's search to files in which *all* of the following conditions are true:

- Files contain the word *computer* or *nerd* in the document summary.

- Files contain *Wanda Granolabar* somewhere in the document.

- Files were revised between April 7, 1992 and May 1, 1993. (To select a revision date or creation date, simply click the Date button next to the option you want to change. When the Find Conditions Date dialog box appears, choose Dates, then select On, Before, After, or Between. Next, type in the date (or date range) you want and choose OK.)

FIGURE 20.10

You can use the
File Manager Find
Conditions dialog box
to set many search
conditions at once.

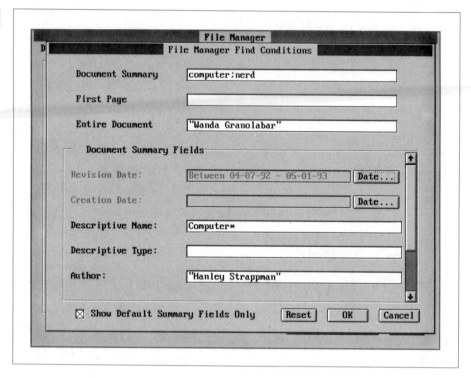

- Files have descriptive names that start with the word *Computer*.
- Files were written by *Hanley Strappman*.

Notice also that I checked the Show Default Summary Fields Only box, so that only the default document summary fields appear. Normally, this box is deselected to let you type in values for any document summary field that WordPerfect offers (there are dozens of them!). You can click the Reset button any time you want to reset all the selection fields back to blank values.

WARNING   Selecting or deselecting the Show Default Summary Fields Only box also resets fields to blank values.

This chapter has shown you many ways to use WordPerfect's File Manager to manage files stored on disk. As you've seen, your options are nearly limitless, far exceeding the capabilities of DOS itself.

Part Six, Office Tools, is the next stop on our tour of WordPerfect. There, you'll learn about the many ways that WordPerfect helps offices run smoothly. I'll start by discussing form letters and mailing labels.

PART SIX

Office Tools

Form Letters, Mailing Labels, and Other Merges

TRACK

To insert a *merge code* into a form   **760**

> to indicate where you want information from the data file to appear after the merge, choose Tools ➤ Merge ➤ Define (Shift+F9). Then choose Field and type the name of the field you want to insert. Or choose List Field Names or press F5 to open the field names in a particular data file.

To prevent blank lines resulting from empty fields in the data file   **764**

> place a question mark (?) after the field name. Or choose Data File Options, then Blank Fields In Data File, and select Remove Resulting Blank Line just before performing the merge.

To prevent extraneous blank spaces caused by empty fields in the data file   **765**

> use the IFBLANK...ENDIF and IFNOTBLANK...ENDIF merge commands in your form.

To access the advanced merge commands while creating your form   **768**

> press Shift+F9 twice.

To merge the data file and form   **769**

> choose Tools ➤ Merge ➤ Run (Ctrl+F9 M). Specify the names of the form and data files, and choose Merge.

F YOU ever need to produce mass mailings, multiple copies of a memo, or other multiple-copy documents, you're sure to love WordPerfect's *merge* feature. Simply stated, it lets you merge a list of things with a formatted document.

For example, you might create a list of names and addresses of people to whom you need to send mail regularly. Later, you create a form letter, with the recipient's name and address left blank. Then you *merge* that letter with your list of names and addresses to create a personalized copy of the letter for everyone in the mailing list. The merge takes only a few seconds, and WordPerfect does all the work.

Whether you have 5 or 500 names and addresses, you need only type the form letter *once*. Then go to lunch and let WordPerfect take care of printing all those personally addressed copies. You can also have WordPerfect print envelopes, mailing labels, a directory, whatever—from that same list of names and addresses. So you'll never need to type the same list of names and addresses more than once. (You'll just need to update them when they change.)

You're not limited to just names and addresses for merges. You can make a list of anything, from titles in a video or CD collection to data gathered in a research project. Then you can display that information in any format you wish, without ever retyping a single item of information.

Understanding Merge Files

There are usually two files involved in a merge:

Data File   A file containing all the information that's unique to each document and that needs to be repeated on each document (such as names and addresses).

Form File   A document (form letter, envelope, mailing labels, fill-in-the-blank form, directory, and so forth) that contains *merge codes* placed where information from the data file will appear.

It doesn't matter which of the above files you create first. Once you create a data file, you can create any number of form files for that data file. We'll start by looking at the data file.

About the Data File

A data file for a merge consists of *records* and *fields*. If you store this information in a table (as I'm going to recommend), it's easiest to think of each column in that table as a *field*, and each row as a *record* (particularly since *row* and *record* both start with the letter *r*).

Figure 21.1 shows an example of a data file stored in a table. I've defined five fields (columns): Name, Address, City, State, and Zip. The field names appear across the top row of the table. This data file contains ten records (rows), but could easily contain hundreds, even thousands, of records.

FIGURE 21.1

Sample data file, in table format, demonstrating *fields* and *records*

Fields

Name	Address	City	State	Zip
Sandi Fête	22 Beach St.	Eugene	OR	87654
Candy Mann	809 Circuit Ct.	Seattle	WA	43930
Doris Knight	Box 11	Boise	ID	74837
Willie Wanna	007 Bond St.	Yippi	OH	40394
Janet Green	543 Myrtle Ave.	Pleasant	VA	20394
Tony Buccio	Box 1234	Bangor	ME	01021
Mimi May Mee	812 Weasel St.	Anywhere	TX	39283
Daniel Tu	Route 22	Kazoo	KY	01234
Freddy Glassy	P.O. Box 228	New York	NY	52919
Wanda Granola	123 Oak Ln.	Leucadia	CA	91234

Records

T I P

If your data file will contain more than a few hundred records, you might consider using a database management system such as dBASE, Paradox, or Access to manage the data. You can still use WordPerfect to merge form letters, mailing labels, and so forth, by exporting data from the database file to a WordPerfect data file. See Chapter 33 for details.

Two Ways to Store Data

Once you've figured out what fields you want in your data file, you need to decide how to *structure* the data file. You have two choices:

Table Method You can use a table to define the table structure, where each field is in a column, and each record is in a row, as in Figure 21.1.

Text Method   As an alternative to a data table, you can just use text and merge codes, where each field ends with an ENDFIELD code, and each record ends with an ENDRECORD code, like this:

Sandi Fète**ENDFIELD**
22 Beach St.**ENDFIELD**
Eugene**ENDFIELD**
OR**ENDFIELD**
87654**ENDFIELD**
ENDRECORD

Besides the general appearance of the data, there are several other differences between these two data file structures:

- The **table** method is limited to 25 fields (columns). The **text** method allows up to 255 fields.

- The **table** method allows a maximum of 32,766 records (rows) in the data file. The **text** method allows as many records as you wish, limited only by the amount of available disk space.

- WordPerfect takes longer to get around in a table than in a regular document. So for a huge data file (several thousand records), you might find the **text** method a more efficient alternative.

- The table method may lead to word-wrapping within the table. This need not be a major inconvenience, however. As long as you let WordPerfect handle the wrapping on its own (that is, you don't force the text to wrap a certain way by pressing ↵), WordPerfect will "unwrap" the line automatically when you merge it into your form.

- The text method is virtually the same as that used by earlier versions of WordPerfect. Therefore, if you already have data stored in a *secondary merge file* (the earlier versions' name for a data file), you may not want to bother converting that file to a table. You'll read more on this later in the chapter.

TIP

Unless your data file is (or will be) huge, your best bet is to use the table method.

Designing a Data File

Here are some tricks for designing a flexible data file that you can use again and again without ever having to retype any of its information:

- Make sure that you have a field for every item of information you'll need in the merge. For example, if you want to send birthday cards to clients every month, include a field for storing the birth date. You might also include a field for fax numbers if you plan to create phone lists from your merge file.

- Every record must have the exact same fields. For example, if you want to store birth dates with *some* of the names and addresses in your data file, then *all* of the records must have a Birth Date field—you just leave the Birth Date field empty for people to whom you don't send birthday cards.

- The more fields you use for your data, the easier it will be to work with the file in the long run.

- Each field must have a unique name. For example, you can't have two fields named Address (though you *could* have one field named Address1 and another named Address2).

It's a good idea to start out by simply making a list of all the fields you think you might need. For example, you'd need a field in your data file for every blank in an income tax form that you're filling in with data.

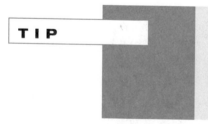

TIP

If your data is already stored on disk by another program, such as a database application, it's easiest to create the data file by *exporting* that information to the WordPerfect data file using techniques covered in Chapter 33.

I'll usually stick with the example of names and addresses in a data file in this chapter, since this is the most common use for a merge operation. The example shown in Figure 21.1 is probably sufficient for a small data file.

However, if you have lots of addresses, including some outside the United States, and you want maximum flexibility in your data file, you might want to use the field names shown in Figure 21.2.

Field Name	Stores
Hon	Honorarium: Mr., Ms., Dr....
First Name	Person's first name
MI	Person's middle initial
Last Name	Person's surname
Dept/ Title	Department or title
Company	Company name
Address	Street address
City	City of residence
State/ Province	State or Province of residence
Zip/ Postal	Zip code or postal code
Country	Country (empty if USA)
Phone	Telephone number
New	✓ if new, No if old

Why Four Fields for a Name?

You may be wondering why you'd want to split names into four separate fields, like this:

HONORARIUM	FIRST NAME	MI	LAST NAME
Dr.	Candy	Q.	Mann

There are several reasons for this arrangement. One is that WordPerfect can sort (or alphabetize) the records based on any field. Thus, you could have WordPerfect alphabetize all the records by last name (or last and first name, as in the phone book), as long as Last Name is in its own, separate field. (See Chapter 22 for information on sorting.)

Second, by breaking the name into four separate fields, you can easily use any portion of a person's name when printing, and you can arrange the parts of the names however you wish. For example, you might display Candy Mann's name in any of these formats when merging her record into a form letter:

Dr. Candy Q. Mann	Dr. Mann
Candy Mann	Mann, Candy Q.
Dear Dr. Mann:	Dear Candy:
Dr. Candy	Yo, Dr. Candy Q.

Granted, this number of fields is probably overkill for a small mailing list of local names and addresses. But as you'll see, this technique can come in handy for larger applications.

TIP

If you don't break names into separate fields, you might consider putting a field named *Salutation* into your data file structure. Then type into that field whatever you want to put next to *Dear* at the top of a letter. For example, if the Name field contains *Ms. Jenny L. Sparta*, your Salutation field could contain *Ms. Sparta* or *Jenny*.

What's That "New" Field For?

Notice the last field in Figure 21.2, which I've named New. This will come in handy if, say, you need to send a welcome letter or catalog to "new people" as soon as they're added to the data file. Just type some unusual character, such as a check mark, into that field (press Ctrl+W and choose a check mark or other unusual character). Later, you can isolate records that have a check mark in the New field, and print welcome letters and labels for those people only.

When you've finished printing the welcome letters and labels, use Search and Replace to change all the check marks to *No* (or to nothing). That way, the next time you want to print welcome letters and envelopes, people who have already received those letters won't be included. And you'll still have their names and addresses on the file for future mailings of other material.

The Order of Fields in the Data File

The order in which you list field names in the data table is not crucial, because you can display them in any desired order and format when you create the form. *However,* it does help to put them into some kind of naturally intuitive order—such as Name, Address, City, State, for instance—rather than using a random order such as City, Name, State, Address, simply because you're less likely to make mistakes when typing data into the file. Similarly, if you (or someone else) will be copying information into the data file from a paper form, it makes sense to order the fields as they appear on the form you're working with, since you'll naturally want to type them in that order.

Alphabetizing and Sorting

Whether you use the table method or text method to store your data, you can use WordPerfect's sorting features to instantly put the records in any order you want, whenever you want. For example, you can sort records into zip code order for bulk mailing. Then re-sort them into alphabetical order by name so you can print a directory or phone list. See Chapter 22 for more information on sorting.

Creating a Data File Structure: Table Method

The *structure* of a data file refers to the quantity of fields and the name of each field—as opposed to the actual *data* (such as specific names and addresses) within the file.

To create a data file structure using the table method, follow these steps:

1. Start with a new document. (Close and save the currently open documents, or use File ➤ New to switch to a new document.)

2. If you *don't* care about maximizing the width of the document (as when your table has only three or four fields), skip to step 6.

3. If you do need to maximize the width of your table, choose Layout ➤ Page ➤ Paper Size/Type. Pick a wide-landscape paper size such as Letter Landscape (11×8.5) or Legal Landscape (14×8.5). Then choose Select and OK to return to your document window.

4. Optionally, choose Layout ➤ Margins and set all four Document Margins to 0 (zero). WordPerfect will automatically adjust, if necessary, for your printer's dead zone. Choose OK to return to the document window.

5. Choose Font ➤ Font ➤ Font and then pick a small font and point size. (In my example, I'll use the Line Printer 16.67cpi font on the LaserJet, but you can use any 8- or 10-point font you want.) Choose OK to return to the document window.

6. Choose Tools ➤ Merge ➤ Define (or press Shift+F9). You'll see the dialog box shown in Figure 21.3.

FIGURE 21.3

The Merge Codes dialog box lets you define the form and data file for a merge.

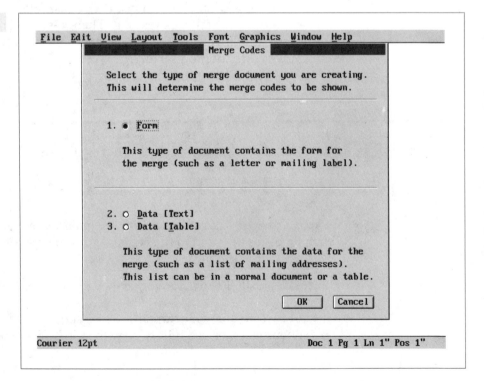

7. Choose Data [Table]. Next you'll see the Merge Codes (Table Data File) dialog box, shown below:

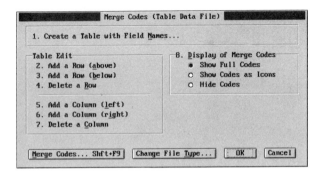

8. Choose Create a Table with Field Names. Next you'll see the Field Names dialog box.

9. Type each field name, pressing the ↵ key after each name. Each time you press ↵, the current field name moves down into the Field Name List, and the Field Name text box clears, ready to accept the next name.

10. After typing the last field name and pressing ↵, choose OK. (Don't worry about mistakes—you can correct them in a moment.)

Figure 21.4 shows the first nine field names from my sample table structure typed into the dialog box. (You can type in more field names—names at the top of the list will just scroll out of view.)

After you choose OK, WordPerfect displays a two-row table, with your field names listed across the top row.

T I P

The data table is nothing more than a WordPerfect table. The steps above are really just a tool to help you create that table. You can use *any* WordPerfect table as a data file, provided you have field names across the top row and have marked that row as a Header Row. See Chapter 7 if you want to learn more about tables.

FIGURE 21.4

The first nine fields from the sample data file structure typed into the Field Names dialog box

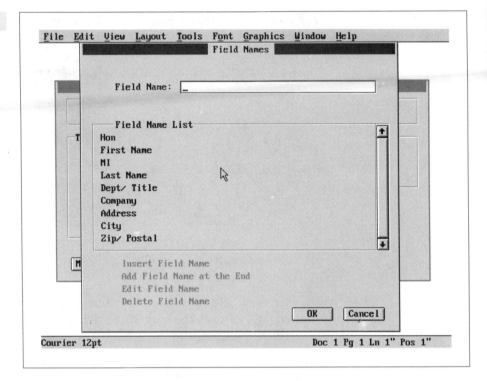

Correcting the Field Names: Table Method

If you make a mistake while typing field names, or you want to add or delete field names, just edit the field names in the first row using standard editing techniques. (As discussed in Chapter 7, you can use the mouse to move the cursor into any cell, or use Tab and Shift+Tab to move across cells.) If the text is too small to read in Graphics or Page mode, increase the magnification (View ➤ Zoom) to 150% or so.

To make a field name wrap differently in its cell, insert a blank space (with the spacebar, *not* with ↵) where you want the name to break. You'll need to remember to put the space in the same place when defining field names in your forms later.

TIP

In the example, I put a space after the slash in Dept/ Title, State/ Province, and Zip/ Postal just to control how the names wrap in the first row of the table. I will then need to remember to include that space whenever referring to the field name in forms that I create later.

If you really make a mess of things and want to start all over, just close the file (File ➤ Close) without saving it, and start over from step 1 above. (Or just delete everything from the [Table Def] to the [Table Off] codes, and start over at step 6.) I'll discuss techniques for inserting and deleting entire fields under "Adding/Changing/Deleting Fields: Tables Method," later in this chapter.

Filling a Data File: Table Method

You can add new records (rows) to your data table at any time. If you have just now created the data table, it's probably still on your screen ready for you to type in data. If you've already closed and saved the data table, just open it as you would any other document (File ➤ Open). Then,

1. Move the cursor into the table. If there's an empty row, move to the first field in that row. Otherwise, move to the very end of the table (Ctrl+Home Home Home ↓ End), then press Tab to insert a new row.

2. Type the information for the field that the cursor is in, and press Tab to move to the next field. Note: Avoid pressing ↵ within a field, unless you want the resulting line break to appear in the merged document. (It's OK to press ↵ if you need two lines within a field—as when entering a two-line street address.)

3. To leave a field empty, just press Tab to move to the next field. But make sure you always put the right information into the right field. For example, don't type a zip code into the City or State Field. See "Why It's So Important to Put Information into the Correct Field," later in this chapter.

4. If you need to insert another record after filling in the last field of a record, press Tab again. WordPerfect will create a new blank record for you to fill in. Repeat steps 2 through 4 to fill in this new record.

Figure 21.5 shows an example of nine records in the table. I zoomed it up to 150% (View ➤ Zoom) so you can see the text, but this means several fields are scrolled off the right edge of the screen. I did fill in those fields, however, and changed some column widths, too.

FIGURE 21.5

My sample data table with nine records. At 150% zoom, several fields are scrolled off the right edge of the screen. These fields are visible in the printed copy shown in Figure 21.6.

| File | Edit | View | Layout | Tools | Font | Graphics | Window | Help |

Hon	First Name	MI	Last Name	Dept/ Title	Company	Address	City	State/ Province	
Mrs.	Janet	L.	Green	President	ABC Corp.	123 A St.	San Diego	CA	9
Ms.	Wanda	B.	Granola	Accts. Payable	Logicon	P.O. Box 123	New York	NY	3
Dr.	José	O.	Menezes	Botanist	Florália	Orquidários Ltda Box n 100541	Niterói	Rio de Janeiro	
Dr.	Candy		Mann	Internist	Ono Pediatric Clinic	1101 Krager	Bangor	ME	0 1
	Cher		Bobo			3232 East Lake	Duarte	CA	9
				Sales Division	Doofdork Corp.	Box 1131	Lakewood	NJ	0
Ms.	Esther	C.	Clauser	Author		1101 Orchard St.	Nepean	ONT	F
Mr.	Stan	J.	Ramdrive	Clerk	Quark County Court	540 Grand Ave.	Orem	UT	8
Ms.	Alberta	J.	Wein	Travel Agent	RSF Travel	12 Paseo Delicias	Saturn	FL	3

C:\WPDOCS\CUSTOMER.DAT   Cell A10 Doc 1 Pg 1 Ln 4.01" Pos 1.52"

Figure 21.6 shows a complete printed copy of my sample data file. I'll talk about how to handle all those empty fields as we go through the chapter.

Hon	First Name	MI	Last Name	Dept/ Title	Company	Address	City	State/ Province	Zip/ Postal	Country	Phone	New
Mrs.	Janet	L.	Green	President	ABC Corp.	123 A St.	San Diego	CA	92000		(619)555-1023	No
Ms.	Wanda	B.	Granola	Accts. Payable	Logicon	P.O. Box 123	New York	NY	32555		(212)555-4049	No
Dr.	José	O.	Menezes	Botanist	Florália	Orquidários Ltda Box n 100541	Niterói	Rio de Janeiro		Brasil	55-21-555800	No
Dr.	Candy		Mann	Internist	Ono Pediatric Clinic	1101 Krager	Bangor	ME	02000-1234		(123)555-1234	No
	Cher		Bobo	Sales Division		3232 East Lake	Duarte	CA	92999		(213)555-3039	✓
					Doofdork Corp.	Box 1131	Lakewood	NJ	08701		(800)555-1030	✓
Ms.	Esther	C.	Clauser	Author		1101 Orchard St.	Nepean	ONT	K2E8A5	Canada	(613)555-4049	✓
Mr.	Stan	J.	Ramdrive	Clerk	Quark County Court	540 Grand Ave.	Orem	UT	84057		(800)555-4049 Ext. 323	✓
	Alberta	J.	Wein	Travel Agent	RSF Travel	12 Paseo Delicias	Saturn	FL	33431		(407)555-5052	✓

FIGURE 21.6

A printed copy of my sample data file

Tips on Typing Dates and Numbers

If you include dates in your data file structure, follow a consistent format when typing each date. For example, *1/1/93* or *Jan 1, 1993*. That way it'll be easier to isolate certain records later. For example, you might want to print letters and/or labels for records that have dates starting with *1/*, or starting with *Jan*. You and I know that 1/1/93 means the same as January 1, 1993, but the computer doesn't know that. So you have to be consistent when typing your dates.

Similarly, if you type in numbers—salaries, for instance—follow a consistent pattern, such as 35,000.00 (a comma separator and two decimal places even if they're both zero; omit the leading dollar sign—you can just type that into the form letter, if you need it). As with dates, this consistency will make it easier to isolate certain types of records in the table.

Deleting a Record: Table Method

To delete a record from your data table, move the cursor into the record that you want to delete, press Ctrl+Del, and choose Yes if you're sure.

Saving Your Data

After typing some or all of the data for your merge data file, close and save it as you would any other document—choose File ➤ Close ➤ Yes when prompted, and enter a valid file name. Choose OK to return to WordPerfect.

TIP   I usually add the extension .DAT to data files, so I can recognize them easily when viewing files in the File Manager. For example, you might name the file you've been working with here CUSTOMER.DAT.

Remember, you can reopen a file, using the standard File ➤ Open command, any time you want to add more records, delete records, correct misspellings, change an address—whatever. Making corrections is simply a matter of putting the cursor where you want to make the change, using

Search (F2), the mouse, Go To (Ctrl+Home), and/or the cursor-positioning keys, and then typing your change using standard WordPerfect typing and editing techniques. You can also use cut-and-paste to move and copy data from one cell to another, as discussed under "Moving or Copying Cells in the Document Window" in Chapter 7.

You can switch to Table Edit mode to alter the structure of the table, as discussed next.

Adding/Deleting/Changing Fields: Tables Method

It's not unusual to create a data file and later realize that you should have included additional fields. Or perhaps you decide you'd like to change some of the column widths so you can see more columns on the screen. Either way, here's all you need to do:

1. If the data table isn't currently on the screen, open it as you would any other document (File ➤ Open).

2. Move the cursor into any table cell, and switch to Table Edit mode (Layout ➤ Tables ➤ Edit or Alt+F11).

   • To **insert a field**, move to the column where you want the field to be, and choose Ins ➤ Columns ➤ How Many. Specify how many columns you want to insert, and choose Before (to the left of) or After (to the right of) Cursor Position. Choose OK and then Close to return to the document window. Type a unique field name into the cell at the top of the new column.

   • To **delete a field**, move to that column, choose Del ➤ Columns, and OK.

   • To **widen or narrow a column**, move the cursor into the column and press Ctrl+→ and Ctrl+←, as appropriate, or choose Column and use the Width and Fixed Width options in the Column Format dialog box to define a specific width (as discussed in Chapter 7).

3. After making your changes to the table structure, choose Close (or press F7) to return to the normal document window.

If you want to change a field name, move the cursor to the field name and make corrections using standard editing techniques.

> **WARNING**
>
> If you change field names *after* creating forms, you'll also need to change the field names within the forms. If you delete a field from the table, you'll also need to delete the reference to that field from any forms you've already created.

Remember, you can use *any* of the techniques described in Chapter 7 to control the appearance of your data table. And don't forget to save the entire document, as usual, when you're done!

Creating a Data File: Text Method

If you need or want to use the text method to store your data, here's how to create the initial data structure:

> **NOTE**
>
> If you've already created a data file using the table method, you can ignore all this. Skip on down to "Creating the Form File" later in this chapter.

1. Start with a new document. (Remember to close and save the currently open documents, or use File ➤ New to open a new document window.)

2. Choose Tools ➤ Merge ➤ Define (or press Shift+F9). You'll be taken to the Merge Codes dialog box shown earlier in this chapter (Figure 21.3).

3. Choose <u>D</u>ata [Text]. Next you'll see the Merge Codes (Text Data File) dialog box, shown below:

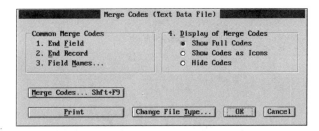

4. Choose Field <u>N</u>ames.

5. Type each field name, pressing ↵ after each name. Don't worry about minor mistakes. When you've finished, your list of field names will look the same as if you had used the table method.

6. Choose OK when you've finished typing all the field names.

After you've chosen OK, you're returned to the document, where you'll see the field names listed between FIELDNAMES...ENDRECORD codes, followed by a hard page break, as shown here:

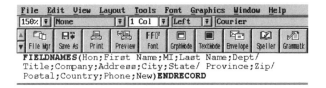

Correcting Field Names: Text Method

If you mistyped a field name while completing the steps above, just position the cursor within the erroneous field names and make your corrections. Note that each field name (except the last) *must be* followed by a single semicolon (;). After making changes to the field names, always close and save the document (File ➤ Close), and then reopen it (File ➤ Open ➤ Yes). That way, WordPerfect can read in your new, modified field name list as it opens the files.

If you just want to start over, close the document without saving it, and start over again at step 1.

Saving the Text Data File

When you're happy with your text data file's field names, you can save the document with the usual File ➤ Save commands. If you like, close it for the time being. As for any data file, you can add new records whenever it's convenient to do so.

Filling a Data File: Text Method

To add new records to your text data file, follow the steps below:

1. If it isn't already open, open the text data file with the usual File ➤ Open command.

2. Move to the end of the document (Home Home ↓), below the last page break (indicated with a double horizontal line across the page and the [HPg] code in Reveal Codes).

3. The name of the field that WordPerfect is expecting you to type appears in the lower-left corner. Type in your data (such as Mr.) and press F9.

4. Repeat step 3 until you've typed in a complete record. If you want to leave a field empty, press F9. Be careful not to put the wrong data into the wrong field—always look at the current field name in the lower-left corner of the screen before typing.

5. After typing the contents of the last field and pressing F9, choose Tools ➤ Merge ➤ Define ➤ End Record, or press Shift+F9 E.

6. Repeat steps 3–5 to add as many records as you wish.

7. Save the file when you're done, using File ➤ Save. Or, if you want to close the file, choose File ➤ Close ➤ Yes, as usual.

NOTE

One of the disadvantages to creating data files with the text method is that it's easy to forget to press F9 when you want to leave a field empty. Also, you're unlikely to notice when you've made a mistake, and (unfortunately) WordPerfect won't complain if you do. As a result, the field will be printed in the wrong place when you merge the documents later. Luckily, you can always go back and correct any mistakes.

To make minor changes to the contents of a text data file, simply open the file if necessary, position the cursor, and make your change.

- If you need to insert an empty field to correct a previous mistake, move the cursor to where the empty field belongs, and press F9.

- To join text that you accidentally divided into two fields, delete the ENDFIELD code and hard return from the end of the first line that you want to join.

As usual, don't forget to save your work after making changes.

Deleting Records: Text Method

To delete a record in a text data table, follow these steps:

1. Turn on Reveal Codes (Alt+F3), and highlight the first character of the record you want to delete (just past the previous record's [HPg] code). You can use Search (F2) to help locate the record if need be.

2. Select all the text (using your mouse, Alt+F4, or F12) in the entire record up to and including the [HPg] code at the end. (The cursor in Reveal Codes will actually be on the first character of the next record.)

3. Press Delete (Del).

Changing the Field Names in a Text Data File

You can change the field names between FIELDNAMES and ENDRE-CORD at the top of the text data file. Just make sure you follow every field name, except the last one, with a semicolon.

Bear in mind that your changes will not take effect until you close and save the file, and then reopen it (because WordPerfect only reads the FIELDNAMES command when you first open the file).

If the text data file already contains records, you'll need to scroll down through records and check the status bar in the lower-left corner of the screen. If the wrong text is in a field, you probably need to insert a blank field above it, or delete the field (depending on how you modified the field name list).

TIP It's much easier to add/delete field names from a data file structure when you use the table method to create the data file.

You may be able to globally insert or delete ENDFIELD commands using Search-and-Replace to locate and change specific codes (see Chapter 9). Again, it all depends on how you've modified the field name list.

Why It's So Important to Put Information into the Correct Field

Several times in previous paragraphs I've emphasized the importance of making sure you type information into the correct field when filling in your data file. This is crucial because (and this often comes as a surprise to beginners) the computer has no brains whatsoever—on the IQ scale, it rates right up there with a blob of mayonnaise.

If you type, say, a zip code into the Last Name field, the computer isn't going to think "Hmmmm, tried to trick me by typing that zip code into the Last Name field," and then correct the error. Nope, it's just going to put the zip code where you told it to: in the Last Name field. Why? Because the computer doesn't know the difference between a zip code, a name, and a cream-cheese bagel. Because the computer does exactly what it's told, it's up to you to tell it *exactly* what to do. I tell you all of this because the most common mistake people make when creating data files is typing the *right* information into the *wrong* field. Then they're surprised when the computer doesn't "figure it out" and correct the mistake on its own—which will never happen (at least, not in this century).

Now this is a true story: Somebody, somewhere, has typed my name as "Author" into the Name field of a database. I now get mail that's addressed to simply "Author, P.O. Box 3384, etc." The letters start with "Dear Author:" and say things such as "Author, it's your lucky day!" My name doesn't appear *anywhere* in this mail. Someone even sent me a sample personalized datebook that I could order printed up to give to friends. The cover announces, in gold embossed letters, "Compliments of Author."

Creating the Form File

Once you've created your data file, in table or text format, you can create as many forms for it as you wish. Any form can use all the fields in the table, or just a few (for instance, just the Last Name, First Name, and Phone for a phone list). The basic technique is fairly simple:

1. Start with a new document window (use File ➤ New if necessary).

2. To change the margins, paper size/type, font, or any other general formatting features of the final document, choose Layout ➤ Document ➤ Document Initial Codes. Then choose your Layout options (including paper size), as described in Chapter 8. Press F7

and choose OK when you're done to return to the document. (Remember that you won't see codes for your selections in Reveal Codes because they're inside that first [Open Style:Initial Codes] code that's at the top of every WordPerfect document you create.)

TIP

If you'll be printing on letterhead stock, be sure to set the top margin large enough so that the letter starts printing below the letterhead.

3. If you want any text to appear before the text that will come from the data file, position the cursor and type that text as you would for any normal document. (You can also select a font, indent, or add any other formatting you want.)

4. If you want a space to precede the text that will come from the data file, press the spacebar. For example, if you've just typed **Dear** in a letter salutation, you'll want to press the spacebar to separate the name in the data file from the word *Dear*.

5. When you're ready to tell WordPerfect where to insert text from the data file, press Shift+F9. If (and only if) this is the first field you're defining in this document, you'll need to choose Form from the Merge Code dialog box that appears. (This dialog box won't appear if you've already defined a field.)

6. Choose Field from the Merge Codes (Form File) dialog box that appears.

7. In the Parameter Entry dialog box shown below, you can type the name of the field *exactly* as you typed it into the data file. Then skip to step 10. Alternatively, to play it safe, pick a valid field name from the list by following steps 8–10.

8. Choose List Field Names (or press F5). If (and only if) this is the first field you're entering into this form, you'll see the Select Data File For Field Names dialog box. Type in the name of your data file, or use File List (F5) to select the data file from a list of file names (for example, CUSTOMER.DAT). Then choose Select.

9. From the List Field Names dialog box (Figure 21.7), choose the name of the field that you want to insert, either by double-clicking it or by highlighting it and choosing Select or pressing ⏎. Notice that the field names are listed in alphabetical order, *not* in the order you typed them into the data file.

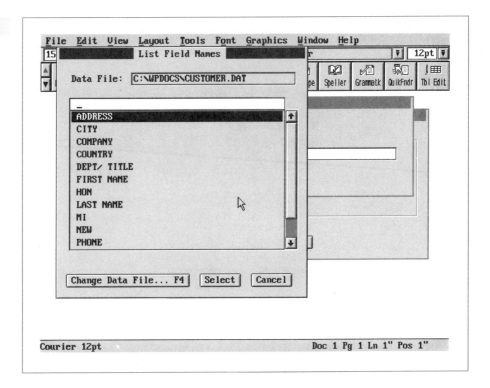

10. Choose OK or press ⏎ to return to your document window.

11. Remember, before you insert the next field, if you want a space to follow the text that will be coming from the data file, you should press the spacebar now to insert that space.

12. Repeat steps 3–11 as necessary until you've completed the entire form, including all text and merge codes (examples are presented in the sections that follow).

13. When you're done, choose File ➤ Close ➤ Yes to save the file, and then give it a file name that will be easy to recognize, such as FRMLTR.FRM (short for Form Letter Form).

Consider the example in Figure 21.8, which shows the top portion of a form letter. Notice that each field name from the data file used in the letter is within a FIELD(...) code. Each of those codes acts as a placeholder that will be replaced by real data from the data file when you actually perform the merge. Notice how I've also put blank spaces between some fields (Hon, First Name, MI, and Last Name).

FIGURE 21.8

The merge codes for printing a name and address at the top of a form letter

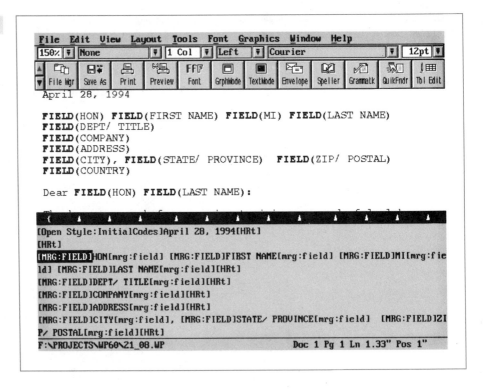

I also put a comma and blank space after the City field, and two spaces after the Zip/ Postal field, so that line is printed in the familiar format:

San Diego, CA 91234

Notice, too, that I used the Hon and Last Name fields twice, once at the top of the inside address, and again in the salutation (next to *Dear*). You can refer to a field as many times as you wish in your form. Finally, notice I didn't use the Phone and New fields (you aren't required to use all the fields).

So how will all of this look after I do the merge? Well, using a record from my sample CUSTOMERS.DAT data file, most letters will be formatted like this:

April 26, 1994

Ms. Wanda B. Granola
Accts. Payable
Logicon
P.O. Box 123
New York, NY 32555

Dear Ms. Granola:

A slight problem may arise, however. In those records where I've left the Hon, MI, Company, and Dept/ Title fields empty, WordPerfect will still print the hard return and any blank spaces surrounding the code. Thus, it's conceivable that a printed name and address could come out looking something like this:

Cher Bobo

3232 East Lake
Duarte, CA 92999

Dear Bobo:

Unless you don't care about first impressions, you won't be happy with this result. Fortunately, there are solutions to the problem, as described in the sections that follow.

Removing Blank Lines

If a field in a data file might be empty, *and* that field appears on a line by itself in your form, you can follow the field name with a question mark (?). This will prevent blank lines.

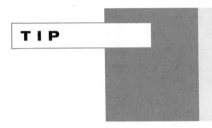

TIP

As an alternative to putting ? next to the field name, you can just tell WordPerfect not to print blank lines in general when doing the merge. I'll talk about that technique under "Controlling Blank Lines throughout the Document" later in this chapter.

Be sure to put the question mark just inside the closing parenthesis for the code. For example, this merge code:

FIELD(COMPANY?)

which looks like this in Reveal Codes:

[MRG:FIELD]COMPANY?[mrg:field][HRt]

tells WordPerfect, "If the Company field *isn't* empty, print the company and a hard return. If the Company field *is* empty, don't print this line at all." Thus, if you were to insert question marks into our sample form letter like so:

FIELD(HON) **FIELD**(FIRST) **FIELD**(MI) **FIELD**(LAST NAME)
FIELD(DEPT/ TITLE?)
FIELD(COMPANY?)
FIELD(ADDRESS?)
FIELD(CITY), **FIELD**(STATE/ PROVINCE) **FIELD**(ZIP/ POSTAL)
FIELD(COUNTRY?)

that record with all the blank fields would come out looking like this:

Cher   Bobo
3232 East Lake
Duarte, CA 92999

Dear Bobo:

Pretty close to perfect, but not quite. The blank spaces in the form that follow the Hon and MI fields are still showing up. And "Dear Bobo" isn't exactly an ideal salutation. Unfortunately, the simple ? option can't help with these problems, because ? is specifically designed to handle blank fields on their own line followed by a hard return ([HRt]).

One simple solution would be to make sure that the HON field in *every* record of the table contains *something* (Ms., Mr., or the like). But that won't help much with the middle initial. For that you'll need to put *advanced merge codes* into the form, so the form can make semi-intelligent decisions on its own when you do the merge.

Removing Blank Spaces

You can use two pairs of advanced merge commands (and they *must* be used in pairs) to control blank spaces in a merged form:

    IFBLANK...ENDIF
    IFNOTBLANK...ENDIF

The first command tells the merge, "If the field is blank (empty), print everything between here and the ENDIF command that follows." The second command says the opposite: "If the field is *not* blank (empty), print everything between here and the ENDIF command that follows."

WARNING

A field is not considered "blank" if it contains even one single space. If your merge seems to be treating a blank field as though it were *not* blank, chances are you accidentally typed a space into the field. Open your data table, move the cursor to the offending field, turn on Reveal Codes, and delete the space (or whatever characters are there), so that the field is truly empty.

Now, let's get back to the original problem: If we tell WordPerfect to print First Name<space>MI<space>Last Name, and MI is blank, we end up with two spaces between the first and last names. To fix that, we can say

"If MI is *not blank*, print MI followed by a blank space." That way, if MI *is* blank, neither the middle initial *nor* the blank space that follows it will be printed. However, you *must* remember to put the blank space that follows the MI field *inside* the ENDIF command. Why? Because anything to the right of the ENDIF command will be printed regardless of whether IFNOT-BLANK was true or false. In other words, IFBLANK and IFNOTBLANK affect *only* text that comes *before* the next ENDIF command.

Let's look at an example. Suppose I modify the opening codes for my sample form letter to look as shown below. (A soft return is automatically wrapping the line after FIELD(FIRST NAME), so the line will unwrap during the merge.)

IFNOTBLANK(HON)**FIELD**(HON) **ENDIF FIELD**(FIRST NAME)
IFNOTBLANK(MI)**FIELD**(MI) **ENDIF FIELD**(LAST NAME)
FIELD(DEPT/ TITLE?)
FIELD(COMPANY?)
FIELD(ADDRESS?)
FIELD(CITY), **FIELD**(STATE/ PROVINCE) **FIELD**(ZIP/ POSTAL)
FIELD(COUNTRY?)

Now, even when I print the record that has empty Hon, MI, Dept/ Title, and Company fields, I get the following clean result:

Cher Bobo
3232 East Lake
Duarte, CA 92999

Dear Bobo:

Let's analyze it more closely. The first line in the merge file puts the Hon and MI fields, and the blank space that follows each field, into its own IF-NOTBLANK...ENDIF codes. Thus, when printing a name that has a blank honorarium and/or middle initial, the blank spaces that normally follow those fields are not printed.

Close, but still not quite right—because *Dear Bobo* is still not exactly what we want. I'll get to that in a moment, but first here's a general little tidbit worth knowing.

Hiding/Displaying Merge Codes

It's sometimes difficult to see how the finished merge will look because the merge codes cause text in the form to wrap differently than it would ordinarily. While you're creating or editing a form, you can choose to hide those merge codes, or display them as icons. Follow these steps:

1. Choose <u>T</u>ools ➤ M<u>e</u>rge ➤ <u>D</u>efine or press Shift +F9.

2. Choose <u>D</u>isplay Of Merge Codes, then select one of the (self-explanatory) options: <u>S</u>how Full Codes, Show Codes As <u>I</u>cons, or <u>H</u>ide Codes.

3. Choose OK.

Your choice affects only the document window. You can still see all the merge codes in Reveal Codes (Alt+F3).

Really Advanced Merge Codes

For the benefit of the truly hard-core whizzes (and aspiring whizzes) out there, I will point out that you can also use an ELSE command between the IF and ENDIF commands. Furthermore, you can nest the commands (put one IF...ENDIF pair inside another IF...ENDIF). For example, suppose you want to set up some fancy logic for the salutation portion of the letter, something like this:

Type **Dear** followed by a space.
If Hon and Last Name are not blank, print Hon and Last Name
   Else, if either of those is blank
      Print the First Name
         Else
            If the First Name is blank too,
               Print "Valued Customer"
            Endif ("Valued Customer" printed)
         Endif (Just the First Name printed)
   Endif (both Hon and Last Name printed)
Type a colon (:) at the end.

In other words, if the Hon and Last Name fields contain data, then we use those in the salutation (*Dear Ms. Bobo:*). If either Hon or Last Name is blank, then test the First Name field. If it's not blank, use it (*Dear Cher:*). If there isn't a First Name either, just print "Valued Customer" (*Dear Valued Customer:*).

Now you may be wondering, "Why would the Last Name and First Name fields be left blank anyway?" The answer is that some records might contain only a company name and address, and not be addressed to any particular person in that company.

So, what would this fancy bit of logic look like when you actually put it into the form letter? Figure 21.9 reveals all.

Note that all the boldfaced codes, such as **FIELD** and **IFNOTBLANK** and **ELSE** and **ENDIF,** *must be* entered as merge codes. You cannot simply type in those commands on your own. The quickest way to get to an advanced merge code is to press Shift+F9 twice, type the first few letters of the command you want, and then use the mouse or arrow keys to zero in and highlight the command you want. Double-click that command, or press ↵ to select it. (When you highlight a command, you'll see a brief description of its purpose near the bottom of the dialog box.)

FIGURE 21.9

Opening to a form letter that uses advanced merge commands to control blank lines, blank spaces, and the appearance of the salutation (the text after *Dear* and before the colon)

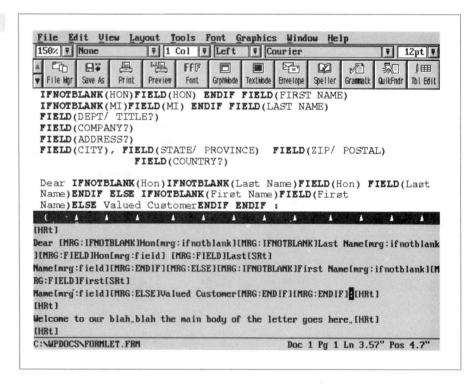

Now, for those of you who hate this kind of stuff (yes, you, with the digital clock that's been flashing 12:00 for years), let me just say that it's rarely necessary to use these advanced merge commands. Most of the time you can get by with simple FIELD commands, as long as your data file isn't too tricky, like Figure 21.1 earlier in this chapter.

For those of you who actually like this kind of stuff (with your digital clock accurate to the second even during daylight savings), let me say this:

- Remember, you *must* select advanced merge commands from the All Merge Codes list that appears when you press Shift+F9 twice. You can't just type the commands into the document. (Each has its own special code that's visible only in Reveal Codes.)

- Every IF… command *must* be followed by an ENDIF command. If you omit the ENDIF, the IF… affects everything to the end of the document, which can produce some weird and confusing results in your merge.

- To learn more about advanced merge commands, refer to the Appendices in the documentation that came with your WordPerfect package.

The sample forms later in this chapter illustrate some good ways to use advanced merge commands—many of which you may be able to copy into your own forms. If something here sparks your curiosity, you can research it further on your own in your official WordPerfect documentation, or in a book that specializes in advanced WordPerfect macro and merge programming techniques. Fair enough?

Running the Merge

Once you've created both a data file and at least one form file, here's how to merge the two:

1. Close all open documents, and start a new Document 1 window.

2. Choose <u>T</u>ools ➤ <u>M</u>erge ➤ <u>R</u>un or press Ctrl+F9 M. You'll see the Run Merge dialog box:

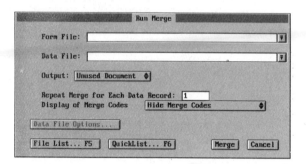

3. Type in the name of your form file, or use the drop-down list to view recently used form files. Or you can use other tools, such as File List (F5) and QuickList (F6), to help you locate the name of your form file. (***Tip:*** If you use the .FRM extension with all your form files, you can press F5 and change the *.* to *.FRM for a quick view of all your form files.) When you've specified your form file, press Tab or click the <u>D</u>ata File box.

4. As you did for the form file, pick the name of the data file.

5. Choose Merge.

If you password-protect the form file and then merge the documents into a file, the resulting merged document will have the same password as the original form file.

The status bar keeps you informed of WordPerfect's progress in the merge, and, after a brief delay, a new document containing all the merged data appears on your screen. The cursor will be at the *bottom* of the document. In most cases, there will be a separate page for each record in your data file. You can use the PgUp key to scroll through each page, or use Home Home ↑ to jump to the top. Figure 21.10 shows the results of merging my sample form letter with my sample data file.

FIGURE 21.10

First few lines of a letter, after merging my sample form letter form with my sample data file

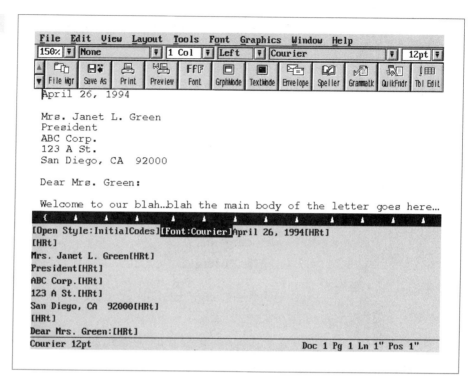

Now you can print the entire document with the regular File ➤ Print/Fax commands. Or save it under a new name, but *don't* use the same name as the data file or form—you don't want to overwrite either of those with this third merged document.

The technique I just described merges the documents into a new, unused document window. There are other ways, and other options, for performing the merge, as I'll discuss in the sections that follow.

Not Enough Memory?!?

WordPerfect usually merges the files in memory, and displays them in a document window on the screen. If your data file is pretty big, and/or your form contains graphics, WordPerfect may run out of memory before it can complete the merge. Don't panic. Here's what you can do about it:

1. Start the merge normally as described above under "Running the Merge."

2. *Before* you choose Merge, choose <u>O</u>utput, and select one of these options:

<u>C</u>urrent Document   Performs the merge in the current document, even if there's already something in that document. This option does require sufficient memory to merge all the data.

<u>U</u>nused Document   Performs the merge in the next available document window. This option requires sufficient memory.

<u>P</u>rinter   Merges one record at a time, then immediately prints each resulting document. The option doesn't require you to have enough memory to store all the merged documents.

<u>F</u>ile   Merges one record at a time, then immediately stores each to a file. This option doesn't require you to have enough memory to store all the merged documents.

NOTE

If your form contains a graphic image (see Chapter 26) such as a logo or signature, it's best to use the Image On Disk feature in the Image Editor when putting the graphics box in the form. That way, WordPerfect won't attempt to store a complete copy of the graphic image in each merged document. This accelerates the merge dramatically, and conserves a lot of memory and disk space.

Printing Multiple Copies of Each Record

Normally, WordPerfect creates one merged page for each record in the data file. If you want to print multiple copies (say, two copies of every form letter), start the merge normally (Ctrl+F9 M), choose <u>R</u>epeat Merge for Each Data Record, and specify the number of copies you want for each record. For example, if you specify two copies, WordPerfect will print all the form letters (once), and then print those same form letters again.

Controlling Blank Lines throughout the Document

Usually when WordPerfect encounters a blank field in the data file and is merging that field into a line that ends with a hard return, it prints the hard return anyway. The result is a blank line in your document.

As mentioned earlier, you can control that on a field-by-field basis by putting a question mark (?) next to the field name. Alternatively, you can just tell WordPerfect never to print blank lines for empty fields in the document. Here's how:

1. Begin the merge normally (Ctrl+F9 M).

2. Before you choose Merge, choose Data File Options. The dialog box expands to show additional options, as in the example in Figure 21.11.

```
File                        Run Merge                        t  ▼
150%                                                            ⊞
  ⌐                                                         Edit
▼ File  1. Form File:    FORMLET.FRM                      ▼

        2. Data File:    C:\WPDOCS\CUSTOMER.DAT           ▼

        3. Output: [Current Document ◆]

        4. Repeat Merge for Each Data Record: [1    ]
        5. Display of Merge Codes      [Hide Merge Codes        ◆]
        6. Blank Fields in Data File  [Leave Resulting Blank Line ◆]
        7. ⊠ Page Break Between Merged Records
        8. ☐ Generate an Envelope for Each Data Record...

       ┌9. Data Record Selection──────┐  [ Default Settings ]
       │  ● All Records               │
       │  ○ Mark Records to Include...│  [ File List... F5 ]
       │  ○ Specify Record Number Range│
       │     From: [0          ]      │  [ QuickList... F6 ]
       │     To:   [0          ]      │
       │                              │  [ Clipboard... Ctrl+F1 ]
       │  ☐ Define Conditions...      │
       └──────────────────────────────┘  [ Merge ] [ Cancel ]

Courier 12pt                          Doc 1 Pg 1 Ln 1" Pos 1"
```

3. Choose <u>B</u>lank Fields in Data File, and then <u>R</u>emove Resulting Blank Line.

4. Now you can choose additional options (described in upcoming sections), if you wish. Or just go ahead and choose the Merge button to start the merge.

Printing Multiple Data Records on a Page

WordPerfect normally inserts a hard page break at the end of every completed form during the merge. That makes sense when you're printing form letters, envelopes, and labels, because you want each record to appear on a separate page (or label). However, if you want to print some kind of a list from your data file, you probably won't want that page break after each record. In that case, just deselect the <u>P</u>age Break Between Merged Records option in the expanded Run Merge dialog box (Figure 21.11) before you start the merge.

Selecting Records to Merge

If you don't want to print a form for every record in your data file, you can start the merge normally (Ctrl+F9 M) and choose the Da<u>t</u>a File Options button to expand the Run Merge dialog box, as shown earlier in Figure 21.11. Then you can choose options under Data Record <u>S</u>election to specify which records to include in the merge. Your options are

<u>A</u>ll Records   (The default) WordPerfect prints a form for every record in the data file.

Mark Records to Include   If you choose this option, you can then select a field to view in your data file (for instance, Last Name). You can then mark the records that you want to include in the merge by typing an asterisk (*) or pressing the spacebar (or choosing <u>M</u>ark Record) next to appropriate records. Figure 21.12 shows an example where I've marked four records to include in the merge.

FIGURE 21.12

Records to include
in the merge are
marked with an
asterisk. Only the first
39 characters of the
selected field appear
in the list.

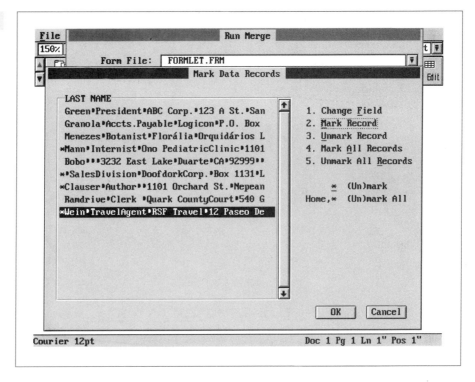

Specify Record Number Range Choose this option if you
want to print a particular set of adjacent records. For example, if
there are 100 records in the data file, but you want to print only
the last 10, choose this option and set From to 91 and To to 100.

Define Conditions This option lets you specify exact conditions for the merge, as discussed in the next section. Choose OK
after defining your condition(s).

Defining Conditions for a Merge

If you choose Define Conditions from the Data Record Selection options
(above), you'll see an (initially blank) dialog box like the one shown in
Figure 21.13.

You can define up to four conditions, each with up to three criteria. (Obviously, this statement needs some explaining...)

FIGURE 21.13

The Define Conditions for Record Selection dialog box lets you specify exactly which records you want to include in the merge.

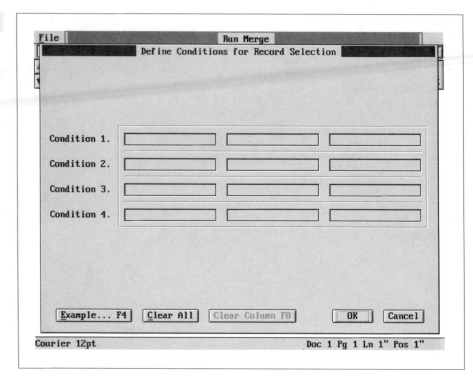

FIGURE 21.13

The Define Conditions for Record Selection dialog box lets you specify exactly which records you want to include in the merge.

Defining Criteria

A *criterion* is basically a field name, followed by whatever it is you're looking for within that field. For example, the criterion

STATE/ PROVINCE
CA

means, "If this record has CA (exactly) in the State/ Province field, include it in the merge."

To enter a criterion, follow these steps:

1. Choose the next available Condition row by entering its number or clicking on its number (for example, type **1** to choose the Condition 1 row).

2. In the List Field Names dialog box that appears, highlight the field name you want to use in the criterion and choose Select (or press ↵), or double-click the name. The selected field name will appear above a newly available text box, as shown below.

```
Use TAB and SHIFT+TAB to move between columns.
Use UP and DOWN arrows to move between rows.

           STATE/PROVINCE

Condition  [              ]  [          ]  [          ]
```

3. Type in whatever you want to find in this field, using options described in the next few sections. A reminder of the special symbols you can use to define your criteria will appear below the Condition rows in the dialog box. These are summarized in Table 21.1. You can also use the Example button or press F4 to see more detailed examples of valid criteria.

4. While the text box is available, you can do any of the following:

   - Press ↵ or double-click the mouse to complete your entry. The text boxes will be dimmed and unavailable again.
   - Press Tab or Shift+Tab to complete your entry and move to another column.
   - Press ↑ or ↓ to complete your entry and move to another row.
   - To clear the column, choose Clear Column or press F8.
   - To clear all columns and start defining criteria from scratch, choose Clear All.

5. If you'd like to make changes when the text boxes are dimmed, you can type or click on the number that appears next to a Condition row or field name column.

6. Choose OK when you're done entering criteria.

So why use rows and columns? Well, when you put two or more criteria on the same line (say, next to Condition 1), then *all* of those criteria must

TABLE 21.1: Symbols You Can Use to Define Criteria for Selecting Records to Be Merged

CRITERION	DESCRIPTION	EXAMPLE
Single value	Only include records that have a specific value	**CA** (only records that have exactly *CA* in the field)
List of Values (;)	Only include records that have one of the listed items	**CA;AZ;TX** (records that have either CA or AZ or TX in the field)
Range of Values (-)	Only include values within the specified range	**10,000.00-20,000.00** (from ten thousand to twenty thousand)
Any one character (?)	Only include records that have exactly one character in place of the question mark	**C?** (any record that starts with the letter C followed by one, and only one, other character)
Zero or more characters (*)	Include any record that has nothing, or any number of characters, in place of the asterisk	**Jan*** (any record that starts with the letters Jan) (Or,**1/*** any record that starts with 1/).
Less than (<)	Only include records that are less than this value	**<N*** (any record that starts with the letters A through M)
Greater than (>)	Only include records that are greater than this value	**>8000** (any record with the value 8001 and above)
Greater than or equal (>=)	Only include records that are greater than or equal to this value	**>=8000** (any record with the value 8000 and above)
Excluded Values (!)	Only include records that *don't* have this value	**!CA** (all records *except* those that have CA in the field)

be true for the record to be included. For example, these criteria mean "Print the record *if* it has CA in the State/ Province field, *and* it also has a check mark in the field named New" (new customers in the state of California):

	STATE/ PROVINCE	NEW	
Condition	CA	/	

Each Condition row, however, represents a "separate question," in a sense—that is, Condition 1 poses one question, Condition 2 poses yet another question, and so forth. If any *one* of those questions proves true, the record *is* included in the merge.

In other words, there's an "and" relationship among criteria across a row, but there's an "or" relationship between the rows. If you're experienced with databases, you'll recognize this as the standard "QBE" (Query By Example) way of doing things. (Otherwise, you may be wondering if the person who thought this up lives on the same planet that you do.)

So now, take a look at the sample Define Conditions... dialog box in Figure 21.14. Here's what it all means.

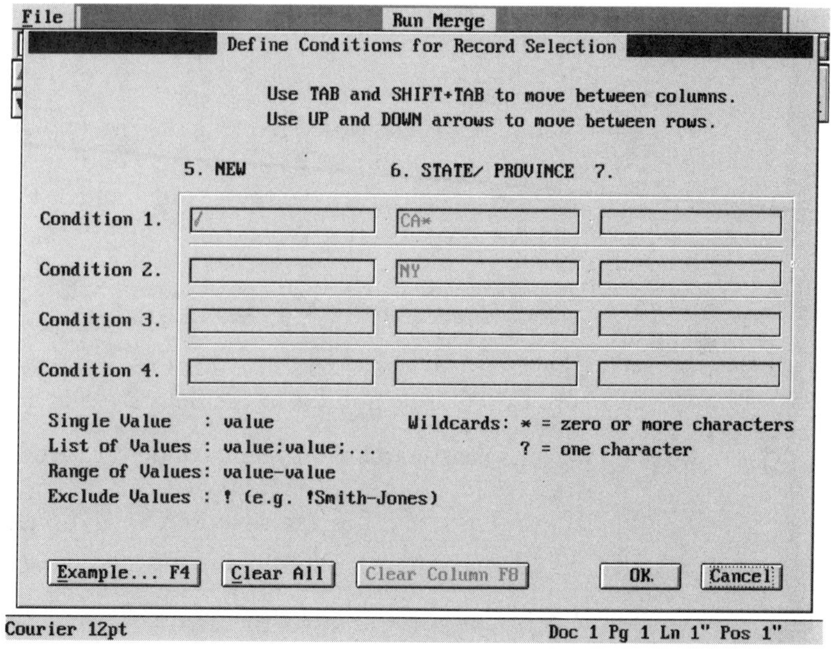

FIGURE 21.14

A sample Define
Conditions dialog box

The first question (Condition 1) asks, "Does this record have a check mark in the New field *and* CA in the State/ Province field?" If the answer to that question is Yes, the record is included in the merge, and WordPerfect can just ignore the next two questions.

If the answer to that first question is No, WordPerfect will ask the second question (Condition 2): "Does this record have NY in the State/ Province field?" If the answer is Yes, the record is included in the merge. If the answer is No, the record is excluded from the merge. There are no more questions in this example, so WordPerfect moves on to the next record in the data file, and poses the same question(s) again. It keeps doing that until it has checked every record in the table (or every record you specified in the From...To options in the Run Merge dialog... Whew!).

Note that because the New field does not include a check mark in Condition 2, *any* record that has NY in the State field will be selected, regardless of what's in the New field. In other words, this dialog box prints records for everyone in the state of New York, and new customers (only) in California.

If you're not accustomed to using queries (which is what this "define conditions" operation really is), you may end up with some surprising, and seemingly incorrect, results in your merge. The next few sections may help you avoid some problems.

Case and Length Sensitivity

Queries are not *case sensitive*. That is, if you search for CA, records that have CA, Ca, ca, and cA in the field *will* match the criterion.

Queries that search for specific values are, however, *length sensitive*. That is, CA *won't* match *Cal* or *California* or *Cat*. You can use the ✶ to overcome length sensitivity. For example, CA✶ *will* match *CA, ca, Ca, Cal, California,* or *Casbah*—anything beginning with the letters *ca*. The >, <, or <= criteria also ignore length sensitivity. Thus the criterion >CA won't match *A, ABC,* or *CA*. But it will match *Cat, Casbah, CB, ZORRO,* and so forth.

Isolating Records with an Empty Field

If you specifically want to isolate records that have nothing in a field, you should search for "less than any character," that is, **<?**. For example, if

you leave the Country field empty for addresses within the United States, this criterion:

```
COUNTRY
<?
```

will pick out only the addresses within the United States (that is, records that have absolutely nothing, not even a blank space, in the field named Country).

To isolate records with nonblank fields (i.e., addresses outside the United States in my example), replace the <? condition with >=? (which means "greater than or equal to any one character").

Isolating Records within an Alphabetical Range

If you want to isolate a range of records within an alphabetical range, such as "everyone whose last name begins with the letters *A* through *M*," set up your condition with the smallest letter first, followed by a hyphen, then the highest letter, followed by an asterisk. For example, this criterion isolates last names starting with the letters *A* through *M*:

```
LAST NAME
A-M*
```

If you forget the ending asterisk, you won't get names that begin with the letter *M*. Why? Because *M* followed by *anything* (as in *MacDonald*) is "larger than" the letter *M* by itself. *A-M* without the asterisk means "everything from *A* up to the letter *M* by itself."

TIP

Maybe this will shed some light: If you look up *M* in the dictionary, where entries are alphabetized, you'll probably find that *M* by itself is the first entry. All other *M* words come after that, because alphabetically they're "larger than" the letter *M* by itself.

Isolating Records for a Specific Month

As long as you type dates into fields in a consistent format, you can isolate records that fall within a range of dates. For example, if you enter all dates in the format *month/day/year*, as in 1/1/93 and 12/31/92, you can fairly easily isolate certain dates using these criteria:

1/*	Dates that start with 1/ (January dates)
*93	Dates that end with 93 (1993 dates)
1/*/93	Dates in January of 1993
1/*;2/*;3/*	Dates that start with 1/ or 2/ or 3/ (first quarter of the year)

Likewise, if you type *all* your dates in the format *Month,Day Year*, you can easily isolate certain dates using criteria such as these:

Jan*	Dates that start with Jan (January)
*93	Dates that end with 93 (1993 dates)
Jan*93	Dates in January of 1993
Jan*;Feb*;/Mar*	Dates that start with Jan, Feb, or March (first quarter of the year)

Okay, let's say you *didn't* follow a consistent format when typing dates into a field—some are in 1/1/93 format, others in Jan 1, 1993 format, and still others in January 1, 1993 format. All is not lost, because this will still isolate all the dates in January of 1993:

1/*/93;Jan/*/93

Notwithstanding, you're better off deciding on a format and sticking to that format throughout your data file.

Defining a Range of Zip Codes

Defining a range of zip codes is like defining a range of letters: You have to be wary of those zip+4 codes at the high end of the range. Suppose you want to isolate records that have a value between 92000 and 92999-9999 in the Zip/ Postal field. This criterion would do the trick:

ZIP/ POSTAL
92000-92999*

The asterisk at the end ensures that you'll get zip codes such as 92999-0123 and 92999-9999 at the high end of the range.

Isolating an Area Code

If your data file contains a Phone field, and you've followed a consistent format when typing in phone numbers, you can easily isolate records within a certain area code. For example, if you typed all phone numbers in the *(xxx)xxx-xxxx* format, as in (619)555-1234, the following criterion will isolate records in the 619 area code:

    PHONE
    (619)*

Isolating Records That Contain a Special Character

In my sample data file, I included a field named New. When I'm typing new records into the data file, I use Ctrl+W to insert a check mark into this field to identify the record as a new one. Later, if I want to print welcome letters and envelopes for new customers only, I can define this criterion:

    New
    ✓

To type in the check mark, simply press Ctrl+W when it's time to enter the text of the criterion. Choose whatever character you've been putting into the New field to identify new records. Use the same code number, such as 5,51—even if the character looks different in the current font. Then perform the merge normally to print your letters, labels, envelopes, whatever.

Once you've printed everything you need for new customers, they no longer need to be marked as "new." Open your data file (CUSTOMER.DAT in my example), and use Search and Replace (Alt+F2) to change all the check marks in the file to *<Nothing>* or *No* or whatever.

By the way, the reason you should use an unusual character, such as a check mark, rather than just Yes or Y, to identify new customers is so that you can do the search-and-replace with confidence. For example, if I tell WordPerfect to change all the Yes entries to No, a person named Yestowsky would have his/her name changed to Notowsky.

Printing an Envelope for Each Merged Letter

If you create a data file and form letter, it's not necessary to run a form file for printing envelopes separately (although, in the long run, you may find it easier just to create a form for envelopes, as discussed under "Envelopes" later in this chapter). Here's how to create an envelope format "on the fly," just before merging your form letter with your data file:

1. If the form letter already has the merge codes for the recipient's name and address at the top, open the form file. Then select those merge codes, as in the example shown in Figure 21.15.

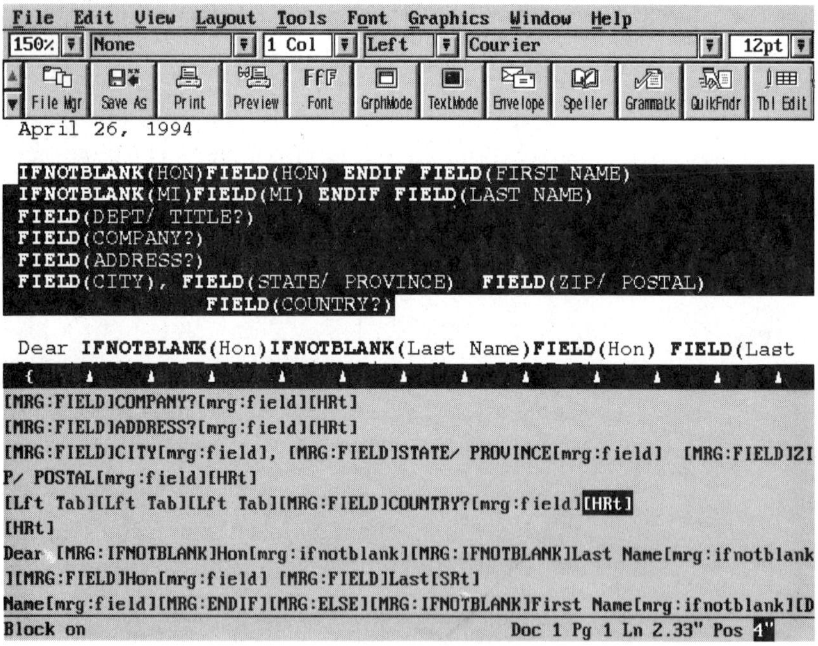

FIGURE 21.15

Merge codes for printing the inside address at the top of a form letter selected.

```
  File   Edit   View   Layout   Tools   Font   Graphics   Window   Help
 150%  None              1 Col     Left       Courier                      12pt
   File Mgr  Save As  Print  Preview  Font  GrphMode  TextMode  Envelope  Speller  Grammatk  QuikFndr  Tbl Edit
 April 26, 1994

 IFNOTBLANK(HON)FIELD(HON) ENDIF FIELD(FIRST NAME)
 IFNOTBLANK(MI)FIELD(MI) ENDIF FIELD(LAST NAME)
 FIELD(DEPT/ TITLE?)
 FIELD(COMPANY?)
 FIELD(ADDRESS?)
 FIELD(CITY), FIELD(STATE/ PROVINCE)   FIELD(ZIP/ POSTAL)
                     FIELD(COUNTRY?)

 Dear IFNOTBLANK(Hon)IFNOTBLANK(Last Name)FIELD(Hon) FIELD(Last
 {         ↓      ↓     ↓     ↓     ↓     ↓     ↓     ↓     ↓     ↓     ↓     ↓
 [MRG:FIELD]COMPANY?[mrg:field][HRt]
 [MRG:FIELD]ADDRESS?[mrg:field][HRt]
 [MRG:FIELD]CITY[mrg:field], [MRG:FIELD]STATE/ PROVINCE[mrg:field]  [MRG:FIELD]ZI
 P/ POSTAL[mrg:field][HRt]
 [Lft Tab][Lft Tab][Lft Tab][MRG:FIELD]COUNTRY?[mrg:field][HRt]
 [HRt]
 Dear [MRG:IFNOTBLANK]Hon[mrg:ifnotblank][MRG:IFNOTBLANK]Last Name[mrg:ifnotblank
 ][MRG:FIELD]Hon[mrg:field] [MRG:FIELD]Last[SRt]
 Name[mrg:field][MRG:ENDIF][MRG:ELSE][MRG:IFNOTBLANK]First Name[mrg:ifnotblank][D
 Block on                                      Doc 1 Pg 1 Ln 2.33" Pos 4"
```

2. Choose Edit ➤ Copy or press Ctrl+C (nothing seems to happen, but a copy of all those codes is sent to the Clipboard).

3. Close and save the current file, if you wish, with the usual File ➤ Close commands.

4. Start your merge as usual (Ctrl+F9 M), and select the names of your form letter and data files.

5. If the data file options aren't visible, choose Data File Options.

6. Choose Generate an Envelope for Each Data Record. You'll see the Envelope dialog box (described shortly).

7. Choose Mailing Address to put the cursor in that text box. Then press Ctrl+V to copy the merge codes from the Clipboard into the address portion of the envelope. Press F7 after the codes appear in the box.

8. Choose Envelope Size, and choose your envelope size.

9. If you're using envelopes that already have your return address printed on them (or if, for whatever reason, you don't want to print a return address), select the Omit Return Address option.

10. If you did not define a return address, and would like to create one that you can use as the default in future sessions, choose Save Return Address as Default.

11. To print a return address, choose Return address. You can choose a font (Ctrl+F8, Chapter 5) and insert a logo or other graphic image (Alt+F9, Chapter 26). Then type your return address as you want it to look on the envelope. Press F7 when you're done.

NOTE   Though I omitted the return address in this example, later in the chapter I'll present an envelope format that includes a return address with a graphic image.

12. If you want to print a POSTNET bar code, choose POSTNET Bar Code. Then press F5 and choose the name of the field that contains the zip code (Zip/ Postal in my example), by double-clicking or by highlighting and pressing ↵. Figure 21.16 shows a sample completed Envelope dialog box.

FIGURE 21.16

Dialog box for defining the format of an envelope, with a sample envelope format typed in

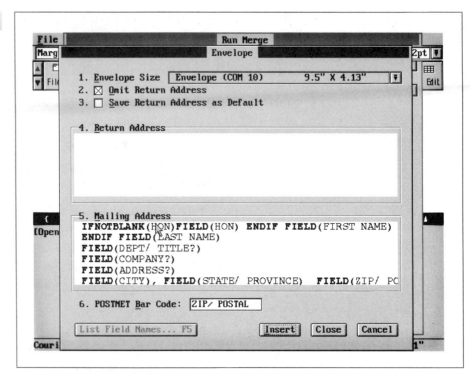

13. Choose <u>I</u>nsert.

14. Choose Merge to start the merge.

WordPerfect will merge all the form letters. Then it will merge all the envelopes at the end of the form letter pages. Print with the usual <u>F</u>ile ➤ Print/Fax commands, and load envelopes when appropriate according to how you've defined the Location and Prompt To Load options of your selected envelope size (see Chapter 8).

TIP

If you have foreign or blank zip codes in your data file, they may not look right on the envelopes. I'll show you how to fix that a little later in the chapter.

If you're using a printer like the newer LaserJet models, which have a message window up front, you might want to keep an eye on the window for instructions on when to load envelopes. Likewise, you can press Shift+F7 C to get to the Control Printer dialog box to watch the progress, and check for instructions as WordPerfect prints the letters and envelopes.

Sample Forms

Now let's take a look at some sample forms that print data from my sample CUSTOMER.DAT data file. You can use these as food for thought when creating your own forms. I'll use some occasional graphics, which aren't discussed until Chapter 26. But these graphics are entirely optional. Just omit them if you don't want them, or haven't yet learned how to create graphics boxes.

NOTE   Don't forget that anything shown in boldface in these examples is a merge code. You cannot simply type those codes in. You must select them as merge codes using Tools ➤ Merge ➤ Define or Shift+F9.

A Form Letter

Figure 21.17 shows a sample form letter, based on fields from my sample CUSTOMER.DAT data file. It uses the fancy IFNOTBLANK merge code I described earlier in the chapter. (I didn't type much in the body of the letter, because I want you to be able to see the signature line. Obviously, the body of *your* letter will probably say more.)

In this example, I'm going to have WordPerfect print the letterhead and signature on each letter for me. I used fonts and graphic images to create the letterhead. I fudged the signature using a script font. But you can use a scanner to scan your own signature and save it to a bitmap file. Then just put that image in a graphics user box where you want your signature to appear. (Beats signing all those form letters!)

FIGURE 21.17

A sample form
letter with its own
letterhead and
signature

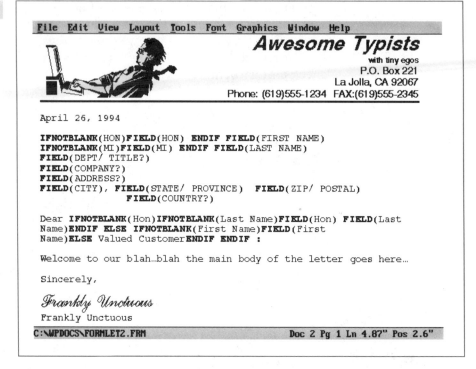

TIP

Don't forget to use the Image On Disk option (Chapter 26) when putting graphic images in a merge file, to speed things up and reduce disk consumption.

Do Yourself a Favor...

To create another form letter, open one you've previously created. Choose File ➤ Save As, and save this copy with a different file name. Then just change the text of the letter under the salutation.

You can also help yourself out by selecting the merge codes that format the inside address of your first form letter, and then use File ➤ Save As to save that block of text to a unique file name, such as MRGADDR.FRM. That way, to create labels or the like, you need not re-create all those codes. Just retrieve your MRGADDR.FRM file into whatever form you're working on.

Mailing Labels

To print mailing labels from your data file, first decide what size and type of label you're going to use. If you're not using one of the standard commercial label sizes, you'll need to create a custom label format, as discussed in Chapter 8. Then...

1. Start with a new document window (File ➤ New).

2. Choose Layout ➤ Document ➤ Document Initial Codes.

3. Choose Layout ➤ Page ➤ Labels, and select your label format by double-clicking, or by highlighting and pressing ↵.

4. If a Labels Printer Info dialog box appears, you can change any options you want, and then choose OK. Then choose OK to return to the Document Initial Codes dialog box. Then press Exit (F7) and choose OK to return to your document window.

5. If you previously saved that MRGADDR.FRM file I mentioned earlier, use File ➤ Retrieve to retrieve it into the current document (*not* a new document). Otherwise, you'll need to insert merge codes to define how you want to format the name and address.

6. You can also move the cursor to the top of the document (Home Home ↑) and center each label vertically by choosing Layout ➤ Page ➤ Center Pages then OK. You can also choose a font in the usual manner (Font ➤ Font ➤ Font).

NOTE

If the address seems to extend past a page break, it may just be that the codes are making it look that way. For a more accurate view of the actual height of the printed label, press Shift+F9, choose Form (if the option presents itself), then Display Of Merge Codes ➤ Show Codes As Icons, and then OK.

7. When you've finished laying out your label format, choose File ➤ Close ➤ Yes, and enter a file name that will be easy to recognize in the future (such as LABELS.FRM).

To use (or test) your label format, merge it with your data file using the regular Tools ➤ Merge ➤ Run commands. Then use File ➤ Print/Fax as usual to print the labels.

T I P

If the text doesn't align properly on the labels, change the margins in the label paper size (Chapter 8), rather than trying to fix the problem in the label form file.

Adding POSTNET to Labels

If you want to print a POSTNET bar code on each merged label, open your label format file (LABELS.FRM in my example). Put the cursor wherever you want the code to appear, and press Shift+F9 twice. Choose POSTNET(string) from the list of merge codes.

In the Parameter Entry dialog box that appears, type a bogus zip code, such as **X,** and choose OK. Move the cursor to the start of the bogus zip code, and delete it using the Delete key.

Make sure the cursor is between the parentheses that follow the POST-NET code. Press Shift+F9 and choose Field. Enter or choose the name of the field in your data file that contains the zip code (Zip/ Postal in my example). Then choose OK. You want it to look something like this in the document window:

POSTNET(FIELD(ZIP/ POSTAL)**)**

and something like this in Reveal Codes:

[MRG:POSTNET][MRG:FIELD]ZIP/ POSTAL[mrg:field]
[mrg:postnet][HRt]

You may need to press ↵ before or after the POSTNET(FIELD (...)) code if you want the code to appear on its own line.

Foreign and Blank Postal Codes

If your data file has non-U.S. addresses in it, that POSTNET code I just had you put into the labels will create problems when you get to a record that has a foreign (or empty) Zip/ Postal code.

As long as you've used a consistent means of identifying U.S. addresses in your data file, you can tell the merge to print the POSTNET code only when it's a U.S. address. I just leave the Country field blank for U.S. addresses in my data file. So we can just insert advanced merge codes that tell the merge to "print the POSTNET code only if the Country field is blank…" On the outside chance that it *is* a U.S. address, but for some reason doesn't have a zip code, we can also add "…but only if the Zip /Postal code isn't blank either."

Move the cursor to the [MRG:POSTNET] code in Reveal Codes. Then press Shift+F9 twice, and choose the IFBLANK(field) command. Enter Country as the field to test, and choose OK.

Press Shift+F9 twice again, but this time choose IFNOTBLANK(field). Enter Zip/ Postal (or whatever your field is named), and choose OK. Finally, move the highlight to just *past* the [mrg:postnet][HRt] codes that end the POSTNET code. Press Shift+F9 twice, and choose ENDIF. Then do it again to insert a second ENDIF code.

If you followed my example, your finished label format should look something like my LABELS.FRM document shown in Figure 21.18. (The soft page break is there only because of all the codes on the form. Each name and address does fit on a label in this example, particularly with the Country field moved up to the end of the last line.)

Envelopes

You can create a merge form for printing envelopes using the same basic technique just described for labels and envelopes. Here are the steps to follow:

1. If you created the MRGADDR.FRM document I mentioned earlier, open that file. Then select the entire document (F12 Home Home ↓) and choose Edit ➤ Copy or press Ctrl+C to copy it to the Clipboard. Choose File ➤ Close.

File Edit View Layout Tools Font Graphics Window Help

```
IFBLANK(Country)IFNOTBLANK(ZIP/
POSTAL)POSTNET(FIELD(ZIP/POSTAL))
ENDIF ENDIF IFNOTBLANK(FIELD(HON)HON
)ENDIF FIELD(FIRST NAME)
IFNOTBLANK(MI)FIELD(MI) ENDIF FIELD(LAST
NAME)
FIELD(DEPT/TITLE?)

FIELD(COMPANY?)
FIELD(ADDRESS?)
FIELD(CITY), FIELD(STATE/PROVINCE)  FIELD(ZIP/
POSTAL)      FIELD(COUNTRY?)
```

```
{     ↑    ↑    ↑    ↑    ↑    ↑       ↑ ]
[Open Style:InitialCodes;[Labels Form:Avery 5162 Address][Paper Sz/Typ:8.5" x 11
",Avery 5162 Address]][Font:Times New Roman][Font Size:11pt][Cntr Pgs][MRG:IFBLA
NK]Country[mrg:ifblank][MRG:IFNOTBLANK]ZIP/[SRt]
POSTAL[mrg:ifnotblank][MRG:POSTNET][MRG:FIELD]ZIP/ POSTAL[mrg:field][mrg:postnet
][HRt]
[MRG:ENDIF][MRG:ENDIF][MRG:IFNOTBLANK][MRG:FIELD]HON[mrg:field]HON[SRt]
[mrg:ifnotblank][MRG:ENDIF][MRG:FIELD]FIRST NAME[mrg:field][SRt]
[MRG:IFNOTBLANK]MI[mrg:ifnotblank][MRG:FIELD]MI[mrg:field]  [MRG:ENDIF][MRG:FIELD
]LAST[SRt]
NAME[mrg:field][HRt]
[MRG:FIELD]DEPT/ TITLE?[mrg:field][HRt-SPg]
C:\WPDOCS\LABELS.FRM                                    Doc 1 Pg 1 Ln 0" Pos 0.064"
```

2. Start with a new document and choose <u>L</u>ayout ➤ En<u>v</u>elope or press Alt+F12.

3. Choose <u>M</u>ailing Address and press Ctrl+V to copy the codes from the Clipboard. (If you skipped step 1, you'll need to insert codes by using Shift+F9.) Press F7 when you're done with the mailing address.

4. Choose the <u>E</u>nvelope Size, <u>O</u>mit Return Address, and <u>S</u>ave Return Address as Default, if you wish.

5. If you wish, choose <u>R</u>eturn Address, fill in the return address (adding fonts, graphics, and other formatting features as needed), and press F7.

6. Choose <u>I</u>nsert.

If you'd like to add a POSTNET bar code, press Shift+F9, choose <u>F</u>orm (if necessary), then press Shift+F9 again. Now, follow the instructions given under "Adding POSTNET to Labels," starting where it says "Choose

"Choose POSTNET(string) from the list of merge codes...". (Alternatively, if you created the labels described above, you can copy and paste the codes from the LABELS.FRM document.)

Figure 21.19 shows my completed envelope format. Notice that like the letterhead described earlier, this example includes a graphic and some fonts in the return address. Each address will be printed on a separate envelope. (Again, the soft page break is caused by all the codes, but won't appear when you merge the addresses later.)

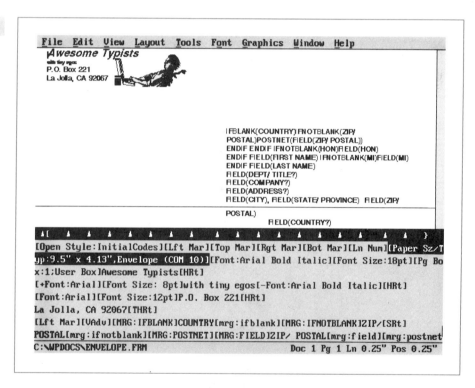

When you're satisfied with your envelope format, choose File ➤ Close ➤ Yes to save and close it (name the file ENVELOPE.FRM). Then use Tools ➤ Merge ➤ Run (Ctrl+F9 M) to start the merge, with ENVELOPE.FRM as the form and CUSTOMER.DAT as the data file (or whatever names you've chosen). Print the envelopes with File ➤ Print/Fax.

If you need to change the bin or feed method for the envelopes, open the ENVELOPE.FRM file again. Choose Layout ➤ Page ➤ Paper Size/Type, highlight the envelope size, and choose Edit as discussed in Chapter 8. When you're done making changes, choose OK to return to the Paper Size/Type dialog box, then choose Select then OK. Now, choose File ➤ Close ➤ Yes and start the merge again from scratch.

Merging to Columns: A Directory Listing

Figure 21.20 shows the sample data from my CUSTOMER.DAT file merged to a directory listing. I used two newspaper-style columns (see Chapter 27) to create that example.

FIGURE 21.20

A sample directory listing created from the CUSTOMER.DAT data file using a merge

FIGURE 21.20

A sample directory listing created from the CUSTOMER.DAT data file using a merge

Customer Directory

Bobo, Cher
     3232 East Lake
     Duarte, CA 92999
     Phone: (213)555-3039

Clauser, Ms. Esther C.
     Author
     1101 Orchard St.
     Nepean, ONT K2E8A5   Canada
     Phone: (613)555-4049

Doofdork Corp.
     Sales Division
     Box 1131
     Lakewood, NJ 08701
     Phone: (800)555-1030

Granola, Ms. Wanda B.
     Logicon
     Accts. Payable
     P.O. Box 123
     New York, NY 32555
     Phone: (212)555-4049

Green, Mrs. Janet L.
     ABC Corp.
     President
     123 A St.
     San Diego, CA 92000
     Phone: (619)555-1023

Mann, Dr. Candy
     Ono Pediatric Clinic
     Internist
     1101 Krager
     Bangor, ME 02000-1234
     Phone: (123)555-1234

Menezes, Dr. José O.
     Florália
     Botanist
     Orquidários Ltda
     Box n 100541
     Niterói, Rio de Janeiro   Brasil
     Phone: 55-21-555800

Ramdrive, Mr. Stan J.
     Quark County Court
     Clerk
     540 Grand Ave.
     Orem, UT 84057
     Phone: (800)555-4049 Ext. 323

Wein, Ms. Alberta J.
     RSF Travel
     Travel Agent
     12 Paseo Delicias
     Saturn, FL 33431
     Phone: (407)555-5052

To create the form for the directory listing, start with a blank, new document window, and choose Layout ➤ Document ➤ Document Initial Codes.

If you want to include a header (like my Customer Directory), use Layout ➤ Header/Footer/Watermark to create a header (Chapter 8). If you want to define columns, choose Layout ➤ Columns ➤ Column Type ➤ Newspaper (or Balanced Newspaper) and define your columns as described in Chapter 27. Press F7 and work your way back to the document window.

The actual merge codes in my sample directory are shown in Figure 21.21. The trickiest part is the first two lines, which look something like this (when not wrapped so tightly in the column):

IFNOTBLANK(Last Name)**FIELD**(Last Name), **FIELD**(Hon)
FIELD(First Name) **FIELD**(MI)*[HRt]*
ENDIF

(The hard return *[HRt]* at the end is only visible in Reveal Codes.) The next IF...ENDIF pair looks like this:

IFNOTBLANK(Last Name)*[Lft Indent]***ENDIF**

where, again, the *[Lft Indent]* code (inserted by pressing F4) appears only in Reveal Codes. That ensures that the Company name will be indented *only* if there is no Last Name in this record. That's why DoofDork Corp in Figure 21.20 is "outdented" like a person's name.

To prevent a person's name and address from being broken across two columns, I selected all the codes in the entire set, including the extra *[HRt]* code at the end (which serves as the blank line between names). Then I turned on Block Protect (Layout ➤ Other ➤ Block Protect).

To prevent each record from being printed on a separate page, move to the bottom of the form and insert a PAGE OFF code (press Shift+F9 and choose Page Off).

Now you can close and save the form. (I named mine DIRECTORY.FRM.) Then, starting from a new document window, you can merge the directory form with your data file as usual.

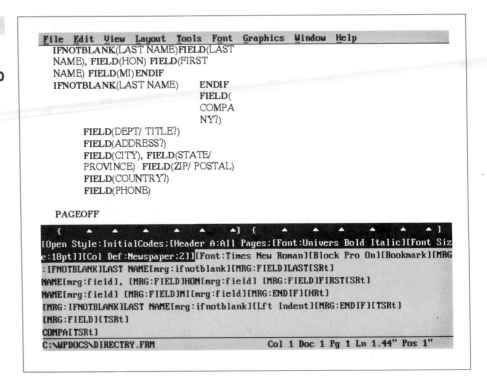

After merging DIRECTORY.FRM with CUSTOMER.DAT, you can put the entries into alphabetical order using the Sort feature, described in Chapter 22. Because of the way this directory is formatted, you can use Paragraph sorting *after* merging to do the job.

NOTE   As discussed in the next chapter, you'll usually want to sort data file records *before* you do the actual merge.

After completing the merge, I chose Tools ➤ Sort then OK. I then set up the Sort dialog box like this:

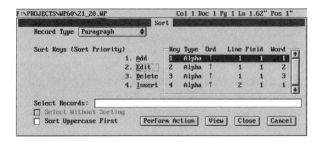

Then I chose Perform Action as usual, to sort the records. Finally, I printed the result.

By the way, a hard return in the data file won't indent in the directory. Here, I manually indented the *Box n 100541* line in the Brazil address prior to printing the document.

Merging to a Table: A Phone List

If you want to merge to a table, you need to start with a two-row table. In the first cell, press Shift+F9, choose Form if necessary, and press Shift+F9 again. Pick the LABEL(Label) command, and make up a name (I used **Top Row**). In the second row, press Shift+F9 twice, and insert a NEXTRECORD command. Then use Shift+F9 twice again, and insert a GO(Label) command, using the same label name you entered before (**Top Row** in my example). For example, if you wanted your table to have two columns, the table would now look like this:

File Edit View Layout Tools Font Graphics Window Help	
LABEL(TopRow)	
NEXTRECORD GO(TopRow)	

Now you can insert the FIELD commands into the top row (only) describing what you want in each column. For example, I inserted the merge commands

IFNOTBLANK(Last Name)**FIELD**(Last Name), **FIELD**(First Name)
ELSE FIELD(Company)**ENDIF**

to print the last and first name from the current record (or, if the Last Name field is blank, the company name). In cell B1, I put in the merge code FIELD(Phone) to display the phone number in that column. Then you can just close and save the form with a name that'll be easy to remember, such as PHONLIST.FRM.

```
 File  Edit  View  Layout  Tools  Font  Graphics  Window  Help
 LABEL(TopRow)IFNOTBLANK(Last    FIELD(Phone)|
 Name)FIELD(Last Name),
 FIELD(First
 Name)ELSE FIELD(Company)ENDIF

 NEXTRECORD GO(TopRow)
```

Perform the merge normally, and it will create a table row for each record in your data file. Then you can use the Table Edit mode (Chapter 7) to customize the table to your liking, changing column widths, adding a header row, and so forth. You can also sort the table rows into alphabetical order, using techniques described for sorting tables in Chapter 22.

Figure 21.22 shows a sample phone list after completing the merge, alphabetizing the rows, modifying the table lines and shading, and typing a title at the top of the page.

Using Merge Files from Previous Versions of WordPerfect

When you merge files that you created in an earlier version of WordPerfect, they're automatically converted to 6.0 format during the merge. Remember, though—once you've converted the files to 6.0 format, earlier

Phone Directory   April 28, 1994

Name/Company	Phone
Bobo, Cher	(213)555-3039
Clauser, Esther	(613)555-4049
Doofdork Corp.	(800)555-1030
Granola, Wanda	(212)555-4049
Green, Janet	(619)555-1023
Mann, Candy	(123)555-1234
Menezes, José	55-21-555800
Ramdrive, Stan	(800)555-4049 Ext. 323
Wein, Alberta	(407)555-5052

versions (such as 5.1) can't open those files unless you first export the 6.0 file to 5.0/5.1 format using Files ➤ Save As ➤ Format first, as explained in Chapter 20.

We've covered merges in some detail here. As mentioned, there's still more territory to explore in the Advanced Merge Codes area. To learn about merges, you can refer to your WordPerfect manual and the Help screens. In the next chapter, you'll learn how to alphabetize (sort) a document.

CHAPTER 22

Alphabetizing, Sorting, and Isolating Text

f a s t TRACK

- **WordPerfect recognizes and lets you sort the following types of records:** 804

  lines (separated by a hard return), paragraphs (separated by two hard returns), merge data files, parallel columns (organized into rows of columns), and tables (organized into rows of cells).

- **The sort key** 810

  defines how the sort takes place. When defining each sort key, you specify its field, line, word, column, or cell position within the record; whether the key is *alphanumeric* or *numeric;* and whether to sort in *ascending* (A to Z) or *descending* (Z to A) order.

- **To perform a sort within a sort** 811

  you define more than one sort key—up to nine. Thus, to sort by last name and then by first name, you'd define two keys: the first key (key 1) for the last name, and the second key (key 2) for the first name.

- **To sort text** 817

  move the cursor into an existing file, table, or column, or select the chunk of text you want to sort. You can also start from an empty document window if you want to sort a file of lines, paragraphs, or merge data. Choose Tools ➤ Sort. If prompted, enter the source of the text to be sorted and an output destination for the sorted text. Define your Sort Keys and other options in the Sort dialog box, and choose Perform Action.

IF YOU work with any kind of tabular or formatted text, including merge data files, chances are you'll want to alphabetize, or in some other way *sort* that information into some kind of meaningful order from time to time. For example, if you have a list of names and addresses, you might want to sort them into alphabetical order by name. Or you might want to sort them into zip-code order for bulk mailing.

You might also occasionally want to isolate (or *select*) certain types of information. For example, you might want to limit a mailing to residents of a particular city or zip-code mailing. You use WordPerfect's Sort feature, described in this chapter, for all these kinds of tasks.

What You Can Sort

You can sort virtually any text that's organized into some consistent format of *records* and *fields*. The exact definition of record and field depends on *what* you want to sort. There are five different types of sorts to choose from:

Line sort   Each record ends with a single hard return, and each field is separated by one tab code (Figure 22.1).

Paragraph sort   Each record ends with two hard returns. The record can contain multiple lines, each ending with a single hard return. Each line can contain one or more fields separated by tab codes (Figure 22.2).

Table sort   Works with any table, including those used as merge data files. Each table row is a record, and each column is a field (Figure 22.3).

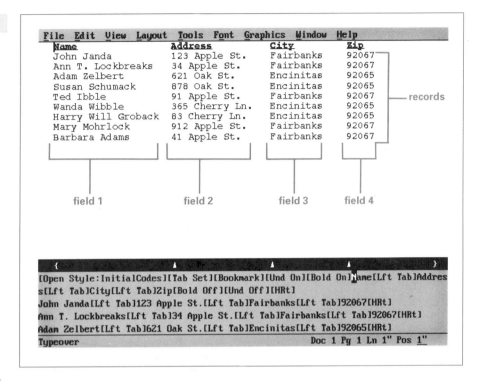

You'd use a Line sort to sort this information, where each record (row) ends with a single hard return.

Parallel column sort   Each record is a row of text, and each field is a column (Figure 22.4).

Merge (text) data file   Each record and field in the data file is also used as a record and field for sorting purposes (Figure 22.5).

Sorting Your Text

Once you have a basic idea of what kind of sort you need to do, the operation is pretty straightforward:

1. Open the document you want to sort. If you want to sort only a portion of the text in the document, select that text. (It's not absolutely necessary to open the document you want to sort, but it's generally easiest that way.)

FIGURE 22.2

You'd use a
Paragraph sort
to alphabetize
this information,
where each "record"
ends with two hard
returns.

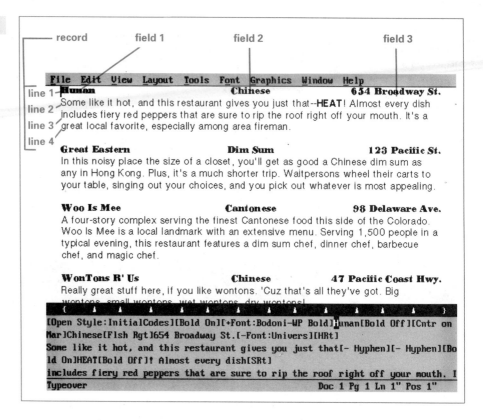

2. To play it safe, choose File ➤ Save to save a copy of the document
   in its current state (just in case your sort doesn't turn out as
   planned).

3. Choose Tools ➤ Sort. Depending on what you're sorting, you
   might see this dialog box. (If you don't see this dialog box, skip to
   the next graphic and step 7.)

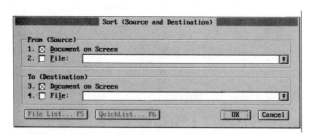

FIGURE 22.3

When sorting a table (even if it's a merge data table), each row is a record, each column a field.

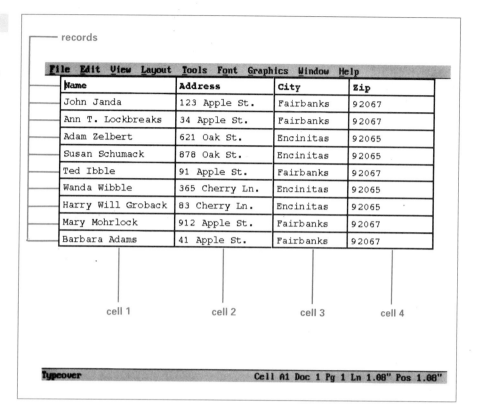

records

Name	Address	City	Zip
John Janda	123 Apple St.	Fairbanks	92067
Ann T. Lockbreaks	34 Apple St.	Fairbanks	92067
Adam Zelbert	621 Oak St.	Encinitas	92065
Susan Schumack	878 Oak St.	Encinitas	92065
Ted Ibble	91 Apple St.	Fairbanks	92067
Wanda Wibble	365 Cherry Ln.	Encinitas	92065
Harry Will Groback	83 Cherry Ln.	Encinitas	92065
Mary Mohrlock	912 Apple St.	Fairbanks	92067
Barbara Adams	41 Apple St.	Fairbanks	92067

cell 1   cell 2   cell 3   cell 4

File Edit View Layout Tools Font Graphics Window Help

Typeover   Cell A1 Doc 1 Pg 1 Ln 1.08" Pos 1.08"

4. If you want to sort the document on your screen, you need not make any changes. If you want to sort a different document, choose File and specify the name of the document that contains the text you want to sort.

5. If you want to store the sorted text under a different file name, choose File, under To (Destination), and enter a name for the file that the sort operation will create.

FIGURE 22.4

Because I used parallel columns to create this document, I'd use a parallel column sort to alphabetize these records.

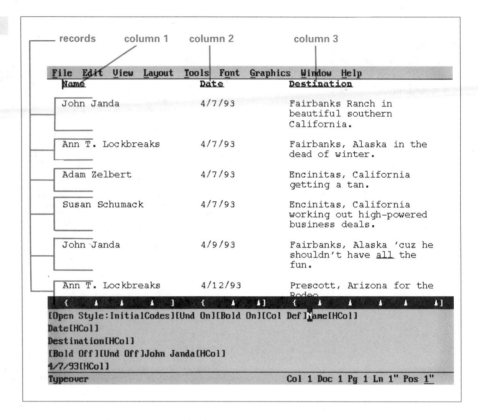

6. Choose OK after making your selection (if any) to get to the Sort dialog box shown below.

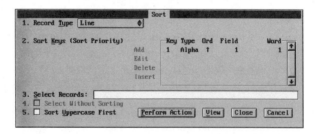

7. If the entry next to Record Type doesn't seem appropriate for the type of sort you want to do, select that option and the appropriate type of sort.

FIGURE 22.5

When sorting a merge data file (text type), each data record and field is also a sorting record and field.

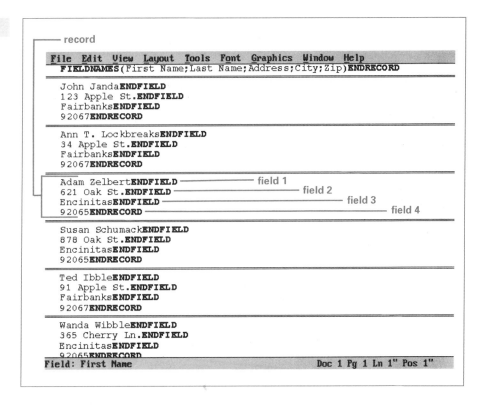

8. Define your sort keys (the text you want to base the sort on), as discussed under "How to Define the Sort Keys" in a few pages.

9. When you're ready to perform the sort, choose Perform Action.

WordPerfect will sort the text and return you to the document window. If you didn't choose any file names in steps 4 and 5, the text that's on your screen will now be sorted. If you did choose any file names, you'll need to open the appropriate file to see the results of the sort.

Undoing a Sort

If the results of your sort are not what you expected, you can (usually) choose Edit ➤ Undo immediately to undo the sort. If that doesn't work (and you followed my advice about saving the document first), you can still undo the sort. Just close the current (sorted) version of the document *without* saving it. Then reopen the copy you saved just before you performed the sort.

About Sort Keys

The key to successful sorting is properly defining the *sort key* (no pun intended). WordPerfect doesn't just intuitively "know" how you want your text arranged. You have to tell it exactly what information you want to base the sort on. In other words, you need to define the sort key(s).

Here's an example. Suppose you have a list of people's names in your document, as below:

Sandy Miller

Zeke Adams

Wanda Miller

Anna Zeeborp

Ted Goofenstein

Lee Miller

If you just performed a sort without first defining your keys, WordPerfect would sort the list by the first word in each row (record). Thus, your list would come out like this:

Anna Zeeborp

Lee Miller

Sandy Miller

Ted Goofenstein

Wanda Miller

Zeke Adams

This might or might not be what you had in mind. Now, had you told WordPerfect that you specifically wanted to sort these records (rows) by the second (or last) word in each row, the names would be alphabetized by that second word. In this example, there's a space in front of each last name. So each person's last name is the second word in the record. The result of such a sort, then, would be records that are alphabetized by peoples' surnames, as below:

Zeke Adams

Ted Goofenstein

Wanda Miller

Sandy Miller

Lee Miller

Anna Zeeborp

Sorts within Sorts

In this tiny list, the order of people with the same last name (e.g. Miller) isn't terribly important. But in a larger list, you might want to alphabetize people by first name within each last name—like the telephone directory.

In that case, you want a sort within a sort. That is, you want to sort by first name within each last name. To accomplish that you need to define two sort keys. The first sort key would be each person's surname. The second sort key would be each person's first name. This would be the result of that sort:

Zeke Adams

Ted Goofenstein

Lee Miller

Sandy Miller

Wanda Miller

Anna Zeeborp

Notice how the second sort key, each person's first name, acts as a tiebreaker. That is, when several people have the same last name (Miller), their records are alphabetized by first name within that group (Lee Miller comes before Sandy Miller, which comes before Wanda Miller).

You can define up to nine sort keys when sorting. That gives you a great deal of flexibility when organizing your text. I'll show you some sample sorts in a moment, to help shed some more light on sort keys. But first, I need to digress for a moment and talk about some other options you have while sorting.

Ascending vs. descending sorts   When you're defining a sort key, you'll be able to choose between ascending order (smallest-to-largest, or A-to-Z) or descending order (largest-to-smallest, or Z-to-A).

Alpha vs. numeric sorts   You can also choose between an alpha (normal alphabetical) or a numeric sort. In general, you want to use a numeric sort only when the field you're basing the sort on is a "true number," such as a quantity or dollar amount. Numbers that contain text and nonnumeric punctuation, such as part numbers (J-123), phone numbers ((415)555-1234), and zip codes (91234-4321), are best sorted as alphas.

T I P

If you're in doubt about whether to use an alpha or numeric sort, experiment with each to see which produces the best result.

How to Define the Sort Keys

Once you've given some thought to how you want to do your sort keys, here's how to set them up in WordPerfect:

1. If you haven't already done so, complete steps 1–7 (listed earlier, under "Sorting Your Text") to get to the Sort dialog box. Then choose Sort Keys (Sort Priority). The highlight moves into the sort key portion of the dialog box.

2. Now you can choose Edit to change an existing key, Add to add a new key to the end of the list, Insert to insert a new key at the current cursor position, or Delete to delete the currently highlighted key.

3. If you choose <u>A</u>dd, <u>E</u>dit, or <u>I</u>nsert, you'll be taken to the Edit Sort Key dialog box shown below.

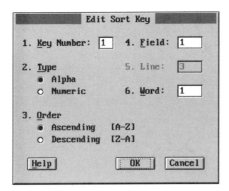

4. You can now choose <u>F</u>ield to define which field you want to sort on, where 1 is the leftmost field, 2 is the next field, and so forth. If you're sorting multiple-line paragraphs, you can also choose which <u>L</u>ine in each paragraph you want to base the sort on. Finally, you can choose which <u>W</u>ord in the field to base the sort on (I'll present some examples in a moment).

5. Optionally, choose a <u>T</u>ype (<u>A</u>lpha or <u>N</u>umeric) and <u>O</u>rder (Ascending or Descending).

6. Choose OK. Repeat steps 2–4 to define up to nine sort keys.

When you're finished defining your keys, choose <u>P</u>erform Action to perform the sort.

Some Sorting Examples

In the next few sections, we'll look at some examples of how to fill in the Sort dialog box for sorting lines, paragraphs, merge data files, parallel columns, and tables.

Sorting Lines

You should use the Line record type when your text is in a simple list format, and each line is broken by a single hard return ([HRt]) code, as in Figures 22.1 and 22.6.

FIGURE 22.6

Sort keys to sort
alphabetically by last
name

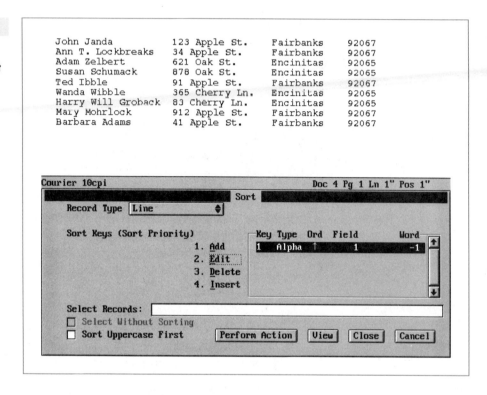

Before choosing Tools ➤ Sort for the records shown in Figure 22.6, I selected all but the first line of the document. (That line, which you can't see in the figure, is the heading for the list and shouldn't be sorted in with the names and addresses.) The sort key shown in the figure will sort the list alphabetically, in ascending order, by each person's last name. Notice that the first field in each line is a person's first and last name. The first word in each name is the person's first name, and the last word in each name is the surname (word −1).

Here are the keys for sorting this same list into zip-code order, then by street name within zip code, and then by street number when several people reside on the same street:

KEY	TYPE	ORD	FIELD	WORD
1	Alpha	↑	4	1
2	Alpha	↑	2	2
3	Num	↑	2	1

TIP

Use an alphanumeric key when sorting zip codes, so that extended zip codes (such as 94803-0011) and foreign zip codes will sort properly.

Sorting Paragraphs

Paragraph sorts are good for—what else?—sorting a series of paragraphs. Figure 22.7 shows the sort keys for arranging our restaurant reviews (Figure 22.2) by type of food, and then by restaurant name within type.

The paragraph sort shown in Figure 22.8 will group each paragraph in the sample bibliography by author's last name. Notice that each bibliography entry is separated by two hard returns (that is, a blank line), like any self-respecting paragraph. However, this is a tricky sort to define, because

FIGURE 22.7

A paragraph sort to organize restaurant reviews by type of food and then by restaurant name

Hunan	**Chinese**	**654 Broadway St.**

Some like it hot, and this restaurant gives you just that--**HEAT**! Almost every dish includes fiery red peppers that are sure to rip the roof right off your mouth. It's a great local favorite, especially among area fireman.

Great Eastern	**Dim Sum**	**123 Pacific St.**

In this noisy place the size of a closet, you'll get as good a Chinese dim sum as any in Hong Kong. Plus, it's a much shorter trip. Waitpersons wheel their carts to your table, singing out your choices, and you pick out whatever is most appealing.

Woo Is Mee	**Cantonese**	**98 Delaware Ave.**

A four-story complex serving the finest Cantonese food this side of the Colorado. Woo Is Mee is a local landmark with an extensive menu. Serving 1,500 people in a

```
Typeover                                    Doc 1 Pg 1 Ln 1" Pos 1"
                                Sort
        Record Type  Paragraph        ⬦

        Sort Keys (Sort Priority)        Key Type  Ord   Line Field Word
                          1. Add        1  Alpha  ↑    1     2    1
                          2. Edit       2  Alpha  ↑    1     1    1
                          3. Delete
                          4. Insert

        Select Records: 
        ☐ Select Without Sorting
        ☐ Sort Uppercase First    [Perform Action] [View] [Close] [Cancel]
```

each paragraph starts with a hanging indent. The hanging indent command (Layout ➤ Alignment ➤ Hanging Indent) inserts [Lft Indent] [Back Tab] codes before the first line of text. Of course, these codes appear only on the Reveal Codes screen (not shown in the figure). For this example, in Reveal Codes the first line in the bibliography would begin like this:

[Lft Indent][Back Tab]Gordon, Barbara, "Art Deco ...

In a paragraph or line sort, the [Lft Tab] and [Back Tab] indent codes create new fields. So, although each author's name appears to be at the start of each line, we must define the sort key as field 3, because the [Lft Tab] and [Back Tab] codes precede the author's last name. In other words, WordPerfect assumes that field 1 is to the left of the [Lft Tab] code, and field 2 is to the left of the [Back Tab] code—even though there is no text in either place. Therefore, field 3 (the author's name) starts at the right of the [Back Tab] code.

FIGURE 22.8

A bibliography with hanging paragraphs, and a sort key to organize the records by author's last name

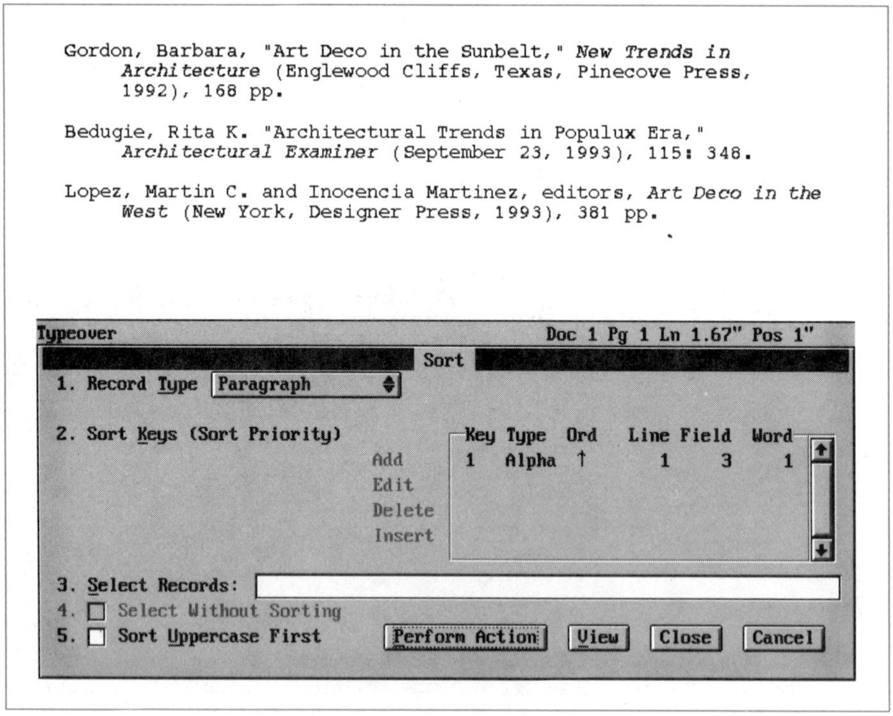

```
Gordon, Barbara, "Art Deco in the Sunbelt," New Trends in
     Architecture (Englewood Cliffs, Texas, Pinecove Press,
     1992), 168 pp.

Bedugie, Rita K. "Architectural Trends in Populux Era,"
     Architectural Examiner (September 23, 1993), 115: 348.

Lopez, Martin C. and Inocencia Martinez, editors, Art Deco in the
     West (New York, Designer Press, 1993), 381 pp.
```

```
Typeover                                  Doc 1 Pg 1 Ln 1.67" Pos 1"
                                     Sort
    1. Record Type  Paragraph        ⬍

    2. Sort Keys (Sort Priority)          ┌Key Type  Ord  Line Field Word┐
                              Add          1  Alpha   ↑     1    3    1
                              Edit
                              Delete
                              Insert

    3. Select Records: _____
    4. ☐ Select Without Sorting
    5. ☐ Sort Uppercase First      Perform Action   View   Close   Cancel
```

Sorting a Text Data File

A merge data file stores information used in form letters and other mass-produced documents. In Chapter 21 you learned that WordPerfect lets you create two types of merge data files: *Text* and *Table*. Text merge data files are the ones I'm talking about here. Recall that each field in a Text merge data file ends with an ENDFIELD code, and each record ends with an ENDRECORD code. If you want to sort a merge data file that's in Table format, simply open the file and sort it as a table, as described later under "Sorting a Table."

To sort a merge data file, make sure that the Record Type in the Sort dialog box is set to Merge Data File. Also remember that you only need to specify the line number for a sort key if a field contains more than one line of text.

The sort key for the merge data file in Figure 22.9 will organize the records into zip-code order (perhaps for bulk mailing). Field 5 identifies the zip code as the fifth field in each record (the name *John Janda* is in the first field).

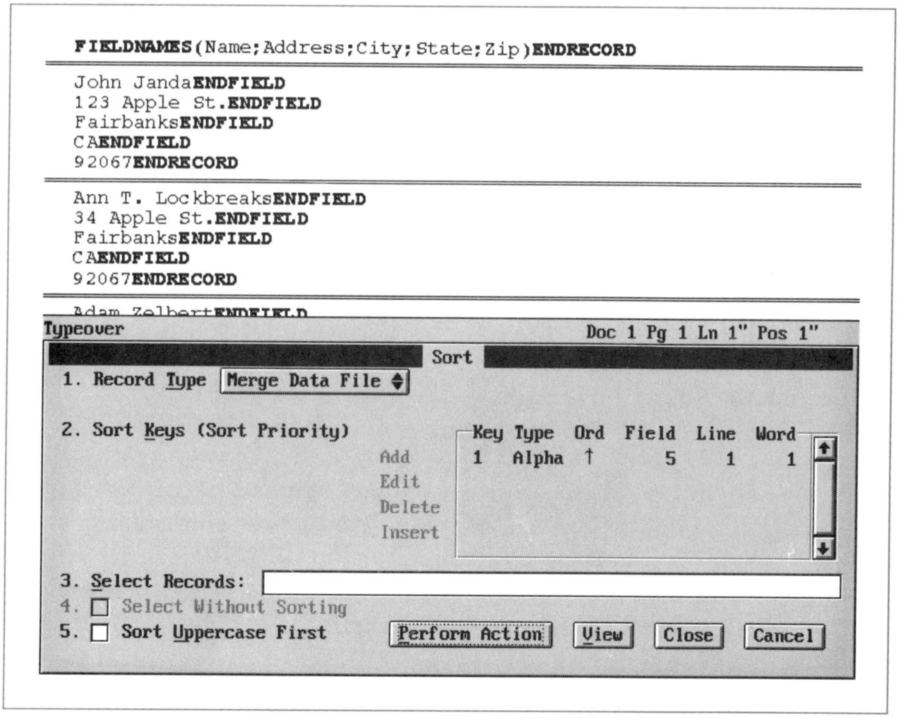

FIGURE 22.9

This sort key will sort the sample merge data file by zip code.

```
FIELDNAMES(Name;Address;City;State;Zip)ENDRECORD

John JandaENDFIELD
123 Apple St.ENDFIELD
FairbanksENDFIELD
CAENDFIELD
92067ENDRECORD

Ann T. LockbreaksENDFIELD
34 Apple St.ENDFIELD
FairbanksENDFIELD
CAENDFIELD
92067ENDRECORD

Adam Zelbert ENDFIELD
```

Typeover   Doc 1 Pg 1 Ln 1" Pos 1"

```
                                      Sort
  1. Record Type  Merge Data File ▲▼

  2. Sort Keys (Sort Priority)            Key Type  Ord  Field  Line  Word
                                  Add      1  Alpha  ↑      5     1     1
                                  Edit
                                  Delete
                                  Insert

  3. Select Records:
  4. ☐ Select Without Sorting
  5. ☐ Sort Uppercase First    Perform Action  View   Close   Cancel
```

If you want to sort the merge data file into name order, like the telephone directory (by last name and then by first name within identical last names), you could define sort keys 1 and 2 like this:

KEY	TYPE	ORD	FIELD	LINE	WORD
1	Alpha	↑	1	1	-1
2	Alpha	↑	1	1	1

Sorting Parallel Columns

To format itineraries, scripts, and other text into parallel columns, you can use the Layout ➤ Columns ➤ Column Type ➤ Parallel (or Parallel With Block Protect) command. (You'll read more about this in Chapter 27.) To sort a document that's organized into parallel columns, first move the cursor into the columns (if you want to sort all the rows), or select the rows you want to sort.

The sort keys in Figure 22.10 illustrate how to sort the sample itineraries shown at the top of the screen by each person's last name, and then by date (year, month, and day) for each person. This grouping tells you where everyone will be on any given date.

In this example, I selected all text except the heading line (not shown in the figure). The first key sorts by last name (word −1 in column 1). The dates in column 2 are divided into three words, separated by slash characters: The second key sorts the dates by year (word 3), the third key sorts the dates by month (word 1), and the fourth key sorts the dates by day (word 2).

N O T E

For sorting purposes, you can use dash (Home −) and slash (/) characters to divide numeric dates such as 4/7/93 into three words. "Sorting Tips and Tricks," later in this chapter, provides more information on sorting dates.

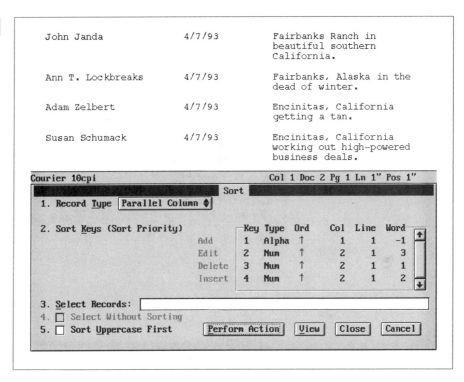

FIGURE 22.10

These settings will sort text in parallel columns by the person's last name, then by date within the same last name.

Sorting a Table

As with parallel columns, table sorts must start with the cursor in the table. To sort the entire table (except for header columns), simply position the cursor anywhere in the table. Or, if you want to sort just a portion of the table, select (block) the rows you want to sort, as shown in Figure 22.11. Then choose Tools ▶ Sort, make sure the Record Type is Table, and pick the sort options you want.

The settings shown in Figure 22.12 will sort the selected rows from Figure 22.11 into descending order from largest to smallest percentage of change (cell 4 of the table).

Here are some points to remember about sorting tables:

- Generally, you don't want to sort column headings, table titles, subtotals, or totals. So be sure to select only the rows that you do want to sort. WordPerfect won't sort header rows, so you don't need to worry about sorting them accidentally. (By the way, the first row of a Table merge data file is automatically created as a header row.)

FIGURE 22.11

Select the rows that you want to sort, and choose Table ➤ Sort.

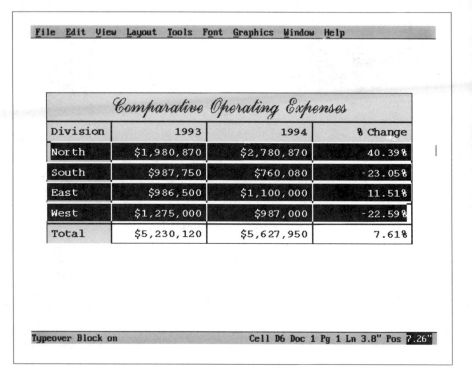

- Try to avoid including rows with more, or fewer, cells than other rows in the sort. For example, if the sort in Figure 22.11 included the "Comparative Operating Expenses" row at the top of the table, that row's position after sorting would be unpredictable.

- The table's lines are sorted with their rows, so you may need to fix the line styles after sorting.

Please see Chapter 7 if you need more information about creating and using tables.

Sorting Tips and Tricks

No, this section isn't about sorting tips and tricks. It's about tips and tricks for sorting. Here are some suggestions that can help you design successful sorts—the first time, every time.

This sort key organizes a table in descending order from largest to smallest percentage of change (column 4).

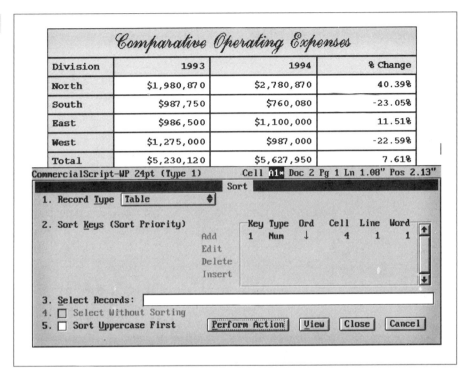

Counting Backwards

The default numbering order for fields, lines, and words is left to right and top to bottom. In a sort key, word 1 is the first word in a field, word 2 is the second word, and so on. However, you can use a negative number in a key to count from right to left or bottom to top. You saw how this backwards-counting trick can help you sort lists that include names such as *Hanley Allen Strappman* and *Gondola Granolabar* by last name. (If you missed that trick, see "Sorting Lines" earlier in this chapter.)

Sorting Several Words as One

Suppose you're sorting a list of names that includes *Harry Durante III* and *Victoria de la Rosa*. An ordinary sort by last name, using word –1 in the sort key, would list these names in the order

Harry Durante III
Victoria de la Rosa

which is backwards. (The records end up in this order because *III* sorts before *Rosa*.)

You probably want *de la Rosa* to appear before *Durante III*. To solve this problem, you must fool WordPerfect into thinking that *Durante III* and *de la Rosa* are both one-word last names. It's easy: Just place a hard space (Home Space) between *Durante* and *III*, and between each of the words in *de la Rosa*. Now the sort keys will correctly alphabetize *de la Rosa* in front of *Durante III*.

Sorting Dates

You can easily sort dates by remembering that WordPerfect recognizes forward slashes (/) and dashes (Home –) as word separators. Just use either of these characters to divide dates into "words" that are the month, day, and year. Then define a separate key for each word.

Suppose you enter a list of dates in the form *07/29/93* or *07–29–93* (with dashes, *not* regular hyphens). To sort these dates in year/month/day order, just set up three *numeric* sort keys and perform a line sort. Define key 1 (the year) as word 3, key 2 (the month) as word 1, and key 3 (the day) as word 2.

Be sure to use *numeric* sort keys for each part of the date. That way, the sort will work properly whether the dates include or omit leading zeros in any position. For example, the dates 7/4/93, 07/02/93, 7/01/93, and 07/5/93 will sort just fine—in the order 7/01/93, 07/02/93, 7/4/93, and 07/5/93—if you define each sort key as numeric. However, if you use alphanumeric sort keys for each word, the list will sort incorrectly as 07/02/93, 07/5/93, 7/01/93, and 7/4/93.

Sorting Codes and Table Lines

WordPerfect sorts codes along with any line that it moves, which can disrupt formatting such as bold and italic and fonts. Your best bet is to use Document Initial Codes or Initial Codes Setup (Chapter 19) to keep page-formatting codes out of the document. If that doesn't do the trick, avoid doing any fancy formatting until after the sort is complete.

You may also need to change a table's line styles after sorting, because lines are sorted with their rows. (Chapter 7 explains how to create and change tables.)

Changing the Sorting Language

One language's alphabetical order can be another language's alphabetical chaos, if the two languages' alphabets differ. Fortunately, you can easily sort text according to the conventions of another language. First, move the cursor to where you want the new language sort order to kick in, or select a block of text. Then choose Layout ➤ Other ➤ Language, or press Shift+F8 OL and select the language you want.

Troubleshooting Sorts

If your sorted text doesn't come out in the order you expected, or if the sort order appears to be random, look for these sure causes of bad sorts:

- You may have defined the wrong text as the sort key. Or you used the wrong sort type (numeric instead of alphanumeric, or vice versa). This is probably the most common error.

- You haven't handled tabs and indents properly (see the suggestions in the section just below).

- You didn't choose the correct record type for the sort. Remember, sorting will work correctly *only* if you assign the proper record type—Line, Paragraph, Table, etc.

- Your records aren't structured uniformly. For example, the Name field of one record contains Address data in another record.

- You forgot to choose Perform Action after defining the sort keys.

N O T E   Some text is impossible to sort simply because it isn't arranged in any kind of field-and-record order.

Troubles with Tab Stops

Tab stops can pose special problems. Always remember to account for tabs and indents between fields in a line or paragraph, keeping in mind that *every* tab or indent defines a new field. For example, if you've indented the first column of text, that text is in field 2, the next field is field 3, and so forth. (The bibliography example in Figure 22.8 illustrates how to handle field numbering when tabs and indents appear at the beginning of a line.)

Another problem can occur if you don't define tab stops before typing text. For example, in the first of the two records shown below, the address is in field 3 because it's preceded by two [Lft Tab] codes. But in the second record, the address is in field 4 because it's preceded by three [Lft Tab] codes (field 3 contains nothing in that record).

John Jones[Lft Tab]   ABC Corporation[Lft Tab]   123 Apple St.
Nancy Wilcox[Lft Tab] XYZ Co.[Lft Tab][Lft Tab]   345 Oak St.

To fix this problem, you must first redefine the tab stops so that you need only one tab code to separate each column of text (see Chapter 5). Then remove any extra tab codes so that text aligns properly in each column. When that's done, you can define your sort keys and perform the sort.

Isolating Information

In Chapter 21 we talked about ways you could select (or isolate) certain records to include in a merge. You can do the same thing with any text by defining selection criteria in the Sort dialog box.

There is one very important point to keep in mind, however, when you define selection criteria using the Sort dialog box. When you define selection criteria during a merge, WordPerfect just *excludes* records that don't meet your selection criteria. But when you define selection criteria using the Sort dialog box, as we'll be discussing in a moment, WordPerfect actually *deletes* the information that doesn't match your selection criteria. The difference is so important, it deserves its own section, which I think I'll write right now.

Warning! WordPerfect Deletes When It Selects!

Let's say you have a list of 500 names and addresses in a WordPerfect document. You use the Sort dialog box to isolate addresses in, say, the city of Cucamonga. When the selection is done, you have a list of, say, 50 Cucamonga residents. Then you print that list.

If you now *save* that list under the same file name, that list of 50 will *replace* your original list of 500—meaning you just sent 450 names and addresses to permanent data heaven. Gone. Unrecoverable. If you didn't do it on purpose, it's a major bummer.

Therefore, I strongly suggest that *before you use the Select capabilities of the Sort dialog box, you open the document you plan to select from and immediately use File* ➤ *Save As to save this copy under a different file name.* If you do that before you even get to the sort dialog box, you don't have to worry about forgetting to later. So even if you do save, on impulse, the document with only selected records in it, you won't accidentally overwrite your original copy.

Steps for Isolating Text

The steps for isolating text are exactly the same as steps 1–7 under "Sorting Your Text" earlier in this chapter. In the Sort dialog box, you can still define any sort keys, if you want to put the text in some kind of sorted order. *You must also define any text that you want to base a selection on as a sort key, even if you don't plan to actually sort on that field.* For example, if you want to alphabetize a mailing list by name, but include only Cucamonga residents in the list, you must define the people's names as the sort key(s), then also define the city as a sort key. Make sure you put the sort keys that you actually want to sort on first in the list.

Once you've defined all your sort and selection keys, you can stay in the Sort dialog box and start defining your *selection criteria.* Just choose Select Records in the Sort dialog box. The dialog box changes to show you Selection Operators, as shown below.

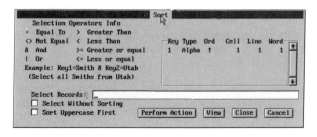

The cursor will also be in the Select Records text box, where you can type a selection criterion using the general format

KeyNumber Operator Value

KeyNumber should be the word *key* followed by the number of the sort key that represents the text you want to search. The *Operator* is one of the Selection Operators shown in the dialog box and summarized in Table 22.1. The *Value* is what you want to search for. For example, if you isolated the city portion of text as the third sort key, you'd type in your selection criterion like this:

key3=Cucamonga

Once you've finished defining your selection criterion (or multiple criteria, as I'll discuss in a moment), don't forget to choose <u>P</u>erform Action to get the job done.

TABLE 22.1: Selection Operators and How They're Used

SYMBOL	PURPOSE	EXAMPLES
=	Selects records that have *exactly the same* information in the indicated key.	**key3=92123** selects only the records in the 92123 zip code.
<>	Selects records that *do not match* the information in the indicated key.	**key3<>92123** selects only the records that *aren't* in the 92123 zip code.
& (AND)	Selects records that meet conditions of *both* keys. You can use the character & or the word AND for this operator.	**key3=92123 and key1<>Smith** selects every record in the 92123 zip code *except* those where key 1 is Smith.
| (OR)	Selects records that meet the conditions of *either* key. You can use the character | or the word OR for this operator.	**key1=Smith or key2=Arizona** selects any records that include Smith in key 1 or Arizona in key 3.
>	Selects records that have values *greater than* the information in the indicated key.	**key4>4700** selects any records where the value in key 4 exceeds 4700.
<	Selects records that have values *less than* the information in the indicated key.	**key4<4700** selects any records where the value in key 4 is less than 4700.
>=	Selects records that have values *greater than or equal to* the information in the indicated key.	**key4>=4700** selects any records where the value in key 4 is greater than or equal to 4700.

TABLE 22.1: Selection Operators and How They're Used (continued)

SYMBOL	PURPOSE	EXAMPLES
<=	Selects records that have values *less than or equal to* the information in the indicated key.	**key4<=4700** selects any records where the value in key 4 is less than or equal to 4700.
g	Global key that means "any key."	**keyg=45** selects records that have the value 45 in any key.
(...)	You can use parentheses to change the selection order (see "Refining Your Selection Criteria with Parentheses").	**key3=92123 & (key1=Jones | key1=Smith)** selects any Jones or Smith who lives in the 92123 zip code area. Without the parentheses, this would select any Jones living in the 92123 zip code, and all Smiths.

Remember, WordPerfect will still *sort* on any sort keys you've defined. In addition, it will *isolate* records for which you've defined selection criteria.

Figure 22.13 illustrates a sort key that will sort a list of names and addresses in zip-code order (key 1, field 4, word 1), then by street name (key 2, field 2, word 2), and then by street number (key 3, field 2, word 1). (If this list included several people at each address, the list would also be sorted by last name—key4, field 1, word –1. You could add a fifth key, field 1 and word 1, to further sort by first name within the same last name.) Thanks to the selection criteria in the Select Records box (*key4<>Schumack*), the sort will retain only those records that don't have *Schumack* as the last name.

Using AND and OR

The AND and OR operators can be a bit difficult to master if you're human (like most people) and don't have the mind of a computer programmer. Fortunately, if your first attempt doesn't do the trick, you can just choose Edit ➤ Undo or press Ctrl+Z to undo your selection. Then choose Tools ➤ Sort again, adjust your criteria, and choose Perform Action to see the improved results. Let's take a quick look at some of the AND and OR traps that might trip you up.

FIGURE 22.13

Sorting records that don't include Schumack by zip, street name, and street number

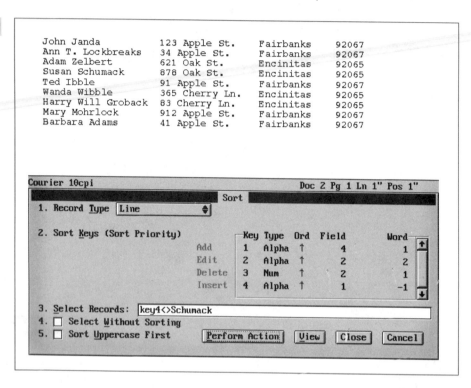

Creating AND and OR Criteria

When combining selection criteria, don't forget to use all three elements—key numbers, selection operators, and search values—on *both* sides of the AND (&) and OR (|) combination characters. For example, you might think that WordPerfect is smart enough to read

    key1>=92000 AND <=92999

as "zip codes that are greater than or equal to 92000 AND less than 92999." But that's simply not the case, because (as we like to point out from time to time) computers have the IQ of toe jam. Instead, this is interpreted as "zip codes that are greater than or equal to 92000 and who-knows-what is less than or equal to 92999."

The same rule holds true for the OR combination operator. Suppose you want to send letters to people in Georgia, Alabama, and Florida, and you've already defined the state field as sort key 1 (*key1* in the selection criteria). What you want to do is delete all records *except* those with GA,

AL, or FL in the state field. But if you incorrectly enter the selection criterion as *key1=GA|AL|FL*, WordPerfect will reject the criteria and display an "Incorrect format" message. The proper way to enter this selection criteria is

key1=GA | key1=AL | key1=FL

NOTE

If you enter a faulty criterion, such as key=GA|AL|FL, you'll get an "Incorrect Format" error on the screen. Choose OK to clear the message, then try again.

Don't Use AND When You Mean OR

It's also important not to confuse the AND and OR operators, because they don't always represent your intent in the same way as you might express it in English. Consider the example of the mailing to residents of Georgia, Alabama, and Florida. You might think that this selection criteria will do the trick:

key1=GA & key1=AL & key1=FL

In English this says, "Keep only those records that have GA in the state field, *AND* AL in the state field, *AND* FL in the state field." WordPerfect, however, interprets this as "Keep records that have GA AL FL in the state field." A single record couldn't possibly have all three states in its state field, so the results of the selection would be no records at all.

Remember that you aren't asking a question in English when you define selection criteria. Instead, you're setting up a screen, or filter, through which some records will pass and some won't. WordPerfect will compare each record, one at a time, with your selection criteria. It retains the record if it can answer Yes to *all* the criteria joined by the AND (&) operator in your selection criteria for that record. Likewise, it retains the record if it can answer Yes to *any* of the criteria joined by the *OR* (|) operator in your selection criteria for that record.

Refining Your Selection Criteria with Parentheses

When selection criteria become rather complicated, you must be careful about how you combine the AND and OR operators. For example, suppose your document contains (among others) a field for the state where each person lives and a field for each person's credit limit. You then decide to write a form letter to all names in Georgia, and to just the people in Florida whose credit limits are $500 or greater, informing them that you've raised their credit limit by $1,000 (perhaps because the value of their real estate has increased). This requires a selection criterion that combines AND logic and OR logic. You must isolate *all* people who live in Georgia and *only* those in Florida who have credit limits of $500 or more.

If you're not careful in a situation like this one, you may end up creating an ambiguous selection criterion. For example, assume that you've already defined the first sort key as the State field, and the second sort key as the Credit Limit field. You might compose the following selection criterion (though it isn't correct):

    key1=GA|key1=FL&key2>=$500

Your selection criteria are evaluated from left to right unless you use parentheses to change the order. Therefore, WordPerfect will interpret the above criteria as "Select records that have GA or FL in the state field. From that list, select records where the credit limit is greater than or equal to $500." The selection result will include those people in both Georgia and Florida whose credit limits are $500 or greater. However, this doesn't do the job, since you want to include *everyone* in Georgia, regardless of their present credit limit.

To avoid potential confusion with such complicated selection criteria, you can use parentheses to control how WordPerfect interprets your criteria. The correct criteria for our Georgia/Florida example,

    key1=GA|(key1=FL&key2>=$500)

says that, to avoid being deleted, a record must have GA in the state field (so all Georgians will be selected), *OR* FL in the state field *AND* have a value that's greater than or equal to $500 in the credit limit field. This resolves the ambiguity and ensures that *all* Georgians (with any credit limit at all) and *only* those Floridians with credit limits of $500 or more will remain after the select operation is finished.

Making Global Selections

The key name *keyg* allows you to search *all* the sort keys for a specific value. Suppose you create a merge data file that includes both a business address and a home address for each person. To mail letters to everyone who has either a home or business address in New York, define both the home and business state fields as sort keys. Then specify **keyg=NY** as the selection criterion. This will delete all records except those with NY in either the home or business state field.

Now you know everything there is to know about sorting and selecting text in your WordPerfect documents. In the next chapter, we'll look at an entirely different topic: techniques for doing math in your documents.

Sending Faxes from WordPerfect

fast TRACK

○ **To have WordPerfect include a cover sheet
with your fax** **844**

choose File ➤ Print/Fax, choose the recipient(s), then choose
Send Fax. Select the Coversheet option, and choose Send Fax
again.

○ **You can speed your faxes by pre-rasterizing
the file** **844**

you want to send. Choose File ➤ Print/Fax and (if necessary)
choose the printer driver you use to send faxes using the Select command button. Choose Fax Services, mark the person
or group you want to send the fax to in the usual manner, and
choose Send Fax. Choose Save As An Image For Fax On
Disk, then enter a file name. Omit the extension, or enter
.FAX as the extension. Choose other options as appropriate,
then choose Send Fax.

○ **To send a rasterized fax file** **845**

start at the WordPerfect document window, and choose File
➤ Print/Fax ➤ Fax Services (or press Shift+F7 X). Mark with
the * character the Phonebook entries that you want to send
the fax to (or choose Manual Dial). Choose Send Fax, then
choose Fax On Disk. Type the name of your rasterized fax file
or use the File List (F5) and/or QuickList (F6) buttons to locate and select the fax file. Choose Send File.

○ **To take a look at a rasterized fax file
before sending it** **845**

choose File ➤ Print/Fax ➤ Fax Services. Choose the View
Fax Files button, and type in or choose the name of the fax
file you want to view. Then choose Print to print (locally) or
View to preview the fax file.

SENDING a fax from WordPerfect is a lot like printing a document. The difference is that the document is printed on someone else's fax machine, rather than on your printer!

Installing Your Fax Board

It's important to understand that WordPerfect doesn't have any built-in fax capability of its own. Instead, WordPerfect can send documents to your existing fax hardware and software rather than to your own printer. WordPerfect supports the following types of fax boards and fax modems:

- Intel SatisFAXtion Board
- FaxBIOS compatible board
- Class I or II fax modem

You must install and test all your fax hardware and software before using WordPerfect's fax service. Follow the fax board manufacturer's instructions to do so.

If you're prompted for a printer driver type while installing your fax software, be sure to select the printer you use most often. If your printer is not included in the list, choose one that most closely matches your printer (for example, if you're using an HP LaserJet 4, the LaserJet II or III is probably the closest choice).

TIP This may seem obvious, but I'll say it anyway. If you have a dedicated fax number in the office, the easiest way to test your fax board is to send yourself a fax.

Once you've finished installing your fax hardware and software, follow the instructions in the fax board's documentation to ensure that the board works correctly before you proceed to the next section.

Installing WordPerfect Drivers

Once you've installed the fax board and fax software, you need to install the WordPerfect fax drivers to make the connection to your installed fax equipment. (You need only do this once, of course—not every time you want to send a fax.) To install the WordPerfect fax drivers, you'll need to grab a copy of your original WordPerfect 6.0 disks, and follow the general instructions under "Installing New Hardware" in Appendix A. You want to install the *Device Files* (option 4) for *Fax Files* (option 3) once you get into the WordPerfect Install program.

Follow all of the instructions on the screen after making your selection, and pay attention to any instructions telling you about additional programs you'll need to load in order to activate the fax software. You'll probably be given the opportunity to add appropriate commands to your AUTOEXEC.BAT program, so that any necessary faxing programs are automatically loaded when you first start your computer.

TIP If you have DOS 6, you might want to run MemMaker after installing your fax drivers, to conserve memory. See your DOS 6 manual for more information.

The Fax Printer Driver

Earlier I mentioned that if you cannot choose a printer driver for your actual printer while installing your fax board, you should choose a driver that resembles your printer (for instance, the Laserjet III if you're using a LaserJet 4). If you need to do that, you should also make sure you have access to that same printer driver from within WordPerfect.

Start WordPerfect in the usual manner, choose File ➤ Print/Fax, then choose Select. If the driver for your selected printer isn't included in the list, you should install that driver into WordPerfect. Choose Add Printer from the Select Printer dialog box, then add the appropriate printer driver to the list. See Chapter 10 if you need more information on selecting and installing printers.

Setting Up a Phonebook

Though you can "manually" dial any phone number that you want to send a fax to, chances are you'll want to set up a personal phonebook of frequently called fax numbers. There are two general ways to set up a WordPerfect phonebook:

- On some fax systems, WordPerfect will let you add, change, and delete numbers in the phonebook *without* leaving WordPerfect.

- Even if your fax software supports its own phonebook, WordPerfect might not be able to give you direct access to that phonebook. You'll need to add, change, and delete phone numbers using the program(s) that came with your fax hardware, according to the instructions in the fax software manual. Skip to "Sending a Fax," later in this chapter.

Using WordPerfect to Manage a Fax Phonebook

To use WordPerfect to manage a fax phonebook, follow the steps below:

1. Starting at the WordPerfect document window, choose File ➤ Print/Fax ➤ Fax Services (or press Shift+F7 X). You'll be taken to the Fax Services dialog box, shown in Figure 23.1. (Your phone list will be empty if you've never added any phone numbers.)

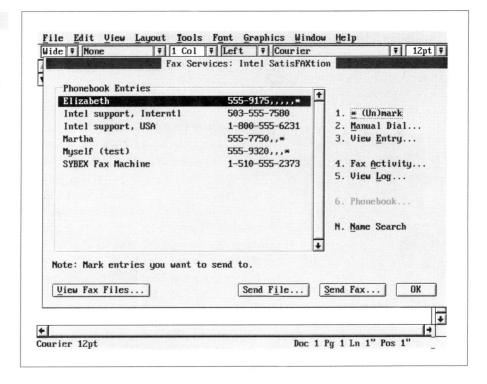

2. Choose Phonebook. (If Phonebook is dimmed and unavailable, you'll need to use your fax software to manage the phonebook.)

3. To add a new recipient to the phonebook, choose Create Entry. Now you'll be taken to the Create Entry dialog box where you can enter the following information for one fax recipient:

> **Name** Enter the fax recipient's name.
>
> **Fax Phone Number** Enter the fax recipient's fax phone number. Use the format recommended in your fax board documentation. Usually, you can include hyphens and commas if you need a pause in the phone number. Here are some examples:
>
> **555–1234** Dials a local fax number.
>
> **1–510–555–1234** Dials a fax number in a different area.
>
> **9,,555–3030** Dials 9 to get an external line, waits four seconds, then dials a local number.

555–9320,,,★ Dials a local number and waits a few seconds for a voice message to complete. Then it presses ★ to switch to fax mode. (Works with certain phones that play the dual role of voice answering machine and fax.)

Voice Phone Number Enter the recipient's voice phone number.

Destination Fax Machine Choose options that define how to send the fax. Higher *resolutions* use more (and smaller) dots to represent the document, giving it a smoother effect. The drawback is that documents with finer resolution take longer to send and can result in higher phone charges. You can usually get away with sending typed or printed documents at the lowest resolutions. *Binary file transfers* let you send your document as a file, so that the recipient can load, edit, and print the document at his or her end. Not all fax modems can handle binary file transfers. See "Binary File Transfers," near the end of this chapter, for more information.

4. Choose OK after adding your phonebook entry.

Other options in the Phonebook dialog box let you change and delete names, create groups, and so forth. These are the options available:

Select Different Phonebook Lets you switch between different phonebooks that you've created (if your fax software supports multiple phonebooks).

Create Group Lets you collect several individual entries into a group. For example, you can create a group called *Newsletter* and add to it all the people on your newsletter mailing list. Once you've defined a group, you can send to all the people in that group simply by selecting the group name in the Phonebook Entries list.

Edit Lets you change the highlighted individual or group entry.

Delete Lets you delete the highlighted individual or group entry.

Name Search Lets you find an entry by typing its name.

Remember that the options available for managing a phonebook really depend on the fax hardware you're using. If you have any problems, you should learn how to manage phonebooks directly from your fax board's documentation.

Sending a Fax

Once you've gotten your fax equipment squared away, sending a Word-Perfect document as a fax is easy:

1. Start WordPerfect as usual, then create or open the document you want to send. If you want to send a block of text, select that text now. If you want to send just a single page, move your cursor anywhere on that page.

2. If you use multiple printers, choose File ➤ Print/Fax ➤ Select and choose the printer driver you installed for sending faxes (for example, LaserJet III even though you are really using a LaserJet 4 locally). If you forget this step, you'll probably see an error message such as "Invalid .DRS File..." or "Unable to access client..." when you try to send the fax.

3. Starting at the document window, choose File ➤ Print/Fax ➤ Fax Services. The Fax Services dialog box will appear.

4. Now, do one of the following to select your recipients:

   - Mark the individual(s) or group(s) who should receive your fax by double-clicking, or by highlighting and pressing ↵ or ★. Then choose Send Fax.
   - To send the fax to someone who is not in your phonebook, choose Manual Dial and enter the recipient's name and fax number. Then choose OK.

5. The Send Fax dialog box, shown in Figure 23.2, will appear. From here, sending a fax is similar to printing a document. Your main choices are described below.

   Full Document   Sends the entire document.

   Page   Sends the current page only.

FIGURE 23.2

The Send Fax
dialog box

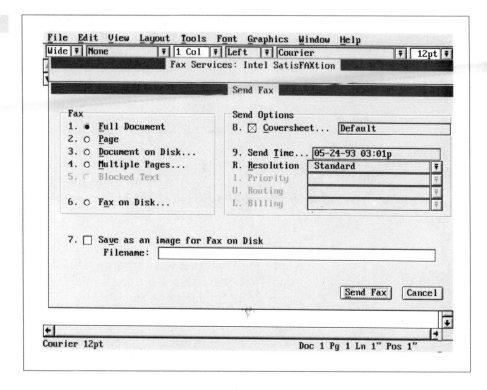

Document on Disk   Lets you send a document that's stored on disk.

Multiple Pages   Lets you send a range of pages.

Blocked Text   Lets you send text that you selected in step 1 (available only if you've already selected text).

Fax on Disk   Lets you send an image that you've previously saved as a rasterized file. (See "About Rasterization," below.)

Save as an Image for Fax on Disk   Saves a rasterized copy of the document. (See "About Rasterization," below.)

Coversheet   If selected, this option sends your cover sheet first. If cleared, it does not send the cover sheet. In most cases, the cover sheet is one you created with your fax software, not WordPerfect.

Send Time   Lets you specify a delivery date and time. The file will be sent automatically when your computer or network calendar and clock match the specified time. This is handy for delaying the delivery until phone rates are cheaper. This feature will work even if you leave WordPerfect, as long as you leave your computer or network on.

Resolution   Lets you choose a resolution quality.

Priority   Lets you specify a priority for your fax (if appropriate for your fax hardware).

Routing   Lets you specify which fax line you want to use (if appropriate for your fax hardware).

Billing   Lets you specify whom to charge for this fax (if appropriate for your fax hardware).

6. When you're done selecting options, choose the Send Fax command button near the bottom of the dialog box.

7. Choose OK as appropriate to return to the document window. WordPerfect will continue to send faxes, even as you create and edit new documents.

That's all there is to it. WordPerfect will send the document through your fax board. If you opted to send the fax immediately, you can choose Fax Activity from the Fax Services dialog box to watch the action as the fax is being sent. The fax Job Status box will inform you of the fax's progress. You can also choose View Log from the Fax Services dialog box to review a list of faxes you've sent or received.

Canceling a Fax

If you need to cancel a fax that you're currently sending, get to the Fax Activity dialog box. (That is, if you're at the document window, choose File ➤ Print/Fax ➤ Fax Services.) Choose Fax Activity from the Fax Services dialog box, then choose Cancel Current Fax.

To cancel a fax you've scheduled for later delivery, you'll probably need to go through your fax software rather than WordPerfect. Check your fax board's faxing documentation for information on canceling pending (or unsent) faxes.

About Fax Cover Sheets

You can choose whether to have WordPerfect automatically send a cover sheet with your fax. Start to send your document in the normal manner (File ➤ Print/Fax), choose your recipient(s), and choose Send Fax. To include a cover sheet, select the Coversheet option. If you don't want a cover sheet, deselect that option. Then choose Send Fax as usual.

For more information on creating, editing, and using fax cover sheets, please refer to the documentation that came with your fax board.

About Rasterization

Before a document can be sent from your computer to a fax machine, it needs to be *rasterized*. When you use the techniques above to send a fax, WordPerfect rasterizes the file before sending it. Though this step is totally automatic, it does take some time.

You can speed up your faxes by pre-rasterizing the file you want to send. Here's how to do it:

1. Choose File ➤ Print/Fax and (if necessary) choose the printer driver you use to send faxes, using the Select command button.

2. Choose Fax Services.

3. Mark the person or group you want to send the fax to, as explained earlier, then choose Send Fax.

4. Choose Save As An Image For Fax On Disk, then enter a file name. Omit the extension, or enter .FAX as the extension (for example, MYFAX.FAX). By default, the document will be stored on the same directory as your other WordPerfect documents.

5. Choose other options as appropriate (such as Coversheet), then choose Send Fax.

6. If you don't want to send the fax right now, choose Fax Activity, then choose Cancel Current Fax. Otherwise, just let the fax board send the file now.

Sending a Rasterized Fax File

Let's assume that you've performed the steps above, and you've created a rasterized fax file named MYFAX.FAX. You have not sent it to anyone yet, but now you want to send it to some group or individual. Starting at the WordPerfect document window, you'd follow these steps:

1. Choose File ➤ Print/Fax ➤ Fax Services (or press Shift+F7 X).

2. Mark with the usual * character the phonebook entries that you want to send the fax to. Or choose Manual Dial as described earlier.

3. Choose Send Fax, then choose Fax On Disk.

WARNING	Don't confuse Fax On Disk, which sends rasterized files, with Document On Disk, which sends unrasterized WordPerfect documents.

4. Type the name of your rasterized fax file (MYFAX.FAX in this example) or use the File List (F5) and/or QuickList (F6) buttons to locate and select the fax file.

5. Choose Send File.

WordPerfect will send the fax without first going through the rasterization process.

Viewing and Printing Faxes

If you rasterize a fax file then want to take a look at it before sending it, choose File ➤ Print/Fax ➤ Fax Services. Choose the View Fax Files button, and type in or choose the name of the fax file you want to view. You can then choose Print to print the fax file (locally) or View to preview it.

You can (probably) use this same technique to view or print a rasterized fax file that someone else sent to your computer. However, you'll need to refer to your fax board documentation for more information on viewing and printing faxes that were sent directly to your computer.

Reversing Black and White

If you view a fax file, and it's shown in negative (white print on a black background), you can choose View ➤ Invert Page to switch to the more normal black-and-white view.

Editing Received Faxes

To convert a fax file that's been sent to you into an editable document, you'll need to buy special OCR software. For example, Omnipage from Caere Corporation (800)535-SCAN can convert from a variety of fax and graphics formats into a text file that you can edit.

You won't need to bother with this conversion, however, if you transfer (or upload/download) the file between computers using a regular data modem and software. Chances are, your fax board can double as a regular data modem. See your fax board documentation to find out, and for instructions on sending and receiving files via modem.

Binary File Transfers

Some fax boards are capable of sending and receiving unrasterized files directly from one computer disk to another. This technique, however, is not the same as transferring a file with a data modem. Rather, it's strictly reserved for fax boards that support BFT, and that can answer a phone and print a file to disk without any input from the person at the receiving end of the transfer.

You should definitely check your fax board's documentation to find out if the board supports BFT. You also need to make sure the recipient's board supports BFT. If they both do, you can use the Binary File Transfer method, which is almost identical to the method for sending a fax:

1. Starting at the WordPerfect document window, choose File ➤ Print/Fax ➤ Fax Services (or press Shift+F7 X).

2. Select your recipient(s) in the usual manner, then choose Send File (rather than Send Fax).

3. Type the name of the file you want to send, or use the File Manager (F5) or QuickList (F6) to select file(s) to send.

4. Choose other options as appropriate, then select the Send File command button.

If you change your mind about sending a file before it's actually sent, you can repeat the general steps above. Then highlight the name of the file you don't want to send, and choose the Remove From List option in the Send File dialog box.

As you've learned in this chapter, using WordPerfect's fax capabilities is a three-step process:

- Install your fax board and software according to the manufacturer's instructions. Learn to use that software well enough to send a fax and test the installation.

- Make the connection between WordPerfect and your fax board by installing the WordPerfect fax drivers (using the WordPerfect 6.0 for DOS Install program).

- To send a fax from WordPerfect, choose File ➤ Print/Fax ➤ Fax Services, choose your recipients, and send the fax.

In the next chapter, I'll focus on another useful office tool: WordPerfect's mail feature.

Sending Interoffice
Mail from WordPerfect

To send a message from the Shell

go to the Shell Message Board dialog box and choose <u>A</u>dd. Choose the <u>S</u>ubject, <u>M</u>essage, <u>A</u>ttachment, and <u>F</u>rom options as appropriate. When you're ready to send the message, choose OK.

To read a message in the Shell

go to the Shell Message Board dialog box, highlight the message you want to look at, and choose <u>R</u>ead. You can view the message or its attachment, list other replies to this message, and enter your own reply to the message. Choose Close when you're done.

FOR YEARS you've probably relied on the infamous "sneak-ernet" to send messages and information to other people in your office or workgroup. That is, you printed a document or copied it to a floppy disk, and then carried the papers to whoever needed them. If you just needed to send a note, you may have scribbled something on a note and stuck it to the recipient's chair.

Those days are long gone for people who use personal computer networks. A *network* is a collection of cables and other hardware, plus the appropriate software, connecting two or more computers. Network users can easily share files, printers, high-speed modems, and other resources. What's more, network users can send electronic messages from one PC to another. Electronic mail, or *e-mail* for short, travels rapidly, doesn't need to be printed before it's read, and can easily be incorporated into reports and other documents.

WordPerfect offers two ways to send electronic information to other people on your network. The first is the Message Board, which is part of the separate Shell 4.0 program that comes with WordPerfect. The Shell is installed automatically when you install WordPerfect. If you are connected to another computer and can share files, you can use the Shell's Message Board features to

- Compose, read, reply to, and delete messages on a central message board.

- Save retrieved messages as text files or WordPerfect 6.0 files.

- Attach files of any type to your messages—including text files, WordPerfect documents, graphics, and sound files.

- View attached files and copy them to another file.

The second e-mail feature is available directly from WordPerfect itself. This feature works by sending your current document to your network's e-mail software. From there, your network mail program takes over, and you use that program's commands to receive messages, reply to messages, and manage them. To send mail from WordPerfect, your network mail software must be active, and it must fall into one of two mail protocol categories: *VIM* or *MAPI*. VIM was developed by Lotus, and MAPI was developed by Microsoft. Please see your network administrator or check the documentation that came with your mail software if you're not sure which protocol the mail program uses.

The main differences between using the Message Board in the Shell and using the e-mail feature in WordPerfect are as follows:

- The Shell's Message Board works without any additional mail software, and it includes all the tools you need to send, read, and reply to messages.

- The Shell's features are generally simpler than those offered by network mail packages. For example, the Shell can't direct mail to specific people or mailboxes; anyone with full access to the message directory can read and delete messages; and there's no automatic notification when messages arrive.

- WordPerfect's mail feature ties into your existing network mail program. Thus, you can use any features of your network mail program to route e-mail to specific people, reply to messages, and manage messages. Typically, the e-mail software will alert the recipient automatically when mail arrives.

Getting Started with Messages and Mail

Both the Message Board and mail features require you to have a network (of some type) installed so you can share files. I'll assume your network is already up and running and that you're connected to it. If you're not sure how to connect to your network, please ask your network administrator for help.

You must also have installed the network version of WordPerfect, by choosing Network Installation from the WordPerfect 6.0 Installation screen. I'll assume that's done, as well. (If you haven't installed WordPerfect for network use, please refer to Appendix A.)

What you do next depends on whether you want to use Message Board features in Shell, or network mail. If you want to use the Message Board, you first need to start Shell (described shortly). If you want to use your network mail program from WordPerfect instead, just go on to the next section.

Sending Mail from WordPerfect

To use WordPerfect's mail features, follow these basic steps:

1. Connect to the network.

2. Start the e-mail system on your computer. Remember, you must have an e-mail system that supports the VIM or MAPI protocol, or you won't be able to use WordPerfect's mail feature.

3. Start WordPerfect. When prompted, type in your network user initials (up to five characters) and press ↵.

4. Open the document that you want to send as mail (File ➤ Open).

5. Choose File ➤ Go To Shell ➤ Mail Current Document As A Message, or press Ctrl+F1 M.

6. From here, the steps for sending mail (or reading it) will depend on the type of e-mail system you're using. If you need help with this, please see your network administrator.

Using Shell

WordPerfect's Shell program lets you run several programs at once (including WordPerfect), and it includes the Message Board feature described in this chapter. The first time you use Shell, you may need to complete some setup steps. After that, it will be smooth sailing.

Here's how to set up Shell:

1. Connect to your network, if you haven't done so already.

2. Normally, Shell resides in the directory C:\WPC6DOS. To launch Shell, start at the DOS prompt, and type these commands:

```
cd \wpc6dos
shell
```

TIP   If you add C:\WPC6DOS to the PATH statement in your AUTOEXEC.BAT file, you can skip the *cd \wpc6dos* command above.

3. If prompted, type your initials (up to five letters) and press ↵.

4. If Shell greets you with a Getting Started screen, choose <u>C</u>reate Menu Manually, type in a description for your startup menu, and choose OK.

5. If you'd like to run WordPerfect from Shell, and you don't see an option for WordPerfect in Shell's menu, press the Insert key to adds a new menu item, and then choose <u>P</u>rogram. In the <u>D</u>escription box, type a description and press ↵ (e.g., **WordPerfect**). In the <u>F</u>ilename box, type the location of your WordPerfect program (for example, **c:\wp60\wp.exe**). Then choose OK.

You only need to do steps 4 and 5 the first time you run Shell. The next time you run Shell, just follow the first three steps.

Here are some additional tips for using Shell:

- To run WordPerfect from Shell, highlight the WordPerfect option you defined in step 5 of the procedure above and press ↵, or double-click the option.

- When you want to return to Shell from WordPerfect, choose <u>F</u>ile ➤ <u>G</u>o To Shell ➤ <u>A</u>ctive Programs (Ctrl+F1 A). Double-click Shell, or highlight Shell in the list and press ↵.

- To exit Shell and any programs that you're running from Shell, return to Shell and choose File ➤ Exit ➤ Yes.

- If you need help using Shell, press the F1 key. Shell's online help is similar to WordPerfect's online help.

- If you don't need to send messages to people on another computer, you can run Shell without connecting to the network first.

Using the Message Board

The Message Board in Shell provides simple e-mail features that you can use regardless of whether you have a fancy mail package installed on your network. The first time you use the Message Board, you'll need to define its location.

Your network administrator may already have designated the message board's location. You should find out where that directory is, and then follow the steps below to give the information to WordPerfect.

Setting Up the Message Board

Here's how to set up the message board:

1. Start Shell as described earlier in "Using Shell."

2. Choose File ➤ Setup ➤ Location Of Files ➤ Messages.

3. Type the directory location of the message board, and press ↵. (If the directory name you entered doesn't exist yet, WordPerfect will ask if you want it to create that directory for you.)

4. Choose OK then Close to return to Shell.

Using the Message Board

Using Shell's message board is easy. Just follow these steps:

1. Choose Tools ➤ Message Board from Shell's menus, or press F8. You'll see the Shell Message Board dialog box, shown in Figure 24.1. (In the example shown in the figure, I've already added one message to the message board.)

FIGURE 24.1

The Shell Message
Board dialog box

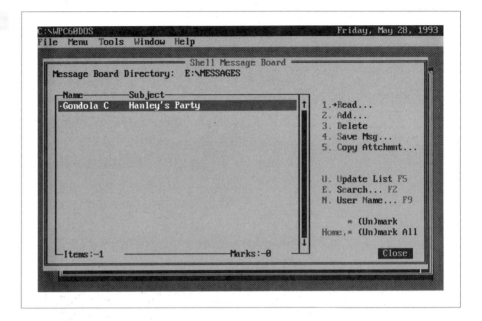

2. To change the user name that will automatically appear in the "From" portion of your messages, choose User Name or press F9. Then enter a user name and choose OK.

3. To update the current list of messages to include any new messages that have arrived since you opened the Message Board dialog box, choose Update List or press F5.

4. If you want to send a new message, choose Add and follow the instructions in "Sending Messages," below. Alternatively, you can highlight an existing message and then read, delete, or save it to a file, or copy its attachment to a file. (The available options are described just below.)

5. When you're finished using the Shell Message Board, choose Close. You'll be returned to Shell's main menus.

Now here's a summary of the options available to you in the Shell Message Board dialog box. In a moment, I'll explain more about the Add and Read options.

Read   Lets you read the highlighted message and reply to it if you wish.

Add   Lets you compose a new message, attach any file to it, and send the message.

Delete   (Also the Delete key) Lets you delete the highlighted message.

Save Msg   Lets you save the highlighted message to a text file, a WordPerfect 6.0 document file, or to the Shell's Clipboard.

Copy Attchmnt   Lets you copy a message's attached file to a new file name.

Update List   (Also F5) Updates the current list of messages to include any new messages that have arrived recently.

Search   (Also F2) Lets you limit the message list to those messages with specific text in their "From" or "Subject" portions. After you choose this option, a Search dialog box will appear. In the Search For text box, type the text you want to search for and press ↵. If you want to search the "From" portion of the message, select (check) Search Name. If you want to search the "Subject" portion, select Search Subject. Choose Search or press F2 to start the search. The resulting message list will show only those messages in which the "From" text or "Subject" text (or both) matches the search text you entered.

User Name   (Also F9) Lets you change the user name that appears in the From portion of your messages or replies.

T I P

You can mark (or unmark) groups of messages by highlighting them and choosing * (Un)mark, or by pressing the spacebar or * key. Then, you can delete the marked set of messages, save them, or copy their attached files in a single step.

Sending Messages

Here are the steps for sending a message to the Message Board:

1. In the Shell Message Board dialog box, choose <u>A</u>dd. You'll then see the Add Message dialog box (Figure 24.2 shows the Add Message dialog box after I filled in a complete message).

2. In the <u>S</u>ubject box, type the subject of your message and press ↵. (If this message is for a specific person, you might want to start the subject entry with that person's name—for example, **Bill G-- Meeting Today at Noon.**)

3. In the <u>M</u>essage box, enter the text of your message. As you type, the message will word-wrap automatically. You only need to press the ↵ key to end a paragraph or a short line, or to insert blank lines. When you're done, press Tab or F7.

FIGURE 24.2

The Add Message dialog box after filling in a message and before sending it

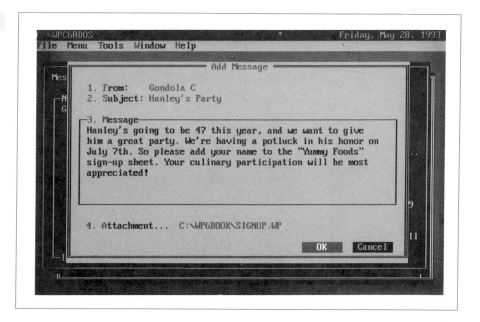

Sorry, no fancy formatting is available when you send a message. However, you *can* send any formatted file as an attachment (see step 4).

4. If you'd like to send a file as an attachment to the message, choose the Attachment option, type the file name of the file you want to attach, and choose OK. (You can attach *any* file you want, including text files, WordPerfect files, graphics files, and sound files.)

5. If you need to revise any information in your message before sending it, choose the From, Subject, Message, or Attachment options as necessary. Then use the mouse or cursor-positioning keys and the usual editing keys to make your changes. When you're finished making a change, press F7. To cancel a change, press Esc.

6. Choose OK to send the message and return to the Message Board.

Reading Messages

Anyone with access to the message board directory can read a message. Here's how:

1. Starting from the main Shell screen, choose Tools ➤ Message Board, or press F8.

2. Highlight the message you want to read and choose Read. Figure 24.3 shows the Read Message dialog box that appeared when I chose to read the message sent from the dialog box shown in Figure 24.2.

You'll be able to see the top part of the message in the Message window. If the message is longer than one window, you'll need to choose Read Msg or click in the Message window to view the rest of it. Once you reach the window, you can use the cursor-positioning keys or the scroll bars to look through the message. When you're done scrolling through the message, press Tab, F7, or Esc.

FIGURE 24.3

The Read Message
dialog box

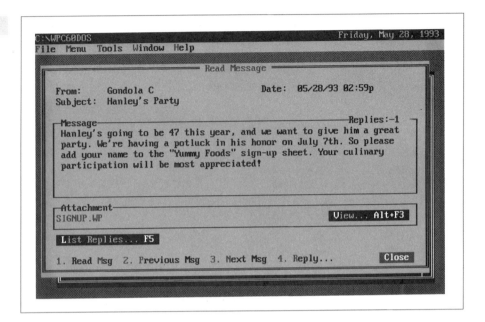

TIP

You can make it easier for recipients to know whether they've reached the end of a message by finishing up with some standard closing like ### *Later Dude!* ###. Whenever recipients see ### *Later Dude!* ### in your message, they'll know there's nothing more to read.

Here are some additional options and buttons you can choose in the Read Message dialog box:

View   (Also Alt+F3) Lets you view the file that's attached to the current message. After choosing this option, you can scroll through the attached message file and even search for specific text in the file. When you're finished viewing the message file, choose Cancel or press Esc.

List Replies (Also F5) If anyone has responded to the current message, choosing this option switches you to the Message Replies dialog box. From here, you can highlight the reply you're interested in and read or delete it. You can also save it as a file, copy its attached file (if it has one), and search for replies based on text in the "From" or "Subject" portion of the messages. When you're ready to return to the current message, choose Close.

NOTE Most options in the Message Replies dialog box are the same as for the Shell Message Board dialog box, discussed in "Using the Message Board," earlier in this chapter.

Previous Msg Displays the previous message and makes it the current message. If no previous message exists, you'll be returned to the Shell Message Board dialog box.

Next Msg Displays the next message and makes it the current message. If no next message exists, you'll be returned to the Shell Message Board dialog box.

Reply Opens the Message Reply dialog box, where you can reply to the current message. When prompted, type a subject (or accept the suggested subject) and press ↵. Then type your reply into the Message window, just as you do when you're adding a new message. Press F7 or Tab when you're done. If you wish to edit the reply further, you can choose the From, Subject, Message, or Attachment options. When you're finished, choose OK. Your reply will appear in the Message Replies dialog box.

When you're done using the Read Message dialog box, you can choose the Close button. You'll return to the Shell Message Board dialog box.

You now know how to set up and use the WordPerfect Message Board and mail features, which let you send interoffice e-mail. Next, we'll look at another handy tool for the office: WordPerfect's impressive ability to do math in tables. Spreadsheet programs beware! You now have a rival in WordPerfect.

Perfect Math: The Built-in Calculator and Spreadsheet

fast **TRACK**

**To exclude a cell from a subtotal, total,
or grand total calculation** 879

go to Table Edit mode, move the cursor to the cell or select the
range of cells that you want to exclude. Then choose Cell and
select the Ignore When Calculating check box.

**If the result of a calculation in your document
looks wrong** 879

chances are that you just need to recalculate. In the document
window, choose Layout ➤ Tables ➤ Calculate All (Alt+F7
TA), or choose the Calc button in Table Edit mode.

To protect cells that contain formulas 883

from being changed accidentally, go to Table Edit mode
(Alt+F11). Select the cells you want to protect. Choose Cell
and then select the Lock check box.

**To name a table cell or group of cells
for easy reference** 884

go to Table Edit mode (Alt+F11) and highlight the cell, group
of cells, row, or column that you want to name. Then choose
the Names button and select options from the dialog boxes
that follow.

To add a floating cell to your document 887

that's useful when you just need a single quick calculation, position the cursor in the regular document window. Then choose
Layout ➤ Tables ➤ Create Floating Cell (Alt+F7 FC). To edit
the floating cell later, move the to cursor to the floating cell and
choose Layout ➤ Tables ➤ Edit Floating Cell (Alt+F7 FE).

WORDPERFECT offers several tools that let you perform math calculations right in your documents. These tools are sure to please the math whizzes as well as the math-a-phobes among you.

First, there's the pop-up Calculator, which is great for doing an occasional quick calculation and copying the results to your document. This handy feature is a macro that comes with WordPerfect, and it works just like the garden-variety pocket or desk calculator that replaced slide rules so long ago.

Second, there's Table Math, perfect for creating invoices, financial statements, and other documents that require spreadsheet-style calculations and formulas.

Finally, you can import or link existing spreadsheets from PlanPerfect, Lotus 1-2-3, Excel, Quattro Pro, and other formats right into your WordPerfect document. I'll cover this last topic in Chapter 33.

Using the Pop-up Calculator

To do a quick calculation on the fly, use the WordPerfect pop-up Calculator, available from the Tools menu:

1. Position the cursor where you want the calculated number to appear in your document.

2. Choose Tools ➤ Macro ➤ Play (Alt+F10).

3. Type **calc,** or choose CALC.WPM from the File List.

4. Choose OK. The Calculator will appear on your screen, as shown here:

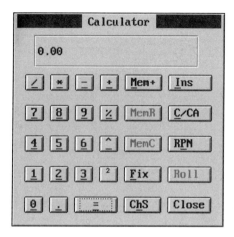

Use the Calculator as you would use any pocket calculator. Click the buttons with your mouse, or type the character that is underlined or highlighted on the button. Once you've got the numeric result you want, just choose the Calculator's Ins button to insert that number into your document. When you're done with the Calculator, choose the Close button.

Suppose you need to calculate a quick 7.75% sales tax on $123.45 and then add that sales tax to the $123.45. Here are the steps to do this using the Calculator:

1. Position the cursor in your document where you want to insert the calculated total.

2. Open the pop-up the Calculator, as described above.

TIP

If the = button isn't visible on your calculator, type n or click the <u>N</u>orm button to switch from the R<u>P</u>N (Reverse Polish Notation) calculator to the normal calculator. (The normal calculator is the default.)

3. Type **123.45** (or click each number button on the Calculator).

4. Type * (for multiplication), or click the * button.

5. Type **1.0775** (or click those numbers on the Calculator).

6. Type **=** (or click the = button).

7. Type **i** or click the <u>I</u>ns button.

8. If you want to do another calculation, type **c** or click the <u>C</u>/CA (Clear/Clear All) button. Otherwise, if you're done with the calculator, choose the Close button or press F7.

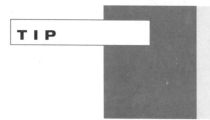

TIP

If you use the calculator often, consider adding it to the Button Bar (Chapter 4) or copying it to an Alt+*key* macro (Chapter 18). The calculator is a macro named CALC.WPM in your WordPerfect macros directory.

After you close the calculator, you can type in dollar signs at the start of the number in your document. Be aware that the number in your document is just typed text. Unlike table formulas, described later in this chapter, there is no way to automatically recalculate a result obtained with the Calculator if you change other numbers in the document. You'll have to delete the number, pop up the calculator, and redo the calculation from scratch.

Using the Built-in Spreadsheet

WordPerfect's built-in spreadsheet features have much in common with spreadsheet applications such as Lotus 1-2-3, Excel, and Quattro Pro. So if you're familiar with spreadsheet basics and WordPerfect tables, you'll have no trouble mastering WordPerfect's Table Math.

You start by creating a table, as explained in Chapter 7. Then, you place your numbers in the table's cells, using the normal document window. When you're ready to define the formulas and functions for your calculations, position the cursor in any table cell and go to Table Edit mode (Layout ➤ Tables ➤ Edit, or Alt+F11). From here, you can define the formulas and functions you want to use, update the calculation results, and customize the format of the numbers.

WordPerfect's built-in spreadsheet is great for creating invoices, financial statements, and other complex documents that require many calculations. You can even create template documents that contain formulas. Then you just fill in the exact numbers you want to work with and tell WordPerfect to calculate the results. The whole setup job takes only a few minutes, and calculations are almost instantaneous.

N O T E

In this chapter, I'll assume you already know the basics of creating and editing tables, as discussed in Chapter 7, and you've created a table to hold your numbers and calculation results. That way we can focus here on the mathematical aspects of tables.

Entering Numbers in Cells

Entering a number into a table cell is easy. Start from the document window (not from Table Edit mode), position the cursor in the appropriate table cell, and type the number just as you would type any text. The number can contain decimal points, comma separators, and a leading dollar sign if you wish. For example, **1000, 1,000, 1,000.00** and **$1,000.00** are all valid ways to type in the number one thousand.

To enter a negative number, precede it with a minus sign (hyphen), or enclose the number in parentheses. For example, you can enter any of the following to express negative one thousand or minus one thousand: **–1000, –1000.00, –1,000.00, –$1,000.00, $–1,000.00, (1,000),** or **$(1,000.00)**. (To type a minus sign, use either the hyphen key or the gray – minus key on the numeric keypad.)

Entering Formulas in Cells

Normally, you'll need to switch to Table Edit mode before you type in a formula. Assuming you've already created the table, you can follow these steps to enter a formula:

1. Position the cursor in any table cell and switch to Table Edit mode by choosing Alt+F11, Layout ➤ Tables ➤ Edit, or Alt+F7 TE. You'll see the Table Edit mode screen, shown in Figure 25.1.

2. Move the cursor into the cell where you want the formula.

FIGURE 25.1

The Table Edit mode screen

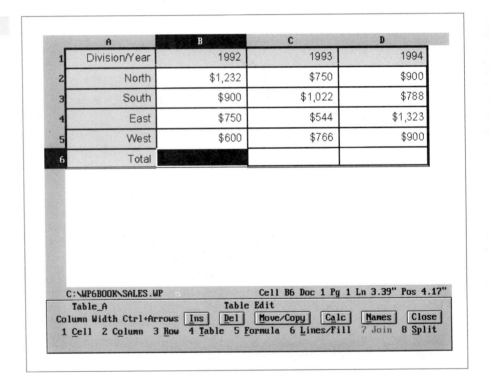

	A	B	C	D
1	Division/Year	1992	1993	1994
2	North	$1,232	$750	$900
3	South	$900	$1,022	$788
4	East	$750	$544	$1,323
5	West	$600	$766	$900
6	Total			

```
C:\WP6BOOK\SALES.WP          Cell B6 Doc 1 Pg 1 Ln 3.39" Pos 4.17"
  Table_A                         Table Edit
Column Width Ctrl+Arrows [Ins] [Del] [Move/Copy] [Calc] [Names] [Close]
  1 Cell  2 Column  3 Row  4 Table  5 Formula  6 Lines/Fill  7 Join  8 Split
```

3. Choose <u>F</u>ormula from the Table Edit options near the bottom of the Table Edit screen. You'll next see the Table Formula dialog box:

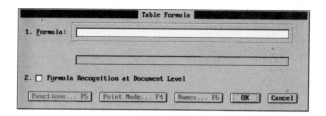

4. Type your formula, including numbers, operators, cell references, and math functions, as discussed in the sections that follow. Then choose OK.

5. Repeat steps 2–4 to enter as many formulas as you wish.

6. When you're done, choose Close to return to the document window.

Using Arithmetic Operators and Precedence in Formulas

You can use any combination of the following arithmetic operators in the formulas you enter:

OPERATOR	MEANING	EXAMPLE
^	Exponent (raise to a power)	3^2 (result is 9)
−	Negation	−3*6 (result is −18)
( )	Change the order of precedence (used for grouping)	(3+5)/2 (result is 4)
*	Multiplication	4*5 (result is 20)
/	Division	10/2 (result is 5)
+	Addition	10+15 (result is 25)
−	Subtraction	53−10 (result is 43)

TIP

When entering math operators in your formulas, you can use either the keys across the top of the keyboard or the gray /, *, –, and + keys on the numeric keypad.

If you're familiar with earlier versions of WordPerfect, be aware that in WordPerfect 6.0 tables now follow the standard *order of precedence*, rather than simple left-to-right calculation. That is, calculations are performed in the order listed in the table above: first exponentiation, then negation, then multiplication, and so forth. So the result of this formula

10+5*2

is 20 (5 times 2 is 10, plus 10 makes 20). The result *is not* 30 (10 plus 5 is 15, times 2 is 30).

When entering formulas, you can use parentheses to group the parts of the formula you want to calculate first. WordPerfect always works from the innermost parentheses outward, just as in standard mathematics. Thus, the result of this formula

(10+5)*2

is indeed 30, because the parentheses force WordPerfect to perform the addition before the multiplication.

You can nest up to seven pairs of parentheses in a formula. This allows you to perform complex calculations within a table. For example, if cell A1 contains the cost of an item, A2 the salvage value of that item, A3 the useful life in years, and A4 the current year, then the formula

(A1–A2)*(A3-A4+1)/(A3*(A3+1)/2)

calculates the current depreciation using the sum-of-the-year's-digits method. However, as I'll discuss next, it would actually be easier to enter this formula as SYD(A1,A2,A3,A4).

Using Math Functions

The Table Formula dialog box includes a Functions button. When you choose that button or press F5, a list of available table functions appears, as shown below:

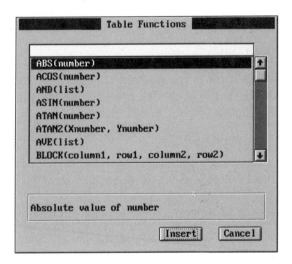

Most functions start with a brief name, such as SQRT (for square root), and are followed by parentheses that indicate which *arguments* the function expects to find in the parentheses. As you scroll through the Table Functions list using ↑ and ↓, you'll see a brief description of the currently highlighted function near the bottom of the dialog box.

The argument is what the function bases its calculation on. The argument can be a number, cell address, list, or text, depending on the function's requirements. For example, the result of the formula below is 9, the square root of 81:

SQRT(81)

This next formula means "display the square root of whatever number is in cell A1":

SQRT(A1)

The following formula uses the AVERAGE function to compute the average of a *list* of numbers (10, 15, 25, and 16). Notice that each item in the list is separated with a comma (,).

AVE(10,15,25,16)

A list might also be a range of cells, where you separate the starting cell from the ending cell with a colon (:). For example, this formula totals the numbers in cells A1 through A4:

SUM(A1:A4)

If a function supports the *list* type argument, you can mix and match arguments. For example, the formula below sums the contents of cells A1 through A3, cell B1, and the number 15.5:

SUM(A1:A3,B1,15.5)

To enter a function into a table formula, start at the Table Formula dialog box (shown earlier) and follow these steps:

1. Choose Functions or press F5 to display the Table Functions list.

2. To select the function you want, use the mouse or PgUp, PgDn, ↑, and ↓ keys to highlight the function, or type the first few characters of the function name. (For example, highlight the SUM() function.)

3. Choose the Insert button or press ↵.

4. The selected function now appears in the Table Formula dialog box, without its argument, like this:

SUM()

5. Between the parentheses, type a valid argument for the function, or use Point Mode (described shortly) to select the cell or range of cells you want to use as the argument. The SUM() function expects a list, so type in a list of numbers to sum, like this:

SUM(15,27,36.5,91)

Or you might type in or point to a range of cells. For example, this formula tells the table to sum all the numbers in cells A2 through A10:

SUM(A2:A10)

After completing your formula, choose OK to leave the Table Formula dialog box. The formula result will appear in its cell.

TIP

The math functions used in tables are virtually identical to the math functions used in spreadsheets. If you have a spreadsheet program, chances are you can find out more about a math function by looking up the function in your spreadsheet documentation.

There are nearly 100 functions, covering everything from financial calculations, such as NPV() (Net Present Value), to trigonometry, as in the COS() (cosine) function. Just scroll through the list to see what's available.

Using Point Mode

Point Mode is an easy, more visual alternative to typing cell addresses into a formula. For example, let's suppose that you want to sum all the numbers in cells A2 through A10 in a table. Here's how to do that using the SUM() function and Point Mode:

1. In Table Edit mode, highlight the cell in which you want to put the formula. (For this example, I highlighted cell B6.)

2. Choose Formula. If you want to use a function, choose Functions (or press F5) and select your function. I'll use SUM() here.

3. With the cursor between the parentheses following the function name (or under the closing parenthesis if you're in Text mode), choose Point Mode (or press F4).

4. Highlight the first cell that you want to include in the range.

5. Choose Start Block or press F4 (or F12), and use the cursor-positioning keys to extend the highlight over all the cells you want to include in the range. Alternatively, you can drag your mouse through the cells you want to highlight. Figure 25.2 shows Point Mode screen after I highlighted cells B2 through B5.

FIGURE 25.2

The Point Mode screen after highlighting cells B2 through B5

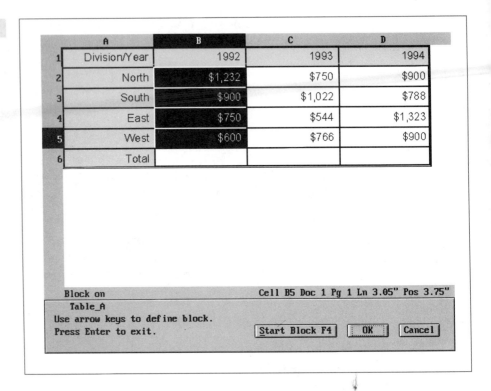

6. Choose OK or press ↵. The starting and ending cell addresses of the highlighted range now appear as the function argument, as in the example below:

SUM(B2:B5)

7. Choose OK to put the formula into its cell and close the Table Formula dialog box.

In Figure 25.3 you can see the results of using Point Mode to enter the formula SUM(B2:B5) into the Table Formula dialog box. To complete the job and show the calculations for the year 1992, choose OK.

Special Functions for Totals and Subtotals

There are three special characters that you can use to have WordPerfect calculate subtotals, totals (the sum of all the subtotals above the current

FIGURE 25.3

FIGURE 25.3

The Table Edit mode screen after using Point Mode to enter arguments for the SUM formula

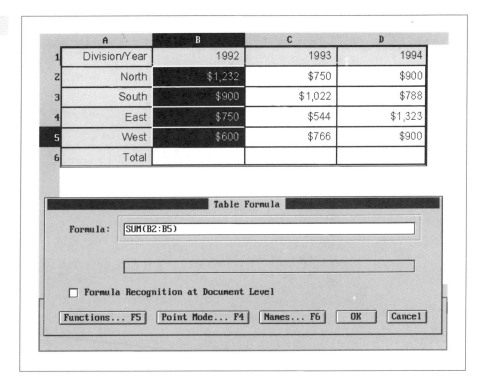

cell), and a grand total (the sum of all the totals above the current cell). These are the three "total" characters that you can use:

+	Subtotal
=	Total
*	Grand Total

To enter one of these characters, start in Table Edit mode and position the cursor in the cell where you want to put the character. Then, choose Formula, type the character you want (+, =, or *) into the Table Formula dialog box, and choose OK. This is much faster than typing a lengthy formula when you want to add a column of numbers.

NOTE

The total function (=) will display zero if there are no subtotals above it, and the grand total function (*) will display zero if there are no totals (=) above it. Therefore, if you simply want to sum a column of numbers, use the subtotal (+) function.

Figure 25.4 shows a table that uses the subtotal (+), total (=), and grand total (*) special functions. The dollar amounts for new and used car sales were entered, complete with dollar signs and decimal points. The calculated results were formatted as Currency, with zero digits, as described back in Chapter 7. (I also removed and changed many of the table lines

FIGURE 25.4

A sample document using the special subtotal (+), total (=), and grand total (*) functions, entered as formulas in Table Edit mode

First Quarter: Eastern Division		
New Cars	$22,500,000	
Used Cars	$7,500,000	
Subtotal	$30,000,000	← + (subtotal)

First Quarter: Western Division		
New Cars	$18,500,000	
Used Cars	$9,500,000	
Subtotal	$28,000,000	← + (subtotal)
Qtr 1 Total	$58,000,000	← = (total)

Second Quarter: Eastern Division		
New Cars	$21,750,000	
Used Cars	$9,675,000	
Subtotal	$31,425,000	← + (subtotal)

Second Quarter: Western Division		
New Cars	$16,000,000	
Used Cars	$8,775,000	
Subtotal	$24,775,000	← + (subtotal)
Qtr 2 Total	$56,200,000	← = (total)

Grand Total	$114,200,000	← * (grand total)

from that example, using techniques discussed in Chapter 7.)

Excluding Cells from Totals

The subtotal, total, and grand total operators base their calculations on all the numbers in the column. If any cell in the column contains a number that should be excluded from the calculation, you must allow for this in order to avoid an incorrect result for the calculation. For example, if the heading of a column is the year 1994, you won't want to add the number 1,994 to the column total.

To exclude a cell from a subtotal, total, or grand total calculation, go to Table Edit mode and move the cursor to the cell that you want to exclude from the calculation (or select a block of cells, if you wish). Then choose Cell ➤ Ignore When Calculating. You won't see a change right away. But when you recalculate the table, as discussed in the next section, WordPerfect will ignore the cell or cells you designated.

Recalculating in a WordPerfect Table

If you've entered a formula into a table and then return to the regular document and add or change some numbers there, you're sure to notice one thing: The results of the formulas are wrong! This happens because a WordPerfect table—unlike a spreadsheet, which recalculates formulas on the fly—recalculates formulas only when you tell it to.

After you've changed text and numbers in the table (and assuming you're still in the regular document window, *not* in Table Edit), there are three ways to recalculate all the formulas in a table.

TIP

If you *are* in Table Edit mode, you can just choose Calc to recalculate the table.

- Choose Layout ➤ Tables ➤ Calculate All, or press Alt+F7 TA.
- If the Tables Button Bar is displayed on your screen, just click the Tbl Calc button.

- Move the cursor into the table and press Alt+F11 A (this also takes you into Table Edit mode).

Assuming that no errors exist in your formulas, your calculations will now be correct.

Changing or Deleting a Formula

If the results of a calculation are incorrect even after you have recalculated the entire table, chances are the formula itself is incorrect. Similarly, if you add or delete table rows and columns, or you move or sort the contents of cells in the table, you may need to adjust cell references in your formulas accordingly. To do so, follow the steps below.

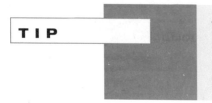

TIP

To see the formula in any cell, just move the cursor into the cell and look at the lower-left corner of the screen. You'll see an equal sign (=), followed by the formula that is in that cell.

1. Go to Table Edit mode (Alt+F11) and move the cursor to the cell that contains the formula you want to change.

2. Choose Formula.

3. To delete the formula, use the Delete key as usual. To change the formula, you can use standard editing techniques or the same techniques you used to create the formula.

4. Choose OK and then choose Calc to recalculate the table. (If you want to return to the document window, choose Close.)

Changing Cells That Contain Formulas and Regular Text

If a cell contains a formula, and you type something into that same cell in the regular document window, you'll see the results of the calculation *and* the other cell contents. To delete extraneous text or numbers, leaving the formula untouched, make the changes in the regular document window, not in Table Edit mode.

A Shortcut for Changing Formulas

If you look back at Figure 25.3, you'll notice that the Table Formula dialog box includes a Formula Recognition At Document Level check box. That's quite a mouthful! Translated into English, it simply means that you can update the formula right from the document window if you check that option.

Suppose you entered the formula SUM(A1:A10) in the Table Formula dialog box and also checked the Formula Recognition...box. After you return to the document window, you decide that this formula should be SUM(B1:B10) instead. To fix the problem, you don't have to switch to Table Edit mode. Instead, you can just move into the cell in the document window and delete its current contents. Then type **SUM(B1:B10)** directly into the cell and press Tab or Shift+Tab to move to another cell and recalculate the result automatically. This is a handy shortcut indeed!

Copying Formulas

When you want several cells to perform similar calculations, you can enter the first formula and then copy it to cells in adjoining rows or columns, using techniques you learned in Chapter 7. Like most spreadsheet programs, WordPerfect will automatically adjust the references in the copied formulas to reflect the pattern of the original formula. For example, suppose you copy the formula SUM(B2:B5) over to columns C and D. The copied formulas in cells C and D will be SUM(C2:C5) and SUM(D2:D5), as demonstrated in the example below. Each formula automatically totals up the numbers in its own column.

East	$750	$544	$1323
West	$600	$766	$900
Total	$3,482	$3,082	$3,911

            ↑   ↑   ↑
    SUM(B2:B5) SUM(C2:C5) SUM(D2:D5)
     (Original)   (Copy)   (Copy)

To copy a formula, just follow these steps

1. Go to Table Edit mode, and move the cursor to the cell that contains the formula you want to copy.

2. Choose the Move/Copy button. You'll see this dialog box:

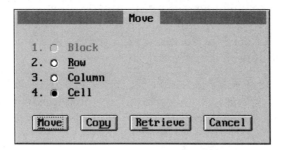

3. Choose the Copy button. You'll see the Copy Cell dialog box, which looks like this:

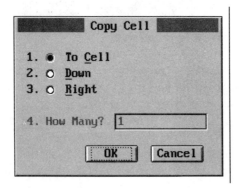

4. Choose whichever option best describes what you want to do. The To Cell option will move or copy the formula to a specific cell. Down or Right will make multiple copies down, or to the right of, the current cell.

5. If you chose the To Cell option in step 4, choose OK, move the cursor to the cell you want to receive the moved or copied formula, and then press ↵, as instructed on the screen. If you chose Down or Right in step 4, indicate how many copies you want to make, and then choose OK.

Now scroll through the copied cells and look to the lower-left corner of the screen, you'll see that each copy has been adjusted to reference its own row or column.

Handy Options to Use with Formulas

In the following sections, I'll explain how to refine the appearance of calculated numbers in the table, lock formula cells so that they can't be changed accidentally, and name individual table cells or cell ranges.

Formatting Calculated Results

You can tailor the alignment and appearance of calculated numbers by changing the column justification and number type format. As usual, you start in Table Edit mode and highlight the cell or cells you want to change. Then choose Cell or Column and select Number Type or Alignment options from the screen that appears. (See "Changing the Horizontal Alignment" and "Changing the Appearance of Numbers" in Chapter 7 for more information.)

If you want other numbers in the table to match the format of calculated values, you must type them in that way, with dollar signs, commas, two decimal places, and so on.

Locking Formula Cells

You can lock any cell in a table to protect it from change or erasure. This is particularly handy for protecting cells that contain numbers, so that text or other numbers aren't accidentally typed in. In the document window, your insertion point will jump right over any locked cells.

If a locked cell contains a formula, it will still be recalculated when you recalculate the table. Also, you can import data from spreadsheets into locked cells.

To lock a cell, follow these steps:

1. Switch to Table Edit mode (Alt+F11) if you're not already there.

2. Move the cursor to the cell you want to lock, or select the range of cells you want to lock.

3. Choose <u>C</u>ell and check the <u>L</u>ock box.

To unlock a cell or cells, repeat steps 1 and 2 above. In step 3, uncheck the <u>L</u>ock box.

Naming Cells

You can name a cell or any group of cells in your table. Once you do, you can use that name, instead of the cell addresses, in your formulas.

To name a cell or range of cells, follow the steps below:

1. If you aren't already there, switch to Table Edit mode (Alt+F11).

2. Move the cursor to the cell you want to name, or select the range of cells you want to name.

3. Choose <u>N</u>ames. If you didn't select a range of cells in step 2, you'll see the Names dialog box, shown below:

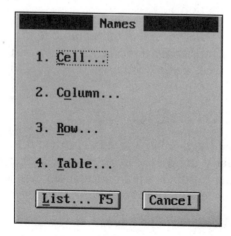

If you did select cells in step 2, you'll see the Name Cells dialog box instead:

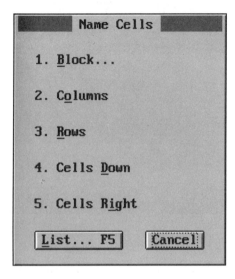

4. Choose what you want to name (for example, Block for selected cells or Cell for the current cell).

5. Type in the name you want to give the cell(s). The name can include letters, numbers, and spaces, but it must begin with a letter.

6. Choose OK or press ↵.

To understand how the named ranges are used, suppose you've named one cell in a table *Subtotal* and another cell *Sales Tax*. You've also placed an appropriate formula in these cells to calculate the subtotal and sales tax amounts. You're now ready to calculate the total for the order in another cell. To do that, start in Table Edit mode, move to the cell where you want the order total to appear, and choose Formula. Now, wherever you'd use Point Mode or type a cell address in the Formula text box, you can choose the Names button or press F6 instead. You'll see a Table Names dialog box like the one shown in Figure 25.5.

If you'd like to display the names of all tables, named cells, cell ranges, and floating cells in your document, check the List All Names In Document option in the List Table Names dialog box. When all names are visible, you can easily pull values into a formula from tables or floating cells located

FIGURE 25.5

The List Table Names dialog box lists named cells and cell ranges. To list all names in the document, check the List All Names In Document box.

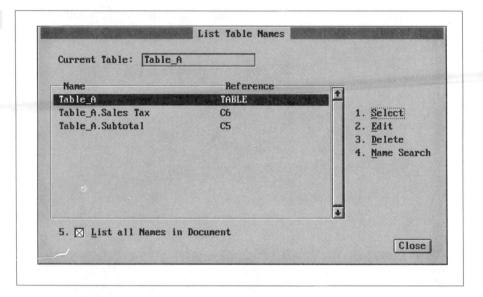

anywhere in your document. This feature is very powerful indeed! (In case you're wondering what a *floating cell* is, I'll explain this shortly.)

When you're ready to select, edit, or delete a name in the List Table Names dialog box, highlight the name and do any of the following:

- To select the highlighted name and enter it into the Formula text box, choose Select or press ↵. Alternatively, you can double-click the name to select it.

- To edit the highlighted name or reference, choose Edit, make your changes in the dialog box that appears, and choose OK.

- To delete the highlighted name or reference, choose Delete or press the Delete key, and then choose Yes.

When you're finished with the List Table Names dialog box, choose Close (or press F7), if necessary.

TIP

You can also display the named cells, ranges, and tables in your document whenever you're defining a new name in the Names or Cell Names dialog box. To do this, choose the List button or press F5.

Figure 25.6 shows a portion of a sample invoice (or receipt) that uses a variety of formulas and named cells. Notice that I've used a function, SUM(), and two named cells, *Subtotal* and *SalesTax*.

FIGURE 25.6

The formulas in this table make it easy to type an invoice or receipt. You just fill in the blanks and recalculate the table, and WordPerfect does all the math.

ID	Description	Qty	Unit Price	Ext. Price	
A-100	Microwave Rice	2	12.50	25.00	← C2*D2
B-200	Wangdoodle Chips	2	7.99	15.98	← C3*D3
C-300	Vermicious Knid	5	1.99	9.95	← C4*D4
				0.00	← C5*D5
				0.00	← C6*D6
				0.00	← C7*D7
				0.00	← C8*D8
			Subtotal	50.93	← SUM(E2:E8) Name: Subtotal
	PLUCKY'S		Sales Tax	3.95	← 1.0775*Subtotal Name: SalesTax
			Total	$54.88	← Subtotal+SalesTax

Floating Cells

If you just need to stick a quick calculation into a document, you can use a single-cell table called a *floating cell*. The advantage to using a floating cell rather than just popping up the Calculator is that you can name each floating cell and refer to the floating cells by name.

For example, your document might contain floating cells used to calculate a billing amount, sales tax, or the like, as in the example shown in Figure 25.7. There I have boldfaced everything that's in a floating cell. In Reveal Codes, you can see [Flt Cell Begin] and [Flt Cell End] codes.

WARNING

Make sure you put *only* numbers and formulas into floating cells (that is, between the [Flt Cell Begin] and [Flt Cell End] codes). Extra spaces, text, or codes are likely to throw the calculations off.

FIGURE 25.7

A sample document that uses floating cells to calculate an order total, but not in tabular format

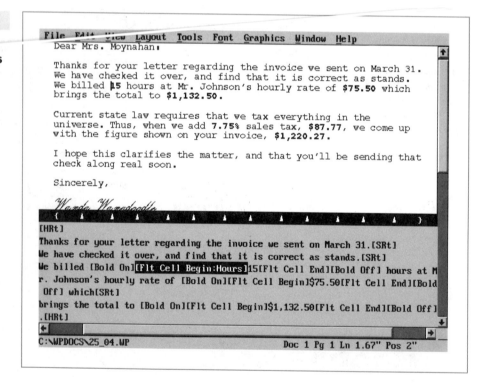

Table 25.1 describes in detail the numbers, formulas, cell names, and format used in the example in Figure 25.7.

TABLE 25.1:   The Numbers, Cell Names, Formulas or Values, and Number Types Used in Figure 25.7

VALUE SHOWN	CELL NAME	FORMULA OR VALUE	NUMBER TYPE
Hours	Hours	15	Fixed, 2
Rate	HourlyRate	75.50	Currency, 2
Subtotal	Subtotal	Hours*HourlyRate	Currency, 2
Sales Tax Rate	TaxRate	7.75	Percent, 2
Sales Tax	SalesTax	TaxRate*Subtotal	Currency, 2
Invoice Total	Total	Subtotal+SalesTax	Currency, 2

The beauty of using floating cells is that if you change the contents of any floating cell, you can instantly recalculate all the floating cell and table cell formulas throughout the document with the usual Layout ➤ Tables ➤ Calculate All commands.

Here's how to create a floating cell:

1. In the regular document window, move the cursor to where you want to put the floating cell.

2. Choose Layout ➤ Tables ➤ Create Floating Cell (or press Alt+F7 FC) to display the Edit Floating Cell dialog box:

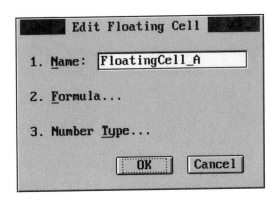

3. In the <u>N</u>ame box, give the cell a name, or accept the suggested name.

4. If you want the cell to contain a formula, choose <u>F</u>ormula and enter your formula. You can also choose Number <u>T</u>ype, and then select a format for the results of the calculation.

5. Choose OK.

Changing the Contents of Floating Cells

Because floating cells have no frames to distinguish them from other text in your document, there's always the chance that you might accidentally type right over a floating cell—in which case both the typed text and the contents of the floating cell will appear in your document. To avoid confusion, keep these tips in mind:

- When your document contains floating cells, leave Reveal Codes (Alt+F3) on, so you can see the codes that start and end the floating cell.

- To type a number or other value (as opposed to a formula) directly into a floating cell, move the cursor between the [Flt Cell Begin] and [Flt Cell End] codes, or highlight the [...End] code, and then type in your number or text.

- To put a formula into a floating cell, move the cursor between the cell's starting and ending codes. Choose <u>L</u>ayout ➤ <u>T</u>ables ➤ Edi<u>t</u> Floating Cell (Alt+F7 FE). Then choose <u>F</u>ormula to change the formula or Number <u>T</u>ype to change the number's format.

- To delete a floating cell, just delete the [Flt Cell Begin] or [Flt Cell End] code in Reveal Codes.

Fixing Rounding Errors

If there's anything that'll drive you crazy about using computers in general (and not just WordPerfect), it's the computer's tendency to miscalculate a total occasionally, by a penny or so. These *rounding errors* are caused by the fact that, behind the scenes, the computer carries out decimal places to about 15 places of accuracy. When you display the result of such a calculation, sometimes it gets rounded off more than it should be.

What can you do about it? There are a couple of things. If you're using a table rather than floating cells, you can take these steps:

1. Move the cursor into the table and switch to Table Edit mode (Alt+F11).

2. Move the cursor into the column that isn't adding up right, and choose Column ➤ Number Type. Then choose some format other than General. (If all the cells in the column don't use the same number type, you can do this on a cell-by-cell basis by selecting a range of cells and choosing Cell instead of Column.)

3. Select Options and check the Round For Calculation check box. Choose OK twice to return to the Table Edit screen.

4. Choose Calc to recalculate the table.

If that doesn't do the trick, or if you're using floating cells, you can use the ROUND() function instead. You need to round the results of all calculations that contribute to the faulty total. Choose the ROUND() function from the Table Functions list described earlier. Enter the formula to round and the number of decimal places of accuracy as arguments. For example, this formula

ROUND(C2*D2,2)

rounds the results of multiplying the contents of cells C2 and D2. Any totals based on those rounded calculations will be accurate to two decimal points.

Ye Olde Math Feature

If you have documents you created using the Math feature in earlier versions of WordPerfect, you can still use those documents in WordPerfect 6.0. The original Math feature is still available in Tools ➤ Math.

In this chapter, you've learned how to use WordPerfect's pop-up calculator, Table Math (spreadsheet), and floating cell features to perform math calculations. In Part Seven, you'll explore WordPerfect's desktop publishing and graphics capabilities. These topics are sure to dazzle the socks off your feet.

PART SEVEN

Desktop Publishing

Dazzle 'Em with Graphics

fast **TRACK**

● **To retrieve a graphic image into your document**   903

choose Graphics ➤ Retrieve Image, then use the Retrieve Image File dialog box to locate the image you want to retrieve.

● **To size and position a graphic using your mouse**   905

use Graphics or Page mode. Click the image once. To move the image, drag the entire image to a new location. To size the image, drag one of the sizing handles.

● **To delete a graphics box**   907

click the box once, then press Delete. Or locate the box's hidden code in Reveal Codes, and delete that code.

● **To edit a graphics box**   907

double-click the box, or choose Graphics ➤ Graphics Boxes ➤ Edit (Alt+F9 BE). Specify the box you want to edit, then choose Edit Box.

● **To put a new or different image into a graphics box**   908

edit the box and choose Filename. Then choose the drive, directory, and file name of the image.

● **To put text, a table, or multiple images into a graphics box**   909

edit the box, then choose Create Text or Edit Text. Insert the text, table or graphics image. Press F7 after filling the box.

NOTHING spruces up a drab document like pictures. You can add virtually any type of graphic to your documents, from commercial clip art and business charts from other programs to scanned photos and other images. Figure 26.1 shows some examples.

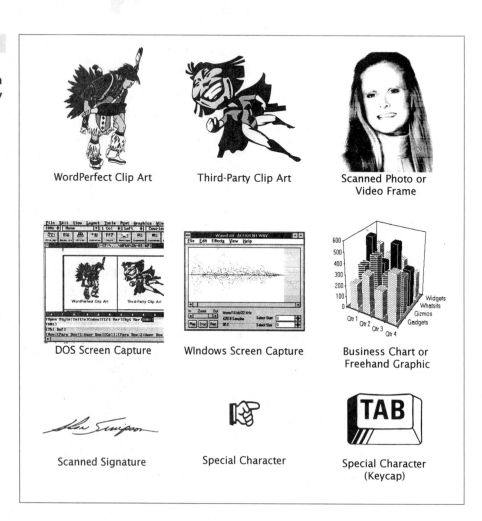

WordPerfect Clip Art   Third-Party Clip Art   Scanned Photo or Video Frame

DOS Screen Capture   Windows Screen Capture   Business Chart or Freehand Graphic

Scanned Signature   Special Character   Special Character (Keycap)

Graphics Boxes

Adding graphics is basically a matter of positioning a *graphics box* in the text, then filling the box. WordPerfect offers eight different styles of graphics boxes: Figure box, Table box, Text box, User box, Equation box, Button box, Watermark Image box, and Inline Equation box.

WordPerfect uses these different types of boxes for two reasons: They make it easy to put all types of elements in their own boxes, and they make it possible to automatically number different styles of boxes independently. For example, in this book we put all captioned figures in one style of box (Figure box), all tables in another style of box (Table box), Notes, Tips and Warnings in yet another style of box, (Text box), and all uncaptioned graphics in still another style of box (User box). Only figures and tables are numbered in this book, and they're numbered independently of one another. By providing different styles of boxes, WordPerfect lets you create your own documents in a similar manner.

Figure 26.2 shows examples of some empty graphics boxes with their default borders, shading, caption positions, and numbering systems. These

FIGURE 26.2

Examples of empty graphics boxes with their default borders, shading, and caption positions

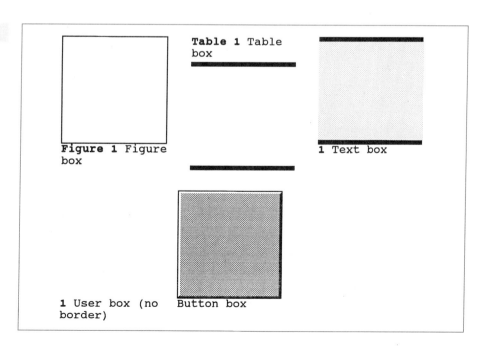

are just the default styles—you can change the appearance and numbering system of any style of box to your liking.

What Can Go in a Box?

Every box you create is initially empty. But you can fill any empty box with a graphic figure, a table, text, or an equation, as described below.

Graphic Images

Graphic images come from files stored outside of your document, which you can read into a box. Your WordPerfect package comes with a selection of sample clip art files, examples of which are shown in Figure 26.3. Each of these files has the file name extension .WPG (for *WordPerfect graphic*).

TIP   You can use any .WPG files from an earlier version of WordPerfect or DrawPerfect.

You can also create your own graphics, using spreadsheet and graphics programs, screen capture programs, and scanners. Or, use commercial clip art in your documents. Regardless of the format of your graphic image, WordPerfect can usually detect what type of file it is and pull it in on the spot. You don't need to convert it yourself. (More on this under "Tips for Building Your Art Collection," later in the chapter.)

Tables

You can display a table in your document with or without the aid of a graphics box. Either way, you still use the Tables feature discussed in Chapter 7 to create and edit the table. However, there are a few advantages to placing tables in boxes:

- You can wrap text around the table.

FIGURE 26.3

Some of
WordPerfect's sample
clip art

Border4.wpg

Border7.wpg

Conduct.wpg

Dragon.wpg

Ecologo.wpg

Factory.wpg

Fishtrop.wpg

Globe.wpg

Grizzly.wpg

FIGURE 26.3

Some of
WordPerfect's sample
clip art (continued)

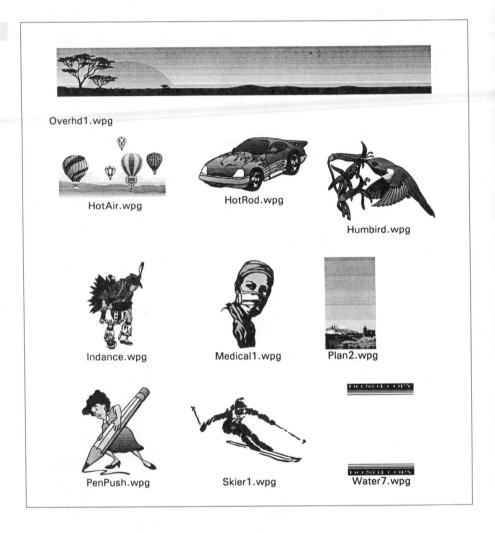

- If the table is in a box and is small enough to fit on one page, WordPerfect will not split the table across two pages.

- You can display two or more tables side by side.

- If you caption and number each table, WordPerfect will handle the numbering automatically. This means you can add, delete, and move Table boxes without having to renumber tables manually.

- You can automatically generate a list of tables for your completed document if all the tables are in Table boxes (see Chapter 31).

Text

A box can contain text, using whichever fonts and printing features your printer offers. Text boxes are commonly used to display quotations, catchy phrases, and sidebars.

Equations

A box can contain an equation that you create using the WordPerfect Equation Editor. Chapter 29 covers the Equation Editor.

Creating a Graphics Box

To create a graphics box, follow the steps below:

1. If you want the graphic to be attached to a specific character or paragraph, move the cursor to that position. If you want to put the graphic at a specific place on the page (say, the center of the page), you can move the cursor to the top of the page instead. (see "Attaching the Box" for details.)

TIP

If you want to put a graphic image in a Figure box, you can take a shortcut: Choose <u>G</u>raphics ➤ <u>R</u>etrieve Image, and then choose the file name of the image you want to retrieve.

2. Choose <u>G</u>raphics ➤ Graphics <u>B</u>oxes ➤ <u>C</u>reate (or press Alt+F9 BC). You'll be taken to the Create Graphics Box dialog box, shown in Figure 26.4.

3. Choose Based On Box St<u>y</u>le near the bottom of the dialog box, and then choose the style of box you want to create (be sure to double-click your selection, or highlight and then choose ↵).

FIGURE 26.4

The Create Graphics Box dialog box. Get here using Graphics ➤ Graphics Boxes ➤ Create (or Edit), or Alt+F9 BC (or BE).

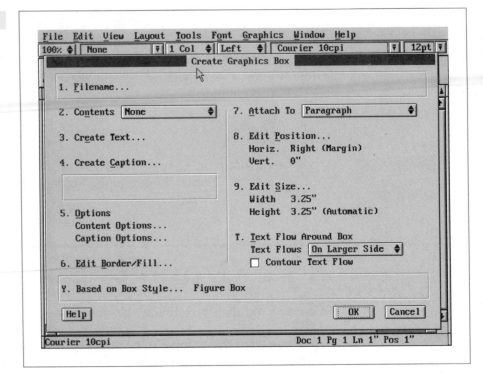

4. If you wish, you can choose OK right now to put the box in your document and take a look at it. (It will look best in Page, Graphics, and Print Preview modes.) Or, select other options in the dialog box (described later in this chapter) to define the box size and contents more specifically.

Hidden Codes for Boxes

In Reveal Codes, boxes are shown as codes. For example, the code for a graphics box might look something like this:

[Box(Page):3; Figure Box]

The little number is useful because, as you'll see, it lets you edit the box when you can't click or double-click it with your mouse.

Incidentally, when you move the highlight right onto a hidden code for a graphics box, the code expands to show you even more information about the box's number and contents. That information can help you identify exactly which code is which.

Moving and Sizing a Box

Once you've created a graphics box and returned to your document, you can easily move and size the box with a mouse, provided you're in Graphics or Page mode. Just click the box once. Sizing handles will appear around the box, as shown below:

To move the box, move the mouse pointer anywhere within the box, hold down the mouse button, drag the box to its new location, then release the mouse button. To size the box, move the mouse to any sizing handle (the little dark squares on the box's border), hold down the mouse button, drag the handle until the outline of the box is the size you want, then release the mouse button.

T I P

You can choose Edit ➤ Undo or press Ctrl+Z to undo your most recent "mouse change" to a graphics box.

As an alternative to using the mouse method described above, you can size and position the box more precisely by editing the box and changing its attachment, position, size, text flow, and other features. I'll describe how as we go along.

N O T E   Once you've selected a graphics box, and it has sizing handles, menu commands and keys that aren't relevant to graphics boxes become unavailable. To get everything working normally again, click anywhere outside the selected box, or press Esc.

Moving or Copying a Box

You can move or copy a box's code just as you would move or copy any other code. Select the code in Reveal Codes, then choose Edit ➤ Cut (Ctrl+X) to move or Edit ➤ Copy (Ctrl+C) to copy. Move the cursor to the new location, and choose Edit ➤ Paste (Ctrl+V). (You can also move a graphics box by deleting its code, moving the cursor to a new location, and then undeleting the code there. See Chapter 4 for more about deleting, moving, and copying codes.)

Keep in mind that several factors determine the exact location of a graphics box, including its size, shape, attachment (anchor point), relative position, and other things that I'll be getting to soon. Therefore, moving a box's hidden code on the page doesn't guarantee that the box itself will move. For the most part, you'll want to use the mouse-dragging technique or attachment methods and positioning techniques described later in this chapter to change the location of the graphics box on the page.

Deleting a Box

Before we get into filling a box, I should point out that if you want to delete a box altogether, all you have to do is this:

- Click the box once (so it shows sizing handles), press Delete, and choose Yes.

- Or, move the highlight to the box's hidden code in Reveal Codes, and press Delete to delete the code.

Editing a Box

You can change anything about a box at any time:

- Double-click the box you want to change.

- Or, choose Graphics ➤ Graphics Boxes ➤ Edit ➤ Document Box Number (or press Alt+F9 BEN), type in the box number (which appears in the box's hidden code), and choose Edit Box.

- Or, in Reveal Codes, move the highlight to just before or after the box you want to edit. Then press Alt+F9 BE, and choose Next Box to edit the box after the highlight, or Previous Box to edit the box to the left of the highlight. Choose Edit Box.

Instead of specifying the box number in either of the last two editing methods listed above, you can identify the box you want to edit by choosing its box type and counter number before choosing Edit Box. I'll describe those numbers (which appear in captions) later in the chapter.

You'll be taken to the Edit Graphics Box dialog box, which offers the same basic options as the Create Graphics Box dialog box shown in Figure 26.4. From there you can fill the box or make whatever other changes suit your fancy.

Once you're in the Edit Graphics Box dialog box, you can choose Previous (or press Home PgUp) or Next (or press Home PgDn) to switch from one graphics box to the next. The file name and caption (if any) for the box you're editing appear near the Filename and Edit Caption commands as you go from box to box.

Filling a Box

Now that you know how to get a box onto the page, how about filling it? As I mentioned earlier, a box can contain just about anything—including text, a table, a graphic image, or an equation. We'll talk about all of these except equations in this chapter (equations are covered in Chapter 29).

Adding a Picture

To put a graphic image in a graphics box, follow the steps below:

1. Create the box, or edit it, to get to the Create Graphics Box or Edit Graphics Box dialog box.

2. Choose Filename. You'll be taken to the Retrieve File dialog box, which looks like this:

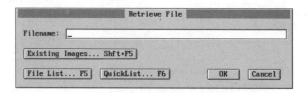

3. Enter the name of the graphic file you want to retrieve. Or use any of the buttons to help you locate a specific file:

> **Existing Images** (Shift+F5) Lists names of images that are already in the document.

> **File List** (F5) Takes you to the Select List dialog box for locating a file. (See Chapter 20.)

> **QuickList** (F6) Takes you to your custom directory names list. (See Chapter 20.)

4. Choose OK.

If the box already has something in it, WordPerfect will prompt you for permission before deleting that image and replacing it with the new one. Otherwise, you'll be returned to the dialog box, and the full path name of the retrieved file will appear next to the Filename option.

If the graphics image is not a .WPG file, you might have to wait a little while as WordPerfect converts the image to a format it can display.

To view the image, you can either return to the document window (by choosing OK) or switch to the Image Editor described a little later in this chapter.

When you have graphics on the screen, it takes the computer a lot longer to redraw the screen as you change text. (It's not WordPerfect's fault—the computer itself needs time to do these things.) If you want to stay focused on your text and speed things along, switch to Text mode (Ctrl+F3 T). In Text mode, all graphics boxes appear to be empty; only their box numbers and a border will be visible. (Use Graphics, Page, or Print Preview mode to view the contents of graphics boxes.)

Adding Text or a Table

Here's how to put text, a table, or multiple images into a box:

1. Create or edit the graphics box, as discussed earlier.

2. Choose Create Text (or Edit Text). You'll be taken to a screen that looks very much like a standard document window, *except...*

- The document area you have to work in is only as large as the box itself. Anything below a page break on this screen indicates stuff that won't appear in the box (unless you increase the size of the box).

- The bottom of the screen shows the instructions "Press (F7) when done. Press Alt+F9 to rotate." (This message in the status bar reminds you that you're editing a graphics box.)

TIP If you forget you're in a graphics box and start typing in text that belongs in the main part of the document, just select and cut the text, then paste it into the document after closing the box editor.

3. Now you can choose fonts, create tables, type text, and do just about anything your heart desires. You can even put some graphics boxes inside the current box, in order to display multiple images within a box. (Don't get too carried away with putting boxes in boxes though, or you'll have a heck of a time finding the boxes later when you're editing from the printed copy.)

4. After creating the box contents, press F7 or click the message at the bottom of the editing window, or choose File ➤ Close.

5. Choose sizing and other options, or choose OK to return to your document and take a look at the box.

NOTE Once you put an image or text in a box, option 3 in the Edit Graphics Box dialog box allows you to change the image or the text. If you want to switch from an image to text, or vice versa, choose Contents and pick the type of content you want. WordPerfect will prompt for permission before deleting the contents of the box.

Moving or Copying Tables, Text, or Files into a Box

If you've already typed some text and/or a table, and you want to move it into a graphics box, select whatever you want to move or copy. (If it's a table, don't forget to include the [Tbl Def] and [Tbl Off] codes in the selected area.) Then choose Edit ➤ Cut (Ctrl+X) to move or Edit ➤ Copy (Ctrl+C) to copy. Create or edit the graphics box, choose Create Text (or Edit Text), and choose Edit ➤ Paste (Ctrl+V). Then work your way back to the document window using F7 and OK.

If you've stored a table, text, or even a document that contains graphic images in a separate file, and you want to display *that* in your graphics box, create or edit the graphics box as usual. Choose Cre̲ate Text (or E̲dit Text), and then choose F̲ile ➤ R̲etrieve. Use the standard techniques to select the name of any file that WordPerfect can read into a normal document window (such as a document you created in WordPerfect or a text file). Then choose OK. Press F7 and choose OK to see the box on your screen. (You may need to resize the box to see all of its contents.)

If you need help retrieving files created in programs other than WordPerfect, please see Chapter 20.

Attaching the Box

Though it's easy enough to position a box simply by dragging it with your mouse, you may find that the box tends to move (or not move) when you edit neighboring text. If you're repositioning a box often, or you want to position a box more precisely, or you want text in columns to flow around the box, you should probably attach (or *anchor*) the box to something other than whatever it's attached to now. Here's how:

1. Create or edit the graphics box as described earlier.

2. Choose A̲ttach To, then choose one of the options described below (see Figure 26.5 for examples).

> **F̲ixed Page Position** The box is attached to a specific place on the page, as measured from the top and left edges of the page, regardless of margins. Changing neighboring text does not move the box at all. (Example: A graphics box in a headline.)
>
> **Paragraph** The box is attached to whichever paragraph its hidden code is in. The box "floats" with its paragraph, meaning that if you insert or delete text above the box, the box will automatically move along with its attached paragraph. (Example: A photo or diagram that needs to stay near its accompanying descriptive text.)

BECOMING ATTACHED

ECOSERVICES
The first text box on this page is a user box containing a logo. It's attached to a Fixed Page Position, .25" from the top and left edges of the page. It's not affected by other page margins.

TED THE TEXT BOX
The text box in the center is the second hidden code on this page. That box is attached to the page, centered both horizontally and vertically. But it's offset Up .5" from the actual vertical center of the page. Outside Spacing is about .04". The silhouette is in a user box within that text box.

TABLE OF CONTENTS
The third hidden code displays the Table of Contents in a table box. That box is attached to the page, Margin Right, and Margin Bottom.

COLUMNS
The code to start these columns begins after the codes just described. Because the first three graphics boxes have already been anchored to the page, the text in the columns will flow around those boxes.

BULLSEYE
The dart board image's user box is attached to the left side of this paragraph, with Contour Text selected. It's offset down .32" from the top of the paragraph. That's why the first line reaches to the left margin. Inside Spacing is 0" all around. Outside Spacing is 0" on top, left, and bottom, 0.167" on Right.

BUTTON BOX
The Button Box below is attached to this paragraph's right margin, and vertically offset Down .325". Text Flow is set to Left Side. All Spacing is set to 0" except Outside Bottom at 0.08" to give a little space here.

ALL THE REST . . . .
The rest of the graphics in this document are each attached to Character Position, centered on the Baseline. Itsy Bitsy went Up the spout. Down came the and washed the out. Out came the and it dried up all the So the itsy bitsy went up the again.

Note to Authors/Publishers of *Itsy Bitsy Spider*.
If that's a copyright infringement, please don't sue. Thanks.

*Hi I'm Ted
I'll be your
Text Box*

Table of Contents

P<u>a</u>ge   As in <u>F</u>ixed Page Position, text always flows around the box, and the box doesn't move as text moves. This option, however, lets you position the box in relation to the margins, rather than in relation to the edges of the page. (Example: A graphic image that's always displayed smack in the middle of the page between the margins.)

<u>C</u>haracter Position   The box is attached to its neighboring character. If that character moves, the box moves too. (Example: An inline equation or a small graphic symbol.)

In summary, the <u>P</u>aragraph and <u>C</u>haracter Position options let you attach the box so that it always floats with its neighboring text. The Page and Fixed Page Position attachments make the box stick to a specific place on the page, regardless of what happens to text on that page.

Putting a Graphic Image in a Repeating Element

If you want to put a graphics box in a repeating design element, such as a header, footer, or watermark, or into a footnote or endnote, create or edit the item in the usual manner. Then, when you get to the screen for editing the item's text, use the standard techniques to create a graphics box within that item. Press F7 and then work your way back to the regular document window. You can then use Print Preview (Shift+F7 V) to see the image on the screen. See Chapter 8 for more about repeating elements.

Putting Pictures in Tables

If you want to put a graphics box in a table cell, just move the cursor to the cell you want the graphic to appear in. Do this in the regular document window, *not* in Table Edit mode. Then create the box normally. You can choose <u>P</u>aragraph as the <u>A</u>ttach To method, and <u>C</u>entered as the <u>H</u>orizontal Position (under Edit Position, described later), to stick the box to the center of the cell.

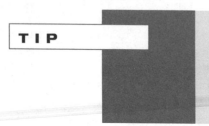

T I P

Putting graphic images in tables is a good way to organize them on the page. For example, I created Figures 26.1, 26.2, 26.3, 26.11, and others in this book by placing graphic images in tables and then removing the table lines.

Putting Graphics in Columns

I'll talk in detail about columns in Chapter 27. But here are some rules of thumb to follow for positioning graphics boxes relative to columns:

- If you want to put the box at a specific position on the page, so that columns and text flow around the box, and/or you want the box to be wider than one column, move the cursor *above* the [Col Def] code that starts the columns. Create the box there, and attach it to the page (or a fixed page position).

- If you want the box to fit within the column, and perhaps move with neighboring text (as when you have a picture that goes with a particular article), move the cursor to exactly where you want to place the box—anywhere *beyond* the [Col Def] code. Create the box there, and attach it to the Paragraph (or to the Character Position, if it's a small inline graphic).

Positioning a Box Relative to Its Anchor

As I mentioned earlier, you can easily position a graphics box by dragging it with your mouse. In many situations, that's all you'll need. But the world is not devoid of anxiety-driven perfectionists, not to mention income-driven perfectionists. Fortunately, WordPerfect offers lots of ways to position a box exactly where you want it, and in relation to whatever it's attached to, down to about a hundredth of an inch.

For experienced typesetters and the truly hardcore, WordPerfect offers Baseline Placement for Typesetters (discussed in Chapter 28).

To position a box precisely, follow these steps:

1. Create or edit the graphics box to get to the Create or Edit Graphics Box dialog box.

2. If you haven't already done so, choose Attach To and the attachment method you want.

3. Choose Edit Position, then choose from among the options presented. Those options depend on what the box is attached to, as described in the following sections.

4. Choose OK after making your selections.

Page-Attached Box

If the box is attached to a Fixed Page Position, your options are to define a specific distance for the upper-left corner of the box in relation to the left and top edges of the page (not the margins). Enter your measurement(s) in inches, points, or whatever units you prefer, then choose OK.

If the box is attached to the Page, you'll be taken to the Page Box Position dialog box, shown in Figure 26.6, instead.

Basically, the Page Box Position options let you put the box anywhere. (If you get confused by all the options, you can always press F1 for help.) When you choose Horizontal Position, your options are as follows:

Set Lets you enter a measurement in inches (or points followed by a *p*).

Left Positions the left edge of the box against the left margin (or columns).

Right Positions the right edge of the box against the right margin (or to the right edge of a column).

FIGURE 26.6

Options for positioning a graphics box that's attached to the page

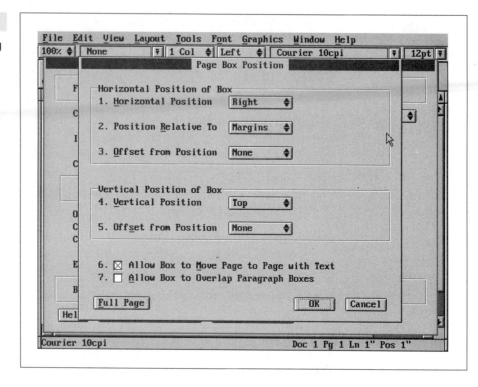

Centered   Centers the box between the margins (or within the column or between columns).

Full   Widens the box to the full width of the margins (or the column(s)).

Depending on your choice for Horizontal Position, you can then choose one of the options below from the Position Relative To option.

WARNING   The cursor must be beyond a [Col Def] code within a column for the column options to work properly (Chapter 27).

Margins   Places the box in relation to the page margins.

Columns   Places the box in relation to two or more columns (you can then specify *which* columns).

Column   Places the box in relation to the current column only. (Presumably the box is small enough to fit within the column.)

If you want to move the box "a little" from its attached position (to increase the space around it perhaps), choose Offset From Position, then choose either Left (to move the box to the left) or Right (to move the box to the right). Then enter a measurement. For example, suppose you set the Horizontal Position of the box to Left and the Position Relative To to Margins. If you then set Offset from Position to Right and enter **.25"**, the left edge of the graphics box will be one-quarter inch to the right of the left margin.

You can also choose Vertical Position and pick one of these options for vertically positioning a box that's attached to the page:

Set   Lets you define an exact measurement from the top margin.

Top   Aligns the top of the box with the top margin.

Bottom   Aligns the bottom of the box with the bottom margin.

Centered   Centers the box between the top and bottom margins.

Full   Expands the box to reach from the top margin to the bottom margin.

If you choose an option other than Set, you can choose Offset From Position, then choose either Up or Down. Next, enter a measurement to define how far up or down you want to move the box. For example, if you choose Vertical Position ➤ Centered, then Offset From Position ➤ Down, and enter 1", the top of the box will be 1 inch down from the center of the page (that might make the box appear to be centered more accurately if there happens to be a 1-inch tall headline at the top of the page).

If you change your mind and no longer want to offset the box, choose Offset From Position (or Offset From Position) ➤ None.

Other options at the bottom of the Page Box Position dialog box are:

Allow Box to Move Page to Page with Text   If selected, the box will move to another page if you insert or delete sufficient text above it. The box will be at the specified position on *that* page. If deselected, the box will never move from its current page.

Allow Box to Overlap Paragraph Boxes   If selected, boxes that are attached to paragraphs can overlap this page-attached box. If deselected, paragraph boxes will automatically move away from this page-attached box so the two don't overlap.

Full Page   Same as setting horizontal position and vertical position each to Full—the box fills the entire page.

Paragraph-Attached Box

Normally, when you attach a graphics box to a paragraph, the box appears at the upper-right corner of that paragraph (or above the paragraph, if the box is as wide as the paragraph). But when you choose Edit Position, you'll have several options for changing those default settings.

First, choosing Horizontal Position presents these options:

Set   Lets you specify how far from the left margin of the paragraph you want the left edge of the box to be.

Left   Aligns the left edge of the box with the left margin of the paragraph.

Right   Aligns the right edge of the box with the right margin of the paragraph.

Centered   Centers the box between the paragraph margins.

Full   Makes the box as wide as the paragraph (text will start *below* the box).

If you choose anything other than Set, you can also choose Offset From Position, choose Left or Right, and then enter a small measurement. Now, suppose you set the <u>H</u>orizontal Position of the box to <u>L</u>eft. If you then set <u>O</u>ffset from Position to <u>R</u>ight and enter **.25″**, the left edge of the graphics box will be one-quarter inch to the right of the left margin.

Under Vertical Position Of Box, you have one option:

> **Distance from Top of Paragraph**   Determines how far from the top of the paragraph the top of the box will be. By default, this is zero, so the top of the box aligns with the top of the paragraph. Entering any number greater than zero moves the box down accordingly.

You also can select <u>A</u>llow Box to Overlap Other Boxes. If the option is selected, neighboring boxes might overlap this one. If the option is *de*selected (the default), WordPerfect will make sure that no other boxes overlap this one.

Character-Attached Box

If you attached the box to a Character Position and then you choose Edit <u>P</u>osition you will have these options to choose from:

> **<u>T</u>op**   The top of the box aligns with the top of the text. If the box is taller than the line, the rest of the box is *below* the line.

> **<u>B</u>ottom**   The bottom of the box aligns with the text. If the box is taller than the line, the rest of the box is above the top of the line.

> **<u>C</u>enter**   The center of the box is in line with the text.

> **Content B<u>a</u>seline**   The bottom of the box is exactly at the baseline of the text (slightly lower than the Bottom option).

You can also use the Box Changes Text <u>L</u>ine Height option. If you select this option, the entire line will become as tall as the box. If you deselect this option, the text will determine the height of the line. (Any part of the box that would have been displayed below the line will be hidden.)

Sizing a Box Precisely

If just dragging the sizing handles of a graphics box doesn't satisfy your need for exactitude, you can use the Edit Size options to size the box more precisely:

1. Create or edit the graphics box normally, and choose Edit Size. You'll see a dialog box like this:

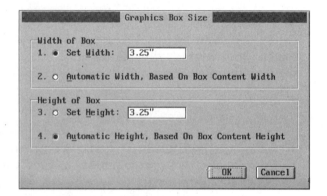

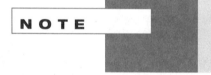

NOTE   If you chose Full when positioning a box that's anchored to the Page or Paragraph, the size will already be set accordingly.

2. Choose either Set Width or Set Height, and enter a measurement.

3. If you want WordPerfect to size the other dimension automatically, based on the dimensions of the original graphic image, choose the Automatic option for that dimension. If you prefer, you can fill in both the height and the width dimensions to size the box to your own specifications.

4. Choose OK (twice if you want to return to the document).

Wrapping Text

You can also choose how you want text to flow around a box, and whether you want the text to flow around the box frame or around the image. Figure 26.7 illustrates your options using a box that's attached to, and centered within, a paragraph. Exactly how the combination of choices you make will pan out depends, in part, on how your graphics box is attached and positioned. But it's easy enough to experiment and see what happens.

To change the text flow and contour, follow these steps:

1. Create or edit the graphics box normally.

2. Choose <u>T</u>ext Flow Around Box ➤ Text <u>F</u>lows, and then choose one of the options below:

> **On Larger Side**   If the box isn't smack against a margin, text will flow on the side of the image that has the most white space.
>
> **On <u>L</u>eft Side**   Text flows on the left side of the box (only if the box isn't already smack up against the left margin).
>
> **On <u>R</u>ight Side**   Text flows on the right side of the box (only if the box isn't already smack up against the right margin).
>
> **On <u>B</u>oth Sides**   Text flows on both sides of the box (only if the box is between the margins, and there's enough room on both sides of the box for the text to flow).
>
> **On <u>N</u>either Side**   Even if there is space along the side of the graphics box, text won't flow next to the box at all. Instead, text flow starts beneath the box.
>
> **<u>T</u>hrough Box**   Text flows right through the box. You can use this option to print white text over a box, or place text "within" a graphic. (See "White Text Over a Graphic" and "Text in a Graphic" in Chapter 28 for examples.)

3. Select <u>C</u>ontour Text Flow if you want the text to flow along the edge of the graphic image (see Figure 26.8). Or clear (deselect) that option if you want the text to flow around the border of the graphics box. (This option is unavailable if <u>T</u>hrough Box is selected, since text flows right over the image.)

FIGURE 26.7

Examples of text
flows and contours
around a graphic
image that's
horizontally centered
within the paragraph
it's attached to

Text here is fully justified. This graphic box is attached to, and horizontally centered within this paragraph. Text Flow is set to Left Side, and Contour Text is turned off.

This graphic box is attached to, and horizontally centered within this para- graph. Text Flow is set to Left Side, Contour Text is turned on.

This graphic box is attached to, and horizontally cen- tered within this paragraph. Text Flow is set to Both Sides, and Contour Text is turned on, causing the border to disappear and the text to follow the shape of the image.

This graphic box is attached to, and horizontally centered within this paragraph. I also moved the box down .25" from the top of the paragraph. Text Flow is set to Both Sides, and Contour Text is turned on. I manu- ally set both the top and bottom spacing to 0" in this example.

TIP

As shown in Figure 26.8, you can change the gap between an image and the contoured text that flows around it by changing the graphics box spacing. (See the next section for details.)

The graphic image shown here is in a user box. It's attached to the left side of this paragraph, .35" vertical (down from the top of the paragraph). Text Flow is set to Larger Side, with Contour Text selected. I knocked out two points of leading (-2p) from of the text here (see Chapter 28). That makes these lines a little tighter, and the contoured shape of the left margin more obvious. Hmm, let's see. What else can I say here to make this paragraph reach around to the bottom of that graphic image. Oh well, never mind, got here anyway. Thanks for waiting.

Same as above except that I edited the graphics box (by double-clicking) and changed the horizontal position from Left to Right. I also went into the Image Editor and flipped the image horizontally. After leaving the Image Editor, I chose Edit Border/Fill ▸ Spacing and cleared the Automatic Spacing check box. Then I set all the spacing measurements to 0". So this text comes in very close to the image. Then I came back to the document, moved the cursor to the top of this paragraph, switched to full justification (Layout ▸ Justification ▸ Full), and turned on automatic hyphenation (Layout ▸ Line ▸ Hyphenation.) Pretty tight squeeze here. To widen the gap between image and text, *increase* that border spacing.

Changing the Appearance of Boxes

As we saw back in Figure 26.2, different types of boxes initially have different default appearances and caption number styles. Different types of boxes also have different default spacing measurements inside and outside the box. WordPerfect lets you change all those defaults to get a different look. You can change the style for one box at a time, or for all the boxes in any given category (for example, all the Figure boxes).

If you want to change the style of a single box, edit that box, by double clicking or by choosing <u>G</u>raphics ➤ Graphics <u>B</u>oxes ➤ <u>E</u>dit as usual.

If you want to change styles for all the boxes in a given category (such as all the Text boxes in your document), follow the steps below:

1. Choose <u>G</u>raphics ➤ Graphics <u>B</u>oxes ➤ St<u>y</u>les (Alt+F9 BY).

NOTE   At the top of the dialog box you can also decide whether you want to change styles for the current Documen<u>t</u> only, your Personal Library of styles, or a Shared Library, as discussed in Chapter 17.

2. Click (or highlight) the type of box you want to restyle and choose <u>E</u>dit. You'll be taken to the Edit Graphics Box Style dialog box, shown in Figure 26.9.

3. Choose options as described in the next section.

NOTE   Many of the options in the Edit Graphics Box Style dialog box shown in Figure 26.9 are exactly the same as those in the Create (or Edit) Graphics Box dialog box. To keep things straight, just remember that the Edit Graphics Box Style options change styles for all boxes in the category you selected. In contrast, the Create (or Edit) Graphics Box options change only the box you're currently editing.

Border, Fill, and Spacing

Regardless of whether you're restyling all the boxes in a category or just the current box, you'll see the option Edit <u>B</u>order/Fill. Choosing that option takes you to the dialog box shown in Figure 26.10.

FIGURE 26.9

The Edit Graphics Box Style dialog box lets you change the style of all the boxes in a given category.

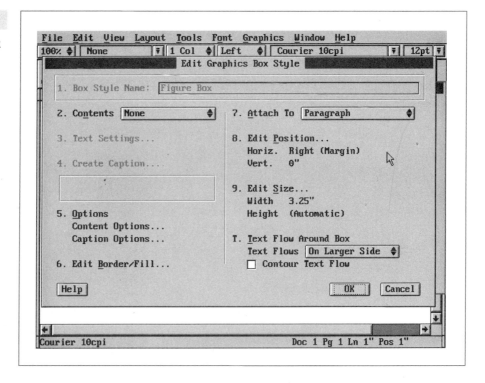

The Border/Fill options are described below. As you make choices, the sample graphics box on your screen will give you a preview of how the box (or boxes) will look in the actual document. This makes it easy to experiment until you get the look you want:

Based on Border Style   Lets you choose any predefined border style from the current document, personal library, or shared library of styles (Chapter 17).

Lines   Lets you define all the lines around the box, or individually define the left, right, top, and bottom lines.

Color   Lets you decide whether you want to use the colors already defined for the current line style, or choose your own color for all the lines in the box.

Spacing   Lets you decide whether to have WordPerfect automatically determine the spacing inside and around the box, or define the spacing yourself from the options provided.

FIGURE 26.10

The dialog box
for defining the
appearance of lines,
colors, fill, spacing,
and other char-
acteristics of graphics
boxes

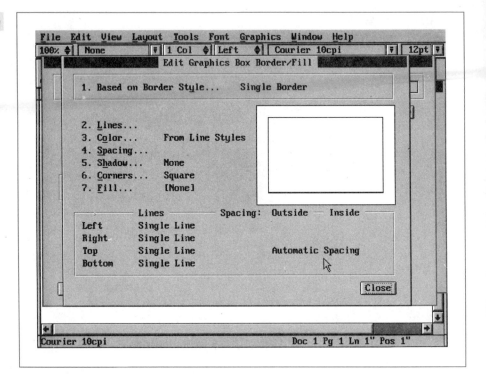

If your boxes have too much white space at the
bottom where text flows across, turn off Automatic
Spacing and try setting the Outside Spacing for Left,
Right, and Top to 0.167", and the Bottom to 0".

Shadow Lets you define a "drop shadow" behind the box, its location (upper-left, lower-left, and so forth), color, and width.

Corners Lets you choose between Square and Rounded corners and, if rounded, the radius of the curve (.325 by default).
The larger the radius, the rounder the edges. Try doubling .325 to
.65 to see what happens.

Fill   Lets you fill in the (empty) box with a foreground color, background color, and a style (% shade or Button fill). For example, Text boxes (Figure 26.1) have a default fill of 10% Shaded Fill based on the color Black (hence the gray background).

Figure 26.11 shows examples of different combinations of border styles, shadows, and corners.

After making your changes in the Edit Graphics Box Border/Fill dialog box, choose Close to return to the previous dialog box and then, if you wish, choose OK to return to the document window.

FIGURE 26.11

Examples of different types of box corners and shadings

Border Style:
Single Border,
Shadow: Lower
Right, Black.
Corners: Square

Border Style: Thin
Thick Border.
Shadow: Upper
Left, Gray, 25"
wide. Corners:
Square.

Border Style:
Single Line Border.
Shadow: Upper
Right, Gray.
Corners: Rounded
0.325" radius.

Border Style:
Single Line Border.
Shadow: Lower
Left, Gray.
Corners: Rounded,
1" radius.

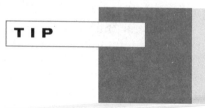

TIP

To color the text within a graphics box, edit the graphics box, choose Edit Text, select the text you want to color, then choose Font ➤ Print Color, and choose a color for the text.

The "Based On" Style

Suppose you create a Figure box, and later you decide it should have been a Text box or a Table box (to match the style of other boxes in that category). How do you change a box type? Here's what to do:

1. Edit the box you want to change the type of (by double-clicking or editing by number, as described earlier).

2. Choose Based On Box Style and double-click the box style you want (or highlight the style and choose Select).

3. Choose OK to return to your document.

The box will be numbered and styled like other boxes in that category.

Positioning Text and Images within Boxes

You can decide how the text or image will align inside a box—or all the boxes of a certain type—by following these simple steps:

1. If you want to realign the contents of the *current box only*, edit that box by double-clicking or by choosing its edit number as described earlier. If you want to realign the contents of a *family of boxes* (for example, all Table boxes), choose Graphics ➤ Graphics Boxes ➤ Styles. Then choose the type of box you want to work with either by double-clicking or by highlighting and choose Edit.

2. Under Options, choose Content Options.

3. Choose either a Left, Right, or Centered horizontal position.

4. Choose either a Top, Bottom, or Centered vertical position.

5. If you want to make sure that the box contents don't get distorted (as when you're showing a photo or a diagram), make sure Preserve Image Width/Height Ratio is selected. If you don't care about the picture being distorted (as might be the case if the image is a cartoon and you prefer that it fill the box at the cost of being distorted), clear (deselect) the Preserve Image…check box.

6. Choose OK.

You won't notice any difference in graphics boxes containing images that already completely fill the box. However, any images that don't completely fill the box, as well as any text in boxes, will take on the new alignment selections.

T I P

You *can* move an image within its box, even if it already fills the box, by using the Move feature of the Image Editor.

This type of positioning has a different effect on boxes that contain text. The alignment of the text within the box will take precedence. If necessary, you can edit an individual graphics box that contains text, choose Edit Text, and use the standard techniques to realign the text (Layout ➤ Margins, Layout ➤ Alignment, Layout ➤ Justification, or the various shortcut keys discussed in Chapter 5). Then use F7 and OK to work your way back to the document window.

Editing Graphic Images

WordPerfect isn't a full-on graphics program for professional artists, and it doesn't let you *create* graphic images. However, its built-in Image Editor does provide enough power and flexibility to control the appearance of an existing graphic image.

Assuming you've already created your graphics box and put an image into it, here's how to get to the Image Editor:

1. Edit the graphic image you want to change by double-clicking or by choosing its edit number.

2. Choose Image Editor. You'll be taken to the Image Editor, with the image ready for editing, as shown in Figure 26.12.

If you don't see the options at the bottom of the screen, but you want to, choose View ➤ Status Box. Similarly, you can choose View ➤ Button Bar to turn the Button Bar on and off. Both the Button Bar and the Edit menu offer alternative paths to many of the features described here.

FIGURE 26.12

The WordPerfect Image Editor lets you change the color, size, position, scale, and appearance of an existing graphic image.

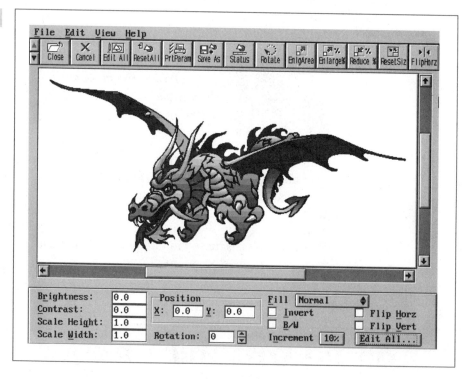

Fortunately, it doesn't take a rocket scientist to figure out how to use the Image Editor. Even those of us who are artistically impaired can work it. You change something, you see the results immediately. If you don't like those results, you change it back. There's even a Reset All option (Edit ➤ Reset All or the ResetAll button in the Button Bar) to return the image to its original state, in case you really make a mess of things.

Here are all the things you can do with the Image Editor:

- **Change the brightness and/or contrast.** Choose Brightness or Contrast (or the Brghtns and Contrast buttons on the Button Bar) and enter positive and negative values (in the range of −1 to +1, where 0 is "normal").

- **Increase or decrease the scale of the image.** Use the PgUp and PgDn keys to increase or decrease the scale, or click the Enlarge % and Reduce % buttons in the Button Bar. To change how much of an effect those keys and buttons have, choose Increment and another value. For example, if Increment is at 25%, each press of the PgUp key will increment the picture size by 25%.

- **Increase or decrease the scale by a specific amount.** You can also increase and decrease the Scale Height and Scale Width by specific values. For example, the close-up dragon face in Figure 26.13 is at 3 times the normal height and width, with the face and claws moved into view on the screen.

Examples of an original image, DRAGON.WPG, and different things you can do to it in the Image Editor

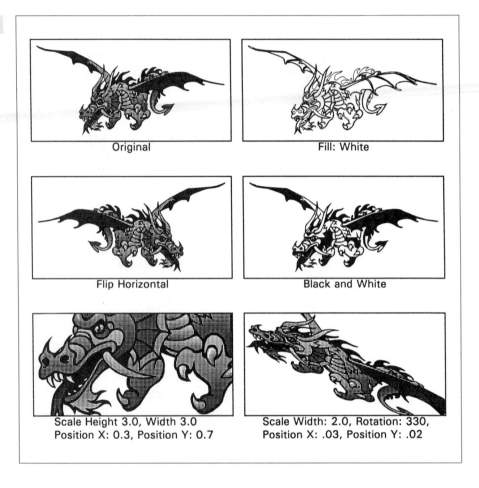

Original

Fill: White

Flip Horizontal

Black and White

Scale Height 3.0, Width 3.0
Position X: 0.3, Position Y: 0.7

Scale Width: 2.0, Rotation: 330,
Position X: .03, Position Y: .02

- **Reset the image to its original size.** Click the ResetSiz button or set the Scale Height and Scale Width back to 1.0.

- **Crop into a particular part of the image**. Click the EnlgArea button in the Button Bar, or choose Edit ➤ Position ➤ Enlarge Area. Then drag a frame around the section you want to crop, and release the mouse button.

- **Move the image within its frame**. Press ←, →, ↑, and ↓. The Increment setting affects these keys in the same way it affects the PgUp and PgDn keys. You can also move the image by using the vertical and horizontal scroll bars, or by changing the Position X and Y settings. (Resetting X and Y to zero (0) returns the image to its original position.)

- **Rotate the image.** To rotate the image, choose Rotation and use the spin box or type in a value. (Press Tab to apply the new rotation.) Or, click the Rotate button in the Button Bar, then drag the perpendicular lines around to the angle you want. To undo rotation, set the Rotation value back to zero (0).

- **Change the color.** Select Fill and then choose Normal, White (opaque), or Transparent (no color). Or, click the equivalent Normal, Trnsprnt, or White button in the Button Bar.

- **Reverse the colors (like a negative).** Choose Invert or click the Invert button.

- **Convert to black and white (no color or gray scale).** Select (check) B/W or click the Blk&Wht button. Deselect B/W or click the Blk&Wht button again to restore color and gray scale.

- **Control the ratio of black to white** in a black-and-white picture. Click the BWThresh button in the Button Bar and enter a number between 1 (very little black) and 255 (maximum black). Alternatively, you can choose Edit All ➤ Attributes ➤ B/W Threshold, enter a number, and then choose OK. The normal setting is 127.

- **Flip the picture over.** Choose Flip Horz and/or Flip Vert, or the FlipHorz and/or FlipVert buttons on the Button Bar.

- **Hide or display background color or gradients** that were saved with the original image (if any). Choose Edit All ➤ Attributes ➤ Show Background (to show the background), or clear Show Background (to hide the background). Then choose OK.

In a pinch, you can always press F1 for help. Figure 26.13 shows examples of a single image, WordPerfect's DRAGON.WPG, in its original state and after playing around with it in the Image Editor.

Image Print Parameters

Depending on your printer, you may also be able to change how WordPerfect prints the image. While you're in the Image Editor, choose Edit

DAZZLE 'EM WITH GRAPHICS

All ➤ Print Parameters (or click the PrtParam button). You'll see this dialog box:

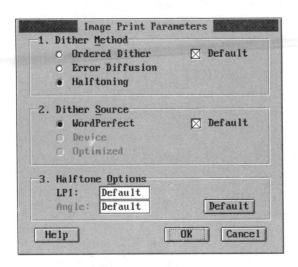

Dither (which used to mean "to be nervously irresolute in acting or doing") is a method of combining several different colored dots (called *pixels*) to create a new color. If you're printing in black and white, the dithering method controls the way your printer handles shades of gray. Dithering mainly affects how images with many gray shades (especially photographs) will look when printed (though it also affects the screen display).

The Image Print Parameters dialog box gives you three choices for the Dither Method: Ordered Dither (which might give the picture a checkerboard texture), Error Diffusion (which might give it a "fingerprint" texture), and Halftoning (the most common technique used in newspapers).

If your printer allows it, you can also choose Dither Source and have WordPerfect handle the dithering or have the printer (Device) handle the dithering. Or you can choose Halftone Options and set Optimized dithering. Depending on which option you pick, you can then choose lines per inch (LPI) and an angle (45% is used in halftoning).

T I P

Photos that were scanned from poor originals, or photos that were poorly scanned, can be retouched online using software specifically designed for that purpose. Some scanners come with photo retouching programs, like Photo Finish from ZSoft.

Your best bet is to stick with the defaults and see what you get. If you're not happy with your printed photographs, experiment with whatever other settings your printer supports. You may want to read about dithering and halftones in your printer manual for more details. You can also click the Help button, or press F1, to learn more about the Dither Method, Dither Source, and Halftone Options selections in this dialog box.

Saving an Imported Image as a WordPerfect Image

If you import an image (such as a TIFF or BMP file) into a graphics box, you can save another copy of that image in WordPerfect's .WPG format. Starting in the Image Editor, just choose File ➤ Save As. Choose a format from the Format drop-down list, and enter a valid file name with the appropriate extension (for example, .WPG). Then choose OK to return to the Image Editor.

Leaving the Image Editor

When you're done using the Image Editor, choose File ➤ Close or press F7, or click the Close button in the Button Bar to leave and save your changes. (If you want to leave without saving your current changes, press Escape, or click Cancel in the Button Bar, and choose Yes.) Then you can choose OK to return to the document and see your masterpiece.

Rotating the Text

If you need to print some text vertically, just put it in a graphics box, then rotate the text within the box. Here's how:

1. Create a graphics box (perhaps a Text box or User box), or edit an existing graphics box.

2. Choose Create Text (or Edit Text if the box already exists).

3. Notice that the status bar says "...Press Alt+F9 to rotate." Press Alt+F9.

4. Choose Rotate Box Contents.

5. Choose the amount of rotation 0° (none), 90° (sideways, first character at the bottom), 180° (upside down), 270° (sideways, first character at the top). Choose OK to return to the text-editing window.

6. If necessary, type or edit the text (for ease of editing, the text won't appear rotated until you return to your document).

7. Press F7, then choose OK, to return to the document window.

Not all fonts can be rotated. If you can't see the rotated text on your screen, try printing it to see if it works. If it doesn't work, check your printer manual to see if your printer can rotate fonts. If it can, try a different font.

Conserving Disk Space

Graphic images can hog a lot of disk space. If you have a non-WordPerfect graphic image on your computer's hard disk, then you put that image in a document and save the document, you're actually saving another copy of the same image. Not a terrific use of disk space.

Assuming that you've already put a non-WordPerfect image into a graphics box, here's how to tell WordPerfect to make a .WPG version of that file and not store another copy of the image in your document:

1. Edit the graphic image as usual (by double-clicking or by choosing the edit number).

2. Choose Contents.

3. Choose Image On Disk.

4. You'll be given an opportunity to save a version of the image in WordPerfect format. If necessary, choose a format from the Format drop-down list. In the Filename text box, change the name of the file so that it has a .WPG extension.

5. Choose OK. If a file with the name you specified already exists, WordPerfect will ask for permission to replace it. You can choose No and think up a different name (but keep the .WPG extension), or you can choose Yes to replace the existing .WPG image with the one in your document.

6. Choose OK to return to your document.

This is also a good time to save the entire document using File ➤ Save. The file should take up less disk space than it used to. You can delete the non-.WPG copy of the graphic image if you won't need that original version in other programs.

Watermark and Button Boxes

Perhaps you've noticed the Watermark and Button Box graphics box styles that WordPerfect offers. If so, you may be curious about what these styles are for. Well, here ya go.

Watermark Graphics

The Watermark Image Box style automatically centers the selected graphic on the page and sets the brightness very high (to about 0.75). This makes the graphic look like a paper watermark (see the large PC centered in Figure 26.14). The Watermark Image Box style lets you type right over the watermark image because it sets Text Flows to Through Box.

To create a watermark image in your document, follow these steps:

1. Move the cursor to the top of the first page that you want the watermark to appear on (the cursor should be *past* any codes that affect the page size and/or margins but *before* any text).

2. Choose Layout ➤ Header/Footer/Watermark ➤ Watermarks.

3. Choose Watermark A or Watermark B, then choose which pages you want the watermark to appear on, for example All Pages (see Chapter 8). Next, choose Create (or Edit if you're changing an existing watermark).

4. To make the watermark a graphic image, choose Graphics ➤ Retrieve Image, and indicate the drive, directory, and file name of the image you want to retrieve. When you get back to the watermark editing window, the graphic will appear in its light tone.

5. Press F7 to return to your document.

You can use Print Preview (Shift+F7 V) to view the watermark. If you want to change the box style for watermarks in the current document, choose Graphics ➤ Graphics Boxes ➤ Styles ➤ Watermark Image Box ➤ Edit. Make your selections in the dialog box, then choose OK and Close to work your way back to the document.

If you want to change something about one particular watermark, choose Layout ➤ Header/Footer/Watermark, then choose either A or B, select a "Pages" option, then choose Edit. Choose Graphics ➤ Graphics Boxes ➤ Edit ➤ Next Box ➤ Edit Box. Use the options in this dialog box (including Image Editor) to make your changes. Then use F7 and choose OK as appropriate to work your way back to the document window.

PC SUPPORT

Independent Support For Computing Professionals
P.O. Box 123
Mongoose, CA 91234
1-800-DNT-ASKM

"It wasn't *my* idea..."

April 1, 1994

Wanda Bea Granolabar
1121 East Pickle St.
Burbank, CA 92123

Dear Ms. Granolabar:

Thanks for your letter dated March 1. Based on what you've told me, you made some menu selections, and a couple of changes to a dialog box. That's fine. Not likely to break anything.

In fact, contrary to what you're thinking, your computer is probably neither "broken" nor "stuck" now. As a general rule, whenever you make changes to a dialog box, you must then "complete the dialog" to proceed. To do so, just click (using the left mouse button) either of these command buttons (on the screen) with your mouse pointer (that little thing that moves on the screen when you roll the mouse around):

OK Tells the program that you're happy with what you've done in the dialog box, and are now ready to proceed.

Cancel Tells the program you've got the willies about this dialog box, and would like to get outta here without saving any changes.

By all means, if we can be of any further assistance, please don't hesitate to ~~call~~ write.

Sincerely,

Willie Frank

Willie B. Frank
Vice President of Technical Details

P.S. Hope you haven't been staring at that same dialog box for the last few weeks while waiting for this letter.

As an alternative to putting a graphic in a watermark, you can use a giant centered character, such as a musical note, dingbat, or any character on the keyboard. You can do this without a graphics box simply by typing the giant character directly into the watermark editing window. If you do want to use a graphics box, choose Layout ➤ Header/Footer/Watermark,

$\underline{A}$ or $\underline{B}$, the pages you want to display the watermark on, then $\underline{C}$reate (or $\underline{E}$dit if you're changing an existing watermark). Then choose $\underline{G}$raphics ➤ Graphics $\underline{B}$oxes ➤ $\underline{C}$reate ➤ Co$\underline{n}$tents ➤ $\underline{T}$ext ➤ Cr$\underline{e}$ate Text.

Next, choose F$\underline{o}$nt ➤ F$\underline{o}$nt ➤ $\underline{F}$ont, a typeface, and a point size, as you wish, then choose OK. For example, given that 1 point is about $1/72$ inch, a point size of 360p will make a 5-inch tall character (more or less, minus the built-in leading). Choose F$\underline{o}$nt ➤ $\underline{P}$rint Color ➤ $\underline{G}$ray (or perhaps Black with Shade % set to 20, or a color if you have a color printer) and choose $\underline{S}$elect. Then choose $\underline{L}$ayout ➤ $\underline{J}$ustification ➤ $\underline{C}$enter. Type the character, or use Ctrl+W to choose a special character. Then press F7 and choose OK to work your way back to the document window. You can use Print Preview (Shift+F7 V) to view the watermark.

Here's a shortcut to use when you just want a watermark-style graphic or text character to appear on the current page (instead of all pages, even pages, or odd pages as for the watermarking procedure given just above). Create or edit the graphics box as usual. In the Create (or Edit) Graphics Box dialog box, choose Based On Box St$\underline{y}$le ➤ Watermark Image Box ➤ $\underline{S}$elect. Now put in your gray text or graphic image. When you're done, choose OK to return to the document. The graphics box will look like a watermark, but it will appear on the current page only.

N O T E   Once you've changed a graphics box to the watermark style, you won't be able to click or double-click it with your mouse. When you need to edit the box, choose $\underline{G}$raphics ➤ $\underline{G}$raphics Boxes ➤ $\underline{E}$dit (or press Alt+F9 BE) and select the graphics box by number.

Button Box Graphics

The Button box graphic image style makes it easy for people who write computer documentation to create buttons that look like the 3-D ones on computer screens. For example, in Figure 26.14 the OK and Cancel buttons are really just text displayed in a Button box graphics box.

Here's how you can create a Button box:

1. Move the cursor to wherever you want to place the button, and choose Graphics ➤ Graphics Boxes ➤ Create.

2. Choose Based On Box Style, then choose Button Box (be sure to double-click or highlight and choose Select).

3. Choose Create Text ➤ Font ➤ Font ➤ Font, and choose the font for the button (perhaps a bold 14pt serif font). Choose OK.

4. If you want to center the text on the button, press Shift+F6.

5. Type the button's text.

6. If you want to simulate the arrows that appear on a pop-up button, as in the example below, try using overstrike special characters 6,29 and 6,30 with very large superscript and subscript attributes. (Here are the exact keystrokes: Alt+F6 Shift+F8 CO Ctrl+F8 SV Ctrl+F8 PP Ctrl+W **6,29** ↵ Ctrl+F8 PP Ctrl+F8 PB Ctrl+W **6,30** ↵ Ctrl+F8 PB Ctrl+F8 SV ↵ ↵. (Whew!) The little arrows should appear flush right in the editing area. If they don't fit in the box when you get back to the document, either make the button taller or reduce the size of the overstrike characters).

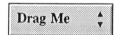

7. Press F7 and choose OK to return to your document. There you can size the button with your mouse, or double-click the button to get to the Edit Graphics Box dialog, where you can size, attach, and position the button.

If you want to create additional, equally-sized buttons, turn on Reveal Codes (Alt+F3), select the button's hidden code, and choose Edit ➤ Copy (Ctrl+C). Then position the cursor and choose Edit ➤ Paste (Ctrl+V) as many times as necessary to create enough duplicate buttons. You can change the text on each duplicate button by double-clicking and choosing Edit Text.

If you need to space the buttons evenly on the page, consider putting each button in a separate table cell (see Chapter 7). Set each Button box's <u>At</u>tach To setting to <u>P</u>aragraph, so that each button sticks to its own cell.

Capturing Buttons

The other way to create buttons is to capture the screen that the button is on and save that screen capture to a file. Then edit the screen capture file, cropping out everything but the button, as shown below:

You can then retrieve the captured button into a graphics box anywhere in your document. (See "Screen Captures," later in this chapter, for more information.)

Using Keycap Fonts

If you write computer documentation, you might consider shopping around for a keycap font, like the one shown below. This is the easiest way to insert keycaps, because you just select the font and then type.

Using Full-Page Graphics

The sample Border, Do Not Copy, and Overhead graphics that come with WordPerfect might strike you as odd at first. After all, why would you want to show one of those in a graphics box? (BORDER7.WPG, WATER7.WPG, OVERHD1.WPG, and PLAN2.WPG are shown in Figure 26.3.)

The value of that kind of clip art is in its ability to act as sort of an on-screen, full-page, preprinted form. All you need to do is size the graphic to full-page and set Text Flow to Through Box. To try this for yourself, start with a new document window and follow these steps:

1. Choose <u>L</u>ayout ➤ <u>M</u>argins and set all four document margins to 0″ (WordPerfect will convert your entries to the smallest possible margins for your printer's dead zone). Choose OK.

2. Chose <u>G</u>raphics ➤ Graphics <u>B</u>oxes ➤ <u>C</u>reate.

3. Choose <u>F</u>ilename and enter the name of the full-page graphic you want (for example, BORDER7.WPG).

4. Return to the Create Graphics Box dialog box and choose Based On Box Style. Then choose User Box (or whatever you want) by double-clicking or by highlighting and choosing <u>S</u>elect. You'll return to the Create Graphics Box dialog box.

5. Choose <u>A</u>ttach To ➤ <u>P</u>age.

6. Choose Edit <u>P</u>osition, choose the <u>F</u>ull Page button, then OK.

7. Choose <u>T</u>ext Flow Around Box ➤ Text <u>F</u>lows ➤ <u>T</u>hrough Box.

8. Choose OK to return to the document window.

If you're in Graphics or Page mode, you should be able to see the background graphic on your screen. You can just type and edit normally now, right on top of the full-page graphic, as shown in Figure 26.15. If necessary, press ↵ at least once to move down a line, then use <u>L</u>ayout ➤ <u>M</u>argins to reset your paragraph margins to 1″ (or whatever you need).

If the typing is going too slowly, use Page or Graphics mode to position the cursor, then switch to Text mode (Ctrl+F3 T) to type. When you print, both the background graphic and your typed text will be on the page.

FIGURE 26.15

The BORDER7.WPG graphic image sized to the full page. Setting Text Flows to Through Box lets you type right on top of the image.

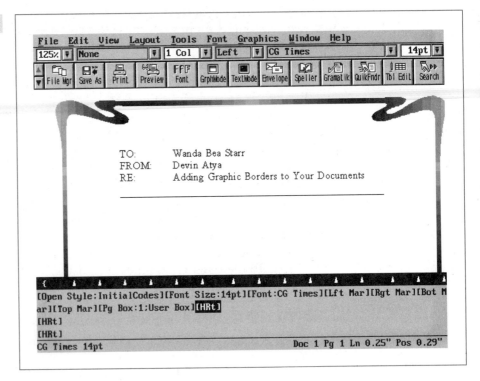

More Examples

For more examples of full-page graphics, borders, and pre-printed backgrounds, browse through the last few pages of Chapter 28. Also, you might want to look at some "semigraphical" full-page documents you can create using Tables, near the end of Chapter 7.

Choosing a Print Quality

If your printer can print graphics, you may also be able to choose from a variety of print qualities for the graphics. The lower the quality the faster the printing (which is fine for drafts). The higher the quality, the longer the printing takes. Here's how to choose a print quality for graphics:

1. Starting at the normal document window, choose File ➤ Print/Fax (or press Shift+F7).

2. Choose Graphics Quality, then choose whichever quality you want from the options displayed.

If Your Printer Runs Out of Memory...

If your printer runs out of memory while trying to print a complex document, first try printing one page at a time using File ➤ Print/Fax ➤ Page ➤ Print.

If a single page alone is too complex for the printer, choose File ➤ Print/Fax, set Graphics Quality to Do Not Print, and set Text Quality to High. Then print the page. After the page is printed, put it back into the printer. Choose File ➤ Print/Fax again, set Text Quality to Do Not Print, set Graphics Quality to High, and then print again.

Storing and Finding Graphic Files

By default, WordPerfect looks for graphics in whatever directory you specify for Graphics File in Location Of Files (File ➤ Setup ➤ Location Of Files). You can change that as you would any other path in the directory. But if you do, don't forget to move to that new location any graphics images that you want easy access to.

I put all my clip art and other graphics files in a single directory on a network drive, named F:\CLIP_ART. In WordPerfect, I used Location Of Files to set the Graphics Files location to that directory. So whenever I retrieve an image, WordPerfect knows to look in the F:\CLIP_ART directory, unless I explicitly tell it to look somewhere else.

Adding Captions

Captions are entirely optional, and certainly not all figures need captions. But WordPerfect lets you caption any graphic in any format you wish. As an added bonus, WordPerfect will automatically number the captions for you. The beauty of automatic numbering is that if you later insert, move, or delete a captioned graphic, WordPerfect will automatically renumber any other captions to reflect the change. This way, graphic numbering stays sequential throughout the document.

To add a caption to a graphics box, follow the steps below:

1. Edit the box by double-clicking or by choosing its number.

2. Choose Create Caption (or Edit Caption, if you want to change an existing caption). You'll be taken to a document window with the message "Box Caption: Press F7 when done" in its status bar. The figure number will already appear in the window. (In Reveal Codes, Alt+F3, you can see that the caption actually contains a couple of [Open Style] codes, which I'll discuss later.)

3. If you *don't* want the automatic number to appear in the caption, press Backspace to delete it. (If Reveal Codes is on, make sure you only delete the second hidden code—not the first one, which controls the general appearance of the caption.) If you do want that number in your caption, you can press the spacebar, colon (:), or any other character you want to put between the number and the text.

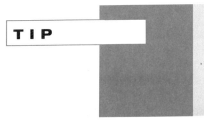

TIP

Pressing ← (or Backspace) and then ↵ *before* typing a caption adds a little white space to the top of the caption. Pressing ↵ *after* typing a caption adds a blank line to the bottom of the caption (which you probably *don't* want).

4. Enter or edit the caption text normally. You can use Center (Shift+F6), Flush Right (Alt+F6), and so forth to align text within the caption.

5. Press F7 or click the "Press F7 when done" message in the window when you've finished typing the caption. Choose OK if you want to return to the document window.

The caption appears near the figure at the default location (and in the default font) on your screen. If you wish, you can choose a different position, font, and so forth for all the captions in a particular type of box. Also, if you're using counters (automatic caption numbers), you can change the starting number if necessary, as I'll explain later under "Controlling the Caption Number Sequence and Style."

Customizing Captions

You can change the appearance of the caption for a single box, or all the boxes in a given category, by changing the box's caption styles. To get started:

- If you want to reposition the caption for *all* the boxes in a given category (for example, all Figure boxes), choose G̲raphics ➤ Graphics B̲oxes ➤ St̲yles, then choose the type of box you want to change (by double-clicking or by highlighting and choosing E̲dit).

- If you want to reposition the caption for a single box only, edit that graphics box.

Under O̲ptions, choose C̲aption Options. You'll be taken to the Caption Options dialog box, shown in Figure 26.16. This dialog box gives you total control over the caption(s). Most of the options are intuitively obvious, but let's run through them anyway.

FIGURE 26.16

The Caption Options dialog box gives you precise control over the appearance of graphics box captions.

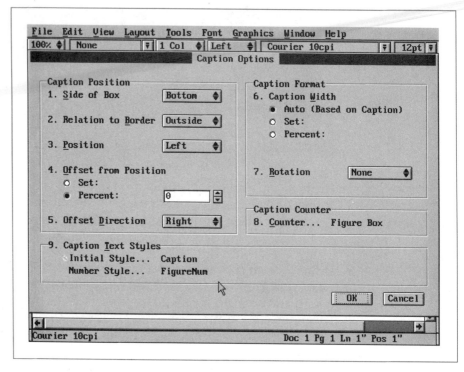

Caption Position Option

The caption positions are:

Side of Box   Lets you choose where the caption is placed.

Relation to Border   Do you want the caption to be Inside, Outside, or On the box's border?

Position   Do you want the caption aligned to the Left, Right, or Center within the space available? Or, if the caption's on the side of the box, do you want to align the caption to the Top, Bottom, or Center of the box?

Offset from Position   Do you want the caption *exactly* at the position you chose above, or do you want to offset it a little? If so, how far in inches (Set) or percent of available space (Percent), and in which direction (Offset Direction)?

Caption Width   Do you want WordPerfect to Auto-size the caption based on its width, or do you want to Set a specific width in inches or define the caption width as a Percent of the width or height of the box?

Rotation   Do you want to rotate the text (so it's sideways), and if so, how much: 90° (sideways with first character at the bottom), 180° (upside down), or 270° (sideways with the first character at top)?

Counter   Which Counter style do you want to use for displaying caption numbers?

Caption Initial Style

You can change the initial caption style for a type of box, instead of an individual box. Choose Graphics ➤ Graphics Boxes ➤ Styles, select a box type (by double-clicking or highlighting and choosing Edit), and then choose Options ➤ Caption Options ➤ Caption Text Styles ➤ Initial Style. You'll see a list of all the system styles, where you can choose a different existing style, or (more likely) edit the currently selected style.

To change the currently selected style, choose Edit to get to the Edit Style dialog box shown in Figure 26.17, and then choose Style Contents.

Now the cursor is inside the Style Contents area, and as the top of the dialog box indicates, you can press Ctrl+F8 to choose a font, Shift+F8 to change the format, and so forth. Choose your font and/or format, and return to the Edit Style dialog box. Press F7, and choose OK and Close, as necessary, to work your way back to the Caption Options dialog box.

Caption Number Style

Different captions have different default titles and numbering styles. For example, Figure box captions start with **Figure 1**. The font of that title and number come from the caption Initial Style discussed in the preceding section. But what if you want to get rid of the boldface? Or you want to number table boxes like this: Table 5.1, Table 5.2, Table 5.3, and so forth.

FIGURE 26.17

The Edit Style dialog box, here showing the contents of the Caption style

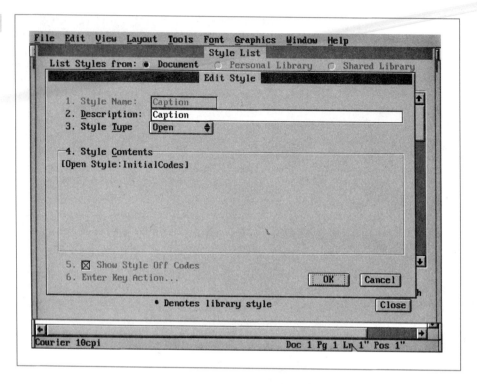

Assuming you're at the Caption Options dialog box, choose <u>N</u>umber Style under Caption <u>T</u>ext Styles. In the Style List dialog box that appears, you can choose <u>C</u>reate to create an entirely new style, or (again, more likely) choose <u>E</u>dit to change the current style. If you choose <u>E</u>dit, you'll see a dialog box like the one in Figure 26.18.

The current codes for the automatic caption number appear in the Style Contents window. For example, let's suppose you're changing the style of Table box numbers. The codes might look something like this:

[Bold On]Table [Box Num Disp][Bold Off]

Now, let's say you're writing Chapter 5 of a book right now, and you want the tables to be titled Table 5.1:, Table 5.2:, and so on. Also, you *don't* want the table captions to be boldfaced. In that case, you would choose Style <u>C</u>ontents and delete the [Bold On] code. Move the cursor to just after the word Table and the space, and type **5.** (including the period).

FIGURE 26.18

Edit Style dialog box, currently showing the style of Table box caption numbers (the style named TblBoxNum)

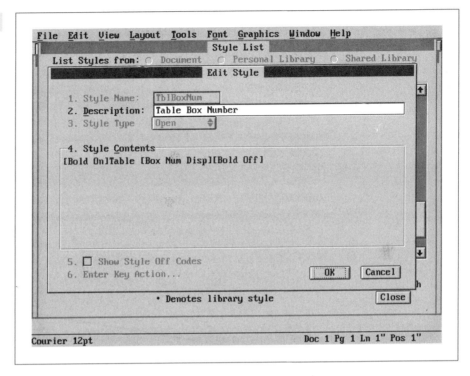

Leave the [Box Num Disp] code in place (that code displays the automatic counter number in the 1, 2, 3, 4 sequence). Press End, and type a colon and a space (:).

So now the style contents look like this instead:

Table 5. [Box Num Disp]:

You then press F7, choose OK, and Close, as necessary, to return to the document window. Any existing captioned boxes of the type you changed will display the new title and numbering scheme. Using my previous example, your table boxes would be titled and numbered like this: Table 5.1:, Table 5.2:, Table 5.3:, and so forth.

WARNING

Remember, the caption numbers won't appear at all if you don't define a caption for the box.

Controlling the Caption Number Sequence and Style

Now let's suppose you want graphics boxes to be numbered using a different method altogether, such as roman numerals (i, ii, iii) or capital letters (Figure A, Figure B, and so forth). Or perhaps you're working on a large document that's broken into several files, and you want the first figure in this file to start out as Figure 10 or Figure 100 or whatever.

To make these types of changes, you don't actually change the box styles. Instead, you move the cursor to the top of the document (or wherever you want to start the new sequence number/numbering method) and insert codes that inform WordPerfect of the change. This is how it's done:

1. Move the cursor to where you want the new numbering sequence or numbering method to start. For example, if you want to start with the first graphics box in a document, make sure the cursor is above (or to the left of) the hidden code for the first graphics box.

2. Choose Graphics ➤ Graphics Boxes ➤ Numbering.

3. Highlight the type of box you want to change (for example, Table box) by clicking or by using the ↑ and ↓ keys.

4. Choose Edit (unless you want to create a new style, which for the moment I'll assume you don't).

5. Choose Numbering Method, and select the type of numbering method you want, for example, Numbers (1,2,3,4), Lower Letter (a,b,c,d), Upper Letter (A,B,C,D), Lower Roman (i,ii,iii,iv), or Upper Roman (I,II,III,IV). Choose OK.

6. If you want the number to start at something other than what's already defined next to Set Value, choose Set Value and enter the new starting value (for example, **10** or **V** or **M**, depending on the method you chose in step 5).

7. Choose OK to return to the document window.

WordPerfect adds a hidden [Count Set] code to the document (visible only in Reveal Codes). Remember that only *captioned* boxes of the type you specified that are *past* the current cursor position will take on the new numbering characteristics.

WARNING If you need to change the numbering method or numbering sequence again, it would be a good idea to delete the existing [Count Set] code(s) first. That way, that existing code won't "cancel out" any new code that you add.

Using Counters with Boxes

WordPerfect uses system counters to increment the box number automatically when you create a graphics box caption. Separate system counters are used for each type of graphics box (Equation, Figure, Table, Text, and User box).

If the automatic numbering scheme that WordPerfect offers for graphics boxes isn't fancy enough for your needs, you can easily create your own counters, and then use them to invent more elaborate numbering schemes. For example, in Chapter 5 of Volume I of your life's story, you might want to number photographs as Figure I-5.1, Figure I-5.2, and so on. Chapter 15 explains how to create and use counters to set up any numbering scheme you want.

Changing the Caption Number for a Single Box

If you want to change the number in the caption for one particular box, you can edit that box by double-clicking or by choosing its box number, as usual. Choose Edit Caption, and delete the hidden code that displays the caption title and number (for example, [Open Style:FigureNum]). Type in your own text and/or number (such as **Fig 5.5:**). Press F7 and choose OK to return to the document window. Keep in mind that because you deleted the code that keeps track of and displays the automatic number, that number *won't* change if you reposition the figure or add or delete figures above it.

Tying a Callout to a Box

When I say "See Figure 1.1" I'm using a *callout*. Presumably, there's a Figure 1.1 nearby for you to look at.

Now, even though WordPerfect automatically renumbers graphics boxes as you shuffle them around, it doesn't automatically renumber the callouts. Thus, if you insert a figure above Figure 1.1, and Figure 1.1 becomes Figure 1.2, your text callout will still say "See Figure 1.1." Trust me: Readers don't like it when that happens, especially if the new Figure 1.1 has nothing to do with what you just told them to go see.

To prevent that sort of mishap, you can use automatic cross-referencing to create a cross-reference in text to a particular graphics box's caption (counter) number. See Chapter 31 for details on cross-referencing.

Labeling Graphics

A *figure label* is text that identifies something within the figure. For example, in Figure 26.19 *Hard Disk* and *Drive Head* are both figure labels.

WordPerfect doesn't have any *special tools* for adding labels to figures. But you can either use a third-party graphics program to do those kinds of labels, or you can use WordPerfect to create a box-within-a-box, as I did in Figure 26.19.

To create that figure, first I created a Figure box that's attached to the paragraph, with a horizontal position of Full. Then, in the Edit Graphics Box dialog box, I chose Create Text (or Contents ➤ Text ➤ Create Text) to get to the graphics box editor. Within that editor, I used Graphics ➤ Graphics Boxes ➤ Create to pull the hard disk image into a User box. I sized that box, centered it, and set Text Flows to Through Box. Then I chose OK to return to the graphics box editor.

FIGURE 26.19

A graphic of a hard
disk, with arrows and
the text labels *Hard
Disk* and *Drive Head*
added

Here we have a paragraph that's followed by a graphic image,
with text and arrows acting as figure labels.

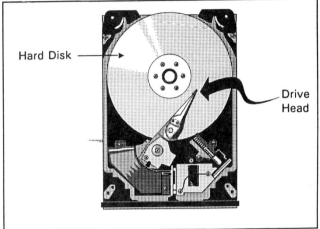

Hard Disk

Drive
Head

Figure 1: The innards of a hard disk.

The whole thing is in one figure box. The hard disk is in a user
box centered within the figure box, The straight arrow I drew
using Line Draw. The curvy arrow is a piece of clip art. The
labels themselves I typed right into the graphics box editor,
using ↵ and Tab to position each label.

TIP

When you want to arrange boxes near each other,
and/or put text near or in boxes, it's important to
set Text Flows to Through Box first.

I used ↵ and Tab to position the cursor to where I wanted to type the first
label. Then I typed the *Hard Disk* label, followed by a blank space.

TIP

If you have trouble positioning the cursor exactly where you want to type a label, choose a small fixed line height (Layout ➤ Line ➤ Line Height ➤ Fixed, as discussed in Chapter 28) at the top of the graphics box, and set the tabs to every .125" or so (Chapter 8).

Next, I switched to a monospaced font (Courier) and used Graphics ➤ Line Draw (Chapter 6) to draw the line that points to the hard disk. Then I left Line Draw (using Close) and deleted the last character from the drawn line (which is only half a space wide) and typed the arrow head by selecting character 6,27 from the WordPerfect Math/Scientific Character Set. (You could also just type a > character.)

For the second arrow, I used Graphics ➤ Graphics Boxes ➤ Create to create another User box and retrieve a piece of clip art (the curvy arrow) into that box. I set that box's Text Flows to Through Box and sized and positioned it to point to the right place. Then I used ↵ and Tab to position the cursor next to that clip art arrow, and I typed the *Drive Head* label.

When it looked right, I pressed F7 to return to the first Create Graphics Box dialog box. I added the caption to the overall figure by choosing Create Caption. Then I chose OK to return to the document window.

TIP

If you'd like to see similar examples of combining text and graphics, browse through Chapter 28, starting at the section "White Text Over a Graphic."

Sizing and Shaping Clip Art Arrows

If you use a graphical clip art arrow, you can use the Image Editor to change it. For instance, you can change its direction using the Flip options. Use Rotate to change its aim. Make it opaque using Fill, Invert and/or B/W. Stretch it using Scale Height and Width. The example below shows the same arrow before and after changing it in the Image Editor.

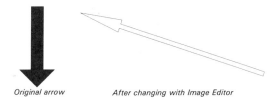

Original arrow   *After changing with Image Editor*

After changing your arrow in the Image Editor, return to the document and use your mouse to resize the arrow's box to match the new shape of the arrow.

Tips for Building Your Art Collection

As I mentioned at the beginning of this chapter and illustrated in Figure 26.1, you can put a picture of just about anything in your document. WordPerfect can automatically convert and read graphics images in most of the common formats. Table 26.1 summarizes those formats.

Converting Other Formats

You can also use the file conversion program called CV that comes with WordPerfect to pre-convert one or more graphics files to WordPerfect Graphic (.WPG) format. The section "The File Conversion Utility" in Chapter 33 provides more information on this topic.

After you finish using CV, you can return to WordPerfect and use Graphics ➤ Retrieve Image to load in any one of those files.

As an alternative, many third-party programs can convert graphics images to and from WordPerfect format to many other formats. Perhaps the most widely used program for this type of work is Hijaak from Inset Systems in Brookfield, CT.

TABLE 26.1: Types of Graphic Images That You Can Read Directly into a Graphics Box

ABBREVIATION	TYPE
BMP	Windows 3.*x* and OS/2 Presentation Manager Bitmap Format
CGM	Computer Graphics Metafile
DHP	Dr. Halo PIC Format
DFX	AutoCAD Format
EPS	PostScript and Encapsulated PostScript
GEM	GEM Draw Format
HPGL	Hewlett-Packard Graphics Language Plotter File
IMG	GEM Paint Format
MSP	Microsoft Windows (2.*x*) Paint Format
PCX	PC Paintbrush Format
PIC	Lotus 1-2-3 PIC Format
PNTG	Macintosh Paint Format
PPIC	PC Paint Plus Format
TIFF	Tagged Image File Format
WMF	Windows Metafile Format
WPG	WordPerfect Graphics Format

About Imported PostScript Images

Imported PostScript Files (.EPS) generally don't appear on the screen—only the frame and a message indicating that the box contains a PostScript image appear. However, when you print the document on a PostScript printer, the graphic will print correctly.

Scanned Images and TV/Video Frames

You can display anything that you see printed on paper in your WordPerfect document by *scanning* that image to a file. That "anything" can be a photo, drawing, signature, company logo—whatever. As long as it's on paper, you can scan it to a file.

TIP

The better you can size and crop an image with your scanning software *while* scanning it (before saving the image as a file), the better it will look in your printed document. Messing with scanned images *after* scanning usually degrades the appearance of the image. The one exception, of course, is using photo retouching software, which is designed to improve scanned images.

To capture video images, TV screens, and so forth, you'll need to purchase additional hardware and software that's specifically designed for video. Check out your local Comput-O-Rama to see what's available.

Screen Captures

Another type of graphic that you can display is the "screen shot"—anything that's on your screen, captured to a file in some format that Word-Perfect can import (see Figure 26.1). If you need to capture many screens, your best bet would be to purchase a third-party program that lets you crop images and save them in a variety of formats. I used Collage Plus by Inner Media (Hollis, NH) for most of the Windows and DOS screen captures in this book.

For the occasional screen capture, you needn't spend the money on an extra program. Below are some tips that will help you out.

DOS Screens

Here's how to capture a DOS screen:

1. If you haven't already done this in the current session, exit Word-Perfect to get to the DOS command prompt. Switch to the WordPerfect 6.0 directory, and type the command **grab**.

TIP You can enter the command *grab /h* at the DOS command prompt to get help with the GRAB program without loading it. Use the Print Screen key to print that information. If necessary, use your printer's form-feed button to eject the last page.

2. Run whatever DOS program you want to run, and do whatever it takes to get the screen looking just the way you want.

3. Press Alt+Shift+F9. You should hear a beep and see a flashing frame on your screen. If you only hear a buzz and/or the flashing frame doesn't appear, chances are you're trying to capture a "pure text" screen. Sorry, you need to use a third-party program, like the aforementioned Collage, or Hot Shot Graphics from SymSoft in Incline Village, NV, to capture pure text screens.

4. Use the →, ←, ↑, and ↓ keys to move that frame, and/or hold down the Shift key while pressing those keys to size the frame. When the flashing frame is surrounding what you want to show in your document, press ↵ and wait for the two-tone beep.

At this point, a copy of the screen is stored in a file named GRAB.WPG in whatever directory you're in at the moment. If you capture more than one screen, subsequent screens will be named GRAB1.WPG, GRAB2.WPG, and so forth.

T I P

If you're not sure where the file is, you're using DOS 5 or later, and you're at the DOS command prompt, you can enter the command dir \ *grab.wpg /s* to search all the directories on the current drive for that file.

To load the captured screen into your WordPerfect document, run Word-Perfect and open the document normally. Then position the cursor where you want the file to appear, choose Graphics ➤ Retrieve Image, and choose the drive, directory, and file name (GRAB.WPG) of the captured image. You can then edit the graphic normally to change its type, size, position, or whatever else you want to change.

Windows Screens

If you need to capture a Windows screen, just run Windows and whatever Windows application you want as usual. Get the screen looking the way you want, then press Print Screen to capture the entire screen, or Alt+Print Screen to capture only the currently selected application window. A copy of the screen is placed in the Windows Clipboard.

N O T E

On some keyboards, you have to press Shift+Print Screen or Alt+Shift+Print Screen to capture the screen. On many keyboards, the Print Screen key is abbreviated (for example, PrtScr).

To copy the image from the Clipboard to a file that you can read into your WordPerfect document, follow these steps:

1. Go to the Windows Program Manager, open the Accessories group, and run Paintbrush.

2. Maximize Paintbrush to full-screen size, then choose Options ➤ Image Attributes ➤ either Colors or Black and White (whichever you prefer) ➤ Default ➤ OK. (If the tool box *isn't* visible, choose View ➤ Tools and Linesize.)

3. Choose View ➤ Zoom Out.

4. Choose Edit ➤ Paste, or press Ctrl+V.

5. Click any tool in the tool box.

6. Choose View ➤ Zoom In. You can now crop, label, or alter the image in any other way using standard Paintbrush techniques.

7. If you want to save *everything* (including the background) that's on the screen, choose File ➤ Save As. If you want to save only a portion of what's on the screen, choose the Pick tool (scissors and square), drag your mouse in the image area to frame the portion you want to save, and choose Edit ➤ Copy To.

8. Choose a drive and directory, enter a file name for the image (for example, **c:\wp60\fig02-01.bmp**), and choose OK.

You can repeat steps 1–8 to capture as many screens as you wish (be sure to give each one a unique file name though).

When you're ready, exit Paintbrush and Windows to get back to DOS. Run WordPerfect normally. Then you can use Graphics ➤ Retrieve Image to retrieve whatever files you saved in the above steps (be sure to specify the complete drive, directory, file name, and extension).

If you need more help with Windows or Paintbrush, or if you run into any problems, please refer to your Windows documentation.

Clip Art

Clip art images are small pieces of art often used to jazz up newsletters and other documents. Thousands of ready-to-use clip art images are available. Much of the clip art is free of copyright restrictions, so you can purchase it for a one-time fee, then use it freely in your work without paying a royalty to the artist.

WARNING

Don't assume *all* clip art is free of copyright. You cannot use copyrighted art without permission. Make sure you understand the terms of the licensing agreement before you buy.

Much of the sample clip art in this book is from the Presentation Task Force collection, published by New Vision Technologies in Nepean, Ontario, Canada. The beauty of this product is that the images are stored in CGM format, which works great in WordPerfect. And, there's both a color copy and a black-and-white copy of every image in the collection. So if the gray shades produced by a color image don't quite fit the bill on your non-color printer, you can use the black-and-white version instead.

But many excellent clip art collections are available, as a trip to your local computer supermarket or a peek in a desktop-publishing magazine will prove. My own preference is to stick with vector (line) formats, particularly CGM. Bitmapped (dot) formats, like PCX, produce jagged edges and are difficult to manage with the WordPerfect Image Editor.

Business and Free-Form Graphics

Most spreadsheet programs let you display data in bar graphs, pie charts, and other business graphic formats. Most graphics programs let you create free-form graphics, as well as business graphs. Specialized graphics programs are also available for scientific, engineering, and other types of applications.

In general, once you create a chart or picture in one of these programs, you can easily "Save As" or "Export" the file to some format that Word-Perfect can read in (as listed in Table 26.1). In some programs, you may need to "Print To Disk." (Check the documentation or help screens for the program you used to create the graph for additional information on those topics.) Or, you can just "screen capture" the graphic while it's on the screen (as discussed earlier).

However you do it, keep track of the drive, directory, and full file name of the saved image. Then you can run WordPerfect, load your document, position the cursor, and use Graphics ➤ Retrieve Image to pull in a copy of the image that you saved to disk.

Special Characters

Don't forget that WordPerfect offers many special characters, including pointing hands, happy faces, musical notes, and so forth. Certain fonts, like PostScript's Dingbats, TrueType's Wingdings, and various keycap fonts, offer even more special characters. To use any one of those special characters as a graphic image, just print it at an enormous size (say 360 points). If you put that giant character in a graphics box, you can then move and size that box in the usual manner and treat it as you would any other graphic image.

Adding graphics to your document is easy, once you've practiced the techniques a bit. You can put any picture anywhere in your document. To make things extra easy, you can size and position your graphic image in Graphics or Page mode just by clicking the image and dragging the image or its sizing handles. When you start adding columns and typesetting features to your document, you can really produce some professional-looking stuff, as you'll learn in the next two chapters.

Creating Multicolumn Documents

fast TRACK

To create newspaper-style columns with a mouse   968

move the cursor to where you want the columns to begin. Turn on the Ribbon if it isn't already on (View ➤ Ribbon), click 1 Col, then type in the number of columns you want and press ↵, or double-click the desired number of columns in the drop-down list.

To create newspaper-style columns without a mouse   970

choose Layout ➤ Columns (or press Alt+F7 C), and choose your column type, number of columns, and other options as appropriate. Choose OK when you're done.

To move the cursor around in columnar text   970

click wherever you want to put the cursor. On most keyboards, you can also press Alt+→ and Alt+← to move left and right across columns. See Table 27.1 for a more complete list of keys used for navigating columns.

To type in newspaper columns   971

just type normally. When you get to the bottom of a column, WordPerfect will automatically move the cursor to the next column. If you want to force text over to the next column, you can press Ctrl+↵.

To delete columns   971

use Reveal Codes to locate and delete the [Col Def] code that defines the columns.

MULTIPLE columns make a document more appealing because people prefer to read across short lines rather than long ones. (At least, that seems to be true when people are reading facts, like the news, rather than fiction.) That's one of the reasons that newspapers and magazines use columns so much.

Newspaper Columns

Newspaper columns (also called *snaking columns*) organize your text like the text in a newspaper: Text runs down the leftmost column to the bottom of the page, wraps to the top of the next column, continues to the bottom of the page, and then wraps either to the next column or, if it has filled the last column on the page, to the leftmost column on the next page. Figure 27.1 shows a newsletter with three newspaper-style columns.

WordPerfect automatically takes care of all the business of wrapping, even as you add, change, and delete text.

Creating Newspaper Columns the Quick and Easy Way

The quick and easy way to create newspaper-style columns, if you're using a mouse, is as follows:

1. If you've already typed the text that you want to put into columns, move the cursor to where you want to begin the columns. Otherwise, just move the cursor to where you plan to start typing text in columns.

FIGURE 27.1

A newsletter
with text in three
newspaper-style
columns

Newsletter

Here da Scoop...

Columns are a lot easier than they look. Especially these newspaper style columns where text flows down one column until it gets to the end. Then, it just picks up again at the top of the next column, automatically.

Some quick-and-dirty tips for making multicolumn documents look good:

✔ Set the tabs to Every .25 at the top of the columns, so each press on Tab only indents a quarter inch.

✔ If you don't want a ragged right margin within the columns, go to the top of the document and turn on full justification and maybe automatic hyphenation as well, to reduce stretching.

✔ You can define your columns either before or after typing your initial text.

✔ In WordPerfect 6.0 you can easily put the lines between all the columns using Layout ▸ Columns ▸ Column Borders ▸ Customize ▸ Lines. Choose a line style for the Separator Lines.

✔ If the columns don't fill the page, and end up uneven

in height, you can use Balanced Newspaper columns instead.

✔ Don't forget that for small columnar documents like itineraries, schedules, and such, you can use the Tables feature (Chapter 7.)

Graphics...

Below is a graphic image in a User Box, that's attached to the paragraph, sized to the Full width of the column.

The big newsletter heading is a graphic named news7.wpg, attached to the page, the full size of the margins, with Text Flows set to through text. See "Using Full Page Graphics" in Chapter 26 for more info on using large graphics.

Tables...

If you want to put a table or graphic image in a columnar document, just put it in a graphics box. If you want text to flow around the box,

or want it to span columns, attach it to the page. If you want the box to fit within a column and float with its neighboring text, attach the box to it paragraph.

Unlike earlier versions, WordPerfect 6.0 won't mind if you just create the table while typing in columns. Rather For example, here's a table I created within these columns. It's not in a grahics box, so WordPerfect just sizes the table to fit within the column.

Size	Capacity
Small	Not much
Medium	Some
Large	Lots

Indents/Aligns...

Indent and alignment play their usual roles, but within the column:

Center (Shift+F6)
Flush Right (Alt+F6)

So do the Layout ▸ Justification and Layout ▸ Alignment commands.

I can't think of any better way to end this little newsletter than on a   ☺♪

TIP   If you've already put page-attached graphics boxes on the page, and you want columns to flow around those boxes, make sure the cursor is *after* the hidden codes for those graphics boxes.

2. If the Ribbon isn't on, turn it on (<u>V</u>iew ➤ <u>R</u>ibbon).

3. Click the "1 Col" drop-down list in the Ribbon (shown at left) and then either type the number of columns you want and press ↵, or double-click the number in the drop-down list.

WordPerfect inserts a hidden [Col Def] code that is visible only in Reveal Codes. All text *beyond* that code will be formatted into equal-width columns. Any paragraph-attached boxes that are past the [Col Def] code might also be resized, if necessary, to fit within the columns. (Tables and page-attached graphics boxes won't automatically be resized.)

"But I Don't Have a Mouse"

If you don't have a mouse, skip steps 2 and 3 above, and instead choose <u>L</u>ayout ➤ <u>C</u>olumns or press Alt+F7 C. Then choose <u>N</u>umber Of Columns, type in the number of columns you want, and choose OK.

Getting around in Newspaper Columns

Once you've defined your columns, you can get the cursor to any place in your text simply by clicking wherever you want to make changes. In addition, you can use Alt+→ and Alt+← (on enhanced keyboards) to move across columns. You can also use any of the keys listed in Table 27.1.

TABLE 27.1: Keys Used for Moving the Cursor in Columns

TO MOVE...	PRESS...
One column right	Alt+→ *or* Ctrl+Home, →
One column left	Alt+← *or* Ctrl+Home, ←
To last column	Ctrl+Home, Home, →
To first column	Ctrl+Home, Home, ←
To top of column	Ctrl+Home, ↑
To bottom of column	Ctrl+Home, ↓
Text to next column	Ctrl+↵
Text to previous column	(Delete the [HCol] code)

Forcing Text to Another Column

If at some point in your document you want to force text from one column over to the next (or from the end of the last column on a page to the first column on the next page), follow these steps:

1. Move the cursor to where you want to break to another column.

2. Press Ctrl+↵.

WordPerfect inserts a horizontal column [HCol] code at the cursor position, which forces text to the next column. If you change your mind, use Edit ➤ Undo (or press Ctrl+Z) right after making the break. Or, later, use Reveal Codes to delete the [HCol] code that's forcing the break.

Deleting Columns

If you change your mind about the number or appearance of columns, the easiest way to "undo" the columns is by deleting the [Col Def] code in Reveal Codes. Edit ➤ Undo will also work if you use it immediately after creating the columns.

Changing and Refining Newspaper Columns

By default, WordPerfect puts about half an inch of space between each column, and it doesn't place any borders around the columns. You can change all that, as well as the number of columns, by following these steps:

1. Move the cursor back to where you first created the columns (just to the right of the existing [Col Def] code is ideal).

2. Choose <u>L</u>ayout ➤ <u>C</u>olumns (or press Alt+F7 C). You'll be taken to a dialog box like the one shown in Figure 27.2.

3. Make your changes (as summarized in the sections that follow), and choose OK.

FIGURE 27.2

The Text Columns dialog box lets you define or change columns. Use <u>L</u>ayout ➤ <u>C</u>olumns or Alt+F7 C to get here.

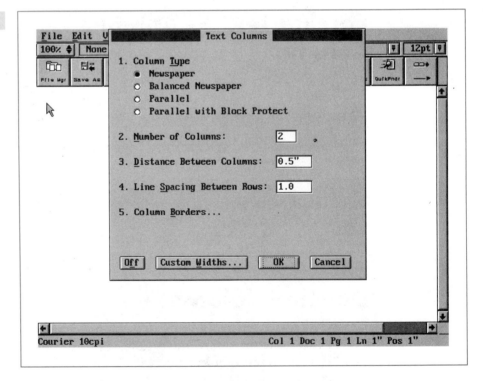

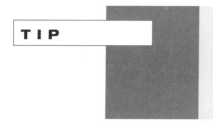

TIP

If WordPerfect ignores your column change, it's probably because the original [Col Def] code is canceling out the new one. Delete that old [Col Def] code. You won't have to worry about this if you followed my advice in step 1 above.

Now let's take a look at what you can do in the Text Columns dialog box:

Column Type   Lets you choose the type of columns: Newspaper, Balanced Newspaper (like newspaper, but with the columns adjusted to be equal in length; see Figure 27.3), Parallel, and Parallel with Block Protect (discussed later in this chapter).

Number of Columns   Indicate how many columns you want across the page, up to the maximum of 24.

Distance Between Columns   How large of a "gutter" (white space) do you want between columns? The default is $1/2''$. Enter a measurement in inches (e.g. .25″) or points (e.g. 10p).

Line Spacing Between Rows   To increase the distance between rows within the columns (especially in parallel columns), you can increase this value. (To change the spacing evenly within the columns, not just between rows, use the Layout ➤ Line ➤ Line Spacing commands to change the line spacing.)

Customizing the Column Borders

You can easily place borders around and shading within columnar text. If you're not already at the Text Columns dialog box (Figure 27.2), follow the first two steps under "Changing and Refining Newspaper Columns," earlier in this chapter. Then choose Column Borders. You'll be taken to this dialog box:

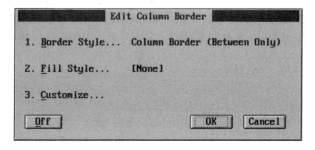

FIGURE 27.3

A comparison of Balanced Newspaper, Newspaper, and "no" columns

Balanced Newspaper Columns

This illustrates the difference between "regular" Newspaper columns, and Balanced Newspaper columns. I chose Balanced Newspaper here, so WordPerfect makes the length of each column (roughly) the same.

So that no extra blank lines end up at the bottom of the last column, make sure you type new text, and press ↵, only *after* the [THCol] and [Col Def:Off] codes that end the column. Any hard breaks or text *above* those codes will end up at the bottom of the second column.

Also, remember that WordPerfect can't always make the columns the *exact* same height because this column might have one line less, or font size differences in the columns might make it impossible for the last line in each column to align along the same baseline. But it does as good a job as you could do manually.

At the end of this passage, I turned columns off before typing the next article (below). Press Alt+F7 CF ↵ when you want to turn off columns.

Newspaper Columns

WordPerfect makes no attempt to equalize the lengths of "regular" newspaper columns. This text just stays in one column because it isn't long enough to reach the next column. I *could* force text to the next column by pressing Ctrl+↵ at the break. But the disadvantage is that if I later add or delete text, I have to rebreak the columns. With Balanced Newspaper columns, WordPerfect takes care of that for you.

No Columns

By the way, if you want to return to no-columns format like this, just press Alt+F7 CF ↵ at the end of the text in the column above. Then don't redefine any new columns.

- To change (or add) lines, choose Border Style, then a line style, then Select.

- To shade the columnar text, choose Fill Style, then a fill style from the options listed, then Select.

- To refine your previous selections, choose Customize to get to the Customize Column Border dialog box, shown in Figure 27.4. Make your selections from the options shown. (The sample box on the screen gives you an idea of how the columnar text will look in the document.) Choose Close when you're done.

Choose OK (twice) to work your way back to the document window.

Customizing the Column Widths

Normally, WordPerfect makes all the columns the same width. But you can change that via the Text Columns dialog box (again, follow the first two steps under "Changing and Refining Newspaper Columns" if you're not already at the dialog box). Choose the Custom Widths button at the bottom of the dialog box. The dialog box expands to include Custom Widths options, as in the example shown in Figure 27.5.

FIGURE 27.4

The Customize Column Border dialog box lets you refine the lines and shading in columnar text. To get here from the document window, press Alt+F7 CBC.

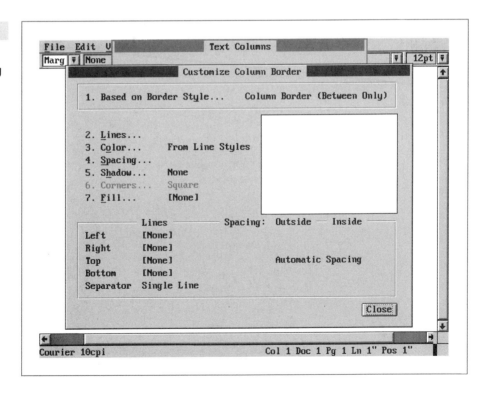

FIGURE 27.5

The Text Columns dialog box expanded to allow you to define column sizes individually. (To get here from the document window, press Alt+F7 CW.)

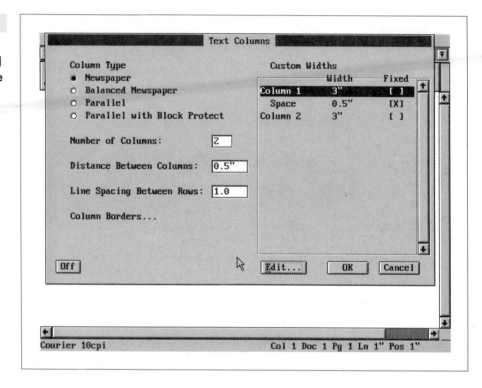

Here's how it works:

1. Click (highlight) the column number you want to change (for example, Column 1, Column 2, and so forth), or any Space option between columns.

2. Choose Edit. A small dialog box like this one appears:

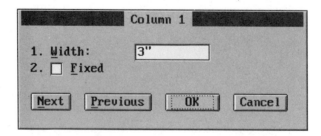

3. Choose Width and type in a width in inches (for example, .25″) or points (for example, 10p). Then press Tab.

4. Normally, WordPerfect will resize other columns as you change column widths, so the columns will fit on the page. If you *don't* want WordPerfect to resize this column (or space between) automatically, check the Fixed box.

5. Choose either Next or Previous to change another column. Or, choose OK when you're done. Then choose OK as necessary to work your way back to the document window.

Figuring Out Column Widths

Unless you're accustomed to doing this sort of thing in your head, you might want to keep a calculator around when trying to determine custom column widths—especially if you want all but one column to be the same size. Let's look at an example.

Your page is 8.5″ wide, and you have 1″ margins at the left and right. That leaves you with 6.5″ across the page. You define three newspaper columns, with .25″ between each column. The gutters required to separate columns 1–2 and columns 2–3, each being .25″, consume another .5″ of space, leaving you with 6″ of "printable" space across the page.

Now you define the first column as being exactly 1″ wide. That leaves you with 5″ of printable space for the remaining two columns, so you make each one 2.5″. (Don't you just love decimal arithmetic?)

Figure 27.6 shows the top half of a sample document using exactly those measurements. The columns begin just under the masthead (main headline). The first column, in this particular example, contains a piece of clip art, rather than text.

T I P

See Chapter 28 for an example of a newsletter format with the masthead placed vertically up the left edge of the first page.

A sample three-column format with a first column that's 1" wide, .25" between columns, and second and third columns that are 2.5" wide. In this example, the first column contains a graphic box with clip art.

'NEAKERS
Word Fun for Grownups

Freedom of Speech

The S Game

What would happen if we all stopped pronouncing the "s" on any word that begins with an "s" followed by a consonant. See if you can guess what these mean:

Eeek. A nake
That's a pretty nappy nare drum
He's as low as a nail
Ha Ha, that's a real thigh lapper
Top it you tupid toad
I've got kabies on my kin
Pleen pasms are ticky
Don't pit on my ponge, ya lob
Sell that tinkin' tock .

Fill In The Blanks

Have you ever seen a sign that says "Will Work for Food"? While the homeless problem is no laughing matter, we can take *any* slogan, and remove the verb and noun (or whatever they are), like this:

    Will _____ for _____

Now you think of fun things to fill in. Here are some ideas to get you started: *laugh/no reason, crawl/contact lens, bowl/dollars, drink/any reason, beg/sex.*

Putting Lines between Columns

Here's how to put lines between columns in your document:

1. Move the cursor to just past the [Col Def] code that starts the columns (use Reveal Codes, Alt+F3, to check your placement).

2. Choose <u>L</u>ayout ➤ <u>C</u>olumns ➤ Column <u>B</u>orders.

3. Choose <u>C</u>ustomize.

4. Choose <u>L</u>ines.

5. Choose Select <u>A</u>ll.

6. Choose [None] by highlighting and choosing <u>S</u>elect.

7. Choose <u>S</u>eparator Line.

8. Choose a Line Style (such as Single Line) by double-clicking, or by highlighting and choosing Select.

9. Choose Close and OK until you've worked your way back to the document window.

Of course, starting at step 4 above, you can choose exactly how and where you want every line. Feel free to experiment. (But I did want to show you this easiest-of-all way to put lines between your columns.)

"But the Line Runs through My Box!"

My easy way of drawing lines between columns has one problem. It draws lines right through any page-attached graphics boxes. The easiest way to fix that problem is to fill the graphics box with opaque white. Here's how:

1. Select the graphic box that has lines running through it, by double-clicking the box or by using the Graphics ➤ Graphics Boxes ➤ Edit commands.

2. Choose Edit Border/Fill.

3. Choose Fill ➤ Fill Style, then choose 100% Shaded Fill by double-clicking or highlighting and choosing Select.

4. Choose Foreground Color, then choose White (by double-clicking, or by highlighting and choosing Select).

5. Choose OK and Close as necessary to get back to the document.

When you print the document now, you'll see that the lines between the columns don't run through the graphics box any more.

Putting a Margin around a Frame

If your graphics box is framed, you may notice that the column lines run right into the frame. If you want to put a little space between the column lines and the box frame, put a larger opaque white User box under the current graphic image. To do that, you'll first need to allow text to run through the graphic image box. Follow these steps to get started:

1. Edit the graphics box again (by double-clicking or by choosing Graphics ➤ Graphics Boxes ➤ Edit and the box's number).

2. Jot down the Attach To, Edit Position, (Horizontal and Vertical) and Edit Size (Width and Height) settings. You'll need this information a little later.

3. Choose Text Flow Around Box ➤ Text Flows ➤ Through Box.

4. Choose Edit Border/Fill ➤ Spacing, deselect Automatic Spacing, and set all the outside spacing to 0".

5. Choose OK and Close, as necessary, to work your way back to the document window.

Now you can add the opaque white User box to the document by following these steps:

1. In the document window, turn on Reveal Codes (Alt+F3) and move the cursor just to the left of the code for the graphic image.

2. Choose Graphics ➤ Graphics Boxes ➤ Create.

3. Choose Based On Box Style then choose User Box (by double-clicking or highlighting and choosing Select).

4. Change the Attach To and Edit Position settings to the same as the previous graphics box (as you jotted down in step 2 in the preceding group of steps).

5. Choose Edit Size, then set the Width and Height options to a size that's slightly larger than your original box size. For example, if your original box size was 3.25×1.62, you might size this box at 3.45×1.82.

6. Choose Edit Border/Fill ➤ Fill ➤ Fill Style, and then choose 100% Shaded Fill by double-clicking or by highlighting and choosing Select.

7. Choose Foreground Color and choose White (again, by double-clicking or by highlighting and choosing Select).

8. Choose OK and Close until you return to the document.

Now when you print the document, the column lines will be cut off at the boundaries of the larger User box. You can fine-tune the spacing around the User box in the usual manner (Chapter 26) to control how closely surrounding text comes to the frame.

WARNING   In your document, the hidden code for the larger opaque white User box must come before the hidden code for the graphic image. Otherwise, the white box will be printed *after* the image, thereby covering the image with solid white!

Even More Exacting Column Lines

If you need even more exacting measurements, such as when you want to bring the column lines close to a contoured image, don't use column separator lines at all. Rather, use Graphics ➤ Graphic Lines (Chapter 6) to create, size, and position each of your vertical graphic lines.

When One Column Hangs Lower Than the Other

If you discover that the left column seems to start a little lower than the right column, it's probably because there's one or more [HRt] codes just after the [Col Def] code that initiates the columns. In Reveal Codes, you can delete the extra [HRt] codes next to or below the [Col Def] code to move that column up. Then, if you like, you can move both columns down. Move the cursor to the left of (or onto) the [Col Def] code, and press ↵ as many times as necessary to move the columns down.

In other words, [HRt] codes above the [Col Def] produce blank lines across the entire page. [HRt] codes below the [Col Def] code produce blank lines across the current column only. It all makes sense when you think about it.

Parallel Columns

In the olden days of WordPerfect, parallel columns were the way to go when you wanted to type text in a columnar format. Now, when you're working with a page or less of text, the Tables feature (Chapter 7) is the easier way to do that. But when you need to create a lengthy document with parallel (as opposed to "snaking") columns, the Parallel Columns feature is still the best alternative.

For example, you might want to use parallel columns to create a document that (like this book) includes a wide left margin that might be used for margin notes, icons, section headings, or whatever. Figure 27.7 shows an example created using the Parallel Columns feature in WordPerfect.

T I P   When using tables, processing slows down dramatically as the table grows. You can use parallel columns instead to create large, multi-column tables.

Figure 27.7 nicely illustrates the difference between parallel and newspaper columns. Text doesn't "snake" from one column to the next. Instead, text (or graphics) in the left column align next to text (or graphics) in the right column. (How well they stick together depends on whether or not you use Block Protect, which I'll describe in a moment.)

Defining Parallel Columns

To set up your parallel columns, follow the steps below:

1. If you've already typed the text that you want to put into columns, move the cursor to where you want to begin the columns. Otherwise, just move the cursor to where you plan to start typing text into columns.

2. Choose Layout ➤ Columns ➤ Column Type. Then choose one of these options:

    Parallel   Text is split into columns, but no effort is made to prevent text in one column from ending up on a different page from text in the other column.

    Parallel With Block Protect   Text in columns is protected, so if text in one column is bumped to the next page, the text directly to the left or right will also be bumped to that page (even if it *could* fit on the current page).

FIGURE 27.7

Sample document
with parallel columns,
using the left column
for margin notes,
icons, and the start of
section titles

THOSE WILD N' CRAZY PARALLEL COLUMNS

To create these columns, I started below the first title and used Layout ▸ Columns ▸ Parallel With Block Protect to create two columns. The first column is 1.5" followed by .25" space, followed by a second column of 4.75". Before typing this paragraph I pressed Ctrl+↵ to move over to this column. At the end of this paragraph I pressed Ctrl+↵ to move over to the left colum.

Danger: This is a margin note with a User box attached to the left, and space around the box reduced.

Pressing Ctrl+↵ after typing the margin note, and resetting the font back to normal brings me back over to here. So I can start typing body text again. I pressed Ctrl+↵ after typing this paragraph to move back over to the left column, so I could put in the next margin icon.

Hot Tip!

After creating that margin icon as a User box with the words *Hot Tip!* as a caption at the top of box, I pressed Ctrl+↵ to once again move over to this column. *The real hot tip here is,* when your document will contain repeating design elements, such as margin notes and margin icons, you should define each of those elements as a style. That way, if you need to change all of them later, you need only change the Style once. At the end of this paragraph, I used Alt+F7 CF ↵ to turn off columns altogether.

> **This Text Box is placed below the [Col Def: Off] code, so it's not impacted by the columns. By anchoring this to the paragraph, with a horizontal position of Center, I'm able to make it span the columns. The box is 6" wide.**

Now I'm back over to this column after turning the parallel columns back on and pressing Ctrl+↵. Once again, I'll turn the columns off (Alt+F7 CF ↵) so I can type the next heading, preceded by a tab for a partial indent from the left margin.

THIS HEAD IS TABBED IN ONE STOP FROM THE LEFT MARGIN

Now I turn columns back on, and press Ctrl+↵ to get back over to this column. Then... Th...Th...Th...Th...Th...*That's All Folks!*

3. Choose <u>N</u>umber Of Columns and enter the number of columns you want across the page (up to 24).

4. Choose <u>D</u>istance Between Columns, Line <u>S</u>pacing Between Rows, Column <u>B</u>orders, and/or Custom <u>W</u>idths, as desired (I described these options earlier in this chapter).

Choose OK to return to the document window.

Initially, any text you start typing will wrap within the first column.

Switching between Columns

As you're typing text into parallel columns, you can break to the next column in the same way you do with Newspaper columns. That is,

- If you want to move existing text over to the next column, move the cursor to the beginning of that text. If there are Tabs, fonts, or other codes at the start of the paragraph, turn on Reveal Codes, using Alt+F3, and make sure the cursor is in front of any codes that you want to move over to the next column. Press Ctrl+⏎.

- If you simply want to move over to the next column to start typing, press Ctrl+⏎.

Once you've typed text into parallel columns, you can use your mouse to click anywhere you want to move the cursor. Or, use the same keys you'd use in newspaper columns (listed earlier in Table 27.1) to move the cursor from column to column.

Distance between Rows

By default, WordPerfect puts one blank line between rows of parallel columns. To change the distance between the rows, move the cursor to wherever you want the new row spacing to start (but to the right of the initial [Col Def] code). Then choose Layout ➤ Columns ➤ Line Spacing Between Rows and enter the amount of spacing you want. For example, type 2 to add two lines between rows. Choose OK to return to your document.

Extra hard returns at the start or end of a paragraph will also force text in the adjacent column down further. To get rid of that extra space, turn on Reveal Codes (Alt+F3) and delete any unwanted [HRt] code from above or below the [HCol] that's splitting the columns. (You can see the result immediately in Graphics and Page modes.)

Spanning Parallel Columns

If you want a heading, graphic box, table, or other element to span the two parallel columns, just follow these steps:

1. Move the cursor to wherever you want to insert the thing that will span the two columns.

2. Choose Layout ➤ Columns ➤ Off (or press Alt+F7 CF) to turn off the columns. (If there's any text below the cursor, it will suddenly be separated by soft page breaks; don't worry about that.)

3. Create and position the text, table, or graphics box that you want to span the columns. When you return to the document window, move the cursor just past the item you created and then press ↵ to start the following text on a new line.

4. To reactivate the parallel columns below that new item, move the cursor down to where you want to resume parallel columns.

5. Then choose Layout ➤ Columns, and choose the type, number, distance between, and other options, as appropriate. Choose OK.

Tables, Graphics, and Columns

When you create a graphics box or table within columns, WordPerfect automatically sizes that object to fit within the column. If you want the table or graphics box to be wider than the column, move the cursor above that item, and turn off the columns as described above. You can then resize the object to your liking.

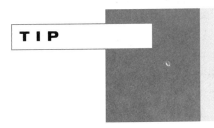

TIP

As described in Chapter 26, if you put graphics boxes *above* the [Col Def] code and attach the box to the page, the columnar text will automatically flow around the box. You can put a table in a table box to get the columns to flow around the table.

For maximum ease of positioning, put the graphic image or table in a graphics box that's attached to the page you want it to appear on. Then drag it around the page using your mouse in Graphics or Page mode.

Turning Columns Off

If you want to go back to typing in noncolumnar format, just turn off the columns (choose Layout ➤ Columns ➤ Off). Type noncolumnar text to the right of or below the [Col Def:Off] code.

Styles and Columns

If you plan on doing anything complex with parallel columns (as in Figure 27.7), you might consider using styles and/or macros to make creating the elements that are repeated throughout the document easier. For example, you might create a style that contains the graphic image and font codes for margin notes (and name it *Margin Notes*).

The beauty of using styles, of course, is that if you decide to change something later, like the graphic image or font of all margin notes, you need only change the style (once, rather than all through the document). For more information on creating and using styles, please refer to Chapter 17.

Preventing Screen Runoff

If you edit columnar text in Text mode, chances are the page will extend wider than the screen, causing all or some of the text in the right columns to run off the edge of the screen. To squeeze the text tighter, choose Layout ➤ Document ➤ Display Pitch ➤ Manual, and increase the display pitch value. For instance, changing that to 0.5″ will tighten the columns.

The downside of this technique is that WordPerfect is likely to cut off text at the right edge of each column. You'll then need to rely on Reveal Codes to make sure you're editing what you think you're editing.

Display Pitch affects only the Text mode. It has no effect on Graphics, Page, or Print Preview modes, or on the printed document. Don't forget that in Graphics and Page modes, you can use Zoom (<u>V</u>iew ➤ <u>Z</u>oom) to widen or narrow the page on your screen.

Adding Page Breaks

If you want text to break to the next page, rather than the next column, press Ctrl+A, then Ctrl+↵. WordPerfect inserts a [HPg] code, which forces the text to go to the next page.

Subdividing Pages

Page subdivision is a means of dividing each page into columns and/or rows. It's particularly useful for printing booklets, where you want to divide each page into two columns, then fold the printed page in half to create a booklet or pamphlet. Here's how to use page subdivision:

1. If you like, you can start by choosing a paper size and margins as discussed in Chapter 8. (Each page subdivision inherits the margins you set. So, in other words, the smaller you make the margins, the closer the subdivided pages will be.)

2. Choose <u>L</u>ayout ➤ <u>P</u>age ➤ Subdivide P<u>a</u>ge, then indicate how many rows and columns you want on the page. (If you're creating a booklet, you'll probably want two columns and one row.) Choose OK twice.

3. If you want to frame each block of text, choose <u>G</u>raphics ➤ B<u>or</u>ders ➤ <u>P</u>age, then use the options presented to define the borders. Then work your way back to the document window.

For the most accurate view of your page, choose <u>V</u>iew ➤ <u>P</u>age Mode (Ctrl+F3 P). Now you can type normally. When you fill a subpage, text naturally flows to the next subpage. Or, you can force the cursor or text to the next page by inserting a hard page break (Ctrl+↵). You can also use PgUp and PgDn to move from subpage to subpage, or use Go To (<u>E</u>dit ➤ <u>G</u>o To or Ctrl+Home) to move to a specific subpage by number.

Figure 27.8 shows a sample document in Print Preview, where I chose a Letter Landscape paper size, subdivided the page into two columns, and put in page borders with rounded corners. The page on the left is the end of one chapter. The page on the right is the start of another.

When you're done creating your document, you can print it normally using <u>F</u>ile ➤ <u>P</u>rint/Fax ➤ <u>P</u>rint. If you want to print the document as a booklet, see "Printing a Booklet," in Chapter 10.

FIGURE 27.8

Two pages for a booklet typed up with Letter Landscape paper size, and subdivided into two columns

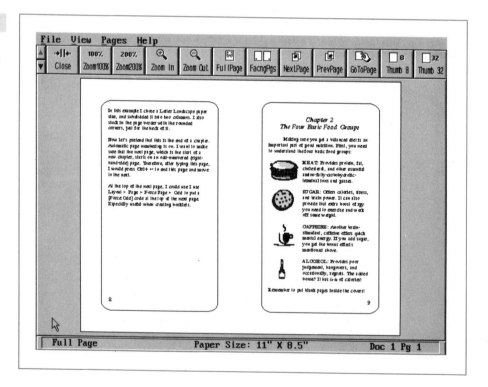

Turning Off Page Subdivision

If you want to subdivide only certain pages in your document, then return to normal pages, move the cursor to where you want the normal pages to begin. Then choose Layout ➤ Page ➤ Subdivide Page, choose the Off button, then choose OK. You might also want to redefine the document margins at that point (Layout ➤ Margins) and/or turn off page borders (Graphics ➤ Borders ➤ Page ➤ Off).

Typing in columns takes a little practice, but it's easy once you get the hang of it. In the next chapter, we'll continue our exploration of WordPerfect's desktop publishing capabilities by looking at its typesetting features and at special effects you can create.

Typesetting, Special Effects, and Fancy Stuff

f a s t TRACK

To advance text to a specific place on the page, or in relation to the cursor position   1002

> choose Layout ➤ Other ➤ Advance, choose your advance method and direction, and enter a measurement.

To change the spacing between characters and words in fully-justified text   1004

> choose Layout ➤ Other ➤ Printer Functions and set the Word Spacing Justification Limits to new compression and expansion percentages.

To prepare a document for professional typesetting   1029

> follow the typesetter's instructions for choosing a printer driver. Then use that printer driver to create the document and print the document to disk. The typesetter will need the copy of the file that you printed to disk.

To display pre-printed forms or other stock on your screen   1031

> scan the form to a file. Then use that file as a full-sized graphic image on the page with Text Flows set to Through Box.

MOST WordPerfect documents look like, well... WordPerfect documents. The reason is that most people just accept the default settings for spacing and measurement, and so their documents all have a certain generic look. For instance, Figure 28.1 shows a sample newsletter that looks—I guess you could say—"WordPerfecty."

What few people realize is that by simply changing some of the default settings, you can give your document a much different look and feel. For instance, Figure 28.2 shows the same newsletter as Figure 28.1 with some changes to the line spacing, character spacing, and other default settings.

The second example has a much "heavier" look to it. And as a matter of fact it is heavier (or denser), because the page has four additional paragraphs squeezed onto it (starting under the *Practical Matters* heading).

Many of the techniques I used in the second example are things I've talked about in previous chapters. For example,

- I reduced the gap between columns from the default .5 inches to .25 inches (Chapter 27).

- I reduced the outside spacing around graphics boxes from the default .167″ to .08″. I moved the caption for the center Figure box inside the frame. I also changed the lines around the Text box showing the Contents (Chapter 26).

- I increased the thickness of the graphic line under the main title from the default .013″ to .1″ (Chapter 6).

- I switched to full justification (Chapter 5) and turned on hyphenation (Chapter 16) to fill in the white space better.

 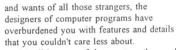

American Fungiblist

This is one of those fake newsletters I use as an example. The text here doesn't have anything to do with the title. Some authors just fill in this part with fake latin. But we can use this space to wrestle with a profound universal question from our own field.

The Big Question

The big question, that almost everyone asks about computers is, "Why don't they just make computers and programs simple, so *anyone* can use them?"

You want to know the answer to that question? Really? Are you sure? OK then brace yourself, here it is... "Because they didn't create the whole technology just for you personally."

Oh the pain of truth. Reality rears its ugly head and faces us with the dreadful conclusion that there are other people in the world. And that those other people have needs and wants that are different from our own. And in meeting the needs

Bet you looked here first

and wants of all those strangers, the designers of computer programs have overburdened you with features and details that you couldn't care less about.

It's all because of the umpteen thousand wisenheimers who learned this program long before you did. They kept sniveling "Why can't it do this?" and "I need it to do that." Software companies want to keep their customers happy. So they put all this extra stuff into their programs.

You wander in at version six-point-something, not having a *clue* as to what's been going on. Suddenly you're faced with a program the size of Louisiana, several pounds of written documentation, and bazillions of help screens that you can't find.

All you want to do is figure out something like, "How do I move this doohickey down to that dingbob there?" But since you can't even phrase the question yet, you're not likely to find the answer soon. Not to mention all the time and brain cell activity required to learn about some obscure feature only to discover that it's of no use to you whatsoever!

It's called being at the bottom (the *dregs* might be a better term) of the learning curve. And there is no fast easy cure.

Practical Matters

Contents

FIGURE 28.2

The same newsletter shown in Figure 28.1 after changing some default measurements

American Fungiblist

This is one of those fake newsletters I use as an example. The text here doesn't have anything to do with the title. Some authors just fill in this part with fake latin. But we can use this space to wrestle with a profound universal question from our own field.

The Big Question

The big question, that almost everyone asks about computers is, "Why don't they just make computers and programs simple, so *anyone* can use them?"

You want to know the answer to that question? Really? Are you sure? OK, then brace yourself, here it is... "Because they didn't create the whole technology just for you personally."

Oh, the pain of truth. Reality rears its ugly head and faces us with the dreadful conclusion that there are other people in the world. And that those other people have needs and wants that are different from our own. And in meeting the needs and wants of all those strangers, the designers of computer programs have overburdened you with features and details that you couldn't care less about.

It's all because of the umpteen thousand wise-nheimers who learned this program long before you did. They kept sniveling "Why can't it do this?" and "I need it to do that." Software companies want to keep their customers happy. So they put all this extra stuff into their programs.

You wander in at version six-point-something, not having a *clue* as to what's been going on. Suddenly you're faced with a program the size of Louisiana, several pounds of written documentation, and bazillions of help screens that you can't find.

All you want to do is figure out something like, "How do I move this doohickey down to that dingbob there?" But since you can't even phrase the question yet, you're not likely to find the answer soon. Not to mention all the time and brain cell activity required to learn about some obscure feature only to discover that it's of no use to you whatsoever!

It's called being at the bottom (the *dregs* might be a better term) of the learning curve. And there is no fast easy cure.

Bet you looked here first

Practical Matters

Now, onto more practical matters. As every writer knows, good writing is accurate, succinct, truthful, and above all, a certain number of words. It's gotta be a certain length because A) Production people have to fit it into some finite space and B) Readers, who always peek ahead, won't read it if they decide that it's too *many* words.

Word count isn't the only way to get stuff to fit on a page. You can use some of WordPerfect's typesetting features to squeeze a little more, or a little less, text on the page. And you can make the whole thing look less "WordPerfecty" in the process.

In this newsletter I changed several of WordPerfect's default measurements. As you can see, there's much less white space, and more text. (These last four paragraphs didn't even fit on the first page in the previous example.)

Look better? I don't know. But it looks *different*. The thing is, you're not stuck with having all your WordPerfect documents look like WordPerfect documents. Play around. You can always change your mind. By the way, *fungible* is a word. ■

Contents	

In addition, I used the techniques below, which I'll cover in this chapter:

- I removed two points of leading between lines, leaving less space between each printed line.

- I reduced the amount of space between characters.

- I altered the word and letter spacing to tighten up text within each line.

- I used *kerning* to tighten up the gap between letters (this let me use a taller font in the main headline without having the text become wider than the space allotted).

- I used Advance to "manually kern" specific letters, making them closer together or farther apart as convenient. (Specifically, I tightened the gap between the *F* and the *U* in the main headline and spread out some of the letters in the figure caption near the center of the page.)

All of this might seem like a bit of overkill to the average computer user. But if you've got to produce a flawlessly formatted newsletter, ad, or other document, you'll want to know how to use some of WordPerfect's typesetting features.

Controlling Text Appearances Exactly

WordPerfect's typesetting features are all geared toward one goal—getting *exact* control of the placement of text on the page. They're mostly bunched together on the menus under Layout ➤ Other (Shift+F8 O) and Layout ➤ Other ➤ Printer Functions (Shift+F8 OP). Two words of caution before we proceed:

- Not all printers, and not all fonts, are created equal. There are few "absolutes" in this realm—sometimes you just have to experiment to see how things will work with your current font and printer.

- WYSIWYG isn't 100% reliable when you're working at this level of exactness. You'll need to make occasional printouts to get an accurate view of your progress.

Changing the Space between Lines (Leading)

Leading (pronounced "ledding") is basically the amount of space between two printed lines. The more leading, the larger the white gap between one printed line and the next.

By default, WordPerfect adds two points of leading to proportionally-spaced fonts and no leading to monospaced fonts. If you want to squeeze a little more text onto the page, you can always remove a little leading. Likewise, if you want to expand the text to fill out the page better, you can increase the leading a little. Here's how:

1. Move the cursor to wherever you want to start the new leading measurement.

2. Choose Layout ➤ Other ➤ Printer Functions ➤ Leading Adjustment.

3. To increase the leading, type in a positive measurement. To decrease the leading, type in a negative value. You can use points by following your entry with a *p*, for example, **2p** to add two points of leading or **-2p** to remove two points of leading.

4. Choose OK twice to return to your document.

WordPerfect adds a [Leading Adj] code, and all subsequent text is reformatted accordingly.

Changing the Line Height

Another way to change the amount of space between lines is to switch to a fixed line height. Normally, WordPerfect determines the height of a line automatically based on the tallest font used in the line. But if you want to determine your own fixed line height, just follow these steps:

1. Move the cursor to where you want to start the new line height.

2. Choose Layout ➤ Line ➤ Line Height.

3. Choose Auto if you want WordPerfect to calculate the line height automatically (as it usually does). Or, choose Fixed and enter a measurement in inches (for example, **.25**) or points (**12p**).

4. Choose OK.

TIP If you want to *increase* the spacing between lines, it's probably easiest to use Layout ➤ Line ➤ Line Spacing, which is discussed in Chapter 5.

All text below the inserted [Ln Height] code will be affected by the change. If you want subsequent text to be printed normally, move the cursor to where you want to resume normal printing. Then repeat the steps to switch back to Auto line height.

Changing the Space between Letters and Words

WordPerfect also puts a little space between each printed character and between each printed word. There are no standards here—different fonts use different spacing. But you can tighten or loosen the space between characters, between words, or both, to squeeze more (or less) text across each line. Here's how:

1. Put the cursor wherever you want the change to take effect.

2. Choose Layout ➤ Other ➤ Printer Functions ➤ Word/Letter Spacing. You'll see this dialog box:

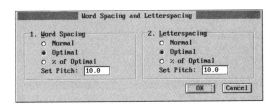

3. To change the spacing between words, choose one of the following options under <u>W</u>ord Spacing. If you want to change the spacing between characters, choose one of the same three options under <u>L</u>etter Spacing:

> **<u>N</u>ormal**   Uses the spacing the printer manufacturer thinks is best.

> **<u>O</u>ptimal**   Uses the spacing that WordPerfect Corporation thinks is best (this is the default, and may be the same as Normal).

> **<u>%</u> of Optimal**   Use this setting to tighten or loosen text yourself. For example, if you enter **75** (for 75%), the text will be 25% tighter. If you enter **125** (for 125%) the text will be 25% looser.

> **<u>S</u>et Pitch**   Lets you enter an exact pitch (in characters per inch).

4. Choose OK until you get back to the document.

Kerning

Kerning provides another way to tighten up the space between letters. When kerning is on, small letters are "tucked under" large letters as space permits. Kerning affects all text, but it's especially apparent with large headline-style text. Figure 28.3 shows an example. The first word *TuTu* is not kerned, and the second example is kerned. Notice how the lowercase *u* tucks under each uppercase T. The last two examples combine automatic kerning with other features that I'll describe a bit later.

To use automatic kerning, follow the steps below:

1. Move the cursor to where you want to activate kerning. Or, if you want to kern a portion of your text, select that text.

2. Choose <u>L</u>ayout ➤ <u>O</u>ther ➤ <u>P</u>rinter Functions.

3. To turn kerning on, select <u>K</u>erning (so it's marked with an ×). To turn it off, deselect <u>K</u>erning so the check box is cleared.

4. Choose OK twice.

TuTu

Normal (no kerning)

TuTu

Automatic kerning

TuTu

Automatic and
"manual" kerning with
Advance

TuTu

Same as above, but at
85% optimal letter spacing

WordPerfect inserts a [Kern On] code where kerning starts and, if you selected text in step 1, a [Kern Off] code where kerning ends. You can also end kerning at any point in your document by moving the cursor there and repeating the steps above, deselecting Kerning in step 3.

Notice that Figure 28.3 also shows an example of "manual" kerning, where I used the Advance feature (described next) to move the second uppercase *T* 12 points to the left, thereby kerning that *T* over the first lowercase *u*. (Automatic kerning isn't quite so fancy.)

Just to show you the possibilities, the fourth *TuTu* illustrates what happens after reducing the letter spacing to 85% Of Optimal. (If you know what you're doing, you can rule your text with an iron fist.)

Using Advance

The Advance feature is the main feature that lets you put your text *exactly* where you want it. It's sort of the laser-printing, obsessive-compulsive Word-Perfectionist's dream-come-true. Here's how to use it:

1. Move the cursor to the character (or, in Graphics mode, to the insertion point just to the left of the character) that you want to reposition on the page.

2. Choose Layout ➤ Other ➤ Advance. You'll see this dialog box:

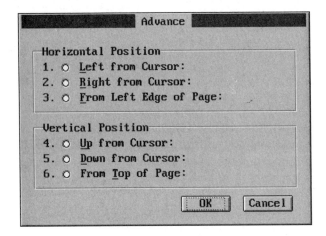

3. Choose the direction you want to advance the text.

4. Type in the amount to move, either in inches (for example, **.0167**) or in points followed by a *p* (for example, **12p**).

5. Choose OK (twice) to return to your document.

WordPerfect inserts a code into the document that will tell the printer how far (or where) to advance the print head before resuming printing.

You can advance text relative to the cursor or to a specific position on the page. For example, in the third example of *TuTu* in Figure 28.3, I advanced the second uppercase *T* 12 points (12p) to the left of the cursor.

If you want to advance text into the margin, or at some other place on the page, you can use one of the "From...Page" options in the Advance dialog box. For example, if while using the Advance feature, you choose From Top Of Page and enter **.25**, the text that follows will start printing .25 inches from the top edge of the page (*not* from the top margin).

Note that *all* the text to the right of the cursor is affected by the Advance. If you want to advance a small amount of text in some direction, you need to start, and follow, that text with the appropriate Advance codes. For instance, suppose you do the following at the start of a page:

1. Choose Layout ➤ Other ➤ Advance ➤ From Top Of Page to .25″.

2. Choose From Left Edge Of Page to 3.5″, then choose OK twice.

3. Type **THIS IS WAY UP HIGH**.

4. Choose Layout ➤ Other ➤ Advance ➤ From Top Of Page to 1″.

5. Choose From Left Edge Of Page to 1″, then choose OK twice.

6. Type **AND THIS IS NORMAL**.

The phrase "THIS IS WAY UP HIGH" will appear near the top of the page ($\frac{1}{4}$″ below the top edge), 3.5″ in from the left edge of the page. The phrase "AND THIS IS NORMAL" will begin at the more "normal" 1″ margins (an inch from the top, and an inch from the left).

You still can't print within that roughly $\frac{1}{4}$″ of white space around the sheet, even with the aid of Advance. That "dead zone" is reserved for the rollers that move the paper through the printer. Ink never touches there because if it did the rollers would surely smudge it.

TIP

You cannot advance text into a graphic box unless that box's Text Flow option is set to Through Box.

It can be a little tricky moving the cursor around advanced text in Graphics or Page mode. You may find it easier to use Reveal Codes and/or Text mode to navigate the cursor through text that's been positioned with Advance. We'll look at some examples of how you can use Advance to achieve special effects in a moment.

Changing the Limits of Justification

Though it sounds like a fancy legal term for a speed trap, *limits of justification* really concerns how much space WordPerfect puts between individual letters versus how much space it puts between words, when fully justifying text across the margins (Layout ➤ Justification ➤ Full, or Layout ➤ Justification ➤ Full, All Lines, or equivalent justification in table cells). It has no effect on left-justified, centered, or flush-right text.

Here's how it works. When you've turned on full justification, and Word-Perfect is about to print a line that doesn't reach over to the right margin (with normal spacing), it starts deciding where to insert spaces to make the stretch:

- First, if it can make the stretch by squeezing one more word from the next line onto the current line, it does so, within the "compression limits."

- If it can't squeeze another word onto the current line, it starts inserting spaces between the words on the line, up to the "expansion limits."

- If it still cannot make the text stretch to the right margin after reaching those limits, it spaces the text evenly between characters.

By default, the most WordPerfect will compress text is to 60% of the current spacing. By default, the farthest it will expand text between words is 400% (four times the number of spaces between each word). After that, it starts spacing characters. Here's how you can change that:

1. Move the cursor to where you want to change the justification limits, or select a block of text. (Presumably, the text here is, or will be, fully justified; otherwise you're wasting your time.)

2. Choose <u>L</u>ayout ➤ <u>O</u>ther ➤ <u>P</u>rinter Functions. The top of the dialog box presents these options:

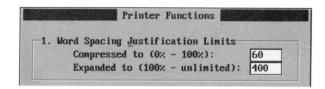

- If you want to squeeze text a little tighter as necessary, *decrease* the Compressed To percentage.

- If you don't want to compress text quite so much, *increase* the Compressed To percentage (for example, 100% means it can't get any tighter than 100% of its current tightness).

- If you want to put *more* space between words, and less space between letters when necessary, *increase* the Expanded To percentage (anything over 1000% is considered unlimited).

- If you want to put *less* space between words, and put more of the spacing between characters (even out the spacing across the line), lower the Expanded To percentage (100% would expand words and characters roughly the same).

3. Choose OK twice.

There are actually situations where these settings can be useful. For an example of compression, take a look back at Figure 28.2, where all the body text is fully justified within the columns. If I were to *decrease* the Compressed To percentage, WordPerfect might be able to squeeze even more text across certain lines. Then there would be even more room on the page, and the document would have an even heavier appearance. If I didn't allow WordPerfect to compress at all (set Compressed To to 100%), there would probably be more white space across some lines, and thus less text and a less heavy appearance.

Figure 28.4 shows a two-word title, *Make Spread*, fully justified between two margins. In the top example, I've minimized the Expanded To justification limit to 100%. Since WordPerfect can't stick all the space between the two words, it spreads the space throughout all the characters. In the bottom example, I maximized the Expanded To ratio to 9999 (unlimited). Therefore, WordPerfect can (and does) put *all* the required extra spacing between the words only.

Make Spread

Make   Spread

Baseline for Typesetters

WordPerfect also has a feature called *Baseline Placement For Typesetters (First Baseline At Top Margin)*. I suppose this one is self-explanatory enough that I can skip it. (Just kidding!) But if you're not a typesetter yourself, *you* might want to skip to the next section.

A typesetter would probably notice that when you use a feature such as Advance to put text at a specific place on the page in relation to the edges of the page, the *baseline* of that text is roughly at the specified position.

If that "roughly" isn't exact enough for you, and you need to ensure that the baseline of the text is at the specified position, you need to

1. Move the cursor to the top of the document and choose <u>L</u>ayout ➤ <u>D</u>ocument ➤ <u>B</u>aseline Placement For Typesetters (First Baseline At Top Margin).

2. Switch to a fixed line height (<u>L</u>ayout ➤ <u>L</u>ine ➤ Line <u>H</u>eight ➤ <u>F</u>ixed), and set the line height you want.

Once you've done this, the first baseline on the page becomes the top margin, rather than the baseline of the first line of text on the page. Then, when you use a feature like Advance, the actual *baseline* of the advanced text will be exactly at the measurement you specified. So there ya go, type-setters. Have a ball.

Special Effects

You can use some of the techniques described in this chapter and previous chapters to spruce up your documents with some special effects. Figure 28.5 shows some examples of what you can do. The next few sections describe the techniques used to create those effects.

Drop Shadow

D rop Cap is what you call that big letter at the start of this paragraph. It's just one big character in a graphics User Box. The box is anchored to the left side of this paragraph. Sizing the graphics box controls space around the cap.

White On Black

STRETCH

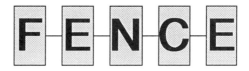

FENCE

Drop Shadow Text

Here's how to do the drop shadow example, as shown in Figure 28.5:

1. Move the cursor to where you're going to type the text, and choose your font. Jot down the Ln and Pos cursor positions indicated in the status bar near the lower-left corner of the screen.

2. Type the text.

3. Type the text again (on the next line if it doesn't fit on the current line).

4. Select the second copy, and use Font ➤ Print Color and Gray (or whatever) from the Palette Colors.

5. Move the cursor to the start of the second (gray) copy of text.

6. Choose Layout ➤ Other ➤ Advance ➤ From Left Edge Of Page. Then enter a number that's slightly larger than the Pos position that you jotted down earlier (about a tenth of an inch). Press ↵.

7. Choose From Top Of Page, and enter a number that's also slightly larger than the Ln position you jotted down earlier.

8. Choose OK to work your way back to the document window, and print the document to see the result.

TIP If you have a PostScript printer, or other printer that prints Outline appearance opaque, try selecting one copy of the dual text and choosing Font ➤ Outline for a different kind of drop-shadow effect.

Note that instead of advancing to a particular place on the page, you can advance left, right, up, or down, as long as you know how far to go. That way, both the text and its drop shadow will move together as you insert and delete neighboring text.

Drop Cap

Drop caps are a common publishing thing, and they're easy to do in WordPerfect. The basic trick is to put the large letter into a graphics User box that's anchored to the left edge of the paragraph.

TIP

Once you've successfully created a couple of drop caps, you can record a macro to do the job. Then, you can just move the cursor to the first line of any paragraph and run the macro whenever you want to create a drop cap.

Here's how to get started with drop caps:

1. Move the cursor to the first character in the paragraph. Make sure it's an uppercase letter. (If there's a tab there, delete the tab.)

2. Select that first character (press Alt+F4 or F12 then →).

3. Choose Edit ➤ Cut (or press Ctrl+X).

4. Choose Graphics ➤ Graphics Boxes ➤ Create ➤ Based On Box Style ➤ User Box ➤ Select.

5. Choose Edit Position ➤ Horizontal Position ➤ Left ➤ OK.

6. Choose Create Text.

7. Use Font ➤ Font ➤ Font to choose the font for the drop cap (I used a bold Sans-Serif font at 72 points), then choose OK.

8. Choose Edit ➤ Paste (or press Ctrl+V) to paste in the first character from the paragraph.

9. Press F7 or choose File ➤ Close.

10. Choose Edit Size ➤ Set Width, and choose a reasonable width (I used .75″ in the example).

11. Choose Set Height and enter a reasonable height (I used .8″). Choose OK.

12. Choose <u>O</u>ptions ➤ Co<u>n</u>tent Options ➤ <u>H</u>orizontal Position Of Contents In Box ➤ <u>C</u>entered ➤ <u>V</u>ertical Position Of Contents In Box ➤ <u>T</u>op ➤ OK. Then choose OK.

13. Choose OK to return to the document.

If there's too much white space around the cap, first reduce the spacing for User boxes:

1. Move the cursor to the left of (or above) the drop cap's [Para Box] code.

2. Choose <u>G</u>raphics ➤ Graphics <u>B</u>oxes ➤ St<u>y</u>les ➤ User Box ➤ <u>E</u>dit.

3. Choose Edit <u>B</u>order/Fill ➤ <u>S</u>pacing ➤ and *de*select <u>A</u>utomatic Spacing.

4. Choose <u>O</u>utside, Set All, and set all the outside spacing to 0".

5. Choose <u>I</u>nside, Set All, and change that setting to 0".

6. Choose OK ➤ Close ➤ OK ➤ Close to return to the document.

You can make any final adjustments to the size of the drop cap's box (in Graphics or Page mode) by clicking the box and then dragging the sizing handles to change its size.

White Text on Black

White text on a black background is also pretty easy, provided your printer can display it.

Begin by creating a one-cell table and setting its fill shade to 100% black. Then type the text inside the cell, select that text, and set the print color to white. Even if it doesn't look right on the screen, print it anyway—it still might work. For more information, look for the same topic toward the end of Chapter 7.

STRETCHING Text

To stretch a title or other passage of text across the margins, just move the cursor to the beginning of the text and choose <u>L</u>ayout ➤ <u>J</u>ustification ➤

Full, All Lines. (At the end of, or beneath the borders, you can use the same basic commands to change the justification to something else.)

If the title has two or more words, and you want to control the spacing between words and characters, set the justification limits at the start of the title, as discussed earlier in this chapter.

"Fenced" Letters

The word *Fence* in Figure 28.5 is really just a table with nine columns and two rows. I vertically joined every other pair of cells starting at cell A1, and then I put a large letter within each joined pair. I also shaded each one of those cells. Finally, I went through the table and removed lines to achieve the appearance you see in the figure.

Rotated Letters

The last example at the bottom of Figure 28.5 is just a table with one row and four columns. Each cell in the table contains a graphics User box. Each User box contains one letter of the alphabet, rotated a bit using Alt+F9 while in the graphics box text editor (Chapter 26).

Drop-Shadowed Boxes

If you want to put a drop shadow behind a table or graphics box to give it a raised look, like the examples shown in Figure 28.6, just customize its border style, as explained below.

- To drop-shadow a table, move the cursor into the table and switch to Table Edit mode (Alt+F11). Choose Lines/Fill ➤ Border/Fill ➤ Customize ➤ Based On Border Style. Highlight any border style *except* [None] and choose Select. Now, choose Shadow.

- To drop-shadow a graphics box, edit the box (just double-click it), choose Edit Border/Fill, then choose Shadow.

FIGURE 28.6

A table and graphics
Figure box, each with
a drop-shadow
giving it a raised
appearance

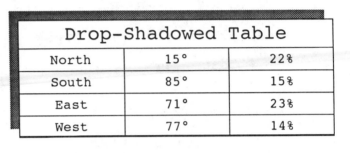

Drop-Shadowed Table		
North	15°	22%
South	85°	15%
East	71°	23%
West	77°	14%

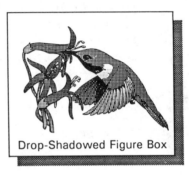

Drop-Shadowed Figure Box

You'll be taken to a dialog box similar to the one below, where you can choose the type of shadow you want:

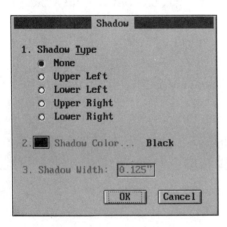

Shadow

1. Shadow Type
   ● None
   ○ Upper Left
   ○ Lower Left
   ○ Upper Right
   ○ Lower Right

2. ■ Shadow Color... **Black**

3. Shadow Width: 0.125"

OK | Cancel

The Shadow Type options lets you decide where to place the shadow (Upper Left, Lower Left, and so forth). After you choose an option (other than None), you can change the Shadow Color, if you wish. Simply choose Shadow Color, choose your color, and choose Close. You can also choose a Shadow Width and specify how thick the shadow should be. Finally, choose OK and/or Close as necessary to work your way back to the document window.

For more information on defining border styles for graphics boxes, please see Chapter 17 and Chapter 26.

White Text over a Graphic

Many PostScript printers (and some others) print text that has the Outline appearance as opaque white. Anything under that text will be covered by the letters. In Figure 28.7 (printed on a PostScript printer) I centered the graphic on the page and set the Text Flows option to Through Box. Then I typed and centered the text *White Text Over A Graphic*. Finally, I selected that text and chose Font ➤ Outline to make it opaque white.

If you want to try to achieve a similar effect using a non-PostScript printer, start with a Bold font (instead of an Outline font), and use Font ➤ Print Color to set the print color of the text to white or some light shade. Then print the job graphically (File ➤ Print/Fax ➤ Print Job Graphically ➤ Print). For more information, see Chapter 10.

FIGURE 28.7

PostScript printers (and some others) print Outline text as opaque white, so that it covers anything behind the text.

Text in a Graphic

To put text "inside" a graphic, first you need to put the graphic on the page, with its Text Flows option set to Through Box. Then you can use the Advance feature to advance text into the graphic box. Alternatively, you can place a second box over the first box. The second box should contain the text that should look as if it's "inside" the graphic in the first box.

In Figure 28.8 the cartoon is in a Figure box that's anchored to its neighboring paragraph. Its Text Flow option is set to Through Box. The words *Text In A Graphic* are in a separate User box that's sized and positioned exactly like the Figure box, but its Text Flow setting is set to On Larger Side. The text within the User box appears to be inside the graphic. The neighboring text outside the box flows around that User box.

FIGURE 28.8

Example of putting text "inside" a graphic box. (The words *Text In A Graphic* are actually in a separate box that overlaps the figure.)

Text
In A
Graphic

In the original Presentation Task Force clip art package, Joe Cool over there is pointing to an empty piece of paper. Right now he's in a Word-Perfect Figure box that's anchored to the left of this paragraph, with Text Flow set to Through Text. Next to the code for that box is a User Box that's the same size as the Figure box. Inside that User box are the words *Text In A Graphic*, stacked and center-aligned as shown. I put some hard returns on top, and a 1-inch left margin inside that User box to get that text to line up on Joe's little sign in there. Text Flow is set to On Right Side for the User box, and *this* text is wrapping around that box.

Free-Form Text and Graphics

For total freedom in combining text and graphics on the page, consider putting all your graphics, arrows, and text labels in graphic User boxes that have

Text Flow set to Through Box. That way, you can just drag boxes around the screen in any manner you wish without worrying about them "bumping" into one another. That's how I created the mishmash of text and graphics in Figure 28.9.

If you need to do a lot of graphics work, a dedicated graphics program is definitely the way to go. But for the occasional blending of text and graphics, WordPerfect will probably do the trick. Here are some pointers that might help you out:

- Use Page mode or Graphics mode at 100% view for the most accurate alignments. (You'll still want to print a hard copy once in a while to check your work.)

- If you have trouble positioning the cursor, consider filling the entire page with hard returns (↵) before you start entering your graphics boxes.

FIGURE 28.9

Miscellaneous chunks of clip art in separate User boxes, sized and arranged in Graphics mode using the mouse

- If you have trouble double-clicking certain boxes once they start overlapping, turn on Reveal Codes so you can edit them by number using Graphics ➤ Graphic Boxes ➤ Edit.

Putting Graphics Boxes inside Graphics Boxes

Suppose you create a mishmash of text and graphics, like the examples in Figure 28.9. Then, you want to take your finished masterpiece and put it into some other document as though it were its own figure.

First, you'd need to save the masterpiece in its own file. Then, in some other document, create a graphics box for storing the entire creation. At the Create Graphics Box dialog box, choose Contents ➤ Text, then choose Filename and enter the name of the masterpiece file.

You won't be able to scale it like a graphic, because it's a graphic box containing text (User box codes in this example). But you will be able to wrap other text around that box and even rotate the contents of the box.

Extreme Special Effects

If you want to do really wild special effects with text, you need to buy a program that's specifically designed for that purpose. Figure 28.10 shows some textual special effects I created in Bitstream's Makeup program.

Once you create a special effect in MakeUp, you can export it to a variety of formats (including WordPerfect's .WPG format) Then you can import that file into your WordPerfect document as a graphic.

Several packages can do this type of text manipulation, though the only one I'm familiar with is the aforementioned MakeUp (which only runs under Windows 3.1 and later). If you're interested, check around your local computer store to see which packages are available for your hardware.

On the simpler and less expensive side, some third-party font packages for DOS offer their own special effects.

FIGURE 28.10

Examples of wild text effects created in Bitstream's MakeUp (requires Windows 3.1)

Sample Layouts

Now let's take a look at some sample desktop publishing layouts. I'll describe the various techniques used to create each one.

Overhead Transparencies, Posters, and Fliers

Creating full-page overhead transparencies, posters, signs, or fliers with WordPerfect is simply a matter of reducing the margins (if appropriate), switching to a landscape paper size (if appropriate), and centering text horizontally and vertically (again, if appropriate). Other than that, it's usually just a matter of using large fonts.

If you have some clip art borders and backgrounds, and you want to use them in a full-page document, bring the clip art into a full-sized User box that's anchored to the page, with Text Flow set to Through Box.

Figure 28.11 shows a sample sign that has a border from the Presentation Task Force clip art collection around its edge. The basic steps needed to bring in the border are explained below.

1. If you'll be printing sideways (landscape), choose Layout ➤ Page ➤ Paper Size/Type ➤ Letter Landscape (or whatever is appropriate) ➤ Select ➤ OK.

2. Choose Layout ➤ Margins ➤ (*set all four document margins to .3"* *each*) ➤ OK.

3. Choose Graphics ➤ Graphics Boxes ➤ Create ➤ Filename ➤ (*choose the file name for your clip art border*).

4. Choose Attach To ➤ Page ➤ Edit Position ➤ Full Page ➤ OK ➤ Text Flow Around Box ➤ Text Flows ➤ Through Box ➤ OK.

5. If you want to center any text that you type within the border, choose Layout ➤ Page ➤ Center Current Page ➤ OK, then choose Layout ➤ Justification ➤ Center. Start choosing your fonts and typing your text.

The best way to see what you're doing as you type is to use Page mode (View ➤ Page Mode). You might want to reduce the magnification, using View ➤ Zoom or the Ribbon.

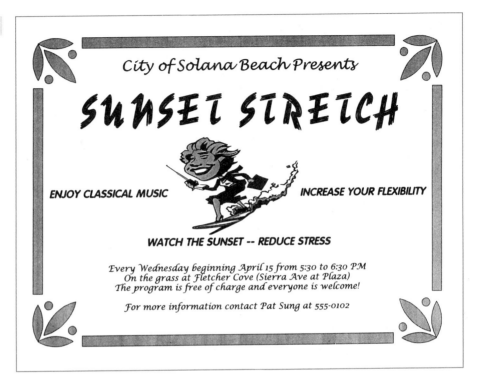

TIP

If you want to print on overhead transparencies, be sure to purchase the kind that will go through your laser printer. Avery makes some, and they're available at many office supply stores.

Tri-Fold Mailers

Figure 28.12 shows a sample blank tri-fold mailer. Figure 28.13 shows how that layout looks with some text added.

Here, in brief, are the basic commands I used to create the layout:

1. Set a landscape (11″ × 8.5″) paper size. Choose <u>L</u>ayout ➤ <u>P</u>age ➤ Paper <u>S</u>ize/Type.

FIGURE 28.12

A sample tri-fold
brochure layout
(blank)

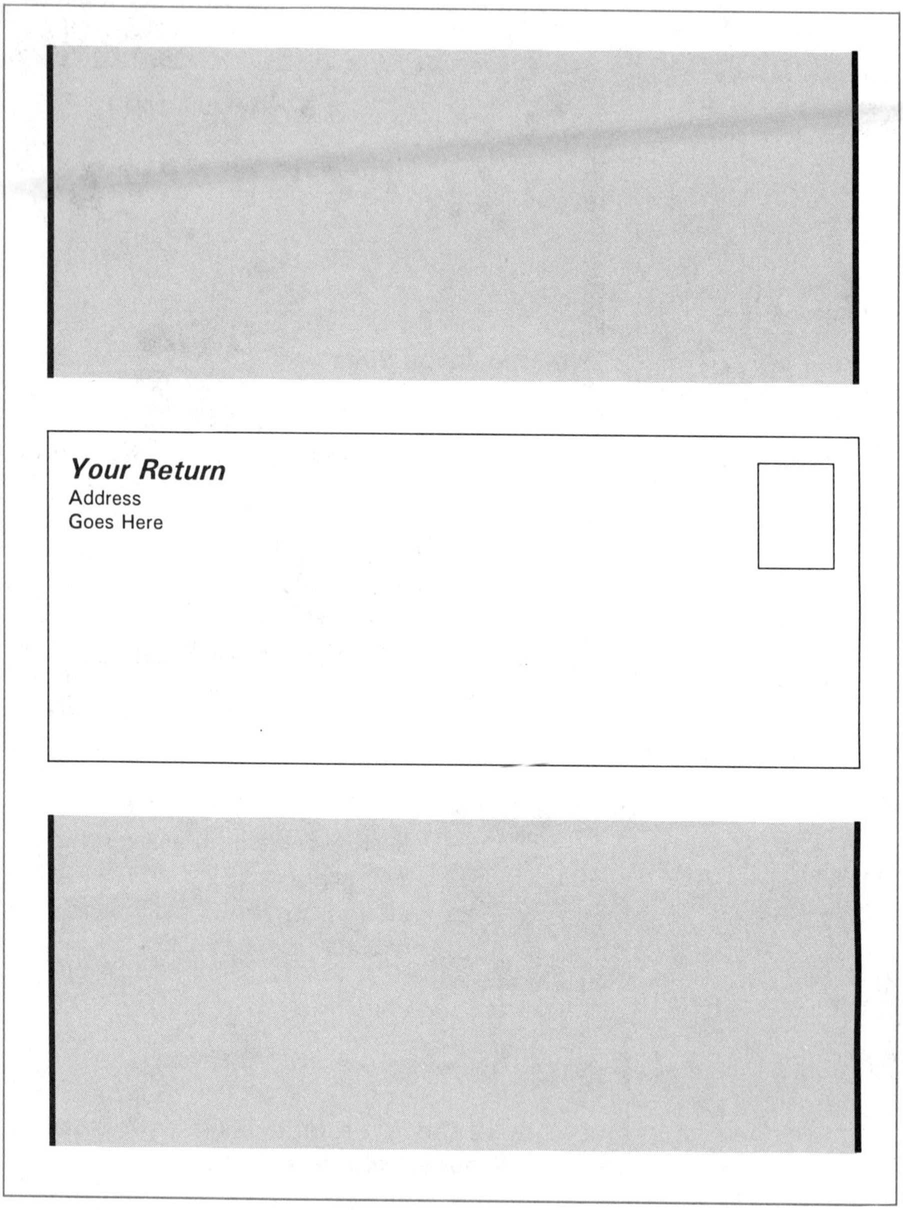

Your Return
Address
Goes Here

2. Make all four document margins as small as possible (each is .3″ in the example). Choose Layout ➤ Margins.

3. Set up three Newspaper columns. Layout ➤ Columns.

FIGURE 28.13

The sample layout in Figure 28.12 with some text typed in

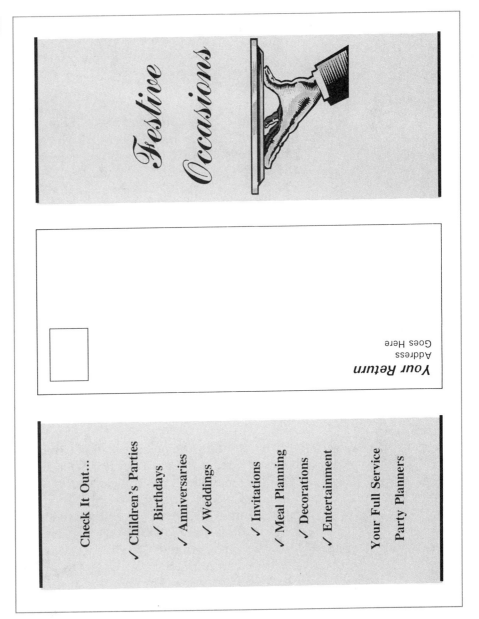

T I P

If you're going to print on pre-printed tri-fold paper stock, as discussed near the end of this chapter, you can stop right here.

4. Create the leftmost shaded panel. Choose Graphics ➤ Graphics Boxes ➤ Create ➤ Based On Box Style ➤ Text Box ➤ Select ➤ Attach To ➤ Page ➤ Edit Position ➤ Horizontal Position ➤ Full ➤ Position Relative To ➤ Column ➤ 1 ➤ Vertical Position ➤ Full ➤ OK ➤ Text Flow Around Box ➤ Text Flows ➤ Through Box ➤ OK.

5. Create the center panel with full border. Choose Graphics ➤ Graphics Boxes ➤ Create ➤ Based On Box Style ➤ Figure Box ➤ Select ➤ Attach To ➤ Page ➤ Edit Position ➤ Horizontal Position ➤ Full ➤ Position Relative To ➤ Column ➤ 2 ➤ Vertical Position ➤ Full ➤ OK ➤ Text Flow Around Box ➤ Text Flows ➤ Through Box ➤ OK.

6. Create the rightmost shaded panel. Choose Graphics ➤ Graphics Boxes ➤ Create ➤ Based On Box Style ➤ Text Box ➤ Select ➤ Attach To ➤ Page ➤ Edit Position ➤ Horizontal Position ➤ Full ➤ Position Relative To ➤ Column ➤ 3 ➤ Vertical Position ➤ Full ➤ OK ➤ Text Flows Around Box ➤ Text Flows ➤ Through Box ➤ OK.

7. Create a spot for the postage stamp. Choose Graphics ➤ Graphics Boxes ➤ Create ➤ Based On Box Style ➤ Table Box ➤ Select ➤ Edit Border/Fill ➤ Lines ➤ Select All ➤ Dotted Line ➤ Select ➤ Close ➤ Close ➤ Attach To ➤ Page ➤ Edit Position ➤ Horizontal Position ➤ Left ➤ Position Relative To ➤ Column ➤ 2 ➤ Offset From Position ➤ Right ➤ .25 ➤ Vertical Position ➤ Top ➤ Offset From Position ➤ Down ➤ .25 ➤ OK ➤ Edit Size ➤ Set Width ➤ 1 ➤ Set Height ➤ .75 ➤ OK ➤ Text Flows Around Box ➤ Text Flows ➤ Through Box ➤ OK.

8. Set up the return address. Choose Graphics ➤ Graphics Boxes ➤ Create ➤ Based On Box Style ➤ User Box ➤ Select ➤ Create Text ➤ (*Here's where you choose fonts and justification and type your own return address exactly how you want it to look on the mailer*) ➤ Alt+F9 ➤ Rotate Box Contents ➤ 90° Rotation ➤ OK ➤ F7 ➤ Attach To ➤ Page ➤ Edit Position ➤ Horizontal Position ➤ Left

➤ Position <u>R</u>elative To ➤ C<u>o</u>lumn ➤ 2 ➤ <u>O</u>ffset From Position ➤ <u>R</u>ight ➤ 0.15 ➤ <u>V</u>ertical Position ➤ <u>B</u>ottom ➤ Off<u>s</u>et From Position ➤ <u>U</u>p ➤ 0.15 ➤ OK ➤ Edit <u>S</u>ize ➤ <u>A</u>utomatic Width... ➤ A<u>u</u>tomatic Height ➤ OK ➤ <u>T</u>ext Flows Around Box ➤ Text <u>F</u>lows ➤ <u>T</u>hrough Box ➤ OK.

Print and save the layout now.

A few tips before you start filling in your own text and graphics:

- When typing directly onto the layout, be sure to start with the cursor beneath all existing codes (press Home End then Home ↑ if you're not sure).

- If you need to change the return address, edit User box #1. Choose <u>G</u>raphics ➤ Graphics <u>B</u>oxes ➤ <u>E</u>dit ➤ <u>C</u>ounter Number ➤ User Box ➤ 1 ➤ <u>E</u>dit Box. Then choose options from the dialog box, or choose <u>E</u>dit Text to change the font or text of the return address.

- The shading in the first and third panels comes from the default fill shading for Text boxes 1 and 2. You can change the borders and fill for either or both Text boxes with the standard <u>G</u>raphics ➤ Graphics <u>B</u>oxes ➤ <u>E</u>dit series of commands.

- Switch to Text mode (Ctrl+F3 T) to make typing into the shaded columns easier.

Newsletter with Vertical Masthead

There are as many different possible formats for newsletters as there are newsletters. Indeed, people have written entire books on the topic of newsletters. Figure 28.14 shows an especially fancy one (and one that might take some patience to create). It uses quite a few advanced features, including rotated fonts, word and letter spacing, graphics, and graphic lines. The commands used to create it are listed below.

1. Set margins. Choose <u>L</u>ayout ➤ <u>M</u>argins ➤ *(Set all four document margins to .5" each)* ➤ OK.

2. Create a Text box for the masthead. Choose <u>G</u>raphics ➤ Graphics <u>B</u>oxes ➤ <u>C</u>reate ➤ Based On Box St<u>y</u>le ➤ Text Box ➤ <u>S</u>elect.

FIGURE 28.14

A sample newsletter format

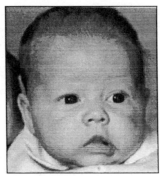

NEWS FLASH!

Rubber Baby Buggy Bulletin

FREE!

All the News in Fits and Starts

January/February 1994

What Makes Us Human?

If you look around a town and a jungle, you'll see one difference between the humans and beasts. All the humans *have* things. None of the beasts do.

Everyone has things, from the lowliest beggar with the clothes on his proverbial back, to the kings and queens with near infinite amounts of stuff.

So ingrained into our being is this concept of ownership that we rarely notice it. For example, you probably didn't even flinch when I attributed "lowness" to the beggar, as though the person with the least stuff naturally *is* the "lower" or "inferior" of the two. We're used to assigning status based on amount of stuff owned.

And speaking of queens, have you noticed how just being the the world's major heavy-hitting thing collectors has made the (otherwise powerless) British royals famous! You always see their faces in check-out stand tabloids. (Though I've often wondered if that's just to remind us the we, too, need to "pick up a few more *things*" while we're out.)

Whole countries are based on this thing-collecting thing. America is the envy of the world because it's based on an unspoken rule that says "You're free to acquire as many *things* as you can in your lifetime. You just can't A)murder or B)deceive (too much) to get them."

For example, you can't walk over and kill your neighbor, then proclaim "all his things are now mine." If that were allowed, the US would have a population of one tough, ruthless dude. And he'd own *everything*.

You can't outright deceive to get things either. Like, you can't trick your neighbor into thinking he's signing an innocent petition, then say "Ha Ha I fooled ya. You just signed over all your earthly possessions to me."

Unfortunately, rules notwithstanding, some people are still just naturally better than others at acquiring things. Over time, those people end up having all the good stuff.

Fortunately, or unfortunately, depending on your own thing-collecting abilities, there is a group out there willing to say "OK, that's enough. You good thing-collectors have too much stuff now. Time to give some back and start over."

That group is called Democrats, and tends to come into power every 10 years or so, after the good thing-collectors have hogged up practically everything. (Apparently, there is no such group in Britain, where the same family has had all the good things for centuries. Maybe that's why our forefathers defected.)

Thing-ownership is so important that we even have legal means of deciding what happens to our things after we're dead. (Heaven forbid they give our ex-stuff to just *anyone*!) Though you may be gone, your will to own things lives on.

None of this has anything to do with rubber baby buggies. I just threw it in as sort of a bonus.

— Alan Simpson

3. Set up border lines for the Text box. Choose Edit B̲order/Fill ➤ Lines ➤ L̲eft Line ➤ Thick Line ➤ Select ➤ R̲ight Line ➤ Thick Line ➤ Select ➤ T̲op Line ➤ [None] ➤ Select ➤ B̲ottom Line ➤ [None] ➤ S̲elect ➤ Close ➤ Close.

4. Attach the Text box to the page and define its position. Choose <u>At</u>-tach To ➤ <u>P</u>age ➤ Edit <u>P</u>osition ➤ <u>H</u>orizontal Position ➤ <u>L</u>eft ➤ <u>V</u>ertical Position ➤ <u>F</u>ull ➤ OK.

5. Define the Text box size. Choose Edit <u>S</u>ize ➤ Set <u>W</u>idth ➤ 1.15″ ➤ OK.

6. Let text flow through the box. Choose <u>T</u>ext Flow Through Box ➤ Text <u>F</u>lows ➤ <u>T</u>hrough Box ➤ OK.

That completes the empty vertical box, which you should be able to see on your screen in Graphics, Page, or Print Preview mode now.

Next comes the tricky part of filling it in:

1. Edit the Text box. Choose <u>G</u>raphics ➤ Graphics <u>B</u>oxes ➤ <u>E</u>dit ➤ Document Box <u>N</u>umber ➤ 1 ➤ <u>E</u>dit Box.

2. Rotate the text. Choose Cr<u>e</u>ate Text ➤ Alt+F9 ➤ Rotate Box <u>C</u>ontents ➤ 90° Rotation ➤ OK.

3. Put a User box inside the Text box. Choose <u>G</u>raphics ➤ Graphics <u>B</u>oxes ➤ <u>C</u>reate ➤ <u>F</u>ilename ➤ (*Enter the name of a graphics file*) ➤ OK ➤ Based On Box Style ➤ User Box ➤ <u>S</u>elect.

4. Define the box position. Choose Edit <u>P</u>osition ➤ <u>H</u>orizontal Position ➤ <u>L</u>eft ➤ <u>V</u>ertical Position ➤ <u>B</u>ottom ➤ OK.

5. Set the box size. Choose Edit <u>S</u>ize ➤ Set <u>W</u>idth ➤ (*about 1″*) ➤ Set <u>H</u>eight ➤ (*about 1″*) ➤ OK ➤ OK.

At this point you've put a User box into the Text box, but you're still editing the Text box. Now you need to pick a font and put the text in:

1. Select a font and size for the masthead title. Choose <u>F</u>ont ➤ <u>F</u>ont ➤ <u>F</u>ont ➤ (*I used Bodoni -WP Bold (Type 1)*) ➤ <u>S</u>ize ➤ (*I used 47pt*) ➤ OK.

2. Squeeze letters closer together and kern. Choose <u>L</u>ayout ➤ <u>O</u>ther ➤ <u>P</u>rinter Functions ➤ <u>W</u>ord/Letter Spacing ➤ <u>L</u>etter Spacing ➤ % Of Optimal ➤ 80 ➤ OK ➤ <u>K</u>erning ➤ OK ➤ OK.

3. Type the vertical title (e.g. **Rubber Baby Buggy Bulletin**).

4. Select a font for the subtitle. Choose <u>F</u>ont ➤ <u>F</u>ont ➤ <u>F</u>ont ➤ (*I chose Courier 10 cpi Bold* ➤ OK

5. Press ↵.

6. Type the second vertical line of text, **January/February 1994,** press Shift+F6, then type **All the News In Fits and Starts**, press Alt+F6, then type **FREE!** and several extra blank spaces (*not* hard returns), to keep it from running clear to the right margin.

If there's a page break within the box, there's too much text. You'll have to reduce font sizes, and remove any extra [HRt] codes until the page break disappears. Then…

7. Choose File ➤ Close or press F7 then choose OK.

You should be back at the document, where you can choose File ➤ Print/Fax ➤ Print to check your progress. If all looks well, this would be a good time to give the document a name and save it, using File ➤ Save.

The rest is relatively easy…

1. Move the cursor to the bottom of the document (Home Home ↓) and press ↵.

2. Set the left margin. Choose Layout ➤ Margins ➤ Left Margin ➤ **1.85″** ➤ OK.

3. Define a font for the horizontal headline ***NEWS FLASH!*** Choose Font ➤ Font ➤ Font (*I used Univers Bold Italic 72pt*) ➤ OK.

4. Tighten the text a little and kern. Choose Layout ➤ Other ➤ Printer Functions ➤ Word/Letter Spacing ➤ Word Spacing ➤ % Of Optimal ➤ **85** ➤ OK ➤ Kerning ➤ OK ➤ OK.

5. Type the headline (***News Flash!*** in my example). If it wraps to two lines, and you don't want that, you'll need to reduce the font size, or % optimal spacing, just to the left of the text.

6. Make sure you're at the end of the text. Press Home End.

7. Select the font for your main body text. Choose Font ➤ Font ➤ Font ➤ (*for example, CG Times 12 pt*) ➤ OK. (Reducing the font prevents a huge break when you press ↵ to move to the next line.)

8. Press ↵ to move down a line.

9. Create the horizontal line below the heading. Choose Graphics ➤ Graphics Lines ➤ Create ➤ OK.

10. On a piece of scratch paper, jot down the vertical position of the cursor right now (it's just to the right of Ln in the status bar—probably about 1.69″).

11. Press ↵ twice to add some space above the columns.

12. Set up the columns. Choose <u>L</u>ayout ➤ <u>C</u>olumns ➤ <u>N</u>umber Of Columns ➤ **2** ➤ <u>D</u>istance Between Columns ➤ *.25″* ➤ OK.

If you want a vertical line between the two columns, here's what to do:

1. Turn on Reveal Codes (Alt+F3) and make sure the cursor is just to the right of the Col Def code.

2. Choose <u>G</u>raphics ➤ Graphics <u>L</u>ines ➤ <u>C</u>reate ➤ Line <u>O</u>rientation ➤ <u>V</u>ertical ➤ <u>H</u>orizontal Position ➤ <u>B</u>etween Columns.

3. Choose <u>V</u>ertical Position ➤ <u>S</u>et, then type in a measurement that's just slightly larger than the one you jotted down a few steps back. For instance, if you jotted down 1.69, type **1.7**).

4. WordPerfect will automatically calculate the <u>L</u>ength of the line from the top of the line to the bottom page margin. You can adjust the length if you wish.

5. Choose OK to return to your document.

That's about it. I'll assume you can type the rest and insert any graphics that you want. By the way, you're still set at 85% optimal spacing. If your text is too tight, go back to the first character within the columns and use <u>L</u>ayout ➤ <u>O</u>ther ➤ <u>P</u>rinter Functions ➤ <u>W</u>ord/Letter Spacing ➤ <u>W</u>ord Spacing to set the spacing back to <u>O</u>ptimal (or whatever you wish).

Coloring Book

In the course of all this writing I end up with a lot of wasted paper that's printed only on one side. I also have a five-year-old daughter who likes to color. So, once in a while I use WordPerfect to create some pictures for her to color in (Figure 28.15), using the backs of otherwise wasted sheets of paper. Starting in a new document window, use the commands below.

1. If you're planning to print a wide picture, you might want to switch to a landscape paper size (<u>L</u>ayout ➤ <u>P</u>age ➤ Paper <u>S</u>ize/Type ➤ Letter (Landscape) ➤ <u>S</u>elect ➤ OK.

2. Choose <u>L</u>ayout ➤ <u>M</u>argins ➤ (*set all document margins to about 0.3"*) ➤ OK.

3. Select a graphics image and box style. Choose <u>G</u>raphics ➤ Graphics <u>B</u>oxes ➤ <u>C</u>reate ➤ <u>F</u>ilename ➤ (*pick an image*) ➤ Based On Box Style ➤ User Box ➤ <u>S</u>elect.

4. Attach and position the box on the page. Choose <u>A</u>ttach To ➤ Page ➤ Edit <u>P</u>osition ➤ <u>F</u>ull Page ➤ OK.

5. Choose Image <u>E</u>ditor ➤ <u>F</u>ill ➤ <u>W</u>hite ➤ F7 ➤ OK.

6. Choose <u>F</u>ile ➤ <u>P</u>rint/Fax ➤ <u>G</u>raphics Quality ➤ (<u>M</u>edium *for thick lines, or <u>H</u>igh for thin lines, depending on your printer*) ➤ P<u>r</u>int.

Be patient…It might take a couple of minutes to print these big graphics.

Preparing a Document for Typesetting

The term "professional typesetting" is a hard one to pinpoint these days, since desktop computers are quickly catching up to many of the high-end (and infinitely more expensive) typesetting machines. Nonetheless, if you don't have a fancy laser (or color) printer, you might want to get your local desktop publishing, typesetting, or pre-publishing service bureau to print some documents for you.

The first thing you need to do is call that service bureau and tell them what you want to do (have them print fancy WordPerfect documents for you). If they can do it, ask them what it will cost so you don't die of fright when you get the bill. (You might want to shop around a little.)

Then ask them which printer driver you should use, ask about any font restrictions, and whether you need to take any other special precautions to be sure the file will print successfully. For the sake of example, let's say they recommend that you use a PostScript printer driver, such as the Apple LaserWriter IINT. Furthermore, let's say that you can then use any of the built-in fonts for that printer.

Your first task is to run the WordPerfect install program, and install that printer driver (even though you don't actually have that printer connected to your computer). When asked for a port during the installation procedure, choose the Prompt For Filename option. Complete the installation normally (refer to Appendix A if you need help). You need only go through this rigmarole once.

Now, whenever you're going to create or work on documents that the service bureau will be printing, you just have to make sure that the new printer driver is selected. That, is, run WordPerfect normally, choose <u>F</u>ile ➤ <u>P</u>rint/Fax ➤ <u>S</u>elect, and then double-click (or select) the name of the printer that the service bureau requires. Create your document normally, using the fonts that are available to you through that printer driver.

You won't actually be able to print the document yourself, but you can see what it's going to look like in Graphics, Page, or Print Preview modes. When you're happy with the document, save it as usual. Then print it to disk. That is, choose File ➤ Print/Fax. Set your Text Quality and Graphics Quality options to High, and choose Print. As prompted, fill in a file name for the file you'll be creating (*don't* use the same name as the original document; save this as a separate copy). For instance, you might name this copy MYFILE.EPS (.EPS is the common extension for Encapsulated PostScript files). Choose OK and wait a couple of minutes.

When WordPerfect seems to be finished, you can copy that file you just created (for example, MYFILE.EPS) to a floppy disk and bring it on down to the printer for printing.

The one possible glitch in the whole thing might be that when you print to disk the resulting file might be too large to fit on a floppy disk. You can use any combination of the following techniques to solve that problem:

- When printing to disk, print each page to a separate file.

- When you're done printing, use a disk compression program to compress the finished files before copying them to floppies.

- Send the finished files to the service bureau by modem, rather than by floppy disk.

- You can also use a program like DOS's Backup (DOS 5 or earlier) or MSBackup (DOS 6) to split the large file into several separate files—but only if your service bureau can restore from the format you use.

For additional information, please talk to the folks at your service bureau.

WARNING

When you're finished printing the file to disk, be sure to return to your normal printer selection (choose File ➤ Print/Fax ➤ Select). If you forget to do this, your printer will ask you for a file name the next time you print a document.

Printing "Color" without a Color Printer

If you're happy with the quality of your printer, but you're looking to brighten up your documents with some color, gold trim, or something nice like that, you might be able to use your own printer. Just use paper that's already preprinted with some fancy colored trim or background.

To get started, contact one of the companies below and ask for a catalog:

Paper Direct
205 Chubb Avenue
Lyndhurst, NJ 07071
(800)-A-Papers (voice); (201)507-0817 (fax)

or...

Premier Papers, Inc.
P.O. Box 64785
St. Paul, MN 55164

You'll be amazed at how many different kinds of paper you can run through your laser printer. Build up your clip art and font collections, and you'll be a veritable one-person publishing firm!

Viewing Preprinted Forms

If you decide to print on preprinted papers, and you want to know what your document is going to look like before you print, try this.

Beg, borrow, or rent time on a flatbed scanner, and scan a copy of the preprinted stock to a bitmap or other file. In your WordPerfect document, set your margins as small as possible, open up that graphic file in a User box, size it to the full height and width of the screen, and set Text Flows to Through Box. To make up for the "dead zone," you might want to use the Image Editor to set the Scale Height and Scale Width to about 1.07 each.

When you get back to the document, you'll be able to see the preprinted background whenever you're in Page, Graphic, or Print Preview mode.

This works for *any* kind of preprinted stock (though, the more complicated the graphic image, the slower WordPerfect will be in redisplaying it on the screen as you type). Figure 28.16 shows a scanned income tax form (ugh) on the current document as a full-size User box. Because text flows through the box, I can type directly in the form. (Lucky me.)

Here are a few tips:

- You can print the text *and* the form simply by printing the finished document (though depending on the size and complexity of the form, this can be sl-o-o-o-o-o-o-w).

- If you want to print on pre-printed forms, set the <u>G</u>raphics Quality in the Print/Fax dialog box to Do <u>N</u>ot Print before you print.

- If you print on preprinted forms, your text might not line up with blanks on the printed form exactly. If necessary, scale the screen image of the preprinted form to match the preprinted form. Increasing the X and Y scales of the form to about 1.07%, using the graphics Image Editor (Chapter 26) will usually do the trick.

FIGURE 28.16

A preprinted form scanned and displayed on the screen

- If you have trouble getting the cursor to line up with blanks on the screen, move to the top of the document and set the Line Height (Layout ➤ Line ➤ Line Height) to some small number (.25″). That way, each time you press ↵ the cursor will move down only slightly.

- *Always* indent with tabs, and for good alignment set the tabs to about every .25″ or so (depending on your form). Use spaces only to make minor horizontal indentations, and use a monospaced font if possible.

- If you found working with the form on the screen to be unbearably slow or difficult, consider switching to Text mode and filling the entire page with tabs and hard returns (↵). Then switch to Graphics mode and use the arrow keys and mouse to move the cursor around the screen. (You might also use View ➤ Screen Setup to increase the % of the window used by Reveal Codes, and turn on Reveal Codes, so less of the graphic image appears in the editing window.)

In this chapter we've looked at some of WordPerfect's more advanced features. If you have a powerful printer, you can use these features to give your documents a more professional, polished look. Most people won't believe that you created them with WordPerfect! Next we'll turn to the Equation Editor, which makes it easy to typeset complex equations.

CHAPTER

29

Adding Equations to Your Documents

f a s t TRACK

To choose commands and mathematical symbols 1043

double-click any command or symbol in the Equation palette. Or press F5, highlight a command or symbol, then press ↵. To use a different palette, select a palette from the Set pop-up list with your mouse. Or press F5 until the list opens, highlight a palette name, then press ↵.

To change an equation 1045

use the same techniques you'd use to edit any graphics box (Chapter 26). For example, just double-click the equation. Or choose Graphics ➤ Graphics Boxes ➤ Edit, and specify the graphics box you want to change. Then use the Edit Equation, Content Options, Attach To, Edit Position, Edit Size, and Text Flows Around Box options, as appropriate, to define the appearance of the equation.

To change the appearance of all the equations 1045

choose Graphics ➤ Graphics Boxes ➤ Styles. Highlight either Equation Box or Inline Equation Box, depending on which type of equations you want to change. Choose Edit.

To change the font and/or size of the equation 1046

while you're in the Equation Editor, click the Settings button or press Shift+F1.

FOR MATHEMATICIANS, scientists, and other people who type mathematical or scientific documents, WordPerfect offers the Equations feature. This feature lets you type complex mathematical equations into a document and print them using all the special symbols and typesetting standards. Note, however, that the Equations feature does not *solve* the equations for you; it just lets you *enter* and *edit* them. A sample equation typed with WordPerfect is shown below:

$$\int_0^\infty x^{n-1}e^{-x}dx \;=\; \int_0^1\left(\log\frac{1}{x}\right)dx \;=\; \frac{1}{n}\prod_{m=1}^\infty \frac{\left(1+\frac{1}{m}\right)}{1+\frac{n}{m}}$$

By default, equations follow standard typesetting guidelines, where variables are printed in italics, and numbers and functions are printed in regular roman font.

Creating Equations

You can place equations in any of the eight types of graphics boxes discussed in Chapter 26, although it's often simplest to use Equation boxes for this purpose. The regular Equation box attaches the equation to a paragraph and displays the equation on its own line. If you want an equation to appear embedded as part of a line of text, use an Inline Equation box type. Be sure the equation you want to include will fit height-wise on a single line.

WordPerfect offers a special Equation Editor for creating, editing, and previewing your equations. To add an equation to a document and access the Equation Editor, follow these steps:

1. If you've already typed some of the text in the document, move the cursor to the line where you want to place the equation.

2. Choose Graphics ➤ Graphics Boxes ➤ Create.

3. Choose Based On Box Style.

4. Double-click Equation Box or Inline Equation Box or highlight and choose Select (or press ↵).

5. Choose Create Equation.

Figure 29.1 shows the Equation Editor. It's divided into three major sections, as shown in the figure:

- The *display pane* in the upper-left portion shows the equation graphically (much as it will be printed).

- The *editing pane* in the lower-left portion is used to type in and edit the equation.

- The *Equation palette* on the right contains commands, symbols, and functions that you can insert in the equation instead of, or in addition to, typing them from the keyboard. There's also a Button Bar that displays equation-related command shortcuts and a status line at the bottom of the screen.

Typing Equations

Typing and editing an equation in the editing pane is much like typing and editing any other text in WordPerfect. There are some differences, however. For the most part, you can type symbols and special operators either from the keyboard or from the various Equation palettes, as I'll explain a little later.

While the cursor is in the editing pane, you can use the usual editing techniques to modify the equation. For example, you can use your mouse and the ← and → keys to position the cursor. You can also use the Backspace and Delete keys to delete characters and the Insert key to switch between Insert and Typeover modes.

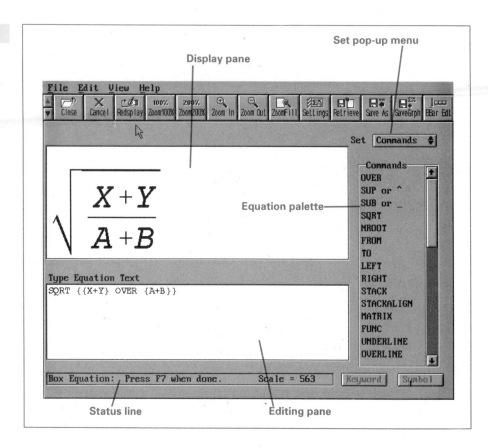

When you're ready to see a graphical representation of the equation you've typed so far, you can choose <u>V</u>iew ➤ <u>R</u>edisplay (Ctrl+F3), or click the Redisplay button, then look at the upper display pane.

When you're satisfied with the equation, choose <u>F</u>ile ➤ <u>C</u>lose (or press F7), or click the Close button. Then choose OK to get back to the document window.

The Role of Curly Braces

When you're entering equations in WordPerfect, you should type them as you would read them aloud and use curly braces ({ }) to group items together. For example, the formula shown in Figure 29.1 could be expressed verbally as "the square root of X + Y over A + B." This equation is expressed in the Equation Editor as

SQRT {{X+Y} OVER {A+B}}

Because everything to the right of the SQRT command must be under the radical, this entire portion of the equation is enclosed in curly braces. And because the entire X + Y portion should be placed over the entire A + B portion, each of these is also contained in its own set of curly braces. Figure 29.2 shows more examples illustrating the important role played by curly braces.

It's important that the curly braces in an equation balance. For example, if you have more open curly braces than closing curly braces, or vice versa, the Equation Editor will not be able to make sense of the grouping. When you choose <u>V</u>iew ➤ <u>R</u>edisplay to view such a formula, you'll see the message "Syntax error" in an error box, and the display pane will not be refreshed.

N O T E

The same error message might appear if your equation uses equation commands improperly, even though the braces are correct.

FIGURE 29.2

The use of braces in equations

$$\text{SQRT X+Y OVER A+B} \qquad \sqrt{X} + \frac{Y}{A} + B$$

$$\text{SQRT \{X+Y\} OVER A+B} \qquad \frac{\sqrt{X+Y}}{A} + B$$

$$\text{SQRT X+Y OVER \{A+B\}} \qquad \sqrt{X} + \frac{Y}{A+B}$$

$$\text{SQRT X+\{Y OVER A\}+B} \qquad \sqrt{X} + \frac{Y}{A} + B$$

$$\text{SQRT \{X+Y OVER A+B\}} \qquad \sqrt{X + \frac{Y}{A} + B}$$

$$\text{SQRT \{\{X+Y\} OVER \{A+B\}\}} \qquad \sqrt{\frac{X+Y}{A+B}}$$

Entering Spaces and Lines

Blanks entered with the spacebar are used to separate equation commands, but these blank spaces are *not* part of the final equation. If you want to include a blank space in an equation, type a tilde (~) where you want the blank space to appear.

You can also insert a thin space (a quarter space) using the backward accent character (`). (It's on the same key as the tilde on most keyboards.) Use one accent to add a quarter space, two accents to add a half space, and so forth. The tilde and the accent appear only in the Edit pane, never in the printed document.

Pressing ↵ while editing an equation moves the cursor to the next line, as in the normal document window. However, this does not insert a line break in the actual equation (it just gives you more room to type the equation and makes the editing pane easier to read). To stack items in an equation, you need to use STACK, STACKALIGN, MATRIX, #, or similar commands from the Equation palette.

Typing Numbers, Variables, and Operators

You will need to type numbers and variables (such as X, Y, A, and B) directly from the keyboard. And because the following operators and symbols aren't on the Equation palette, you'll also need to type them directly from the keyboard:

$$- + * / = < > ! ? . | @ \text{ '' } , ;$$

NOTE   When typing a real number containing a decimal point or negative sign, you must surround the number in curly braces.

In addition, you can type commands like SQRT and OVER directly from the keyboard, in either upper- or lowercase letters, provided that you know the exact command to use. Be sure to enter a space before and after the command keyword so that WordPerfect recognizes it as a command. Similarly, you can type special symbols with the WordPerfect characters key by pressing Ctrl+W. However, when first learning to use the Equation Editor, you'll probably prefer to choose most commands and symbols from the Equation palette.

Using the Equation Palettes

You can choose commands or special symbols from the Equation palette any time you are in the Equation Editor by following these steps:

1. With the cursor in the editing pane, move the cursor to where you want to place an item from a palette.

2. Press F5 or click in the Equation palette. Or choose a different group of symbols or special characters from the Set pop-up menu:

3. When you click or highlight a symbol, its name appears near the bottom of the screen. Choose the symbol or word you want by double-clicking, or by highlighting and pressing ↵.

Remember, the equation won't be updated until you click the Redisplay button or press Ctrl+F3.

Figure 29.3 shows several examples of equations created with the Equation Editor. Keywords in the examples that don't come directly from the Commands palette were chosen from other palettes. For example, ALPHA, OMEGA, and THETA were chosen from the Greek palette; SUM and INT were chosen from the Large palette; INF and THEREFORE were chosen from the Symbols palette. Numbers, letters, and operators (as in m + n = 0) were typed directly from the keyboard.

FIGURE 29.3

Examples of equation commands and symbols

BINOM ALPHA OMEGA	$\binom{A}{\Omega}$
SUM FROM {x=0} TO INF	$\displaystyle\sum_{x=0}^{\infty}$
LEFT ({1^x} OVER m RIGHT)	$\left(\dfrac{1^x}{m}\right)$
LEFT DLINE MATRIX {a & b & c # x & y & z} RIGHT DLINE	$\left\Vert\begin{matrix} a & b & c \\ x & y & z \end{matrix}\right\Vert$
NROOT 3 {-{x OVER y}}	$\sqrt[3]{-\dfrac{x}{y}}$
tan \`\`THETA\`=\`{sin\`\`THETA} OVER {cos\`\`THETA}	$\tan\Theta = \dfrac{\sin\Theta}{\cos\Theta}$
STACK {m+n=0 # m PHANTOM {+n}=2}	$\begin{matrix} m+n=0 \\ m=2 \end{matrix}$
LEFT. {X^1} OVER {Y_2} RIGHT LINE	$\left.\dfrac{X^1}{Y_2}\right\vert$
SQRT {a^2 + b^2}\`\`=c	$\sqrt{a^2+b^2}=c$
x SUB y SUP 1 (or x_y^1)	x_y^1
INT SUB 0 SUP INF	$\displaystyle\int_0^{\infty}$

The ways in which you can combine equation commands and symbols are nearly endless. When you're first learning, it may take some trial-and-error practice to get everything just right. You should build your formula gradually, choosing View ➤ Redisplay (or clicking Redisplay) often to see how things are progressing. That way, you can correct mistakes and refine the equation as you type it. If you need additional help or information while you're in the Equation Editor, just press Help (F1).

Changing an Equation

After completing your equation and returning to the document window, the equation appears in a graphics box. You can edit the equation, if necessary, using the standard techniques used for editing any graphics box (see Chapter 26). For example, in Graphics or Page mode, you can just double-click the equation. Or, choose Graphics ➤ Graphics Boxes ➤ Edit and specify the box to edit. Then choose Edit Equation if you want to go back to the Equation Editor.

Controlling the Appearance of Equations

You can control the font, size, alignment, and position of equations by editing a single equation's graphics box, or by changing the style of all Equation Boxes, or all Inline Equation boxes, in the document. Use the same general techniques described in Chapter 26 and summarized below:

- If you want to change the appearance of a single equation, start at the document window and edit that equation's graphics box by double-clicking the box, or by choosing Graphics ➤ Graphics Boxes ➤ Edit and choosing the equation box to edit.

- To change the appearance of all the equations, start at the document window and choose Graphics ➤ Graphics Boxes ➤ Styles. Highlight the type of box you want to change (Equation Box or Inline Equation Box), then choose Edit.

You'll be taken to the Edit Graphics Box (or Edit Graphics Box Style) dialog box, where you can control the general size and alignment of equation graphics boxes using the Options ➤ Content Options, Edit Border/Fill, Attach To, Edit Position, Edit Size, and Text Flow Around Box options, as described in Chapter 26.

To change the font or size of a single equation, starting from the Edit Graphics Box dialog box, choose Edit Equation. When you get to the Equation Editor, click the Settings button or press Shift+F1. If you're editing a graphics box style, choose Equation Settings instead. Either way, you'll be taken to this dialog box:

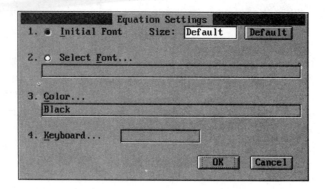

Here you can choose Initial Font to use the same font for your equations that you chose as the initial font for the rest of the document. Or, you can choose a different font, size, or print color. (You can also switch to another keyboard from this dialog box, as discussed in Chapter 19.)

After making your changes, choose OK and Close, as appropriate, to work your way back to the document window.

Changing the Print Quality

Most equation characters are printed graphically. Therefore, if parts of equations are missing from your document, or are too rough, try changing the graphics quality just before printing the document. That is, starting at the document window, choose File ➤ Print/Fax ➤ Graphics Quality, and choose a higher print quality. If some characters from your equations still don't appear, choose Print Job Graphically from the Print/Fax dialog box, and try again.

Using an Equation in Multiple Documents

You can use the same equation in multiple documents simply by using standard copy-and-paste techniques to copy the equation's hidden code from one document to another. You can also save an equation in its own file, and retrieve previously saved equations into the Equation Editor by following these steps:

1. Edit the graphics box that contains the equation you want to save, by double-clicking or choosing Graphics ➤ Graphics Boxes ➤ Edit. Or, if you want to retrieve a previously saved equation into the current document, create an Equation (or Inline Equation) graphics box in the current document.

2. Choose Edit Equation (or Create Equation) to get to the Equation Editor.

3. Choose File from the menu bar, then choose whichever option is appropriate:

   Retrieve   Retrieves an equation you previously saved using Save As (below) into the Equation Editor.

   Save As   Saves the equation, or a selected portion of the equation, in its own file.

   Save As Image   Saves the equation as a Bitmap Graphics (BMP), WordPerfect Graphic, or WordPerfect Presentations image, with the default .WPG extension. (Later, you can retrieve this type of image using Graphics ➤ Retrieve, starting from the document window.)

Equations are stored in graphics boxes, but they are unique in that they offer an Equations Editor in place of the Image Editor (and Text Editor) described in Chapter 26. In the next chapter, we'll take a look at a couple of features you can use to create interactive multimedia documents—sound and hypertext.

CHAPTER 3

Creating Interactive Documents with Sound and Hypertext

fast **TRACK**

Hypertext lets you put "hot spots" in your document   1065

which the reader can click on-screen to jump to another topic or to initiate some other action.

To create a Hypertext link   1065

first create the text you want the link to jump *to* and mark it with a named bookmark (Chapter 9). Or, create the macro (Chapter 18) that you want the hot spot to run.

Once you've created the item you want the hot spot to link to   1066

select the text in your document that defines the hot spot. Then choose Tools ➤ Hypertext ➤ Create Link. Define the action and appearance of the hot spot in the Create Hypertext Link dialog box that appears.

To activate hypertext in a document that contains links   1067

Choose Tools ➤ Hypertext and select the Hypertext Is Active check box and OK. Then just click any hot spot in your document to activate it.

To return to normal editing   1068

do the same as in the entry above, but clear the Hypertext Is Active check box. The mouse resumes its normal editing role.

AN INTERACTIVE document is one that the reader uses on the screen, as opposed to on paper. Two advantages of using the screen rather than the printed page are

Sound   If the computer has sound capabilities, you can add voice, such as spoken instructions, pronunciations, and greetings to a document. In fact, you can add *any* sound, from bird calls to musical notes to zany cartoon-like sound effects.

Hypertext   Lets you put *jump words* and command buttons (collectively called *hot spots*) into your document. You can then assign an action such as "go to topic *X*," "open document *Y*," or "play macro *Z*" to each hot spot. For example, you might have the hot spot jump to some related topic or display the definition of a term. You could even have it play a sound. When the reader clicks a hot spot, its action is played out instantly.

Multimedia WordPerfect!

The Sound and Hypertext features of WordPerfect let you take advantage of today's multimedia capabilities. As an example of a multimedia document with both sound and hypertext, take a look at Figure 30.1. The reader of this sample document could

- Click on any bird command button to hear the bird's song.

- Click on an underlined bird name to jump directly to the entry for that bird.

FIGURE 30.1

A sample interactive document. Clicking any bird button plays the bird's song.

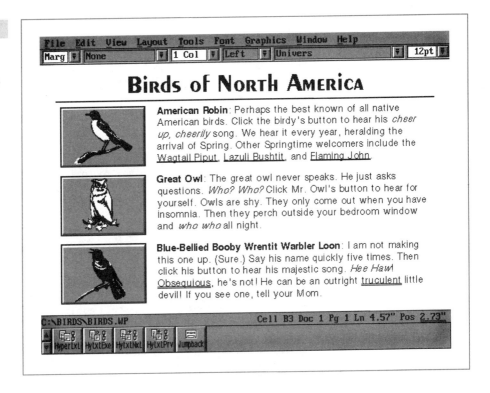

- Click on any underlined word to look up the definition for that term in a separate dictionary (see Figure 30.2), then click the JumpBack button at the bottom of the screen to get back to the birds.

Later in this chapter, I'll talk about the techniques I used to create that sample document. But first let's discuss the basic techniques required to add sound and hypertext to your own WordPerfect documents.

Getting into Sound

You can use WordPerfect's sound capabilities only if your computer has sound capabilities built in. For example, you could purchase and install a Sound Blaster card or an entire multimedia upgrade kit, including sound

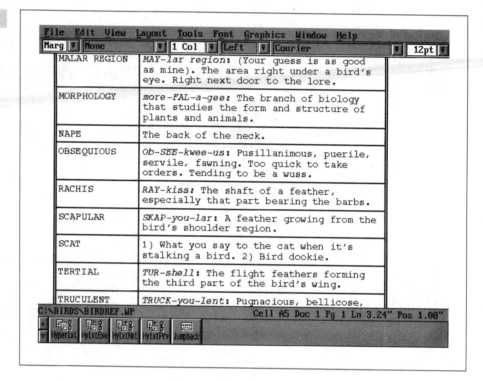

and CD-ROM. Some computers now come with multimedia capabilities, including sound, built right in.

Regardless of which type of sound system your computer uses, you need to "tell" WordPerfect that the sound capability is there before you can use sounds in your WordPerfect documents.

Step 1: Install the Sound Hardware

If your computer doesn't already have sound built into it, you need to purchase and install the appropriate hardware. You can get as fancy as you want with your sound system. But a good, solid system with speakers, headphones, and microphones will probably run you about $250.00. (Yeah, I know, you already paid half/twice that. When I quote prices, they're ballpark figures.)

You must completely install the sound device so that it works on its own. Most sound systems come with a test program. Be sure you can play sounds with that test program before you even bother getting WordPerfect linked up to the sound system.

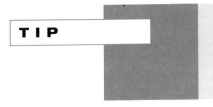

TIP

If you install the sound system yourself, keep track of the *base address* and *interrupt request level* you use. If you have someone else install the system, ask them to jot that information down for you.

Some Can Listen Too

Before we get to the next step, I want to fill you in on a little-known fact that's worth knowing if you haven't bought a sound system yet. Most systems can record sound, but some can use your spoken voice as commands. For example, my Microsoft Windows Sound System comes with a tiny microphone and a program named *Voice Pilot*. While I'm working, I can bark simple commands like "SAVE" or "OPEN" at the microphone. Windows obeys and does whatever I say. No need for messy mouse clicks or menu commands.

Supposedly (though I haven't tried this yet), an add-on program will allow me to record virtually my entire vocabulary. That means I could type up an entire document with my hands tied behind my back. I just talk, and the computer types what I say. (I already see one potential problem though. When I say "there," how will it know if I mean *there, their,* or *they're*. Hmmm, maybe the grammar checker could fix those kinds of mistakes.)

I should point out that the Voice Pilot in that particular sound system only works with Windows applications. It won't do you much good with a DOS program. Though I suspect that there are, or will be, similar types of systems for DOS. The technology is all a little rough around the edges still. But it's a harbinger of good things to come!

Step 2: Install the WordPerfect Sound Driver

If you already had your sound system in place when you installed WordPerfect 6.0 for DOS, and you chose your sound driver at that time, you can now skip to step 3. If you added your sound capabilities *after* you installed WordPerfect 6.0, you need to install the WordPerfect driver for your sound system now. See "Installing New Hardware" in Appendix A if you need help with that.

Keep in mind that this step merely copies the WordPerfect Corporation sound driver for your system from the floppies to your hard disk. You must still complete the next step, below, after that.

Step 3: Tell WordPerfect Where to Send Sounds

Now you need to tell WordPerfect how to communicate with your sound system:

1. Run WordPerfect as usual to get to a document window.

2. Choose <u>T</u>ools ➤ Sound <u>C</u>lip ➤ <u>S</u>ound Setup.

3. Choose <u>T</u>ype. You should see a list containing the sound drivers that you installed using the WordPerfect 6.0 installation program.

4. Highlight the name of the appropriate driver and choose <u>S</u>elect.

5. Choose <u>H</u>ardware Setup. If you know for certain that your Interrupt Request Level (IRQ) and Base Address are different from what appears in those settings, make the appropriate changes. If you installed a MIDI-capable sound card and wish to use an external synthesizer through the sound board's MIDI port, select the <u>E</u>xternal Synthesis (Via MIDI Port) check box. Choose OK.

6. Choose <u>R</u>ecording Quality Setup. If you know for certain that you need to change something in the dialog box, choose your options accordingly. Here's the general rule of thumb: The slower the sampling rate, the lower the quality of the recording, and the less disk space the recording will require. Note that you can also choose between Stereo and Mono modes in this dialog box. Choose OK when you've finished making your changes (if any).

WARNING

If memory is limited, you may not be able to use Stereo mode. When you test the system, you'll see an error message stating that you'll need to go back to the Recording Quality Setup dialog box and change the mode back to Mono. Also, a stereo-recorded sound will use up twice as much disk space as a mono sound.

7. Choose Close to leave the Sound Setup dialog box.

At this point, you should be at a WordPerfect document window, which means it's time for step 4.

Step 4: Test Your Sound System

To test your system, add a sound clip to a document and play it:

1. Choose <u>T</u>ools ➤ Sound <u>C</u>lip ➤ <u>A</u>dd.

2. Use the File List (F5) to locate a sound file, which will have a .MID or .WAV extension. Directories that are likely to contain sound include your WordPerfect graphics directory (typically C:\WP60\GRAPHICS), the directory that your sound system software is on, and if you have Windows, your C:\WINDOWS (or C:\WINDOWS\SYSTEM) directory. When you've found a sound file, double-click its name, or highlight its name and choose <u>S</u>elect.

3. If you wish, choose <u>D</u>escription and type in a brief description, such as **This is a test**.

Choose OK to return to your document window. You should now see a box with a musical icon in it, like the example below. In Reveal Codes, you'll see a [Sound] code. (The box is never printed, since there's no way to play a sound from a printed page!)

```
♩ Sound (Ctrl+S): This is a test
```

WARNING

If you're using headphones, hold them away from your ears when you're testing a sound card. The volume might be high enough to damage your eardrums!

5. To play the sound, choose Tools ➤ Sound Clip ➤ Play.

6. In the dialog box that appears, choose the Play/Pause button. (Note that you can also adjust the volume in this dialog box.)

You should hear the sound being played now, assuming everything is plugged in, turned on, and properly installed. If you don't, try playing a different type of file. For example, if you just tried a MIDI file (.MID), add another sound clip, but this time try a sound wave (.WAV) file.

If you still have trouble, make sure your headphones and speakers are plugged in correctly. Then try playing the sound at a higher volume. If it *still* doesn't work, the culprit is probably the IRQ and Base Address settings in the Hardware Setup dialog box. You'll need to determine the correct settings, then repeat Step 3, "Tell WordPerfect Where to Send Sounds," earlier in this chapter. (Or, if you're in the Sound Clips In Document dialog box, just press Shift+F1 or choose the Setup button to correct the hardware settings.)

TIP

The MSD.EXE (Microsoft Diagnostics) program that comes with some versions of DOS and Windows might help you identify your sound card's IRQ.

Adding Sound Clips

Assuming you get everything working and together, you can now start adding sound clips to your document. You can use the same general technique that you used to test your sound system. But let's take a look at some alternatives and options that you can choose along the way.

To add a sound clip to your document, follow these steps:

1. Move the cursor to wherever you want to put the sound clip and choose <u>T</u>ools ➤ Sound <u>C</u>lip ➤ <u>A</u>dd, or press Ctrl+F7 SA. You will be taken to the Add Sound Clip To Document dialog box, shown below.

2. Choose <u>F</u>ilename, and then choose the name of the sound clip file you want to add to your document. (Tip: Use the QuickList to define a path for sounds, such as C:\MYSOUNDS*.WAV.)

3. After selecting the file name, choose <u>D</u>escription and, if you wish, type in a brief description. Whatever you type will appear in your document next to the sound icon.

4. If you'll be using this document only on computer(s) that already have the sound clip on disk, you can choose <u>L</u>ink To File On Disk to conserve disk space. If you're likely to distribute the document to people who might not have that sound clip on disk, choose <u>S</u>tore In Document. A copy of the sound clip will be saved with the document (of course, this makes the document much larger).

5. Choose OK to return to your document.

Playing a Sound

There are a couple of different ways you can play a sound:

- Move the cursor to just before the sound you want to play, then press Ctrl+S. After hearing the sound, you can choose Exit or press F7 to close the Listen And Type dialog box that appears. (More on this dialog box under "Using Sound for Dictation," later in this chapter.)

- Choose Tools ➤ Sound Clip ➤ Play. You'll be taken to the Sound Clips In Document dialog box, as in the example shown in Figure 30.3. Highlight the name of the sound clip you want to play, then click the Play/Pause button.

FIGURE 30.3

The Sound Clips In Document dialog box lists all the sound clips in the current document. Choose Tools ➤ Sound Clip ➤ Play to get to this dialog box.

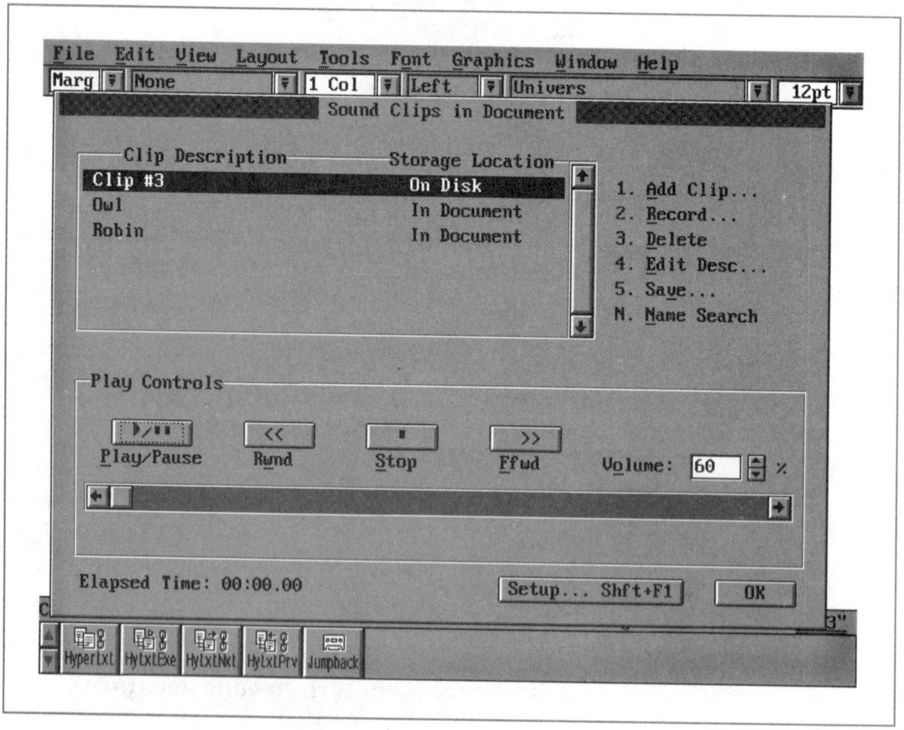

As you can see in the figure, the Sound Clips In Document dialog box lets you Add, Record, Delete, Edit the description of, Save, and search for a clip in the current document (Name Search). The Play Controls buttons let you Play/Pause, Rwnd (Rewind), Stop, and Ffwd (Fast Forward) the sound, just as you would on a tape recorder or VCR. The Volume option lets you increase or decrease the volume.

When you've finished with the Sound Clips In Document dialog box, choose OK or press F7 to return to your document.

Recording a Sound Clip

If you have a microphone, and your sound system has the capability, you can record sounds of your own. This might be handy if, for example, you want to put a personal message or instructions into a document.

To record your own sound, first make sure your microphone is properly connected to your sound device, according to the manufacturer's instructions. Then,

1. Place the cursor where you want the sound clip to appear in your document.

2. Choose Tools ➤ Sound Clip ➤ Record to get to the Record Sound Clip dialog box, shown in Figure 30.4.

3. Choose a Recording Quality, depending on what you're recording: Good (Speech), Better (Music), Other (a specific sample rate, size, and mode). Remember, the better the quality, the larger the resulting file.

4. When you're ready to record, choose the Rec button and speak your message or play the sound you want to record.

5. As you record, you can keep an eye on the elapsed time of your recording and the size of the file you're creating. The Level Meter will also keep you posted on how strongly your sound is coming in.

FIGURE 30.4

The Record Sound Clip dialog box lets you record your own sounds. You need a microphone and sound equipment with recording capability to use it. Choose <u>T</u>ools ➤ Sound <u>C</u>lip ➤ <u>R</u>ecord to get here.

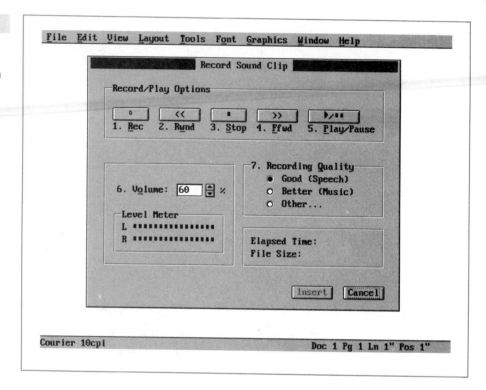

WARNING

Elapsed time plus *quality* equals *size*. For example, a 10-second recording in Best quality with stereo can easily be 400 KB in size. That's almost half a megabyte!

6. When you're done recording, choose the <u>S</u>top button.

7. To hear your recording, choose the <u>P</u>lay/Pause button.

TIP

In some sound systems, the recording level is set in an external program. If it's off, you won't be able to record. See the section on recording sounds in your sound card documentation if you have problems.

8. To insert the recording into your document, choose <u>I</u>nsert.

9. To save the recording to its own file, choose <u>T</u>ools ➤ Sound <u>C</u>lip ➤ <u>P</u>lay. Highlight the name of the clip you just recorded, and choose Sa<u>v</u>e. Choose a directory and enter a file name (for example, **c:\wp60\graphics\myvoice.wav**).

10. When you're ready to return to your document, choose OK or press F7.

If you saved the recorded sound in its own file in step 9, you can add that sound to any document with the <u>T</u>ools ➤ Sound <u>C</u>lip ➤ <u>A</u>dd commands. You can also choose the <u>L</u>ink To File On Disk option described earlier if you want to avoid storing a copy of the sound clip in the document.

Using Sound for Dictation

The techniques I've talked about so far are fine for creating interactive documents. But if your sound card has recording capabilities (and you have an enormous amount of free disk space), you can also use your sound card to record and play dictation.

Recording Dictation

To record dictation, follow the steps below:

1. Make sure your microphone is hooked up and ready to receive.

2. Press Ctrl+D. You'll be taken to the Record Sound Clip dialog box, shown below.

3. If you want to minimize the size of the recorded clip, choose <u>O</u>ptions and set Recording <u>Q</u>uality. Use the <u>G</u>ood (Speech) setting. You can also press Setup (Shift+F1), choose <u>R</u>ecording Quality Setup, and set Mo<u>d</u>e to <u>M</u>ono. If you do either of these, choose OK and Close, as appropriate, to return to the Record Sound Clip dialog box.

4. If you wish, choose <u>D</u>esc and enter a new description for your sound clip. Then press ↵.

5. When you're ready, choose <u>R</u>ec and start talking. Keep an eye on the Elapsed Time and Clip Size odometers. And try not to faint.

6. When you're done recording, choose <u>S</u>top.

Now you can use the <u>P</u>lay/Pause, R<u>w</u>nd, and other buttons to listen to your dictation, or choose <u>I</u>nsert to insert it into the document. Use <u>F</u>ile ➤ <u>S</u>ave or <u>F</u>ile ➤ Save <u>A</u>s to save the current document with the sound clip in it.

Typing from Dictation

To type from a recorded sound clip, follow these steps:

1. If you (or someone else) closed the document that was saved in the preceding steps, use <u>F</u>ile ➤ <u>O</u>pen to open it.

2. Move the cursor to just above the sound clip, then press Ctrl+S. The Listen And Type dialog box appears, as in the example below, and you can start typing as you hear the dictated message.

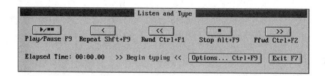

3. You can also use buttons and shortcut keys displayed in the dialog box to stop, rewind, repeat, and change the volume of the dictation. For example, press Alt+F9 or click the Stop button to stop. Click the Repeat button, or press Shift+F9, to repeat the passage you just played.

4. When you've finished typing the dictation, press F7 to leave the Listen And Type dialog box.

Expanding Your Sound Clip Collection

WordPerfect Corporation has chosen Voyetra Technologies Sound Factory to provide audio enhancements to your WordPerfect 6.0 for DOS documents. For more information about Voyetra's WordPerfect-compatible sound programs and clip files, contact Voyetra Technologies, 333 Fifth Ave., Pelham, NY 10802. Phone numbers are (800) 233-9377 (from within the U.S.) and (914) 738-4500 (from outside the U.S.). The fax number is (914) 738-9646.

There are also many freebie sound clips out and about. If you have a modem and know how to access bulletin boards, chances are you can always find and download some public domain sound clips.

Hypertext—The Ultimate in Interactive Documents

Hypertext is totally independent of sound. You can use it on any computer. As I mentioned at the beginning of this chapter, *hypertext* is a technique that allows you to put *hot spots* into a document. You can then assign an action to that hot spot. Specifically, you can link any phrase or term to a bookmark in the current document, any part of another document, or to a macro (Chapter 18). When the reader of your document clicks the hot spot, the action you assigned to it is triggered instantly.

Before You Link Hypertext

Before you create hypertext links, you should create all the text, as well as any macros that you want to link to hot spots. That is, you want to...

1. Create the text that includes the hot spots you want to jump *from*.

2. Create the text (or document) that you want the hot spot to jump *to*. Then use Edit ➤ Bookmark ➤ Create (Chapter 9) to identify the text you want to jump to. Give the bookmark a descriptive name that will be easy to remember later.

3. If you want the hypertext to run a macro, create and test the appropriate macro(s) (Chapter 18).

You might want to consider putting documents, macros, sounds, and clip art that make up the interactive document in one directory. For example, I put everything for my sample "Birds" interactive document in a separate directory named C:\BIRDS. Using one directory is easier than using the separate default directories for documents, graphics, and macros.

Creating Hypertext

Once you've created all your document(s) and any macros you want to activate with hypertext, here's how to create a hypertext link:

1. Select the text that you want to jump *from*, using your mouse or the Alt+F4 or Alt+F12 keys.

2. Choose Tools ➤ Hypertext ➤ Create Link. You'll be taken to the Create Hypertext Link dialog box, shown below.

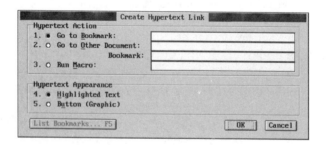

3. Choose one of the Hypertext Action options listed below:

> **Go to Bookmark** Choose this option if you want to link to a bookmark in this same document. Then type the bookmark name or press F5 and choose its name from the list of

available bookmarks.

Go to Other Document   Choose this option if you want
to link to another document. You can use F5 to select the
document's name from a list. If you want to jump to a particular bookmark in that other document, choose Bookmark and then type the name of the bookmark, or press
F5 to choose it from a list.

Run Macro   If you want the link to run a macro, choose
Run Macro, then type the name of the macro, or press F5
to choose a macro name from the macros directory.

4. You can also choose the appearance of the hypertext, as either
Highlighted Text or Button (Graphic).

5. Choose OK to return to your document.

You can repeat the steps above to create as many links as you want.

Using Hypertext

Using a Hypertext document is easiest if you first turn on the Hypertext
Is Active switch. Once you've switched on hypertext, you can use your
mouse to click the hot spots.

Activating Hypertext

Before you test your Hypertext link(s), *save the document.* Then, activate
hypertext and give it a whirl:

1. Choose Tools ➤ Hypertext.

2. Select the Hypertext Is Active check box, if it isn't already selected. Then choose OK.

Once you've completed these steps, the mouse changes its role. From
now on, it will activate hot spots that you click.

To test and use your hypertext document, just click any hot spot. The action you assigned to that hot spot will be activated instantly.

TIP

If you want to edit the hypertext document and use the mouse in its normal editing role, you'll need to clear the Hypertext Is Active check box.

One thing to keep in mind is that if a hot spot takes you to a different document, you must use Hypertext Return to get back to the original document. That is, choose Tools ➤ Hypertext ➤ Return From Jump (or press Alt+F5 HR). If hypertext opens a document, then you try to use the Window and File menus to get around, things are likely to become confusing very quickly.

If you look at my sample document in Figure 30.1, you'll notice that I put a JumpBack button in the Button Bar. That gives my reader a quick and easy way back to the previous document.

Of course, an even simpler approach might be to put *all* the text in one document. Then you don't need to think about jumping around from document to document.

Using Hypertext from the Menus

Clicking hot spots with the mouse is certainly the most natural and intuitive way to use a hypertext document. But you can also use the menus:

1. Choose Tools ➤ Hypertext, or press Alt+F5 H. You will be taken to the Hypertext dialog box, shown below.

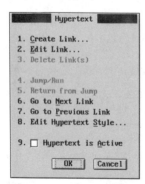

2. Choose whichever option is appropriate to what you want to do:

Jump/Run   Activates the hot spot that the cursor is on.

Return from Jump   Moves the cursor back to the hot spot that sent you to your current place.

Go to Next Link   Moves the cursor to the next hot spot in the document.

Go to Previous Link   Moves the cursor to the previous hot spot in the document.

Editing Your Hypertext

As I mentioned earlier under "Activating Hypertext," when you want to make changes to your hypertext document, you're best bet is probably to clear the Hypertext Is Active check box. That way, the mouse will return to its normal editing functions, and you can edit graphics boxes normally. If you want to add a new hot spot, use the basic procedure described under "Creating a Hypertext Link," earlier in this chapter.

Here's how to change or delete a hot spot:

1. Turn on Reveal Codes (Alt+F3) and move the cursor anywhere between the [Hypertext Begin] and [Hypertext End] codes or just after the [Box(Char)...] code of the hot spot you want to change.

2. To change the hot spot, choose Tools ➤ Hypertext ➤ Edit Link, make your changes in the dialog box that appears, and choose OK.

3. If you want to delete the link, choose Tools ➤ Hypertext ➤ Delete Link(s).

Changing the Appearance of Hot Spots

By default, WordPerfect uses bold and underline to identify jump words. If you prefer to use color or some other feature to make your jump words stand out, follow these steps:

1. Move the cursor anywhere in the document, and choose Tools ➤ Hypertext ➤ Edit Hypertext Style. You will be taken to the Hypertext Style dialog box, where you can see the codes that define the appearance of the jump word.

2. Use the Delete key to delete any unwanted codes.

3. Use the menus or shortcut keys (Font or Ctrl+F8) to select new formatting codes.

4. When you're done, press F7 until you get back to the document.

All the jump words that you've already created in the current document, plus any new ones you create, will adhere to your new Hypertext Style format. You can change that style any time you wish. (Please see Chapter 17 for more general information on styles if you have any problems.)

The Sample Document

If you've read everything in the chapter up to this point, you may be wondering how I got from what's described here to command buttons with pictures of birds on them that you can click to hear a bird song. The answer to that is *macros*. In case you'd like to try creating a similar document on your own, I'll run through the steps I went through to create the sample hypertext document shown in Figure 30.1.

The Initial Documents

I started out by creating a table (Chapter 7) with bird names in the left column and bird descriptions in the right column, as in Figure 30.5. The table is entirely optional. I just used it to set up the two-column format.

File Edit View Layout Tools Font Graphics Window Help

Birds of North America

ROBIN	**American Robin**: Perhaps the best known of all native American birds. Click the birdy's button to hear his *cheer up, cheerily* song. We hear it every year, heralding the arrival of Spring. Other Springtime welcomers include the Wagtail Piput, Lazuli Bushtit, and Flaming John.
OWL	**Great Owl**: The great owl never speaks. He just asks questions. *Who? Who?* Click Mr. Owl's button to hear for yourself. Owls are shy. They only come out when you have insomnia. Then they perch outside your bedroom window and *who who* all night.
BOOBY	**Blue-Bellied Booby Wrentit Warbler Loon**: I am not making this one up. (Sure.) Say his name quickly five times. Then click his button to hear his majestic song. *Hee Haw*! Obsequious, he's not! He can be an outright truculent little devil! If you see one, tell your Mom.

Typeover   Cell B3 Doc 1 Pg 1 Ln 5.5" Pos 6.95"

I named this document BIRDS.WP.

Though not shown in the figure, some of the entries have bookmarks of their own. For example, when I created the table row for Wagtail Piput (not shown), I added a bookmark, ingeniously named WAGTAIL PIPUT, to that table row. I created a bookmark entry for every bird that's cross-referenced from some other bird.

I also created the dictionary shown in Figure 30.2 as a separate document. It's just a standard WordPerfect document, using the Tables feature to keep text aligned. What you can't see in the figure is the hidden bookmark that's next to each dictionary entry. For example, the hidden bookmark for the *Obsequious* entry is OBSEQUIOUS.

I saved the dictionary under its own file name, BIRDREF.WP. I could just as easily have put the dictionary at the end of the original BIRDS.WP document. Doing so would actually speed up the hypertext jumping.

The Sounds

Next, I spent months in the wild recording bird sounds for my document. Just kidding. I faked them with my own voice, and they're awful. I suspect that there are some copyright-free pre-recorded bird sounds out there that I could have used. But since I know next to nothing about birds, and you can't hear the sounds anyway, my faked ones were sufficient for getting this chapter written.

I inserted all the sounds at the *end* of the document. That is, if you were to scroll to the end of the BIRDS.WP document, you'd see the sound clips stacked up looking something like this:

♫ **Sound (Ctrl + S):** Robin

♫ **Sound (Ctrl + S):** Owl

♫ **Sound (Ctrl + S):** Booby

Next, I hid those sound clips using F<u>o</u>nt ➤ <u>H</u>idden Text. That way, my reader won't ever see them unless he or she happens to be sneaking around with Reveal Codes turned on.

The Hypertext Jump Words

With documents created and bookmarks in place, the next job was simply to select a hot spot (for example *Wagtail Piput*) and create the hypertext link to the appropriate bookmark. I used the basic technique described earlier in this chapter, under "Creating Hypertext."

I used the Go To <u>B</u>ookmark option for cross-references to the same document and the Go To <u>O</u>ther Document option for references to the separate dictionary, BIRDREF.WP. The appearance of all the hot spots in column B is Highlighted Text, as opposed to Button (Graphic).

The Macros

Next I needed a way to make a hot spot play a sound. That was easy enough. I just turned on Macro Record (Ctrl+F10) and gave the macro an obvious name (ROBIN.WPM). Then I chose <u>T</u>ools ➤ Sound <u>C</u>lip ➤

Play and double-clicked the name of the sound I wanted the macro to play (ROBIN). After the sound was played, I chose OK to return to the document window, then I stopped recording the macro (Ctrl+F10).

I created such a macro for every one of my recorded sounds. Thus, I ended up with a macro named ROBIN.WPM to play the Robin sound, a macro named OWL.WPM to play the Owl sound, and so forth.

The Sound Buttons

To create a sound button, I selected the text in column A for one row (for example, ROBIN). Then I chose ➤ Tools Hypertext ➤ Create Link. The action I chose was Run Macro, followed by the name of the macro the button is to play (ROBIN.WPG). Then I choose Button (Graphic) as the Hypertext Appearance and chose OK to return to the document.

My ROBIN button ended up looking something like this:

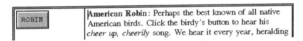

With Hypertext active, I could then click that button and, sure enough, it ran the macro and played the appropriate sound.

I relied on my Presentation Task Force clip art collection to come up with the picture for each button. To put the picture on a button, I first turned off Hypertext Is Active. Then I could double-click the button to get to the button's Edit Graphics Box dialog box (discussed in Chapter 26).

There I chose Filename and retrieved the picture that I wanted to put onto the button. Then I used Edit Size to size the button to my liking, 1.45″ wide by 1″ high in this example. I used the Image Editor to scale and position the graphic nicely within that size, and then I used F7 to work my way back to the document. The result is a button with a picture on it, as in the example below (and back in Figure 30.1).

American Robin. Perhaps the best known of all native American birds. Click the birdy's button to hear his *cheer up, cheerily* song. We hear it every year, heralding the arrival of Spring. Other Springtime welcomers include the Wagtail Piput, Lazuli Bushtit, and Flaming John.

I repeated that basic procedure for every entry in the first column of the table. (Actually, I created another macro to do most of the steps involved in sizing the button and putting the picture on it.)

The Button Bar

The Button Bar at the bottom of the screen is just a standard WordPerfect Button Bar (Chapter 4). That is, I created a blank Button Bar using View ➤ Button Bar Setup ➤ Select ➤ Create. Then I used Add Feature to create each button. (All the hypertext features are listed in the general vicinity of "Hy..." in the Feature Button List.) I did, however, create a macro to choose Tools ➤ Hypertext ➤ Return From Jump, but only because I wanted the button to say "JumpBack" rather than "HyperRet." (You could do that for all the buttons if you like. For instance, create a macro named *NextLink* to replace the HyperNxt button.)

For no reason other than personal preference, I also used View ➤ Button Bar Setup ➤ Options to put the Button Bar at the bottom of the screen.

General Format

For the finishing touches, I set all the table lines to None (Chapter 7). I also changed the hypertext style to double-underline and a red print color (though that's not apparent in Figure 30.1). To keep other people from messing up my document, I saved it, exited WordPerfect, and used the DOS ATTRIB command to set its status to read only (+r). You can learn more about that from the your DOS documentation.

Hypertext lets you create interactive documents that the reader can operate on-screen. By creating Hypertext hot spots and links, you can make cross-referencing within that document as simple as clicking the mouse.

Sound only works on computers that have WordPerfect-compatible sound equipment installed. But if you do have that capability, you can jazz up your interactive documents with voice, sounds, or musical fanfares. Sound and hypertext add a whole new dimension to the author's craft. What's more, they're easy to use and a lot of fun. Keep in mind that, because a hypertext link can run a macro, you can create a hot spot in your document to do virtually anything imaginable—not just jump to a bookmark or play a sound.

PART EIGHT

Managing the
Big Jobs

Automatic Indexing and Referencing

fast TRACK

● **To type a footnote or an endnote** 1082

place the cursor where you want the note number to appear in your text. Choose either Layout ➤ Footnote ➤ Create (Ctrl+F7 FC) or Layout ➤ Endnote ➤ Create (Ctrl+F7 EC). Type the text of your note. Press F7.

● **To edit an existing footnote or endnote** 1083

place the cursor on the page that contains the note. Choose either Layout ➤ Footnote ➤ Edit (Ctrl+F7 FE) or Layout ➤ Endnote ➤ Edit (Ctrl+F7 EE).

● **To change the note numbering** 1084

choose either Layout ➤ Footnote ➤ New Number (Ctrl+F7 FN) or Layout ➤ Endnote ➤ New Number (Ctrl+F7 EN).

● **To change note spacing, placement, and other options** 1086

choose either Layout ➤ Footnote ➤ Options (Ctrl+F7 FO) or Layout ➤ Endnote ➤ Options (Ctrl+F7 EO).

● **To mark lists** 1089

select the items you want to reference. Choose Tools, then a list type (Index, Table Of Contents, List, or Table Of Authorities), and then a Mark option. Or press Alt+F5 and select options under Mark Text. Complete the dialog box that appears.

To define the list and cross-reference location
and format   1096

>   position the cursor where you want the list to appear. If you
>   want to start the list on a new page, press Ctrl+⏎, and type a
>   title or page header for the list. Choose Tools, select a list type,
>   and choose Define (or press Alt+F5 and select options under
>   Define). Complete the dialog box that appears. If necessary,
>   adjust the starting number of the document text (press
>   Shift+F8 PNNN).

To mark a cross-reference and target   1105

>   place the cursor where you want the reference to appear and
>   type any introductory text. Choose Tools ➤ Cross-Reference
>   ➤ Both (or press Alt+F5 MB). Choose the type of target you
>   want to reference, enter a target name, and choose OK. Posi-
>   tion the cursor at the target and press ⏎. (You can also mark
>   references and targets individually.)

To generate lists and cross-references   1108

>   choose Tools ➤ Generate (or press Alt+F5 G) and then OK.

To compare two documents   1109

>   open one of the documents to be compared. Choose File ➤
>   Compare Documents ➤ Add Markings (or press Alt+F5 K).
>   Specify the document you want to compare against the open
>   document, select a comparison option, and then choose OK.

MANY documents require *references*, such as footnotes and endnotes, tables of contents, indexes, figure and table lists, cross-references, and more. As you'll see in this chapter, WordPerfect makes it easy to create and manage all these document references and, in true WordPerfect style, will automatically update them as you add, change, and delete text in your document.

Footnotes and Endnotes

Many scholarly, scientific, and technical documents use *footnotes* and *endnotes* to reference additional reading material or to provide parenthetical or related information that need not be included in the main body of the text. Footnotes appear at the bottom of the page, and endnotes generally appear at the end of the document.

Figure 31.1 shows a printed page with two footnotes at the bottom. The superscript numbers 1 and 2 in the body of the page are the note numbers that refer to these footnotes. Figure 31.2 shows the same parenthetical information, this time used as endnotes.

NOTE   Except for their positions when printed, footnotes and endnotes are virtually the same in WordPerfect, so from here on I'll just refer to both as *notes* and indicate any differences where appropriate.

FIGURE 31.1

WordPerfect footnotes

Only two of Archie Medees' works on mechanics have been handed down to us. These are titled *On Why Mechanics Charge a Lot to Fix Our Cars* and *On Why Cars Have Top Speeds*. Both were published in 1955 by Clickety Clack Publishers, specialists on automotive matters. In *Why Mechanics Charge*, Medees dealt with mechanical price structures, which, along with the diminishing value of the dollar and the high price of fuel, serve to undermine the basic American freedom to drive cars as fast and as far as they want to. Archie Medees used the concept of the *center of gravity* to discuss these topics, but he never explicitly defined this notion.[1]

Great progress in the theory of mechanics followed Archie Medees time. In 1965 Johann Andretti proposed the principle of *virtual reality*[2] as the fundamental law of roadworthiness. The law states that

> *in roadworthiness, no work is needed to achieve an infinitesimal*
>
> *displacement of a given mechanic's ability to mess up an engine.*

The rule captures both stable and unstable mechanics. That is, imagine a car

---

[1] Many have speculated about why Archie Medees never defined the center of gravity. Most scholars believe that the concept had already been defined elsewhere, either by Archie or earlier writers. However, the real reason may be that the center of gravity has absolutely nothing to do with the topic that Mr. Medees was addressing.

[2] This principle is a well-known buzzword in the computer industry, but it applies to cars as well. People who drive them think the posted speed limit is virtually real--that is, they can define it to mean virtually anything they want.

♪   **N   O   T   E   S**   ♪

1. Many have speculated about why Archie Medees never defined the center of gravity. Most scholars believe that the concept had already been defined elsewhere, either by Archie or earlier writers. However, the real reason may be that the center of gravity has absolutely nothing to do with the topic that Mr. Medees was addressing.

2. This principle is a well-known buzzword in the computer industry, but it applies to cars as well. People who drive them think the posted speed limit is virtually real--that is, they can define it to mean virtually anything they want.

Adding and Editing Notes

All notes consist of two elements: a superscript *note number* that appears in the text to alert the reader to the note, and the note itself. Typing a note is a simple procedure:

1. Move the cursor to where you want the note number to appear in the text (usually after the period in a sentence).

2. Choose either Layout ➤ Footnote ➤ Create (Ctrl+F7 FC) or Layout ➤ Endnote ➤ Create (Ctrl+F7 EE). The note editing window that appears looks just like a normal document window, except that it includes the superscripted number of the note and displays either "Footnote: Press F7 when done" or "Endnote: Press F7 when done" near the lower-left corner.

3. Type the text of your note, just after the superscript note number that WordPerfect inserted automatically. You can use any of WordPerfect's editing features, as usual.

4. Press F7 (or click the "Press F7 when done" message in the lower-left corner of the window) to return to your document.

To view the text of a note, switch to Page mode, display the Print Preview screen, or print the document. (Footnotes appear in Page mode once there's enough text to extend to a second page, or when you've *deselected* Layout ➤ Footnote ➤ Options ➤ Footnotes At Bottom Of Page.)

Editing the text of a note is easy. Just follow these steps:

1. Place the cursor on the page that contains the note.

2. Choose either Layout ➤ Footnote ➤ Edit (Ctrl+F7 FE) or Layout ➤ Endnote ➤ Edit (Ctrl+F7 EE).

3. When prompted, type the number of the note you want to change and press ↵. A note editing window appears with the text of your original note.

4. Edit the note as you wish.

5. Press F7 or click the "Press F7 when done" message in the lower-left corner of the window when you're done.

Here are some tips you can use when you're editing a note in the note editing window:

- To add a space or indent after the note number, press the space-bar or use indenting techniques such as Tab, F4, and Shift+F4.

- To add space between notes, you can press ↵, or use the Footnote Options or Endnote Options, described later, to add a uniform amount of space between notes.

- If you accidentally delete a note number while entering or editing a note, you can restore it easily. Press Ctrl+F7 in the note editing window, choose either Footnote or Endnote, and then select Insert Style In Note.

- To switch to the editing window for the next note, press Home PgDn. To edit the previous note, press Home PgUp.

Here are some tips for moving, deleting, and converting notes:

- To move the superscript note number from one place in your document to another, simply move the [Footnote] or [Endnote] code for that note. (See Chapter 4 for help on moving codes.)

- To delete a note, use Reveal Codes to locate its [Footnote] or [Endnote] code, and delete the code.

- To convert footnotes to endnotes, or endnotes to footnotes, use WordPerfect's NOTECVT macro. First move the cursor to where you want note conversion to begin, press Alt+F10, type **NOTECVT**, choose OK, and follow the on-screen instructions.

Renumbering Notes

Normally, the first note in a document is numbered 1, and any other notes are numbered consecutively and automatically whenever you create them. You can customize the note numbering method easily and change the starting note number at any point in your document. Here's how:

1. Place the cursor before the first note that you want to renumber.

2. Choose either <u>L</u>ayout ➤ <u>F</u>ootnote ➤ <u>N</u>ew Number (Ctrl+F7 FN) or <u>L</u>ayout ➤ <u>E</u>ndnote ➤ <u>N</u>ew Number (Ctrl+F7 EN). The Set Footnote Number dialog box appears:

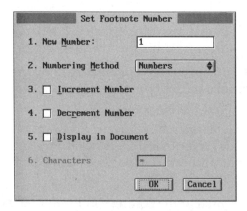

3. Choose any options you want (described below), and then choose OK to return to the document window.

You can choose from these note-numbering options:

New <u>N</u>umber   Lets you restart the note numbering at a new number.

TIP If you need to change the note starting numbers in several files, try using the Master Document feature discussed in Chapter 32 to number notes consecutively in multiple documents.

Numbering <u>Method</u>   Which numbering method do you want (numbers, letters, roman numerals, or characters)?

Increment Number   Select this option to increment the next note number manually.

De<u>c</u>rement Number   Select this option to decrement the next note number manually.

<u>D</u>isplay in Document   Select this option to display the current note number at the cursor position in the document (the note won't contain any text).

<u>C</u>haracters   Which character(s) do you want for character-style note numbering? You can type up to five characters or WordPerfect Characters (entered with Ctrl+W). WordPerfect will recycle and repeat each character in the list whenever it reaches the end of the list. To understand how this works, suppose you've entered the characters * and + in the <u>C</u>haracters text box. In this case, the number for note 1 is *, note 2 is +, note 3 is **, note 4 is ++, note 5 is ***, note 6 is +++, and so on.

TIP When you use characters to mark footnotes, it's best to restart note numbers on each page, to avoid long strings of characters. This way, your numbering characters will recycle on each page, starting again with one instance of the first character. You'll learn how to restart note numbers in the next section.

Changing the Format of Notes

Footnotes usually appear in the format shown in Figure 31.1. Endnotes usually are single-spaced, with a blank line between each note. You can change these defaults, as follows:

1. Move the cursor to where you want the new note format to take effect.

2. Choose either <u>L</u>ayout ➤ <u>F</u>ootnote ➤ <u>O</u>ptions (Ctrl+F7 FO) or <u>L</u>ayout ➤ <u>E</u>ndnote ➤ <u>O</u>ptions (Ctrl+F7 EO). The Footnote Options dialog box is shown below. (The Endnote Options dialog box has just two options: <u>S</u>pacing Between EndNotes and <u>Mini</u>mum Amount of Endnote to Keep Together.)

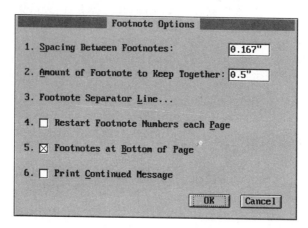

3. Choose any of the options that apply, and then choose OK.

The note formatting options are as follows:

<u>S</u>pacing Between Footnotes or **<u>S</u>pacing Between Endnotes**
How much space do you want between notes on the current and following pages?

Amount of Footnote to Keep Together or **Minimum Amount of Endnote to Keep Together**   For lengthy notes, how much note text do you want to keep at the bottom of a page before the text spills onto the next page?

Footnote Separator Line   What should the horizontal line that separates the document text from footnotes look like?

Restart Footnote Numbers Each Page   Select this option to restart footnote numbers at 1 (or the first numbering character) on each page. Deselect the option to number footnotes consecutively.

Footnotes at Bottom of Page   Select this option to place footnotes at the bottom of each page, whether the page is filled or not. Deselect this option to place footnotes immediately after the text on a partially filled page.

Print Continued Message   Select this option to print the message "(Continued...)" for footnotes that continue to another page. Deselect to remove the continuation messages. Continuation messages appear as the last line of a footnote that is continued to the next page and as the first line of a footnote that is continued from the previous page.

T I P

To change the language of the "(Continued...)" message—perhaps to "(continuación...)" for a document in Spanish—move the cursor to where the language change should take effect, choose Layout ➤ Other ➤ Language, and select a language.

Where Endnotes Will Appear

WordPerfect endnotes are automatically numbered and placed at the end of a document by default. But you can place them anywhere you want, with these steps:

1. Position the cursor where you want the endnotes to appear.

2. To start endnotes on a new page, press Ctrl+↵. Type in a page heading or title, such as **The Living EndNotes**, if you wish, and press ↵.

3. Choose <u>L</u>ayout ➤ <u>E</u>ndnote ➤ <u>P</u>lacement (Ctrl+F7 P).

4. When prompted with "Restart endnote numbering," choose <u>Y</u>es if you want to renumber any remaining endnotes, starting with 1, or <u>N</u>o to continue with consecutive numbering.

If you're in Graphics or Text mode, a comment box with the message "Endnote Placement" will show where the endnotes will appear. You'll see the actual endnote text in Page mode, Print Preview, and when you print the document.

Changing the Note Styles

WordPerfect uses predefined styles to format notes and note numbers. You can customize these styles, with the following techniques:

- To change the style of all the note numbers in the document body, choose either <u>L</u>ayout ➤ <u>F</u>ootnote ➤ Edit Style In <u>D</u>oc (Ctrl+F7 FS) or <u>L</u>ayout ➤ <u>E</u>ndnote ➤ Edit Style In <u>D</u>oc (Ctrl+F7 ES).

- To change the style of the text of all notes, choose either <u>L</u>ayout ➤ <u>F</u>ootnote ➤ Edit <u>S</u>tyle In Note (Ctrl+F7 FT) or <u>L</u>ayout ➤ Endnote ➤ Edit <u>S</u>tyle In Note (Ctrl+F7 ET).

- To change the style starting at the *current* note, edit the note as described earlier under "Adding and Editing Notes." Then press Ctrl+F7 and choose either <u>F</u>ootnote or <u>E</u>ndnote. Now pick either Edit <u>S</u>tyle in Document (to change the note number style) or Edit Style in Note (to change the note text style).

In the style editing dialog box that appears, go ahead and customize the style as you would any other style (see Chapter 17). When you're finished, press F7 to work your way back to the document window.

Automatic Reference Lists

A *reference list* is a list of items in a document and the page numbers on which they appear. WordPerfect documents can have four types of reference lists: *indexes, general lists* (useful for lists of figures and tables), *tables of contents,* and *tables of authorities* (bibliographies in legal documents).

You can generate lists in a single document, or use the Master Document feature (Chapter 32) to generate reference lists from multiple documents that are stored in separate files.

Here are the basic steps for creating any of these lists:

1. Mark all the items that belong in the list (press Alt+F5 M).

2. Insert a page break before the list and add a title, if you wish.

3. Define the format and position for the list (press Alt+F5 D).

4. To ensure proper page numbering, adjust the page numbers for text below the list, if necessary.

5. Generate the lists and cross-references (choose Tools ➤ Generate, or press Alt+F5 G, and choose OK).

Because you can do any of these steps at any time, you can create the lists as you write the document or after the document is completed. I'll explain in detail how to mark items and define each type of list in the sections that follow. You'll learn more about generating and editing the lists near the end of this chapter.

Marking Table of Contents Entries

To mark entries for a table of contents (ToC), follow these steps:

1. Select (block) the text for which you want to have entries in the table of contents.

2. Choose <u>T</u>ools ➤ Ta<u>b</u>le Of Contents ➤ <u>M</u>ark (or press Alt+F5 C).

3. Enter the level of indentation (1–5) you want, where 1 is the left-most position. For example, you might assign chapter headings to level 1, main headings to level 2, subheadings to level 3, and so on.

4. Choose OK or press ↵.

WordPerfect will mark the selected text with [Mrk Txt ToC Begin] and [Mrk Txt ToC End] codes, which you can see in Reveal Codes (Alt+F3).

Figure 31.3 shows a sample table of contents, after marking the entries, defining the list, and generating it.

FIGURE 31.3

A sample generated table of contents

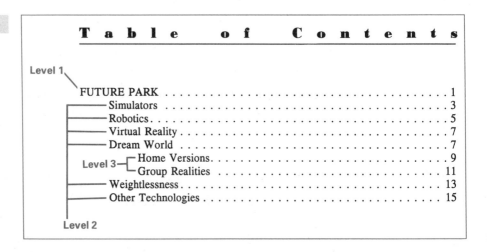

Table of Contents

Level 1

FUTURE PARK 1
Simulators 3
Robotics 5
Virtual Reality 7
Dream World 7
Level 3 ┌ Home Versions 9
        └ Group Realities 11
Weightlessness 13
Other Technologies 15

Level 2

Defining a Table of Contents

Here's how to define the position and format of your table of contents:

1. Move the cursor to where you want to place the table of contents (press Home Home Home ↑ to start the table at the very top of your document).

2. To start the table on a new page, press Ctrl+↵. Press ↑ to move the cursor before the [HPg] code. If you wish, enter a title or page heading for the ToC, such as **Table of Contents,** and press ↵.

3. Choose Tools ➤ Table Of Contents ➤ Define (press Alt+F5 DC). You'll see the Define Table Of Contents dialog box, shown here:

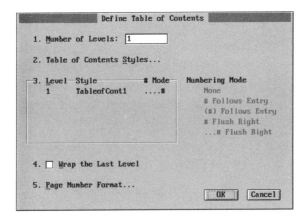

4. Specify the format for your ToC (the options are described just below). Then choose OK.

5. To ensure proper page numbering, move the cursor to the top of the first numbered page (the first page that follows any front matter, such as the table of contents). Press Shift+F8 PNNN and set the page number to 1 (see Chapter 8) if you need help.

You can now generate the table of contents if you wish. Choose Tools ➤ Generate, or press Alt+F5 G, and choose OK.

You can use these options to customize your table of contents:

Number of Levels   How many levels do you want in your table of contents, in the range 1 to 5? Suppose you've marked chapter titles as level 1 and main headings as level 2. If you want the table of contents to include both levels, enter **2** as the number of levels. If you want to include only the chapter titles, enter **1** as the number of levels.

Table of Contents Styles   Lets you customize the appearance of the text in each table of contents level.

Numbering Mode   Where do you want to place page numbers in each level in the table of contents? Highlight the level you want to change and choose one of the five numbering options. The #Mode column will reflect your current selections.

Wrap the Last Level   Select this option to word-wrap the last level in the ToC if it's longer than one line.

Page Number Format   Lets you customize the page number format with text, page numbers, secondary page numbers, volume numbers, and chapter numbers.

Marking Index Entries

WordPerfect indexes offer two levels of index entries: the index *heading* and the *subheading*. In Figure 31.4 the index headings are *Amusement*, *Questor*, *Robotics*, *Simulators*, and so on. Only the *Amusement* and *Robotics* headings have subheadings. Here are the steps to mark your index entries:

1. Select the word or phrase you want to include in the index.

2. Choose Tools ➤ Index ➤ Mark (or press Alt+F5 I). You'll see the Mark dialog box.

3. In the Heading text box, type a new heading if you wish. Or, to copy the heading and subheading quickly from another index entry in your document, choose the List Index Marks button (or press F5), select the entry you want to copy, and choose either Select Complete Mark or Select Heading Only.

4. In the Subheading text box, enter a subheading if you wish.

5. Choose OK to return to the document window.

Using an Index Concordance File

As an alternative (or supplement) to marking each index entry, you can create a *concordance file* that lists all the words you want to index. When you generate the index, WordPerfect will automatically create an entry for any word or phrase in your document that matches a corresponding entry in the concordance file. Each entry in the concordance file must end with a hard return ([HRt]) code.

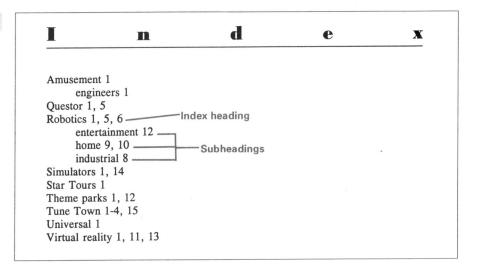

By default, each entry in the concordance file is an index heading entry.
To convert an entry to a subheading, mark it as a subheading in the concordance file. If you want WordPerfect to match the entry both as a heading and a subheading, mark the entry twice: once as a heading and once
as a subheading. After creating your concordance file, save it as you would
any other WordPerfect document.

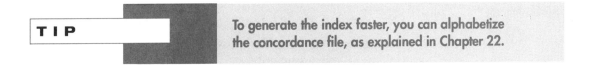

TIP   To generate the index faster, you can alphabetize
the concordance file, as explained in Chapter 22.

Defining the Index

Here are the steps to define the location and appearance of your index:

1. Place the cursor where you want the index to appear. (Press
   Home Home ↓ to start the index at the end of the document.)

2. To start the index on a new page, press Ctrl+↵. Type in a title or
   page heading, such as **Index**, if you wish, and press ↵.

3. Choose <u>T</u>ools ➤ <u>I</u>ndex ➤ <u>D</u>efine (or press Alt+F5 DI). You'll see the Define Index dialog box, shown here:

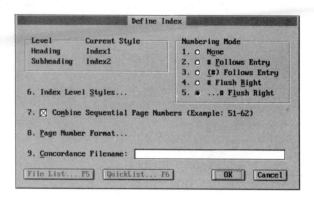

4. Define the index format and concordance file (if you've created one), using the options described just below.

5. Choose OK to return to your document.

You can now generate the index if you wish, by choosing <u>T</u>ools ➤ <u>G</u>enerate (Alt+F5 G) and then OK.

Here are the options you can use to customize your index:

> **Numbering Mode**   Where should the page numbers appear?
>
> **Index Level <u>S</u>tyles**   What style do you want for the index heading and subheading entries?
>
> **Com<u>b</u>ine Sequential Page Numbers**   Select this option to have WordPerfect list sequential page numbers as a range (for instance, 4–7). Deselect the option to print sequential page numbers separately (for instance, 4, 5, 6, 7).
>
> **<u>P</u>age Number Format**   Lets you customize the page number format with text, page numbers, secondary page numbers, volume numbers, and chapter numbers.
>
> **<u>C</u>oncordance Filename**   Lets you specify the concordance file name. Leave this blank if you're not using a concordance file.

Marking List Entries

General lists show page numbers for items that don't necessarily fit into the index or table of contents format. For example, you might want to make a list of words or phrases as a glossary or make a list of books and articles as a bibliography. A general list can also contain references to figure boxes, text boxes, and table boxes.

Figure 31.5 shows a sample list of figure captions. (In this example, I tweaked the style to print a blank line between entries.)

Here's how to mark an item that you want to include in a list:

1. Select the text that you want to put in the list.

2. Choose <u>T</u>ools ➤ <u>L</u>ist ➤ <u>M</u>ark (or press Alt+F5 L). You'll see the Mark Text For List dialog box.

3. In the List <u>N</u>ame text box, type a name for the list or accept the suggested name. You can also choose the Lists button (or press F5) to assign the text to an existing list.

4. Choose OK to return to the document window.

T I P

You don't need to mark captions for graphics boxes. WordPerfect will do this for you automatically.

FIGURE 31.5

A list of figures

L i s t   o f   F i g u r e s

1. WordPerfect sports the Windows-like "drag 'n drop" feature. 1

2. Right on Target! The appearance of all WordPerfect "objects" is defined with styles. 5

3. Something fishy this way comes. 8

4. Save a tree! Use the File ▸ Print Preview feature! 12

Defining a General List

Here's how to define the location and format of a general list:

1. Move the cursor to where you want the list to appear.

2. To place the list on its own page, press Ctrl+↵. (If you're placing the list at the top of the document, press ↑ next to move the cursor before the [HPg] code.) Type a title or page header for the list, such as **List of Figures**, if you wish, and press ↵.

3. Choose Tools ➤ List ➤ Define (or press Alt+F5 DL). The Define List dialog box, shown below, will appear. (In this example I've already defined three lists.)

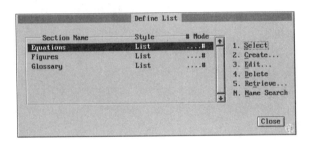

4. If the list you want to define appears in the Define List dialog box, skip to step 5. If you want to create a list for captioned Equation, Figure, Table, Text, or User boxes (or any other list that doesn't appear), choose Create to open this Create List dialog box:

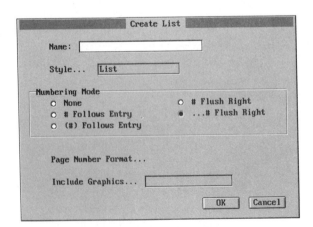

- In the <u>N</u>ame text box, type a name for the list (such as **Fig-ures**) and press ↵.
- To customize the list's appearance, choose the <u>S</u>tyle, Numbering Mode, and <u>P</u>age Number Format options as appropriate (these options are the same as described earlier for tables of contents).
- To include graphics box captions in the list, choose <u>I</u>nclude Graphics. When the Graphics Box Counters dialog box appears, highlight the type of graphics box caption you want, and choose Select.
- Choose OK to return to the Define List dialog box.

5. In the Define List dialog box, highlight the list you want to place in the document and choose <u>S</u>elect, or double-click the name you want. (Other options in this dialog box are explained below.)

6. If you want a page break to appear after the list, press Ctrl+↵.

7. If you've placed the list in the front matter, move the cursor to the first numbered page. Press Shift+F8 PNNN and set the page number to 1 (see Chapter 8). This step will ensure proper page numbering of the text below the list. Press F7 until you return to your document.

Repeat steps 1–5 for each list that you want to define. When you're finished defining the lists, you can generate them by choosing <u>T</u>ools ➤ <u>G</u>enerate (Alt+F5 G) and then OK.

The Define List dialog box includes the options summarized below. Before you choose the <u>S</u>elect, <u>E</u>dit, or <u>D</u>elete options, be sure to highlight the list you want to work with first.

<u>S</u>elect   Places the highlighted list definition in your document at the cursor position.

<u>C</u>reate   Lets you create a new list, as described above.

<u>E</u>dit   Lets you change the format of the highlighted list.

<u>D</u>elete   (or the Delete key) Deletes the highlighted list.

Re<u>t</u>rieve   Lets you retrieve list definitions from another file.

<u>N</u>ame Search   Lets you highlight a list name quickly, by typing a few characters of the name.

You'll usually need to follow the steps given earlier in "Marking List Entries" to mark each item that you want to include in a general list. However, you *don't* have to mark graphics boxes. As long as a box has a caption, WordPerfect will include it automatically in the general list defined for that box type. (Graphics boxes without captions won't be included in the list.)

For example, suppose you've added captions to several Figure boxes, using techniques discussed in Chapter 26. To create a list of figures for your document, follow the first three steps given just above. When you get to step 4, choose Create, enter a name such as **Figures** in the Create List dialog box, and press ↵. Then choose Include Graphics. Highlight Figure Box, choose Select, and then choose OK. When you return to the Define List dialog box, highlight the name of your new list and choose Select.

Marking Table of Authorities Entries

A table of authorities (ToA) is a list of citations in a legal document (see Figure 31.6). This table is typically divided into several sections, such as *Cases, Authorities, Constitutional Provisions, Statutory Provisions, Regulatory Provisions,* and *Miscellaneous.* Each section usually has a different format, which you can customize as needed (though you will want to follow accepted legal practices to avoid strange glances from the legal community).

The document itself (typically a legal brief) generally contains two types of citations: a *full form,* which is usually the first reference in the document, and a *short form,* which is an abbreviated way to show all subsequent references to the same authority. For each authority that you cite, you must complete these basic steps:

1. Use the full form procedure to mark the first citation of any authority, edit the text of the full citation (if necessary), and assign a "nickname" (the short form) to that authority.

2. Use the short form method to mark all remaining references to the same authority.

FIGURE 31.6

A sample table of
authorities

```
                    TABLE OF CASES AND AUTHORITIES

Cases                                                              Page

Association of General Contractors v.
City and County of San Francisco
      813 F.2d 922 (9th Cir. 1993) . . . . . . . . . . . . . 1, 9

City of Richmond v. Croson
      _____ U.S. _____
      109 S. Ct. 706
      _____ L. Ed. 2d (1993). . . . . . . . . . . . . . . . 1, 13

Fullilove v. Klutznick
      448 U.S. 488
      100 S. Ct. 2758
      65 L. Ed. 2d 902 (1993). . . . . . . . . . . . . . . 1, 13

Gregory Construction Co v. Blanchard
      691 F. Supp. 17 (W.D. Mich. 1993). . . . . . . 1, 12, 14, 15

Jackson v. Conway
      472 F. Supp. 896 (D. C. Mont. 1993). . . . . . . . . 8, 11

London v. Coopers & Lybrand
      644 F.2d 811 (C.A. Cal. 1993). . . . . . . . . . . . 12

Authorities

California Rules of Civil Procedure
      Rule 58(a) . . . . . . . . . . . . . . . . . . . . . 12

California Rules of Evidence
      Rule 704 . . . . . . . . . . . . . . . . . . . . . . 40
```

These basic steps are explained fully in the sections that follow.

After you've marked all the authorities, you can define the appearance
and location of each section of the table and generate the entire table.

Marking the Full Form

Follow these steps to create and mark the full form citation for an entry
in a table of authorities:

1. Select the long form of the citation, as shown in Figure 31.7.

2. Choose Tools ➤ Table Of Authorities ➤ Mark Full (or press
   Alt+F5 A). You'll see a ToA Full Form dialog box.

FIGURE 31.7

A long-form ToA entry selected in the document window

```
 File  Edit  View  Layout  Tools  Font  Graphics  Window  Help
      Construing plaintiff's claims liberally, especially in light

of the United States Supreme Court's decision in City of

Richmond v. Croson, _____ U.S. _____, 109 S. Ct. 706, ____ L. Ed.

2d (1993), plaintiff has established the patent invalidity of the

"quotas," since such quotas have been found to violate 42 U.S.C.

§ § 1981, 1983 and 2000(d).  See, e.g., Association of General

Contractors v. City and County of San Francisco, 813 F.2d 922

(9th Cir. 1993).

                              VI.

      PLAINTIFF'S CAUSE OF ACTION FOR DECLARATORY RELIEF IS
      IDENTICAL TO THE CASE PRESENTED IN GREGORY
      CONSTRUCTION CO. V. BLANCHARD.¹

      Plaintiff's remaining cause of action is for declaratory

relief.  Relying upon City of Richmond v. Croson, _____

U.S. at ____, 109 S. Ct. at 707, _____ L. Ed. 2d at ____, and

Fullilove v. Klutznick, 448 U.S. 488, 100 S. Ct. 2758, 65 L. Ed.

 Typeover Block on                          Doc 1 Pg 1 Ln 2" Pos 1.9"
```

3. In the Section Name text box, type a name for a ToA section. Or, to copy the section name from an existing section quickly, choose the List Sections button (or press F5), highlight the entry you want to copy, and choose Select.

4. In the Short Form text box, enter the short form "nickname" that you'll use to mark subsequent ToA entries for this authority. Be sure to assign a unique short name, since each short name will identify a separate authority.

5. If you'd like to change the text of the full form citation, choose Edit Full Form. An editing window will appear. You can use all the usual WordPerfect techniques, including shortcut keys and pull-down menus, to edit and format the text of your full form citation as you want it to appear in the final table of authorities. When you're finished editing, press F7 or click the "Press F7 when done" message at the lower-left corner of the window.

6. Choose OK to return to the document window.

If you need to update an existing ToA entry, choose Tools ➤ Table Of Authorities ➤ Edit Full. Highlight the entry you want to change, and choose an option from the Edit Table Of Authorities Marks dialog box:

- To change the entry's short name, choose Short Form.
- To change the section this entry is assigned to, choose Section.
- To change the text of the entry's full form, choose Full Form.

Marking the Short Forms

Once you have marked the full form of the citation, use the short form procedure below to mark all the subsequent citations of the same authority. Here are the steps:

1. Position the cursor just after the text that you want to mark.

2. Choose Tools ➤ Table Of Authorities ➤ Mark Short (or press Alt+F5 MA).

3. If you want to change the suggested short name, type it in the Short Form text box. Or choose the List Short Forms button or press F5, highlight the name you want, and choose Select.

4. Choose OK to return to the document.

5. Repeat steps 1–4 for each remaining short form of this citation in the document.

And that's the long and short (form) of it. Once you've marked the citations for one authority in a particular section, simply repeat the procedure to mark the full and short forms for each authority in the document.

Defining the Table of Authorities

You define a table of authorities one section at a time, as follows:

1. Place the cursor where you want the Table of Authorities section to appear (usually at or near the start of the document).

2. To insert a hard page break, press Ctrl+↵. Press ↑ to move the cursor above the [HPg] code. If you wish, type in a title or page heading, such as **Cases**, and press ↵.

3. Choose <u>T</u>ools ➤ Table Of <u>A</u>uthorities ➤ <u>D</u>efine (or press Alt+F5 DA). You'll see the Define Table Of Authorities dialog box.

4. Highlight the ToA section you want to define.

5. If you want to use the default ToA format, skip to step 6. If you'd like to change the format, choose <u>E</u>dit. The Edit Table Of Authorities dialog box appears, as shown below:

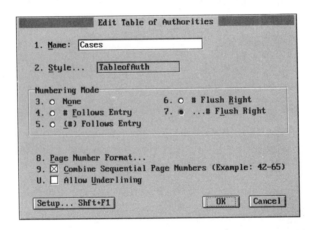

You can adjust the following elements of the ToA format:

- You can change <u>S</u>tyle and Numbering Mode, and you have the same <u>P</u>age Number Format and <u>C</u>ombine Sequential Page Numbers options described earlier for indexes.

- If you want to include underlining from the original document entries, select the Allow <u>U</u>nderlining check box.

- If you want to change the default settings for sequential pages and underlining in this and future tables of authorities, choose the Setup button or press Shift+F1. Then select (or deselect) the options you want and choose OK.

6. In the Define Table of Authorities dialog box, highlight the entry you want and choose <u>S</u>elect, or double-click the entry.

7. Repeat steps 1–6 for each section in the ToA.

8. To ensure proper page numbering, move the cursor to page 1 (beyond the ToA and any other front matter), press Shift+F8 PNNN, and set the page number to 1 (see Chapter 8). Press F7 until you return to the document.

Now you can generate the Table of Authorities by choosing Tools ➤ Generate (Alt+F5 G) and then OK.

Cross-Referencing

You can use WordPerfect's powerful *cross-referencing* features to keep track of cross-references in your documents—such as "see Table 3.7 on page 14." And if the referenced page or table number changes—as is often the case—no problem! WordPerfect will update the cross-references automatically.

The item referred to is the *target* (in the foregoing example, the target is Table 3.7 on page 14). The place where you mention the target is the *reference*. You'll have no trouble keeping these two terms straight if you remember that a *reference* always points to its *target*.

Generating cross-references involves two simple processes:

1. Setting up the references and targets. You can define your references and targets separately, or both at once. You need to mark a target only once. Then, you can mark as many references to that target as you need.

2. Generating the cross-references.

Marking a Reference

To mark a reference, follow these steps:

1. Place the cursor where you want the reference to appear.

2. Type any introductory text and then enter a blank space, if necessary. For example, type **[see page** and then press the spacebar. When generating references later, WordPerfect will automatically insert text from the caption number style of any graphics box. For

example, if you mark Table 1 as a target, WordPerfect will automatically insert the words *Table 1* in the reference. Therefore, you don't have to include text from the caption number style in your introductory text.

3. Choose Tools ➤ Cross-Reference ➤ Reference (or press Alt+F5 MR) to display the Mark Cross Reference dialog box, shown here:

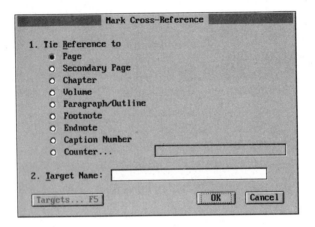

4. Choose Tie Reference To and select the type of item you're referencing. (For graphics boxes, choose Caption Number.)

5. In the Target Name box, type a descriptive name for the target that will be easy to remember when you mark the target later. Or choose Targets (or press F5), highlight an existing target, and choose Select.

6. Choose OK. Don't worry if the reference appears as a question mark (?). That character will be replaced by the correct reference when you generate the lists and references.

7. Finish typing any introductory text for the reference. For instance, to finish the example started in step 2, type a space and then **]**; the full reference will be **[see page 10]** after it's generated.

Marking a Target

Here's how to mark a referenced target in your document:

1. Move the cursor just past the target. (Use Reveal Codes to help you position the cursor.)

2. Choose Tools ➤ Cross-Reference ➤ Target (Alt+F5 MT).

3. Enter the target name. *Be sure to use the exact spelling you used when defining the reference.* Or choose Targets (or press F5), then highlight the target name you want and choose Select.

4. Choose OK.

Marking a Reference and Target at the Same Time

Instead of marking references and targets independently, you can save some steps and mark them both at the same time. This is especially useful when you only have one reference to a single target. Here are the steps:

1. Place the cursor where you want the *reference* to appear and type the introductory text (as explained in step 2 of the reference-marking procedure above).

2. Choose Tools ➤ Cross-Reference ➤ Both (Alt+F5 MB). The Mark Cross-Reference and Target dialog box will appear. This dialog box is nearly identical to the Mark Cross-Reference example shown in step 3 of the reference-marking procedure above.

3. Choose Tie Reference To and then select the type of item you're referencing.

4. Choose Target Name. Then type the target name. Or choose Targets (or press F5), highlight an existing target, and choose Select.

5. Choose OK. You'll see a special window that shows text in your document. The prompt "Position cursor and press Enter to insert target" appears at the bottom of the screen.

6. You can scroll through the window with the cursor keys to locate the target text, or press Ctrl+Home and enter a page number to view a specific page in your document. Place the cursor just to the right of the target text and press ↵.

7. Finish typing any introductory text for the reference.

If you need to mark additional references to the same target, just follow the earlier procedure under "Marking a Reference."

Page X of Y Numbering

It's very easy to define "page *x* of *y*" page numbering in your page headers or footers (where *x* is the current page of your document, and *y* is the last page in your document). For example, on page 30 of a 100-page document, your page header might say *Page 30 of 100*. If that document increased to 102 pages, WordPerfect would automatically adjust the header on page 30 to read *Page 30 of 102* the next time you generated lists and cross-references. In this example, the current page number would be the reference, and the last page of the document would be the target.

All this will become clearer as you follow the steps below:

1. Move the cursor to the last page of the document (Home Home ↓).

2. Choose Tools ➤ Cross-Reference ➤ Target (Alt+F5 MT). Type an obvious target name, such as **LAST PAGE**, and choose OK.

3. Move back to the top of the document (Home Home Home ↑).

4. Choose Layout ➤ Header/Footer/Watermark and follow the usual steps for creating a new header or footer (see Chapter 8).

5. When you get to the header or footer editing window, move the cursor to where you want the current page number to appear. Type any introductory text, such as **Page**, and a space, and choose Layout ➤ Page ➤ Page Numbering ➤ Insert Formatted Page Number (Shift+F8 PNI).

6. Press the spacebar, type **of**, and press the spacebar again.

7. Choose Tools ➤ Cross-Reference ➤ Reference (Alt+F5 R) and then choose OK. (The reference will be tied to the page number.)

8. Finish typing the header or footer, and press F7 to return to the document window.

Generate the cross-references (choose Tools ➤ Generate then OK), and then print your document.

WARNING

If you add new text to the end of the document, be sure to place that text *above* the [Target(LAST PAGE)] code that identifies the last page number. Also, if you lengthen or shorten your document by a page or more, be sure to generate the cross-references again.

Using Styles to Mark Reference Entries

You can use the Styles feature (Chapter 17) to format and automatically mark entries for tables of contents and general lists. The trick is to include the marking codes right in the style.

To help you understand how this works, take a look at the steps below. These create a style that automatically marks chapter titles in a table of contents as ToC level 1 entries.

1. Choose Layout ➤ Styles ➤ Create (Alt+F8 C), and define a new Paragraph (or Character) style for the element you want to format, in this case, the chapter titles.

2. In the Edit Style dialog box, select Show Style Off Codes.

3. Choose Style Contents and enter the formatting codes you want.

4. Select (block) all the codes and text in the Style Contents area (above and below the style on/style off comment box).

5. Choose Tools ➤ Table Of Contents ➤ Mark (Alt+F5 C) and enter the level for this style (in this example, **1** for chapter titles). Choose OK.

6. Press F7, choose OK, and then choose Close to save the style.

Use your new style to format the chapter titles. Then define the ToC, and generate the list as described next.

Generating and Editing Lists

Once you've marked your lists and cross-references, generating them is easy. Simply choose Tools ➤ Generate (or press Alt+F5 G), and choose OK. WordPerfect will generate all reference lists in the document and will replace any previously generated reference lists with new lists.

NOTE WordPerfect *does not* update the lists automatically when you change your document. Therefore, be sure to choose Tools ➤ Generate again to regenerate your lists after making changes. (When you print a document, WordPerfect will let you know if it contains lists that might be out of date.)

If you decide to edit a generated list, pay special attention to the codes that define the list and its contents. You'll typically see codes like these after you generate a list:

[Def Mark][Begin Gen Txt]...*the list goes here*...[End Gen Txt]

Each list begins at the [Def Mark] code that WordPerfect inserts when you define the list. The generated list appears between [Begin Gen Txt] and [End Gen Txt] codes. Each time you generate a list, WordPerfect will completely replace any text between the [Begin Gen Txt] and [End Gen Txt] codes. You should, therefore, keep the following points in mind.

- Always place list titles and page headers *before* the [Def Mark] code (otherwise, they'll simply disappear—poof!)

- If you edit the generated list only, your changes will be lost when you regenerate the list. Therefore, it's best to edit your references within the main document, and then generate the lists anew.

Comparing Documents

Suppose you want to know what's different about two versions of a document, but you don't want to suffer through comparing them manually. This job is a piece of computer cake with WordPerfect's Document Compare feature.

WordPerfect can show differences between documents in three ways:

Added Text   Added text is placed between *redline* codes ([Redln On] and [Redln Off]).

Deleted Text   Deleted text is placed between *strikeout* codes ([StkOut On] and [StkOut Off]), with lines drawn through the deleted text.

Moved Text   "THE FOLLOWING TEXT WAS MOVED" appears *before* text that you've moved, and "THE PRECEDING TEXT WAS MOVED" appears *after* text you've moved.

NOTE   WordPerfect will mark changes to footnotes, endnotes, and tables, but not changes in graphics boxes, headers, footers, and comments.

Follow these steps to compare two documents:

1. Open one of the documents that you want to compare. For added safety, make a backup copy of this document.

2. Choose <u>F</u>ile ➤ Compare <u>D</u>ocuments ➤ <u>A</u>dd Markings (Alt+F5 K) to display the Compare Documents dialog box, shown here:

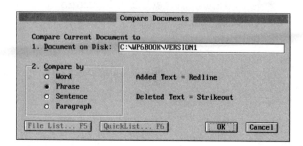

3. Choose <u>D</u>ocument On Disk, type the name of a document that you want to compare against the open document, and press ↵.

4. Choose <u>C</u>ompare By, and then choose the chunk of text you want:

   <u>W</u>ord   Compares text that ends with a space, period, comma, colon, semicolon, question mark, exclamation point, hard return, or hard page break.

   <u>P</u>hrase   Same as the Word option, except that spaces *do not* end the phrase. (This is the default setting.)

   <u>S</u>entence   Compares text that ends with a period, question mark, exclamation point, hard return, or page break.

   Pa<u>r</u>agraph   Compares text that ends with a hard return or hard page break.

5. Choose OK to begin comparing the documents.

The comparison results will appear in the current document window. After looking at the results, you can remove the markings from the current document using any of these techniques:

- To remove all markings quickly, choose <u>E</u>dit ➤ <u>U</u>ndo (Ctrl+Z) or <u>F</u>ile ➤ <u>C</u>lose ➤ <u>Y</u>es. If it's too late for these options to work (because you've saved the document or done some other operation), choose <u>F</u>ile ➤ Compare <u>D</u>ocuments ➤ <u>R</u>emove Markings ➤ <u>Re</u>move Redline Markings And Strikeout Text and choose OK.

- To remove the strikeout text only, choose <u>F</u>ile ➤ Compare <u>D</u>ocuments ➤ <u>R</u>emove Markings ➤ Remove <u>S</u>trikeout Text Only and choose OK.

In the next chapter, you'll learn about WordPerfect's Master Document feature, which makes it easy to assemble many small files into one big document for editing, formatting, list generation, and printing.

Using Master Document to Manage Many Files

fast TRACK

● **To create a master document**   1117

place the cursor where you want the subdocument link to appear, choose File ➤ Master Document ➤ Subdocument (Alt+F5 AS), and enter the subdocument's file name. Repeat these steps for each subdocument that you want to include in the master document.

● **To expand the master document**   1119

choose File ➤ Master Documents ➤ Expand, or press Alt+F5 AE. Mark or unmark the subdocuments that you want to expand. Choose OK, then Yes.

To generate lists for the master document and subdocuments   1121

open the master document and choose <u>T</u>ools ➤ <u>G</u>enerate or press Alt+F5 G. If you don't want to save changes to subdocuments, deselect <u>S</u>ave Modified Subdocuments. Choose OK.

To condense a master document and save all your changes   1124

choose <u>F</u>ile ➤ <u>M</u>aster Document ➤ <u>C</u>ondense (or press Alt+F5 AC), and select the subdocuments that you want to condense and save. Choose OK, then choose <u>Y</u>es.

IF YOU write large documents, such as books with several chapters or reports with many large sections, you'll undoubtedly find it easier to store each chapter or section in a separate file. This helps prevent any file from becoming so large that it's unwieldy to work with in a document window.

You can use WordPerfect's Master Document feature to *link* these individual files (called *subdocuments*) into one large *master document*. Then, when you want to assemble and work with all the subdocuments at once, you can *expand* the master document to its full size. Once you are done using the master document, you can *condense* it back to its small size and save any subdocuments that you've changed.

About Master Documents

A master document is pretty much like any other WordPerfect document. And, like any other document, it can contain text and hidden codes. The only difference is that the master document contains links to other documents, called *subdocuments*. Each subdocument is also just a regular WordPerfect document that you've created and saved in the usual manner.

Keep the following points in mind before using the Master Document feature to number pages, notes, or boxes, or to generate cross-references:

- If your document requires front matter before page number 1, place a [Pg Num Set:1] code after the front matter to start numbering at page 1. To do this, move the cursor to the page that should be numbered as page 1 (after the table of contents and other front matter). Then press Shift+F8 PNNN. Type **1,** and then choose OK until you return to the document window. Use additional [Pg Num Set] codes in the subdocuments *only* if you want to interrupt the consecutive numbering sequence. For instance, if each section is numbered separately (1-1, 2-1, and so forth), you could restart the page numbering at the beginning of each section.

- To start each chapter or section on an odd-numbered page, include a [Force:Odd] code at the top (with Layout ➤ Page ➤ Force Page ➤ Odd ➤ OK).

- You can define automatic lists in separate documents if you wish. For example, you could define front matter (such as tables of contents and lists of figures) in a file named FRONTMAT.WP. Then put definitions for back matter, such as indexes, in another file named BACKMAT.WP. Be sure to use hard page breaks between various lists (see Chapter 31).

- Instead of storing list definitions in separate documents, you can put them right in the master document itself. Simply define the appropriate lists above the first subdocument (for front matter) and below the last subdocument (for back matter).

Creating a Master Document

To create your master document, open a new document window and follow these steps:

1. Position the cursor where you want to place the subdocument link.

2. Choose File ➤ Master Document ➤ Subdocument (Alt+F5 AS).

3. Type the file name of the subdocument that you want to link. You can use the File List (F5) or QuickList (F6) buttons to help you locate the file (see Chapter 20). Note that the subdocument doesn't have to exist at the moment.

4. Choose OK. A comment box will indicate the position of the sub-document within the master document, and a [Subdoc] code will appear in Reveal Codes.

5. To start the next document on a new page, press Ctrl+↵.

Repeat steps 1–5 for each subdocument you want to include in the master document, making sure to link the files in proper order (for instance, FRONTMAT.WP, CHAP1.WP, CHAP2.WP, and so forth). When you're done, you'll see comments in the document window for each subdocument, along with any hard page breaks you added, as shown in Figure 32.1.

Here are some useful tips for working with master documents:

- You can use a master document as a subdocument in other master documents. WordPerfect will automatically expand this file when you expand the master document that includes it.

- To delete a subdocument link from the master document, delete the [Subdoc] code in Reveal Codes.

FIGURE 32.1

Several subdocuments in the document window

File Edit View Layout Tools Font Graphics Window Help

Subdoc: FRONTMAT.WP

Subdoc: CHAP1.WP

Subdoc: CHAP2.WP

Subdoc: CHAP3.WP

Subdoc: BACKMAT.WP

Typeover   Doc 2 Pg 5 Ln 1" POS 1"

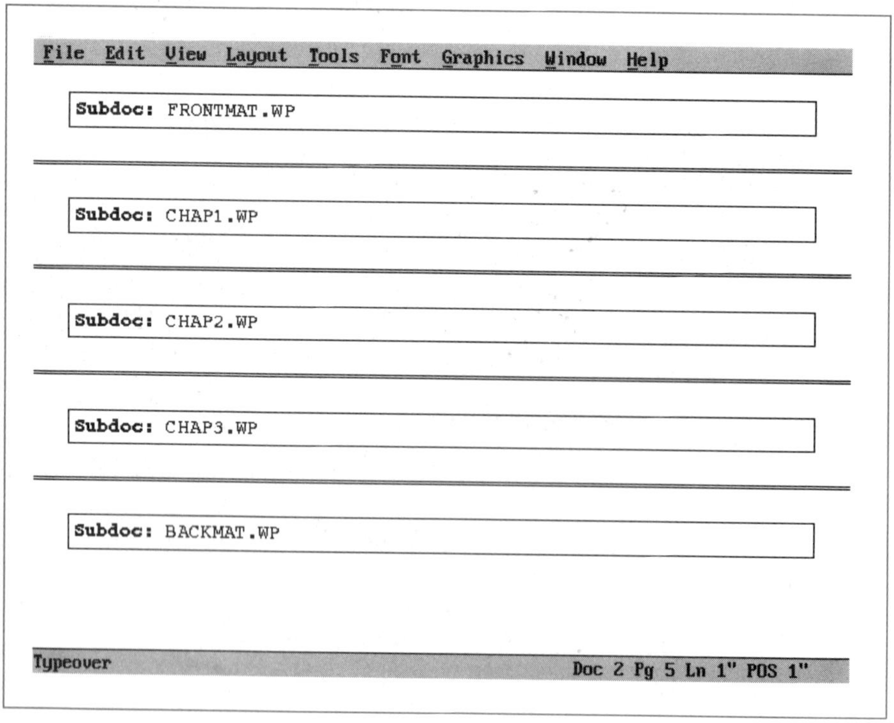

- To move a subdocument link to another place in the master document, simply move the [Subdoc] code, using techniques discussed in Chapter 4.

- It's easiest to move and delete subdocument links when the master document is condensed.

Expanding the Master Document

You can edit and save subdocuments individually, just like any other WordPerfect files. Often, however, you'll want to see and work with all your subdocuments at once. To do this, you need to *expand* the master document. Although you don't need to expand the master document to generate reference lists, you must do so for most other types of operations (for example, making global changes and printing).

Follow these steps to expand the master document:

1. Open the master document, and choose File ➤ Master Document ➤ Expand (or press Alt+F5 AE). You'll see the Expand Master Document dialog box, shown below:

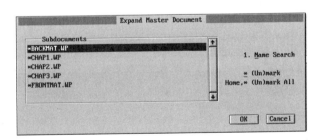

2. Initially, all subdocuments are marked for expansion. To unmark a subdocument (or to mark an unmarked subdocument), choose Subdocument. Then highlight the subdocument and press the spacebar or the * key. To mark or unmark all subdocuments at once, press Home *.

3. Choose OK, then <u>Y</u>es.

4. If WordPerfect can't find a subdocument, you'll have a chance to <u>S</u>kip on to the next one, specify a <u>N</u>ew Filename, or Cancel the operation.

Your retrieved subdocuments will appear as one large file on the document window, and you can edit this file as you would any other. Each subdocument is placed between a Subdoc Begin and Subdoc End comment, and corresponding [Subdoc Begin] and [Subdoc End] codes will appear in Reveal Codes. Figure 32.2 shows a bird's-eye view of a master document after expanding it. Notice the comment boxes that surround each expanded subdocument, and the [Subdoc Begin] and [Subdoc End] codes in Reveal Codes.

FIGURE 32.2

A master document after expanding it

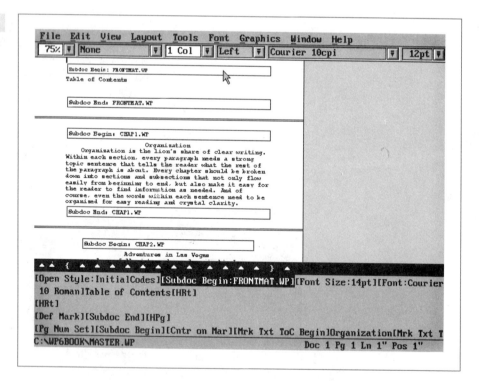

WARNING   Don't delete the [Subdoc Begin] code or [Subdoc End] code, unless you want to break the links to a subdocument.

Generating References

You can define lists either in the master document or the subdocuments (see Chapter 31). Normally, you'll mark text in the subdocuments, but you can also mark text in the master document, if necessary.

When you're ready to generate the lists, follow these steps:

1. Open the master document and choose Tools ➤ Generate (Alt+F5 G) to reach the Generate dialog box.

2. Normally, WordPerfect will generate and update lists and cross-references in subdocuments automatically. (It can do this even if you haven't expanded the master document yet.) If, for some reason, you don't want to take the time to generate and save lists and cross-references, you can deselect the Save Modified Subdocuments in the Generate dialog box. However, to be sure that all your lists are up to date, it's best to leave this option checked.

3. Choose OK.

4. If WordPerfect can't find a subdocument, you'll have a chance to Skip to the next one, specify a New Filename, or Cancel the operation.

WordPerfect will expand and condense the subdocuments automatically—behind the scenes—and generate your lists.

TIP

If page numbers or other automatic numbers in your generated lists aren't accurate, check to see whether any subdocuments contain codes that restart numbering incorrectly. Also, make sure that you've inserted hard page breaks whenever text needs to start on a new page.

Editing a Master Document

You can use any of WordPerfect's editing features to change subdocuments within the expanded master document. However, keep these points in mind:

- Any codes *outside* the [Subdoc Begin] and [Subdoc End] codes are part of the master document and will be saved in the master document only.

- Any codes *inside* the [Subdoc Begin] and [Subdoc End] codes are part of that subdocument and will be saved only in that subdocument when you condense the master document (see "Condensing a Master Document," later in this chapter).

- Changes made within a subdocument are saved *only* if you condense and save the subdocument (discussed later).

- As with single documents, later codes take precedence over earlier ones. For example, if you set the left and right margins to 2 inches at the top of the master document, all the subdocuments will have 2-inch margins, unless one of the documents contains codes that set the margins differently.

- Codes in subdocuments have no effect until you expand the master document. You won't know if the codes conflict until you expand the master document.

- When you expand a master document, WordPerfect deletes all redundant codes in the subdocuments, as long as Auto Code Placement is on (see Chapter 4). When you later condense the master document and save the subdocuments, WordPerfect deletes the redundant codes from the subdocuments.

- When the master document is expanded, initial codes and styles in the master document take precedence over initial codes and styles in the subdocuments (see Chapter 19).

- If both the master document and any subdocument contain styles with the same name, the master document's style will replace the subdocument's style when you condense the master document and save that subdocument. See the next section for more on using styles with master documents.

Updating Styles

You can use the Master Document feature to bring all the styles in various subdocuments up to date, in case you suspect that they're out of sync. When you expand the master document, WordPerfect combines all styles in the subdocuments and any styles defined in the master document. If two styles have the same name, WordPerfect uses the style from the master document, or from the document nearest the top of the master document (whichever appears first).

If you know which document has the most recent, "correct" set of styles, you can use that document to create an up-to-date style library for the first subdocument, before expanding the master document. This assumes, of course, that the master document *does not* contain any styles by the same name. If it does, be sure to delete those same-named styles in the master document before continuing.

Suppose a document named CHAP20.WP has the most recent, complete set of styles for the overall project. Follow these steps to create a new document with these latest (most fashionable) styles:

1. Open the document that has the most recent set of styles (CHAP20.WP in this example).

2. Choose Layout ➤ Styles ➤ Save, enter a file name for the new style library (for example LATEST.STY), and return to the document window.

3. Open the first subdocument that's linked to the master document (for example, FRONTMAT.WP).

4. Choose Layout ➤ Styles ➤ Retrieve, enter the name of the file you saved in step 2 (LATEST.STY), and choose OK. If you're asked about replacing existing styles, choose Yes.

5. Return to the document window and close the current document.

Now you can create (or open) your master document and expand it. Because the topmost subdocument now has the most recent set of styles, all documents beneath it will share these styles. When you condense the master document and save the subdocuments again, each document will inherit this style library. (See Chapter 17 for more on styles.)

Printing a Master Document

To print the entire master document, expand it first, and then print as you normally do with File ➤ Print/Fax (Chapter 3). You can print the entire document, select multiple pages, or select text before printing, as for any other document.

Condensing a Master Document

Once you're done working with an expanded master document, you should condense it before saving it again. Condensing preserves disk space, ensures that your subdocuments are updated properly, and forces you to generate a fresh master document before printing and editing.

To condense a master document, follow these steps:

1. Choose <u>F</u>ile ➤ <u>M</u>aster Document ➤ <u>C</u>ondense (or press Alt+F5 AC). You'll see the Condense Master Document dialog box:

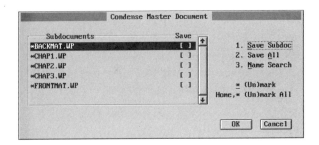

2. Initially, all subdocuments in the <u>S</u>ubdocuments list are marked for condensing, but none will be saved. You can change this by choosing <u>S</u>ubdocuments, and then...

   • To unmark a subdocument for condensing (or to mark an unmarked subdocument), highlight it and press the spacebar or the * key. To mark or unmark all subdocuments at once, press Home *.

   • If you want to save changes that you've made to a subdocument, double-click that document's name, or highlight it and choose <u>S</u>ave Subdoc. This will place an × in the Save check box for the document. (Repeat this step if you change your mind about saving a document.)

   • To mark (or unmark) *all* subdocuments for saving, choose Save <u>A</u>ll.

3. Choose OK, and then <u>Y</u>es.

WordPerfect removes the subdocuments from the master document, but retains the links to those subdocuments for future use.

NOTE If you try to save a master document that you've changed without condensing it first, WordPerfect will remind you that the document is expanded and give you a choice to condense it.

This chapter has shown you how to manage large documents that consist of smaller subdocuments. In the next chapter, you'll learn how to import and export information between WordPerfect and other programs.

Passing Information
between Programs

fast **TRACK**

WORDPERFECT makes it easy to convert documents and data to and from dozens of program formats. All you need to know is which formats you're using and where you've stored the files that you want to import or export. WordPerfect does the rest.

Converting Files

Converting a file in another format to WordPerfect's format is very simple. Just choose File ➤ Open or File ➤ Retrieve, type the name of the document, and choose OK. When prompted, highlight the foreign format in the File Format list (in most cases WordPerfect will do this for you), and choose Select.

Exporting is just as easy. Choose File ➤ Save As, type in a document name, choose Format, specify the foreign format, and choose OK.

Table 33.1 lists the formats that WordPerfect can recognize automatically when you open or save a file. Please see Chapter 20 for additional information about opening and saving files.

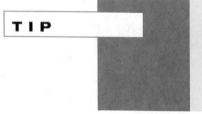

TIP

The Look feature in the File Manager (discussed in Chapter 20) can display many types of files, including graphics files, word processing files, spreadsheets, and databases. The files may not look "perfect," but you can usually get a good idea of what's in them.

TABLE 33.1:   Foreign Formats That WordPerfect Recognizes

FORMAT	WORDPERFECT CAN OPEN	WORDPERFECT CAN SAVE
Ami Pro (Windows)	x	x
ASCII Text (CR/LF → SRt)	x	
ASCII Text (Standard)	x	x
ASCII Text (Stripped)		x
Bitmap Graphics (BMP)	x	
CGM Graphics	x	
CompuServe GIF	x	
DisplayWrite	x	x
DOS Delimited Text	x	x
Encapsulated PostScript (EPS)	x	
Excel	x	
Hewlett Packard Plotter (HPGL)	x	
IBM DCA FFT	x	x
IBM DCA RFT	x	x
Lotus .PIC Graphs	x	
Lotus 123	x	
Macintosh PICT	x	
MS Word	x	x
MS Word for Windows	x	x
PC Paintbrush Graphic (PCX)	x	
PlanPerfect	x	
Quattro Pro	x	
Quattro Pro for Windows	x	
Rich Text Format (RTF)	x	x

TABLE 33.1:   Foreign Formats That WordPerfect Recognizes (continued)

FORMAT	WORDPERFECT CAN OPEN	WORDPERFECT CAN SAVE
Tagged Image File Format (TIFF)	x	
Windows Metafile (WMF)	x	
WordPerfect 2.0, 2.1 (Macintosh)	x	
WordPerfect 4.2	x	x
WordPerfect Graphics 1.0, 2.0	x	
WordPerfect 5.0, 5.1/5.2, 6.0	**	x
WordStar	x	x

** Automatically converted when you open the document

Keep the following points in mind when you convert files from one format to another:

- Your document won't always look the same after conversion. Therefore, you'll get the best results if you keep the formatting in your files as simple as possible.

- When WordPerfect 6.0 formatting features aren't available in the program or format to which you're exporting, they are usually replaced by a space.

- Most files that you import will be saved in WordPerfect 6.0 format automatically when you choose File ➤ Save.

- ASCII text files are *not* converted to WordPerfect 6.0 format when you save them. See Chapter 20 for more information on opening and saving text files.

- If you want to use WordPerfect 6.0 files in older versions of Word-Perfect—including WordPerfect 4.2, 5.0, 5.1, and 5.2—you'll need to convert them to the old version's format first. Just go through the usual File ➤ Save As steps, and select the appropriate "old" WordPerfect format from the Format list.

- Special techniques for importing spreadsheets and delimited-text database files are described later in this chapter.

Choosing an Intermediate Data Format

If WordPerfect doesn't offer a way to convert a particular file directly to or from the WordPerfect format, try to find an *intermediate data format* that is common to both programs. The documentation that comes with the program will list the formats that the program can export. If those formats include one that WordPerfect can import, your problem is solved.

Many programs can export data in these formats:

- IBM DCA Revisable Form Text (RFT)
- IBM DCA Final Form Text (FFT)
- DOS Delimited Text (discussed later in this chapter)

WordPerfect 6.0 can handle all of these easily. And practically every program, including WordPerfect, can export and import ASCII text files. (However, ASCII files have no formatting codes, just text.)

Using ASCII Text Files

DOS, Windows, and many application programs handle ASCII text files. You can edit and print these files from WordPerfect simply by opening them in ASCII Text (Standard) format. Here are some additional points to consider when you work with ASCII files in WordPerfect:

- You can use the > redirection symbol at the end of a DOS command to send its output to an ASCII text file. For example, the command below sends output from the DIR command to a file named WPLIST.TXT:

  dir *.wp > wplist.txt

- Many programs let you "print" or save reports to disk in ASCII text format. These files often have the extension .PRN or .TXT.

- WordPerfect keeps ASCII text files in their original format when you save them.

- Beware of saving system files (files with .TXT, .BAT, .INI, or .SYS extensions) in WordPerfect format. Doing so can damage them and prevent your system from working properly (see Chapter 20 for additional information).

The File Conversion Utility

The CV utility that comes with WordPerfect allows you to convert a whole bunch of files from one format to another in just a few easy steps. You can also use CV to convert the occasional file that's too large for WordPerfect's built-in converter to handle.

Because CV can recognize dozens of file formats automatically, including those listed in Table 33.1, there's no guesswork involved. You don't even have to know what format a file is in—simply tell CV the file's name and sit back while the utility does all the work.

Here's how to convert files from one format to another using the file conversion utility:

1. Exit WordPerfect (if you're in WordPerfect) and return to the DOS prompt.

2. Switch to the WordPerfect directory (if you're not already there), then type **cv** and press ↲. You'll see the ConvertPerfect dialog box.

N O T E

If you'd like some help while you're using CV, choose the Help button in the ConvertPerfect dialog box, or press F3 in any dialog box.

3. Choose Insert Job.

4. In the Source Filename box, type the full path name of the input file or files to be converted and press ↲. For example, if you want to convert all the .BMP (Bitmap) files in your C:\WINDOWS directory, type **c:\windows*.bmp** as the source file name.

5. In the Target Filename box, type the full path name of the file or files you want to create and press ↵. For example, if you want to convert the bitmap (.BMP) files described in step 4 to WordPerfect Graphics (.WPG) files stored in your C:\WP60\GRAPHICS directory, type **c:\wp60\graphics*.wpg** as the target file name.

6. If you'd like to convert the input files to a *non-WordPerfect* format, choose Target File Format. Then highlight the format you want and choose Select.

7. Choose OK.

8. Repeat steps 3–7 until you've entered all the input and output files you want.

9. When you're ready to convert the files, choose Convert. If an output file already exists, CV will ask whether you want to replace it. If you want to replace the file, choose Yes. If you don't want to replace the file, choose No, type in another file name, and choose OK.

10. As it works, CV will display a progress report on the screen. When the conversion is complete, you can choose Exit to return to the DOS prompt.

You can also run CV by specifying all the options you want on the command line. The general format is

CV *inputfile outputfile /switch /switch...*

where *inputfile* is the name of the file you want to convert, *outputfile* is the new name for the converted file, and */switch* is a switch that the CV file conversion program recognizes.

To display a complete list of switches that you can use on the CV command line, type this command at the DOS prompt:

cv /?

If you'd like a printed list of the command line switches, type this command instead:

cv /? > prn

After typing this command, you may need to press the ↵ key a few times until the DOS prompt reappears. If you're using a laser printer, be sure to eject the last page of the listing.

Importing Data into Merge Files

Many programming languages and database management systems, as well as some spreadsheets, let you export data to *delimited* text files, also known as *CSV (comma-separated value)* files. Typically, each field in a delimited file is separated by a comma, each record ends with a CR/LF (carriage return /line feed), and character strings (textual data) are enclosed in quotation marks. Figure 33.1 shows a sample delimited file, displayed with the File Manager's Look feature.

In general, database management programs provide a more flexible way to store large quantities of data than WordPerfect does. However, with just a few simple steps, you can convert some or all of your database information

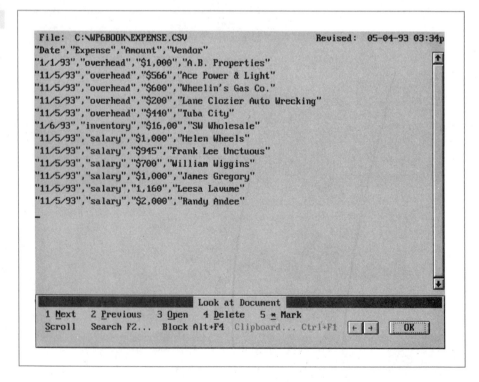

to a WordPerfect merge data file. (You learned to create form letters, mailing labels, and other merge documents in Chapter 21.)

To convert a database file to a merge data file in WordPerfect, first use whatever tools your database program offers to export the data you need to a comma-delimited file. (Check your database documentation to find out how to do it.) Then follow the steps below to create a merge data file from the delimited text file:

1. Choose File ➤ Open, enter the name of the file that contains the delimited text (for example, **EXPENSE.CSV**), and choose OK.

2. When the File Format dialog box appears, highlight the DOS *Delimited Text* option, and choose Select. You'll see the Delimited Text Options dialog box:

```
┌──────────────────────────────────────────────────────┐
│          ░░░░░  Delimited Text Options  ░░░░░          │
│                                                        │
│   1. Field Delimiter:            ┌────────────────────┐│
│                                  │,                   ││
│                                  └────────────────────┘│
│   2. Record Delimiter:           ┌────────────────────┐│
│                                  │[CR][LF]            ││
│                                  └────────────────────┘│
│   3. Field Encapsulate Character:┌────────────────────┐│
│                                  │"                   ││
│                                  └────────────────────┘│
│   4. Strip Characters:           ┌────────────────────┐│
│                                  │                    ││
│                                  └────────────────────┘│
│   5. ☐ Save Setup Options                              │
│                                                        │
│   ┌───────────┐              ┌──────┐  ┌────────┐      │
│   │ Codes... F5│              │  OK  │  │ Cancel │      │
│   └───────────┘              └──────┘  └────────┘      │
└──────────────────────────────────────────────────────┘
```

3. If you want to change the characters used to control the import process, select one of the options below.

> **Field Delimiter**   Text that separates each field.
>
> **Record Delimiter**   Text that separates each record.
>
> **Field Encapsulate Character**   Text that surrounds each field. WordPerfect won't try to convert the surrounded text.
>
> **Strip Characters**   Text that WordPerfect should remove from the data file.

4. If you chose an option in step 3, type the character or characters that you want to use. You can enter keyboard characters, or press Ctrl+W and select a WordPerfect Character. If you want to use a tab, line feed, form feed, or carriage return as the character, choose Codes (or press F5) and then choose the appropriate code.

5. Repeat steps 3 and 4 as necessary.

6. If you want to save the current settings for future merges, select (check) Save Setup Options. (Alternatively, you can choose File ➤ Setup ➤ Environment ➤ Delimited Text Options to change the default delimited text options.)

7. Choose OK to begin converting the file.

WordPerfect will convert field delimiters to ENDFIELD codes and the record delimiters to ENDRECORD codes, as shown in Figure 33.2.

The final step is to create your merge form (if you haven't done so already) and run the merge as described in Chapter 21.

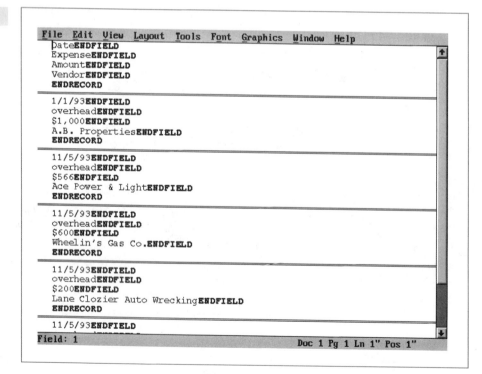

FIGURE 33.2

The WordPerfect merge data file, converted from a comma-delimited database file

Converting Imported Dates

Sometimes your merge data files will contain dates in the YYYYMMDD format, such as 19931115 (for November 15, 1993). To convert this YYYYMMDD format to a more readable one, such as 11/15/93, use the SUBSTR command in your merge form to isolate specific parts of the date. The SUBSTR command extracts a portion of a string from a larger string (called the *expression*), given a *start* position and a *length*.

Characters in a string are numbered from left to right, starting at 1. Therefore, the month number in a YYYYMMDD date starts at character 5 and is two characters long. The day starts at character 7 and is two characters long. The year starts at character 1 and is four characters long. The last two digits of the year start at character 3.

Now, let's assume that FIELD 1 in the merge data file contains a date in YYYYMMDD format. To show that date in MM/YY/DD format, you'd enter the series of SUBSTR commands that are shown next to "Date:" in Figure 33.3. Entering those commands is a bit tricky, because you can't just type in **SUBSTR(FIELD(1)**...) at the keyboard. Instead, you must enter appropriate merge codes and commands.

To start the document shown in Figure 33.3, open a new document window, press Shift+F9, and choose OK twice. This establishes your file as a merge data form. Now, you can enter the first SUBSTR command:

1. Type **Date:** and press Tab.
2. Press Shift+F9 twice.

FIGURE 33.3

SUBSTR commands used in a merge form to convert YYYYMMDD dates to MM/DD/YY format

File	Edit	View	Layout	Tools	Font	Graphics	Window	Help

Date: SUBSTR(FIELD(1);5;2)/SUBSTR(FIELD(1);7;2)/SUBSTR(FIELD(1);3;2)

No: FIELD(4)

Name: FIELD(3)

3. Highlight the SUBSTR command in the All Merge Codes list box, and choose Select. You'll see the Parameter Entry dialog box.

4. In the Expression text box, type **X** (or any other letter); you'll replace this in a later step.

5. In the Start text box, type **5**.

6. In the Length text box, type **2**.

7. Choose OK to return to the document window.

8. Move the cursor to the X (or whatever character you typed in step 4) and delete it.

9. Press Shift+F9 F, type **1** in the Field text box, and choose OK.

Now move the cursor to the end of the line and type a slash (*I*), which separates the month from the day. To enter the SUBSTR commands for the day and the year, just repeat steps 2–9, adjusting the Start value in step 5 and the Length value in step 6 accordingly. Type another slash at the end of the line, and repeat steps 2–9 once more (again adjusting the values in steps 5 and 6).

Importing and Linking Spreadsheets

WordPerfect can import or link to spreadsheets created in PlanPerfect, Lotus 1-2-3, and Quattro Pro (3.0 and 4.0).

There is a difference between importing and linking:

- If you *import* the spreadsheet, subsequent changes made to the spreadsheet in your spreadsheet program *are not* reflected in your WordPerfect document, unless you import the spreadsheet again.

- If you *link* to the spreadsheet, subsequent changes made to the spreadsheet in your spreadsheet program are reflected in the WordPerfect document.

WordPerfect imports only the *results* of formulas—not the formulas themselves—when you link or import a spreadsheet. You can edit the spreadsheet in WordPerfect as you would any other document; this has no effect on the underlying spreadsheet file. However, if you change some numbers in the imported spreadsheet and then try to recalculate the math, nothing will happen, because the imported spreadsheet doesn't contain any formulas.

To import or link a spreadsheet file, follow these steps:

1. Position the cursor where you want the spreadsheet to appear.

2. Choose Tools ➤ Spreadsheet (or press Alt+F7 S).

3. Choose Import (to import a copy of the spreadsheet without a link) or Create Link (to link to the spreadsheet). Depending on your choice, you'll see either the Import Spreadsheet or Create Spreadsheet Link dialog box, shown in Figures 33.4 and 33.5.

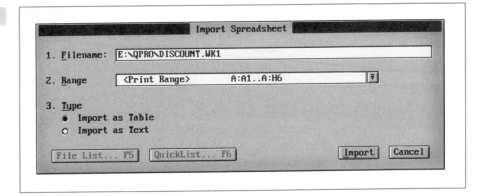

FIGURE 33.4

The Import Spreadsheet dialog box

FIGURE 33.5

The Create Spreadsheet Link dialog box

(I've already filled in the dialog boxes in these examples.)

4. In the <u>F</u>ilename text box, enter the name of the spreadsheet file you're importing. You can use the File List (F5) or QuickList (F6) buttons to help locate the file, as described in Chapter 20.

5. If you want to select and import a range (or block) of cells instead of the entire spreadsheet, choose <u>R</u>ange, and then type in a range (such as **A1.B5**) or a range name (such as **<PRINT RANGE>**), or select a range from the <u>R</u>ange drop-down list. See "Specifying a Range," just below, for information on specifying ranges.

6. Choose <u>T</u>ype, and then choose either Import As <u>T</u>able or Import As Te<u>x</u>t. When you choose Import As <u>T</u>able, WordPerfect copies each cell in the spreadsheet to a cell in a WordPerfect table. When you choose Import As Te<u>x</u>t, WordPerfect uses tab codes to separate columns and hard return ([HRt]) codes to separate rows.

7. Finally, do one of the following:

   - If you're *importing* the spreadsheet, choose the <u>I</u>mport button.
   - If you're *linking* to a spreadsheet, choose either the <u>L</u>ink or the Link & <u>I</u>mport button. <u>L</u>ink brings in the link codes *only*, and you'll need to update the link (via the Link Options, which are described a little later) to display the spreadsheet. Link & <u>I</u>mport brings in the link codes *and* displays the spreadsheet in a single step.

If you linked the spreadsheet, you'll see Link and Link End messages indicating where the link begins and ends (these messages are never printed). In Reveal Codes, you'll see [Link] and [Link End] codes.

Changing a Link

You can easily change the file name, range, or type of a spreadsheet after you've linked it. Simply move the cursor between the [Link] and [Link End] codes (or messages), and then choose <u>T</u>ools ➤ <u>S</u>preadsheet ➤ <u>E</u>dit Link (or press Alt+F7 SE). The resulting Edit Spreadsheet Link dialog box has the same options as Create Spreadsheet Link (see Figure 33.5). Make your selections, as described in the previous section, and choose OK to update the link and return to your document.

TIP

To quickly import an entire spreadsheet as a WordPerfect table, choose File ➤ Open, or position the cursor at the place where you want the table to appear and choose File ➤ Retrieve. Now enter the spreadsheet's file name and choose OK. Highlight the spreadsheet's file format in the File Format list and choose Select or press ↵.

Specifying a Range

When entering a range in step 5 of the importing/linking procedure above, you can specify either a range of cell *addresses* or a range *name* that you've assigned within your spreadsheet program.

In a two-dimensional spreadsheet, the range extends from the upper-left cell to the lower-right cell. Use a period or colon to separate the two range addresses, as in A1.C10 or A1:C10. In a three-dimensional spreadsheet, each cell address also includes a letter followed by a colon, indicating which sheet the cell is from. Thus the range A1 to C10 in spreadsheet A is expressed as A:A1.A:C10.

A range name provides a shortcut method for referring to a range of cell addresses. For example, you could use your spreadsheet program to assign the name TO_WP to the range A1.C10. Later, when you link or import the spreadsheet to WordPerfect, you enter the name **TO_WP** instead of typing the range as A1.C10.

Fixing Imported Spreadsheets

Sometimes the imported table or text columns are too wide to fit between the current page margins. Cells in tables that extend beyond the right edge of the page will be invisible, and text imported as columns will wrap to the next line. To solve "too wide" problems like these, you can

- Change the font, margins, and paper size.
- Adjust the width of the table's columns in the Table Editor (Chapter 7).

- Remove extra tab codes and adjust the tab stops to bring text columns closer together and improve their alignment (Chapter 5).

Managing Linked Spreadsheets

Once you've linked a spreadsheet to your document, you can hide the Link and Link End messages on the screen. You can also control when WordPerfect updates the link with actual data from the spreadsheet. Here's how:

1. Place the cursor between the [Link] and [Link End] codes or messages.

2. Choose Tools ➤ Spreadsheet ➤ Link Options (or press Alt+F7 SL) to display the Spreadsheet Link Options dialog box.

3. If you want to update the spreadsheet whenever you retrieve the document, select (check) Update On Retrieve.

4. If you want to display the comment boxes that indicate the name and range of the linked spreadsheet, select Show Link Codes. (Deselect the option to hide the link messages.)

5. When you're ready to return to the document window, do one of the following:

   - To update (and display) every linked spreadsheet in your document with the most recently saved version in your spreadsheet program, choose Update All Links.
   - To return to the document without updating links, choose OK.

Importing Spreadsheets to Graphics Boxes

It's easy to import a spreadsheet into a graphics box so that you can wrap text around it. First, move the cursor where you want the box to appear in the document. Choose Graphics ➤ Graphics Boxes ➤ Create ➤ Edit Position ➤ Horizontal Position ➤ Full, and then choose OK. Next, choose Create Text and follow the steps outlined above for importing or linking a spreadsheet. (You may also wish to hide the Link and Link End messages.)

Adjust the appearance of your spreadsheet in the Table Editor, if necessary, and press F7 to return to the Create Graphics Box dialog box. Finally, adjust the graphics box settings to get the look you want and press F7 to return to your document. (See Chapter 26 for more on graphics.)

Using DOS from WordPerfect

Sometimes you'll want to use DOS for a single command or several commands, without exiting WordPerfect. For example, you might want to format a floppy disk, so that you can copy some files to it. Or you might want to start a communication program, sign onto another computer's electronic bulletin board, and retrieve a file.

Start by choosing File ➤ Go To Shell (or press Ctrl+F1). Then do one of the following:

- To exit to DOS temporarily, choose Go To DOS. Enter the necessary commands at the DOS prompt. Then—*and this is crucial*—return to WordPerfect by typing **EXIT** and pressing ↵.
- To enter a single DOS command and return to WordPerfect automatically, choose DOS Command, type the command you want to run, and press ↵.

WARNING

Do not turn off your computer while you are temporarily exited to DOS, or you may lose unsaved work in WordPerfect. Also, be aware that loading memory-resident programs may prevent you from returning to WordPerfect, and these programs may hog memory that WordPerfect needs in order to work properly.

Using Other Programs from WordPerfect

WordPerfect comes with its own "Shell" program that lets you set up menus from which to run your favorite commands and programs (including WordPerfect, of course). You can fire up a bunch of programs from Shell, and then switch between those programs as needed.

Shell is completely optional, but definitely worth a look-see. Here are some of the more interesting things you can do with Shell:

- Set up menus of commands, programs, and macros.
- Start several programs, and switch between running programs.
- Record, edit, and play back Shell macros that can automate your work in Shell and programs running under Shell.
- Manage files. The File Manager in Shell is similar to the WordPerfect File Manager, discussed in Chapter 20.
- Transfer information between programs running under Shell.
- Exchange electronic messages with users on a network.

Chapter 24 explains how to start Shell, set up simple menus, and use Message Boards to exchange electronic messages. If you'd like to learn more about this fun addition to WordPerfect, please see the *WordPerfect Shell Version 4.0 User's Guide* that comes with WordPerfect.

That's all folks!

APPENDICES

APPENDIX

A

Installing WordPerfect

THIS appendix summarizes hardware requirements and installation procedures for WordPerfect 6.0 for DOS. For more technical information, please refer to the appendices in your WordPerfect software documentation.

Hardware Requirements

You'll need the following hardware to run WordPerfect 6.0 for DOS:

- A PC or PC-compatible computer with *at least* 520 KB of RAM
- DOS Version 2.0 or later
- A hard disk with at least 14.5 MB of available disk space
- To use the graphics modes, at least an EGA or VGA graphics adapter and display

First-Time Installation

Your best bet for installing WordPerfect 6.0 for DOS is to refer to the documentation that came with your WordPerfect program. This is especially true if you're a beginner or you're installing to a network. In general, the procedure goes like this:

1. Insert the WordPerfect 6.0 for DOS Install 1 disk in drive A or B.

2. At the DOS command prompt, type **a:install** if you put the disk in drive A or **b:install** if you put the disk in drive B. Then press ↲.

3. Answer any questions that appear on the screen.

4. When you see the installation options, either choose <u>S</u>tandard Installation to install the full program on your hard disk, select <u>C</u>ustom Installation to define your own files and directories, or select <u>N</u>etwork Installation to install WordPerfect on a network.

5. Answer questions and respond to prompts as they appear on the screen. Here are a few pointers:

   - You only need to install additional graphics drivers if you're using a display adapter that offers more than standard EGA and VGA features.

   - When you're asked about adding printer drivers, if this is the first time you're installing WordPerfect 6.0 for DOS choose <u>Y</u>es. Then select and install the appropriate printer driver(s) according to the instructions on the screen.

   - When asked about installing a sound driver, choose <u>Y</u>es only if you've already installed a sound card in your system.

6. When the installation is complete, and you're returned to the DOS prompt (C:>), remove all floppy disks from their drives.

7. You'll probably want to reboot (press Ctrl+Alt+Del) to activate any changes the installation program made to your AUTOEXEC.BAT file.

If you didn't install a driver for a graphics board, sound board, or whatever, and you later want to install such a driver in your computer, you can do a "partial installation" to install that device with WordPerfect. See "Installing New Hardware," later in this appendix.

Verifying the Installation

If you're an absolute beginner, you might want to skip the rest of this appendix and proceed to Chapter 1. Otherwise, if you know your way around your system and want to verify your WordPerfect installation, do the following:

1. Starting at the DOS command prompt, switch to the WordPerfect directory and run WordPerfect (for example, enter **cd \wp60** ↲ and then **wp** ↲).

2. To verify your printer selections, press Shift+F7 S. You should see the names of all your installed printers. Press F7 twice to leave the dialog box.

3. To check out your font list, press Ctrl+F8 F. You should see your built-in printer fonts (if any). If you're using a graphics printer, you should also see some bonus graphics fonts (Type 1 and Speedo) that WordPerfect Corporation has provided for your printing pleasure. Press F7 twice to return to your document.

NOTE For information on installing additional printer or graphics fonts, see Chapter 10.

4. To try out various screen modes, press Ctrl+F3 and then choose Text, Graphics, or Page. You can also set up your screen by pressing Ctrl+F3, then Shift+F1, and choosing whatever options tickle your fancy. You can learn about these options in Chapter 4.

5. If you want to exit WordPerfect and go back to DOS without saving anything, press F7, type **n,** and then type **y** (to answer No, then Yes).

Installing New Hardware

Suppose you install WordPerfect, then you get a new printer or graphics adapter. Or maybe you decide to add a fax board or a sound board to your system. You'll need to inform WordPerfect of this change in hardware. To do so, follow these general steps:

1. Install the hardware and any device drivers, following the manufacturer's instructions. (Also, check to see if that documentation includes instructions for WordPerfect, which will probably be more specific than what I can offer here.)

2. If and when instructed to by the installation documentation, be sure to reboot (press Ctrl+Alt+Del).

3. Starting at the DOS command prompt, switch to your WordPerfect 6.0 directory (typically by typing **cd \wp60** ↵) and run the Install program (type **install** ↵). If all goes well and you get to the WordPerfect 6.0 Install program, skip to step 5.

4. If the WordPerfect 6.0 Install program doesn't start, you'll need to run it from the floppies. Put your original WordPerfect 6.0 Install 1 disk in drive A or B. Then type **a:install** ↵ (for drive A), or **b:install** ↵ (for drive B).

5. Answer any initial prompts. When you get to the Installation Options screen, choose <u>D</u>evice Files (Sound, Graphics, Fax, Printer).

6. The screen will now prompt you for necessary information. Follow all instructions that appear on the screen.

That's all there is to it. The next time you start WordPerfect, your new device should be available.

N O T E　Remember, if you specifically want to install new fonts, you can do so without using the Install program. See Chapter 10.

Startup Switches

You can use any combination of the optional startup switches that WordPerfect uses, to solve startup problems or to take advantage of special hardware. For a quick summary of those switches, enter the command

    wp /?

at the DOS prompt. For example, the command below starts WordPerfect and automatically runs the macro named MYMACRO.WPM:

    wp /m-mymacro

If you want DOS to add the startup switch to the WP command automatically, so you don't have to type it yourself, add the switch to the DOS environmental variables. For example, suppose you want WordPerfect to run a macro named MYMACRO.WPM every time you (or anyone else) starts WordPerfect from the DOS prompt on your computer. Using the DOS Edit command or a similar ASCII text editor (or even WordPerfect, as long as you remember to save the file in ASCII text format), add this command to your C:\AUTOEXEC.BAT file:

```
set wp=wp /m-mymacro
```

For more information on the AUTOEXEC.BAT file, environmental variables, and the SET command, refer to your DOS documentation. For more information on WordPerfect's optional startup switches, refer to Appendix O in the Reference manual that came with your WordPerfect 6.0 for DOS program.

Summary of New Features: For Experienced Users

THIS appendix offers a quick overview of the hottest new features in WordPerfect 6.0 for DOS. The material here is specifically written for

- People who are *considering* upgrading to 6.0 and want to know if it's worth the effort.
- People who have upgraded to 6.0 already and want to find the good stuff in a hurry.

What's Involved in Upgrading?

Before we get into specific new features, let's take a look at what's involved in upgrading to WordPerfect 6.0 for DOS.

How compatible is 6.0 with 5.x?   WordPerfect 6.0 will read, without conversion, any document created in WordPerfect 5.x for DOS or Windows. However, Version 6.0 has many new features not available in earlier versions. So once you save a document in WordPerfect 6.0, you cannot retrieve it back into an earlier version of WordPerfect—*unless* you remember to save your 6.0 document specifically in WordPerfect 5.x format. This step is no trouble—it's just a simple menu selection—but, of course, any features that are specific to Version 6.0, such as rounded-corner Figure boxes, won't carry down to the earlier-format file.

WordPerfect 6.0 uses an entirely new macro language, which is much more like the version of WordPerfect for Windows than previous DOS versions. You cannot run 5.x macros in 6.0; however, there is a conversion utility named MCV.EXE that will convert most 5.x macros to 6.0 format automatically. See Chapter 18 for more information.

NOTE   In my opinion, the macro capability is so vastly improved that any energy you put into converting 5.x macros to 6.0 format is time well spent.

What kind of hardware do I need for 6.0?   I recommend that you have *at least* a 386 machine with a VGA monitor, and 640 KB of RAM. I also recommend that you have DOS 5, DOS 6, or a third-party utility that can help you conserve conventional memory. Plan on setting aside at least 15 MB of hard disk space if you want to install the whole kit and caboodle. You'll find the "official" hardware specifications in Appendix A.

How much trouble is the upgrade?   No trouble at all. You put the Install disk in drive A or B, run the Install program, and follow the instructions on the screen. See Appendix A.

WordPerfect 6.0's Hottest New Features

For the remainder of this appendix, I'll summarize the hottest new features and point you to the chapters that discuss them. I'll categorize and alphabetize the main features, and I'll mark the start of each one with a Hot Stuff icon. That should help you find the features you're most interested in quickly.

Documents and Files

9 Docs at a Time   Edit up to nine documents at a time, each in its own sizable, movable window (Chapter 4).

Cut-and-Paste   It's easier than ever to move and copy text from one document to another using the Clipboard (Chapter 3).

File Manager, QuickList, and QuickFinder Make quick work of storing and finding files (Chapter 20).

 FAX and Mail

HOT STUFF

Fax from the Keyboard If you have a compatible fax board, you can send a fax right from WordPerfect. No need to print the document first. And it looks better at the other end (Chapter 23)!

Send Mail from WordPerfect If you have e-mail, you can send a document to somebody else without printing and without exiting WordPerfect (Chapter 24).

 Fonts

HOT STUFF

Cheap, Great-Looking Scalable Fonts Not only are the new graphics fonts flexible, but they're also cheap. You can build a complete font library for under $100.00 (Chapter 10).

Total Font Integration You can use all your original printer fonts, plus new graphics fonts (TrueType, Type 1, Speedo, and so forth), for DOS *and* Windows, in WordPerfect 6.0 for DOS (Chapter 10). (You'll still need Windows to *install* most Windows fonts.)

Use the Same Fonts with *Any* Printer Graphics fonts work with *any* printer that can print graphics. So you don't need to change fonts every time you switch to another printer (Chapters 6 and 10).

 Formatting/General

HOT STUFF

Automatic Code Placement This feature moves certain codes where they most likely belong on the page or line and automatically deletes the old code, if any. It eliminates code clutter and the confusion caused by competing codes (Chapter 4).

Bookmarks You can find your place in a jiffy with the press of a key (Chapter 9).

Columns Working with columns is easier than ever, especially with the addition of optional built-in separator lines and Balanced Newspaper columns (Chapter 27).

Delay Codes   You can define headers, footers, and other repetitive elements at the top of the document and then delay the codes so they don't print until you get to a specific page (Chapter 8).

Initial Caps   Quickly convert selected text to *UPPERCASE*, *lowercase*, or *Initial Caps* with Edit ➤ Convert Case or Shift+F3 (Chapter 3).

Drag-and-Drop   To move text, just select the text and drag it to its new location. To copy, hold down the Ctrl key while dragging (Chapter 3).

Labels, Envelopes, Pamphlets, and Booklets   These are easier than ever to create (Chapters 8 and 10).

Outlines   There's a special Outline Bar that makes creating and editing outlines a snap. And the outlines are collapsible now (Chapter 14).

Search and Replace   You can find, and optionally replace, *specific codes*—such as a particular font—throughout your document. Also, you can change paired codes throughout a document without using a macro (Chapter 9).

Select (Block) Text   Before selecting virtually any format or font, you can block text to affect only that block (Chapter 4).

Special Characters   These are now much easier to add to your document, using the instant pop-up dialog box (Ctrl+W) (Chapter 6).

Undo   Reverse your most recent change with a simple Ctrl+Z keypress (Chapter 3).

Vertically Center Text   You can do this on every label or every page with Layout ➤ Page ➤ Center Pages (Chapter 8).

HOT STUFF

Graphics

Borders and Shading   Now you can easily draw borders around pages and paragraphs, and shade them if you like, using Graphics ➤ Borders (Chapter 6). You can shade cells within a table individually, as well (Chapter 7).

Contoured Text   You can now wrap text around the image *inside* a graphics box, rather than just around the square box itself (Chapter 26).

Drop Shadows and Rounded Corners   You can now round the corners of graphics boxes, and you have complete control over the size, location, and color of drop shadows (Chapter 26).

Easy Sizing and Placement   Move and size graphics boxes and graphics lines interactively, just by dragging them with your mouse (Chapter 26).

Watermarks   You can print a light watermark on every page of your text (Chapters 8 and 26).

Help

Coaches   These aids let you learn a new feature while you're actually getting some real work done (Chapter 4).

Find What You Need, Quickly   Help includes a Table of Contents, Index, "How Do I...?" list, Glossary, and jump words to help you find the information you need in a flash (Chapter 2).

Tutorial   Run the WordPerfect 6.0 tutorial right from your Help menu (Chapter 1).

Interactive Documents

Hypertext   Use hypertext to build instant cross-referencing capability into a document, just like the jump words in a help screen (Chapter 30).

Voice and Sound   If you have a compatible sound card, you can make your on-screen documents talk, play music, or make any kind of sound you want (Chapter 30).

Macros

Macro Command Language   For macro mavens, the new macro command language offers the capabilities of a real programming language (Chapter 18).

On-line Macro Reference   Extensive macro documentation is now available on disk. Just choose <u>H</u>elp ➤ <u>M</u>acros (Chapter 18).

Run Macros with a Mouse Click   You can copy a macro to the Button Bar, and run that macro with a simple click of the mouse (Chapters 4 and 18).

Smarter Macros   Macros now record only your *completed* actions, ignoring false starts and mistakes you make along the way (Chapter 18).

Math

Built-in Spreadsheet   The Tables feature is now virtually a complete spreadsheet (*sans* graphics), making it easy for you to do any kind of math, from financial calculations to trigonometry (Chapter 25).

Pop-up Calculator   Need to do a quick calculation on the fly? Just pop up the on-screen calculator (Chapter 25).

Mass Mailings/Merges

Envelopes   Automatically print an envelope (with POSTNET bar codes!) for every form letter you print (Chapter 21).

POSTNET Bar Codes   Automatically print a POSTNET bar code on every mailing label or envelope, to get your mail there fast (Chapters 8 and 21).

Store Merge Data in a Table   You can kiss goodbye those old "secondary merge files" with their weird coding. Now you can put merge data into a plain old WordPerfect table, making the whole job *much* easier (Chapter 21).

Printing

Create a Booklet or Pamphlet   You can subdivide pages and then print them as a booklet. When printing is done, just fold the pages in half, and the booklet is ready for binding. No need to figure out page numbering or reshuffle pages (Chapters 10 and 27).

HP LaserJet 4 Fans   Your printer driver is ready and included with your package (Appendix A).

Print Light Text over a Dark Background   You can do this with virtually any printer using graphics fonts and the Print Job Graphically option (Chapters 10 and 28).

Print Preview   This used to be View Document. It can display thumbnail sketches of up to 255 pages at a time (Chapter 4).

Screen/Interface

HOT STUFF

Button Bars, et al   If you have a mouse, you can use the optional Button Bar, Ribbon, scroll bars, and other great shortcut tools to make your on-screen life easier (Chapter 4).

Dialog Boxes   WordPerfect 6.0 for DOS now has the more natural and intuitive kind of interface formerly available only in Windows applications (Chapter 2).

Graphics and Page Modes   You can work in the familiar Text mode, or switch to Graphics or Page modes. In these WYSIWYG (what-you-see-is-what-you-get) modes, it's like being able to edit in the old View Document mode—only better (Chapter 4).

Zoom   In Graphics and Page modes, you can zoom in for a close-up view or zoom out for an arm's-length view—even while editing your document (Chapter 4).

Spelling and Grammar

HOT STUFF

Auto-Replace   Automatically replace common misspellings, such as replacing *hte* with *the*, without being prompted (Chapter 11).

Check Your Grammar   The built-in grammar checker checks grammar as well as spelling (Chapter 12).

Document Statistics   Get complete document statistics, not just a word count (Chapter 4).

Styles

Put *Anything* in a Style   Styles can now include columns, graphics boxes, and even other styles (Chapter 17)!

Shared Style Libraries   Let network users share styles stored on a network drive/directory (Chapter 17).

Tables

Drop Shadows   No need any more to put a table in a graphics box if all you want is a nice drop shadow (Chapter 28).

Recalculate All   With Layout ➤ Tables ➤ Calculate All, you can recalculate the formulas in *all* the document's tables (Chapter 25).

Shade Cells Individually   Individual cells can now have their own Shading % (Chapter 7).

Spreadsheet   The built-in spreadsheet makes table math a breeze (Chapter 25).

First Aid for Common Problems

THIS appendix is loaded with first aid: helpful solutions for the most common WordPerfect problems, questions, and confusions. The problems are categorized and alphabetized into the following sections for easy reference, and the start of each section is marked with a First Aid icon:

- Document/File Problems
- Formatting Problems
- Keyboard/Shortcut Key Problems
- Menu/Command Problems
- Mouse Problems
- Printer/Font Problems
- Screen Problems
- Startup Problems
- Undo/Undelete Problems

How to Use This Appendix

Go to any section and browse through the problems explained there. Your problem may be solved right on the spot. If not, you can always get more in-depth information by looking up the appropriate topic in the index at the back of this book. (Or maybe by pressing F1 in WordPerfect!)

In this appendix I'll assume you already have your most basic WordPerfect skills down pat. If you don't, you'll do yourself a favor if you go back and read Chapter 1. Or at least browse through any unfamiliar topics in Part One, just to get your bearings.

Using WordPerfect's Built-in Troubleshooter

Some situations and problems will result in an error message on your screen, briefly describing the problem—for example, "Access Denied" or "No Predefined Fonts." To get more information about an error message, you can look it up right on your screen. Here's how:

1. Choose the OK or Close button or press Escape (as appropriate) to remove the error message from the screen.

2. Choose Help ➤ Contents.

3. Double-click on the Error Messages topic, or highlight that topic and choose Look (or press ↵).

Now you can look up the error message in the alphabetized list that appears. Choose the message you need help with by double-clicking, or by highlighting and pressing ↵. When you've finished viewing the possible causes and solutions, choose Cancel or press Escape to return to your document.

First Aid

Document and File Problems

I Can't Find My Document!

First of all, are you sure you *saved* the file before you exited WordPerfect and turned off the computer? If you don't know what I'm talking about here, see "Before Shutting Down," in Chapter 2.

If the screen says "File not found" when you try to open a document, then either (1) you didn't save the file, (2) you just now misspelled its name,

(3) the file you're trying to open is not on the current directory, or (4) you or somebody else has deleted the file.

If it's the first problem, you're plain out of luck. Next time, remember to save your work. If it's just a spelling problem, choose OK, retype the name, and choose OK again.

If you're in the wrong directory, try using the File Manager (F5) or QuickList (F6) to find the file. These tools are explained in Chapter 20.

If someone deleted the file, you *may* not be completely out of luck. See "I Just Deleted My Document (or Reformatted My Disk) by Mistake!" at the end of this section.

If you've forgotten the name of the file you want to open, the File Manager can help you find the file based on its contents. See Chapter 20.

If the Open and Retrieve commands are dimmed on the File menu, see "The Command I Need Is Dimmed," later in this appendix.

It Says the File Is "Read-Only"

If, when you try to open a file, you see a message indicating that the "file is in use or is read-only," you or someone else may already have opened that document in this session. Choose Window ➤ Cascade, or Window ➤ Switch To (or press F3) to review your currently open documents. Chapters 4 and 20 offer more information on managing windows and files.

Another possibility is that the file really *is* a read-only file. This is a feature you can turn on and off in DOS, using the ATTRIB command (see your DOS manual or local DOS whiz).

My Whole Document Disappeared

Maybe it has just scrolled out of view. Press Home Home Home ↑ or Ctrl+Home. If it still doesn't reappear, redraw the screen (press Ctrl+F3 and type **r**).

Still no document? Choose Window ➤ Switch To or press F3. If you see the name of the missing document in the list, click that name, or highlight the name using the ↑ and ↓ keys and then press ↵. (If you don't see the name, you can just press Escape.)

If you still can't find the document, you've probably just closed it. Use File ▶ Open to reopen the file (Chapter 3).

I Just Deleted My Document (or Reformatted My Disk) by Mistake!

Once you have deleted a file or reformatted a disk, WordPerfect won't be able to recover your data. If you're using DOS 5 or 6, or you have a third-party utility program that can do the job, look up UNDELETE (if you deleted a file) or UNFORMAT (if you reformatted a disk) for help. You'll need to exit WordPerfect before using these programs.

First Aid

Formatting Problems

Boldface/Italic/Other Formatting Has Gone Too Far

If you turn on a formatting feature such as Boldface or Italic, and then you forget to turn it off, the formatting feature will go on...and on...and on... To correct this situation, move the cursor to where the attribute first took effect, turn on Reveal Codes (Alt+F3), and delete the [... On] or [... Start] code that started the formatting. Then select the text you really do want to format, and choose your print attribute or other feature. See "Revealing the Hidden Codes," in Chapter 4, and "Selecting (Blocking) Text," in Chapter 3.

WordPerfect Just Completely Ignored My Formatting Change

Chances are, there's a code right after the one you just inserted that's canceling out your new code. For example, in this pair of codes

[Ln Spacing: 2.0]*some text here*[Ln Spacing: 1.0]

the first line spacing code, which is supposed to start double-spacing, has no effect because the code for single-spacing immediately cancels it out. Your task is to turn on Reveal Codes and seek-and-destroy (delete) the code that's interfering with the code you want. See "Revealing the Hidden Codes," in Chapter 4.

My Codes Just Up and Disappeared (or Moved)

WordPerfect 6.0 uses *Auto Code*, a feature that automatically moves and replaces certain formatting codes. You can turn Auto Code on or off. See "Using Auto Code Placement," in Chapter 4.

Numbers (4488222) Are Appearing in My Document for No Reason

You're using the cursor-positioning keys with the Num Lock toggle turned on. Press Num Lock (once only!), and try those cursor-positioning keys again. Then move the cursor over to the offending numbers and delete them with the Backspace or Delete keys. See "Using Your Keyboard," in Chapter 2.

mY tEXT lOOKS lIKE tHIS

pRESS THE cAPS lOCK kEY (oNCE oNLY!) and try again. See "Using Your Keyboard" in Chapter 2.

My Header/Footer Starts on the Wrong Page

WordPerfect needs to plan for a header, footer, or watermark on a page before it can print any of those items. If any text exists *before* the [Header] or [Footer] code on the current page, the header or footer won't start until the *next* page.

Make sure the code is the first thing on the page. Or put the code at the top of the document and use Delay Codes to determine exactly which page the header or footer should start on.

Likewise, be sure to put any new page numbering code at the *top* of a newly numbered page. See "Revealing the Hidden Codes," in Chapter 4, and the sections on headers, footers, and page numbering in Chapter 8.

I Don't Want WordPerfect to Hyphenate Those Words

If you type something like a phone number (555-1234) or Zip+4 code (92067-3384), and it ends up at the end of a line, WordPerfect might divide the number at the hyphen that is part of the number. If you don't want that to happen, delete the existing hyphen and replace it with a dash character (hard hyphen). To type a dash character, press Home then press the hyphen key.

My Text Refuses to Align at the New Tab Stops

There are four reasons why existing text might refuse to align at new tab stops you create using Layout ➤ Tab Set:

- Only text *after* the new [Tab Set] code is affected by the new tab ruler. Make sure you position the cursor properly before you change the tab stops.

- Any [Tab Set] code that comes *after* the one you just inserted will override that new [Tab Set] code. Delete old [Tab Set] codes that are canceling out any new ones.

- Text may be aligning at the wrong tab stop because there are two or more [Tab] codes to its left (or no tab code).

- Hard tab codes such as [LFT TAB], as opposed to soft tab codes such as [Lft Tab], don't realign when you change the tab stop. Replace any hard codes with soft ones, using Search and Replace (Chapter 9).

For more information on hard and soft tab codes, see "Tab Codes" in Appendix D.

Keyboard and Shortcut Key Problems

First Aid

My Keys Don't Work the Way You Said They Would

Are you sure you're using WordPerfect 6.0 for DOS? If you are, you should be able to choose Help ➤ WP Info to verify the version number. (Choose OK to leave that dialog box.) Once you're sure you're using Version 6.0 for DOS, check to see if you're using a different keyboard layout. Choose File ➤ Setup ➤ Keyboard Layout. Highlight [ORIGINAL] in the Keyboard Layout list and then choose Select. Try again. Your keys should now work as I've described them. (See the next problem, as well.)

My Cursor-Positioning Keys Don't Work

If you're using the cursor-positioning keys that are on the numeric keypad, press Num Lock once and try again—this may solve the problem.

If you've switched to another keyboard, such as CUAWPW52, the keyboard will follow Windows instead of WordPerfect standards. To get to the WordPerfect standard, go back to the [ORIGINAL] keyboard, as described in the tip just above.

You should also choose File ➤ Setup ➤ Environment (or press Shift+F1 E). Then clear (deselect) the check boxes for the WordPerfect 5.1 Keyboard (F1 = Cancel) and WordPerfect 5.1 Cursor Movement options, to use the same keyboard defaults I used while writing this book.

Some shortcut keys, such as Next Paragraph (Ctrl+↓) and Previous Paragraph (Ctrl+→), require a keyboard with an enhanced BIOS. If those shortcut keys don't work, you're probably using an older keyboard. You'll have to make do with alternative keys such as ↑, ↓, PgUp, and PgDn.

My Keyboard Just Beeps at Me

Most likely, you're typing too fast for WordPerfect to keep up. Wait a few seconds, and try again. Tip: Text mode (Alt+F3 T) can usually handle even the speediest keyboard moguls. If that doesn't work, check to see if

"Block on" appears in the status bar near the lower-left corner of the screen. If so, press Alt+F4 to turn off the block function. Then try again (see "Selecting (Blocking) Text," in Chapter 3, for more information).

If you're still hearing the beep, you may be hung up due to a crash with some other program (this is most likely to occur if you start WordPerfect from Windows rather than DOS). In this situation, your only alternative may be to reboot (press Ctrl+Alt+Del), in which case you'll lose your work. (A good reason to *save your work often* using File ➤ Save!)

I Want to Select Text with the Shift Key, as I Do in Windows

Choose File ➤ Setup ➤ Keyboard Layout, highlight CUAWPW52, and then choose Select. Many shortcut and cursor-positioning keys change roles to adhere to the Windows Common User Access (CUA) Standards. For example, with the CUA keyboard selected, pressing Ctrl+Home (rather than Home Home ↑) will take you to the top of the document. (Just pretend you're in Windows!)

First Aid

Menu and Command Problems

The Command I Need Is Dimmed

Commands are dimmed (grayed out) when they are not appropriate for the current context. For example, Edit ➤ Cut is available only when text is selected. Edit ➤ Paste is available only when there's something in the Clipboard to paste.

Conversely, when you're selecting text and "Block on" appears in the lower-left corner of the screen, certain commands won't be accessible. Press Escape until "Block on" goes away. Then try again.

It Seems Like Almost Everything in This Book Is Wrong!

Are you sure you're using WordPerfect 6.0 for DOS? If so, follow the tips in the foregoing section on "Keyboard and Shortcut Key Problems."

Mouse Problems

Help! My Mouse Is Dead!

If your mouse doesn't work at all in WordPerfect 6.0 for DOS, but it does work in other programs, you probably just need to tell WordPerfect what kind of mouse you're using. Choose File ➤ Setup ➤ Mouse ➤ Type. Highlight the type of mouse you've installed, and choose Select. (If you're not sure, try choosing Auto Select instead of Select.) Then choose OK, and try the mouse again.

My Mouse Buttons Are Backwards

If your left mouse button does what the right button is supposed to do (and vice versa), choose File ➤ Setup ➤ Mouse. Then deselect (clear) the Left-Handed Mouse check box (if you want to use the mouse with your right hand), or select the check box (if you're a lefty mouse user), and try the mouse again.

How Do I Do That without a Mouse?

Some features, such as the Ribbon and Button Bar, cannot be used without a mouse. But you *can* manage with dialog boxes alone. If a button has a shortcut key, you can just press that key. You can usually press Escape for the Cancel button, F7 for Close, and ↵ for OK. Or just press Tab or Shift+Tab until the button you want is highlighted, and then press ↵. For other options, see "Getting Along with Dialog Boxes," in Chapter 2.

Printer and Font Problems

My Printer Doesn't Do Anything

First, look around the screen. If WordPerfect is waiting for you to respond to some question, do so.

Next, make sure you've selected the appropriate printer (Shift+F7 S), as discussed near the beginning of Chapter 10. Check to make sure the printer is plugged in (to the wall and to the computer), turned on, and online (according to the instructions in your printer manual).

If you still need help, go to the Control Printer dialog box (Shift+F7 C) and check the Status, Message, and Action prompts for clues on what to do. Do whatever the Action prompt tells you to do. See "Controlling Print Jobs," in Chapter 10.

If you're using a manual-feed paper size or paper type, the printer may be waiting for an envelope, sheet of labels, or whatever type of paper you chose. If there is a message window on the front of the printer, it will probably show you what type of paper it's waiting for. Insert the paper into the manual feed (usually on the top of the paper bin), until the printer pulls it in. You may have to feed each page manually. See "Printing on Nonstandard Page Sizes" and "Adding a Paper Size," in Chapter 8 for more information. (See also "Printing One Page at a Time," in Chapter 10.)

Text Doesn't Align Properly on the Page

If you're using a dot-matrix or other tractor-feed printer, the paper may have been misaligned to begin with. You can change the left-to-right position of paper in the printer on most dot-matrix printers. Read the first few sections in Chapter 10, and refer to your printer's manual for additional information if necessary.

The Quality of My Printed Graphics or Text Is Awful

Try a higher print quality. See "Step 6: Tell WordPerfect How to Print," in Chapter 10.

My Printer Runs Out of Memory

Try printing the graphics and text separately. See "If Your Printer Runs Out of Memory..." in Chapter 26 and "Step 6: Tell WordPerfect How to Print," in Chapter 10.

The Printer Isn't Using the Right Font

You've probably designed the document with one printer selected, and you're trying to print it with another printer. Use File ➤ Print/Fax ➤ Select to display the list of installed printers. Double-click the name of the printer you used to create this document, or highlight its name and choose Select. Choose Print from the Print dialog box and try again.

To see which fonts WordPerfect is using, turn on Reveal Codes and take a look at the [Font:] codes. Any font name with an asterisk next to it is one that WordPerfect has chosen because it's the font in *this* printer that most closely matches your original font selection. See "Step 4: Select Your Printer" and "Understanding Font Substitution Codes," in Chapter 10.

If you use font cartridges, you might have put the wrong font cartridge into the printer. Turn off the printer, correct the cartridge problem, turn the printer back on, and try again.

If you use soft (printer) fonts, you might have forgotten to download those fonts to the printer. Choose File ➤ Print/Fax ➤ Initialize Printer and wait for the downloading to finish. (You can press Shift+F7 C to watch its progress.) Then try printing the document again.

If none of these suggestions works, maybe you accidentally deleted graphics fonts from your hard disk. When you install WordPerfect with a graphics printer driver, it automatically installs some sample Speedo fonts in the directory named \BTFONTS and sample Type 1 fonts in the \PSFONTS directory. In addition, you may have added some graphics fonts, such as TrueType, on your own. Use the File Manager (F5) to ensure that the font files are still in the proper directories. If you deleted them without realizing what they were, you may be able to undelete them using the DOS 5 or DOS 6 UNDELETE command (see your DOS manual). Or, you can just reinstall those fonts from their original floppies. To reinstall the fonts on \BTFONTS and \PSFONTS, just perform a partial installation, following the instructions in Appendix A.

Special Characters Aren't Printing or Are Coming Out Wrong

Individual fonts offer their own special characters. If you've changed fonts or printers, chances are you're just using the wrong font to print the special character. To remedy the problem, start at your regular document window and select (block) the special character. Then choose Font ➤ Font and look at the currently selected font in the Font text box. If you indeed need to use a different font, open the font list (choose Font) and select your font and point size as usual. Then choose OK to work your way back to the document window and print the page again.

Another possible cause for the problem stems from the fact that some special characters are printed as tiny graphics rather than as text. Go to the Print/Fax dialog box (Shift+F7), and try setting the Graphics Quality to High. Then print the page, and the special character might print. In addition, you can choose Print Job Graphically in the Print/Fax dialog box, and the entire job will be printed graphically (this takes longer).

How Can I See Which Special Characters Are Available?

If you're not sure which special characters are available for a particular font, open the CHARMAP.TST or CHARACTER.DOC file that came with your WordPerfect program. (They may be stored in your C:\WP60 directory rather than with your other documents.) Both these files will open faster if you use Text mode rather than Graphics mode.

Position the cursor somewhere before the first special character in CHARMAP.TST or CHARACTER.DOC (just after the word *ASCII*), and choose the font you're interested in (with the usual Font ➤ Font ➤ Font commands). Choose OK.

Next, choose File ➤ Print/Fax, and set the Graphics Quality to Medium or High if you want the printout to include graphically drawn characters. Choose Print, and wait. You can press Shift+F7 C to speed the printing a little, and watch its progress. (Warning: CHARACTER.DOC is over 50 pages long; CHARMAP.TST is about 5 pages long.)

Compare the printed copy with the document on your screen to see which codes printed each character. For example, if you turn on Reveal Codes and move the highlight directly onto the "happy face" character, you'll see its identifying number (for example, 5,7). Later, when you want to type that character into a document, you can press Ctrl+W and enter 5,7 in the Number option of the WordPerfect Characters dialog box.

Some Fonts Disappeared from My Font List

Your graphics fonts may just be temporarily hidden from view. See "But I Don't See My Newly Installed Graphics Fonts" and "Speeding Up the Font List," in Chapter 10 for information on hiding and displaying graphics font names.

If the printer fonts are missing, you may have inadvertently deleted their names. The names of fonts for the current printer are stored in the printer .PRS file. All possible fonts for a printer, including third-party cartridges and soft fonts, are stored in the printer .ALL file.

If you reinstall a printer, you'll replace the .PRS and/or .ALL file, thereby erasing all those font names (and custom paper sizes) from the font list. You'll need to reinstall those fonts to WordPerfect. See "Installing Printer Fonts," in Chapter 10.

First Aid

Screen Problems

The Text Is Just Too Small, Spread Out, or Slow

In Graphics or Page modes, you can change the magnification setting, using View ➤ Zoom, to increase or decrease the size of the text. See "Zooming In for a Closer Look," in Chapter 4.

If you want to speed things up, and you're just trying to concentrate on writing or editing text, switch to Text mode (Ctrl+F3 T).

If you're in Text mode and your text and tab stops suddenly spread out, forcing some text off the right edge of the screen, try changing the display pitch (see Chapter 5).

I Can't Get to Graphics or Page Mode

You need at least an EGA or VGA adapter and monitor to use Graphics and Page modes, as well as about 520 KB of *available* memory. If you have 640 KB, but WordPerfect claims there isn't enough memory for graphics, you need to free up some conventional memory.

In DOS 6, you can use the MEMMAKER command to do that. In DOS 5, you can use the DEVICEHIGH and LOADHIGH commands. See your DOS manual.

WARNING

If you're not familiar with memory management techniques, you may need to get someone to help you with this problem. You'll be in dangerous waters if you don't know what you're doing!

I Don't See the Scroll Bars, Menu Bar, Button Bars...

Switch to Graphics or Page mode if you can (Ctrl+F3 G or Ctrl+F3 P). Then choose <u>V</u>iew ➤ Scree<u>n</u> Setup, or press Ctrl+F3 then Shift+F1. Select the elements you want to see on your screen. You can also select or clear the first two options, to hide or display the pull-down menus all the time, and to decide whether or not the Alt key alone turns the menus on and off. Choose OK or press F7 after making your choices.

For more information, see "Instant Screen Setup" and "Turning the Button Bar On and Off," in Chapter 4. You can also select many features directly from the View menu.

My Screen Looks Ridiculous

This should do the trick: Press Ctrl+F3 and then choose <u>R</u>ewrite (or type **r**). Or, press Ctrl+F3 twice.

First Aid

Startup Problems

WordPerfect Won't Start at All

First of all, understand that WordPerfect will run on a computer only if you, or someone else, has *installed* WordPerfect on the computer (Appendix A). Also, don't forget to press ↵ *after* you type **wp**.

If you try to start WordPerfect and see the message "Bad command or file name," that means DOS couldn't find the program you asked for. Try again, and make sure you correctly type **wp** and press ↵.

If you still see the "Bad command..." message, it's possible that you need to switch to the WordPerfect directory. Start by typing **cd \wp60** at the DOS prompt and press ↵. Notice that it's a backslash (\), *not* a forward slash (/), between the **cd** and **wp60** in this command. Then type **wp** and press ↵ to try again.

If that doesn't work, either WordPerfect isn't installed on your computer, or it's in an unusual directory. You might have to ask someone who is familiar with the computer for help.

Incidentally, if the CD \WP60 command solves the problem, and you're not a DOS whiz but you do know one, ask him or her to show you how to add the WordPerfect 6.0 directory (typically it's C:\WP60) to your AUTOEXEC.BAT file, so you can start WordPerfect from any directory.

If the solution to this problem is more elusive, and you already know about everything I just suggested, you might need to experiment with some of the optional startup switches discussed in Appendix A.

It Says "Backup File Exists..."

From time to time, WordPerfect puts a *temporary backup* copy of your current document on disk. When you save the file and exit WordPerfect properly, the temporary backup file is erased.

If you don't exit WordPerfect properly before turning off the computer, the temporary backup file will not be erased. The next time you start WordPerfect, it will recognize that a temporary backup file is there, and it will ask if you want to open it, delete it, or rename it. In most cases, you'll probably want to choose Open each time you're prompted, to see what's in the file before you decide. In the future, always remember to exit WordPerfect properly, and save your work, as discussed under "Before Shutting Down," in Chapter 2.

To control how often WordPerfect saves that temporary file, use File ➤ Setup ➤ Environment ➤ Backup Options (see Chapter 19). In situations where the computer reboots arbitrarily (because of electrical storms, lots of static electricity, commercial airline radar, and so forth), you might want WordPerfect to make that temporary backup every minute or so.

First Aid

Undo and Undelete Problems

Undo Doesn't Work at All

Somebody may have turned off the Undo feature, perhaps because Word-Perfect runs a little faster without it. Choose File ➤ Setup ➤ Environment. If the check box next to Allow Undo isn't marked, select the option. Chose OK to return to your document.

If Allow Undo was already enabled, chances are you performed another operation *after* the action you want to undo. Undo can only reverse your most recent action. If you need more information, see "Controlling the Environment," in Chapter 19, and "Undoing a Recent Change," in Chapter 3.

Undelete Puts Text in the Wrong Place

The Undo function puts deleted text back in at its original position (if it can undo the deletion at all). The Undelete function always places the un-deleted text at the current cursor position. See "Undo vs. Undelete," in Chapter 3.

APPENDIX

D

Hidden Codes
Revealed

AS DISCUSSED in Chapter 4, you can use Reveal Codes (View ➤ Reveal Codes or Alt+F3) to see the codes that WordPerfect uses to format your document. Most of the codes are self-explanatory. For example, [Ln Spacing: 2.0] is the code that WordPerfect inserts when you change the line spacing to 2.

In this appendix, I'll talk about some of the not-so-obvious codes, such as [TSRt], that seem to "just appear" in your document. For a complete listing of codes, consult Appendix B in your WordPerfect documentation.

Tab Codes

Tab codes generally appear in mixed case, as in [Lft Tab], or in all uppercase, as in [LFT TAB].

The mixed-case codes like [Lft Tab] are normal soft codes that you put in by pressing the Tab key. If you change the tab stop above that code to something else, such as a center tab, the code itself will change to [Cntr Tab], and text to the right of the code will be aligned accordingly.

In contrast, [LFT TAB] is a hard code, which you can insert by pressing Home, then Tab. WordPerfect, too, might add these hard codes when, say, you convert a certain table to text.

A hard code is different from a soft code, in that the hard code's neighboring text is left-aligned to the tab stop—regardless of whether it's aligned to a left, center, right, or decimal tab stop. This can drive you batty when you're trying to change the tab stops above some hard tab codes, and they refuse to realign on the new tab stop. The simple solution? Use Search and Replace (Chapter 9) to convert the hard tab codes to soft tab codes. Then change the tab ruler above the codes.

All the tab codes come in soft and hard versions. If you add dot leaders to a tab stop, the word *(Dot)* is added to the code. Thus, there are actually four types of tab codes for center tabs [Cntr Tab], decimal tabs [Dec Tab], and right tabs [Rgt Tab]. For example, here are the four possible codes for a decimal tab:

[Dec Tab]   Decimal-aligned tab

[DEC TAB]   Hard decimal-aligned tab

[Dec Tab (Dot)]   Decimal-aligned tab with dot leader

[DEC TAB (DOT)]   Hard decimal-aligned tab with dot leader

You can insert hard tab codes into your document by choosing Layout ➤ Special Codes from the main menu bar.

The [Dorm HTt] Code

The mysterious [Dorm HRt] *(dormant hard return)* code appears when the first line at the top of a page contains only a [HRt] (hard return) code. The code is "dormant" because WordPerfect assumes that you don't really want a blank line at the top of the page. If you add or delete text above the [Dorm HRt] code, and that line moves to somewhere else other than the top of a page, the code will revert back to the regular [HRt] code.

The [Ignore:...] Code

The word Ignore at the beginning of a code indicates that the code no longer makes sense and is therefore being ignored. For example, suppose you have five tabs across a line. Then you change the tab ruler so that there are only four tab stops. The last tab code on that line will probably have an Ignore indicator in it, to let you know that the original tab code is being ignored because it doesn't make sense.

If you change the tab ruler again, and insert five or more tab stops, the [Ignore:...] is removed and the code takes on its original meaning.

[Font:*...] Codes

A [Font:] code that contains an asterisk indicates that the font specified in that code is not the one you originally selected—most likely because you changed to a different printer after creating the document, and the current printer doesn't have the font you originally selected. Therefore, WordPerfect has substituted the font you see in the [Font:] code. For more information, see "Understanding Font Substitution Codes" in Chapter 10.

Codes to Break and Hyphenate Lines

WordPerfect uses several codes to break lines at the right margin, as well as to prevent lines from being broken. The most common codes are the soft return, [SRt], and hard return, [HRt]. WordPerfect inserts soft returns automatically to word-wrap lines within a paragraph. You insert a hard return whenever you press ↵.

Many other codes are used to control whether text breaks at the end of a line, including the hard hyphens, soft hyphens, hard spaces, and so forth. You can insert these codes by choosing Layout ➤ Special Codes as you type your document. For more information on these special codes, please see Chapter 16.

[T...]: Temporary Codes

A *temporary code* is typically used to break text that won't fit within the margins or the current column. For example, if you're using narrow columns and you type a word that's wider than the column, WordPerfect will insert a temporary soft return [TSRt] code at the beginning of the word to ensure that it starts on a new line. If you later divide the wide word with a hyphen or reduce its font size so that it fits within the space available, the temporary code will disappear.

Temporary codes that are likely to change if you change font sizes, column widths, margins, and so forth include the following:

[THCol]   Temporary hard column break

[THCol-SPg]   Temporary hard column break-soft page break

[THPg]   Temporary hard page break

[THRt]   Temporary hard return

[THRt-SCol]   Temporary hard return-soft column break

[THRt-SPg]   Temporary hard return-soft page break

[TSRt]   Temporary soft return

[TSRt-SCol]   Temporary soft return-soft column break

[TSRt-SPg]   Temporary soft return-soft page break

The [Unknown] Code

An [Unknown] code indicates that the current document contains a code that was created in another version of WordPerfect or in another word processing program. WordPerfect cannot interpret the code but leaves it in as an "unknown." If you convert the document back to the original word processor's format, that [Unknown] code will (usually) regain its original meaning.

GLOSSARY

IN ADDITION to the glossary provided here, you can use the one that's built into WordPerfect. Here's how:

1. Choose Help ➤ Contents.

2. Double-click on Glossary, or highlight Glossary and choose Look.

3. To get to the word you want to look up, you may want to start by choosing Name Search and typing in the first few letters of the word you want. This will bring you to the word or to its general vicinity. You can use the ↑ and ↓ keys if necessary to highlight the exact word that you want.

4. Double-click the word you want to look up, or highlight it and choose Look.

5. After reading the definition, choose OK and Cancel or press F7 twice to return to your document.

+ (as in Ctrl+Z or Shift+F7): Denotes a combination of keystrokes, meaning "Hold down the first key, tap the second key, and then release both keys" (Chapter 2).

*: In a [Font] code, indicates a font that WordPerfect has substituted for your original selection. WordPerfect only does this when you change printers, and the current printer doesn't have the font you originally selected (Chapter 10).

↵: The symbol used to indicate the Enter key, also called the Return key (Chapter 2).

➤: In this book, this is the symbol separating the commands or options that you select in a series. For example, "Choose Help ➤ WP Info" is a shortcut (and better way) to say "Choose WP Info from the Help pull-down menu" (Chapter 2).

.ALL file: File containing information about all the printer fonts and paper sizes for a family of printers (Chapter 10).

Alt: Abbreviation for the Alternate key; usually pronounced "allt," like the first three letters in the word *alternate* (Chapter 2).

Argument: The number or text on which a *function* operates. In the function SQRT(81), for instance, SQRT() is the function, and 81 is the argument (Chapter 25).

Attribute: The way a font is printed, such as Boldface or Extra Large size (Chapter 6).

Baseline: The invisible line on which text is printed (Chapter 28).

Block: A selected chunk of text, or the act of selecting text. See *Select* in this glossary (and Chapter 3).

Built-in font: A font that comes with the printer, and therefore need not be installed separately (Chapter 10).

Byte: Approximately one character of information; for example, the word *cat* takes up three bytes of disk space.

Cartridge font: A collection of fonts stored on a cartridge that goes in a slot in the printer (Chapter 10).

Case-sensitive: Indicates that a function or application distinguishes between uppercase and lowercase. Very few features and programs are case-sensitive, so in most situations, "Smith" is the same as "SMITH," "smith," and "SmItH."

Cell: In a table, the place where a column and row intersect. For example, cell B2 is the intersection of column B and row 2 (Chapter 7).

Check box: An option in a dialog box that can either be selected (contains an ×) or deselected (is empty). To select or deselect the option, you click it with the mouse or highlight it and press the spacebar (Chapter 2).

Click: Move the mouse pointer to the item, and then press and release the mouse button—usually the left mouse button, but this is reversed on a left-handed mouse (Chapter 2).

Code: An item visible only in the Reveal Codes window, and enclosed in square brackets ([ ]); codes control the format of the document (Chapter 4).

Ctrl: Abbreviation for the Control key; pronounced "control" (Chapter 2).

Current directory: The directory that WordPerfect is currently using to store and search for files (Chapter 20).

Current document: When several documents are open on the screen, the current document is the one that's in the active window and is perhaps covering other documents (Chapter 4).

Cursor: The (usually) blinking character on the screen that indicates where the next character you type will appear. Also called the *insertion point* (Chapter 2).

Data file: Information that's used to "fill in the blanks" during a merge. Example: a list of names and addresses used for printing form letters and mailing labels (Chapter 21).

Dead zone: An area around the edge of the page, about $\frac{1}{4}$-inch wide, where the print rollers touch the paper to move it through the printer. You cannot print anything within the dead zone (Chapter 10).

Default: The setting or option WordPerfect uses if you don't make any changes on your own (Chapter 19).

Design element: Anything that's repeated throughout your document, such as section headings (Chapters 8 and 17).

Dialog box: A box or window that appears on your screen and presents options for you to choose (Chapter 2).

Dimmed: A menu or dialog box command that's not relevant at the moment, and therefore cannot be selected (Appendix C, Chapter 2).

Directory: A place on the disk (hard or floppy) where files are grouped together (Chapter 20).

Document: Any body of text or other information created with a computer program. Letters, essays, mailing labels, newsletters, and spreadsheets are all examples of documents (Chapters 2 and 33).

Document window: The part of the screen where you do your typing and editing. Also called the *edit screen* or *editing screen* (Chapter 4).

DOS: (Rhymes with "floss.") An acronym for *Disk Operating System,* the program that gets your computer running and controls the computer's operations. The DOS command prompt looks something like

    C:\> *or* C>

followed by a blinking cursor. You can run DOS commands and other programs from the prompt by typing a valid command and pressing ↵. For example, typing **ver** ↵ tells you which version of DOS you're using. Typing **wp** ↵ starts WordPerfect.

Dot leader: A line of dots that connects a piece of text with a page number or other information. To type the dot leader below, I pressed Alt+F6 twice, right after typing **Introduction** (Chapter 5).

    Introduction...................12

Double-click: A technique that selects an option or highlights a word of text. This means, "Move the mouse pointer to the item, and then press and release the mouse button twice, as quickly as possible"; usually refers to the left mouse button (Chapter 2).

Drag: A technique that usually selects a block of text or moves or resizes a graphic. This means, "Move the mouse pointer to the item, hold down the mouse button, move the mouse pointer to another location, and then release the mouse button"; usually refers to the left mouse button (Chapter 2).

Drag-and-drop: A technique for moving or copying text with the mouse, where you place the mouse pointer on selected text, drag the mouse pointer to another location, and then release the mouse button to drop the selected text at that location (Chapter 3). Not to be confused with "dragon drops," which don't exist.

Drive: Short name for *disk drive*, the place where files are stored (Chapter 20).

Driver: A small program that enables WordPerfect to communicate with a piece of equipment that's attached to your computer. For example, a *printer driver* helps WordPerfect send text and graphics to your printer correctly (Chapter 10).

Drop cap: A large capital letter at the start of a paragraph (Chapter 28).

Drop-down list: A list of alternatives available for a text box. To open a drop-down list, you click the downward-pointing triangle next to the text box. You can also press the ↓ key to open the list (Chapter 2).

Drop shadow: A darkened, offset patch behind a figure or text, used to give a raised or floating appearance (Chapter 28).

Editing screen: Same as *edit screen* and *document window*—the place on the screen where you type and edit text (Chapters 3 and 4).

Extension: The optional suffix that follows a file name. The extension is preceded by a period, up to three characters in length. Example: In MYLETTER.WP (pronounced "my letter dot w p"), the .WP is the extension (Chapter 20).

Field: One column or type of information in a merge data file. Example: A data file of names and addresses usually has a field for name, a field for address, a field for city, and so forth (Chapter 21).

Figure box: A type of graphics box, typically used to hold graphic images (Chapter 26).

File: A document or program stored on a computer disk with a unique name (Chapter 20).

Flush right: Aligns the right edge of text with the right margin (Chapter 5).

Font: A combination of typeface, size, and any additional attributes (Chapter 6).

Footer: A section of text and/or graphics that's repeated at the bottom of every page (Chapter 8).

Form: In merge terminology, this is the "primary merge file" used to fill out and format data from a data file. Example: a form letter (Chapter 21).

Function: In Tables math, a command that performs some action on a number or text. Example: The square root function SQRT() can determine the square root of any positive number (Chapter 25).

Function keys: The keys that are named F1 through F12 (or F1 through F10 on some keyboards) across the top or at the left side of the keyboard (Chapter 2).

Graphics box: A container for storing a graphic image, table, or text in a document. Styles of graphics boxes include Figure box, Table box, Text box, User box, and others (Chapter 26).

Graphics font: A font that's stored on disk and can be used with any printer that prints graphics. Examples: TrueType, Speedo, and Type 1 (Chapter 10).

Hang/hanging indent: An "outdent" that reaches out into the margin, or sticks out from the rest of the paragraph (Chapter 5).

Hard return: An intentional line break that's inserted when you press ↵; appears as [HRt] in Reveal Codes (Chapters 1, 2, 3, 4).

Header: Text and/or graphics repeated at the top of every page (Chapter 8).

Hidden code: See *Code*.

Insertion point: See *Cursor*.

KB (or K or Kilobyte): 1,024 bytes, or roughly one thousand characters (see *Byte*).

Landscape: An orientation for printing in which the long edge of the page runs horizontally and printing appears between the short sides of the paper. Landscape is the opposite of *Portrait* (Chapter 8).

Leading: Pronounced "ledding;" this is the amount of white space between printed lines (Chapter 28).

Macro: A collection of actions that can be played back with a single keystroke (Chapter 18).

MB (or M or Megabyte): 1,024 kilobytes, or roughly a million characters (see *Byte*).

Memory: The chips in the computer hardware that store the program(s) and document(s) you're working on at the moment. Also called RAM, for Random Access Memory (Chapter 2).

Menu/menu bar: The bar across the top of the screen that offers commands for you to choose (Chapters 2, 4).

Merge: To join data, such as names and addresses, from a data file to a form, such as a form letter or envelopes. Typically used for mass mailings (Chapter 21).

Mouse: A point-and-click alternative to the keyboard as a means of interacting with a computer (Chapter 2, Appendix C).

Mouse pointer: The arrow or other symbol that moves on the screen when you roll the mouse (Chapter 2; Appendix C for troubleshooting).

Path: The location of a file. For example: **c:\wpdocs\myletter.wp** refers to the file named MYLETTER.WP on the directory named WPDOCS on drive C. The **c:\wpdocs** part is the path the computer needs to follow to get to the file (Chapter 20).

Personal directory: Typically a directory of files on your local hard disk that only you can access.

Point: *For fonts*, a point represents about $\frac{1}{72}$ of an inch. *For the mouse*, to point means to move the mouse pointer so that the mouse pointer is touching the object.

Pop-up: A list that pops up when you use certain buttons. If you click the button itself, you must then keep the mouse button depressed, highlight the option you want in the pop-up list, and then release the mouse button. If you choose the option instead of the button, the pop-up list stays open until you make a selection (Chapter 2).

Portrait: The standard way of printing on the page, where text and graphics appear between the two long edges of the paper. Portrait is the opposite of *Landscape* (Chapter 8).

Printer font: Unlike graphics fonts, printer fonts are designed for use with a particular type of printer. Printer fonts include built-in, cartridge, and soft fonts (Chapter 10).

RAM: See *Memory*.

Read-only file: A file that can be viewed but not changed (see "Document/File Problems" in Appendix C).

Record: *For merges,* this is a single row of information in a data table (pronounced like "phonograph record"). Example: the complete name and address of one person in a mailing list (Chapter 21). *For macros,* this means to save actions as you perform them, so that you can play them back again later (pronounced like "tape recorder") (Chapter 18).

Reveal Codes: The window that allows you to see WordPerfect's hidden codes (Chapter 4).

Right-justify: See *Flush right.*

Screen Font: A font that's used to display text on the screen so that the text looks the way it will look when printed (Chapter 10).

Select: *For documents,* the phrases *select text* and *select the text* refer to "blocking" or "highlighting" the text you want to work with, by dragging the mouse pointer through it or by using Edit ➤ Block, Alt+F4, F12, or Edit ➤ Select (Chapter 3). *For a dialog box or menu,* select means to mark a check box with an × or mark a radio button option in a dialog box, by clicking the mouse or pressing the spacebar (Chapter 2). *When sorting or merging,* selecting refers to the ability to isolate certain types of information, such as customers in the state of California, or a certain zip code area (Chapter 22).

Shared directory: Typically a directory of files on a network drive or workgroup directory that all (or some) users in a workgroup can access.

Shared library: A collection of *styles,* typically stored on a network drive so that multiple users can share the same set of styles (Chapter 17).

Sheet-feed: See *Tractor-feed.*

Shift: The key used to capitalize a single letter, or used in a combination keystroke such as Shift+F1 (Chapter 2).

Shortcut (key): An alternative to going through the menus and/or dialog boxes to get to a frequently used feature. Often appears next to the command name in the menu, and often requires a *combination keystroke* (Chapter 2).

Soft font: A printer font (*not* a graphics font) that's stored on disk and *downloaded* (sent) to the printer when needed, or when the printer is initialized (Chapter 10).

Soft return: The [SRt] code that WordPerfect uses to break text at the right margin between words, rather than between characters. You can see [SRt] in Reveal Codes (Chapter 4).

Sort: To put text or numbers into a specific order, such as alphabetical or numerical (Chapter 22).

Specific codes: Codes with a specific setting, such as [Font:CG Times], as opposed to a general code such as [Lft Tab] or [HRt] (Chapter 9).

Status bar (status line): The bar that appears (usually) across the bottom of the screen. You can use View ➤ Screen Setup (Ctrl+F3, Shift+F1) to change the appearance of the status bar (Chapter 19).

Style: A set of codes that defines the format and appearance of a design element in your text, such as all the chapter titles or all the section titles (Chapter 17).

Style library: A collection of styles that can be used in any document. A *personal library* is usually stored on a local hard disk. A *shared library* is stored on a network drive so that multiple users at various workstations can use the same set of styles (Chapter 17).

Tab: The key used to move to the next tab stop (Chapter 2), or the result of pressing that key (Chapter 5).

Tab stop: The place where the cursor stops when you press Tab, Indent, or any other key that indents or outdents. Use Layout ➤ Line ➤ Tab Set to change the tab stops (Chapter 5).

Text box: *In dialog boxes,* this is a box into which you enter information related to a selected option or command. You can type the information into a text box, or open a drop-down list and select the information for the text box (Chapter 2). *In graphics,* this is the type of box used to display elements such as sidebars and quotations separately from the main text (Chapter 26).

Toggle: A key or option that turns a feature on and off every time you press the key or select the option. Example: Each time you press it, the Insert key toggles between Insert and Typeover modes (Chapter 2).

Tractor-feed: A means of feeding paper into a printer by using paper with perforations along the left and right edges. The opposite of *sheet-feed*, where individual, nonperforated sheets are fed to the printer from a bin (Chapter 10).

User box: A graphics box which, by default, has no frame (Chapter 26).

Watermark: Text or a graphic that's usually printed on every page, most often in a light shade of gray (Chapters 8, 26).

Wildcard: A special character that stands for something else. For example, **?** stands for any single character, and ★ stands for zero or more characters (Chapter 20).

Window: A section of the screen that displays a document. Also called a *document window* (Chapter 4).

Word-wrap: To end a line by automatically breaking it between two words rather than in the middle of a word (Chapter 3).

WYSIWYG: An acronym, pronounced "wizzy wig," that stands for What You See Is What You Get. WordPerfect's Graphics and Page modes, as well as Print Preview, are all somewhat WYSIWYG. Text mode is not (Chapter 4).

Zoom: To increase or decrease the magnification of a document on the screen (Chapter 4).

INDEX

Note: Boldfaced page numbers indicate definitions of terms and principal discussions of topics. Italicized page numbers indicate illustrations.

T

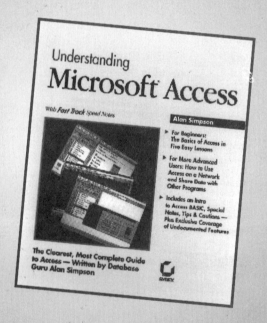

Alan Simpson's Mastering WordPerfect 6.0 for DOS Companion Disks

If you want to use the example documents, styles, and macros presented in this book without keying them in yourself, you can send for the companion disks containing all the files (excluding the files that came with your WordPerfect package). You can use each file as it is, or as a starting point for creating your own document, style, or macro.

To purchase the optional companion disks, please complete the order form below and return it with your VISA or MasterCard number, a check, international money order, or purchase order for $20.00 U.S. currency (plus sales tax for California residents) to the address shown on the coupon. Or, we can bill you later.

If you prefer, you can return the coupon without making a purchase to receive free periodic newsletters and updates about Alan Simpson's latest books.

> Alan Simpson Computing
> P.O. Box 945
> Cardiff-by-the-Sea, CA 92007
> Phone (619) 943-7715   FAX (619) 943-7750

☐ Please send the companion disks for *Mastering WordPerfect 6.0 for DOS*.

☐ No disk thanks, but please send free newsletters from Alan Simpson Computing.

_____
Name

_____
Company

_____
Address

_____
City, State, Zip

_____
Country   P.O. Number (if applicable)

_____
Phone Number (Required for VISA/MC orders)

Check one:

☐ Payment enclosed ($20.00, plus sales tax for California residents), made payable to Alan Simpson Computing

☐ Bill me later   ☐ Bill my VISA or MasterCard

_____
Card Number   Exp. Date

Check one disk size:

☐ 5$\frac{1}{4}$-inch disk   ☐ 3$\frac{1}{2}$-inch disk

SYBEX is not affiliated with Alan Simpson Computing and assumes no responsibility for any defect in the disk or files.

SYBEX

FREE BROCHURE!

Complete this form today, and we'll send you a full-color brochure of Sybex bestsellers.

Please supply the name of the Sybex book purchased.

_____

How would you rate it?

_____ Excellent   _____ Very Good   _____ Average   _____ Poor

Why did you select this particular book?

_____ Recommended to me by a friend
_____ Recommended to me by store personnel
_____ Saw an advertisement in _____
_____ Author's reputation
_____ Saw in Sybex catalog
_____ Required textbook
_____ Sybex reputation
_____ Read book review in _____
_____ In-store display
_____ Other _____

Where did you buy it?

_____ Bookstore
_____ Computer Store or Software Store
_____ Catalog (name: _____)
_____ Direct from Sybex
_____ Other: _____

Did you buy this book with your personal funds?

_____ Yes   _____ No

About how many computer books do you buy each year?

_____ 1-3   _____ 3-5   _____ 5-7   _____ 7-9   _____ 10+

About how many Sybex books do you own?

_____ 1-3   _____ 3-5   _____ 5-7   _____ 7-9   _____ 10+

Please indicate your level of experience with the software covered in this book:

_____ Beginner   _____ Intermediate   _____ Advanced

Which types of software packages do you use regularly?

_____ Accounting   _____ Databases   _____ Networks

_____ Amiga   _____ Desktop Publishing   _____ Operating Systems

_____ Apple/Mac   _____ File Utilities   _____ Spreadsheets

_____ CAD   _____ Money Management   _____ Word Processing

_____ Communications   _____ Languages   _____ Other _____
                                                                                           (please specify)

Which of the following best describes your job title?

_____ Administrative/Secretarial _____ President/CEO

_____ Director Manager/Supervisor

_____ Engineer/Technician _____ Other _____

(please specify)

Comments on the weaknesses/strengths of this book: _____

_____

_____

_____

_____

Name _____

Street _____

City/State/Zip _____

Phone _____

PLEASE FOLD, SEAL, AND MAIL TO SYBEX

SYBEX, INC.
Department M
2021 CHALLENGER DR.
ALAMEDA, CALIFORNIA USA
94501

SYBEX

SEAL

FEATURE	SHORTCUT	FEATURE	SHORTCUT
Language	Shift+F1 EL or Shift+F8 OL	Outline (appearance)	Ctrl+F8 AO
Leading Adjustment	Shift+F8 OPL	Outline Bar	Alt+V O
Letterspacing	Shift+F8 OPWL	Overstrike	Shift+F8 C O or E
Line (graphic)	Alt+F9 L	Page Mode	Ctrl+F3 P
Line Draw	Ctrl+F3 L	Page Numbering	Shift+F8 PN
Line Height	Shift+F8 LH	Paper Size/Type	Shift+F8 PS
Line Numbering	Shift+F8 LN	Password Protect	F10 F8
Line Spacing	Shift+F8 LS	Paste from Clipboard	Ctrl+V
Lists	Alt+F5 M or D	POSTNET Bar Code	Shift+F8 OR
Location of Files	Shift+F1 L	Print Document	Shift+F7 R
Macro (control and commands)	Ctrl+PgUp	Print Preview	Shift+F7 V
Macro (play)	Alt+F10	Print Quality	Shift+F7 T or G
Macro (record)	Ctrl+F10	Printer Control	Shift+F7 C
Mail (from Shell)	F8	Pull-Down Menus	Alt+V P
Mail (from WordPerfect)	Ctrl+F1 M	QuickMark (set)	Ctrl+Q
		QuickMark (find)	Ctrl+F
Margin Release	Shift+Tab	Redline	Ctrl+F8 AR
Margins	Shift+F8 M	Redline (add to text)	Alt+F5 K
Mass Mailings	Shift+F9		
Master Document	Alt+F5 A	Redline Method	Shift+F7 Shift+F1 R
Math (floating cell)	Alt+F7 F	Registration Number	Alt+H W
Math (no table)	Alt+F7 M	Repeat Next	Ctrl+R
Merge Codes	Shift+F9	Replace	Alt+F2
Merge Documents	Ctrl+F9 M	Retrieve (insert) Document	Shift+F10 Shift+F10
Move (Cut) Text to Clipboard*	Ctrl+X	Reveal Codes	Alt+F3 or F11
New Document	Alt+F N	Reveal Codes (size/detail)	Ctrl+F3 C
Open Document	Shift+F10	Rewrite Screen	Ctrl+F3 R
Outline	Ctrl+F5	Ribbon	Alt+V R
		Save Document	Ctrl+F12

Quick Reference on pages 35–36.
Problem? See First Aid, pages 1167–1181.
Select (block) text first.